6th Workshop on Representation Learning for NLP (RepL4NLP-2021)

Held online due to COVID-19

Bangkok, Thailand
6 August 2021

ISBN: 978-1-7138-3384-0

Printed from e-media with permission by:

Curran Associates, Inc.
57 Morehouse Lane
Red Hook, NY 12571

Some format issues inherent in the e-media version may also appear in this print version.

Association for Computational Linguistics
209 N. Eighth Street
Stroudsburg, Pennsylvania 18360

Phone: 1-570-476-8006
Fax: 1-570-476-0860

acl@aclweb.org

Additional copies of this publication are available from:

Curran Associates, Inc.
57 Morehouse Lane
Red Hook, NY 12571 USA
Phone: 845-758-0400
Fax: 845-758-2633
Email: curran@proceedings.com
Web: www.proceedings.com

RepL4NLP 2021

The 6th Workshop on Representation Learning for NLP

Proceedings of the Workshop

August 6, 2021
Bangkok, Thailand (online)

Introduction

Welcome to the 6th Workshop on Representation Learning for NLP (RepL4NLP-2021)! The workshop was co-located with the Joint Conference of the 59th Annual Meeting of the Association for Computational Linguistics and the 11th International Joint Conference on Natural Language Processing (ACL-IJCNLP 2021), and was held on August 6, 2021 as an online workshop. The workshop was organised by Anna Rogers, Iacer Calixto, Ivan Vulić, Naomi Saphra, Nora Kassner, Oana-Maria Camburu, Trapit Bansal, and Vered Shwartz; and advised by Chris Dyer, Ed Grefenstette, Isabelle Augenstein, Karl Moritz Hermann, Kyunghyun Cho, and Laura Rimell. The workshop is annually organised by the ACL Special Interest Group on Representation Learning (SIGREP).

The 6th Workshop on Representation Learning for NLP aims to continue the success of the previous editions, and remains a strong and established venue for representation learning in NLP, attracting more than 60 submissions this year. This edition continued to invite papers of a theoretical or experimental nature describing recent advances in vector space models of meaning, compositionality, and the application of deep neural networks and spectral methods to NLP. A strong focus was put on topics of developing new representations, evaluating existing representations, efficient and sustainable learning and inference, and representation learning beyond the English language and text only (e.g., multi-modal, cross-lingual, knowledge-informed learning).

We take this opportunity to thank the RepL4NLP-2021 program committee for their help and thorough reviews. We also thank the authors who presented their work at the workshop, and the workshop participants for the valuable feedback and discussions. Finally, we are deeply honored to have four excellent talks from our invited speakers Sameer Singh, Karen Livescu, Noah Smith, and Lena Voita.

The RepL4NLP-2021 Workshop organizers

Organizers:

Anna Rogers, University of Copenhagen
Iacer Calixto, New York University & University of Amsterdam
Ivan Vulić, University of Cambridge & PolyAI
Naomi Saphra, New York University
Nora Kassner, LMU Munich
Oana-Maria Camburu, University of Oxford
Trapit Bansal, UMass Amherst
Vered Shwartz, Allen Institute for AI & University of Washington

Senior Advisers:

Chris Dyer, DeepMind
Edward Grefenstette, Facebook AI Research & University College London
Isabelle Augenstein, University of Copenhagen
Karl Moritz Hermann, Saiga
Kyunghyun Cho, New York University
Laura Rimell, DeepMind

Keynote Speakers:

Sameer Singh, University of California Irvine
Karen Livescu, Toyota Technological Institute at Chicago
Noah Smith, Allen Institute for AI & University of Washington
Lena Voita, University of Edinburgh & University of Amsterdam

Program Committee:

Muhammad Abdul-Mageed
Guy Aglionby
Roee Aharoni
Nicholas Andrews
Mikel Artetxe
Federico Bianchi
Andrew Caines
Helena Caseli
Yue Chen
Mingda Chen
Alexandra Chronopoulou
Manuel Ciosici
Paula Czarnowska
Giuseppe Antonio Di Luna
Philipp Dufter
Javid Ebrahimi
Vladimir Eidelman
Yanai Elazar
Sergey Feldman
Eraldo Fernandes
Elisabetta Fersini
Orhan Firat
Thibault Févry
Rainer Gemulla

Eleonora Giunchiglia
Hongyu Gong
Kartik Goyal
Robin Jia
Aishwarya Kamath
Santosh Kesiraju
Ekaterina Kochmar
Vid Kocijan
Shankar Kumar
Andrey Kutuzov
Matthieu Labeau
John P. Lalor
Jey Han Lau
Carolin Lawrence
Xiang Lorraine Li
Tao Li
Yitong Li
Bill Yuchen Lin
Peng Liu
Olga Majewska
Sabrina Mielke
Victor Milewski
Jeff Mitchell
Daichi Mochihashi
Ashutosh Modi
Nicholas Monath
Lili Mou
Maximilian Mozes
Khalil Mrini
Nikita Nangia
Jason Naradowsky
Thien Huu Nguyen
Truc-Vien T. Nguyen
Jekaterina Novikova
Tsuyoshi Okita
Ankur Padia
Letitia Parcalabescu
Matthew Peters
Tiago Pimentel
Vipul Raheja
Surangika Ranathunga
Abhilasha Ravichander
Subendhu Rongali
Frank Rudzicz
Ehsan Shareghi
Hao Tang
Shuai Tang
Dung Thai
Jörg Tiedemann
Nadi Tomeh
Marcos Treviso

Adam Trischler
Lifu Tu
Shikhar Vashishth
Hai Wang
Hua Wang
Rodrigo Wilkens
Adina Williams
Yuexin Wu
Yuxiang Wu
Wenpeng Yin
Yordan Yordanov
Hong Yu
Wei Zhang
Xiangyang Zhou
Dong Zhou
Yi Zhu
Imed Zitouni
Robert Östling

Table of Contents

Conference Program

Improving Cross-lingual Text Classification with Zero-shot Instance-Weighting
Irene Li, Prithviraj Sen, Huaiyu Zhu, Yunyao Li and Dragomir Radev

Probing Multilingual Language Models for Discourse
Murathan Kurfalı and Robert Östling

Comprehension Based Question Answering using Bloom's Taxonomy
Pritish Sahu, Michael Cogswell, Ajay Divakaran and Sara Rutherford-Quach

Larger-Scale Transformers for Multilingual Masked Language Modeling
Naman Goyal, Jingfei Du, Myle Ott, Giri Anantharaman and Alexis Conneau

Learning Sparse Sentence Encoding without Supervision: An Exploration of Sparsity in Variational Autoencoders
Victor Prokhorov, Yingzhen Li, Ehsan Shareghi and Nigel Collier

Temporal-aware Language Representation Learning From Crowdsourced Labels
Yang Hao, Xiao Zhai, Wenbiao Ding and Zitao Liu

Structure-aware Sentence Encoder in Bert-Based Siamese Network
Qiwei Peng, David Weir and Julie Weeds

Preserving Cross-Linguality of Pre-trained Models via Continual Learning
Zihan Liu, Genta Indra Winata, Andrea Madotto and Pascale Fung

Text Style Transfer: Leveraging a Style Classifier on Entangled Latent Representations
Xiaoyan Li, Sun Sun and Yunli Wang

Inductively Representing Out-of-Knowledge-Graph Entities by Optimal Estimation Under Translational Assumptions
Damai Dai, Hua Zheng, Fuli Luo, Pengcheng Yang, Tianyu Liu, Zhifang Sui and Baobao Chang

Revisiting Pretraining with Adapters
Seungwon Kim, Alex Shum, Nathan Susanj and Jonathan Hilgart

Knodle: Modular Weakly Supervised Learning with PyTorch
Anastasiia Sedova, Andreas Stephan, Marina Speranskaya and Benjamin Roth

August 6, 2021 (continued)

August 6, 2021 (continued)

Improving Cross-lingual Text Classification with Zero-shot Instance-Weighting

Irene Li[1]*, Prithviraj Sen[2], Huaiyu Zhu[2], Yunyao Li[2], Dragomir Radev[1]
[1]Yale University, USA
{irene.li,dragomir.radev}@yale.edu
[2]IBM Research Almaden, USA
{senp,huaiyu,yunyaoli}@us.ibm.com

Abstract

Cross-lingual text classification (CLTC) is a challenging task made even harder still due to the lack of labeled data in low-resource languages. In this paper, we propose zero-shot instance-weighting, a general model-agnostic zero-shot learning framework for improving CLTC by leveraging source instance weighting. It adds a module on top of pre-trained language models for similarity computation of instance weights, thus aligning each source instance to the target language. During training, the framework utilizes gradient descent that is weighted by instance weights to update parameters. We evaluate this framework over seven target languages on three fundamental tasks and show its effectiveness and extensibility, by improving on F1 score up to 4% in single-source transfer and 8% in multi-source transfer. To the best of our knowledge, our method is the first to apply instance weighting in zero-shot CLTC. It is simple yet effective and easily extensible into multi-source transfer.

1 Introduction

Natural language processing (NLP) has largely benefited from recent advances in deep learning and large-scale labeled data. Unfortunately, such labeled corpora are not available for all languages. Cross-lingual transfer learning is one way to spread the success from high-resource to low-resource languages. Cross-lingual text classification (CLTC) (Prettenhofer and Stein, 2010; Ni et al., 2011) can learn a classifier in a low-resource *target* language by transferring from a resource-rich *source* language (Chen et al., 2018; Esuli et al., 2019).

Previous work has learned a classifier in the target language using a very small sample of labeled target instances or external corpora of unlabeled instances (Wang et al., 2019; Xu and Wan, 2017). In addition, other resources that may be utilized to achieve the same include, but are not limited to, parallel corpora of unlabeled instances in the target language (Xu and Wan, 2017). In this work, we address the most challenging setting, zero-shot CLTC (Arnold et al., 2007; Joachims, 2003), where no resource in the target language is given. Among the many methods for transfer learning that have been successfully employed in NLP (Mogadala and Rettinger, 2016; Zhou et al., 2016; Eriguchi et al., 2018), instance (re-) weighting is perhaps one of the oldest and most well known (Wang et al., 2017, 2019). It is best illustrated when we are given access to a few target labeled instances (few-shot learning). For example, both Dai et al. (2007) and Wang et al. (2019) learn a classifier iteratively by assigning weights to each instance in the source training data. While Dai et al. (2007) assigns weights to both source and target instances, Wang et al. (2019) pre-trains a classifier on the source training data and then re-weights the target labeled instances. Crucially, the weights are set to be a function of the error between the prediction made for the instance by the current classifier and the instance's gold label.

In a few-shot case, it is easy to see the appeal of re-weighting target language instances, since an instance that incurs a higher prediction loss can be given a larger weight, so as to improve the classifier. But in a zero-shot case, it seems impossible to compute instance weights based on prediction loss. In this work, we make it possible to assign such weights on instances in zero-shot CLTC. To the best of our knowledge, this is the first attempt to apply such a method to NLP tasks.

Our contributions are two-fold: First, we introduce **zero-shot instance-weighting**, a simple but effective, and extensible framework to enable instance weighted transfer learning for zero-shot CLTC. Second, we evaluate on three cross-lingual

*Work done as an intern at IBM Research Almaden.

Proceedings of the 6th Workshop on Representation Learning for NLP (RepL4NLP-2021), pages 1–7
Bangkok, Thailand (Online), August 6, 2021.

classification tasks in seven different languages. Results show that it improves F1 score by up to 4% in single-source transfer and 8% in multi-source transfer, identifying a promising direction for utilizing knowledge from unlabeled data.

2 Proposed Method

We illustrate the zero-shot CLTC framework in Figure 1. The source and target language inputs are x_s and x_t respectively, during training, only the source label y_s is available and the task is to predict the target label y_t. We first apply the pre-trained model as an encoder to encode the inputs, the encoded representations are denoted by h_s and h_t. The figure illustrates four instances for each language in the mini-batch. Then there is an *Instance Weighting* module to assign weights to source language instances by considering the hidden representations h_s and h_t. Note that these layers are shared. We train the task layer and fine-tune the pre-trained language model layers.

2.1 Pre-trained Models

We compare two multilingual versions of pre-trained models for the pre-trained models: multilingual BERT (mBERT)[1] (Devlin et al., 2019) and XLM-Roberta (XLMR)[2] (Conneau et al., 2020).

We evaluate on multiple tasks in Section 3, so there are different ways to utilize the pre-trained models. For the sentiment and document classification task, we train a fully-connected layer on top of the output of the `[CLS]` token, which is considered to be the representation of the input sequence. For the opinion target extraction task, we formulate it as sequence labeling task (Agerri and Rigau, 2019; Jebbara and Cimiano, 2019). To extract such opinion target tokens is to classify each token into one of the following: **B**eginning, **I**nside and **O**utside of an aspect. We follow a typical IOB scheme for the task (Toh and Wang, 2014; San Vicente et al., 2015; Álvarez-López et al., 2016). In this case, each token should have a label, so we have a fully-connected layer that is shared for each token. We note that it may be possible to improve all the results even further by employing more powerful task layers and modules such as conditional random fields (Lafferty et al., 2001), but keep things relatively simple since our main goal is to evaluate instance weighting with zero-shot CLTC.

[1] `github.com/google-research/bert/blob/master/multilingual.md`

[2] `huggingface.co/XLMRoberta-base`

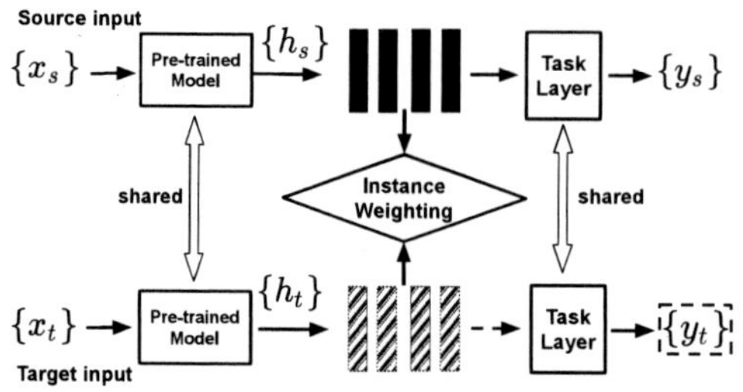

Figure 1: Framework Illustration: we illustrate 4 instances for each domain here.

2.2 Instance Weighting

The intuition behind instance weighting is the following: if the difference between a source instance and the target language is small, then it shares more common features with the target language, so it should make a larger contribution. For each instance in the source language, a large weight indicates a large contribution by the instance during training. Ideally, when deciding an instance weight, we should compare it with *all* instances from the target language. But doing so would incur prohibitively excessive computational resources. We thus approximate in small batches and calculate the weights by comparing how similar the instances are to the target ones within a small batch in each training step.

Instance Weighting-based Gradient Descent Vanilla mini-batch gradient descent is defined as:

$$\theta \leftarrow \theta - \alpha \sum_{i=1}^{k} \nabla_\theta f\left(y_i, g_\theta\left(x_i\right)\right) \quad (1)$$

where α is the learning rate, θ is the parameter that we want to update, $g_\theta(x_i)$ is the model prediction for x_i , ∇_θ is the partial derivative, and $f(\cdot)$ is the loss function.

We modify Equation 1 to include instance weights:

$$\theta \leftarrow \theta - \alpha \sum_{i=1}^{k} w_i \cdot \nabla_\theta f\left(y_i, g_\theta\left(x_i\right)\right) \quad (2)$$

where we assign a weight w_i to each instance within a mini-batch, and there is a weighted summation of the gradients in the mini-batch for all the instances and then update the parameter θ. It can be easily extended to multiple source languages, in this case, x_s may be training samples from more than one languages.

Unsupervised Weighting Metrics In each batch, to obtain weight w_i for each source instance i, we follow a similarity-based approach. We define a scoring function to calculate a score between the current source instance representation h_i and the target instance representation h_j. Then we conduct a summation as the final score for source instance i to the *set* of target instances within this batch D_t. For $i \in D_s$:

$$w_i = score(i, D_t) = \sum_{j \in D_t} score(i, j).$$

We normalize each w_i in this batch to make sure the summation is 1, and they are plugged into Eq. 2.

Multiple ways exist to define a scoring function $score(i, j)$, and a Cosine-Similarity based scoring function is defined as:

$$score(i, j) = \frac{1}{2}(\frac{h_i \cdot h_j}{||h_i|| \, ||h_j||} + 1).$$

We also investigate two other ways for scoring function: Euclidean-Distance based and the CORAL Function (Sun et al., 2016). While Cosine scoring function performs the best, so we report it in our main experiments and ignoring the other two.

3 Evaluation

We test on three tasks: opinion target extraction, document classification, and sentiment classification [3]. English is the source language for all the experiments. We evaluate four settings: 1) direct adaptation with mBERT-base (mBERT), 2) mBERT with Instance Weighting (mBERT+IW), 3) direct adaption of XLMR-base (XLMR), and 4) XLMR with Instance Weighting (XLMR+IW).

Opinion Target Extraction We choose SemEval 2016 Workshop Task 5 (Pontiki et al., 2016) for opinion target extraction. It includes restaurant reviews in five languages[4]: English, Spanish (`es`), Dutch (`nl`), Russian (`ru`) and Turkish (`tr`). Given a sentence as input, one needs to classify each token into one of the three classes according to the IOB scheme. The training and testing size varies from 144 to 3,655. We compare against a list of models. Pontiki et al. (2014) and Kumar et al. (2016) are supervised and require extra corpora or resources to train. Agerri and Rigau exploits additional resources like unlabeled corpora. Jebbara and Cimiano (2019) applies multi-source (including the target) languages to train a classifier using cross-lingual embeddings and evaluates in a zero-shot manner. We summarize the results in Table 1.

Method	es	nl	ru	tr
Pontiki et al. (2014)★	0.520	0.506	0.493	0.419
Kumar et al. (2016)★	0.697	0.644	-	-
Jebbara and Cimiano (2019)	0.687	0.624	0.567	0.490
Agerri and Rigau (2019)★	0.699	0.664	0.655	0.602
mBERT	0.697	0.677	0.652	0.598
mBERT+IW	0.692	0.691	0.671	0.620
XLMR	0.690	0.700	0.664	0.674
XLMR+IW	**0.704**	**0.714**	**0.706**	**0.682**

Table 1: F1 scores on SemEval for Opinion Target Extraction. ★ indicates a supervised or semi-supervised learning method.

Cross-lingual Document Classification We conduct cross-lingual document classification task on the MLDoc dataset (Schwenk and Li, 2018). It is a set of news articles with balanced class priors in eight languages; Each language has 1,000 training documents and 4,000 test documents, and splits into four classes. We select a strong baseline (Schwenk and Li, 2018), which applies pre-trained MultiCCA word embeddings (Ammar et al., 2016) and then trained in a supervised way. Another baseline is a zero-shot method proposed by Artetxe and Schwenk (2019), which applies a single BiLSTM encoder with a shared vocabulary among all languages, and a decoder trained with parallel corpora. Artetxe and Schwenk (2019) apply mBERT as a zero-shot language transfer. Table 2 shows the results of our comparison study.

Sentiment Classification Finally, we evaluate sentiment classification task on Amazon multilingual reviews dataset (Prettenhofer and Stein, 2010). It contains positive and negative reviews from 3 domains, including `DVD`, `Music` and `Books`, in four languages: English (`en`), French (`fr`), German (`de`), and Japanese (`ja`). For each domain, there are 1,000 positive samples and 1,000 negative samples in each language for both training and testing. We choose the following baselines: translation baseline, UMM (Xu and Wan, 2017), CLDFA (Xu and Yang, 2017) and MAN-MoE (Chen et al., 2019). For the translation baseline, we translate the training and testing data for each target language into English using Watson Language Translator[5], and trained on the mBERT model, which is more

[3] We release our code in `https://github.com/IreneZihuiLi/ZSIW/`.

[4] The download script was broken and failed to obtain French data, so we do not report results for French.

[5] `https://www.ibm.com/watson/services/language-translator/`, version `2018-05-01`

Method	en	de	es	fr	it	ja	ru	zh
Schwenk and Li (2018) ★	0.9220	0.8120	0.7250	0.7238	0.6938	0.6763	0.6080	0.7473
Wu and Dredze (2019)	0.9420	0.8020	0.7260	0.7260	0.6890	0.5650	0.7370	0.7690
Artetxe and Schwenk (2019)	0.8993	0.8478	0.7733	0.7795	0.6943	0.6030	0.6778	0.7193
mBERT	0.8981	0.8680	0.7519	0.7492	0.6952	0.7222	0.6797	0.7937
mBERT+IW	-	0.8766	0.7532	0.7527	0.7122	0.7264	0.6949	0.8277
XLMR	**0.9295**	0.9245	0.8462	0.8710	0.7322	0.7824	0.6892	0.8580
XLMR+IW	-	**0.9265**	**0.8612**	**0.8797**	**0.7464**	**0.7942**	**0.7024**	**0.8712**

Table 2: F1 scores on MLDoc for Cross-lingual Document Classification. ★ indicates a supervised or semi-supervised learning method.

Method	Books	DVD	Music
Translation Baseline	0.7993	0.7789	0.7877
UMM★ (Xu and Wan, 2017)	0.7772	0.7803	0.7870
CLDFA★ (Xu and Yang, 2017)	0.8156	0.8207	0.7960
MAN-MoE (Chen et al., 2019)	0.7543	0.7738	0.7688
mBERT	0.7497	0.7378	0.7575
mBERT+IW	0.7573	0.7565	0.7553
XLMR	0.8248	0.8268	**0.8425**
XLMR+IW	**0.8452**	**0.8362**	0.8400

Table 3: F1 scores on Amazon Review for Sentiment Classification group by domains: Each cell shows the average accuracy of the three languages.★ indicates a supervised or semi-supervised learning method.

Method	es	nl	ru	tr
XLMR	0.690	0.700	0.664	0.674
Single-source	0.704	0.714	0.706	0.682
Multi-source	**0.735**	**0.738**	**0.745**	**0.688**

Table 4: Multi-source F1 scores on SemEval for Opinion Target Extraction: transfer from single-source and multi-source using XLMR+IW model.

confident in English[6]. Both UMM and CLDFA utilized more resources or tools like unlabeled corpora or machine translation. MAN-MoE is the only zero-shot baseline method. It applies MUSE (Lample et al., 2018) and VecMap (Artetxe et al., 2017) embeddings. We summarize the results in Table 3 for each domain.

Results Among the three tasks, both base models achieve competitive results for all languages thanks to the choice of pre-trained models. Instance weighting produces consistent improvements over the base models for nearly all target languages. Especially, in Table 1, the best model XLMR+IW beats the best baseline by 4.65% on average, improving from XLMR by 4% on Russian and gaining substantially on the other target languages; in Table 2, XLMR+IW outperforms the baselines, and surpassing XLMR steadily, with impressive gains on Russian, Chinese and Spanish. In Table 3, the best model shows the same trend in most cases. While our approach is model-agnostic, when the base model or the embedding improves, instance weighting will still help, as we can see the improved results obtained by switching from mBERT to XLMR. Again, the framework is simple but effective given these observations. Most importantly, it requires no additional external data and is easily adaptable into any deep models.

[6]`https://github.com/google-research/bert/blob/master/\multilingual.md` explains the pre-training.

4 Discussion

Multi-source Expansion Studies show that multilingual transfer outperforms bilingual transfer (Guo et al., 2018). We run an experiment on the opinion extraction task to illustrate how our approach can be easily extended to enable multi-source transfer, (see Table 5). Here, we take the SemEval dataset, and for each target language, we train on the union of all other available languages. We can observe that by easily expanding into multi-source language training, we get a significant boost across the board in all target languages. Specifically, there is a 8.1% improvement on Russian. With easy adaptation, we show the extensibility and that multilingual transfer in zero-shot learning is a promising direction.

Case Study Intuitively, we should focus on the source instances with a smaller difference with target language, because they contain more common features with the target language. Thus, if we let those instances contribute more, it is possible that the model may perform better on the target language. As an example, Table 5 shows a positively-labeled French review containing adjectives with positive emotions (e.g., "exceptionnel", "superbe") and the instance weights for two English reviews, where the weights are generated using our best model XLMR+IW. Since English instance

Language	Score	Content	Label
English Instance 2	0.5056	...I liked the book. Kaplan has consistently been one of my favorite authors (Atlantic Monthly) His theme is consistent: many nation states are not really nation states... Kaplan had great hope for the future of Iran as they struggle with theocracy...	Pos
English Instance 1	0.3647	One start , for some very acurate dramatic and terrorific facts about the Ebola, but very weak regarding origin of the virus, very unconvincing about possible "theories". sound more like that old music of desinformation, he almost blame another monkey for the Ebola...	Neg
French		**Origin**: ...ce livre est exceptionnel..La construction du livre est superbe, l'écriture magique... **Translation**: ...this book is outstanding..The construction of book is superb, magical writing ...	Pos

Table 5: A positive scenario: score comparison within the same batch.

1 contains adjectives with positive emotions (e.g. "favorite", "great"), it has a higher score than English instance 2 containing adjectives with negative emotions (e.g., "weak", "unconvincing").

5 Conclusion

We proposed instance weighting for CLTC and evaluated on 3 fundamental tasks. The benefits of our approach include simplicity and effectiveness by ensuring wide applicability across NLP tasks, extensibility by involving multiple source languages and effectiveness by outperforming a variety of baselines significantly. In the future, we plan to evaluate on more tasks such as natural language inference (Conneau et al., 2018) and abstract meaning representation (Blloshmi et al., 2020).

References

Rodrigo Agerri and German Rigau. 2019. Language independent sequence labelling for opinion target extraction. *Artificial Intelligence*, 268:85–95.

Tamara Álvarez-López, Jonathan Juncal-Martínez, Milagros Fernández-Gavilanes, Enrique Costa-Montenegro, and Francisco Javier González-Castaño. 2016. GTI at SemEval-2016 task 5: SVM and CRF for aspect detection and unsupervised aspect-based sentiment analysis. In *Proceedings of the 10th International Workshop on Semantic Evaluation (SemEval-2016)*, pages 306–311, San Diego, California. Association for Computational Linguistics.

Waleed Ammar, George Mulcaire, Yulia Tsvetkov, Guillaume Lample, Chris Dyer, and Noah A Smith. 2016. Massively multilingual word embeddings. *arXiv preprint arXiv:1602.01925v2*.

Andrew Arnold, Ramesh Nallapati, and William W Cohen. 2007. A comparative study of methods for transductive transfer learning. In *Proceedings of the Seventh IEEE International Conference on Data Mining Workshops*, pages 77–82.

Mikel Artetxe, Gorka Labaka, and Eneko Agirre. 2017. Learning bilingual word embeddings with (almost) no bilingual data. In *Proceedings of the 55th Annual Meeting of the Association for Computational Linguistics (Volume 1: Long Papers)*, pages 451–462, Vancouver, Canada. Association for Computational Linguistics.

Mikel Artetxe and Holger Schwenk. 2019. Massively multilingual sentence embeddings for zero-shot cross-lingual transfer and beyond. *Transactions of the Association for Computational Linguistics*, 7:597–610.

Rexhina Blloshmi, Rocco Tripodi, and Roberto Navigli. 2020. XL-AMR: Enabling cross-lingual AMR parsing with transfer learning techniques. In *Proceedings of the 2020 Conference on Empirical Methods in Natural Language Processing (EMNLP)*, pages 2487–2500, Online. Association for Computational Linguistics.

Xilun Chen, Ahmed Hassan Awadallah, Hany Hassan, Wei Wang, and Claire Cardie. 2019. Multi-source cross-lingual model transfer: Learning what to share. In *Proceedings of the 57th Annual Meeting of the Association for Computational Linguistics*, pages 3098–3112, Florence, Italy. Association for Computational Linguistics.

Xilun Chen, Yu Sun, Ben Athiwaratkun, Claire Cardie, and Kilian Weinberger. 2018. Adversarial deep averaging networks for cross-lingual sentiment classification. *Transactions of the Association for Computational Linguistics*, 6:557–570.

Alexis Conneau, Kartikay Khandelwal, Naman Goyal, Vishrav Chaudhary, Guillaume Wenzek, Francisco Guzmán, Edouard Grave, Myle Ott, Luke Zettlemoyer, and Veselin Stoyanov. 2020. Unsupervised cross-lingual representation learning at scale. In *Proceedings of the 58th Annual Meeting of the Association for Computational Linguistics*, pages 8440–8451, Online. Association for Computational Linguistics.

Alexis Conneau, Ruty Rinott, Guillaume Lample, Adina Williams, Samuel Bowman, Holger Schwenk, and Veselin Stoyanov. 2018. XNLI: Evaluating cross-lingual sentence representations. In *Proceedings of the 2018 Conference on Empirical Methods in Natural Language Processing*, pages 2475–2485, Brussels, Belgium. Association for Computational Linguistics.

Wenyuan Dai, Qiang Yang, Gui-Rong Xue, and Yong Yu. 2007. Boosting for transfer learning. In *Machine Learning, Proceedings of the Twenty-Fourth International Conference (ICML 2007), Corvallis, Oregon, USA, June 20-24, 2007*, volume 227 of *ACM International Conference Proceeding Series*, pages 193–200. ACM.

Jacob Devlin, Ming-Wei Chang, Kenton Lee, and Kristina Toutanova. 2019. BERT: Pre-training of deep bidirectional transformers for language understanding. In *Proceedings of the 2019 Conference of the North American Chapter of the Association for Computational Linguistics: Human Language Technologies, Volume 1 (Long and Short Papers)*, pages 4171–4186, Minneapolis, Minnesota. Association for Computational Linguistics.

Akiko Eriguchi, Melvin Johnson, Orhan Firat, Hideto Kazawa, and Wolfgang Macherey. 2018. Zero-shot cross-lingual classification using multilingual neural machine translation. *arXiv preprint arXiv:1809.04686v1*.

Andrea Esuli, Alejandro Moreo, and Fabrizio Sebastiani. 2019. Funnelling: A new ensemble method for heterogeneous transfer learning and its application to cross-lingual text classification. *ACM Transactions on Information Systems (TOIS)*, 37(3):37.

Jiang Guo, Darsh Shah, and Regina Barzilay. 2018. Multi-source domain adaptation with mixture of experts. In *Proceedings of the 2018 Conference on Empirical Methods in Natural Language Processing*, pages 4694–4703, Brussels, Belgium. Association for Computational Linguistics.

Soufian Jebbara and Philipp Cimiano. 2019. Zero-shot cross-lingual opinion target extraction. In *Proceedings of the 2019 Conference of the North American Chapter of the Association for Computational Linguistics: Human Language Technologies, Volume 1 (Long and Short Papers)*, pages 2486–2495, Minneapolis, Minnesota. Association for Computational Linguistics.

Thorsten Joachims. 2003. Transductive learning via spectral graph partitioning. In *Machine Learning, Proceedings of the Twentieth International Conference (ICML 2003), August 21-24, 2003, Washington, DC, USA*, pages 290–297. AAAI Press.

Ayush Kumar, Sarah Kohail, Amit Kumar, Asif Ekbal, and Chris Biemann. 2016. IIT-TUDA at SemEval-2016 task 5: Beyond sentiment lexicon: Combining domain dependency and distributional semantics features for aspect based sentiment analysis. In *Proceedings of the 10th International Workshop on Semantic Evaluation (SemEval-2016)*, pages 1129–1135, San Diego, California. Association for Computational Linguistics.

John D. Lafferty, Andrew McCallum, and Fernando C. N. Pereira. 2001. Conditional random fields: Probabilistic models for segmenting and labeling sequence data. In *Proceedings of the Eighteenth International Conference on Machine Learning (ICML 2001), Williams College, Williamstown, MA, USA, June 28 - July 1, 2001*, pages 282–289. Morgan Kaufmann.

Guillaume Lample, Myle Ott, Alexis Conneau, Ludovic Denoyer, and Marc'Aurelio Ranzato. 2018. Phrase-based & neural unsupervised machine translation. In *Proceedings of the 2018 Conference on Empirical Methods in Natural Language Processing*, pages 5039–5049, Brussels, Belgium. Association for Computational Linguistics.

Aditya Mogadala and Achim Rettinger. 2016. Bilingual word embeddings from parallel and non-parallel corpora for cross-language text classification. In *Proceedings of the 2016 Conference of the North American Chapter of the Association for Computational Linguistics: Human Language Technologies*, pages 692–702, San Diego, California. Association for Computational Linguistics.

Xiaochuan Ni, Jian-Tao Sun, Jian Hu, and Zheng Chen. 2011. Cross lingual text classification by mining multilingual topics from wikipedia. In *Proceedings of the Forth International Conference on Web Search and Web Data Mining, WSDM 2011, Hong Kong, China, February 9-12, 2011*, pages 375–384. ACM.

Maria Pontiki, Dimitris Galanis, Haris Papageorgiou, Ion Androutsopoulos, Suresh Manandhar, Mohammad AL-Smadi, Mahmoud Al-Ayyoub, Yanyan Zhao, Bing Qin, Orphée De Clercq, Véronique Hoste, Marianna Apidianaki, Xavier Tannier, Natalia Loukachevitch, Evgeniy Kotelnikov, Nuria Bel, Salud María Jiménez-Zafra, and Gülşen Eryiğit. 2016. SemEval-2016 task 5: Aspect based sentiment analysis. In *Proceedings of the 10th International Workshop on Semantic Evaluation (SemEval-2016)*, pages 19–30, San Diego, California. Association for Computational Linguistics.

Maria Pontiki, Dimitris Galanis, John Pavlopoulos, Harris Papageorgiou, Ion Androutsopoulos, and Suresh Manandhar. 2014. SemEval-2014 task 4: Aspect based sentiment analysis. In *Proceedings of the 8th International Workshop on Semantic Evaluation (SemEval 2014)*, pages 27–35, Dublin, Ireland. Association for Computational Linguistics.

Peter Prettenhofer and Benno Stein. 2010. Cross-language text classification using structural correspondence learning. In *Proceedings of the 48th Annual Meeting of the Association for Computational Linguistics*, pages 1118–1127, Uppsala, Sweden. Association for Computational Linguistics.

Iñaki San Vicente, Xabier Saralegi, and Rodrigo Agerri. 2015. EliXa: A modular and flexible ABSA platform. In *Proceedings of the 9th International Workshop on Semantic Evaluation (SemEval 2015)*, pages 748–752, Denver, Colorado. Association for Computational Linguistics.

Holger Schwenk and Xian Li. 2018. A corpus for multilingual document classification in eight languages. In *Proceedings of the Eleventh International Conference on Language Resources and Evaluation (LREC 2018)*, Miyazaki, Japan. European Language Resources Association (ELRA).

Baochen Sun, Jiashi Feng, and Kate Saenko. 2016. Return of frustratingly easy domain adaptation. In *Proceedings of the Thirtieth AAAI Conference on Artificial Intelligence, February 12-17, 2016, Phoenix, Arizona, USA*, pages 2058–2065. AAAI Press.

Zhiqiang Toh and Wenting Wang. 2014. DLIREC: Aspect term extraction and term polarity classification system. In *Proceedings of the 8th International Workshop on Semantic Evaluation (SemEval 2014)*, pages 235–240, Dublin, Ireland. Association for Computational Linguistics.

Rui Wang, Masao Utiyama, Lemao Liu, Kehai Chen, and Eiichiro Sumita. 2017. Instance weighting for neural machine translation domain adaptation. In *Proceedings of the 2017 Conference on Empirical Methods in Natural Language Processing*, pages 1482–1488, Copenhagen, Denmark. Association for Computational Linguistics.

Zhi Wang, Wei Bi, Yan Wang, and Xiaojiang Liu. 2019. Better fine-tuning via instance weighting for text classification. In *Proceedings of the AAAI Conference on Artificial Intelligence*, volume 33, pages 7241–7248.

Shijie Wu and Mark Dredze. 2019. Beto, bentz, becas: The surprising cross-lingual effectiveness of BERT. In *Proceedings of the 2019 Conference on Empirical Methods in Natural Language Processing and the 9th International Joint Conference on Natural Language Processing (EMNLP-IJCNLP)*, pages 833–844, Hong Kong, China. Association for Computational Linguistics.

Kui Xu and Xiaojun Wan. 2017. Towards a universal sentiment classifier in multiple languages. In *Proceedings of the 2017 Conference on Empirical Methods in Natural Language Processing*, pages 511–520, Copenhagen, Denmark. Association for Computational Linguistics.

Ruochen Xu and Yiming Yang. 2017. Cross-lingual distillation for text classification. In *Proceedings of the 55th Annual Meeting of the Association for Computational Linguistics (Volume 1: Long Papers)*, pages 1415–1425, Vancouver, Canada. Association for Computational Linguistics.

Guangyou Zhou, Zhao Zeng, Jimmy Xiangji Huang, and Tingting He. 2016. Transfer learning for cross-lingual sentiment classification with weakly shared deep neural networks. In *Proceedings of the 39th International ACM SIGIR conference on Research and Development in Information Retrieval*, pages 245–254.

Probing Multilingual Language Models for Discourse

Murathan Kurfalı
Linguistics Department
Stockholm University
Stockholm, Sweden
murathan.kurfali@ling.su.se

Robert Östling
Linguistics Department
Stockholm University
Stockholm, Sweden
robert@ling.su.se

Abstract

Pre-trained multilingual language models have become an important building block in multilingual natural language processing. In the present paper, we investigate a range of such models to find out how well they transfer discourse-level knowledge across languages. This is done with a systematic evaluation on a broader set of discourse-level tasks than has been previously been assembled. We find that the XLM-RoBERTa family of models consistently show the best performance, by simultaneously being good monolingual models and degrading relatively little in a zero-shot setting. Our results also indicate that model distillation may hurt the ability of cross-lingual transfer of sentence representations, while language dissimilarity at most has a modest effect. We hope that our test suite, covering 5 tasks with a total of 22 languages in 10 distinct families, will serve as a useful evaluation platform for multilingual performance at and beyond the sentence level.

1 Introduction

Large-scale pre-trained neural language models have become immensely popular in the natural language processing (NLP) community in recent years (Devlin et al., 2019; Peters et al., 2018). When used as contextual sentence encoders, these models have led to remarkable improvements in performance for a wide range of downstream tasks (Qiu et al., 2020). In addition, multilingual versions of these models (Devlin et al., 2019; Conneau and Lample, 2019) have been successful in transferring knowledge across languages by providing language-independent sentence encodings.

The general usefulness of pre-trained language models has been convincingly demonstrated thanks to persistent creation and application of evaluation datasets by the NLP community. Discourse-level analysis is particularly interesting to study, given that many of the currently available models are trained with relatively short contexts such as pairs of adjacent sentences.

Wang et al. (2019) use a diverse set of natural language understanding (NLU) tasks to investigate the generality of the sentence representations produced by different language models. Hu et al. (2020) use a broader set of tasks from across the NLP field to investigate the ability of multilingual models to transfer various types of knowledge across language boundaries.

Our goal in this paper is to systematically evaluate the multilingual performance on NLU tasks, particularly at the discourse level. This combines two of the most challenging aspects of representation learning: multilinguality and discourse-level analysis. A few datasets have been used for this purpose before, most prominently the XNLI evaluation set (Conneau et al., 2018) for Natural Language Inference (NLI), and recently also XQuAD (Artetxe et al., 2020) and MLQA (Lewis et al., 2020) for Question Answering (QA). We substantially increase the breadth of our evaluation by adding three additional tasks:

1. Penn Discourse TreeBank (PDTB)-style implicit discourse relation classification on annotated TED talk subtitles in seven languages (Section 3.1.1)

2. Rhetorical Structure Theory (RST)-style discourse relation classification with a custom set consisting of treebanks in six non-English languages (Section 3.1.2)

3. Stance detection with a custom dataset in five languages (Section 3.1.3)

We investigate the cross-lingual generalization capabilities of seven multilingual sentence encoders with considerably varying model sizes

Proceedings of the 6th Workshop on Representation Learning for NLP (RepL4NLP-2021), pages 8–19
Bangkok, Thailand (Online), August 6, 2021.

through their cross-lingual zero-shot performance[1] which, in this context, refers to the evaluation scheme where sentence encoders are tested on the languages that they are not exposed to during training. The complied test suite consists of five tasks, covering 22 different languages in total.

We specifically focus on zero-shot transfer scenario where a sufficient amount of annotated data to fine-tune a pre-trained language model is assumed to be available only for one language. We believe that this is the most realistic scenario for a great number of languages; therefore, zero-shot performance is the most direct way of assessing cross-lingual usefulness in a large scale.

Our contributions are as follows: (i) we provide a detailed analysis of a wide range of sentence encoders on large number of probing tasks, several of which have not previously been used with multilingual sentence encoders despite their relevancy, (ii) we provide suitably pre-processed versions of these datasets to be used as a multilingual benchmark for future work with strong baselines provided by our evaluation, (iii) we show that the zero-shot performance on discourse level tasks are not correlated with any kind of language similarity and hard to predict, (iv) we show that knowledge distillation may selectively destroy multilingual transfer ability in a way that harms zero-shot transfer, but is not visible during evaluations where the models are trained and evaluated with the same language.

2 Background

The standard way of training a multilingual language model is through a large non-parallel multilingual corpora, e.g. Wikipedia articles, where the models are not provided with any explicit mapping across languages which renders cross-lingual performance of such models puzzling. Pires et al. (2019) and Wu and Dredze (2019) are the earliest studies to explore that puzzle by trying to uncover the factors that give multilingual BERT (henceforth, mBERT) its cross-lingual capabilities. Pires et al. (2019) perform a number of probing tasks and hypothesize that the shared sentence pieces across languages gives mBERT its generalization ability by forcing other pieces to be mapped into the same space. Similarly, Wu and Dredze (2019) evaluate the performance of mBERT in five tasks and report that while mBERT shows a strong zero-shot performance, it also retains language-specific information in each layer.

Chen et al. (2019a) proposes a benchmark to evaluate sentence encoders specifically on discourse level tasks. The proposed benchmark consists of discourse relation classification and a number of custom tasks such as finding the correct position of a randomly moved sentence in a paragraph or determining if a given paragraph is coherent or not. The benchmark is confined to English, hence, only targets monolingual English models.

Two very recent studies, XTREME (Hu et al., 2020) and XGLUE (Liang et al., 2020), constitute the first studies on the cross-lingual generalization abilities of pre-trained language models via their zero-shot performance. The tasks in both studies largely overlap, where XTREME serves as cross-lingual benchmark consisting of well-known datasets, e.g. XNLI, XQuAD. On the other hand, while covering the most of XTREME tasks[2], XGLUE offers new datasets which either focus on the relation between a pair of inputs, such as web page–query matching, or on text generation via question/news title generation. In addition to the mBERT and certain XLM and XLM-R versions, XTREME includes MMTE (Arivazhagan et al., 2019) whereas XGLUE evaluates Unicoder (Huang et al., 2019) among its baselines.

3 Cross-lingual Discourse-level Evaluation

In discourse research, sentences/clauses are not understood in isolation but in relation to one another. The semantic interactions between these units are usually regarded as the backbone of coherence in various prominent discourse theories including that underlying the Penn Discourse TreeBank (PDTB) (Prasad et al., 2007), and Rhetorical Structure Theory (RST) (Mann and Thompson, 1988) used in the RST Discourse Treebank (Carlson and Marcu, 2001). Modelling such interactions requires an understanding that is beyond sentence-level and, from this point-of-view, determining any kind of relation between sentences/clauses can be associated with discourse.

Although paraphrase detection or natural language inference may not strike as discourse-level tasks at first glance, they both deal with semantic

[1]In the remainder of the paper, *cross-lingual zero-shot performance* is simply referred as *zero-shot performance* for brevity. Similarly, source language performance denotes the performance of the respective model on the test set of the training language.

[2]Except parallel sentence retrieval tasks.

relations between sentences. Tonelli and Cabrio (2012) show that textual entailment is, in fact, a subclass of *Restatement* relations of the PDTB framework whereas Nie et al. (2019) report an increase in discourse relation classification accuracy when NLI is used as the intermediate fine-tuning task. In a similar vein, a stance against a judgement, *Favor* or *Against*, can be seen as *CONTINGENCY: Cause: reason* and *COMPARISON: Contrast* in PDTB; *Explanation* and *Antithesis* in RST, respectively.

Therefore, these NLU tasks can be seen as special subsets of discourse relation classification; only a model with a good understanding beyond individual sentences can be expected to solve these tasks. Finally, since question answering requires an understanding on discourse level in order to be solved, so we also believe classifying this as a discourse-level task should be uncontroversial.

3.1 Tasks & Datasets

In this section, we present our task suite and the datasets used for training and zero-shot evaluation. For the sake of clarity, we name each task after the dataset used for training.

3.1.1 Implicit Discourse Relation Classification (PDTB)

Implicit discourse relations hold between adjacent sentence pairs but are not explicitly signaled with a connective such as *because, however*. Implicit discourse relation classification is the task of determining the sense conveyed by these adjacent sentences, which can be easily inferred by readers. Classifying implicit relations constitutes the most challenging step of shallow discourse parsing (Xue et al., 2016).

The training is performed on PDTB3 (Webber et al., 2016) where sections 2–20, 0–1 are used for training and development respectively. The zero-shot evaluation is performed on the TED-MDB corpus (Zeyrek et al., 2019)[3], which is a PDTB-style annotated parallel corpus consisting of 6 TED talk transcripts, and the recent Chinese annotation effort on TED talk transcripts that however are mostly not parallel to TED-MDB (Long et al., 2020). Due to the small size of the test sets, we confine ourselves to the top-level senses: *Contingency, Comparison, Expansion, Temporal* which is also the most common setting for this task. Despite the limited size of TED-MDB, zero-shot transfer is possible and yields meaningful results as shown in (Kurfalı and Östling, 2019). In total, seven languages are evaluated in this task: English, German, Lithuanian[4], Portuguese, Polish, Russian and Chinese.

3.1.2 Rhetorical Relation Classification (RST)

Rhetorical relations are just another name for discourse relations but this term is most commonly associated with Rhetorical Structure Theory (RST) (Mann and Thompson, 1988). Similar to PDTB's discourse relations, rhetorical relations also denote links between discourse units, but are considerably different from the former. The difference largely stems from the take of the respective theories on the structure of the discourse. RST conceives discourse as one connected tree-shaped structure assuming hierarchical relations among the discourse relations. On the other hand, PDTB does not make any claims regarding the structure of the discourse and annotates discourse relations only in a local context (i.e. adjacent clauses/sentences) without assuming any relation on higher levels. Hence, evaluation on RST and PDTB relations can be seen as complementary to each other as the former focuses on both global and local discourse structure whereas PDTB focuses only on local structure.

We use English RST-DT (Carlson and Marcu, 2001) for training where a randomly selected 35 documents are reserved for development. However, unlike PDTB, there is not any compact parallel RST corpus; RST annotations across languages usually differ from each other in several ways. Therefore, we follow Braud et al. (2017) and create a custom multilingual corpus for the zero-shot experiments which consists of the following languages: Basque (Iruskieta et al., 2013), Brazilian Portuguese (Cardoso et al., 2011; Collovini et al., 2007; Pardo and Seno, 2005), Chinese (Cao et al., 2018), German (Stede, 2004), Spanish (Da Cunha et al., 2011), Russian (Pisarevskaya et al., 2017). We perform a normalization step on each treebank which includes binarization of non-binary trees and mapping all relations to 18 coarse grained classes described in (Carlson and Marcu, 2001). The normalization step is performed via the pre-processing scripts of (Braud et al., 2017). Due to memory constraints, we limit the sequence lengths to 384. Hence, we only keep those relations where the first discourse unit is shorter than 150 words so that both units can

[3]https://github.com/MurathanKurfali/Ted-MDB-Annotation

[4]Lithuanian is the latest addition to the Ted-MDB corpus, as documented in (Oleskeviciene et al., 2018).

be equally represented which lead to omission of only 5% of all non-English relations.

3.1.3 Stance Detection (X-Stance)

The stance detection is task of determining the attitude expressed in a text towards a target claim. For experiments, we mainly use the X-stance corpus which consists of 60K answers to 150 questions concerning politics in German, Italian and French (Vamvas and Sennrich, 2020). Unlike other tasks, we select German as the training language for stance detection as it is the largest language in X-Stance. Following the official split, we use the German instances in the training and development sets during fine-tuning and non-German instances in the test set for evaluation. Furthermore, we enrich the scope of our zero-shot evaluation by two additional dataset, one in English (Chen et al., 2019b) and other one in Chinese (Yuan et al., 2019), which also consist of stance annotated claim–answer pairs, despite in different domains.

3.1.4 Natural Language Inference (XNLI)

Natural language inference (NLI) is the task of determining whether a premise sentence entails, contradicts or is neutral to a hypothesis sentence. MultiNLI and the mismatched part of the development data (Williams et al., 2018) are used for training and validation, respectively. The evaluation is performed on the test sets of the XNLI (Conneau et al., 2018) corpus which covers the following 14 languages in addition to English: French, Spanish, German, Greek, Bulgarian, Russian, Turkish, Arabic, Vietnamese, Thai, Chinese, Hindi, Swahili and Urdu.

3.1.5 Question Answering (XQuAD)

Question answering is the task of identifying span in a paragraph which answers to a question. We use the SQuAD v1.1 (Rajpurkar et al., 2016) for training. We evaluate the models on the popular XQuAD dataset which contains the translation of SQuAD v1.1 development set into ten languages (Artetxe et al., 2020): Spanish, German, Greek, Russian, Turkish, Arabic, Vietnamese, Thai, Chinese, and Hindi.

3.2 Languages

The proposed task suite covers the following 22 languages representing 10 language families: Indo-European (Bulgarian *bg*, German *de*, Greek *el*, English *en*, Spanish *es*, French *fr*, Hindi *hi*, Italian *it*, Lithuanian *lt*, Polish *pl*, Portuguese *pt*, Russian *ru*, Urdu *ur*), Afroasiatic (Arabic *ar*), Basque (*eu*), Japonic (Japanese *ja*), Koreanic (Korean *ko*), Niger-Congo (Swahili *sw*), Tai-Kadai (Thai *th*), Turkic (Turkish *tr*), Austroasiatic (Vietnamese *vi*), Sino-Tibetan (Chinese *zh*). Seven of these languages are evaluated in at least three different tasks.

4 Experiments

We evaluate a wide range of multilingual sentence encoders which learn contextual representations. The evaluated models represent a broad spectrum of model sizes, in order to allow practitioners to estimate the trade-off between model size and accuracy.

4.1 Sentence Encoders

The sentence encoders evaluated in the current paper are described in detailed below, and their characteristics summarized in Table 2.

Multilingual BERT (mBERT): mBERT is a transformer-based language model trained with masked language modelling and next sentence prediction objectives similar to the original English BERT model (Devlin et al., 2019)[5]. mBERT is pretrained on the Wikipedias of 104 languages with a shared word piece vocabulary. As discussed in Section 2, its input is not marked with any language-specific signal and mBERT does not have any objective to encode different languages in the same space.

distilmBERT: distilmBERT is a compressed version of mBERT obtained via model distillation (Sanh et al., 2019). Model distillation is a compression technique where a smaller model, called *student*, learns to mimic the behavior of the larger model, called *teacher*, by matching its output distribution. distilmBERT is claimed to reach 92% of mBERT's performance on XNLI while being two times faster and 25% smaller.[6] However, to the best of our knowledge, there is not any comprehensive analysis of distilmBERT's zero-shot performance.

XLM: XLM is a transformer-based language model aimed at extending BERT to cross-lingual setting (Conneau and Lample, 2019). To this end,

[5] https://github.com/google-research/bert/blob/master/multilingual.md

[6] https://github.com/huggingface/transformers/tree/master/examples/distillation

Task	Training data	$|train|$	$|test|$	#langs	metric
RST	RST DT	17K	603 – 6,902	6	acc
PDTB	PDTB3	17K	194 – 1,366	7	F_1
X-stance	X-stance-DE	33K	1,446 – 6,153	4	F_1
NLI	MultiNLI	433K	5,010	14	acc
Q/A	Squad 1.1	100K	1,190	11	ex. match/F_1

Table 1: Summary of the datasets used in experiments. "Corpus name-(lang.code)" refers to the part of the corpus belonging to the respective language. #langs refers to the number of *zero-shot* languages, excluding the training language.

XLM increases the shared vocabulary across languages via shared byte pair encoding (BPE) vocabulary. Moreover, unlike BERT, the input sentences are accompanied by language embeddings. There are several different XLM models which differ at either number of training languages or training objectives. In the current study, we consider the following three:

- *XLM-mlm*: The XLM model which is trained with BERT's masked language model (MLM) objective on the Wikipedias of the 15 XNLI languages.
- *XLM-tlm*: In addition to the MLM, this XLM model has a novel training objective which is called Translation Language Model (TLM). In TLM, the model receives a pair of translationally equivalent sentences and tries to predict the masked word by attending both sentences. Hence, the model tries to predict the masked word by looking at its context in another language which encourages representations of different languages to be aligned. TLM is shown to lead a significant increase on XNLI (Conneau and Lample, 2019). XLM-tlm is also trained for 15 XNLI languages but only on parallel data.
- *XLM-100*: This version is trained, like mBERT, on Wikipedia data covering 100 languages using only an MLM objective. Unlike previous XLM models, this version does not utilize language embeddings.

XLM-RoBERTa (XLM-R): XLM-RoBERTa is not an XLM model, in spite of what its name suggests. XLM-R does not use language embeddings, applies sentence-piece tokenization instead of BPE and is not trained on a parallel corpus unlike the XLM-tlm. Instead, it is a RoBERTa model (Liu et al., 2019), which is an optimized version of BERT, trained on 2.5 TB of cleaned CommonCrawl data covering 100 languages (Conneau et al., 2020). There are two released XLM-R models, XLM-R_{base} and XLM-R_{large}, named after the BERT-architecture they are based on. Compared to original multilingual-BERT, XLM-RoBERTa models have a considerably larger vocabulary size which results in larger models.

4.2 Experimental Setup

A summary of the datasets used in the experiments is provided in Table 1. Except PDTB, all datasets are publicly available. As stated earlier, the training language is English for all tasks except stance detection where German is preferred due the size of the available data. In the spirit of real zero-shot transfer, the validation sets only consist of instances in the training language; hence, no cross-lingual information whatsoever is utilized during training/model selection. For the evaluation metrics, we stick to the default metrics of each task (Table 1).

We set the sequence length to 384 for question answering and RST relation classification; to 250 for stance detection and to 128 for the remaining tasks. At evaluation time, we keep the same configuration. For all models, adam epsilon is set to 1e-8 and maximum gradient norm to 1.0. The learning rate of 2×10^{-5} is used for all the models except XLM-R-large and XLM-100 where it is set to 5×10^{-6}. We adopt the standard fine-tuning approach and fine-tune all models for 4 epochs. We do not apply any early stopping and use the model with the best validation performance during zero-shot experiments. All tasks are implemented using Huggingface's Transformers library (Wolf et al., 2019). As fine-tuning procedure is known to show high variance on small training datasets, all models are run for 4 times with different seeds and the average performance is reported. For XLM and XLM-tlm models, we fall back to English lan-

Model	Langs	Parameter count	Vocab. size	# of layers
distilmBERT	104	134M	30K	6
mBERT	104	177M	30K	12
XLM-mlm	15	250M	95K	12
XLM-tlm	15	250M	95K	12
XLM-100	100	570M	200K	16
XLM-R$_{base}$	100	270M	250K	12
XLM-R$_{large}$	100	550M	250K	24

Table 2: The characteristics of the sentence encoders evaluated in the experiments

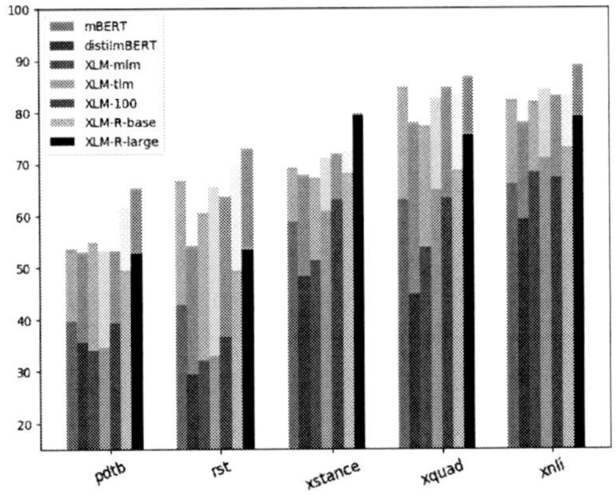

Figure 1: Overview of performance of each sentence encoder on all Disco-X tasks. The semi-transparent bars represent source language performance (German for X-stance, English for the rest) while the solid bars represent the zero-shot performance, i.e. the mean performance across all languages *except* the training language. All values are averages over independent training runs.

guage embeddings for non-XNLI languages. All experiments are run on a single TITAN X (12 GB) GPU.

5 Results and Discussion

We provide an overview of the main results in Figure 1. The detailed results with per-language breakdown are provided in the Appendix A.

Overall, there is a clear difference between the training and zero-shot performance of all models. When averaged over all tasks, the performance loss in zero-shot transfer ranges from 15.58% (XLM-R-large) to 34.96% (distilmBERT) which clearly highlights the room for improvement, especially with smaller model sizes. In the rest of the section, we discuss the results in terms of the encoder type, task and the languages.

Model-wise analysis The ranking of the encoders displays relatively little variation across tasks, with XLM-R$_{large}$ exhibiting the best zero-shot performance across all tasks by outperforming the second best model (XLM-R$_{base}$) by 5.98%. distillmBERT, on the other hand, fails to match the performance of other encoders.[7]

The Translation Language Model (TLM) objective is proved to be a better training objective than MLM by consistently outperforming the vanilla XLM in all tasks. XLM-tlm outperforms XLM-100 on XNLI languages as well which is possibly because of the 'curse of multilinguality' (Conneau et al., 2020), the degradation of the overall performance in proportion to the number of languages in the training. However, training setting (e.g. training data, hyperparameters) outplays the 'curse of multilinguality' as XLM-R$_{base}$ clearly outperforms XLM-tlm even on XNLI languages. It would be interesting to see how an XLM-R trained with TLM objective on small set of languages, e.g. XNLI languages, would perform.

DistillmBERT is the lightest model evaluated in the current investigation. It is shown to retain 92% of the mBERT's performance on certain XNLI languages.[8] The results suggest that distillmBERT delivers its promise, although to a lesser extent. When averaged over all tasks, distillmBERT retains 93% of the source language performance of mBERT. However, its relative performance significantly drops to 82% on zero-shot transfer. That is, distillmBERT is not as successful when it comes to copying mBERT's cross-lingual abilities. Furthermore, its performance (relative to mBERT) is not stable across tasks either. It only achieves 69% of

[7]The only exception is the XLM and XLM-tlm's performance on non-XNLI languages where distillmBERT manages to outperform them but not always by a large margin.

[8]https://github.com/huggingface/transformers/tree/master/examples/distillation

mBERT's zero-shot performance on RST whereas 89% on XNLI. The low memory requirement and its speed (with the same batch size, it is x2 faster than mBERT and x5 than XLM-R$_{large}$) definitely makes distillmBERT a favorable option; however, the results show that its zero-shot performance is considerably lower than its source language performance and is highly task-dependent, hence, hard to predict.

Task-wise Analysis Table 3 shows to what extent encoders manage to transfer their source language performance to zero-shot languages. Overall, the zero-shot performances show high variance across tasks which is quite interesting given that all tasks are on the same linguistic level. It is also surprising that mBERT manages a better zero-shot transfer performance than all XLM models while being almost as consistent as XLM-R$_{base}$.

Overall, the results show that even modern sentence encoders struggle to capture inter-sentential interactions in both monolingual and multilingual settings, contrary to the what the high performances on well-known datasets (e.g. PAWS (Hu et al., 2020)) may suggest. We believe that this finding supports our motivation to propose new probing tasks to have a fuller picture of the capabilities of these encoders.

Language-wise Analysis: In all tasks, regardless of the model, training-language performance is better than even the best zero-shot performance. The only exception is the XLM-R-large's performance on the X-stance where the zero-shot performance is on par with its performance on the German test set.

An important aspect of cross-lingual research is predictability. The zero-shot performance of a certain language do not seem to be stable across tasks (e.g. German is the language with the worst RST performance; yet it is one of the best in XNLI). We further investigate this following Lauscher et al. (2020), who report high correlation between syntactic similarity and zero-shot performance for low-level tasks, POS-tagging and dependency parsing. We conduct the same correlation analysis using Lang2Vec (Littell et al., 2017). However, syntactic and geographical similarity only weakly correlates with zero-shot performances across the tasks (Pearson's $r = .46$ and Spearman's $r = .53$ on average for syntactic; Pearson's $r = .30$ and Spearman's $r = .45$ for geographical similarity). Such low correlations are important as it further supports the claim that the tasks are beyond the sentence level and also highlights a need for further research to reveal the factors at play during zero-shot transfer of discourse-level tasks.

6 Conclusion

As pre-trained multilingual sentence encoders have become prevalent in natural language processing, research on cross-lingual zero-shot transfer gains increasing importance (Hu et al., 2020; Liang et al., 2020). In this work, we evaluate a wide range of sentence encoders on a variety of discourse-level tasks in a zero-shot transfer setting. Firstly, we enrich the set of available probing tasks by introducing three resources which have not been utilized in this context before. We systematically evaluate a broad range of widely used sentence encoders with considerably varying sizes, an analysis which has not been made before.

The main variable we look at is the performance gap between training-language evaluation and zero-shot evaluation. Unsurprisingly, nearly always there is such a gap, but its magnitude depends on a number of factors:

- **Distillation**: the distilled mBERT model has a larger gap than the full mBERT model, indicating loss of multilingual transfer ability during distillation.
- **Language similarity**: the gap correlates only weakly with measures of language similarity (syntactic and geographical), indicating that sentence encoders generally transfer discourse-level information about as well between similar and dissimilar languages.
- **High variance**: apart from the above, we also observe a generally high variance in the gap magnitude between different tasks in our benchmark suite.

These observation provide several starting points for future work: investigating why knowledge distillation seems to hurt zero-shot performance to a much greater extent than same-language sentence encoding ability and what can be done to solve this problem, and explaining the large variations in the zero-shot transfer gap between different discourse-level NLP tasks.

Model	PDTB	RST	X-stance	XQuAD	MNLI	Average ± std
mBERT	74.49	64.18	84.75	74.22	80.28	75.58 ± 6.92
distilmBERT	66.13	54.37	71.34	57.35	75.9	65.02 ± 8.15
XLM-mlm	60.32	52.93	76.4	69.68	83.47	68.56 ± 10.93
XLM-tlm	63.49	50.36	85.57	78.76	84.26	72.49 ± 13.56
XLM-100	73.76	57.54	87.62	74.89	81.01	74.96 ± 10.02
XLM-R_{base}	78.96	70.75	94.29	82.44	88.1	82.91 ± 8.00
XLM-R_{large}	79.91	73.33	100.4	86.81	89	85.89 ± 9.11

Table 3: Relative zero-shot performance of each encoder to the source language performance (metrics differ between tasks but higher is better in all cases). The figures shows what percentage of the source language performance is retained through zero-shot transfer in each task. Hu et al. (2020) refer to this as the *cross-lingual transfer gap*. A score above 100 indicates that a better zero-shot performance than that of training.

References

Naveen Arivazhagan, Ankur Bapna, Orhan Firat, Dmitry Lepikhin, Melvin Johnson, Maxim Krikun, Mia Xu Chen, Yuan Cao, George Foster, Colin Cherry, et al. 2019. Massively multilingual neural machine translation in the wild: Findings and challenges. *arXiv preprint arXiv:1907.05019*.

Mikel Artetxe, Sebastian Ruder, and Dani Yogatama. 2020. On the cross-lingual transferability of monolingual representations. In *Proceedings of the 58th Annual Meeting of the Association for Computational Linguistics*, pages 4623–4637, Online. Association for Computational Linguistics.

Chloé Braud, Maximin Coavoux, and Anders Søgaard. 2017. Cross-lingual RST discourse parsing. In *Proceedings of the 15th Conference of the European Chapter of the Association for Computational Linguistics: Volume 1, Long Papers*, pages 292–304, Valencia, Spain. Association for Computational Linguistics.

Shuyuan Cao, Iria da Cunha, and Mikel Iruskieta. 2018. The rst spanish-chinese treebank. In *Proceedings of the Joint Workshop on Linguistic Annotation, Multiword Expressions and Constructions (LAW-MWE-CxG-2018)*, pages 156–166.

Paula CF Cardoso, Erick G Maziero, Maria LC Jorge, Eloize MR Seno, Ariani Di Felippo, Lucia HM Rino, Maria das Gracas Volpe Nunes, and Thiago AS Pardo. 2011. Cstnews-a discourse-annotated corpus for single and multi-document summarization of news texts in brazilian portuguese. In *Proceedings of the 3rd RST Brazilian Meeting*, pages 88–105.

Lynn Carlson and Daniel Marcu. 2001. Discourse tagging reference manual. *ISI Technical Report ISI-TR-545*, 54:56.

Mingda Chen, Zewei Chu, and Kevin Gimpel. 2019a. Evaluation benchmarks and learning criteria for discourse-aware sentence representations. In *Proceedings of the 2019 Conference on Empirical Methods in Natural Language Processing and the 9th International Joint Conference on Natural Language Processing (EMNLP-IJCNLP)*, pages 649–662.

Sihao Chen, Daniel Khashabi, Wenpeng Yin, Chris Callison-Burch, and Dan Roth. 2019b. Seeing things from a different angle: Discovering diverse perspectives about claims. In *Proceedings of the 2019 Conference of the North American Chapter of the Association for Computational Linguistics: Human Language Technologies, Volume 1 (Long and Short Papers)*, pages 542–557.

Sandra Collovini, Thiago I Carbonel, Juliana Thiesen Fuchs, Jorge César Coelho, Lúcia Rino, and Renata Vieira. 2007. Summ-it: Um corpus anotado com informaç oes discursivas visandoa sumarizaç ao automática. *Proceedings of TIL*.

Alexis Conneau, Kartikay Khandelwal, Naman Goyal, Vishrav Chaudhary, Guillaume Wenzek, Francisco Guzmán, Edouard Grave, Myle Ott, Luke Zettlemoyer, and Veselin Stoyanov. 2020. Unsupervised cross-lingual representation learning at scale. In *Proceedings of the 58th Annual Meeting of the Association for Computational Linguistics*, pages 8440–8451, Online. Association for Computational Linguistics.

Alexis Conneau and Guillaume Lample. 2019. Cross-lingual language model pretraining. In *Advances in Neural Information Processing Systems*, pages 7059–7069.

Alexis Conneau, Ruty Rinott, Guillaume Lample, Adina Williams, Samuel Bowman, Holger Schwenk, and Veselin Stoyanov. 2018. XNLI: Evaluating cross-lingual sentence representations. In *Proceedings of the 2018 Conference on Empirical Methods in Natural Language Processing*, pages 2475–2485, Brussels, Belgium. Association for Computational Linguistics.

Iria Da Cunha, Juan-Manuel Torres-Moreno, and Gerardo Sierra. 2011. On the development of the rst spanish treebank. In *Proceedings of the 5th Linguistic Annotation Workshop*, pages 1–10.

Jacob Devlin, Ming-Wei Chang, Kenton Lee, and Kristina Toutanova. 2019. Bert: Pre-training of deep bidirectional transformers for language understanding. In *Proceedings of the 2019 Conference of the North American Chapter of the Association for Computational Linguistics: Human Language Technologies, Volume 1 (Long and Short Papers)*, pages 4171–4186.

Junjie Hu, Sebastian Ruder, Aditya Siddhant, Graham Neubig, Orhan Firat, and Melvin Johnson. 2020. Xtreme: A massively multilingual multi-task benchmark for evaluating cross-lingual generalisation. In *International Conference on Machine Learning*, pages 4411–4421. PMLR.

Haoyang Huang, Yaobo Liang, Nan Duan, Ming Gong, Linjun Shou, Daxin Jiang, and Ming Zhou. 2019. Unicoder: A universal language encoder by pre-training with multiple cross-lingual tasks. In *Proceedings of the 2019 Conference on Empirical Methods in Natural Language Processing and the 9th International Joint Conference on Natural Language Processing (EMNLP-IJCNLP)*, pages 2485–2494.

Mikel Iruskieta, Mara Jesus Aranzabe, Arantza Diaz de Ilarraza, Itziar Gonzalez, Mikel Lersundi, and Oier Lopez de la Calle. 2013. The rst basque treebank: an online search interface to check rhetorical relations. In *4th Workshop" RST and Discourse Studies", Brasil, October*, pages 21–23.

Murathan Kurfalı and Robert Östling. 2019. Zero-shot transfer for implicit discourse relation classification. In *Proceedings of the 20th Annual SIGdial Meeting on Discourse and Dialogue*, pages 226–231.

Anne Lauscher, Vinit Ravishankar, Ivan Vulić, and Goran Glavaš. 2020. From zero to hero: On the limitations of zero-shot language transfer with multilingual transformers. In *Proceedings of the 2020 Conference on Empirical Methods in Natural Language Processing (EMNLP)*, pages 4483–4499.

Patrick Lewis, Barlas Oguz, Ruty Rinott, Sebastian Riedel, and Holger Schwenk. 2020. MLQA: Evaluating cross-lingual extractive question answering. In *Proceedings of the 58th Annual Meeting of the Association for Computational Linguistics*, pages 7315–7330, Online. Association for Computational Linguistics.

Yaobo Liang, Nan Duan, Yeyun Gong, Ning Wu, Fenfei Guo, Weizhen Qi, Ming Gong, Linjun Shou, Daxin Jiang, Guihong Cao, et al. 2020. Xglue: A new benchmark datasetfor cross-lingual pre-training, understanding and generation. In *Proceedings of the 2020 Conference on Empirical Methods in Natural Language Processing (EMNLP)*, pages 6008–6018.

Patrick Littell, David R Mortensen, Ke Lin, Katherine Kairis, Carlisle Turner, and Lori Levin. 2017. Uriel and lang2vec: Representing languages as typological, geographical, and phylogenetic vectors. In *Proceedings of the 15th Conference of the European Chapter of the Association for Computational Linguistics: Volume 2, Short Papers*, pages 8–14.

Yinhan Liu, Myle Ott, Naman Goyal, Jingfei Du, Mandar Joshi, Danqi Chen, Omer Levy, Mike Lewis, Luke Zettlemoyer, and Veselin Stoyanov. 2019. Roberta: A robustly optimized bert pretraining approach. *arXiv preprint arXiv:1907.11692*.

Wanqiu Long, Xinyi Cai, James Reid, Bonnie Webber, and Deyi Xiong. 2020. Shallow discourse annotation for chinese ted talks. In *Proceedings of The 12th Language Resources and Evaluation Conference*, pages 1025–1032.

William C. Mann and Sandra A. Thompson. 1988. Rhetorical structure theory: Toward a functional theory of text organization. *Text & Talk*, 8(3):243 – 281.

Allen Nie, Erin Bennett, and Noah Goodman. 2019. Dissent: Learning sentence representations from explicit discourse relations. In *Proceedings of the 57th Annual Meeting of the Association for Computational Linguistics*, pages 4497–4510.

Giedre Valunaite Oleskeviciene, Deniz Zeyrek, Viktorija Mazeikiene, and Murathan Kurfalı. 2018. Observations on the annotation of discourse relational devices in ted talk transcripts in lithuanian. In *Proceedings of the workshop on annotation in digital humanities co-located with ESSLLI*, volume 2155, pages 53–58.

Thiago Alexandre Salgueiro Pardo and Eloize Rossi Marques Seno. 2005. Rhetalho: um corpus de referência anotado retoricamente. *Anais do V Encontro de Corpora*, pages 24–25.

Matthew Peters, Mark Neumann, Mohit Iyyer, Matt Gardner, Christopher Clark, Kenton Lee, and Luke Zettlemoyer. 2018. Deep contextualized word representations. In *Proceedings of the 2018 Conference of the North American Chapter of the Association for Computational Linguistics: Human Language Technologies, Volume 1 (Long Papers)*, pages 2227–2237, New Orleans, Louisiana. Association for Computational Linguistics.

Telmo Pires, Eva Schlinger, and Dan Garrette. 2019. How multilingual is multilingual bert? In *Proceedings of the 57th Annual Meeting of the Association for Computational Linguistics*, pages 4996–5001.

Dina Pisarevskaya, Margarita Ananyeva, Maria Kobozeva, Alexander Nasedkin, Sofia Nikiforova, Irina Pavlova, and Alexey Shelepov. 2017. Towards building a discourse-annotated corpus of russian. In *Proceedings of the International Conference on Computational Linguistics and Intellectual Technologies" Dialogue*.

Rashmi Prasad, Eleni Miltsakaki, Nikhil Dinesh, Alan Lee, Aravind Joshi, Livio Robaldo, and Bonnie L Webber. 2007. The penn discourse treebank 2.0 annotation manual.

Xipeng Qiu, Tianxiang Sun, Yige Xu, Yunfan Shao, Ning Dai, and Xuanjing Huang. 2020. Pre-trained models for natural language processing: A survey. *Science China Technological Sciences*, pages 1–26.

Pranav Rajpurkar, Jian Zhang, Konstantin Lopyrev, and Percy Liang. 2016. Squad: 100,000+ questions for machine comprehension of text. In *Proceedings of the 2016 Conference on Empirical Methods in Natural Language Processing*, pages 2383–2392.

Victor Sanh, Lysandre Debut, Julien Chaumond, Thomas Wolf, and Hugging Face. 2019. Distilbert, a distilled version of bert: smaller, faster, cheaper and lighter. *arXiv preprint arXiv:1910.01108*.

Manfred Stede. 2004. The potsdam commentary corpus. In *Proceedings of the Workshop on Discourse Annotation*, pages 96–102.

Sara Tonelli and Elena Cabrio. 2012. Hunting for entailing pairs in the penn discourse treebank. In *Proceedings of COLING 2012*, pages 2653–2668.

Jannis Vamvas and Rico Sennrich. 2020. X-Stance: A multilingual multi-target dataset for stance detection. In *Proceedings of the 5th Swiss Text Analytics Conference (SwissText) & 16th Conference on Natural Language Processing (KONVENS)*, Zurich, Switzerland.

Alex Wang, Amanpreet Singh, Julian Michael, Felix Hill, Omer Levy, and Samuel R Bowman. 2019. Glue: A multi-task benchmark and analysis platform for natural language understanding. In *7th International Conference on Learning Representations, ICLR 2019*.

Bonnie Webber, Rashmi Prasad, Alan Lee, and Aravind Joshi. 2016. A discourse-annotated corpus of conjoined vps. In *Proceedings of the 10th Linguistic Annotation Workshop held in conjunction with ACL 2016 (LAW-X 2016)*, pages 22–31.

Adina Williams, Nikita Nangia, and Samuel Bowman. 2018. A broad-coverage challenge corpus for sentence understanding through inference. In *Proceedings of the 2018 Conference of the North American Chapter of the Association for Computational Linguistics: Human Language Technologies, Volume 1 (Long Papers)*, pages 1112–1122.

Thomas Wolf, L Debut, V Sanh, J Chaumond, C Delangue, A Moi, P Cistac, T Rault, R Louf, M Funtowicz, et al. 2019. Huggingface's transformers: State-of-the-art natural language processing. *ArXiv, abs/1910.03771*.

Shijie Wu and Mark Dredze. 2019. Beto, bentz, becas: The surprising cross-lingual effectiveness of bert. In *Proceedings of the 2019 Conference on Empirical Methods in Natural Language Processing and the 9th International Joint Conference on Natural Language Processing (EMNLP-IJCNLP)*, pages 833–844.

Nianwen Xue, Hwee Tou Ng, Sameer Pradhan, Attapol Rutherford, Bonnie Webber, Chuan Wang, and Hongmin Wang. 2016. Conll 2016 shared task on multilingual shallow discourse parsing. In *Proceedings of the CoNLL-16 shared task*, pages 1–19.

Jianhua Yuan, Yanyan Zhao, Jingfang Xu, and Bing Qin. 2019. Exploring answer stance detection with recurrent conditional attention. In *Proceedings of the AAAI Conference on Artificial Intelligence*, volume 33, pages 7426–7433.

Deniz Zeyrek, Amália Mendes, Yulia Grishina, Murathan Kurfalı, Samuel Gibbon, and Maciej Ogrodniczuk. 2019. Ted multilingual discourse bank (tedmdb): a parallel corpus annotated in the pdtb style. *Language Resources and Evaluation*, pages 1–27.

A Task-wise Results

Model	en	de	es	eu	pt	ru	zh	AVG
mBERT	66.7	29.2	39.3	31.1	58.6	48.0	50.7	42.8
distilmBERT	54.1	16.3	25.7	21.4	44.5	32.2	36.5	29.4
XLM-mlm	60.6	25.5	33.2	14.1*	40.4*	39.8	39.4	32.1
XLM-tlm	65.5	26.0	35.2	13.3*	42.0*	39.9	41.3	33.0
XLM-100	63.8	24.3	34.6	26.2	55.2	40.0	39.8	36.7
XLMR-b	69.8	37.6	44.7	39.4	61.9	56.2	56.7	49.4
XLMR-l	72.9	44.8	46.8	47.0	65.6	59.3	57.3	53.5

Table 4: RST zero-shot results (Accuracy) for each language. * denotes that the language is not one of the training languages of the respective sentence encoder.

Model	en	de	lt	pl	pt	ru	tr	zh	AVG
mBERT	53.6	42.7	39.2	33.9	46.7	33.1	40.3	43.5	39.9
distilmBERT	53.1	42.7	30.0	34.7	41.1	32.6	29.4	35.4	35.1
XLM-mlm	54.9	44.9	19.5*	20.6*	28.9*	33.8	43.5	40.5	33.1
XLM-tlm	53.3	45.9	20.1*	21.3*	26.8*	37.1	41.9	43.6	33.8
XLM-100	54.6	41.9	41.6	32.5	44.5	34.2	35.9	40.4	38.7
XLMR-b	61.8	49.5	49.6	40.4	53.5	42.7	54.4	51.4	48.8
XLMR-l	65.4	53.4	49.4	42.8	59.5	48.9	53.8	58.1	52.3

Table 5: PDTB zero-shot results (F_1) for each language. * denotes that the language is not one of the training languages of the respective sentence encoder.

Model	de	en	fr	it	zh	AVG
mBERT	69.3	60.2	60.7	63.2	50.8	58.7
distilmBERT	67.7	49.8	48.7	59.5	35.2	48.3
XLM-mlm	67.3	52.6	55.0	56.2*	41.8	51.4
XLM-tlm	71.2	60.4	62.5	59.6*	61.1	60.9
XLM-100	71.8	62.3	64.8	64.0	60.6	62.9
XLMR-b	72.3	65.8	70.4	69.9	66.7	68.2
XLMR-l	79.3	80.9	79.0	78.9	79.5	79.6

Table 6: X-stance zero-shot results (F_1) for each language. * denotes that the language is not one of the training languages of the respective sentence encoder.

Model	en	ar	bg	de	el	es	fr	hi	ru	sw	th	tr	ur	vi	zh	AVG
mBERT	82.3	65.7	69.4	72.1	68.2	75.9	75.3	60.6	69.8	51.3	54.7	62.2	58.8	70.9	69.7	66.1
distilmBERT	77.9	60.3	63.9	65.7	61.4	70.1	69.9	54.7	63.6	46.6	39.1	57.3	54.1	59.2	62.4	59.2
XLM-mlm	81.9	68.5	73.7	73.0	73.3	75.3	75.2	64.4	72.0	64.9	49.2	67.3	62.8	70.3	67.3	68.4
XLM-tlm	84.2	71.1	76.5	76.2	74.3	78.3	77.9	66.5	75.3	67.4	53.9	70.8	62.7	72.8	69.3	70.9
XLM-100	83.1	67.9	72.6	73.3	72.4	76.6	75.5	64.7	71.3	58.4	39.7	68.2	62.0	72.7	67.0	67.3
XLMR-b	82.8	71.0	77.3	75.7	75.3	78.2	76.9	68.6	75.2	66.4	71.6	72.4	65.2	74.6	73.0	73.0
XLMR-l	88.8	78.6	83.0	82.9	81.8	84.5	82.7	76.0	79.3	71.6	77.0	78.7	71.5	79.5	79.3	79.0

Table 7: XNLI zero-shot results (Accuracy) for each language

Model	en	ar	de	el	es	hi
mBERT	84.8/72.9	62.6/46.0	72.5/56.8	64.4/47.1	75.3/56.3	58.6/45.1
distilmBERT	78.0/65.9	44.6/28.3	57.6/41.0	37.6/21.2	60.5/40.0	34.9/20.5
XLM-mlm	77.2/64.5	59.9/43.2	66.0/50.4	57.8/39.5	67.7/49.8	47.5/33.0
XLM-tlm	82.5/70.4	68.1/51.6	73.7/57.6	69.5/51.2	77.1/59.2	65.6/50.2
XLM-100	84.6/73.4	67.6/50.3	73.6/58.3	63.9/45.1	77.3/59.1	60.2/44.5
XLMR-b	83.3/72.4	65.0/47.1	73.4/57.6	71.9/54.5	75.5/57.1	68.3/50.9
XLMR-l	86.8/75.5	74.1/55.6	79.5/62.6	79.8/61.4	82.0/62.3	75.4/58.6
Model	ru	th	tr	vi	zh	AVG
mBERT	71.4/54.9	43.3/34.4	54.8/40.8	68.1/48.9	58.3/48.2	62.9/47.8
distilmBERT	58.9/40.2	20.9/13.9	37.9/21.8	47.5/28.2	46.9/33.8	44.7/28.9
XLM	64.1/47.0	24.9/12.4	50.2/34.6	60.3/41.3	39.8/30.1	53.8/38.1
XLM-tlm	72.6/55.3	33.3/21.9	65.0/47.5	71.8/51.3	53.4/43.8	65.0/48.9
XLM-100	73.7/57.6	22.4/13.6	66.7/49.9	73.9/54.8	54.1/44.5	63.3/47.8
XLMR-b	73.3/56.9	67.1/55.5	67.5/50.4	73.0/53.4	51.6/41.7	68.7/52.5
XLMR-l	79.4/62.9	73.7/62.6	74.7/58.5	79.4/59.4	55.5/46.7	75.4/59.1

Table 8: XQuAD results (F_1/Exact-match) for each language

Comprehension Based Question Answering using Bloom's Taxonomy

Pritish Sahu[1,2] * **Michael Cogswell**[1] * **Sara Rutherford-Quach**[1] **Ajay Divakaran**[1]

[1]SRI International

[2]Rutgers University

Abstract

Current pre-trained language models have lots of knowledge, but a more limited ability to use that knowledge. Bloom's Taxonomy helps educators teach children how to use knowledge by categorizing comprehension skills, so we use it to analyze and improve the comprehension skills of large pre-trained language models. Our experiments focus on zero-shot question answering, using the taxonomy to provide proximal context that helps the model answer questions by being relevant to those questions. We show targeting context in this manner improves performance across 4 popular common sense question answer datasets.

1 Introduction

Recent large language models such as GPT-3 (Brown et al., 2020) have made a giant leap forward in knowledge acquisition and even generalize this knowledge to a new tasks. But when less narrow tasks are considered they fail to understand as much as these benchmarks suggest. They turn out to be "stochastic parrots" (Bender et al., 2021) or "smart/super parrots." (Dunietz et al., 2020) that just memorize without all of the comprehension we want from a Natural Language Understanding system. We focus on a particular kind of failure mode where the model knows (has memorized) the information it needs, but is not able to apply that information correctly, and we do so in a zero-shot fashion to control for what the model knows.

For example, in Fig. 1 the model is asked if a mixture of grape juice and cranberry juice is safe to drink (Marcus and Davis, 2020). GPT-3 declares that it is a deadly poison, even though it appears to "know" that grape juice and cranberry juice are safe to drink by themselves (Fig. 1, Level 1, dark purple). It even knows that cranberry juice with grape juice is not poisonous, but it still thinks the result is death (Fig. 1, Level 2, light blue). The model has memorized the necessary information from large amounts of text, but does not use its knowledge appropriately. Following (Shwartz et al., 2020), we extract this knowledge as explicit language then feed it back as additional context during inference, forcing the model to use what it already knows but in our case targeting specifically useful knowledge.

To formalize this distinction we drew inspiration from elementary school classrooms, where teachers (Miller, 2002; Harvey and Goudvis, 2007) have a schema based approach in which they teach children to demonstrate multiple levels of comprehension, making complex inferences and direct recall from memory. They use a hierarchy of comprehension skills called Bloom's Taxonomy (Anderson et al., 2000) (*c.f.* Fig. 1) with memorization is at the bottom (requiring children to recall facts) followed by understanding (requiring children to grasp semantics) application (requiring children to solve problems), and more complex skills. For us, these comprehension skills describe ways our language model might fail to use its knowledge.

In this paper we address our failure mode by relying on commonly understood relationships between the skills of Bloom's Taxonomy which we term *proximal context*. In order to *understand* whether the cranberry grape mixture is poisonous the model needs to *remember* whether grape juice is poisonous. In order to *apply* its knowledge to figure out what will happen next it needs to *understand* whether the cranberry grape mixture is poisonous or not. In general, the *proximal context* for a particular task T at level L is given by those tasks implicitly required by T, which are mostly at level $L - 1$ of the taxonomy. We guide our language to answer questions more accurately by providing it not just any context, but proximal context [1]. In performing zero-shot question answering our language model asks itself additional clarifica-

* These two authors contributed equally.

[1] Proximal context is not defined for level 1 questions, so we only address questions at level 2 or above.

Proceedings of the 6th Workshop on Representation Learning for NLP (RepL4NLP-2021), pages 20–28
Bangkok, Thailand (Online), August 6, 2021.

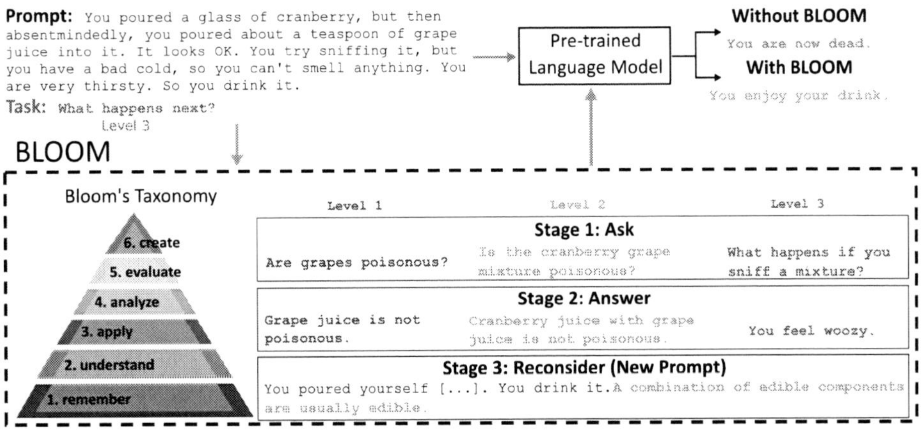

Figure 1: Our approach incorporates context into question answering guided by Bloom's Taxonomy.

tion questions, choosing those most likely to result in proximal context.

Our contributions in this paper are:

- We use Bloom's Taxonomy to choose proximal clarifying context that improves question answering performance using only what the model already knows.
- We show proximal context is better than other levels of context on four different commonsense question answering tasks.
- By observing how different levels of clarification impact our language model we also explain how the model answers questions.

2 Related Works

Question Answering from External Supervision. Several approaches has been proposed to improve question-answering by adding external knowledge source. Recent large pre-trained language models (Peters et al., 2018; Radford et al., 2019; Devlin et al., 2018; Liu et al., 2019; Joshi et al., 2020; Clark et al., 2020) learn general purpose text encoders from a huge text corpus. (Petroni et al., 2019) recently used a language model as knowledge base to unmask a token given an entity and a relation in a predefined template. Shwartz et al. (2020); Bosselut et al. (2019a,b) used pretrained language models to improve zero-shot question answering performance by extracting context from the language model itself, using self-talk or a knowledge graph. We add context via self-talk, with structure provided by Bloom's Taxonomy.

Bloom's Taxonomy. The original work (Bloom, 1956) defined taxonomies for learning in the cognitive (intellectual), affective (interests, attitudes, values), and psychomotor domains, though the cognitive domain is what we usually refer to today. Almost half a century later the cognitive domain taxonomy was revised (Anderson et al., 2000) to reflect more active thinking and improve usability by adding verbs to describe levels. Teachers use this taxonomy, for example in computer science education (Whalley et al., 2006; Thompson et al., 2008; Oliver et al., 2004), and our inspiration is from this revised version of the cognitive taxonomy. Machine learning has been applied to automatically classify questions (Mohammed and Omar, 2020; Zhang et al., 2021; Nafa et al., 2016) into Bloom's Taxonomy levels, but the taxonomy has not been applied to analyze or improve machine learning models themselves. We use it to help our model think about what it knows.

3 Approach

Our approach builds on the zero-shot question answering approach of Shwartz et al. (2020) to answer questions (Section 3.1) by adding clarifications with self-talk (Section 3.2). We describe this approach then we use Bloom's Taxonomy to select better clarifications (Section 3.2).

3.1 Question Answering with Language Models

Given a prompt p, a question q, and answer options a_o $\forall o \in [1, K]$ we use a pre-trained language model LM to pick the correct answer a_{o^*}. This

Dataset	Question Prefix	Sample Clarification Question	Sample Clarification Answer
COPA	What is the definition of : 1	(a) What is the definition of an accident? (b) What is the definition of a flat tire?	(a) The definition of an accident is the crash of collusion caused by the vehicle. (b) The definition of a flat tire is that the tire does not hold air.
	What is the main purpose of : 2	(a) What is the main purpose of this investigation? (b) What is the main purpose of this post?	(a) The purpose of this investigation is to provide information about how and why he was shot. (b) The purpose of this post is to share my thoughts and feelings on his death.
CommonsenseQA	What is the main function of a : 2	(a) What is the main function of a teacher in this area? (b) What is the main function of a farmer?	(a)The main function of a teacher in this area is to teach them about life and love. (b) The main function of a farmer is to provide food for his family and the community.
	What might have caused : 3	(a) What might have caused this problem? (b) What might have caused the animal to flee?	(a) the cause of this problem was that his wife's husband didn't have enough money. (b) The cause of the animal to flee was a predator.
Social IQA	What did [NAME] do? : 1	(a) What did Kendall do? (b) What did Kendall do?	(a) What Kendall did was make sure that he wasn't going anywhere else. (b) What Kendall did was so horrible, that it was hard to believe.
	How would you describe [NAME]? : 3	(a) How would you describe Riley? (b) How would you describe Riley?	(a) Riley is a big brother, he's an awesome dad. (b) Riley is a very sensitive person and has a lot of anxiety.
Winogrande	What are the properties of a : 1	(a) What are the properties of a diet that is not healthy? (b) What are the properties of a home?	(a) The property of a diet that is not healthy are that it has high cholesterol (a good idea). (b) The properties of a home are that which makes it comfortable and pleasant for the occupants.
	What does it mean to : 2	(a) What does it mean to be an explorer? (b) What does it mean to be sophisticated?	(a) Be an explorer means to explore and make sense of things. (b) Be sophisticated means to be classy, elegant and smart.

Table 1: This table shows some of the question prefixes we used for different datasets in our experiments. We assign each prefix a level in Bloom's Taxonomy. We show generated clarifications questions and answers for both Distil-GPT2 (a) and GPT-Neo (b) for their corresponding question prefixes.

approach simply concatenates each (prompt, question, answer) tuple into into a single string of text $T_o = [p, q, a_o]$ and feeds this string to the language model to assign each choice a score $s_o = LM(T_o)$. The language model's answer is just the answer with the highest score: $\hat{o} = \text{argmax}_o\, s_o$.

3.2 Self-talk Clarifications

Self-talk (Shwartz et al., 2020) has a language model ask itself clarifying questions then answer those questions to generate clarifications.

Stage 1: Ask clarification questions. To produce clarifications we start with a set of clarification question prefixes $r_1, \ldots, r_J$ that are designed specifically for each question answering dataset. "What happens if" is a sample prefix for the clarifications, shown in Fig. 1, and in Tab. 1 we present examples for all the datasets we use. In this stage the language model completes each of these prefixes, using its generator function LM_G to ask one question $R_j = LM_G(r_j)$ per prefix.

Stage 2: Answer the questions. Next we use the model to answer each of these questions, possibly prompted with an answer prefix b_j corresponding to question prefix r_j. The results are the clarifications $c_j = LM_G([R_j, b_j])$.

Stage 3: Reconsider with a new prompt. To use the clarifications we pick one from the list then append it to the original prompt. This approach simply considers all combinations of clarifications questions and answers $T_{j,o} = [p, q, c_j, a_o]\ \forall o, j$, first chooses the clarification which maximizes model score per answer option, then chooses the final answer $o^* = \text{argmax}_o \max_j LM(T_{j,o})$. This can improve question answering performance on its own, but in the next section we more carefully choose clarifications using our notion of proximal context and Bloom's Taxonomy.

3.3 Using Bloom's Taxonomy to Choose Clarifications with Proximal Context

To test our idea of proximal context we consider the level L of task give by each dataset then allow only proximal clarifications of level $L - 1$. We label each question prefix with the level of Bloom's Taxonomy that it falls into, and then force the model to choose from the set $\mathcal{C}_L$ of clarifications of level L. This results in a final choice for each level $o^*_L = \text{argmax}_o \max_{j \in \mathcal{C}_L} LM(T_{j,o})$. We also provide a *Choice Baseline* that allows the model to choose any level of clarification to show the model would have difficulty choosing proximal clarifications itself. Note that the annotation of questions along Bloom's taxonomy requires special skills typically found only among educators. While a layperson can be trained to annotate such questions, our experience was that it takes much more time than we could afford for a preliminary study such as this one. We therefore relied on our co-author, Sara Rutherford-Quach, who is a researcher at SRI's Education Division and has also worked as a teacher at the kindergarten-elementary level to provide us the annotations. Two other co-authors, Sahu and Cogswell, went through those annotations and made sure that each label had a three way consensus among Rutherford-Quach, Sahu and Cogswell. There might be some ambiguity about which level a particular prefix fits into, but this is also true of other applications of the taxonomy (Thompson et al., 2008). In future work, we plan to carry out a more rigorous annotation with more than one skilled annotator so we can measure inter-annotator agreement through measures such as Kappa scores.

4 Experiments

4.1 Datasets

We evaluate our study on four datasets that can each be thought of in terms of multiple choice question answering, all measuring some kind of common sense: COPA (Roemmele et al., 2011) measures common sense causal reasoning, CommonSenseQA (Talmor et al., 2019) asks questions that require prior knowledge, Social IQA (Sap et al., 2019) asks about social common sense, and WinoGrande (Sakaguchi et al., 2020) adversarially measures semantic common sense. Perhaps surprisingly, all of the datasets we used asked questions that fell into just one level of the taxonomy (Tab. 2). These datasets do focus on very specific problems, but the result is still disappointing because it would be more useful to see variations in both task and clarification level. It may be interesting to develop datasets that can better express the range of abilities described by Bloom's Taxonomy.

4.2 Language Model

We use distill-GPT2 (Sanh et al., 2019) and the publicly released GPT-Neo2.7B(Black et al., 2021) (based on EleutherAI's replication of the GPT-3 architecture) as the language models throughout our experiments. Our clarification question prefixes and hyperparameter settings for both models are

Table 2: Question answering accuracy and std. dev. using different levels ofclarification over multiple clarification samples. Results on the dev sets of each dataset.(* = level of proximal context \wrt the dataset)

Task	Model	Level	Accuracy
Winogrande (1267 total) (2: Understand)	Distil-GPT2 (235±5 valid)	0A: Choice Baseline	53.2 ± 1.8
		1A: Remember*	**54.7 ± 3.6**
		2A: Understand	52.5 ± 3.1
	GPT-Neo (1230±7 valid)	0A: Choice Baseline	54.62 ± 0.5
		1A: Remember*	**54.77 ± 0.5**
		2A: Understand	54.76 ± 0.3
SocialIQA (1954 total) (3. Apply)	Distil-GPT2 (58±5 valid)	0B: Choice Baseline	44.5 ± 0.1
		1B: Remember	43.7 ± 2.1
		2B: Understand*	**48.0 ± 1.1**
		3B: Apply	44.4 ± 1.8
	GPT-Neo (1334±9 valid)	0B: Choice Baseline	**48.74 ± 0.4**
		1B: Remember	47.31 ± 0.1
		2B: Understand*	**48.44 ± 0.5**
		3B: Apply	48.1 ± 0.1
COPA (100 total) (3: Apply)	Distil-GPT2 (11±2 valid)	0C: Choice Baseline	**54.9 ± 0.9**
		1C: Remember	46.0 ± 14.7
		2C: Understand*	**53.1 ± 12.5**
		3C: Apply	40.8 ± 15.2
	GPT-Neo (96±0 valid)	0C: Choice Baseline	**70.83 ± 0.0**
		1C: Remember	65.62 ± 0.0
		2C: Understand*	**70.83 ± 1.4**
		3C: Apply	**70.83 ± 0.0**
CommonsenseQA (1221 total) (3: Apply)	Distil-GPT2 (68±1 valid)	0D: Choice Baseline	**29.9 ± 2.7**
		1D: Remember	26.5 ± 3.3
		2D: Understand*	**28.1 ± 1.2**
		3D: Apply	25.6 ± 3.4
	GPT-Neo (1118±4 valid)	0D: Choice Baseline	40.59 ± 3.6
		1D: Remember	38.00 ± 6.0
		2D: Understand*	**43.19 ± 0.2**
		3D: Apply	42.30 ± 0.8

from (Shwartz et al., 2020). For each question prefix, we generate 5 clarification questions using nucleus sampling threshold probability $p = 0.2$ and adding at most 6 words to the clarification question prefix. We then generate 10 answers to each clarification question using $p = 0.5$ and maximum answer length 10. Some changes were necessary to accurately measure the impact of clarification level. Instead of always including *no clarification* as a choice we do not allow this option as it defeats our goal of measuring clarification level impact. Furthermore, we do not use the clarification questions which were manually completed without input from the model (as in COPA and Winogrande).

In order to compare performance across different levels of clarifications we only consider examples where the model was able to generate at least one clarification from each level. To increase the number of viable examples we found it necessary to remove some restrictions relative to the implementation of (Shwartz et al., 2020). In particular, we kept all clarifications that had no overlapping words with the context and did not allow the model to chose the "no clarification" option. Even with these constraints it was still often the case that distil-GPT2 could not generate a short clarification sentence that was plausible enough to use whereas GPT-Neo was able to generate clarifications for almost the entire dataset. This indicates larger scale models may be more able to take advantage of clarifying questions. The number of examples with valid clarifications for all levels is indicated for each model in column 2 of Tab. 2. These changes help us more accurately measure the impact of Bloom's Taxonomy, but mean our approach is not directly comparable to Shwartz et al. (2020).

4.3 Results

Table 2 reports the performance of our Bloom's Taxonomy infused zero-shot question answering method. Each row shows question answering accuracy for a particular dataset and level of clarification. If our hypothesis is correct then the level of available clarifications should matter and clarifications that provide proximal context –one level below the dataset level– should be most helpful.

Clarification Level Makes a Difference. All levels of clarification questions and answers provide some amount of extra information that changes how a language model processes the entire string it is presented with. This is often helpful information, but it may be that all levels of Bloom's Taxonomy provide equally useful information. We find that is not the case. Different levels of clarification help more or less, as evidenced by the large gap between minimum and maximum accuracy for each dataaset. Furthermore, when the model can choose any clarification (rows 0A/B/C/D) it either does a worse job than proximal context or its performance similar to proximal context, so enforcing a particular kind of context should be helpful.

Proximal Context Helps Most. Proximal context, as we've defined it with respect to Bloom's Taxonomy is context from the clarification level directly below the dataset question level. The proximal clarification level for each dataset is marked by a * in Tab. 2. In all cases proximal clarifications are better than using clarifications of a lower level. For the datasets that ask level 3 questions the proximal (level 2) clarifications also outperform level 1 clarifications (2B/C/D greater than 1B/C/D). Proximal clarifications are also about as good as or better than using clarifications of a higher level. You can see this for Winogrande by noting row 1A is greater than 2A and for the other datasets by noting rows 2B/C/D usually have greater performance than 3B/C/D. Overall, proximal context is most consistent in efficacy.

4.4 Qualitative Results

In Tab. 1 we show samples of question answer pairs generated for each model and in Tab. 5 of the appendix we show complete examples (with context and choices) for each model and dataset. GPT-Neo is much larger than distil-GPT2 and is expected to generalize to slightly new tasks like the clarification generation task better than the smaller model. This expectation is clearly met by the observed quality of clarifications. Distil-GPT2 clarification questions and answers often do not have meaningful semantics, are not correct, or are not relevant. GPT-Neo is much more likely to generate questions and answers which are meaningful, correct, and relevant. This suggests the greater number of valid clarifications generated by GPT-Neo may be due to an increase in clarification quality. Furthermore, it fails in an intuitive fashion: when it fails to generate meaningful answers it often has also failed to generate a meaningful clarification question in the first place.

Also note that the performance differences observed for distil-GPT2 occur despite its relatively poor interpretability. This indicates that context which is somewhat relevant to the topic even if it does not precisely make sense can still be useful.

5 Conclusion

Large pre-trained language models sometimes have the right information, but they just do not know how to use it. We used Bloom's taxonomy to pick questions with the right amount of proximal context. This helped the language models use their knowledge to more effectively answer questions. In the future we would like to extend our work on tasks that present a wide range of questions that fall under different levels of the taxonomy. Similarly, we also would like to study and improve upon the current limited set of prefix questions used.

Acknowledgments

The authors thank Yunye Gong, Stephanie Nunn, and the anonymous reviewers for the helpful discussions and comments.

References

L. Anderson, D. Krathwohl, and B. Bloom. 2000. A taxonomy for learning, teaching, and assessing: A revision of bloom's taxonomy of educational objectives.

Emily M. Bender, Timnit Gebru, Angelina McMillan-Major, and Shmargaret Shmitchell. 2021. On the dangers of stochastic parrots: Can language models be too big? . *Proceedings of the 2021 ACM Conference on Fairness, Accountability, and Transparency.*

Sid Black, Leo Gao, Phil Wang, Connor Leahy, and Stella Biderman. 2021. GPT-Neo: Large scale autoregressive language modeling with mesh-tensorflow.

B. Bloom. 1956. Taxonomy of educational objectives: The classification of educational goals.

Antoine Bosselut, Ronan Le Bras, and Yejin Choi. 2019a. Dynamic neuro-symbolic knowledge graph construction for zero-shot commonsense question answering. *arXiv preprint arXiv:1911.03876.*

Antoine Bosselut, Hannah Rashkin, Maarten Sap, Chaitanya Malaviya, Asli Celikyilmaz, and Yejin Choi. 2019b. Comet: Commonsense transformers for automatic knowledge graph construction. *arXiv preprint arXiv:1906.05317.*

T. Brown, Benjamin Mann, Nick Ryder, Melanie Subbiah, J. Kaplan, Prafulla Dhariwal, Arvind Neelakantan, Pranav Shyam, Girish Sastry, Amanda Askell, Sandhini Agarwal, Ariel Herbert-Voss, Gretchen Krueger, T. Henighan, R. Child, A. Ramesh, Daniel M. Ziegler, Jeffrey Wu, Clemens Winter, Christopher Hesse, Mark Chen, Eric Sigler, Mateusz Litwin, Scott Gray, Benjamin Chess, J. Clark, Christopher Berner, Sam McCandlish, A. Radford, Ilya Sutskever, and Dario Amodei. 2020. Language models are few-shot learners. *ArXiv*, abs/2005.14165.

Kevin Clark, Minh-Thang Luong, Quoc V Le, and Christopher D Manning. 2020. Electra: Pre-training text encoders as discriminators rather than generators. *arXiv preprint arXiv:2003.10555.*

Jacob Devlin, Ming-Wei Chang, Kenton Lee, and Kristina Toutanova. 2018. Bert: Pre-training of deep bidirectional transformers for language understanding. *arXiv preprint arXiv:1810.04805.*

Jesse Dunietz, Greg Burnham, Akash Bharadwaj, Jennifer Chu-Carroll, Owen Rambow, and D. Ferrucci. 2020. To test machine comprehension, start by defining comprehension. In *ACL*.

Stephanie Harvey and Anne Goudvis. 2007. *Strategies that work: Teaching comprehension for understanding and engagement.* Stenhouse Publishers.

Mandar Joshi, Kenton Lee, Yi Luan, and Kristina Toutanova. 2020. Contextualized representations using textual encyclopedic knowledge. *arXiv preprint arXiv:2004.12006.*

Yinhan Liu, Myle Ott, Naman Goyal, Jingfei Du, Mandar Joshi, Danqi Chen, Omer Levy, Mike Lewis, Luke Zettlemoyer, and Veselin Stoyanov. 2019. Roberta: A robustly optimized bert pretraining approach. *arXiv preprint arXiv:1907.11692.*

Gary Marcus and Ernest Davis. 2020. Gpt-3, bloviator: Openai's language generator has no idea what it's talking about. *MIT Technology Review.*

Debbie Miller. 2002. *Reading with meaning: Teaching comprehension in the primary grades.* Stenhouse Publishers.

Manal Mohammed and N. Omar. 2020. Question classification based on bloom's taxonomy cognitive domain using modified tf-idf and word2vec. *PLoS ONE*, 15.

Fatema Nafa, S. Othman, and J. Khan. 2016. Automatic concepts classification based on bloom's taxonomy using text analysis and the naïve bayes classifier method. In *CSEDU*.

D. Oliver, Tony Dobele, Myles Greber, and Tim S. Roberts. 2004. This course has a bloom rating of 3.9. In *ACE*.

Matthew Peters, Mark Neumann, Mohit Iyyer, Matt Gardner, Christopher Clark, Kenton Lee, and Luke Zettlemoyer. 2018. Deep contextualized word representations. In *Proceedings of the 2018 Conference of the North American Chapter of the Association for Computational Linguistics: Human Language Technologies, Volume 1 (Long Papers)*, pages 2227–2237.

Fabio Petroni, Tim Rocktäschel, Patrick Lewis, Anton Bakhtin, Yuxiang Wu, Alexander H Miller, and Sebastian Riedel. 2019. Language models as knowledge bases? *arXiv preprint arXiv:1909.01066.*

Alec Radford, Jeffrey Wu, Rewon Child, David Luan, Dario Amodei, and Ilya Sutskever. 2019. Language models are unsupervised multitask learners. *OpenAI blog*, 1(8):9.

Melissa Roemmele, Cosmin Adrian Bejan, and Andrew S Gordon. 2011. Choice of plausible alternatives: An evaluation of commonsense causal reasoning. In *AAAI Spring Symposium: Logical Formalizations of Commonsense Reasoning*, pages 90–95.

Keisuke Sakaguchi, Ronan Le Bras, Chandra Bhagavatula, and Yejin Choi. 2020. Winogrande: An adversarial winograd schema challenge at scale. In *Proceedings of the AAAI Conference on Artificial Intelligence*, volume 34-05, pages 8732–8740.

Victor Sanh, Lysandre Debut, Julien Chaumond, and Thomas Wolf. 2019. Distilbert, a distilled version of bert: smaller, faster, cheaper and lighter. *ArXiv*, abs/1910.01108.

Maarten Sap, Hannah Rashkin, Derek Chen, Ronan Le Bras, and Yejin Choi. 2019. Social iqa: Commonsense reasoning about social interactions. In *Proceedings of the 2019 Conference on Empirical Methods in Natural Language Processing and the 9th International Joint Conference on Natural Language Processing (EMNLP-IJCNLP)*, pages 4453–4463.

Vered Shwartz, Peter West, Ronan Le Bras, Chandra Bhagavatula, and Yejin Choi. 2020. Unsupervised commonsense question answering with self-talk. In *Proceedings of the 2020 Conference on Empirical Methods in Natural Language Processing (EMNLP)*, pages 4615–4629.

Alon Talmor, Jonathan Herzig, Nicholas Lourie, and Jonathan Berant. 2019. Commonsenseqa: A question answering challenge targeting commonsense knowledge. In *Proceedings of the 2019 Conference of the North American Chapter of the Association for Computational Linguistics: Human Language Technologies, Volume 1 (Long and Short Papers)*, pages 4149–4158.

E. Thompson, Andrew Luxton-Reilly, J. Whalley, M. Hu, and Phil Robbins. 2008. Bloom's taxonomy for cs assessment. In *ACE '08*.

J. Whalley, R. Lister, E. Thompson, T. Clear, Phil Robbins, P. Kumar, and C. Prasad. 2006. An australasian study of reading and comprehension skills in novice programmers, using the bloom and solo taxonomies.

James Zhang, Casey Wong, Nasser Giacaman, and Andrew Luxton-Reilly. 2021. Automated classification of computing education questions using bloom's taxonomy. *Australasian Computing Education Conference*.

A Prefixes and Examples

In the appendix we provides more details about the question prefixes we used in Tab. 3 and provide more examples of outputs from our models in Tab. 5.

Table 3: All the prefix questions with its corresponding taxonomy level used in our zero shot question answering evaluation.

Question Prefix	Answer Prefix	Bloom's Taxonomy Level
	CommonsenseQA & COPA	
What is the definition of	The definition of _ is	1
What is the main purpose of	The purpose of _ is to	2
What is the main function of a	The main function of a _ is	2
What are the properties of a	The properties of a _ are that	1
What is a	_ is	1
What happened as a result of	As a result of _,	3
What might have caused	The cause of _ was	3
	SocialIQA	
What will [NAME] want to do next?	NAME] wanted	3
What will [NAME] want to do after?	[NAME] wanted	3
How would [NAME] feel afterwards?	[NAME] felt	3
How would [NAME] feel as a result?	[NAME] felt	3
How would [NAME] feel after?	[NAME] felt	3
How would you describe [NAME]?	[NAME] is a	2
What kind of person is [NAME]?	[NAME] is a	2
How would you describe [NAME] as a person?	[NAME] is a	2
Why did [NAME] do that?	[NAME] did this because they wanted	3
Why did [NAME] do this?	[NAME] did this because they wanted	3
Why did [NAME] want to do this?	[NAME] did this because they wanted	3
What does [NAME] need to do beforehand?	Before doing that, [NAME] first had to	2
What does [NAME] need to do before?	Before doing that, [NAME] first had to	2
What does [NAME] need to do before this?	Before doing that, [NAME] first had to	2
What did [NAME] need to do before this?	Before doing that, [NAME] first had to	2
What will happen to [NAME]?	[NAME]	3
What will happen to [NAME] next?	[NAME]	3
What will [NAME] do next?	[NAME]	3
What did [NAME] do?	What [NAME] did was	1
	Winogrande	
What is the definition of	The definition of _ is	1
What is the main purpose of	The purpose of _ is to	2
What is the main function of a	The main function of a _ is	2
What are the properties of a	The properties of a _ are that	1
What is	_ is	1
What does it mean to	_ means	2

Table 4: Example contexts, questions, choices, clarification questions and clarification answers for each dataset. We present results for both Distil-GPT2 and GPT-Neo.

COPA	Generated Clarifications	
(Context, Question, Choice)	**Distil-GPT2**	**GPT-Neo**
C:The man turned on the faucet. Q: effect Ch: [The toilet filled with water., **Water flowed from the spout.**]	Q: What might have caused it to be so hot? A: The cause of it to be so hot was that he would have a big fire in his face and then immediately had an explosion, which killed all but one person.	Q: What happened as a result of that? A: As a result of that, he was forced to drink water.
C: The woman retired. Q: effect Ch: [**She received her pension.**, She paid off her mortgage.]	Q: What happened as a result of this? A: As a result of this, the government has announced that it will pay Rs 7 crore to her family for compensation and legal expenses related thereto as part-time payments.	Q: What happened as a result of her retirement? A: As a result of her retirement, she had been receiving a pension for life.
C: I wanted to conserve energy. Q: effect Ch: [I swept the floor in the unoccupied room., **I shut off the light in the unoccupied room.**]	Q: What is the main function of a plant? A: The main function of a plant is the growth and maintenance of nutrients, so that we can increase our food intake by 10% or more per year, he said.	Q: What might have caused this? A: The cause of this was the lack of electricity in my home.
Winogrande	**Generated Clarifications**	
(Sentence, Context, Choice)	**Distil-GPT2**	**GPT-Neo**
S: The home that my parents had when I was in school was a lot nicer than my house now because the _ was sophisticated. C: home Ch: [**home**, house]	Q: What is the main function of a building? A: The main function of a building is to keep people happy and healthy.	Q: What are the properties of a home? A: he properties of a home are that which makes it comfortable and pleasant for the occupants.
S: He had enough time between classes to go to a cafe or to the library. He went to the _ because his paper could wait. C: classes Ch: [**cafe**, library]	Q: What is the definition of a book? A: The definition of a book is an article written in order for it be read.	Q: What is the definition of cafe? A: cafe is defined as a place where people gather for refreshment.
S: They had to eat a lot to gain the strength they had lost and be able to work, the _ was too much. C: strength Ch: [**work**, strength]	Q: What is the main function of a good diet? A: The main function of a good diet is not for food or health but also on exercise.	Q: What is the definition of strength? A: strength is defined as : having power or ability to do something.
SocialIQA	**Generated Clarifications**	
(Context, Question, Choice)	**Distil-GPT2**	**GPT-Neo**
C: Kendall got a new sports car and could not wait to show friends. Q: What will Kendall want to do next? Ch: [drive that sports car, **show off his new sports car**, clean and wax her legs]	Q: Why did Kendall want to do this? A: Kendall did this because they wanted her, too.	Q: What will Kendall want to do next? A: Kendall wanted to impress them with his new ride."
C: Kendall was really into house plants and often pour water in to jars so the fluoride would evaporate out. Q: What will Kendall want to do next? Ch: [**watered a few of the plants**, gather jars, watered a few of her pets]	Q: Why did Kendall do that? A: Kendall did this because they wanted him at home, he said.	Q: Why did Kendall do this? A: Kendall did this because they wanted to get a lot of water for their plants.
C: Remy gave birth to a baby girl on a Saturday afternoon. Q: What does Remy need to do before this? Ch: [leave her husband, did this to start a family, **go to the hospital**]	Q: What did Remy need to do before this? A: Before doing that, Remy first had to tell her he was too old.	Q: What does Remy need to do before? A: Before doing that, Remy first had to go to the hospital to deliver her baby.
CommonsenseQA	**Generated Clarifications**	
(Context, Question, Choice)	**Distil-GPT2**	**GPT-Neo**
C: In what Spanish speaking North American country can you get a great cup of coffee? Q: cup of coffee Ch: [mildred's coffee shop, **mexico**, diner, kitchen, canteen]	Q: What is the definition of coffee? A: The definition of coffee is the word that comes from Latin for espresso.	Q: What is the definition of mexico? A: mexico is defined as the country that produces the best coffee.
C: Unlike a spider and his many sight seers, people only have what? Q: people Ch: [tongues, names, brains, feelings, **two eyes**]	Q: What is the main purpose of this article? A: The purpose of this article is to explain the basic characteristics that are characteristic of spiders.	Q: What is the definition of two eyes? A: two eyes is defined as the organs by which we see.
C: The artist was sitting quietly pondering, then suddenly he began to paint when what struck him? Q: sitting quietly Ch: [sadness, anxiety, **inspiration**, discomfort, insights]	Q: What is a man who can do that? A: Man who can do that is a really great painter.	Q: What is the definition of inspiration? A: inspiration is defined as a sudden flash of inspiration that comes from within.

Larger-Scale Transformers for Multilingual Masked Language Modeling

Naman Goyal Jingfei Du Myle Ott Giri Anantharaman Alexis Conneau
{naman, jingfeidu, myleott, giriman, aconneau}@fb.com

Facebook AI

Abstract

Recent work has demonstrated the effectiveness of cross-lingual language model pretraining for cross-lingual understanding. In this study, we present the results of two larger multilingual masked language models, with 3.5B and 10.7B parameters. Our two new models dubbed XLM-R_{XL} and XLM-R_{XXL} outperform XLM-R by 1.8% and 2.4% average accuracy on XNLI. Our model also outperforms the RoBERTa-Large model on several English tasks of the GLUE benchmark by 0.3% on average while handling 99 more languages. This suggests larger capacity models for language understanding may obtain strong performance on both high- and low-resource languages. We make our code and models publicly available.[1]

1 Introduction

The goal of this paper is to present a study of the impact of larger capacity models on cross-lingual language understanding (XLU). We scale the capacity of XLM-R by almost two orders of magnitude while training on the same CC100 dataset (Wenzek et al., 2019). Our two new multilingual masked language model dubbed XLM-R_{XL} and XLM-R_{XXL}, with 3.5 and 10.7 billion parameters respectively, significantly outperform the previous XLM-R model on cross-lingual understanding benchmarks and obtain competitive performance with the multilingual T5 models (Raffel et al., 2019; Xue et al., 2020). We show that they can even outperform RoBERTa-Large (Liu et al., 2019) on the GLUE benchmark (Wang et al., 2018).

Recent multilingual masked language models (MLM) like mBERT (Devlin et al., 2018) or XLM (Lample and Conneau, 2019) improved cross-lingual language understanding by pretraining large Transformer models (Vaswani et al., 2017) on multiple languages at once. The XLM-R model (Conneau et al., 2019) extended that approach by scaling the amount of data by two orders of magnitude, from Wikipedia to Common-Crawl and training longer, similar to RoBERTa (Liu et al., 2019). These models are particularly effective for low-resource languages, where both labeled and unlabeled data is scarce. They enable supervised cross-lingual transfer, where labeled data in one language can be used to solve the same task in other languages, and unsupervised cross-lingual transfer, where low-resource language self-supervised representations are improved using additional unlabeled data from higher-resource languages. Furthermore, they reduce the need for training one model per language, and allows the use of a single - potentially much larger - pretrained model that is then fine-tuned on annotated data from many languages.

The better performance of self-supervised cross-lingual models on low-resource languages comes however at the cost of lower performance on higher-resource languages (Arivazhagan et al., 2019). When the number of languages becomes large, Conneau et al. (2019) even observed an overall decrease of performance on all languages. It was hypothesized that when multilingual models get more capacity, they may showcase strong performance on both high-resource languages and low-resource languages. With only 550M parameters, the XLM-R model is now relatively small compared to new standards. Recent work scaled language models to hundreds of billions (Brown et al., 2020) or even multiple trillion parameters (Fedus et al., 2021), showing consistent gains in doing so. Recently, multilingual T5 showed impressive increase in performance by scaling the model capacity to tens of billions of parameters. Our study complements these findings by showing the impact of larger capacity models on the important pretraining task of *multilingual* masked language model-

[1] https://github.com/anonymous

Proceedings of the 6th Workshop on Representation Learning for NLP (RepL4NLP-2021), pages 29–33
Bangkok, Thailand (Online), August 6, 2021.

ing. We show promising results for cross-lingual understanding: XLM-R_{XXL} can both obtain a new state of the art on some cross-lingual understanding benchmarks and outperform the RoBERTa-Large model on the English GLUE benchmark (Wang et al., 2018). This suggests that very large-scale multilingual models may be able to benefit from the best of both worlds: obtaining strong performance on high-resource languages while still allowing for zero-shot transfer and low-resource language understanding. We make the following contributions:

- We scale XLM capacity by two orders of magnitude, and publicly release XLM-R_{XL} and XLM-R_{XXL} with 3.5B and 10.7B parameters.
- We show that those two models obtain very strong performance on cross-lingual benchmarks while outperforming $\text{RoBERTa}_{\text{Large}}$ on the GLUE benchmark.

2 Pretraining and evaluation

In this section, we describe the model we use and how we scale it, as well as the data and tasks we use for pretraining and evaluation.

2.1 Multilingual masked language models

We use a Transformer model (Vaswani et al., 2017) trained with the multilingual MLM objective (Devlin et al., 2018; Lample and Conneau, 2019) using only monolingual data. We sample streams of text from each language and train the model to predict the masked tokens in the input. We use the same learning procedure as XLM-R. We apply subword tokenization directly on raw text data using Sentence Piece (Kudo and Richardson, 2018) with a unigram language model (Kudo, 2018) just like in XLM-R. We sample batches from different languages using the same sampling distribution as Conneau et al. (2019), with $\alpha = 0.3$, and without language embeddings. We use a large vocabulary size of 250K with a full softmax and train two different models: XLM-R_{XL} (L = 36, H = 2560, A = 32, 3.5B params) and XLM-R_{XXL} (L = 48, H = 4096, A = 32, 10.7B params). We pretrain the models on the CC100 dataset, which corresponds to 167B tokens in 100 languages. We compare our approach to previous results as well as the mT5 baselines, which were pretrained on the larger mC4 corpus of 6.4T tokens.

2.2 Evaluation

We consider three evaluation benchmarks. For cross-lingual understanding, we use cross-lingual natural language inference and question answering, and use the GLUE benchmark to evaluate the English performance.

Cross-lingual Natural Language Inference. The XNLI dataset (Conneau et al., 2018) comes with ground-truth dev and test sets in 15 languages, and a ground-truth English training set. The training set has been machine-translated to the remaining 14 languages, providing synthetic training data for these languages as well. We evaluate our model on cross-lingual transfer from English to other languages. We also consider two machine translation baselines: (i) *translate-test*: dev and test sets are machine-translated to English and a single English model is used (ii) *translate-train-all*: the English training set is machine-translated to each language and we fine-tune a multilingual model on all training sets. For translations, we use the original XNLI data for consistency.

Cross-lingual Question Answering. We use the MLQA and XQuad benchmark from Lewis et al. (2019) and Artetxe et al. (2019), which extends the English SQuAD benchmark to more languages. We report the F1 score as well as the exact match (EM) score for cross-lingual transfer from English.

The English GLUE Benchmark. Finally, we evaluate the English performance of our model on the GLUE benchmark (Wang et al., 2018) which gathers multiple classification tasks, such as MNLI (Williams et al., 2017), SST-2 (Socher et al., 2013), or QNLI (Rajpurkar et al., 2018).

2.3 Training details

We use model parallelism based on tensor parallel (Shoeybi et al., 2019) for scaling models. XLM-R_{XL} uses model parallel size of 2 and XLM-R_{XXL} used 8. Compared to previous XLM-R models, we reduce the batch size and number of updates significantly to keep the compute of the new models similar (see Table 5). For both models, we use batch size of 2048 and train for 500,000 updates. We use pre-LayerNorm setting for both the models which was more stable during training.

For all the tasks in finetuning, we use batch size of 32 and train for 10 epochs. We do early stopping based on the average valid metrics across all languages and report test results.

Model	Data (#tok)	en	fr	es	de	el	bg	ru	tr	ar	vi	th	zh	hi	sw	ur	Avg
Fine-tune multilingual model on English training set (Cross-lingual Transfer)																	
mBERT	Wikipedia	80.8	64.3	68.0	70.0	65.3	73.5	73.4	58.9	67.8	49.7	54.1	60.9	57.2	69.3	67.8	65.4
XLM		83.2	76.5	76.3	74.2	73.1	74.0	73.1	67.8	68.5	71.2	69.2	71.9	65.7	64.6	63.4	71.5
mT5-Base	mC4 (6.4T)	84.7	73.3	78.6	77.4	77.1	80.3	79.1	70.8	77.1	69.4	73.2	72.8	68.3	74.2	74.1	75.4
mT5-Large		89.4	79.8	84.1	83.4	83.2	84.2	84.1	77.6	81.5	75.4	79.4	80.1	73.5	81.0	80.3	81.1
mT5-XL		90.6	82.2	85.4	85.8	85.4	81.3	85.3	80.4	83.7	78.6	80.9	82.0	77.0	81.8	82.7	82.9
mT5-XXL		91.6	84.5	87.7	87.3	87.3	87.8	86.9	83.2	85.1	80.3	81.7	83.8	79.8	84.6	83.6	84.5
XLM-R_{Base}	CC100 (167B)	85.8	79.7	80.7	78.7	77.5	79.6	78.1	74.2	73.8	76.5	74.6	76.7	72.4	66.5	68.3	76.2
XLM-R_{Large}		89.1	84.1	85.1	83.9	82.9	84.0	81.2	79.6	79.8	80.8	78.1	80.2	76.9	73.9	73.8	80.9
XLM-R_{XL}		90.7	85.5	86.5	84.6	84.0	85.2	82.7	81.7	81.6	82.4	79.4	81.7	78.5	75.3	74.3	82.3
XLM-R_{XXL}		91.6	86.2	87.3	87.0	85.1	85.7	82.5	82.0	82.5	83.0	79.5	82.6	79.8	76.2	74.9	83.1
Translate everything to English and use English-only model (TRANSLATE-TEST)																	
RoBERTa	CC-En	91.3	82.9	84.3	81.2	81.7	83.1	78.3	76.8	76.6	74.2	74.1	77.5	70.9	66.7	66.8	77.8
Fine-tune multilingual model on all training sets (TRANSLATE-TRAIN-ALL)																	
mT5-Base	mC4 (6.4T)	82.0	74.4	78.5	77.7	78.1	79.1	77.9	72.2	76.5	71.5	75.0	74.8	70.4	74.5	76.0	75.9
mT5-Large		88.3	80.3	84.1	84.0	83.7	84.9	83.8	79.8	82.0	76.4	79.9	81.0	75.9	81.3	81.7	81.8
mT5-XL		90.9	84.2	86.8	86.8	86.4	87.4	86.8	83.1	84.9	81.3	82.3	84.4	79.4	83.9	84.0	84.8
mT5-XXL		**92.7**	87.2	**89.4**	**89.8**	**89.5**	**90.0**	**89.1**	**86.5**	**87.6**	84.3	**85.6**	**87.1**	83.8	**87.5**	**86.5**	**87.8**
XLM-R_{Base}	CC100 (167B)	85.4	81.4	82.2	80.3	80.4	81.3	79.7	78.6	77.3	79.7	77.9	80.2	76.1	73.1	73.0	79.1
XLM-R_{Large}		89.1	85.1	86.6	85.7	85.3	85.9	83.5	83.2	83.1	83.7	81.5	83.7	81.6	78.0	78.1	83.6
XLM-R_{XL}		91.1	87.2	88.1	87.0	87.4	87.8	85.3	85.2	85.3	86.2	83.8	85.3	83.1	79.8	78.2	85.4
XLM-R_{XXL}		91.5	**87.6**	88.7	87.8	87.4	88.2	85.6	85.1	85.8	**86.3**	83.9	85.6	**84.6**	81.7	80.6	86.0

Table 1: **Results on cross-lingual classification (XNLI).** We report the accuracy on each of the 15 XNLI languages and average accuracy, and specify the dataset and its corresponding size in number of tokens. We report results of XLM-R models with increasing capacity, from 270M (Base), 550M (Large), 3.5B (XL) to 10.7B (XXL) parameters.

3 Analysis and Results

In this section, we present our results and compare XLM-R_{XL} and XLM-R_{XXL} performance to other methods from previous work.

Cross-lingual understanding results. On XNLI, we observe in Table 1 that scaling the capacity from XLM-R_{Large} to XLM-R_{XL} leads to an average accuracy improvement of 1.4 on zero-shot cross-lingual transfer and 1.8 on multilingual fine-tuning. When scaling even further to XLM-R_{XXL}, we observe a total improvement of 2.2 on zero-shot and 2.4 on translate-train-all compared to XLM-R_{XL}, with a new state of the art on French, Vietnamese and Hindi. On MLQA, in Table 4, we observe even larger gains for cross-lingual zero-shot transfer, where scaling from XLM-R_{Large} to XLM-R_{XXL} leads to improvements of 4.1 F1 and 3.9 EM scores on average. Similarly, on XQuad we observe improvements of 4.4 F1 and 5.5 scores, with new state-of-the-art results on Arabic, German, Greek and Russian (see Table 3).

Comparison to monolingual English model. For smaller-capacity models like the Base and Large version of XLM-R, it was shown that the more languages are considered the lower the performance (Conneau et al., 2019), in particular on high-resource languages. For instance, XLM-R_{Large} was outperformed by RoBERTa$_{Large}$ by 1% accuracy on average on several downstream tasks from the GLUE benchmark, as illustrated in Table2. With larger capacity, we now observe that XLM-R_{XXL} is able to outperform RoBERTa$_{Large}$ by 0.3 dev points, going from 92.9 to 93.2 average accuracy, while handling 99 more languages. While a RoBERTa$_{XXL}$ model may outperform XLM-R_{XXL}, we believe it interesting to notice that with more capacity, a multilingual model can get strong high-resource performance while not losing its cross-lingual transfer ability for lower-resource languages. Given the compute needed for training such large-scale models, the possibility of training a single very large model on hundreds of languages with state-of-the-art performance on high-resource languages is an encouraging and positive result.

Model	#lgs	MNLI	QNLI	QQP	SST	MRPC	Avg
RoBERTa[†]	1	90.2	94.7	92.2	96.4	**90.9**	92.9
XLM-R_{Large}	100	88.9	93.8	92.3	95.0	89.5	91.9
XLM-R_{XL}	100	90.4	94.9	92.5	96.6	90.4	93.0
XLM-R_{XXL}	100	**90.9**	**95.0**	**92.6**	**96.7**	90.7	**93.2**

Table 2: GLUE dev results

Model	en	ar	de	el	es	hi	ru	th	tr	vi	zh	avg
Cross-lingual zero-shot transfer (models fine-tune on English data only)												
mT5-Large	88.4 / 77.3	75.2 / 56.7	80.0 / 62.9	77.5 / 57.6	81.8 / 64.2	73.4 / 56.6	74.7 / 56.9	73.4 / 62.0	76.5 / 56.3	79.4 / 60.3	75.9 / 65.5	77.8 / 61.5
mT5-XL	88.8 / 78.1	77.4 / 60.8	80.4 / 63.5	80.4 / 61.2	82.7 / 64.5	76.1 / 60.3	76.2 / 58.8	74.2 / 62.5	77.7 / 58.4	80.5 / 60.8	80.5 / 71.0	79.5 / 63.6
mt5-XXL	**90.9 / 80.1**	**80.3** / 62.6	**83.1** / 65.5	83.3 / **65.5**	**85.1 / 68.1**	**81.7 / 65.9**	79.3 / 63.6	**77.8 / 66.1**	**80.2** / 60.9	**83.1 / 63.6**	**83.1 / 73.4**	**82.5 / 66.8**
XLM-R_{Large}	86.5 / 75.7	68.6 / 49.0	80.4 / 63.4	79.8 / 61.7	82.0 / 63.9	76.7 / 59.7	80.1 / 64.3	74.2 / 62.8	75.9 / 59.3	79.1 / 59.0	59.3 / 50.0	76.6 / 60.8
XLM-R_{XL}	89.5 / 79.0	78.4 / 61.6	81.3 / 64.1	82.3 / 63.9	84.6 / 66.2	78.8 / 63.2	81.5 / 65.0	76.0 / 65.5	73.9 / 57.9	81.7 / 61.8	72.3 / 66.1	80.0 / 64.9
XLM-R_{XXL}	89.3 / 79.4	80.1 / **63.7**	82.7 / **65.8**	**83.4 / 65.5**	83.8 / 66.0	80.7 / 65.4	**82.4 / 65.4**	76.6 / 65.6	76.8 / **61.7**	82.2 / 63.0	74.1 / 67.4	81.1 / 66.3

Table 3: XQuad results (F1/EM) for each language.

Model	en	es	de	ar	hi	vi	zh	Avg
Cross-lingual zero-shot transfer (models fine-tune on English data only)								
mT5-Large	84.9 / 70.7	65.3 / 44.6	68.9 / 51.8	73.5 / 54.1	66.9 / 47.7	72.5 / 50.7	66.2 / 42.0	71.2 / 51.7
mT5-XL	85.5 / 71.9	68.0 / 47.4	70.5 / 54.4	75.2 / 56.3	70.5 / 51.0	74.2 / 52.8	70.5 / 47.2	73.5 / 54.4
mT5-XXL	**86.7 / 73.5**	**70.7 / 50.4**	**74.0 / 57.8**	**76.8 / 58.4**	**75.6 / 57.3**	**76.4 / 56.0**	**71.8** / 48.8	**76.0 / 57.4**
XLM-R_{Large}	80.6 / 67.8	74.1 / 56.0	68.5 / 53.6	63.1 / 43.5	69.2 / 51.6	71.3 / 50.9	68.0 / 45.4	70.7 / 52.7
XLM-R_{XL}	85.1 / 72.6	66.7 / 46.2	70.5 / 55.5	74.3 / 56.9	72.2 / 54.7	74.4 / 52.9	70.9 / 48.5	73.4 / 55.3
XLM-R_{XXL}	85.5 / 72.4	68.6 / 48.4	72.7 / **57.8**	75.4 / 57.6	73.7 / 55.8	76.0 / 55.0	71.7 / **48.9**	74.8 / 56.6

Table 4: MLQA results (F1/EM) for each language.

Discussion and comparison to mT5. Both mT5 and XLM-R models obtain strong performance on cross-lingual understanding benchmarks, as well as high performance on English benchmarks (see the score of 91.6 of mT5$_{XXL}$ on English XNLI). Many hyperparameters are however different between mT5 and XLM-R models which makes difficult an apple-to-apple comparison. First, as shown in Table 5, the mT5 models are pretrained on the much larger mC4 dataset which contains around 6.4T tokens, which is 38 times bigger than CC100 (167B tokens). While XLM-R_{Large} was pretrained with more updates (6T tokens), the XLM-R_{XL} and XLM-R_{XXL} models have seen less tokens (0.5T) during pretraining than their mT5 counterparts, although it also uses a bigger batch size (2048 over 1024 for mT5). Another difference is the context sequence length of 512 for XLM-R and 1024 for mT5. The mT5-XXL model also has slightly more parameters (13B over 10.7B). The larger number of updates combined with the larger dataset size may explain the larger improvement from the XL model to the XXL model in the case of mT5 (+3 average accuracy on XNLI), in which the additional capacity can exploit the large quantity of unlabeled mC4 data. We note however that the mT5$_{XL}$ is outperformed by XLM-R_{XL} on XNLI by 0.6% on average, on XQuad by 1.3% and on MLQA by 0.9% when considering average EM score. In comparison, gains of XLM-R from the XL to the XXL architecture are only of 0.6 on average. Another explanation may be that generative models scale better than masked language models. The difference in the nature of the pretraining dataset is particularly striking when looking at the variance of performance across languages. For example the mT5$_{XXL}$ outperforms XLM-R_{XXL} by 8.4 points on Swahili on XNLI zero-shot, while it only outperforms XLM-R_{XXL} by 1.4 average accuracy. These results may suggest that the CC100 dataset gets saturated with current larger-capacity models.

Model	Number of parameters	Dataset name	Dataset size	Number of training tokens	Batch size	Sequence length
XLM-R_{Large}	550M	CC100	167B	6T	8192	512
XLM-R_{XL}	3.5B	CC100	167B	0.5T	2048	512
XLM-R_{XXL}	10.7B	CC100	167B	0.5T	2048	512
mt5-XL	3.7B	mC4	6.4T	1T	1024	1024
mt5-XXL	13B	mC4	6.4T	1T	1024	1024

Table 5: Comparison of datasets and pretraining details between XLM-R and mT5. We report dataset sizes and number of updates in terms of number of tokens.

4 Conclusion

In this study, we scaled the model capacity of the XLM-R model up to 10.7B parameters and obtained stronger performance than previous XLM-R models on cross-lingual understanding benchmarks. We also show that the additional capacity allows a multilingual model to outperform a the RoBERTa$_{Large}$ baseline on English benchmarks. Our technical study thus suggests that larger capacity multilingual model can obtain state-of-the-art cross-lingual understanding results while maintaining strong performance on high-resource languages. Our work provides an alternative to mT5 models, with new state-of-the-art performance on some languages. We release our code and models publicly.

References

Naveen Arivazhagan, Ankur Bapna, Orhan Firat, Dmitry Lepikhin, Melvin Johnson, Maxim Krikun, Mia Xu Chen, Yuan Cao, George Foster, Colin Cherry, et al. 2019. Massively multilingual neural machine translation in the wild: Findings and challenges. *arXiv preprint arXiv:1907.05019*.

Mikel Artetxe, Sebastian Ruder, and Dani Yogatama. 2019. On the cross-lingual transferability of monolingual representations. *arXiv preprint arXiv:1910.11856*.

Tom B Brown, Benjamin Mann, Nick Ryder, Melanie Subbiah, Jared Kaplan, Prafulla Dhariwal, Arvind Neelakantan, Pranav Shyam, Girish Sastry, Amanda Askell, et al. 2020. Language models are few-shot learners. *Proc. of NeurIPS*.

Alexis Conneau, Kartikay Khandelwal, Naman Goyal, Vishrav Chaudhary, Guillaume Wenzek, Francisco Guzmán, Edouard Grave, Myle Ott, Luke Zettlemoyer, and Veselin Stoyanov. 2019. Unsupervised cross-lingual representation learning at scale. *arXiv preprint arXiv:1911.02116*.

Alexis Conneau, Ruty Rinott, Guillaume Lample, Adina Williams, Samuel R. Bowman, Holger Schwenk, and Veselin Stoyanov. 2018. Xnli: Evaluating cross-lingual sentence representations. In *EMNLP*. Association for Computational Linguistics.

Jacob Devlin, Ming-Wei Chang, Kenton Lee, and Kristina Toutanova. 2018. Bert: Pre-training of deep bidirectional transformers for language understanding. *NAACL*.

William Fedus, Barret Zoph, and Noam Shazeer. 2021. Switch transformers: Scaling to trillion parameter models with simple and efficient sparsity. *arXiv preprint arXiv:2101.03961*.

Taku Kudo. 2018. Subword regularization: Improving neural network translation models with multiple subword candidates. In *ACL*, pages 66–75.

Taku Kudo and John Richardson. 2018. Sentencepiece: A simple and language independent subword tokenizer and detokenizer for neural text processing. *EMNLP*.

Guillaume Lample and Alexis Conneau. 2019. Cross-lingual language model pretraining. *NeurIPS*.

Patrick Lewis, Barlas Oğuz, Ruty Rinott, Sebastian Riedel, and Holger Schwenk. 2019. Mlqa: Evaluating cross-lingual extractive question answering. *arXiv preprint arXiv:1910.07475*.

Yinhan Liu, Myle Ott, Naman Goyal, Jingfei Du, Mandar Joshi, Danqi Chen, Omer Levy, Mike Lewis, Luke Zettlemoyer, and Veselin Stoyanov. 2019. Roberta: A robustly optimized BERT pretraining approach. *arXiv preprint arXiv:1907.11692*.

Colin Raffel, Noam Shazeer, Adam Roberts, Katherine Lee, Sharan Narang, Michael Matena, Yanqi Zhou, Wei Li, and Peter J. Liu. 2019. Exploring the limits of transfer learning with a unified text-to-text transformer. *arXiv preprint arXiv:1910.10683*.

Pranav Rajpurkar, Robin Jia, and Percy Liang. 2018. Know what you don't know: Unanswerable questions for squad. *ACL*.

Mohammad Shoeybi, Mostofa Patwary, Raul Puri, Patrick LeGresley, Jared Casper, and Bryan Catanzaro. 2019. Megatron-lm: Training multi-billion parameter language models using model parallelism. *arXiv preprint arXiv:1909.08053*.

Richard Socher, Alex Perelygin, Jean Wu, Jason Chuang, Christopher D Manning, Andrew Ng, and Christopher Potts. 2013. Recursive deep models for semantic compositionality over a sentiment treebank. In *EMNLP*, pages 1631–1642.

Ashish Vaswani, Noam Shazeer, Niki Parmar, Jakob Uszkoreit, Llion Jones, Aidan N. Gomez, Lukasz Kaiser, and Illia Polosukhin. 2017. Attention is all you need. In *Advances in Neural Information Processing Systems*, pages 6000–6010.

Alex Wang, Amanpreet Singh, Julian Michael, Felix Hill, Omer Levy, and Samuel R Bowman. 2018. Glue: A multi-task benchmark and analysis platform for natural language understanding. *arXiv preprint arXiv:1804.07461*.

Guillaume Wenzek, Marie-Anne Lachaux, Alexis Conneau, Vishrav Chaudhary, Francisco Guzman, Armand Joulin, and Edouard Grave. 2019. Ccnet: Extracting high quality monolingual datasets from web crawl data. *arXiv preprint arXiv:1911.00359*.

Adina Williams, Nikita Nangia, and Samuel R Bowman. 2017. A broad-coverage challenge corpus for sentence understanding through inference. *Proceedings of the 2nd Workshop on Evaluating Vector-Space Representations for NLP*.

Linting Xue, Noah Constant, Adam Roberts, Mihir Kale, Rami Al-Rfou, Aditya Siddhant, Aditya Barua, and Colin Raffel. 2020. mt5: A massively multilingual pre-trained text-to-text transformer. *arXiv preprint arXiv:2010.11934*.

Learning Sparse Sentence Encoding without Supervision: An Exploration of Sparsity in Variational Autoencoders

Victor Prokhorov[♣] **Yingzhen Li**[◇*] **Ehsan Shareghi**[♠♣] **Nigel Collier**[♣]
[♣] Language Technology Lab, University of Cambridge
[♠] Department of Data Science & AI, Monash University
[◇] Department of Computing, Imperial College London
vp361@cam.ac.uk, yingzhen.li@imperial.ac.uk,
ehsan.shareghi@monash.edu, nhc30@cam.ac.uk

Abstract

It has been long known that sparsity is an effective inductive bias for learning efficient representation of data in vectors with *fixed dimensionality*, and it has been explored in many areas of representation learning. Of particular interest to this work is the investigation of the sparsity within the VAE framework which has been explored a lot in the image domain, but has been lacking even a basic level of exploration in NLP. Additionally, NLP is also lagging behind in terms of learning sparse representations of large units of text e.g., sentences. We use the VAEs that induce sparse latent representations of large units of text to address the aforementioned shortcomings. First, we move in this direction by measuring the success of unsupervised state-of-the-art (SOTA) and other strong VAE-based sparsification baselines for text and propose a hierarchical sparse VAE model to address the stability issue of SOTA. Then, we look at the implications of sparsity on text classification across 3 datasets, and highlight a link between performance of sparse latent representations on downstream tasks and its ability to encode task-related information.[1]

1 Introduction

Representation learning has been pivotal in many success stories of modern days NLP. Observing its success, two fundamental questions arise: *How is the information encoded in them?* and *What is encoded in them?* While the latter has received a lot of attention by designing probing tasks, the former has been vastly neglected. In this work, we take small steps in this non-trivial direction by building on the knowns: One property we know about the encoding of information is that different data points embody different characteristics (e.g. statistically, semantically, or syntactically) which should ideally utilise different sub-regions of the representation space. Therefore, the high-dimensional learned representations should ideally be sparse (Bengio et al., 2013; Burgess et al., 2018; Tonolini et al., 2019). In other words it allows us to have varying number of active dimension per sentence[2] (Bengio, 2009) in a fixed dimensional vector[3]. But *if sparsity*[4] *is expected, could it be learned from data without supervision?*

A handful of studies in NLP that have delved into building sparse representations of words either during the learning phase (Faruqui and Dyer, 2015; Yogatama et al., 2015) or as a post-processing step on top of existing representations (e.g., word2vec embeddings) (Faruqui et al., 2015; Sun et al., 2016; Subramanian et al., 2018; Arora et al., 2018; Li and Hao, 2019). These methods have not been developed for sentence embeddings, with the exception of Trifonov et al. (2018) which makes a strong assumption by forcing the latent sentence representation to be a sparse categorical distribution.

In parallel, Variational Autoencoders (VAEs) (Kingma and Welling, 2014) have been effective in capturing semantic closeness of sentences in the learned representation space (Bowman et al., 2016; Prokhorov et al., 2019; Xu et al., 2019; Balasubramanian et al., 2020). Furthermore, methods have been developed

* Work done while at Microsoft Research Cambridge.

[1] The code is available on https://github.com/VictorProkhorov/HSVAE.

[2] This, for example, may allow us to cluster sentences' representations not only based on similarity of their active features (as it is the case for dense vectors) but also on active/inactive dimensions.

[3] More on speculative side, sparse representations may be a more natural way of modelling sentences of a language in a fixed dimensional vector. Sentences vary in length and an amount of information that they convey. As such it makes sense to reflect this property in a vector representation of the sentence.

[4] As in (Mathieu et al., 2019), we induce sparse representations for each data point.

Proceedings of the 6th Workshop on Representation Learning for NLP (RepL4NLP-2021), pages 34–46
Bangkok, Thailand (Online), August 6, 2021.

to encourage sparsity in VAEs via learning a deterministic selection variable (Yeung et al., 2017) or sparse priors (Barello et al., 2018; Mathieu et al., 2019; Tonolini et al., 2019). However, the success of these is yet to be examined on text domain.

To bridge this gap, we make a sober evaluation of existing state-of-the-art (SOTA) VAE-based sparsification model (Mathieu et al., 2019) against several VAE-based baselines on two experimental tasks: text classification accuracy, and the level of representation sparsity achieved. Additionally, we propose Hierarchical Sparse Variation Autoencoder (HSVAE), to improve the stability issue of existing SOTA model and demonstrate its performance on both experimental tasks.

Our experimental findings demonstrate that: (I) neither the simpler baseline models nor the SOTA manage to impose a satisfactory level of sparsity on text, (II) as expected, sparsity level and task performance have a negative correlation, while giving up task performance and having sparse codes helps with the analysis of the representations, (III) presence/absence of task related signal in the sparsity codes affects the task performance, (IV) the success of capturing the task related signal in the sparsity codes depends on the strength of the signal presented in a corpus, and representation dimensionality, (V) the success of SOTA in image domain does not necessarily transfer to inducing sparse representations for text, while HSVAE addresses this shortcoming.

2 Background

VAE. Given an input x, VAEs, Figure 1 (left), are stochastic autoencoders that map x to a corresponding representation z using a probabilistic encoder $q_\phi(z|x)$ and a probabilistic decoder $p_\theta(x|z)$, implemented as neural networks. Optimisation of VAE is done by maximising the ELBO:

$$\mathbb{E}_{q_\phi(z|x)} \log p_\theta(x|z) - \mathbb{D}_{KL}\big(q_\phi(z|x)||p_\theta(z)\big) \quad (1)$$

where the reconstruction maximises the expectation of data likelihood under the posterior distribution of z, and the Kullback-Leibler (KL) divergence acts as a regulariser and minimises the distance between the learned posterior and prior of z.

Spike-and-Slab Distribution. This is a mixture of two Gaussians with mixture weight γ_i, where the *slab* component is a standard Gaussian while the *spike* component is a Gaussian with $\sigma \to 0$:

$$p(z) = \prod_i^{D} (1-\gamma_i)\,\mathcal{N}(z_i; 0, 1) + \gamma_i\,\mathcal{N}(z_i; 0, \sigma\to 0)$$

where i denotes the ith dimension of z and D is the total number of dimensions of z.

Figure 1: Graphical Models of VAE (left) and HSVAE (right). Solid and dashed lines represent generative and inference paths, respectively.

3 Hierarchical Sparse VAE (HSVAE)

We propose the hierarchical sparse VAE (HSVAE), Figure 1 (right), to learn sparse latent codes automatically. We treat the mixture weights $\gamma = (\gamma_1, ..., \gamma_D)$ as a random variable and assign a factorised Beta prior $p_\theta(\gamma_i) = \text{Beta}(\alpha, \beta)$ on it. The latent code z is then sampled from a factorised Spike-and-Slab distribution $p_\theta(z|\gamma)$ conditioned on γ, and the observation x is generated by decoding the latent variable $x \sim p_\theta(x|z)$ using a GRU (Cho et al., 2014) decoder. This returns a probabilistic generative model $p_\theta(x, z, \gamma) = p_\theta(x|z)p_\theta(z|\gamma)p_\theta(\gamma)$.

For posterior inference, the encoder distribution is defined as $q_\phi(z, \gamma|x) = q_\phi(\gamma|x)q_\phi(z|\gamma, x)$, where $q_\phi(\gamma|x)$ is a learnable and factorised Beta distribution, and $q_\phi(z|\gamma, x)$ is a factorised Spike-and-Slab distribution with mixture weights γ_i and learnable "slab" components for each dimension. The q distribution is computed by first extracting features from the sequence using a GRU, then applying MLPs to the extracted feature (and γ for $q_\phi(z|\gamma, x)$) to produce the distributional parameters.

ELBO: We derive the ELBO, $\mathcal{L}(\theta, \phi; x)$:

$$\mathbb{E}_{q_\phi(z,\gamma|x)}[\log p_\theta(x|z)] - \psi\mathbb{E}_{q_\phi(\gamma|x)}[\mathbb{D}_{KL}\big(q_\phi(z|\gamma, x), p_\theta(z|\gamma)\big)] - \lambda\mathbb{D}_{KL}\big(q_\phi(\gamma|x)||p_\theta(\gamma)\big),$$

where $\psi \in \mathbb{R}$ and $\lambda \in \mathbb{R}$ are the coefficients for the KL terms. This ELBO is approximated with Monte Carlo (MC) in practice, $\mathcal{L}(\theta, \phi; x)$:

$$\frac{1}{N}\sum_{\gamma\sim q_\phi(\gamma|x)}^{N}\left[\frac{1}{M}\sum_{z\sim q_\phi(z|x,\gamma)}^{M}\log p_\theta(x|z)\right] - \frac{\psi}{N}\sum_{\gamma\sim q_\phi(\gamma|x)}^{N}\left[\mathbb{D}_{KL}(q_\phi(z|x,\gamma)||p_\theta(z|\gamma))\right] - \lambda\mathbb{D}_{KL}(q_\phi(\gamma|x)||p_\theta(\gamma)), \quad (2)$$

where M and N are scalar numbers corresponding to a number of samples taken from $q_\phi(z|x,\gamma)$ and $q_\phi(\gamma|x)$ respectively. In this work, we set both M and N to 1. Similar to the vanilla VAE, the first term is the reconstruction, the second and the third KL terms control the distance between the posteriors and their corresponding priors. The parameters of the priors are fixed to some constant values (can be also thought as the hyperparameters) during the training. Also, see *Appendix* for ELBO derivation.

Control of Sparsity. The random variable γ_i, in our model, can be viewed as a "probabilistic switch" that determines how likely is for the ith dimension of z to be turned off. Intuitively, since for both generation and inference the latent code z is sampled from a Spike-and-Slab distribution with the mixture weights γ, $\gamma_i \rightarrow 1$ means z_i is drawn from a delta mass centered at $z_i = 0$. As the switch follows a Beta distribution $\gamma_i \sim Beta(\gamma_i; \alpha, \beta)$, we can select the parameters α and β to control the concentration of the probability mass on $\gamma_i \in [0, 1]$ interval.

There are three typical configurations of the (α, β) pair: (1) $\alpha < \beta$: density is shifted towards $\gamma_i = 0$ hence ith unit is likely to be on and dense representation is expected, (2) $\alpha = \beta$: the density is centered at $\gamma_i = 0.5$, and (3) $\alpha > \beta$: density is shifted towards $\gamma_i = 1$, hence the unit is likely to be off, leading to sparsity. The magnitude of these parameters also plays a role as it controls the spread and uni/bi-modal structure of the density.

4 Experiments

We conduct a set of experiments on three text classification corpora: Yelp (sentiment analysis - 5 classes) (Yang et al., 2017), DBpedia and Yahoo (topic classification - 14 and 10 classes respectively) (Zhang et al., 2015). First, we compare performance of the sparse latent representations with their dense counterpart on the text classification tasks (§4.2). Second, the stability of sparsification of HSVAE is compared with the state-of-the-art MAT-VAE (§4.3). Then, to better understand performance of our model on the downstream task, we examine the sparsity patterns (§4.4).

Remark. An integral part of the experiments is the analysis of the learned representations. In this sense, tasks that rely on understanding of semantics (e.g., GLUE (Wang et al., 2018)) or syntax (e.g., (Marvin and Linzen, 2018)) would be non-trivial to analyse due to their inherent complexity. We consider classification tasks because the distribution of words alone could be a good indicator of class labels. Given the unsupervised nature of the models, we explore if this surface-level distribution of words could be captured by the sparsity patterns in the learned representation.

4.1 Experimental Setup

4.1.1 Corpora Preprocessing

We use Yelp[5] as it is, without any additional preprocessing. As for DBpedia[6] and Yahoo[7], the preprocessing is as follows: (1) removing all non-ASCII characters, quotations marks, and hyperlinks, (2) tokenising with spaCy[8], (3) lower-case conversion for all tokens, then (4) **for each class** we randomly sample 10,000 sentences for the training corpus and 1,000 sentences for the test and validation respectively. The vocabulary size of the both corpora is reduced to the first 20,000 most frequent words.

4.1.2 Baselines and Models

To ground the performance of HSVAE we use 4 baselines: 1) VAE is a version of the vanilla VAE used in Higgins et al. (2017), 2) the same VAE model but the activation of μ and σ of $q_\phi(z|x)$ regularised by either L^1 (VAE$_{L^1}$) or L^2 (VAE$_{L^2}$) norms, 3) MAT-VAE is a VAE framework introduced by Mathieu et al. (2019) and 4) simple classifier which is simply a text encoder with a classifier on top of it. For all these models we use a GRU network (Cho et al., 2014) to encode and decode text sequences. We set the dimesnionality of the both encoder and the decoder GRU's to 512D and the dimensionality of the word embeddings is 256D. The decoder and the encoder share the word embeddings. To train the model we use the Adam optimiser (Kingma and Ba, 2014) with the learning rate: 0.0008.

BERT vs GRU Encoder. Inspired by Li et al. (2020b), we replace the GRU network used in VAE and HSVAE encoders with a pretrained BERT[9] (Devlin et al., 2019), while keeping the GRU decoder. We refer to these models as B-VAE and B-HSVAE, respectively. Also, we compare the

[5] https://github.com/jxhe/vae-lagging-encoder/blob/master/prepare_data.py.

[6] https://github.com/srhrshr/torchDatasets/blob/master/dbpedia_csv.tar.gz

[7] https://github.com/jxhe/vae-lagging-encoder/blob/master/prepare_data.py.

[8] https://spacy.io

[9] After extracting features from a sequence with BERT, we then applying MLPs to extract features for the posterior distributions, as it is the case for the encoder with GRU network.

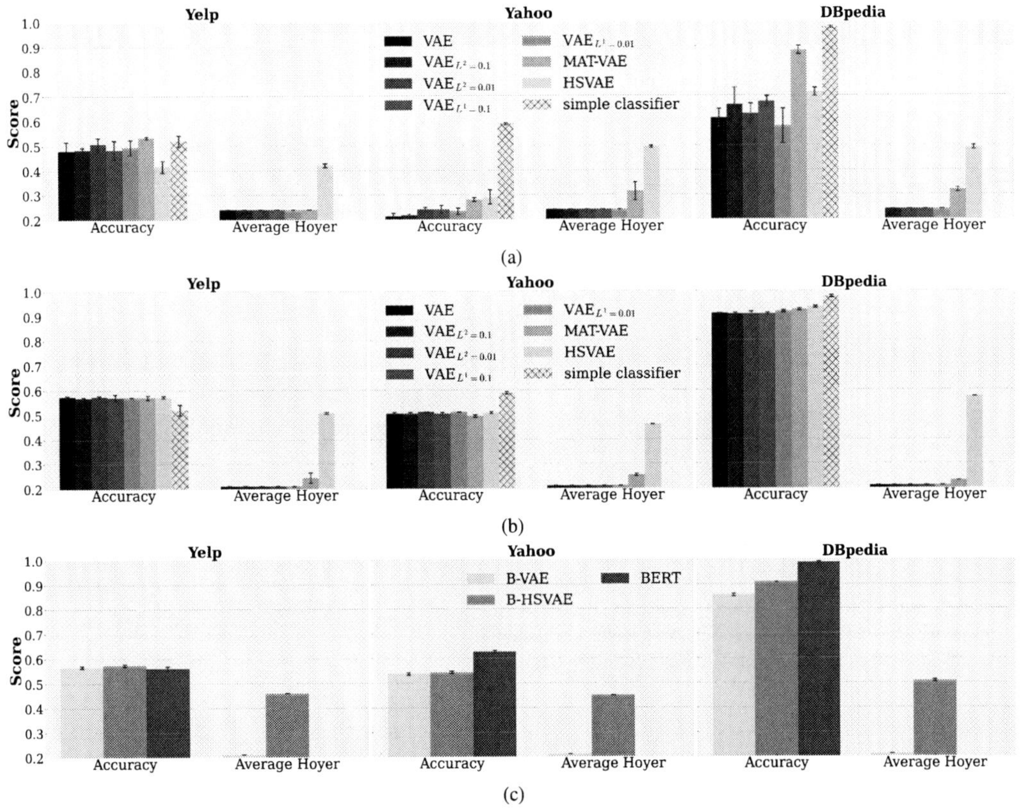

Figure 2: Classification Accuracy and Average Hoyer (higher means sparser z) for various VAE variants and the two baselines: simple classifier and BERT evaluated on Yelp, Yahoo or DBpedia test. The latent code of the VAEs is 32 D Figure (a) and 768 D Figures (b) and (c). Hoyer metric is not applicable to the simple classifier in the panels (a) and (b) and to the vanilla BERT model in the panel (c). The weights of the VAE encoders and BERT are **frozen** during the training of the classifiers. While the encoder of the simple classifier is updated during the training.

task performance of these VAE models with the plain pretrained base-BERT[10]. To train B-VAE and B-HSVAE, we use the Adam optimiser with the learning rate: 0.00008.

Dimensionality of z. We use the following two dimensions: 32D and 768D. Since, HSVAE and MAT-VAE induce sparse latent representations we want to make sure that they perform robustly regardless of the number of the dimensions.

KL-Collapse. None of the used VAE models is immune to the KL-collapse (Bowman et al., 2016) - when the KL term becomes zero and the decoder ignores the information provided by the encoder through z. To address this issue, in all the models, we put a scalar value $\psi, \lambda < 1$ on the KL terms of the VAE's objective function (He et al., 2019).

[10]https://huggingface.co/transformers/model_doc/bert.html

Coupling Encoder with Decoder. To connect the encoder with the decoder we concatenate the latent variable z, sampled from the posterior distribution, to word embeddings of the decoder at each time step (Prokhorov et al., 2019). Also, for GRU encoders we take the last hidden state to parameterise the posterior distribution. For BERT encoder, we take average pooling of all token's embeddings produced by the last layer of BERT.

4.1.3 Evaluation Metrics

Text Classification. To report the classification performance we use accuracy as a metric.

Sparsity. We measure Hoyer (Hurley and Rickard, 2009) on the representations of all data points in a corpus and report its average as our sparsity metric (Mathieu et al., 2019). Hoyer, in a nutshell, is ratio of the L^2 to L^1 norm, normalised by the number of dimensions. Higher indicates

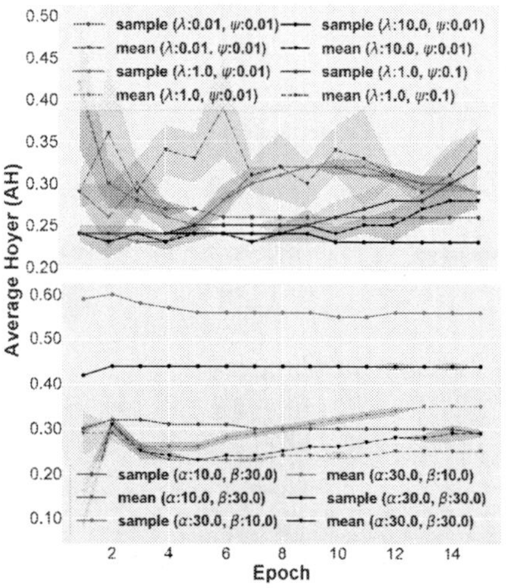

Figure 3: Average Hoyer (AH) on DBpedia corpus dev set for different parameterisations of Mathieu et al. (2019) (Top) vs. HSVAE (Bottom). Same is observed on Yelp and Yahoo (see *Appendix*). Lines are an average over the 3 runs of the models, the shaded area is the standard deviation. The dimensionality of the latent variable of the models is 32D.

more sparsity. More specifically, to evaluate the average Hoyer, or as we refer to it as Average Hoyer (AH) in the experiments, either on a validation or test corpus we employ the following procedure. First, for each x_i in the corpus $\{x_1, ..., x_n\}$ we obtain its corresponding z_i by sampling it from a probabilistic encoder of a VAE model, such that for each x_i we sample one z_i: e.g. $x_1 \rightarrow z_1$. Then we normalise $\bar{z}_i = z_i/\sigma(z)$, where $z = \{z_1, ..., z_n\}$, and $\sigma(.)$ is the standard deviation. Finally, for each $\bar{z}_i$ we compute Hoyer as follows:

$$Hoyer(\bar{z}_i) = \frac{\sqrt{d} - ||\bar{z}_i||_1/||\bar{z}_i||_2}{\sqrt{d} - 1}, \quad (3)$$

where d is the dimensionality of $\bar{z}_i$. To report the Hoyer for the whole corpus we compute the Average Hoyer $= \frac{1}{N}\sum_i^N Hoyer(\bar{z}_i)$, where N is the number of data points in a test or validation corpus.

4.2 Text Classification

Prior to use of a VAE encoder in the classification experiment, we pretrained it using the full VAE model with the corresponding VAE's objective function on one of the target corpus: Yelp, Yahoo or DBpedia. We compare performance of the sparse latent representations with their dense counterparts on the three text classification tasks (Figure 2). The classifier that we use comprises of the two dense layer of 32D each with the Leaky ReLU (Maas, 2013) activation function. To establish whether the performance gain or loss on the tasks is achieved thanks to the sparsity inductive bias, for all the VAE models and BERT we freeze the parameters of the encoder and only train the classifier which we put on top of the encoder. However, for the simple classifier model its text encoder is being trained together with the classifier. When the classifier, $p(y|x)$, is trained with a probabilistic VAE encoder we marginalise the latent variable(s). This is done for instance for HSVAE as,

$$p(y|x) = \int_{z,\gamma} p(y|z)q(z|x,\gamma)q_\phi(\gamma|x)dzd\gamma$$

We approximate the integral with MC by taking $K = 5$ samples from the probabilistic encoder both to train and to test the classifier: For each x_i in a batch $\{x_1, ..., x_p\}$:

1. sample K of $\gamma_{i,j}$ from $q_\phi(\gamma|x_i)$ i.e. a set of sampled γ's is $\{\gamma_{i,1}, ..., \gamma_{i,K}\}$
2. sample K of $z_{i,j}$ from $q_\phi(z|x_i, \gamma_{i,j})$ i.e. a set of sampled tuples of $z_{i,j}$ and $\gamma_{i,j}$ is $\{(z_{i,1}, \gamma_{i,1}), ..., (z_{i,K}, \gamma_{i,K})\}$ in other words for each $\gamma_{i,j}$ we sample only one $z_{i,j}$.

For the other VAEs the procedure is similar. With the MC approximation : $p(y|x) \approx 0.2 \times \sum_i^5 p(y|z_i)$.

For a systematic comparison of various VAEs, we collate classification performance of VAEs with comparable reconstruction loss - which indicates how informative the latent code is for the decoder during reconstruction. In other words the reconstruction loss serves as an intrinsic metric. Thus, for an example, in Figure 2a, for the Yelp corpus all the VAE models have a similar reconstruction loss. The same applies to Figure 2b and Figure 2c.

Comparing the accuracy of the classifiers that are trained with the different latent representations i.e. sparse and dense (Figure2), shows that in general the performance of the sparse latent representations induced by HSVAE or MAT-VAE is on par with their dense latent counterparts inferred by the VAEs. However, the performance of HSVAE slightly lagging behind on the Yelp corpus when the dimensionality of the latent representation is 32D (Figure 2a). We put forward a hypothesis that may explain this in Section 4.4. Also, when the dimensionality of the latent representation is 32D, the accuracy of

MAT-VAE is slightly better than of HSVAE, but this performance is reached at lower levels of sparsity. Additionally, we found that regularising the posterior parameters of the VAE model with either L^1 or L^2 norm, in some cases, helps to increase the classification accuracy, but does not reach AH higher than the vanilla VAE. Notably, the classification performance of all the VAE models becomes almost identical when the dimensionality of the latent space is increased from 32D to 768D, with HSVAE slightly outperforming all other VAEs on the DBpedia corpus (Figure 2b). We further elaborate on it in Section 4.4.

Use of BERT as an encoder, in our settings, only gives an improvement on the Yahoo corpus with B-HSVAE performing on par with B-VAE, but does not reach the classification accuracy of the plain BERT. We hypothesise that to reach the full potential of the use of a pretrained encoder in a VAE model one needs to pair it with a powerful decoder such as GPT-2 (Radford et al., 2019) as it is the case in the Li et al. (2020b) VAE model. Further exploration of this was beyond our compute resource.

Finally, one can observe that the simple classifier model performs on a par (in Figure 2a) or even worse (Figure 2b) than the VAE models on the Yelp corpus. Putting it into the context that the VAE encoders are not being trained with a supervision signal while the encoder of the simple classifier is, we speculate that this can be explained by the discussion put forward in Valpola (2014). A classifier in nature tries to remove all the information that is not relevant to the supervision signal, while an autoencoder tries to preserve as much as possible information in the latent code in order to reconstruct the original input data reliably. Thus, if the distribution of class related words in a text alone (see §4.4.1) is not indicative enough of a class then the classifier may perform poorly. In our case, we hypothesise that the VAE models capture some additional information other than class distribution of words in text that allows it to better discriminate the classes. For example, some class may have shorter sentences, on average, than the sentences presented in the other classes. This may provide an additional bias that allows the VAE models to discriminate sentences from this class from the sentences from the other classes. Thus, with this additional bias VAEs can perform better than the simple classifier. We leave this investigation for a future work.

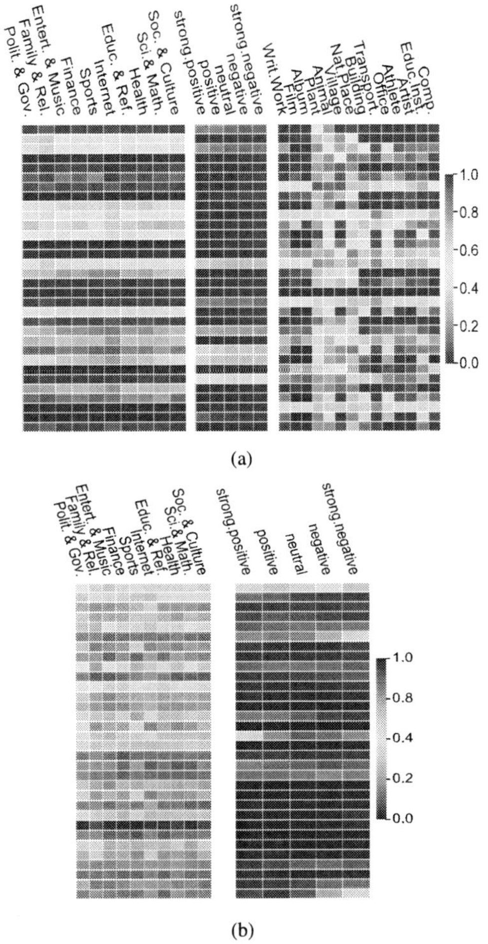

Figure 4: Heat maps of γ_{class} (Section §4.4). (a) γ_{class} of 32D - from left to right: Yahoo, Yelp, DBpedia. (b) contiguous 32D out of 768D of γ_{class} - from left to right: Yahoo, Yelp.

4.3 Representation Sparsity

In Figure 7 we compare HSVAE with MAT-VAE. We report AH both on the mean and samples from the posterior distributions. As illustrated, MAT-VAE struggles to achieve steady and consistent AH regardless of the configurations of its hyperparameters (ψ, λ). However, HSVAE stably controls the level of sparsity with α and β parameters, a positive effect of its more flexible posterior distribution and the learnable distribution over γ.

4.4 Can Sparsity Patterns Encode Classes?

In order to identify pertinent features, the unsupervised representation learning models are typically trained/fine-tuned on corpora that are closely related to the downstream task. As such, without a supervisory signal, the model can only rely on the distribution of words in a text in order to identify these relevant features for the task. Ideally, compared to their dense counterparts, an unsupervised sparsification model such as HSVAE could result in performance improvement on downstream tasks if they capture the task-related features and discard the noisy features. However, if the sparsification model fail to capture the task related signal in its sparsity pattern; it can hurt the performance of the model on the downstream task as the task-related information can be removed. In what follows we investigate this direction by analysing the sparsity patterns and relate this analysis to the classification performance of the model (§4.2).

Analysis of γ. We hypothesise that if γ captures a class of a sentence then the sentences that belong to the same class should have a similar sparsity patterns in γ. To obtain a class specific γ_{class}, first, for each sentence x we obtain the mean of the posterior distribution: $q_\phi(\gamma|x)$ and we denote it as $\mu_{\gamma(x)}$. Then we binarise the mean such as $\mu^b_{\gamma(x)} = \text{Binarise}(\mu_{\gamma(x)})$, where Binarise($\cdot$) is defined as: 0 if $\mu_{\gamma(x)} < 0.5$ and 1 otherwise. Finally, for each class we average its $\mu^b_{\gamma(x)}$ vectors to obtain a single vector that represent this class: $\gamma_{class} = \frac{1}{M}\sum_{x \in class} \mu^b_{\gamma(x)}$, where M is a number of sentences in the class. The averaging removes the information that differentiate these sentences, while preserving the class information that is shared among them. A similar approach was also used in Mathieu et al. (2019).

Figure 4 reports the magnitudes of the γ_{class} vectors as heat maps for the three corpora. One would expect that γ_{class} of different classes should differ. For 32D γ_{class} (Figure 4a) this is the case when HSVAE is trained on the DBpedia and Yahoo but not on Yelp. Taking into account the unsupervised nature of these models, this difference is echoing the distribution of words in the classes, which is more distinct in DBpedia and Yahoo, but not in Yelp (see §4.4.1). We also hypothesis that this observation can explain inferior performance of the model on the Yelp corpus (Figure 2a).

In contrast, for γ_{class} in 768D (Figure 4b) one can observe that the different classes have different activation patterns even when HSVAE is trained on the Yelp corpus.[11] Also, the distributedness of the activation patterns now becomes more apparent when HSVAE is trained on the Yahoo corpus. This observation is also related to the distribution of words in the text (further elaborated in §4.4.1).

Intuitively, to reconstruct a sentence a VAE model first captures aspect of data that are the most conducive for reconstruction error reduction (Burgess et al., 2018). Therefore, given the limited dimensionality of the latent vector, the model will prioritised aspects of data during encoding. As such, if the information such as sentence class is not strongly presented in the corpus the model could potentially ignore it during encoding. However, when the dimensionality of the latent space is increased, the model has more capacity to represent various aspects of data that may otherwise be ignored in the smaller dimensionality. We speculate this could explain the presence of distributedness of γ_{class} on Yelp for 768D as opposed to 32D, which also translates into matching the task performance of its dense counterpart (Figure 2b).

4.4.1 Class Kullback–Leibler Divergence

The question that has yet not been addressed is why in some cases the HSVAE model is more successful at capturing the class distribution when trained on DBpedia compared to Yelp. We previously hypothesised that the reason for this can be a word distribution in a text. To empirically test our hypothesis, we calculate the add-1 smoothed probabilities of words in the classes and measure the pairwise KL divergence across them. The magnitudes of the pairwise KL divergences are shown in Figure 5. As demonstrated, the magnitude of the KL divergence is the largest for DBpedia and smallest for Yelp. This indicates that separating classes in Yelp would rely on more subtle aspects of data, whereas surface-level cues are more present in DBpedia and allow for an easier discrimination.

5 Related Work

Learning sparse representations of data can be dated back to Olshausen and Field (1996). This work motivates encoding of images in sparse linear codes for its biological plausibility and efficiency. It was later argued by Bengio (2009) that compared to the dimensionality reduction approaches, sparsity is a more efficient method for representation learning on vectors with fixed dimensionality.

[11] In Figure 4b we only show 32D out of 768D. This is one of the subsets of the 768 dimensions where the distributedness is present. It is not unique and the distributedness is also present in other dimensions of the 768D code.

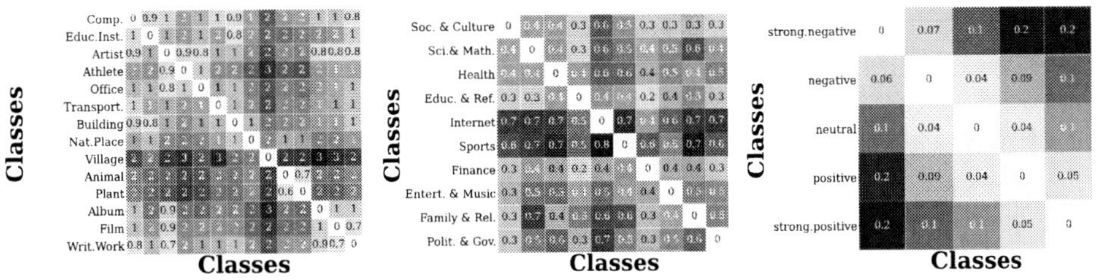

(a) (b) (c)

Figure 5: Experimental results for KL between classes on the three corpora: DBpedia (a), Yahoo (b) and Yelp (c).

Representation Sparsity. In NLP, learning sparse representations has been explored for various units of text with most of the focus placed on sparse representation of words. As the earliest work that moved in this direction, Murphy et al. (2012) looked into sparse representations for ease of analysis, performance, and being more cognitively plausible. This idea was further developed by many other researchers (Faruqui and Dyer, 2015; Yogatama et al., 2015; Faruqui et al., 2015; Sun et al., 2016; Subramanian et al., 2018; Arora et al., 2018; Li and Hao, 2019). Sparsification of the large units of text (i.e., sentences) has not received a lot of attention, perhaps due to inherent complexity of sentence/phrase representations: i.e., encoding and analysing syntactic and semantic information in a sentence embedding is rather a non-trivial task. To the best of our knowledge, the only model that sparsifies sentence emebeddings is introduced by Trifonov et al. (2018). The authors introduced a Seq2Seq model (Sutskever et al., 2014) with the Sparsemax layer (Martins and Astudillo, 2016) between the encoder and the decoder which induces sparse latent codes of text. This layer allows to learn codes that can be easier to analyse compared to their dense counterparts, but it is limited to modelling the categorical distribution. Thus restricts a type a sentence representations that can be learned.

VAE-based Representation Sparsity. VAE-based sentence representation learning has shown superior properties compared to their deterministic counterparts on tasks such as text generation (Bowman et al., 2016), Semantic Textual Similarity (Li et al., 2020a) and other wide range of language tasks (Li et al., 2020b). While a handful of VAE-based sparsification methods have been proposed recently Mathieu et al. (2019) (MAT), Tonolini et al. (2019) (TON), they have been only evaluated on image domain. We summarise the similarity and key differences with HSVAE model:

PRIOR AND POSTERIOR. All three frameworks use the Spike-and-Slab distribution to construct the prior on z. While the posterior distribution in MAT remains as a Gaussian, both TON and HSVAE opt for Spike-and-Slab. However, TON controls the sparsity level in an indirect way via "pseudo data" (Tomczak and Welling, 2018) used in prior, whereas HSVAE's probabilistic treatment of γ enables direct control on the target sparsity level.

OBJECTIVE. HSVAE is trained with a principled ELBO (eq. 3), while the other two add additional regularisers to the ELBO of VAE (eq. 1). For instance, MAT add a *maximum mean discrepancy* (MMD) divergence between z's aggregated posterior and prior $\text{MMD}(q_\phi(z), p_\theta(z))$ and include scalar ψ and λ weights to the KL and MMD term, respectively, see *Appendix*.

Model Sparsity. Concurrent to the widespread use of large models such as Transformers (Vaswani et al., 2017) in NLP, sparsification of these models is also becoming popular (Zhang et al., 2020; Zhao et al., 2019; Correia et al., 2019; Ye et al., 2019; Child et al., 2019). The most common approach to sparsify a Transformer is to reduce a number of connection between the words/tokens in the self attention kernel e.g. Correia et al. (2019). However, these approaches still learn dense continuous representations of token/word/sentence embeddings.

6 Conclusion

We provided an objective analysis of several unsupervised sparsification frameworks based on VAEs, both in terms of the impact on downstream tasks and the level of sparsity achieved. Also, we presented a novel VAE model - Hierarchical Sparse Variational Autoencoder (HSVAE), outperforming existing SOTA model (Mathieu et al., 2019). Ideally, sparse representations should be capable of encoding the underlying characteristics of a corpus (e.g. class), in activation patterns as shown to be the case for HSVAE. Moreover, using the text classification corpora as a testbed, we established how statistical properties of a corpus such as word distribution in a class affect the ability of learned sparse codes to represent task-related information.

Moving forward, HSVAE model along with the analysis provided in this paper can serve as a good basis for the design of sparse models that induce continuous sparse vectors of text. For example, a potential extension of HSVAE could be an incorporation of explicit linguistic biases into the learned representations with the group sparsity (Yogatama et al., 2015). Furthermore, as we discussed in Section 5, sparsity found its application in the Transformers, but it, mainly, has been used to reduce the number of connection between the words/tokens. With the HSVAE framework one can also learn sparse continuous representations of token/word/sentence embeddings.

Acknowledgments

The first author would like to thank Yi Zhu for providing his feedback on the earlier vesrsion of the paper. The authors, also, would like to thank the three anonymous reviewers for their helpful suggestions.

References

Sanjeev Arora, Yuanzhi Li, Yingyu Liang, Tengyu Ma, and Andrej Risteski. 2018. Linear algebraic structure of word senses, with applications to polysemy. *Transactions of the Association for Computational Linguistics*, 6:483–495.

Vikash Balasubramanian, Ivan Kobyzev, Hareesh Bahuleyan, Ilya Shapiro, and Olga Vechtomova. 2020. Polarized-vae: Proximity based disentangled representation learning for text generation. *arXiv preprint arXiv:2004.10809*.

Gabriel Barello, Adam S. Charles, and Jonathan W. Pillow. 2018. Sparse-coding variational auto-encoders. *bioRxiv*.

Yoshua Bengio. 2009. Learning deep architectures for ai. *Found. Trends Mach. Learn.*, 2(1):1–127.

Yoshua Bengio, Aaron C. Courville, and Pascal Vincent. 2013. Representation learning: A review and new perspectives. *IEEE Trans. Pattern Anal. Mach. Intell.*, 35(8):1798–1828.

Samuel R. Bowman, Luke Vilnis, Oriol Vinyals, Andrew M. Dai, Rafal Józefowicz, and Samy Bengio. 2016. Generating sentences from a continuous space. In *CoNLL*.

Christopher P. Burgess, Irina Higgins, Arka Pal, Loïc Matthey, Nick Watters, Guillaume Desjardins, and Alexander Lerchner. 2018. Understanding disentangling in β-vae. *CoRR*, abs/1804.03599.

Rewon Child, Scott Gray, Alec Radford, and Ilya Sutskever. 2019. Generating long sequences with sparse transformers.

Kyunghyun Cho, Bart van Merrienboer, Çaglar Gülçehre, Fethi Bougares, Holger Schwenk, and Yoshua Bengio. 2014. Learning phrase representations using RNN encoder-decoder for statistical machine translation. *CoRR*, abs/1406.1078.

Gonçalo M. Correia, Vlad Niculae, and André F. T. Martins. 2019. Adaptively sparse transformers. In *Proceedings of the 2019 Conference on Empirical Methods in Natural Language Processing and the 9th International Joint Conference on Natural Language Processing (EMNLP-IJCNLP)*, pages 2174–2184, Hong Kong, China. Association for Computational Linguistics.

Jacob Devlin, Ming-Wei Chang, Kenton Lee, and Kristina Toutanova. 2019. BERT: Pre-training of deep bidirectional transformers for language understanding. In *Proceedings of the 2019 Conference of the North American Chapter of the Association for Computational Linguistics: Human Language Technologies, Volume 1 (Long and Short Papers)*, pages 4171–4186, Minneapolis, Minnesota. Association for Computational Linguistics.

Manaal Faruqui and Chris Dyer. 2015. Non-distributional word vector representations. In *Proceedings of the 53rd Annual Meeting of the Association for Computational Linguistics and the 7th International Joint Conference on Natural Language Processing (Volume 2: Short Papers)*, pages 464–469, Beijing, China. Association for Computational Linguistics.

Manaal Faruqui, Yulia Tsvetkov, Dani Yogatama, Chris Dyer, and Noah A. Smith. 2015. Sparse overcomplete word vector representations. In *Proceedings of the 53rd Annual Meeting of the Association for Computational Linguistics and the 7th International Joint Conference on Natural Language Processing (Volume 1: Long Papers)*, pages 1491–1500, Beijing, China. Association for Computational Linguistics.

Michael Figurnov, Shakir Mohamed, and Andriy Mnih. 2018. Implicit reparameterization gradients. In *Proceedings of the 32nd International Conference on*

Neural Information Processing Systems, NIPS'18, page 439–450, Red Hook, NY, USA. Curran Associates Inc.

Junxian He, Daniel Spokoyny, Graham Neubig, and Taylor Berg-Kirkpatrick. 2019. Lagging inference networks and posterior collapse in variational autoencoders. In *Proceedings of ICLR*.

Irina Higgins, Loïc Matthey, Arka Pal, Christopher Burgess, Xavier Glorot, Matthew Botvinick, Shakir Mohamed, and Alexander Lerchner. 2017. beta-vae: Learning basic visual concepts with a constrained variational framework. In *5th International Conference on Learning Representations, ICLR 2017, Conference Track Proceedings*, Toulon, France.

N. Hurley and S. Rickard. 2009. Comparing measures of sparsity. *IEEE Transactions on Information Theory*, 55(10):4723–4741.

Diederik Kingma and Jimmy Ba. 2014. Adam: A method for stochastic optimization. *International Conference on Learning Representations*.

Diederik P. Kingma and Max Welling. 2014. Auto-encoding variational bayes. In *2nd International Conference on Learning Representations, ICLR 2014, Banff, AB, Canada, April 14-16, 2014, Conference Track Proceedings*.

Bohan Li, Hao Zhou, Junxian He, Mingxuan Wang, Yiming Yang, and Lei Li. 2020a. On the sentence embeddings from pre-trained language models. In *Proceedings of the 2020 Conference on Empirical Methods in Natural Language Processing (EMNLP)*, pages 9119–9130, Online. Association for Computational Linguistics.

Chunyuan Li, Xiang Gao, Yuan Li, Baolin Peng, Xiujun Li, Yizhe Zhang, and Jianfeng Gao. 2020b. Optimus: Organizing sentences via pre-trained modeling of a latent space.

Wenye Li and Senyue Hao. 2019. Sparse lifting of dense vectors: Unifying word and sentence representations. *CoRR*, abs/1911.01625.

Andrew L. Maas. 2013. Rectifier nonlinearities improve neural network acoustic models.

Chris J. Maddison, Andriy Mnih, and Yee Whye Teh. 2016. The concrete distribution: A continuous relaxation of discrete random variables. *International Conference on Learning Representations, ICLR*.

Andre Martins and Ramon Astudillo. 2016. From softmax to sparsemax: A sparse model of attention and multi-label classification. In *Proceedings of The 33rd International Conference on Machine Learning*, volume 48 of *Proceedings of Machine Learning Research*, pages 1614–1623, New York, New York, USA. PMLR.

Rebecca Marvin and Tal Linzen. 2018. Targeted syntactic evaluation of language models. In *Proceedings of the 2018 Conference on Empirical Methods in Natural Language Processing*, pages 1192–1202, Brussels, Belgium. Association for Computational Linguistics.

Emile Mathieu, Tom Rainforth, N Siddharth, and Yee Whye Teh. 2019. Disentangling disentanglement in variational autoencoders. In *Proceedings of the 36th International Conference on Machine Learning*, volume 97 of *Proceedings of Machine Learning Research*, pages 4402–4412, Long Beach, California, USA. PMLR.

Brian Murphy, Partha Talukdar, and Tom Mitchell. 2012. Learning effective and interpretable semantic models using non-negative sparse embedding. In *Proceedings of COLING 2012*, pages 1933–1950, Mumbai, India. The COLING 2012 Organizing Committee.

Bruno Olshausen and David Field. 1996. Emergence of simple-cell receptive field properties by learning a sparse code for natural images. *Nature*, 381:607–9.

Victor Prokhorov, Ehsan Shareghi, Yingzhen Li, Mohammad Taher Pilehvar, and Nigel Collier. 2019. On the importance of the Kullback-Leibler divergence term in variational autoencoders for text generation. In *Proceedings of the 3rd Workshop on Neural Generation and Translation*, pages 118–127, Hong Kong. Association for Computational Linguistics.

Alec Radford, Jeff Wu, Rewon Child, David Luan, Dario Amodei, and Ilya Sutskever. 2019. Language models are unsupervised multitask learners.

Anant Subramanian, Danish Pruthi, Harsh Jhamtani, Taylor Berg-Kirkpatrick, and Eduard H. Hovy. 2018. SPINE: sparse interpretable neural embeddings. In *Proceedings of the Thirty-Second AAAI Conference on Artificial Intelligence, (AAAI-18), the 30th innovative Applications of Artificial Intelligence (IAAI-18), and the 8th AAAI Symposium on Educational Advances in Artificial Intelligence (EAAI-18), New Orleans, Louisiana, USA, February 2-7, 2018*, pages 4921–4928. AAAI Press.

Fei Sun, Jiafeng Guo, Yanyan Lan, Jun Xu, and Xueqi Cheng. 2016. Sparse word embeddings using l1 regularized online learning. In *Proceedings of the Twenty-Fifth International Joint Conference on Artificial Intelligence, IJCAI 2016, New York, NY, USA, 9-15 July 2016*, pages 2915–2921. IJCAI/AAAI Press.

Ilya Sutskever, Oriol Vinyals, and Quoc V. Le. 2014. Sequence to sequence learning with neural networks. In *Proceedings of the 27th International Conference on Neural Information Processing Systems - Volume 2*, NIPS'14, page 3104–3112, Cambridge, MA, USA. MIT Press.

Jakub M. Tomczak and Max Welling. 2018. Vae with a vampprior. In *Proceedings of the International Conference on Artificial Intelligence and Statistics, pp. 1214–1223.*

Francesco Tonolini, Bjorn Sand Jensen, and Roderick Murray-Smith. 2019. Variational sparse coding. In *Proceedings of the Thirty-Fifth Conference on Uncertainty in Artificial Intelligence (UAI).*

Valentin Trifonov, Octavian-Eugen Ganea, Anna Potapenko, and Thomas Hofmann. 2018. Learning and evaluating sparse interpretable sentence embeddings. In *Proceedings of the Workshop: Analyzing and Interpreting Neural Networks for NLP, BlackboxNLP@EMNLP 2018, Brussels, Belgium, November 1, 2018*, pages 200–210. Association for Computational Linguistics.

H. Valpola. 2014. From neural pca to deep unsupervised learning. *ArXiv*, abs/1411.7783.

Ashish Vaswani, Noam Shazeer, Niki Parmar, Jakob Uszkoreit, Llion Jones, Aidan N. Gomez, Lukasz Kaiser, and Illia Polosukhin. 2017. Attention is all you need.

Alex Wang, Amanpreet Singh, Julian Michael, Felix Hill, Omer Levy, and Samuel Bowman. 2018. GLUE: A multi-task benchmark and analysis platform for natural language understanding. In *Proceedings of the 2018 EMNLP Workshop BlackboxNLP: Analyzing and Interpreting Neural Networks for NLP*, pages 353–355, Brussels, Belgium. Association for Computational Linguistics.

Peng Xu, Jackie Chi Kit Cheung, and Yanshuai Cao. 2019. On variational learning of controllable representations for text without supervision. *arXiv preprint arXiv:1905.11975.*

Zichao Yang, Zhiting Hu, Ruslan Salakhutdinov, and Taylor Berg-Kirkpatrick. 2017. Improved variational autoencoders for text modeling using dilated convolutions. In *Proceedings of the 34th International Conference on Machine Learning*, volume 70 of *Proceedings of Machine Learning Research*, pages 3881–3890, International Convention Centre, Sydney, Australia. PMLR.

Zihao Ye, Qipeng Guo, Quan Gan, Xipeng Qiu, and Zheng Zhang. 2019. Bp-transformer: Modelling long-range context via binary partitioning.

Serena Yeung, Anitha Kannan, Yann Dauphin, and Li Fei-Fei. 2017. Tackling over-pruning in variational autoencoders. *International Conference on Machine Learning: Workshop on Principled Approaches to Deep Learning.*

Dani Yogatama, Manaal Faruqui, Chris Dyer, and Noah A. Smith. 2015. Learning word representations with hierarchical sparse coding. In *Proceedings of the 32nd International Conference on Machine Learning, ICML 2015, Lille, France, 6-11 July 2015*, volume 37, pages 87–96. JMLR.org.

Biao Zhang, Ivan Titov, and Rico Sennrich. 2020. On sparsifying encoder outputs in sequence-to-sequence models.

Xiang Zhang, Junbo Zhao, and Yann LeCun. 2015. Character-level convolutional networks for text classification. In *Proceedings of the 28th International Conference on Neural Information Processing Systems - Volume 1*, NIPS'15, page 649–657, Cambridge, MA, USA. MIT Press.

Guangxiang Zhao, Junyang Lin, Zhiyuan Zhang, Xuancheng Ren, Qi Su, and Xu Sun. 2019. Explicit sparse transformer: Concentrated attention through explicit selection.

A Derivations of ELBO

Starting from the $\mathbb{D}_{KL}(q_\phi(z,\gamma|x)||p_\theta(z,\gamma|x))$, we derive the Evidence Lower Bound (ELBO) as follows:

$$\mathbb{D}_{KL}(q_\phi(z,\gamma|x)||p_\theta(z,\gamma|x)) = \int_{z,\gamma} dz d\gamma \, q_\phi(z,\gamma|x) \log \frac{q_\phi(z,\gamma|x)}{p_\theta(z,\gamma|x)}, \tag{4}$$

after rearranging terms in equation 4 we can obtain:

$$\log p_\theta(x) - \mathbb{D}_{KL}(q_\phi(z,\gamma|x)||p_\theta(z,\gamma|x)) = \underbrace{\int_{z,\gamma} dz d\gamma \, q_\phi(z,\gamma|x) \log \frac{p_\theta(z,\gamma,x)}{q_\phi(z,\gamma|x)},}_{\text{ELBO}} \tag{5}$$

Based on the independence assumption that we make in our graphical model (Figure 1) the generative model factorises as: $p_\theta(z,\gamma,x) = p_\theta(x|z)p_\theta(z|\gamma)p_\theta(\gamma)$ and the inference model factorises as: $q_\phi(z,\gamma|x) = q_\phi(z|\gamma,x)q_\phi(\gamma|x)$. Therefore, we can rewrite the ELBO as follows:

$$\int_{z,\gamma} dz d\gamma \, q_\phi(z|\gamma,x)q_\phi(\gamma|x) \log \frac{p_\theta(x|z)p_\theta(z|\gamma)p_\theta(\gamma)}{q_\phi(z|\gamma,x)q_\phi(\gamma|x)}, \tag{6}$$

We can further rewrite the ELBO as a sum of the three separate terms. Where the first term is:

$$\int_{z,\gamma} dz d\gamma \, q_\phi(z|x,\gamma)q_\phi(\gamma|x) \log p_\theta(x|z)$$
$$\int_\gamma d\gamma \, q_\phi(\gamma|x) \int_z dz \, q_\phi(z|x,\gamma) \log p_\theta(x|z) \therefore \tag{7}$$
$$\left\langle \int_z dz \, q_\phi(z|x,\gamma) \log p_\theta(x|z) \right\rangle_{q_\phi(\gamma|x)} \therefore$$

The second term is:

$$
\begin{aligned}
&\int_{z,\gamma} dzd\gamma\ q_\phi(z|x,\gamma)q_\phi(\gamma|x)[\log q_\phi(z|x,\gamma) - \log p_\theta(z|\gamma)] \\
&\left\langle \int_z dz\, q_\phi(z|x,\gamma)[\log q_\phi(z|x,\gamma) - \log p_\theta(z|\gamma)] \right\rangle_{q_\phi(\gamma|x)} \therefore \\
&\left\langle \mathbb{D}_{KL}(q_\phi(z|x,\gamma)||p_\theta(z|\gamma)) \right\rangle_{q_\phi(\gamma|x)} \therefore
\end{aligned} \tag{8}
$$

Finally, the third term is:

$$
\begin{aligned}
&\int_{z,\gamma} dzd\gamma\ q_\phi(z|x,\gamma)q_\phi(\gamma|x)[\log q_\phi(\gamma|x) - \log p_\theta(\gamma)] \\
&\int_\gamma d\gamma\ q_\phi(\gamma|x)[\log q_\theta(\gamma|x) - \log p_\theta(\gamma)] \underbrace{\int_z dz\, q_\phi(z|x,\gamma)}_{\text{sums to 1 for each}:\gamma} \therefore \\
&\int_\gamma d\gamma\ q_\phi(\gamma|x)[\log q_\phi(\gamma|x) - \log p_\theta(\gamma)] \therefore \\
&\mathbb{D}_{KL}(q_\phi(\gamma|x)||p_\theta(\gamma)) \therefore
\end{aligned} \tag{9}
$$

Collecting all the three terms into the single ELBO:

$$
\begin{aligned}
&\left\langle \int_z dz\, q_\phi(z|x,\gamma) \log p_\theta(x|z) \right\rangle_{q_\phi(\gamma|x)} - \\
&-\left\langle \mathbb{D}_{KL}(q_\phi(z|x,\gamma)||p_\theta(z|\gamma)) \right\rangle_{q_\phi(\gamma|x)} - \\
&-\mathbb{D}_{KL}(q_\phi(\gamma|x)||p_\theta(\gamma)),
\end{aligned} \tag{10}
$$

B Objective Functions of Mathieu et al. (2019) and Tonolini et al. (2019) Models

The objective function of Mathieu et al. (2019) is:

$$
\begin{aligned}
&\left\langle \log p_\theta(x|z) \right\rangle_{q_\phi(z|x)} - \psi KL(q_\phi(z|x)||p_\theta(z)) - \\
&-\lambda \mathbb{D}(q_\phi(z), p_\theta(z)),
\end{aligned}
$$

where ψ and λ are the scalar weight on the terms and Tonolini et al. (2019) is:

$$
\begin{aligned}
&\left\langle \log p_\theta(x|z) \right\rangle_{q_\phi(z|x)} - KL(q_\phi(z|x)||q_\phi(z|x_u) - \\
&-J \times \mathbb{D}_{KL}(\bar{\gamma}_u||\alpha)),
\end{aligned}
$$

where J is the dimensionality of the latent variable z, x_u is a learnable pseudo-input (Tomczak and Welling, 2018) and α is prior sparsity.

C Deriving Marginal of (Univariate) Spike-and-Slab Prior

We derive the Spike-and-Slab distribution by integrating out the index component which is distributed as a Bernoulli variable. This result is quite well-known in machine learning, however for the ease of the reader we present it here as a quick reference.

The derivation: assume 1) $\pi \sim p(\pi;\gamma)$ is a $Bernoulli(\gamma)$ and 2) $p(z|\pi) = (1-\pi) \times p_1(z) + \pi \times p_2(z)$, where $p_1(z) \sim \mathcal{N}(z;0,1)$ and $p_2(z) \sim \mathcal{N}(z;0,\sigma \to 0)$ is a Spike-and-Slab model. The the marginal Spike-and-Slab prior over z can be obtained in the following way:

$$
\begin{aligned}
&p(z;\gamma) = \sum_{i=0}^{1} p(z|\pi=i)p(\pi=i;\gamma) \\
&p(z|\pi=0)p(\pi=0;\gamma) + p(z|\pi=1)p(\pi=1;\gamma) \therefore \\
&[(1-0) \times p_1(z) + 0 \times p_2(z)]p(\pi=0;\gamma) + \\
&+ [(1-1) \times p_1(z) + 1 \times p_2(z)]p(\pi=1;\gamma) \therefore
\end{aligned}
$$

Expanding brackets:

$$
\begin{aligned}
&p_1(z)p(\pi=0;\gamma) + p_2(z)p(\pi=1;\gamma) \therefore \\
&\mathcal{N}(z;0,1)p(\pi=0;\gamma) + \mathcal{N}(z;0,\sigma \to 0)p(\pi=1;\gamma) \therefore \\
&(1-\gamma)\mathcal{N}(z;0,1) + \gamma\mathcal{N}(z;0,\sigma \to 0) \therefore
\end{aligned}
$$

Therefore,

$$
p(z;\gamma) = (1-\gamma)\mathcal{N}(z;0,1) + \gamma\mathcal{N}(z;0,\sigma \to 0).
$$

D End-to-end Differentiable

Sampling a value from the Spike-and-Slab posterior distribution $q(z|x,\gamma)$ is a two step process. First a spike or slab component is sampled which is a binary decision, we use Binary Concrete distribution (Maddison et al., 2016) to make this sampling step end-to-end differentiable. Then the value is sampled from the corresponding component, for this we employ the reparameterization trick (Kingma and Welling, 2014). Also, samples from the Beta distribution are pathwise differentiable (Figurnov et al., 2018).

E Hoyer

This section reports Average Hoyer, for the two corpora Yelp and Yahoo, both on the mean and samples from the posterior distributions of the HSVAE and MAT-VAE models.

E.1 MAT-VAE

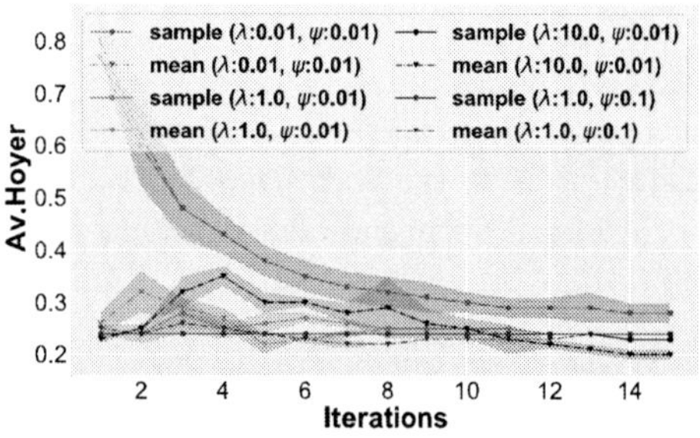

Figure 6: Average Hoyer (Av.Hoyer) on Yelp corpus dev set for MAT-VAE. Lines are an average over the 3 runs of the models, the shaded area is the standard deviation. The dimensionality of the latent variable of the models is 32D.

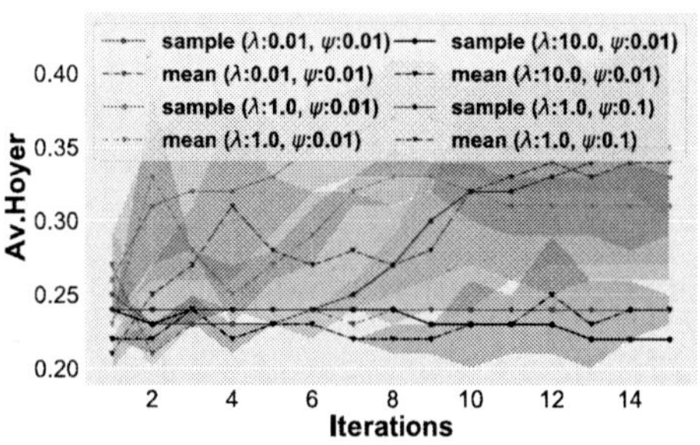

Figure 7: Average Hoyer (Av.Hoyer) on Yahoo corpus dev set for MAT-VAE. Lines are an average over the 3 runs of the models, the shaded area is the standard deviation.

E.2 HSVAE

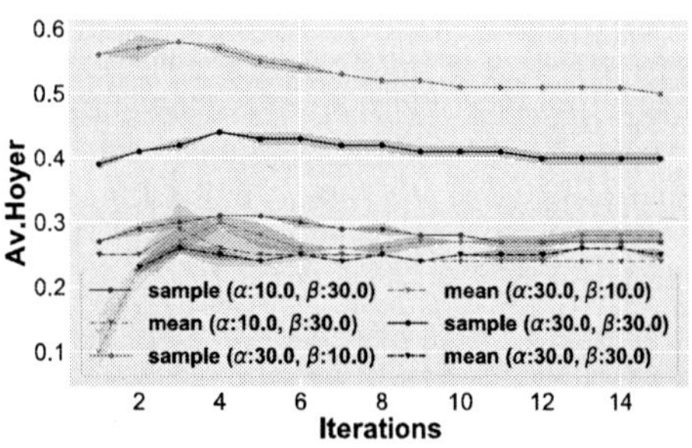

Figure 8: Average Hoyer (Av.Hoyer) on Yelp corpus dev set for HSVAE. Lines are an average over the 3 runs of the models, the shaded area is the standard deviation. The dimensionality of the latent variable of the models is 32D.

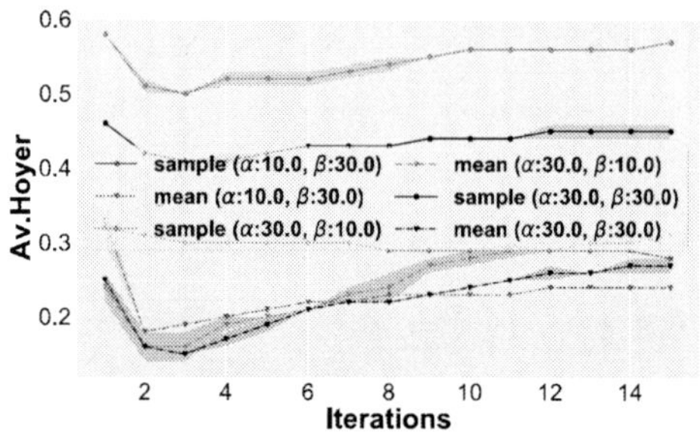

Figure 9: Average Hoyer (Av.Hoyer) on Yahoo corpus dev set for HSVAE. Lines are an average over the 3 runs of the models, the shaded area is the standard deviation. The dimensionality of the latent variable of the models is 32D.

F Hardware

Please refer to Table 1 for the hardware that we use.

hardware	specification
CPU	Intel® Xeon E5-2670V3, 12-cores, 24-threads
GPU	NVIDIA® TITAN RTX™ (24 GB) x 1
RAM	CORSAIR® Vengeance LPX DDR4 2400 MHz (8 GB) x 4

Table 1: Computing infrastructure.

G Datasets

	Yelp	DBpedia	Yahoo
# sent. (train corpus)	100K	140K	100K
# sent. (valid corpus)	10K	14K	10K
# sent. (test corpus)	10K	14K	10K
vocabulary size	19,997	20K	20K
min sent. length.	20	1	5
av. sent. length.	96	35	12
max. sent. length.	200	60	30
# classes	5	14	10
# sent. in each class (train/test corpus)	20K/2K	10K/1K	10K/1K

Table 2: Statistics of corpora. Vocabulary size excludes the ⟨pad ⟩and ⟨EOS ⟩symbols.

Temporal-aware Language Representation Learning From Crowdsourced Labels

Yang Hao Xiao Zhai Wenbiao Ding Zitao Liu*
TAL Education Group, Beijing, China
{haoyang2, zhaixiao, dingwenbiao, liuzitao}@tal.com

Abstract

Learning effective language representations from crowdsourced labels is crucial for many real-world machine learning tasks. A challenging aspect of this problem is that the quality of crowdsourced labels suffer high intra- and inter-observer variability. Since the high-capacity deep neural networks can easily memorize all disagreements among crowdsourced labels, directly applying existing supervised language representation learning algorithms may yield suboptimal solutions. In this paper, we propose *TACMA*, a temporal-aware language representation learning heuristic for crowdsourced labels with multiple annotators. The proposed approach (1) explicitly models the intra-observer variability with attention mechanism; (2) computes and aggregates per-sample confidence scores from multiple workers to address the inter-observer disagreements. The proposed heuristic is extremely easy to implement in around 5 lines of code. The proposed heuristic is evaluated on four synthetic and four real-world data sets. The results show that our approach outperforms a wide range of state-of-the-art baselines in terms of prediction accuracy and AUC. To encourage the reproducible results, we make our code publicly available at https://github.com/CrowdsourcingMining/TACMA.

1 Introduction

Crowdsourcing offers the ability to utilize the power of human computation to generate data annotations that are needed to train various AI systems. For many practical supervised learning applications, it may be infeasible (or very expensive) to obtain objective and reliable labels due to many reasons such as varying skill-levels and biases of crowdsourced workers. Instead, to improve the quality of labels, we can collect subjective and inconsistent labels from multiple heterogeneous crowdsourced workers. In practice, there is a substantial amount of disagreement between the crowdsourced workers (Nie et al., 2020), i.e., inter-observer variability or even between a worker and the same worker looking at the same example some time later (Guan et al., 2018), i.e., intra-observer variability. Hence, it is of great practical interest to address supervised learning problems in this scenario.

Meanwhile, with the recent advances of deep neural networks (DNNs), supervised representation learning (SRL) has led to rapid improvements in the ability of learning intrinsic nonlinear embeddings using DNNs that preserves the distance between similar examples close and dissimilar examples far on the embedding space. In spite of the significant progress for SRL applications such as face recognition (Schroff et al., 2015), image retrieval (Xia et al., 2014), directly applying existing deep language representation learning approaches on crowdsourced labels may yield poor generalization performance (Han et al., 2018). Because of the high capacity, DNNs could entirely memorize the inconsistency within crowdsourced labels sooner or later during the modeling training process. Besides, this phenomenon does not change with the choice of training optimizations or network architectures (Han et al., 2018).

A large spectrum of approaches have been successfully developed in either estimating true labels from crowdsourced labels, a.k.a., truth inference or label aggregation (Dawid and Skene, 1979; Whitehill et al., 2009), learning via adversarial data generation (Wang et al., 2020a), or learning language representations discriminatively from large-scale consistent labeled data with complicated neural architectures (Rodrigues and Pereira, 2018). However, learning effective neural embeddings directly from crowdsourced labels of real-world data poses

*Corresponding author: Zitao Liu.

Proceedings of the 6th Workshop on Representation Learning for NLP (RepL4NLP-2021), pages 47–56
Bangkok, Thailand (Online), August 6, 2021. ©2021 Association for Computational Linguistics

numerous challenges. First, crowdsourced workers conduct labeling tasks sequentially, i.e., they label samples one after another. Such sequential labeling behavior is a process of learning, and the expertise of the workers is not stable but gradually changing even without feedback (Elliott and Riach, 1965). According to Miller's Law (Miller, 1956), humans retain what they just learned in their short-term working memory with a limited span of 7 ± 2. Temporal factors such as fatigue (Zhang et al., 2018) and intrinsic motivation (Kaufmann et al., 2011) implicitly influence the crowdsourcing quality, which are different from existing well-studied factors, such as the quality of crowdsourced workers, the difficulty of data samples, the price of annotation tasks, etc. In the following, such unconscious temporal behaviors are referred to as *"temporal labeling effects"*. How to model such sample-level temporal information for each individual worker undoubtedly poses a hard modeling problem. Second, a large number of real-world crowdsourced data sets have a substantial amount of disagreement among labels and a relatively small sample size. The majority of existing SRL approaches are discriminatively trained on large-scale consistent labeled data to learn their complicated neural architectures, which may easily overfit the inconsistent crowdsourced data.

In this paper we study and develop solutions that are applicable and can learn effective neural language representations from crowdsourced labels in an end-to-end manner. Our work focuses on the refinements of a popular deep language representation learning paradigm: the deep metric learning (DML) (Koch et al., 2015; Xu et al., 2019; Wang et al., 2020b). We aim to develop an algorithm to automatically learn a nonlinear language representation of the crowdsourced data from multiple workers using DNNs.

Briefly, the DML is a classical and widely used approach for language representation learning that preserves the distance between similar examples close and dissimilar examples far on the embedding space. The majority of existing DML techniques restricted to just noise-free labels appropriately. However, learning effective representation from highly inconsistent crowdsourced data sets from multiple workers gives rise to numerous important questions: (1) since in practice, annotation performance is affected and varied over time (Boksem et al., 2005; Zhang et al., 2018), *how do we capture such temporal labeling effects in the DML learning framework?* (2) while in some cases the problem may be alleviated by pre-processing methods, such as filtering(Li et al., 2016), label correction(Li et al., 2019a), truth inference (Dawid and Skene, 1979; Raykar et al., 2010), etc., the number of remained instances is often significantly reduced or such pre-processing errors for many problems will be propagated to the downstream representation learning tasks. *How to capture the label uncertainties from multiple workers and at the same time prevent the overfitting problem in an end-to-end framework?*

In this work we address the above issues by presenting a temporal-aware language representation learning heuristic for crowdsourced labels with multiple annotators (TACMA), that

- utilizes the attention mechanism to capture the temporal influence among sequential labeling tasks according to each worker's short-term working memory.
- estimates and aggregates the annotation confidence from disagreements among multiple workers for each sample.
- supports language representation learning with DML into an end-to-end fashion, and is extremely easy to implement based on existing DML framework with crowdsourced labels i.e., RLL (Xu et al., 2019), in around 5 line of codes.

2 Related Work

2.1 Truth Inference in Crowdsourcing

A large body of research has focused on inferring true labels from crowdsourced labels from multiple workers (Dawid and Skene, 1979; Whitehill et al., 2009; Li et al., 2019c; Rodrigues and Pereira, 2018). The majority of truth inference approaches are inspired by the classic Expectation-Maximization learning paradigm that iterates between estimating the expertise of annotators given true labels inferred and inferring true labels given the expertise of annotators (Dawid and Skene, 1979; Whitehill et al., 2009; Zhang et al., 2014; Li et al., 2019c). Some improvements include modeling the difficulty of items and the expertise of annotators jointly (Whitehill et al., 2009), applying spectral methods to initialize worker confusion matrix (Zhang et al., 2014), and modeling correlations of workers (Li et al., 2019c), etc.

In spite of the successful applications of the truth inference techniques, the majority of aforementioned approaches do not consider the temporal effects of labeling tasks of each individual worker and they cannot seamlessly integrate into deep SRL frameworks.

2.2 Learning from Noisy Labels

Learning with noisy labels has been an important research topic since the beginning of machine learning (Frénay and Verleysen, 2013) and a large spectrum of models have been developed and successfully applied in improving the model prediction performance in noisy settings from different perspectives such as effective label cleaning (Lee et al., 2018), robust model architectures (Vahdat, 2017) and loss functions (Ghosh et al., 2017), sample reweighting (Ren et al., 2018), and carefully designed training procedures (Zhong et al., 2019).

However, in this work, different from above approaches of robust learning from noisy labels that assume certain percentage of labels are corrupted, our scenario focuses on noisy labels obtained from multiple annotators where the disagreement (corruption) proportion might be surprisingly high and sometimes even 100%, i.e., no completely agreement on every single sample from all crowd workers.

2.3 Deep Metric Learning

DML approaches automatically learn nonlinear metric spaces (Schroff et al., 2015). Many approaches have achieved promising results in many tasks such as face recognition (Schroff et al., 2015), person re-identification (Yi et al., 2014), and collaborative filtering (Hsieh et al., 2017) etc. Recently a body of works have attempted to learn effective embeddings from crowdsourced labels by using DML approaches (Xu et al., 2019; Wang et al., 2020b). For example, Xu et al. estimated crowdsourced label confidence and adjust the DML loss function accordingly (Xu et al., 2019). An exhaustive review of previous work is beyond the scope of this paper. We refer to the survey of (Schroff et al., 2015) on works of DML. Although DML approaches are able to learn effective representations, they heavily rely on comparisons within pairs or triplets, which is very sensitive to ambiguous examples and may be easily misled by inconsistent crowdsourced labels.

Please note that models from the above three categories are complementary and they can be combined. For example, learning representation from crowdsourced labels can be conducted in two stages where the truth inference algorithms in Section 2.1 is applied to get estimated labels and then the standard DML approaches in Section 2.3 are used to output the learned embeddings. Details are discussed in Section 4.

3 The Proposed Approach

3.1 Notations

Without loss of generality, we consider crowdsourcing scenarios that each data sample is annotated by multiple workers. Following the crowdsourcing practice and to avoid the order effect (Hogarth and Einhorn, 1992) and cheating, each worker will annotate the same set of samples but with shuffled orders. Let $\boldsymbol{\alpha}^j$ be the sample order index set for the jth worker and α_i^j be the index of ith sample for worker j. Let $\mathbf{x}_{\alpha_i^j}$ and $y_{\alpha_i^j}$ be the feature vectors and the worker's assigned label for sample α_i^j. Let $\mathcal{F}(\cdot)$ represent the learned language representation. Let $(\cdot)^+$ and $(\cdot)^-$ be the indicators of positive and negative examples.

3.2 Temporal-Aware Memory Confidence

According to Miller's Law (Miller, 1956), humans can only hold a very limited number of objects in their short-term working memories. When workers conduct labeling tasks, they tend to make relative comparisons in their memory spans and the annotation quality of one sample is largely influenced by its preceding samples. Therefore, in this work, we focus on studying and modeling the effects of unconscious human behaviors during the labeling process that may implicitly influence the overall crowdsourcing quality. We design an approach to explicitly capture such unconscious temporal human behaviors, i.e., temporal labeling effects. We aim to ensure that *the newly annotated samples should obtain the consistent label with similar samples that have already been annotated recently.* Here we first define the short-term labeling memory as follows:

Definition 1. (SHORT-TERM LABELING MEMORY) *A short-term labeling memory of ith sample, i.e., indexed as α_i^j, is composed of a sequence of the current item and k most recent historical items that have been labeled by worker j, i.e.,* $\mathbf{M}_i^j = \{< \mathbf{x}_{\alpha_i^j}, y_{\alpha_i^j} >, < \mathbf{x}_{\alpha_{i-1}^j}, y_{\alpha_{i-1}^j} >, \cdots, < \mathbf{x}_{\alpha_{i-k}^j}, y_{\alpha_{i-k}^j} >\}$.

When the new labeling task arrives, i.e., the ith sample, we compute a weight for every element in worker j's short-term labeling memory $\mathbf{M}_i^j$ as the dot product of their learned language representations. This weight might be viewed as an attention over the short-term labeling memory per sample per worker.

To form a proper probability distribution over the elements in $\mathbf{M}_i^j$, we normalize the weights using the softmax function. This way we model probability $s_{\alpha_{i-l}^j}$ that represents the similarity between the ith sample and the sample appears at position l in $\mathbf{M}_i^j$. In a functional form this is:

$$s_{\alpha_{i-l}^j} \propto \exp\left(\mathcal{F}(\mathbf{x}_{\alpha_{i-l}^j}), \mathcal{F}(\mathbf{x}_{\alpha_i^j})\right), \quad l = 0, \cdots, k$$

Then we define a memory confidence score, i.e., c_i^j, to represent the probability that how likely the sample i is positive ($y_{\alpha_i^j} = 1$) solely considering similar samples in the short-term labeling memory. The memory confidence score of c_i^j is computed as follows:

$$c_i^j = \Pr(y_{\alpha_i^j} = 1) \propto \sum_{l=0}^{k} \mathbb{1}\left[y_{\alpha_{i-l}^j} = 1\right] s_{\alpha_{i-l}^j}$$

Please note that our attention based temporal-aware memory confidence scores are not limited to binary crowdsourcing tasks and it can be easily extended to multi-class tasks.

3.3 Multi-Worker Confidence Aggregation

For each sample i, after collecting the memory confidence scores from all workers, we conduct the mean pooling as our aggregation operation, and the final aggregated multi-worker confidence is computed as follows: $c_i = \text{MeanPooling}(c_i^1, c_i^2, \cdots, c_i^m)$, where m is the number of workers.

3.4 Representation Learning Framework

We use DML as our representation learning framework. Specifically, following the suggestion of (Xu et al., 2019), instead of using pair and triplet comparisons, we use group, a.k.a., n-tuplet, as our comparison unit. A group is made up of two positive and n negative examples. Similar to (Xu et al., 2019), we choose to learn our model parameters by maximizing the conditional likelihood of retrieving the positive example $\mathbf{x}_j^+$ given the positive example $\mathbf{x}_i^+$ from a given group.

Importantly, we do not assume that we know the ground truth label of items in the training set and the validation set. During the training stage of the representation learning framework, after obtaining the aggregated multi-worker confidence c_i of an item with methods introduced in Section 3.3, its label is estimated by $\arg\max c_i$.

Given a collection of groups, we optimize the DML model parameters by maximizing the sum of log conditional likelihood of finding a positive example $\mathbf{x}_j^+$ given the paired positive example $\mathbf{x}_i^+$ within every group $\mathbf{g}$, which will push items of the same class close and items of different classes far in the embedding space. Furthermore, we incorporate the aggregated temporal-aware multi-worker confidence scores from Section 3.3 into the loss function to capture the inconsistency of crowd-sourced labels. The loss function is defined as $\mathcal{L}(\Omega) = -\sum \log p(\mathbf{x}_j^+|\mathbf{x}_i^+)$,

$$p(\mathbf{x}_j^+|\mathbf{x}_i^+) = \frac{\exp\left(\eta \cdot c_j \cdot r_{ij}\right)}{\sum_{\mathbf{x}_* \in \mathbf{g}, \mathbf{x}_* \neq \mathbf{x}_i^+} \exp\left(\eta \cdot c_* \cdot r_{i*}\right)}$$

where Ω is the parameter set of the DNN. r_{i*} represents the cosine similarity score between the representations of $\mathbf{x}_i^+$ and $\mathbf{x}_*$ in the embedding space. η is a smoothing hyper parameter in the softmax function, which is set empirically on a held-out data set in our experiment. Since $\mathcal{L}(\Omega)$ is differentiable with respect to Ω, we use gradient based optimization approach to train the DNN.

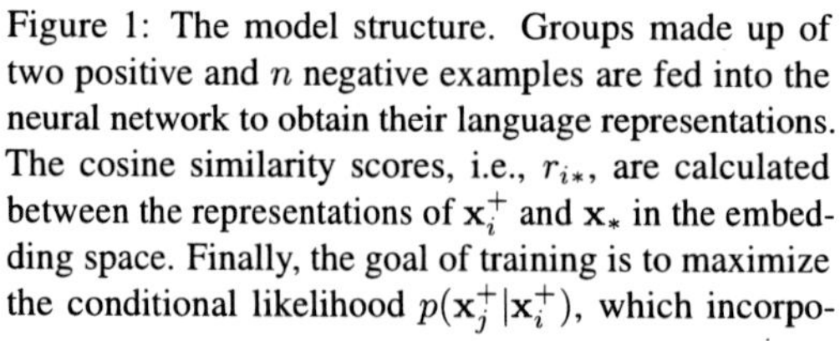

Figure 1: The model structure. Groups made up of two positive and n negative examples are fed into the neural network to obtain their language representations. The cosine similarity scores, i.e., r_{i*}, are calculated between the representations of $\mathbf{x}_i^+$ and $\mathbf{x}_*$ in the embedding space. Finally, the goal of training is to maximize the conditional likelihood $p(\mathbf{x}_j^+|\mathbf{x}_i^+)$, which incorporates temporal-aware memory confidence scores c_i^j.

4 Experiments

Experiments are conducted on both real-world and synthetic data sets. The internal cross validation approach is used to select hyper parameters when optimizing models' predictive performances. Means as well as standard deviations of both accuracy and AUC scores are reported, to comprehensively evaluate the performance of our proposed method, i.e. *TACMA*.

4.1 Real-World Data Sets

Experiments are first conducted on 4 real-world data sets and the corresponding descriptive statistics can be found in Table 1.

- *Emotion*: A vocal emotional speech data set with binary labels indicating whether the voice fragment is exciting or not.
- *Concluding*: A linguistic data set where each item is labeled on whether it is a conclusion of a lesson.
- *Commending*: A linguistic data set of ASR transcripts from real-world classroom recordings. Each item is labeled on whether it's a commending instruction from the instructors.
- *Question*: A vocal speech data set where each item is labeled on whether it is an interrogative sentence.

Acoustic features of the *Emotion* data set are extracted using OpenSmile[1] with the computational paralinguistic challenge's (COMPARE-2013) feature set (Schuller et al., 2013). Sentence embedding features are extracted with a Chinese RoBERTa pretrained model [2]. Again we emphasize that the ground truth labels of items in the training and validation set are not observed. In order to evaluate the performance of each model objectively, the labels of items in test sets are labeled by experts and they have reached an agreement on the labels of items.

Inter-observer variability of each data set is measured with Fleiss-kappa score (Fleiss, 1971). Intra-observer variability, i.e., the level of consistency of an annotator when labeling items from the same class, is hard to directly measure without ground truth labels. We will explore the effect of intra-observer variability using temporal-aware memory confidence in Section 4.8.

4.2 Synthetic Data Sets

In real-world scenarios, annotators are not guaranteed to be serious about their annotating work, and one may assign random labels in order to get paid quickly. Methods designed for crowdsourcing scenarios should be able to get rid of the influence of these noisy annotations. Hence we build synthetic data sets to evaluate the robustness to irresponsible annotators of each method. Starting from the original *Question* data set, we gradually add 2, 4, 6 and 8 simulated irresponsible annotators. They make random judgments regardless of the features of items. Hence in the worst case, 8 out of 13 workers are making random judgments, resulting in an extreme low kappa of 0.02. Experiments conducted on these synthetic data sets are helpful to examine the robustness of methods.

4.3 Baselines

We carefully selected several groups of baselines as follows:

Group 1: Truth Inference. A wide range of label aggregation methods are chosen as our baselines. Some widely-used methods according to the survey (Zheng et al., 2017) are included, i.e., *EM* (Dawid and Skene, 1979), *Spectral-EM*(Zhang et al., 2014), *GLAD* (Whitehill et al., 2009), *IBCC* (Kim and Ghahramani, 2012), *VI-BP* (Qiang et al., 2012), *VI-MF* (Qiang et al., 2012), *KOS* (Karger et al., 2011), *ZenCrowd* (Demartini et al., 2012), *LFC* (Raykar et al., 2010), *PM* (Li et al., 2014), and the implementation of these algorithms can mostly be found in the website[3]. Meanwhile some more recent works are also included: *EBCC* (Li et al., 2019c), *BWA* (Li et al., 2019b).

Group 2: Representation Learning. Our proposed method is compared with representation learning methods via deep metric learning, including Triplet with semi-hard example mining (Schroff et al., 2015), i.e., *Triple*, and Triplet networks with Center Loss (He et al., 2018), i.e., *Center*. Recent works of learning effective embeddings from crowdsourced labels using DML approaches are also important baselines: RLL-MLE (Xu et al., 2019), RLL-Bayesian (Xu et al., 2019), RECLE (Wang et al., 2020b).

Group 3: Learning from Noisy Data. Group 3 contains methods of learning with noisy labels: *LC* (Arazo et al., 2019) use a two-component beta mixture model to perform unsupervised noise mod-

[1]https://www.audeering.com/opensmile/

[2]https://github.com/ymcui/Chinese-BERT-wwm

[3]https://zhydhkcws.github.io/crowd_truth_inference/index.html

Table 1: Data sets statistics.Data sets statistics. It should be noted that the class ratio of each training set is estimated by majority voting since the ground truth labels are not observed. The labels of items in each test set are annotated by experts and they have reached an agreement on the label of each item.

Data Sets	Emotion	Commending	Question	Concluding	Syn-2	Syn-4	Syn-6	Syn-8
# of annotators	5	7	5	5	7	9	11	13
# of train samples	3067	1200	3140	1208	3140	3140	3140	3140
# of validation samples	766	299	785	302	785	785	785	785
# of test samples	800	1300	2000	648	2000	2000	2000	2000
kappa	0.84	0.69	0.82	0.37	0.35	0.2	0.12	0.08
train class ratio (majority voting)	0.42	0.50	0.63	0.42	0.63	0.63	0.63	0.63

eling, and *DivideMix* (Li et al., 2019a) leverages semi-supervised learning techniques. *CrowdLayer* (Rodrigues and Pereira, 2018) is an end-to-end approach learning a DNN from noisy labels with a crowd layer.

Group 4: Combining Group 1 with Groups 2 & 3. Some methods of Group 2 & 3, i.e. *Triple*, *Center*, *LC*, *DivideMix*, are not specifically designed for crowdsourcing scenarios. Although majority-voting labels are served as a default choice, these models should be trained with labels inferred by methods of Group 1 as stronger baselines, since methods of Group 1 are likely to provide more accurate inferred labels than majority voting. These methods are therefore trained with labels inferred by *EBCC*, which achieves the best performances of Group 1 in all data sets.

4.4 Setup and Implementation Details

Experimental codes are implemented in Tensorflow 1.8 available at https://github.com/CrowdsourcingMining/TACMA. Experiments are conducted on a server with a GTX 1080 Ti GPU. We set the tuplet size n to 5 for all the experiments, as suggested in (Xu et al., 2019). The representation learning network has a simple structure, i.e., 2 fully-connected layers with a drop-out rate of 0.2, a learning rate of 1e-3, and hyper-parameters including sizes of each layer and scale of ℓ_2 regularization searched via grid searching with cross validation. The network weights are initialized with a normal distribution initializer and updated with Adadelta optimizer (Zeiler, 2012). For all the representation learning methods, the downstream classifier is set to be a logistic regression classifier with ℓ_2 penalty containing the only hyper-parameter C as penalty strength ranging from 1e-2 to 1e4.

4.5 Performance Comparison

We compare performance of *TACMA* with existing methods on 4 real-world data sets and the results are summarized in Table 2. *TACMA* outperforms all the 4 groups of baselines, and here are some observations:

- The advantage of *TACMA* over truth inference methods gets bigger on the *Concluding* data set than other data sets. The *Concluding* data set has a low kappa score of 0.37, indicating that there are more disagreements among workers, which makes it hard to inference correct labels regardless of items' features. By contrast, *TACMA* makes full use of representations of items to gain more information resulting in the best performance.
- Although labels inferred by *EBCC* boost the performances of representation learning models, e.g., *Triple+EBCC*, they still perform inferior to *TACMA*, a possible explanation is that these two-stage methods give equal weight to each item and ignores temporal labeling effects. *TACMA* is able to discover potential conflicts in the short-term working memory, by applying the attention mechanism and gives low weights to the conflicting judgments.
- *TACMA* shares the same representation network structures with other methods of representation learning with crowdsourced labels i.e., *RLL-MLE*, *RLL-bayesian* and *RECLE*. The learned representations are compared in Figure 2 by feeding the raw features into representation network and performing dimension reduction into 2-dimensional space with t-SNE method (Van and Hinton, 2008). In the raw feature space, items of different classes are interleaved with each other. By contrast, learned representations of *TACMA* are more

Table 2: Prediction accuracy and AUC scores on 4 real-world data sets. The experiments are repeated 5 times and the means and standard deviations are reported.

	Commending		Emotion		Question		Concluding	
	ACC	AUC	ACC	AUC	ACC	AUC	ACC	AUC
EM	0.794±0.019	0.871±0.008	0.883±0.012	0.967±0.005	0.877±0.010	0.941±0.005	0.681±0.004	0.720±0.015
Spectral-EM	0.794±0.017	0.870±0.007	0.886±0.010	0.964±0.003	0.876±0.009	0.941±0.004	0.681±0.004	0.720±0.013
GLAD	0.794±0.017	0.870±0.007	0.886±0.010	0.964±0.003	0.878±0.009	0.942±0.004	0.689±0.009	0.742±0.014
IBCC	0.794±0.017	0.870±0.007	0.889±0.004	0.964±0.004	0.876±0.009	0.941±0.004	0.681±0.004	0.720±0.013
VI-BP	0.794±0.017	0.870±0.007	0.892±0.012	0.968±0.005	0.877±0.008	0.941±0.004	0.681±0.004	0.720±0.013
VI-MF	0.799±0.013	0.874±0.003	0.786±0.000	0.898±0.000	0.876±0.009	0.941±0.004	0.685±0.003	0.725±0.009
KOS	0.799±0.013	0.874±0.003	0.786±0.000	0.898±0.000	0.878±0.009	0.942±0.004	0.694±0.005	0.747±0.010
ZenCrowd	0.794±0.019	0.871±0.008	0.895±0.011	0.971±0.004	0.877±0.010	0.941±0.005	0.689±0.010	0.742±0.016
LFC	0.794±0.019	0.871±0.008	0.883±0.009	0.967±0.004	0.877±0.010	0.941±0.005	0.681±0.004	0.720±0.015
PM	0.799±0.014	0.867±0.008	0.887±0.010	0.966±0.003	0.874±0.010	0.940±0.004	0.677±0.009	0.730±0.013
EBCC	0.812±0.006	0.874±0.003	0.895±0.012	0.970±0.005	0.878±0.007	0.941±0.008	0.694±0.003	0.748±0.006
BWA	0.794±0.020	0.867±0.008	0.888±0.005	0.965±0.004	0.875±0.009	0.939±0.004	0.689±0.007	0.741±0.013
Triple	0.793±0.012	0.871±0.006	0.804±0.005	0.876±0.002	0.888±0.002	0.941±0.001	0.725±0.014	0.821±0.008
Center	0.806±0.002	0.859±0.001	0.701±0.007	0.780±0.007	0.840±0.006	0.905±0.008	0.705±0.015	0.797±0.007
RLL-MLE	0.800±0.008	0.866±0.001	0.854±0.016	0.961±0.008	0.853±0.013	0.919±0.006	0.735±0.004	0.828±0.009
RLL-Bayesian	0.816±0.000	0.861±0.001	0.877±0.006	0.954±0.004	0.877±0.004	0.932±0.003	0.725±0.001	0.839±0.001
RECLE	0.812±0.002	0.858±0.000	0.746±0.001	0.836±0.001	0.880±0.024	0.934±0.012	0.729±0.003	0.838±0.005
LC	0.560±0.085	0.700±0.028	0.611±0.046	0.715±0.007	0.715±0.018	0.720±0.007	0.701±0.018	0.790±0.011
DivideMix	0.515±0.016	0.733±0.014	0.535±0.000	0.730±0.000	0.734±0.009	0.720±0.014	0.654±0.025	0.710±0.007
CrowdLayer	0.802±0.008	0.878±0.007	0.757±0.008	0.798±0.009	0.852±0.003	0.920±0.002	0.676±0.014	0.722±0.011
LC+EBCC	0.581±0.070	0.687±0.029	0.825±0.024	0.845±0.019	0.758±0.010	0.830±0.012	0.705±0.018	0.784±0.004
DivideMix+EBCC	0.515±0.018	0.730±0.014	0.726±0.039	0.832±0.028	0.760±0.012	0.833±0.014	0.659±0.006	0.720±0.005
Triple+EBCC	0.814±0.004	0.872±0.000	0.893±0.003	0.968±0.004	0.890±0.001	0.938±0.003	0.737±0.003	0.825±0.007
Center+EBCC	0.814±0.004	0.866±0.003	0.826±0.016	0.884±0.018	0.844±0.005	0.909±0.005	0.742±0.006	0.848±0.003
TACMA	**0.831±0.002**	**0.882±0.004**	**0.904±0.002**	**0.973±0.001**	**0.899±0.005**	**0.945±0.003**	**0.765±0.006**	**0.855±0.010**

separated than the other methods, reducing the difficulty of downstream classification tasks.

4.6 Robustness to Irresponsible Workers

We select some representatives from Groups 1-4 and draw the curves of accuracy on synthetic data sets containing different number of irresponsible workers in Figure 3. We can find that:

- Truth inference methods such as *EBCC* stay stable facing different numbers of irresponsible workers. On the other hand, the accuracy of other methods decreases when increasing the number of irresponsible workers. This result may be explained by the fact that for methods including *RLL-Bayesian*, *Triple*, learning effective representations of items heavily relies on correct labels, and hence becomes harder as the labels become more noisy.
- *TACMA* maintains the highest accuracy of all the methods. Unlike the two-stage method i.e., *Triplet + EBCC*, which gives equal weight to each item and ignores *temporal labeling effects*, *TACMA* is able to discover potential conflicts in the short-term working memory using the attention mechanism, and give low training weights to the conflicting judgments.

4.7 Effect of Working Memory Sizes

We set the working memory size ranging from 3 to 11 to find the optimized length and at the same time explore its influence on performance, shown in Figure 4. The accuracy of our proposed method goes up at the beginning with the increasing working memory size, and the standard deviations gradually become smaller at the same time. It is reasonable because potential inconsistent judgments among similar items cannot be found without observing enough historical annotations. As the working memory size continues extending, the accuracy scores become relatively stable, indicating that there is sufficient evidence to estimate the time-aware confidence of the current annotation.

4.8 Relations between Temporal-aware Memory Confidence and Worker's Expertise

In this part we further explore the relations between worker's expertise and temporal-aware memory confidence. To evaluate a worker's expertise, a Logistic Regression classifier is trained with labels annotated by this same person, and the accuracy on the corresponding test set is recorded. On the other hand, the temporal-aware confidence of all

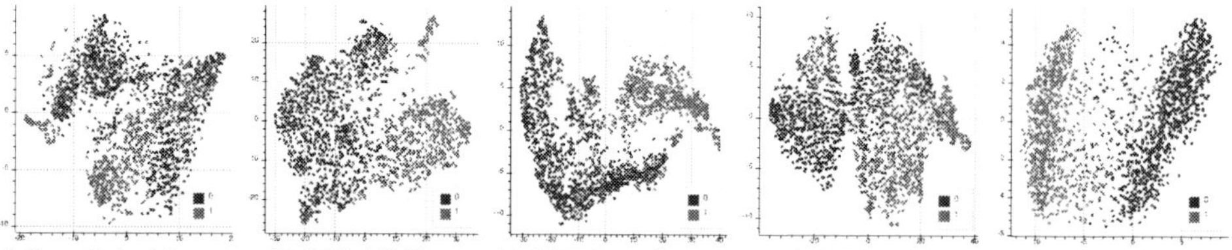

(a) Raw Embedding (b) RLL-MLE (c) RLL-Bayesian (d) RECLE (e) TACMA

Figure 2: Visualization of learned representations on the test set of Question data. The raw features of items are fed into the representation network to obtain the semantic representations, and dimension reduction using t-SNE method is performed for visualization.

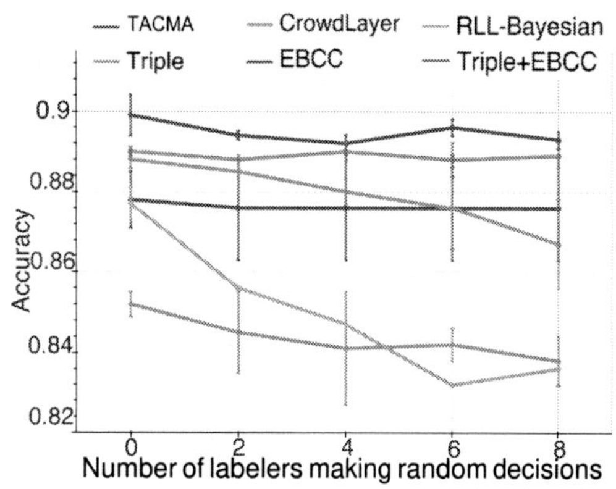

Figure 3: Accuracy curves on synthetic data sets containing different number of irresponsible annotators who make random decisions.

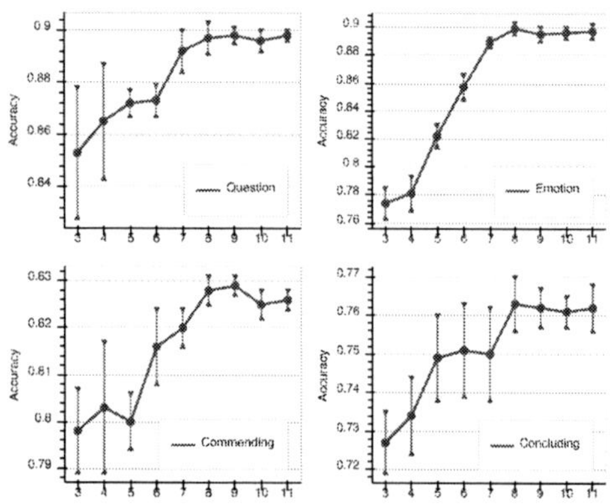

Figure 4: The effect of different working memory sizes on prediction accuracy on real-world data sets.

the judgments made by this worker is averaged.

We perform standardization on both accuracy scores and the averaged temporal-aware confidence scores within the corresponding data set, and put the standardized values of all the 62 workers from 4 real-world data sets and 4 synthetic data sets together in Figure 5, to reveal the universal relation between temporal-aware confidence and the worker's expertise. We can find a wide range of intra-observer variability among different workers, estimated by their temporal-aware confidence scores. A strong positive correlation is found between averaged confidence and prediction accuracy ($pearson\ r = 0.844$). Specifically, synthetic irresponsible annotators, colored in blue, are automatically clustered in the lower left corner, indicating that the poor performances of the classifiers trained with their labels derive from huge inner inconsistencies in their judgments.

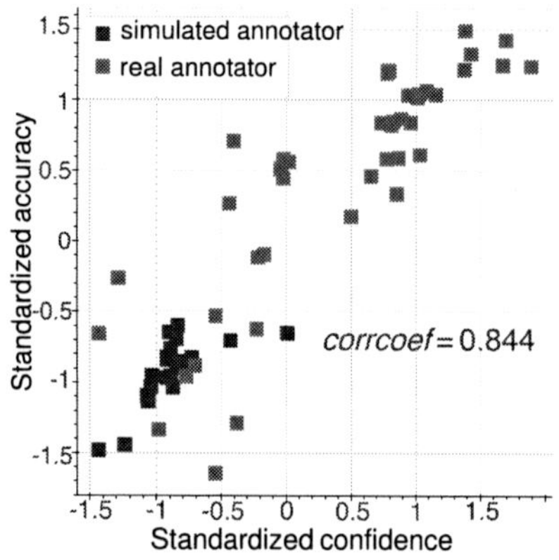

Figure 5: The relations between standardized temporal-aware memory confidence and standardized prediction accuracy of annotators in both real and synthetic data sets. Most of the irresponsible annotators appear in the lower left corner, indicating that there are internal conflicts in their judgments (low confidence), and therefore LR models trained with these labels perform worse than average.

5 Conclusion

We presented TACMA, an end-to-end framework for language representation learning from crowdsourced labels. Comparing with traditional SRL approaches, the advantages of our framework are: (1) it is able to consider temporal labeling effects within sequences of sample-level labeling tasks for each worker; (2) it automatically computes and aggregates sample-level confidence scores from multiple workers which makes the training process more effective. Experimental results on both synthetic and real-world data sets demonstrates that our approach outperforms other state-of-the-art baselines in terms of accuracy and AUC scores.

References

Eric Arazo, Diego Ortego, Paul Albert, Noel O'Connor, and Kevin Mcguinness. 2019. Unsupervised label noise modeling and loss correction. In *ICML*, pages 312–321.

Maarten AS Boksem, Theo F Meijman, and Monicque M Lorist. 2005. Effects of mental fatigue on attention: an erp study. *Cognitive brain research*, 25(1):107–116.

Alexander Philip Dawid and Allan M Skene. 1979. Maximum likelihood estimation of observer error-rates using the em algorithm. *Journal of the Royal Statistical Society: Series C (Applied Statistics)*, 28(1):20–28.

Gianluca Demartini, Djellel Difallah, and Philippe Cudre-Mauroux. 2012. Zencrowd: Leveraging probabilistic reasoning and crowdsourcing techniques for large-scale entity linking. pages 469–478.

DN Elliott and WD Riach. 1965. Effect of repeated practice with and without feedback upon discrimination performance. *The Journal of the Acoustical Society of America*, 37(6):1194–1194.

Joseph L Fleiss. 1971. Measuring nominal scale agreement among many raters. *Psychological Bulletin*, 76(5):378.

Benoît Frénay and Michel Verleysen. 2013. Classification in the presence of label noise: a survey. *IEEE transactions on neural networks and learning systems*, 25(5):845–869.

Aritra Ghosh, Himanshu Kumar, and PS Sastry. 2017. Robust loss functions under label noise for deep neural networks. In *AAAI*, volume 31.

Melody Guan, Varun Gulshan, Andrew Dai, and Geoffrey Hinton. 2018. Who said what: Modeling individual labelers improves classification. In *AAAI*, volume 32.

Bo Han, Quanming Yao, Xingrui Yu, Gang Niu, Miao Xu, Weihua Hu, Ivor Tsang, and Masashi Sugiyama. 2018. Co-teaching: Robust training of deep neural networks with extremely noisy labels. In *NeurIPS*, pages 8527–8537.

Xinwei He, Yang Zhou, Zhichao Zhou, Song Bai, and Xiang Bai. 2018. Triplet-center loss for multi-view 3d object retrieval. In *CVPR*, pages 1945–1954.

Robin M Hogarth and Hillel J Einhorn. 1992. Order effects in belief updating: The belief-adjustment model. *Cognitive psychology*, 24(1):1–55.

Cheng-Kang Hsieh, Longqi Yang, Yin Cui, Tsung-Yi Lin, Serge Belongie, and Deborah Estrin. 2017. Collaborative metric learning. WWW '17, page 193–201, Republic and Canton of Geneva, CHE. WWW Steering Committee.

David R. Karger, Sewoong Oh, and Devavrat Shah. 2011. Iterative learning for reliable crowdsourcing systems. In *NIPS*, pages 1953–1961.

Nicolas Kaufmann, Thimo Schulze, and Daniel Veit. 2011. More than fun and money. worker motivation in crowdsourcing-a study on mechanical turk. In *Amcis*, volume 11, pages 1–11. Detroit, Michigan, USA.

Hyun-Chul Kim and Zoubin Ghahramani. 2012. Bayesian classifier combination. In *Artificial Intelligence and Statistics*, pages 619–627.

Gregory Koch, Richard Zemel, and Ruslan Salakhutdinov. 2015. Siamese neural networks for one-shot image recognition. In *ICML Deep Learning Workshop*, volume 2. Lille.

Kuang-Huei Lee, Xiaodong He, Lei Zhang, and Linjun Yang. 2018. Cleannet: Transfer learning for scalable image classifier training with label noise. In *CVPR*, pages 5447–5456.

Chaoqun Li, Victor S Sheng, Liangxiao Jiang, and Hongwei Li. 2016. Noise filtering to improve data and model quality for crowdsourcing. *Knowledge-Based Systems*, 107:96–103.

Junnan Li, Richard Socher, and Steven CH Hoi. 2019a. Dividemix: Learning with noisy labels as semi-supervised learning. In *ICLR*.

Qi Li, Yaliang Li, Jing Gao, Bo Zhao, Wei Fan, and Jiawei Han. 2014. Resolving conflicts in heterogeneous data by truth discovery and source reliability estimation. In *SIGMOD*, pages 1187–1198.

Yuan Li, Benjamin IP Rubinstein, and Trevor Cohn. 2019b. Truth inference at scale: A bayesian model for adjudicating highly redundant crowd annotations. In *WWW*, pages 1028–1038.

Yuan Li, Benjamin Rubinstein, and Trevor Cohn. 2019c. Exploiting worker correlation for label aggregation in crowdsourcing. In *ICML*, pages 3886–3895.

George A Miller. 1956. The magical number seven, plus or minus two: Some limits on our capacity for processing information. *Psychological review*, 63(2):81.

Yixin Nie, Xiang Zhou, and Mohit Bansal. 2020. What can we learn from collective human opinions on natural language inference data? *EMNLP*.

Liu Qiang, Peng Jian, and Alexander Ihler. 2012. Variational inference for crowdsourcing. *NIPS*, 25.

Raykar, Vikas, C., Shipeng, Yu, Zhao, Linda, H., Valadez, and Gerardo. 2010. Learning from crowds. *JMLR*.

Mengye Ren, Wenyuan Zeng, Bin Yang, and Raquel Urtasun. 2018. Learning to reweight examples for robust deep learning. *arXiv preprint arXiv:1803.09050*.

Filipe Rodrigues and Francisco Pereira. 2018. Deep learning from crowds. In *AAAI*, volume 32.

Florian Schroff, Dmitry Kalenichenko, and James Philbin. 2015. Facenet: A unified embedding for face recognition and clustering. In *CVPR*, pages 815–823.

Björn Schuller, Stefan Steidl, Anton Batliner, Alessandro Vinciarelli, Klaus Scherer, Fabien Ringeval, Mohamed Chetouani, Felix Weninger, Florian Eyben, Erik Marchi, et al. 2013. The interspeech 2013 computational paralinguistics challenge: Social signals, conflict, emotion, autism. In *Proceedings INTERSPEECH 2013, 14th Annual Conference of the International Speech Communication Association, Lyon, France*.

Arash Vahdat. 2017. Toward robustness against label noise in training deep discriminative neural networks. In *NIPS*, pages 5596–5605.

L Van, der Maaten and Ge Hinton. 2008. (visualizing high-dimensional data using t-sne. *Journal of Machine Learning Research*, 9(2):2579–2605.

Wentao Wang, Tyler Derr, Yao Ma, Suhang Wang, Hui Liu, Zitao Liu, and Jiliang Tang. 2020a. Learning from incomplete labeled data via adversarial data generation. In *2020 IEEE International Conference on Data Mining (ICDM)*, pages 1316–1321. IEEE.

Wentao Wang, Guowei Xu, Wenbiao Ding, Yan Huang, Guoliang Li, Jiliang Tang, and Zitao Liu. 2020b. Representation learning from limited educational data with crowdsourced labels. *TKDE*.

Jacob Whitehill, Ting-fan Wu, Jacob Bergsma, Javier R Movellan, and Paul L Ruvolo. 2009. Whose vote should count more: Optimal integration of labels from labelers of unknown expertise. In *NIPS*, pages 2035–2043.

Rongkai Xia, Yan Pan, Hanjiang Lai, Cong Liu, and Shuicheng Yan. 2014. Supervised hashing for image retrieval via image representation learning. In *AAAI*.

Guowei Xu, Wenbiao Ding, Jiliang Tang, Songfan Yang, Gale Yan Huang, and Zitao Liu. 2019. Learning effective embeddings from crowdsourced labels: An educational case study. In *ICDE*, pages 1922–1927. IEEE.

Dong Yi, Zhen Lei, Shengcai Liao, and Stan Z Li. 2014. Deep metric learning for person re-identification. In *ICPR*, pages 34–39. IEEE.

Matthew D Zeiler. 2012. Adadelta: an adaptive learning rate method. *arXiv preprint arXiv:1212.5701*.

Ying Zhang, Xianghua Ding, and Ning Gu. 2018. Understanding fatigue and its impact in crowdsourcing. In *CSCWD*, pages 57–62. IEEE.

Yuchen Zhang, Xi Chen, Dengyong Zhou, and Michael I Jordan. 2014. Spectral methods meet em: A provably optimal algorithm for crowdsourcing. In *NIPS*, pages 1260–1268.

Yudian Zheng, Guoliang Li, Yuanbing Li, Caihua Shan, and Reynold Cheng. 2017. Truth inference in crowdsourcing: Is the problem solved? *PVLDB*, 10(5):541–552.

Yaoyao Zhong, Weihong Deng, Mei Wang, Jiani Hu, Jianteng Peng, Xunqiang Tao, and Yaohai Huang. 2019. Unequal-training for deep face recognition with long-tailed noisy data. In *CVPR*, pages 7812–7821.

Structure-aware Sentence Encoder in BERT-Based Siamese Network

Qiwei Peng David Weir Julie Weeds
University of Sussex
Brighton, UK
{qiwei.peng, d.j.weir, j.e.weeds}@sussex.ac.uk

Abstract

Recently, impressive performance on various natural language understanding tasks has been achieved by explicitly incorporating syntax and semantic information into pre-trained models, such as BERT and RoBERTa. However, this approach depends on problem-specific fine-tuning, and as widely noted, BERT-like models exhibit weak performance, and are inefficient, when applied to unsupervised similarity comparison tasks. Sentence-BERT (SBERT) has been proposed as a general-purpose sentence embedding method, suited to both similarity comparison and downstream tasks. In this work, we show that by incorporating structural information into SBERT, the resulting model outperforms SBERT and previous general sentence encoders on unsupervised semantic textual similarity (STS) datasets and transfer classification tasks.

1 Introduction

Pre-trained models like BERT (Devlin et al., 2018) and RoBERTa (Liu et al., 2019) have demonstrated promising results across a variety of downstream NLP tasks. Though BERT-like models have been shown to capture hidden syntax structures (Clark et al., 2019; Hewitt and Manning, 2019; Jawahar et al., 2019), recent works have achieved performance improvements on various natural language understanding (NLU) tasks through the use of a graph network that captures syntax and semantics information. Xu and Yang (2019) demonstrate the value of syntax information for pronoun resolution tasks, using Relational Graph Convolutional Networks (RGCNs) (Schlichtkrull et al., 2018) to incorporate syntactic dependency graphs. Wu et al. (2021) argue that semantics has not been brought to the surface of pre-trained models and propose to introduce semantic label information into RoBERTa via RGCNs. Similar ideas have been applied to information extraction (Santosh et al., 2020), sentence-pair classification (Liu et al., 2020) and sentiment analysis (Wang et al., 2020; Yin et al., 2020) tasks. Though problem-specific fine-tuning is required, these improvements suggest that structural supervision is useful, and that RGCNs serve as an effective structure encoder.

BERT can also be used as a general sentence encoder, either by using the CLS token (the first token of BERT output) or applying pooling over its outputs. However, this fails to produce sentence embeddings that can be used effectively for similarity comparison. Furthermore, this method of using BERT for similarity comparison is extremely inefficient, requiring sentence pairs to be concatenated and passed to BERT for every possible comparison. In response, Sentence-BERT (SBERT) has been proposed to alleviate this by fine-tuning BERT on natural language inference (NLI) datasets using a siamese structure (Reimers and Gurevych, 2019). General-purpose sentence embeddings are generated which outperform previous sentence encoders on both similarity comparison and transfer tasks.

In this paper, we show that it is possible to improve the SBERT sentence encoder through the use of explicit syntactic or semantic structure. Inspired by SBERT's success in producing general sentence representations and previous efforts on introducing structural information into pre-trained models, we propose a model that combines the two by training a BERT-RGCN model in a siamese structure. Under specific structural supervision, the proposed model is able to produce structure-aware, general-purpose sentence embeddings. Our empirical results show that it outperforms SBERT and previous sentence encoders on unsupervised similarity comparison and transfer classification tasks. Furthermore, we find that the produced sentence representation generalises better especially

Proceedings of the 6th Workshop on Representation Learning for NLP (RepL4NLP-2021), pages 57–63
Bangkok, Thailand (Online), August 6, 2021.

on fine-grained classification tasks.

2 Related Work

Sentence encoders have been studied extensively in years. Skip-Thought (Kiros et al., 2015) has been trained to predict its surrounding sentences by using current sentence in a self-supervised fashion. Hill et al. (2016) proposed a sequential denoising autoencoder (SDAE) to reconstruct given sentence representations. InferSent (Conneau et al., 2017), on the other hand, used labelled NLI datasets to train a general-purpose sentence encoder in a BiLSTM-based siamese structure. Cer et al. (2018) proposed the Universal Sentence Encoder (USE) model based on transformers (Vaswani et al., 2017), and trained it with both unsupervised tasks and supervised NLI tasks. Inspired by InferSent, Sentence-BERT (SBERT) (Reimers and Gurevych, 2019) produces general-purpose sentence embeddings by fine-tuning BERT on NLI datasets in a siamese structure, showing improved performance on a variety of tasks.

Hidden syntax structures in pre-trained models have been well explored. Various probing methods have been used to investigate hidden structures (Clark et al., 2019; Hewitt and Manning, 2019; Jawahar et al., 2019). The impact of external structures on pre-trained models has also been questioned. Glavaš and Vulić (2021) examined the benefits of incorporating universal dependencies into pre-trained models. Dai et al. (2021) showed that the tree induced from pre-trained models could produce competitive results compared with external trees. However, recent improvements have still been observed on various NLU tasks by incorporating structural information into pre-trained models. Yin et al. (2020) proposed SentiBERT to incorporate constituency tree into BERT for sentiment analysis. Xu and Yang (2019) modelled each sentence as a directed dependency graph by using RGCNs, and achieved large improvements on pronoun resolution. Zhang et al. (2020) proposed a semantics-aware BERT model by further encoding semantic information with BERT using a GRU (Chung et al., 2014). RGCNs have also been used by Wu et al. (2021) to introduce semantic information into RoBERTa, and achieved consistent improvements when fine-tuned on problem-specific datasets. Similar efforts can be seen where researchers try to provide syntax information via self-attention mechanism (Bai et al., 2021; Li et al., 2020).

3 Model

Inspired by Reimers and Gurevych (2019), we train our model in a siamese network to update weights so as to produce similarity-comparable sentence representations. The model we propose consists of two components, as shown in Figure 1.

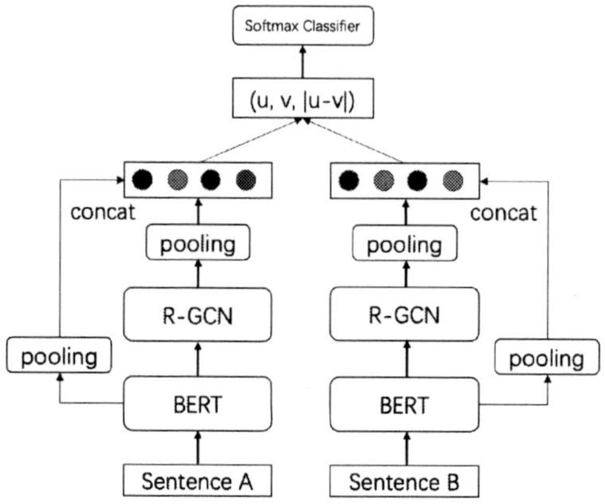

Figure 1: The proposed model in siamese structure

BERT: Each sentence is first fed into the pre-trained BERT-base model to produce both a sentence representation, by applying mean-pooling, and an original contextualised sequence-length token representation, which is used to initialise a RGCN.

Structure Information: We use Spacy dependency parser (Honnibal et al., 2020) with its middle model to obtain dependency parse trees for all input sentences. We also experimented with the use of semantic graphs[1], since Wu et al. (2021) has shown that semantic information benefits pre-trained models. However, we found semantic graphs to be less effective than syntactic dependency trees when evaluated on our development set, and as a result, in the experiments below, we restrict our attention to the use of syntactic dependency graphs.

RGCN: RGCNs, proposed by (Schlichtkrull et al., 2018), can be viewed as a weighted message passing process. At each RGCN layer, each node's representation will be updated by collecting information from its neighbours and applying edge-specific weighting:

$$h_i^{l+1} = ReLU(W_0^l h_i^l + \sum_{r \in R} \sum_{j \in N_i^r} \frac{1}{c_{i,r}} W_r^l h_j^l) \quad (1)$$

[1]For semantic graphs, we use the semantic parser produced by Che et al. (2019).

where N_i^r and W_r^l are the neighbours of node i and the weight of relation $r \in R$, respectively. $c_{i,r}$ is the normalisation constant and normally set to be $|N_i^r|$ which is the number of neighbours under relation r. W_0^l is the self-loop weight. In our case, each sentence is first parsed into a dependency tree, then modelled as a labelled directed graph by an RGCN, where nodes are words and edges are dependency relations. Following Schlichtkrull et al. (2018), we allow information to flow in both directions (from head to dependent and from dependent to head). Following Wu et al. (2021), we pass BERT output through an embedding projection which is made of an affine transformation and ReLU nonlinearity, then use the transformed representations to initialise RGCN's node representations. Since BERT and Spacy use different tokenisation strategies, we align them by taking the first subtoken as its word representation from BERT for each word in the RGCN. A structure-aware sentence representation is derived from RGCN's output by applying a mean-pooling over its node representations. During training, rather than using $c_{i,r} = |N_i^r|$, we found it best to apply the normalisation factor across relation types, $c_{i,r} = c_i = \sum_r |N_i^r|$, the number of neighbours. We use a one-layer RGCN, as we find that a deeper network lowers the performance.

Connect BERT and RGCN: The concatenation of BERT and RGCN's sentence representations are then passed through a layer normalisation layer to form the final sentence representation. Sentence embeddings of given sentence-pair are then interacted before passing to the final classifier for training. As for the interaction, we use the concatenation of sentence embedding u, v and the element-wise difference $|u - v|$, which has been found to be the best concatenation mode by Reimers and Gurevych (2019). In this siamese structure, all parameters are shared and will be updated correspondingly. We use cross-entropy loss for optimisation.

4 Experiments

We compare our model with SBERT[2], InferSent[3], USE[4], average GloVe vectors, and also two strategies using pre-trained BERT to produce sentence representations (BERT-CLS and BERT-AVG). For all experiments on these models, we use released pre-trained models and scripts to produce sentence embeddings.

4.1 Training Details

In order to produce general-purpose sentence embeddings, we follow SBERT in training the model on a combination of the SNLI (Bowman et al., 2015) and the MNLI datasets (Williams et al., 2018). They contain $570,000$ and $430,000$ sentence pairs, respectively, which are annotated as contradiction, entailment, or neutral. Our model is trained for one epoch, and we use a batch-size of 16, the Adam optimizer with learning rate 2e$-$5, and a linear learning rate warm-up over 10% of the training data. For RGCN layer, we use dropout of 0.2 and hidden dimension of 512. Following SBERT, we evaluate our model on the STS benchmark development set in Spearman rank correlation for every $1,000$ steps during training, and save the best model.

4.2 Evaluation - Unsupervised STS

First, we evaluate our model on semantic textual similarity (STS) datasets. Here we use STS12-16 tasks (Agirre et al., 2012, 2013, 2014, 2015, 2016), SICK-Relatedness (SICK-R) (Marelli et al., 2014) test set and STS benchmark (STSb) (Cer et al., 2017) test set. These datasets are labelled from 0 to 5 on semantic relatedness of sentence pairs. We obtain these datasets via SentEval (Conneau and Kiela, 2018). In this evaluation, we test different encoders' performance without using any task-specific training data.

Model	STS12	STS13	STS14	STS15	STS16	STSb	SICK-R	AVG
GloVe AVG	52.24	49.91	43.36	55.91	47.67	46.00	55.02	50.02
InferSent	48.42	67.37	61.41	72.87	66.12	64.33	62.95	63.35
USE	63.42	67.50	64.16	76.99	73.23	74.60	**76.67**	70.94
BERT-AVG	30.87	59.89	47.73	60.29	63.73	47.29	58.22	52.57
BERT-CLS	21.54	32.11	21.28	37.89	44.24	20.29	42.42	31.40
SBERT	70.97	76.53	73.19	79.09	74.30	76.98	72.91	74.85
Ours	**72.51**	**77.05**	**74.06**	**80.90**	**76.20**	**78.50**	73.58	**76.11**

Table 1: Results on STS12-16, STSb and SICK-R. Spearman rank correlation ρ between the cosine similarity of sentence representations and the gold labels is calculated. $\rho \times 100$ is reported

The results are given in Table 1, and show that our model outperforms SBERT on all 7 tasks, obtaining the highest average score, and demonstrating the benefits of including explicit syntax structure during supervision. Both SBERT and

[2]https://github.com/UKPLab/sentence-transformers, we use its BERT-base-nli-mean model

[3]https://github.com/facebookresearch/InferSent

[4]https://tfhub.dev/google/universal-sentence-encoder-large/3

our model perform worse than USE on SICK-R. However, as observed by Reimers and Gurevych (2019), USE is trained on various datasets including question-answering pairs, NLI, online forums and news, which appears to be particularly suitable to the data of SICK-R. Both BERT-AVG and BERT-CLS perform poorly which reflects their weakness as general-purpose sentence encoders.

4.3 Evaluation - Transfer Tasks

While the best results for BERT-like models is achieved with problem-specific fine-tuning, an evaluation on transfer tasks provides a way to test the encoder's generalisation ability and representation quality. Following Reimers and Gurevych (2019), we use SentEval with logistic regression to test different encoders on 8 classification tasks: sentiment analysis, MR (Pang and Lee, 2005); CR (Hu and Liu, 2004); SST-5/SST-2 (Socher et al., 2013); question-type, TREC (Li and Roth, 2002); subjectivity-objectivity, SUBJ (Pang and Lee, 2004); phrase-level opinion polarity, MPQA (Wiebe et al., 2005); and paraphrase detection, MRPC (Dolan et al., 2004). These datasets are provided by SentEval.

As shown in Table 2, the proposed model outperforms previous encoders in general though the difference between SBERT and our model is relatively small. Our model performs significantly worse than USE on TREC, which may be due to the fact that USE is pre-trained on question-answering data, which appears to be beneficial to the TREC question-type classification task. Unlike previous poor performance on STS datasets, BERT-CLS and BERT-AVG produce good results on classification tasks. This shows that the relevant information is encoded in BERT-CLS and BERT-AVG, they just lack the ability to produce similarity-comparable sentence embeddings. Both SBERT and our model perform worse than BERT-AVG and BERT-CLS on SUBJ task, which suggests that, while gaining on sentiment analysis tasks, fine-tuning on NLI datasets leads to information loss on recognising the subjectivity of a sentence.

Extraction Difficulty As we have seen, the difference between SBERT and our model in our previous transfer comparison is small. Our hypothesis is that, since we concatenate the outputs of BERT and RGCN, the representations produced by our model are more complex, and that simple logistic regression lacks the ability to extract useful information from such complex embeddings. To assess this, we replace the logistic regression with a single hidden layer MLP (128 hidden units) which is widely used as a probing classifier. We focus on the comparison between our model and SBERT, re-running these two models with 5 random seeds, and report accuracy in the same fashion, except we adopt a more strict bold strategy to mark the difference (as explained in the caption).

As shown in Table 3, for some tasks, e.g. MR and CR, both models show stable performance cross different classifiers, and their performance remains similar when this more powerful extractor is used. However, for SST-5 (5-way sentiment classification) and TREC (6-way question-type classification), we see that clear improvements are obtained by our model, suggesting that the additional syntax supervision that we bring in through RGCNs is beneficial for fine-grained classification tasks. A similar pattern of results was found when we experimented with a 2 hidden layer MLP.

	GloVe AVG	BERT-AVG	BERT-CLS	InferSent	USE	SBERT	Ours
MPQA	87.64±0.11	87.84±0.08	88.17±0.05	**90.32±0.12**	86.52±0.09	89.81±0.06	89.75±0.12
SST-5	44.35±0.11	47.33±0.22	48.03±0.45	44.93±1.14	47.67±0.06	48.57±0.53	**49.19±1.01**
SST-2	80.02±0.24	85.69±0.09	87.21±0.17	84.15±0.33	85.78±0.11	87.8±0.28	**87.99±0.28**
SUBJ	91.26±0.11	95.29±0.05	**95.48±0.1**	92.47±0.1	93.85±0.16	94.03±0.12	93.81±0.16
TREC	80.36±2.13	90.24±0.8	91.36±0.83	87.94±0.56	**92.36±0.32**	86.4±0.83	87.8±0.68
MRPC	72.79±0.21	73.43±0.77	71.68±0.48	**75.33±0.37**	71.2±0.61	74.68±0.75	74.9±0.74
MR	77.26±0.19	81.38±0.08	82.12±0.15	81.71±0.23	79.48±0.1	**82.77±0.22**	82.59±0.13
CR	78.9±0.1	87.12±0.31	87.33±0.23	86.34±0.52	86.03±0.23	88.99±0.16	**89.02±0.13**
AVG	76.57	81.04	81.42	80.40	80.36	81.63	**81.88**

Table 2: Results on SentEval evaluation with logistic regression. For MR, CR, MPQA and SUBJ, we use 10-fold cross validation and report accuracy on test-fold. For remaining tasks, results are reported on test set. We run 5 times with random seeds and report mean with standard deviation.

	SBERT	Ours
MPQA	89.98±0.16	90.11±0.13
SST-5	49.1±0.56	**50.5±0.3**
SST-2	88.51±0.71	88.39±0.39
SUBJ	94.1±0.12	94.05±0.17
TREC	86.96±0.32	**88.4±0.58**
MRPC	74.79±1.28	75.01±0.85
MR	82.7±0.16	82.56±0.14
CR	88.89±0.24	88.94±0.26
AVG	81.88	**82.25**

Table 3: Results on SentEval evaluation with MLP. Cells marked as bold only when the mean minus std is no worse than the mean plus std of the other model

5 Conclusion

In this work, we show that SBERT can be improved by explicitly incorporating structural information. By using RGCNs to incorporate syntactic structure into supervision, our model is able to produce structure-aware, general-purpose sentence embeddings that achieve improved results on both unsupervised similarity comparison and transfer classification tasks, when compared against previous sentence encoders. By extending probing classifiers, we further show that our syntax-informed supervision method is particularly beneficial for fine-grained tasks such as SST-5 and TREC.

6 Acknowledgement

We thank all anonymous reviewers for their helpful comments, and NVIDIA for the donation of the GPU that supported our work.

References

Eneko Agirre, Carmen Banea, Claire Cardie, Daniel Cer, Mona Diab, Aitor Gonzalez-Agirre, Weiwei Guo, Iñigo Lopez-Gazpio, Montse Maritxalar, Rada Mihalcea, German Rigau, Larraitz Uria, and Janyce Wiebe. 2015. SemEval-2015 task 2: Semantic textual similarity, English, Spanish and pilot on interpretability. In *Proceedings of the 9th International Workshop on Semantic Evaluation (SemEval 2015)*, pages 252–263, Denver, Colorado. Association for Computational Linguistics.

Eneko Agirre, Carmen Banea, Claire Cardie, Daniel Cer, Mona Diab, Aitor Gonzalez-Agirre, Weiwei Guo, Rada Mihalcea, German Rigau, and Janyce Wiebe. 2014. Semeval-2014 task 10: Multilingual semantic textual similarity. In *Proceedings of the 8th international workshop on semantic evaluation (SemEval 2014)*, pages 81–91.

Eneko Agirre, Carmen Banea, Daniel Cer, Mona Diab, Aitor Gonzalez-Agirre, Rada Mihalcea, German Rigau, and Janyce Wiebe. 2016. SemEval-2016 task 1: Semantic textual similarity, monolingual and cross-lingual evaluation. In *Proceedings of the 10th International Workshop on Semantic Evaluation (SemEval-2016)*, pages 497–511, San Diego, California. Association for Computational Linguistics.

Eneko Agirre, Daniel Cer, Mona Diab, and Aitor Gonzalez-Agirre. 2012. SemEval-2012 task 6: A pilot on semantic textual similarity. In **SEM 2012: The First Joint Conference on Lexical and Computational Semantics – Volume 1: Proceedings of the main conference and the shared task, and Volume 2: Proceedings of the Sixth International Workshop on Semantic Evaluation (SemEval 2012)*, pages 385–393, Montréal, Canada. Association for Computational Linguistics.

Eneko Agirre, Daniel Cer, Mona Diab, Aitor Gonzalez-Agirre, and Weiwei Guo. 2013. *SEM 2013 shared task: Semantic textual similarity. In *Second Joint Conference on Lexical and Computational Semantics (*SEM), Volume 1: Proceedings of the Main Conference and the Shared Task: Semantic Textual Similarity*, pages 32–43, Atlanta, Georgia, USA. Association for Computational Linguistics.

Jiangang Bai, Yujing Wang, Yiren Chen, Yaming Yang, Jing Bai, Jing Yu, and Yunhai Tong. 2021. Syntax-BERT: Improving pre-trained transformers with syntax trees. In *Proceedings of the 16th Conference of the European Chapter of the Association for Computational Linguistics: Main Volume*, pages 3011–3020, Online. Association for Computational Linguistics.

Samuel R. Bowman, Gabor Angeli, Christopher Potts, and Christopher D. Manning. 2015. A large annotated corpus for learning natural language inference. In *Proceedings of the 2015 Conference on Empirical Methods in Natural Language Processing*, pages 632–642, Lisbon, Portugal. Association for Computational Linguistics.

Daniel Cer, Mona Diab, Eneko Agirre, Iñigo Lopez-Gazpio, and Lucia Specia. 2017. SemEval-2017 task 1: Semantic textual similarity multilingual and crosslingual focused evaluation. In *Proceedings of the 11th International Workshop on Semantic Evaluation (SemEval-2017)*, pages 1–14, Vancouver, Canada. Association for Computational Linguistics.

Daniel Cer, Yinfei Yang, Sheng-yi Kong, Nan Hua, Nicole Limtiaco, Rhomni St John, Noah Constant, Mario Guajardo-Cespedes, Steve Yuan, Chris Tar, et al. 2018. Universal sentence encoder for english. In *Proceedings of the 2018 Conference on Empirical Methods in Natural Language Processing: System Demonstrations*, pages 169–174.

Wanxiang Che, Longxu Dou, Yang Xu, Yuxuan Wang, Yijia Liu, and Ting Liu. 2019. HIT-SCIR at MRP 2019: A unified pipeline for meaning representation parsing via efficient training and effective encoding. In *Proceedings of the Shared Task on Cross-Framework Meaning Representation Parsing at the 2019 Conference on Natural Language Learning*, pages 76–85, Hong Kong. Association for Computational Linguistics.

Junyoung Chung, Caglar Gulcehre, Kyunghyun Cho, and Yoshua Bengio. 2014. Empirical evaluation of gated recurrent neural networks on sequence modeling. In *NIPS 2014 Workshop on Deep Learning, December 2014*.

Kevin Clark, Urvashi Khandelwal, Omer Levy, and Christopher D Manning. 2019. What does bert look at? an analysis of bert's attention. In *Proceedings of the 2019 ACL Workshop BlackboxNLP: Analyzing and Interpreting Neural Networks for NLP*, pages 276–286.

Alexis Conneau and Douwe Kiela. 2018. SentEval: An evaluation toolkit for universal sentence representations. In *Proceedings of the Eleventh International Conference on Language Resources and Evaluation (LREC 2018)*, Miyazaki, Japan. European Language Resources Association (ELRA).

Alexis Conneau, Douwe Kiela, Holger Schwenk, Loïc Barrault, and Antoine Bordes. 2017. Supervised learning of universal sentence representations from natural language inference data. In *Proceedings of the 2017 Conference on Empirical Methods in Natural Language Processing*, pages 670–680.

Junqi Dai, Hang Yan, Tianxiang Sun, Pengfei Liu, and Xipeng Qiu. 2021. Does syntax matter? a strong baseline for aspect-based sentiment analysis with roberta. In *Proceedings of the 2021 Conference of the North American Chapter of the Association for Computational Linguistics: Human Language Technologies*, pages 1816–1829.

Jacob Devlin, Ming-Wei Chang, Kenton Lee, and Kristina Toutanova. 2018. Bert: Pre-training of deep bidirectional transformers for language understanding. *arXiv preprint arXiv:1810.04805*.

Bill Dolan, Chris Quirk, and Chris Brockett. 2004. Unsupervised construction of large paraphrase corpora: exploiting massively parallel news sources. In *Proceedings of the 20th international conference on Computational Linguistics*, pages 350–es.

Goran Glavaš and Ivan Vulić. 2021. Is supervised syntactic parsing beneficial for language understanding tasks? an empirical investigation. In *Proceedings of the 16th Conference of the European Chapter of the Association for Computational Linguistics: Main Volume*, pages 3090–3104, Online. Association for Computational Linguistics.

John Hewitt and Christopher D Manning. 2019. A structural probe for finding syntax in word representations. In *Proceedings of the 2019 Conference of the North American Chapter of the Association for Computational Linguistics: Human Language Technologies, Volume 1 (Long and Short Papers)*, pages 4129–4138.

Felix Hill, Kyunghyun Cho, and Anna Korhonen. 2016. Learning distributed representations of sentences from unlabelled data. In *Proceedings of the 2016 Conference of the North American Chapter of the Association for Computational Linguistics: Human Language Technologies*, pages 1367–1377.

Matthew Honnibal, Ines Montani, Sofie Van Landeghem, and Adriane Boyd. 2020. spaCy: Industrial-strength Natural Language Processing in Python.

Minqing Hu and Bing Liu. 2004. Mining and summarizing customer reviews. In *Proceedings of the tenth ACM SIGKDD international conference on Knowledge discovery and data mining*, pages 168–177.

Ganesh Jawahar, Benoît Sagot, and Djamé Seddah. 2019. What does bert learn about the structure of language? In *Proceedings of the 57th Annual Meeting of the Association for Computational Linguistics*, pages 3651–3657.

Ryan Kiros, Yukun Zhu, Ruslan Salakhutdinov, Richard S Zemel, Antonio Torralba, Raquel Urtasun, and Sanja Fidler. 2015. Skip-thought vectors. In *Proceedings of the 28th International Conference on Neural Information Processing Systems-Volume 2*, pages 3294–3302.

Xin Li and Dan Roth. 2002. Learning question classifiers. In *COLING 2002: The 19th International Conference on Computational Linguistics*.

Zhongli Li, Qingyu Zhou, Chao Li, Ke Xu, and Yunbo Cao. 2020. Improving bert with syntax-aware local attention. *arXiv preprint arXiv:2012.15150*.

Tao Liu, Xin Wang, Chengguo Lv, Ranran Zhen, and Guohong Fu. 2020. Sentence matching with syntax- and semantics-aware bert. In *Proceedings of the 28th International Conference on Computational Linguistics*, pages 3302–3312.

Yinhan Liu, Myle Ott, Naman Goyal, Jingfei Du, Mandar Joshi, Danqi Chen, Omer Levy, Mike Lewis, Luke Zettlemoyer, and Veselin Stoyanov. 2019. Roberta: A robustly optimized bert pretraining approach. *arXiv preprint arXiv:1907.11692*.

Marco Marelli, Stefano Menini, Marco Baroni, Luisa Bentivogli, Raffaella Bernardi, and Roberto Zamparelli. 2014. A SICK cure for the evaluation of compositional distributional semantic models. In *Proceedings of the Ninth International Conference on Language Resources and Evaluation (LREC'14)*, pages 216–223, Reykjavik, Iceland. European Language Resources Association (ELRA).

Bo Pang and Lillian Lee. 2004. A sentimental education: Sentiment analysis using subjectivity summarization based on minimum cuts. In *Proceedings of the 42nd Annual Meeting of the Association for Computational Linguistics (ACL-04)*, pages 271–278.

Bo Pang and Lillian Lee. 2005. Seeing stars: Exploiting class relationships for sentiment categorization with respect to rating scales. In *Proceedings of the 43rd Annual Meeting of the Association for Computational Linguistics (ACL'05)*, pages 115–124, Ann Arbor, Michigan. Association for Computational Linguistics.

Nils Reimers and Iryna Gurevych. 2019. Sentence-BERT: Sentence embeddings using Siamese BERT-networks. In *Proceedings of the 2019 Conference on Empirical Methods in Natural Language Processing and the 9th International Joint Conference on Natural Language Processing (EMNLP-IJCNLP)*, pages 3982–3992, Hong Kong, China. Association for Computational Linguistics.

T.y.s.s Santosh, Debarshi Kumar Sanyal, Plaban Kumar Bhowmick, and Partha Pratim Das. 2020. SaSAKE: Syntax and semantics aware keyphrase extraction from research papers. In *Proceedings of the 28th International Conference on Computational Linguistics*, pages 5372–5383, Barcelona, Spain (Online). International Committee on Computational Linguistics.

Michael Schlichtkrull, Thomas N Kipf, Peter Bloem, Rianne Van Den Berg, Ivan Titov, and Max Welling. 2018. Modeling relational data with graph convolutional networks. In *European semantic web conference*, pages 593–607. Springer.

Richard Socher, Alex Perelygin, Jean Wu, Jason Chuang, Christopher D. Manning, Andrew Ng, and Christopher Potts. 2013. Recursive deep models for semantic compositionality over a sentiment treebank. In *Proceedings of the 2013 Conference on Empirical Methods in Natural Language Processing*, pages 1631–1642, Seattle, Washington, USA. Association for Computational Linguistics.

Ashish Vaswani, Noam Shazeer, Niki Parmar, Jakob Uszkoreit, Llion Jones, Aidan N Gomez, Łukasz Kaiser, and Illia Polosukhin. 2017. Attention is all you need. In *Proceedings of the 31st International Conference on Neural Information Processing Systems*, pages 6000–6010.

Kai Wang, Weizhou Shen, Yunyi Yang, Xiaojun Quan, and Rui Wang. 2020. Relational graph attention network for aspect-based sentiment analysis. In *Proceedings of the 58th Annual Meeting of the Association for Computational Linguistics*, pages 3229–3238.

Janyce Wiebe, Theresa Wilson, and Claire Cardie. 2005. Annotating expressions of opinions and emotions in language. *Language resources and evaluation*, 39(2):165–210.

Adina Williams, Nikita Nangia, and Samuel Bowman. 2018. A broad-coverage challenge corpus for sentence understanding through inference. In *Proceedings of the 2018 Conference of the North American Chapter of the Association for Computational Linguistics: Human Language Technologies, Volume 1 (Long Papers)*, pages 1112–1122, New Orleans, Louisiana. Association for Computational Linguistics.

Zhaofeng Wu, Hao Peng, and Noah A Smith. 2021. Infusing finetuning with semantic dependencies. *Transactions of the Association for Computational Linguistics*, 9:226–242.

Yinchuan Xu and Junlin Yang. 2019. Look again at the syntax: Relational graph convolutional network for gendered ambiguous pronoun resolution. In *Proceedings of the First Workshop on Gender Bias in Natural Language Processing*, pages 96–101.

Da Yin, Tao Meng, and Kai-Wei Chang. 2020. Sentibert: A transferable transformer-based architecture for compositional sentiment semantics. In *Proceedings of the 58th Annual Meeting of the Association for Computational Linguistics*, pages 3695–3706.

Zhuosheng Zhang, Yuwei Wu, Hai Zhao, Zuchao Li, Shuailiang Zhang, Xi Zhou, and Xiang Zhou. 2020. Semantics-aware bert for language understanding. In *Proceedings of the AAAI Conference on Artificial Intelligence*, volume 34, pages 9628–9635.

Preserving Cross-Linguality of Pre-trained Models via Continual Learning

Zihan Liu, Genta Indra Winata, Andrea Madotto, Pascale Fung
Center for Artificial Intelligence Research (CAiRE)
Department of Electronic and Computer Engineering
The Hong Kong University of Science and Technology, Clear Water Bay, Hong Kong
zihan.liu@connect.ust.hk

Abstract

Recently, fine-tuning pre-trained language models (e.g., multilingual BERT) to downstream cross-lingual tasks has shown promising results. However, the fine-tuning process inevitably changes the parameters of the pre-trained model and weakens its cross-lingual ability, which leads to sub-optimal performance. To alleviate this problem, we leverage continual learning to preserve the original cross-lingual ability of the pre-trained model when we fine-tune it to downstream tasks. The experimental result shows that our fine-tuning methods can better preserve the cross-lingual ability of the pre-trained model in a sentence retrieval task. Our methods also achieve better performance than other fine-tuning baselines on the zero-shot cross-lingual part-of-speech tagging and named entity recognition tasks.

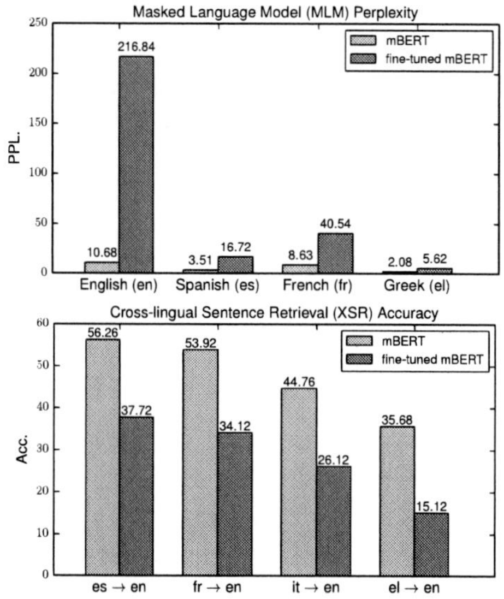

Figure 1: Masked language model and cross-lingual sentence retrieval results before and after fine-tuning mBERT to the English part-of-speech tagging task.

1 Introduction

Recently, multilingual language models (Devlin et al., 2019; Conneau and Lample, 2019), pre-trained on extensive monolingual or bilingual resources across numerous languages, have been shown to enjoy surprising cross-lingual adaptation abilities, and fine-tuning them to downstream cross-lingual tasks has achieved promising results (Pires et al., 2019; Wu and Dredze, 2019). Taking this further, better pre-trained language models have been proposed to improve the cross-lingual performance, such as using larger amounts of pre-trained data with larger pre-trained models (Conneau et al., 2019; Liang et al., 2020), and utilizing more tasks in the pre-training stage (Huang et al., 2019).

However, we observe that multilingual BERT (mBERT) (Devlin et al., 2019), a pre-trained language model, forgets the masked language model (MLM) task that has been learned and partially loses the cross-lingual ability (from a cross-lingual sentence retrieval (XSR)[1] experiment) after being fine-tuned to the downstream task in English, as shown in Figure 1, which results in sub-optimal cross-lingual performance to target languages.

In this paper, we consider a new direction to improve the cross-lingual performance, which is to preserve the cross-lingual ability of pre-trained multilingual models in the fine-tuning stage. Motivated by the continual learning (Ring, 1994; Rebuffi et al., 2017; Kirkpatrick et al., 2017; Lopez-Paz and Ranzato, 2017) that aims to learn a new task without forgetting the previous learned tasks, we adopt a continual learning framework to constrain the parameter learning in the pre-trained multilingual model when we fine-tune it to downstream

[1]This task is to find the correct translation sentence from the target corpus given a source language sentence.

Proceedings of the 6th Workshop on Representation Learning for NLP (RepL4NLP-2021), pages 64–71
Bangkok, Thailand (Online), August 6, 2021.

tasks in the source language. Specifically, based on the results in Figure 1, we aim to maintain the cross-linguality of pre-trained multilingual models by utilizing MLM and XSR tasks to constrain the parameter learning in the fine-tuning stage.

Experiments show that our methods help pre-trained models better preserve the cross-lingual ability. Additionally, our methods surpass other fine-tuning baselines on the strong multilingual model mBERT and XLMR (Conneau et al., 2019) on zero-shot cross-lingual part-of-speech tagging (POS) and named entity recognition (NER) tasks.

2 Related Work

Cross-lingual methods, which alleviate the need for obtaining large amounts of annotated data in target languages, have been applied to multiple NLP tasks, such as task-oriented dialogue systems (Chen et al., 2018; Liu et al., 2019), part-of-speech tagging (Wisniewski et al., 2014; Zhang et al., 2016; Kim et al., 2017), named entity recognition (Mayhew et al., 2017; Ni et al., 2017; Xie et al., 2018; Liu et al., 2021), abstractive summarization (Duan et al., 2019; Zhu et al., 2019), and dependency parsing (Schuster et al., 2019; Ahmad et al., 2019). Recently, multilingual language models (Devlin et al., 2019; Conneau and Lample, 2019; Huang et al., 2019; Conneau et al., 2019), pre-trained on a large-scale data corpus across a great many languages, have significantly improved the cross-lingual performance. However, the corresponding fine-tuning techniques have been less studied. Wu and Dredze (2019) investigated the effectiveness of fine-tuning mBERT by freezing its partial bottom layers, and Muller et al. (2021) further analyzed the fine-tuning of mBERT.

3 Methodology

In this section, we first describe the gradient episodic memory (GEM) (Lopez-Paz and Ranzato, 2017), a continual learning framework, which we adopt to constrain the fine-tuning process. Then, we introduce how we fine-tune the pre-trained multilingual model with GEM.

3.1 Gradient Episodic Memory (GEM)

We consider a scenario where the model has already learned $n-1$ tasks and needs to learn the n-th task. The main feature of GEM is an episodic memory $\mathcal{M}_k$ that stores a subset of the observed examples from task k ($k \in [1, n]$). The loss at the memories from the k-th task can be defined as

$$\mathcal{L}(f_\theta, \mathcal{M}_k) = \frac{1}{|\mathcal{M}_k|} \sum_{(x_i,k,y_i)\in\mathcal{M}_k} \mathcal{L}(f_\theta(x_i, k), y_i), \tag{1}$$

where the model f_θ is parameterized by θ. In order to maintain the performance of the model in the previous $n-1$ tasks while learning the n-th task, GEM utilizes the losses for the previous $n-1$ tasks in Eq. (1) as inequality constraints, avoiding their increase but allowing their decrease. Concretely, when observing the training samples (x, y) from the n-th task, GEM solves the following problem:

$$\begin{aligned}&\text{minimize}_\theta\ \mathcal{L}(f_\theta(x, n), y)\\ &\text{subject to}\\ &\mathcal{L}(f_\theta, \mathcal{M}_k) \le \mathcal{L}(f_\theta^{n-1}, \mathcal{M}_k) \text{ for all } k < n,\end{aligned} \tag{2}$$

where f_θ^{n-1} is the model before learning task n.

3.2 Fine-tuning with GEM

We consider two tasks ($n = 2$) in total by applying GEM to the fine-tuning of pre-trained multilingual models, namely, mBERT and XLMR. The first task is either what the pre-trained models have already learned (MLM) or the ability that they already possess (XSR), and the second task is the fine-tuning task. We follow Eq. (2) when we fine-tune the pre-trained models:

$$\begin{aligned}&\text{minimize}_\theta\ \mathcal{L}(f_\theta(x, \mathcal{T}_2), y)\\ &\text{subject to } \mathcal{L}(f_\theta, \mathcal{T}_1) \le \mathcal{L}(f_\theta^*, \mathcal{T}_1),\end{aligned} \tag{3}$$

where $\mathcal{T}_1$ and $\mathcal{T}_2$ denote the first and second tasks, respectively, and f_θ^* represents the original pre-trained model. When the MLM task is considered as the first task, we constrain the fine-tuning process of the pre-trained model by preventing it from forgetting its original task after fine-tuning so as to better preserve the original cross-lingual ability. When the XSR task is considered as the first task, on the other hand, we prevent the pre-trained model from losing its cross-lingual ability after fine-tuning. We also consider incorporating both MLM and XSR as the first task.

4 Experiments

4.1 Dataset

For the POS task, we use Universal Dependencies 2.0 (Nivre et al., 2017) and select English (en), French (fr), Spanish (es), Greek (el) and Russian (ru) to evaluate our methods. For the NER task,

Model	MLM					XSR (Spanish to English)			XSR (Italian to English)		
	en	es	fr	el	ru	P@1	P@5	P@10	P@1	P@5	P@10
mBERT	10.68	3.51	8.63	2.08	2.70	56.26	68.80	73.92	44.76	61.32	66.70
Naive Fine-tune	216.80	16.72	40.54	5.62	8.61	37.72	52.20	58.43	26.12	37.46	46.69
w/ frozen layers	95.17	9.33	30.04	3.44	5.34	38.16	53.92	59.16	28.69	42.74	48.76
Multi-Task Learning											
MTF w/ MLM	9.50	5.10	8.62	2.56	3.47	35.93	50.41	56.20	24.79	37.18	45.46
MTF w/ XSR	121.50	100.10	96.50	773.00	180.80	75.40	80.88	85.76	75.94	85.44	88.29
MTF w/ Both	9.89	9.45	11.30	3.80	4.16	77.84	82.57	87.97	74.38	83.29	86.95
Continual Learning											
GEM w/ MLM	12.99	6.62	11.39	2.87	4.22	**42.90**	**57.26**	**63.58**	**31.66**	**44.16**	**50.16**
GEM w/ XSR	252.9	26.73	55.95	11.84	16.46	63.65	75.45	80.56	63.56	78.18	83.42
GEM w/ Both	12.16	6.40	10.62	3.40	4.30	64.34	76.23	81.42	64.12	79.35	84.59

Table 1: Experiments on MLM and XSR tasks based on mBERT. Models other than mBERT are fine-tuned to the English POS task. The underlined numbers in the MLM task denote that the performance is close to mBERT's. The bold numbers in the XSR task denote the best performance after fine-tuning without using the XSR supervision.

we use CoNLL 2002 (Tjong Kim Sang, 2002) and CoNLL 2003 (Sang and De Meulder, 2003), which contain English (en), German (de), Spanish (es) and Dutch (nl), to evaluate our methods. For both tasks, we consider English as the source language and other languages as target languages.

4.2 Baselines

We compare our methods to several baselines. **Naive Fine-tune** (Wu and Dredze, 2019) is to add one linear layer on top of the pre-trained model while fine-tuning with L2 regularization. **Fine-tune with Partial Layers Frozen** (Wu and Dredze, 2019) is to fine-tune pre-trained multilingual models by freezing the partial bottom layers. And **Multi-Task Fine-tune (MTF)** is to fine-tune pre-trained multilingual models on both the fine-tuning task and additional tasks (MLM and XSR).

4.3 Training Details

We conduct the MLM task with two settings. First, we only utilize the English Wikipedia corpus (**MLM (en)**) since we observe the catastrophic forgetting in the English MLM task as in Figure 1. Second, we utilize both the source and target languages Wikipedia corpus (**MLM (all)**). The first setting is used in our main experiments. Note that we do not use all pre-trained languages in mBERT for the MLM task because it would make the fine-tuning process very time-consuming. For the XSR task, we leverage the sentence pairs between the source and target languages from the Europarl parallel corpus (Koehn, 2005).[2]

[2]More training details are in the appendix.

5 Results & Analysis

Does GEM preserve the cross-lingual ability? From Table 1, we can see that naive fine-tuning mBERT significantly decreases the MLM performance, especially in English. Since mBERT is fine-tuned to the English task, the English subword embeddings are fine-tuned, which makes mBERT lose more MLM task information in English. Naive fine-tuning also makes the XSR performance of mBERT drop significantly. We observe that fine-tuning with partial layers frozen is able to somewhat prevent the MLM performance from getting worse, while fine-tuning with GEM based on that task almost preserves the original MLM performance of mBERT. Although we only use English data in the MLM task, using GEM based on the MLM task still preserves the task-related parameters that are useful for other languages. Correspondingly, we can see that *GEM w/ MLM* achieves better XSR performance than *Naive Fine-tune w/ frozen layers*, which shows that GEM helps better preserve the cross-lingual ability of mBERT.

In addition, although *GEM w/ XSR* aggravates the catastrophic forgetting in the MLM task, it is able to significantly improve the XSR performance due to the usage of the XSR supervision. Furthermore, incorporating both the MLM and XSR tasks can better preserve the performance in both tasks.

Does GEM improve the cross-lingual performance? From Table 2, we can see that our methods consistently surpass the fine-tuning baselines on all target languages in the POS and NER tasks. In terms of the average performance, our methods outperform the baselines by an around or more

Model	POS						NER				
	en	es	fr	el	ru	avg†	en	es	de	nl	avg†
Naive Fine-tune	96.23	82.95	89.12	84.21	85.45	85.43	**91.97**	74.96	69.56	77.57	74.03
w/ frozen layers	96.07	83.41	89.41	85.54	85.17	85.88	91.90	75.27	70.23	77.89	74.46
Multi-Task Learning											
MTF w/ MLM	94.47	83.01	88.08	84.48	80.46	84.01	91.82	71.47	67.90	74.91	71.43
MTF w/ XSR	96.39	82.41	87.05	72.51	86.09	82.01	91.85	74.02	68.55	75.67	72.75
MTF w/ Both	95.63	83.52	89.07	85.21	83.10	85.28	91.74	71.87	68.12	74.86	71.62
Continual Learning											
GEM w/ MLM	**97.39**	84.65	89.74	86.04	**86.93**	86.84‡	91.93	**76.45**	70.48	78.61	75.18‡
GEM w/ XSR	96.97	84.53	89.83	**86.53**	86.36	86.81‡	91.89	76.29	70.74	78.77	75.27‡
GEM w/ Both	97.04	**84.91**	**90.32**	86.44	86.13	**86.95**‡	91.45	76.20	**70.98**	**79.19**	**75.46**‡

Table 2: Zero-shot results on POS and NER tasks based on mBERT. †The average scores excluding en. ‡The results are statistically significant compared to all baselines with $p < 0.01$ by t-test.

Task	Models	en	es	fr	el	ru	avg
MLM	mBERT	10.7	**3.51**	8.63	**2.08**	**2.70**	5.52
	MTF w/ MLM (en)	9.50	5.10	8.62	2.56	3.47	5.85
	MTF w/ MLM (all)	**9.33**	4.19	**4.89**	2.34	3.04	**4.76**
	GEM w/ MLM (en)	13.0	6.62	11.4	2.87	4.22	7.62
	GEM w/ MLM (all)	11.8	4.18	6.83	2.29	2.99	5.62
POS	Naive Fine-tune	96.2	82.9	89.1	84.2	85.5	85.4
	MTF w/ MLM (en)	94.5	83.0	88.1	84.5	80.5	84.0
	MTF w/ MLM (all)	94.7	77.5	83.3	81.9	77.0	79.9
	GEM w/ MLM (en)	97.4	**84.7**	**89.7**	**86.0**	86.9	**86.8**
	GEM w/ MLM (all)	97.2	83.9	89.2	85.9	**87.1**	86.5

Table 3: Ablation study on the two settings of using the MLM task based on mBERT.

than 1% improvement.[3] In addition, constraining mBERT fine-tuning on the MLM task shows similar performance to constraining it on the XSR task. We conjecture that the effectiveness of both methods is similar, although they come from different angles. When the information of both tasks is utilized, GEM is able to slightly improve the performance. We find that the experimental results on XLMR are consistent with mBERT.

GEM vs. MTF From Table 1, we notice that using the MLM task, MTF achieves lower perplexity than GEM since it aggressively trains mBERT on this task. However, we observe that *MTF w/ MLM* makes the performance of the XSR, POS and NER tasks worse than *Naive Fine-tune*, and we speculate that MTF pushes mBERT to be overfit on the MLM task, instead of preserving its cross-lingual ability. Meanwhile, we can see that GEM regularizes the loss of the training on the MLM task to avoid catastrophic forgetting of previously trained languages, and conserve the cross-linguality of the pre-trained multilingual models.

In addition, we observe that adding XSR objective to the training cause the MLM performance worse. Although MTF achieves the best performance in the XSR task since it directly fine-tunes mBERT on that task, we can see from Table 2 that *GEM w/ XSR* boosts the cross-lingual performance of downstream tasks, while *MTF w/ XSR* has the opposite effect. We speculate that brutally fine-tuning mBERT on the XSR task (*MTF w/ XSR*) just makes mBERT learn the XSR task, while using GEM to constrain the fine-tuning on the XSR task can preserve its cross-lingual ability of mBERT. Incorporating both the MLM and XSR tasks further improves the performance for GEM, while MTF still performs worse than *Naive Fine-tune*.

Ablation Study From Table 3, we can see that using GEM to constrain fine-tuning on MLM with all languages (*GEM w/ MLM (all)*) achieves better performance than it does with only English (*GEM w/ MLM (en)*) on the MLM task since more MLM supervision signals are provided, while their performances in the POS task are similar. Intuitively, since *GEM w/ MLM* is able to improve the cross-lingual performance, constraining on more languages should give better performance. We conjecture, however, that the constraint with all languages could be too aggressive, so mBERT might tend to be overfit to the monolingual MLM task in all languages instead of preserving its original cross-lingual ability. In addition, we observe that fine-tuning mBERT on the MLM task (MTF) would get worse when more languages are utilized.

6 Conclusion

In this paper, we propose to preserve the cross-linguality of pre-trained language models in the fine-tuning stage. To do so, we adopt a continual

[3]The results of XLMR are included in the appendix.

learning framework, GEM, to constrain the parameter learning in pre-trained multilingual models based on the MLM and XSR tasks when we fine-tune them to downstream tasks. Experiments on the MLM and XSR tasks illustrate that our methods can better preserve the cross-lingual ability of pre-trained models. Furthermore, our methods achieve better performance than fine-tuning baselines for the strong multilingual models mBERT and XLMR on the zero-shot cross-lingual POS and NER tasks.

Acknowledgement

We want to say thanks to the anonymous reviewers for the insightful reviews and constructive feedback. This work is partially funded by ITF/319/16FP and MRP/055/18 of the Innovation Technology Commission, the Hong Kong SAR Government.

References

Wasi Ahmad, Zhisong Zhang, Xuezhe Ma, Eduard Hovy, Kai-Wei Chang, and Nanyun Peng. 2019. On difficulties of cross-lingual transfer with order differences: A case study on dependency parsing. In *Proceedings of the 2019 Conference of the North American Chapter of the Association for Computational Linguistics: Human Language Technologies, Volume 1 (Long and Short Papers)*, pages 2440–2452.

Wenhu Chen, Jianshu Chen, Yu Su, Xin Wang, Dong Yu, Xifeng Yan, and William Yang Wang. 2018. Xl-nbt: A cross-lingual neural belief tracking framework. In *Proceedings of the 2018 Conference on Empirical Methods in Natural Language Processing*, pages 414–424.

Alexis Conneau, Kartikay Khandelwal, Naman Goyal, Vishrav Chaudhary, Guillaume Wenzek, Francisco Guzmán, Edouard Grave, Myle Ott, Luke Zettlemoyer, and Veselin Stoyanov. 2019. Unsupervised cross-lingual representation learning at scale. *arXiv preprint arXiv:1911.02116*.

Alexis Conneau and Guillaume Lample. 2019. Cross-lingual language model pretraining. In *Advances in Neural Information Processing Systems 32*, pages 7059–7069. Curran Associates, Inc.

Jacob Devlin, Ming-Wei Chang, Kenton Lee, and Kristina Toutanova. 2019. Bert: Pre-training of deep bidirectional transformers for language understanding. In *Proceedings of the 2019 Conference of the North American Chapter of the Association for Computational Linguistics: Human Language Technologies, Volume 1 (Long and Short Papers)*, pages 4171–4186.

Xiangyu Duan, Mingming Yin, Min Zhang, Boxing Chen, and Weihua Luo. 2019. Zero-shot cross-lingual abstractive sentence summarization through teaching generation and attention. In *Proceedings of the 57th Annual Meeting of the Association for Computational Linguistics*, pages 3162–3172.

Haoyang Huang, Yaobo Liang, Nan Duan, Ming Gong, Linjun Shou, Daxin Jiang, and Ming Zhou. 2019. Unicoder: A universal language encoder by pre-training with multiple cross-lingual tasks. In *Proceedings of the 2019 Conference on Empirical Methods in Natural Language Processing and the 9th International Joint Conference on Natural Language Processing (EMNLP-IJCNLP)*, pages 2485–2494.

Joo-Kyung Kim, Young-Bum Kim, Ruhi Sarikaya, and Eric Fosler-Lussier. 2017. Cross-lingual transfer learning for pos tagging without cross-lingual resources. In *Proceedings of the 2017 conference on empirical methods in natural language processing*, pages 2832–2838.

James Kirkpatrick, Razvan Pascanu, Neil Rabinowitz, Joel Veness, Guillaume Desjardins, Andrei A Rusu, Kieran Milan, John Quan, Tiago Ramalho, Agnieszka Grabska-Barwinska, et al. 2017. Overcoming catastrophic forgetting in neural networks. *Proceedings of the national academy of sciences*, 114(13):3521–3526.

Philipp Koehn. 2005. Europarl: A parallel corpus for statistical machine translation. Citeseer.

Yaobo Liang, Nan Duan, Yeyun Gong, Ning Wu, Fenfei Guo, Weizhen Qi, Ming Gong, Linjun Shou, Daxin Jiang, Guihong Cao, et al. 2020. Xglue: A new benchmark dataset for cross-lingual pre-training, understanding and generation. *arXiv preprint arXiv:2004.01401*.

Zihan Liu, Jamin Shin, Yan Xu, Genta Indra Winata, Peng Xu, Andrea Madotto, and Pascale Fung. 2019. Zero-shot cross-lingual dialogue systems with transferable latent variables. In *Proceedings of the 2019 Conference on Empirical Methods in Natural Language Processing and the 9th International Joint Conference on Natural Language Processing (EMNLP-IJCNLP)*, pages 1297–1303.

Zihan Liu, Genta I Winata, Samuel Cahyawijaya, Andrea Madotto, Zhaojiang Lin, and Pascale Fung. 2021. On the importance of word order information in cross-lingual sequence labeling. In *Proceedings of the AAAI Conference on Artificial Intelligence*, volume 35, pages 13461–13469.

David Lopez-Paz and Marc'Aurelio Ranzato. 2017. Gradient episodic memory for continual learning. In *Advances in Neural Information Processing Systems*, pages 6467–6476.

Stephen Mayhew, Chen-Tse Tsai, and Dan Roth. 2017. Cheap translation for cross-lingual named entity recognition. In *Proceedings of the 2017 conference on empirical methods in natural language processing*, pages 2536–2545.

Benjamin Muller, Yanai Elazar, Benoît Sagot, and Djamé Seddah. 2021. First align, then predict: Understanding the cross-lingual ability of multilingual bert. *arXiv preprint arXiv:2101.11109*.

Jian Ni, Georgiana Dinu, and Radu Florian. 2017. Weakly supervised cross-lingual named entity recognition via effective annotation and representation projection. In *Proceedings of the 55th Annual Meeting of the Association for Computational Linguistics (Volume 1: Long Papers)*, pages 1470–1480.

Joakim Nivre, Željko Agić, Lars Ahrenberg, et al. 2017. Universal dependencies 2.0. lindat/clarin digital library at the institute of formal and applied linguistics, charles university, prague.

Telmo Pires, Eva Schlinger, and Dan Garrette. 2019. How multilingual is multilingual bert? In *Proceedings of the 57th Annual Meeting of the Association for Computational Linguistics*, pages 4996–5001.

Sylvestre-Alvise Rebuffi, Alexander Kolesnikov, Georg Sperl, and Christoph H Lampert. 2017. icarl: Incremental classifier and representation learning. In *Proceedings of the IEEE conference on Computer Vision and Pattern Recognition*, pages 2001–2010.

Mark Bishop Ring. 1994. *Continual learning in reinforcement environments*. Ph.D. thesis, University of Texas at Austin Austin, Texas 78712.

Erik Tjong Kim Sang and Fien De Meulder. 2003. Introduction to the conll-2003 shared task: Language-independent named entity recognition. In *Proceedings of the Seventh Conference on Natural Language Learning at HLT-NAACL 2003*, pages 142–147.

Tal Schuster, Ori Ram, Regina Barzilay, and Amir Globerson. 2019. Cross-lingual alignment of contextual word embeddings, with applications to zero-shot dependency parsing. In *Proceedings of the 2019 Conference of the North American Chapter of the Association for Computational Linguistics: Human Language Technologies, Volume 1 (Long and Short Papers)*, pages 1599–1613.

Erik F Tjong Kim Sang. 2002. Introduction to the conll-2002 shared task: language-independent named entity recognition. In *proceedings of the 6th conference on Natural language learning-Volume 20*, pages 1–4.

Guillaume Wisniewski, Nicolas Pécheux, Souhir Gahbiche-Braham, and François Yvon. 2014. Cross-lingual part-of-speech tagging through ambiguous learning. In *Proceedings of the 2014 Conference on Empirical Methods in Natural Language Processing (EMNLP)*, pages 1779–1785.

Shijie Wu and Mark Dredze. 2019. Beto, bentz, becas: The surprising cross-lingual effectiveness of bert. In *Proceedings of the 2019 Conference on Empirical Methods in Natural Language Processing and the 9th International Joint Conference on Natural Language Processing (EMNLP-IJCNLP)*, pages 833–844.

Jiateng Xie, Zhilin Yang, Graham Neubig, Noah A Smith, and Jaime G Carbonell. 2018. Neural cross-lingual named entity recognition with minimal resources. In *Proceedings of the 2018 Conference on Empirical Methods in Natural Language Processing*, pages 369–379.

Yuan Zhang, David Gaddy, Regina Barzilay, and Tommi Jaakkola. 2016. Ten pairs to tag–multilingual pos tagging via coarse mapping between embeddings. In *Proceedings of the 2016 Conference of the North American Chapter of the Association for Computational Linguistics: Human Language Technologies*, pages 1307–1317.

Junnan Zhu, Qian Wang, Yining Wang, Yu Zhou, Jiajun Zhang, Shaonan Wang, and Chengqing Zong. 2019. Ncls: Neural cross-lingual summarization. In *Proceedings of the 2019 Conference on Empirical Methods in Natural Language Processing and the 9th International Joint Conference on Natural Language Processing (EMNLP-IJCNLP)*, pages 3045–3055.

A Training Details

We utilize the Wikipedia corpus for the MLM task. Given that using all the Wikipedia corpus will greatly lower the training speed, we randomly sample 1M sentences for each language for the training of *MTF w/ MLM* and *GEM w/ MLM*, and we use another 100K sentences for each language to evaluate the model performance on the MLM task. We take the English-Spanish (en-es), English-Italian (en-it), English-French (en-fr), English-Greek (en-el), English-German (en-de), and English-Dutch (en-nl) parallel datasets from the Europarl parallel corpus. We ramdomly select 90% of them for the training of *GEM w/ MLM* and *GEM W/ XSR*, and the rest 10% of them are used for evaluating the model performance on the XSR task. We use accuracy for evaluating the POS task, BIO-based F1-score for evaluating the NER task, perplexity for evaluating the MLM task, and P@k for evaluating the XSR task. Concretely, P@k (k=1,5,10) accounts for the fraction of pairs for which the correct translation of the source language sentence is in the k-th nearest neighbors. We use an early stop strategy which is based on the average performance over the target languages to select the model. We use the Adam optimizer with a learning of 1e-5. We use batch size 16 for the all tasks, namely, POS, NER, MLM and XSR. In each iteration, we use GEM to constrain the fine-tuning on a batch of data samples from the MLM and XSR tasks. Our models are trained on V100. The number of parameters for the mBERT-based model is around 178.6 million and for the XLMR-based model is around 278.9 million.

# samples	en	es	de	nl
Train	14,040	8,319	12,152	15,802
Validation	3,249	1,914	2,867	2,895
Test	3,452	1,516	3,005	5,194

Table 4: Number of samples for each language in the CoNLL 2002 and CoNLL 2003 NER datasets.

# samples	en	es	fr	el	ru
Train	12,543	14,187	14,450	1,662	3,850
Validation	2,002	1,400	1,476	403	579
Test	2,007	426	416	456	601

Table 5: Number of samples for each language in the Universal Dependencies 2.0 dataset for the POS task.

B Data Statistics

The data statistics of the NER and POS datasets are shown in Table 4 and Table 5, respectively.

C Results

C.1 XLMR Experiments

Experiments on POS and NER tasks for $\text{XLMR}_{\text{base}}$ are illustrated in Table 6 (in the next page). The results on XLMR are consistent with mBERT.

C.2 XSR Experiments

Experiments on more language pairs are illustrated in Table 7 (in the next page). The results on French to English, Greek to English, German to English and Dutch to English are consistent with the XSR results shown in the main paper (i.e., Spanish to English and Italian to English).

Model	POS						NER				
	en	es	fr	el	ru	avg†	en	es	de	nl	avg†
Naive Fine-tune	96.55	84.61	90.37	87.23	89.32	87.88	91.95	75.86	69.59	77.83	74.42
w/ frozen layers	96.40	84.63	90.33	86.27	89.44	87.67	91.53	76.12	68.79	78.26	74.39
Multi-Task Learning											
MTF w/ MLM	96.43	82.37	89.70	83.90	86.73	85.68	91.90	74.55	67.70	78.13	73.46
MTF w/ XSR	96.93	84.94	89.08	86.93	89.27	87.55	91.93	75.35	70.58	77.65	74.53
MTF w/ Both	96.31	83.55	89.90	87.01	84.94	86.35	91.67	75.45	67.80	77.91	73.72
Continual Learning											
GEM w/ MLM	96.87	**85.90**	90.57	87.25	89.43	88.29	91.93	76.43	70.98	78.77	75.39
GEM w/ XSR	96.86	85.01	89.87	88.14	89.90	88.23	91.94	**76.61**	**71.19**	79.28	**75.69**
GEM w/ Both	96.10	85.63	**90.99**	**89.02**	**91.36**	**89.25**	91.91	76.48	70.53	**79.86**	75.62

Table 6: Zero-shot results on POS and NER tasks based on XLMR. †The average scores excluding en.

Model	XSR (French to English)			XSR (Greek to English)			XSR (German to English)			XSR (Dutch to English)		
	P@1	P@5	P@10	P@1	P@5	P@10	P@1	P@5	P@10	P@1	P@5	P@10
mBERT	53.92	65.44	72.12	35.68	59.40	65.31	52.10	64.71	69.43	54.56	66.69	72.54
Naive Fine-tune	34.12	50.03	57.90	15.12	33.35	42.69	33.68	49.23	56.45	34.79	51.13	58.01
w/ frozen layers	35.50	52.23	59.87	16.98	35.63	44.74	34.20	50.97	58.11	35.29	53.24	59.77
Multi-Task Learning												
MTF w/ MLM	32.49	48.67	56.23	14.67	32.29	40.64	32.37	47.45	55.48	32.86	50.35	56.55
MTF w/ XSR	74.20	78.65	83.69	73.94	77.59	83.47	75.48	80.67	85.44	75.83	85.28	88.35
MTF w/ Both	75.30	79.34	84.86	74.25	78.39	84.63	77.93	82.67	87.86	74.42	83.57	86.68
Continual Learning												
GEM w/ MLM	**39.79**	**55.62**	**63.34**	**21.33**	**39.60**	**47.36**	**37.70**	**53.44**	**60.53**	**38.35**	**54.89**	**63.06**
GEM w/ XSR	63.11	67.81	71.92	61.79	65.37	70.43	63.14	75.52	80.85	63.90	78.33	83.46
GEM w/ Both	63.84	68.50	72.05	61.54	64.38	69.50	64.41	76.39	81.70	64.36	79.65	84.72

Table 7: Experiments on XSR tasks based on mBERT. Models other than mBERT are fine-tuned to the English POS task. The bold numbers in the XSR task denote the best performance after fine-tuning without using the XSR supervision.

Text Style Transfer: Leveraging a Style Classifier on Entangled Latent Representations

Xiaoyan Li
Department of Computer Science
University of Toronto
Toronto, Canada
xiaoy.li@mail.utoronto.ca

Sun Sun **Yunli Wang**
Digital Technologies Research Centre
National Research Council Canada
Waterloo, Ottawa, Canada
Sun.Sun,Yunli.Wang@nrc.gc.ca

Abstract

Learning a good latent representation is essential for text style transfer, which generates a new sentence by changing the attributes of a given sentence while preserving its content. Most previous work adopt disentangled latent representation learning to realize style transfer. We propose a novel text style transfer algorithm with entangled latent representation, and introduce a style classifier that can regulate the latent structure and transfer style. Moreover, our algorithm for style transfer applies to both single-attribute and multi-attribute transfer. Extensive experimental results show that our method generally outperforms state-of-the-art approaches.

1 Introduction

Text generation, which leverages knowledge in computational linguistics and artificial intelligence for automatically generating natural language texts, is the core problem for a number of Natural Language Processing (NLP) applications such as speech to text, conversational/dialogue system (Banchs and Li, 2012; Kim et al., 2007), and text summarization (Ozsoy et al., 2011; Liu et al., 2018). Text style transfer can be thought of as a controllable text generation task, which aims to restyle a given sentence by changing specific attributes (sentiment, tense, formality, or politeness) while preserving the remaining attributes and the content. Successful applications of text style transfer include paraphrasing (Han et al., 2017), formality transfer (Rao and Tetreault, 2018), and text simplification (Cao et al., 2020).

A good latent representation is essential to the performance of text style transfer. Regarding the structure of the latent representation, the current work for text style transfer can be generally categorized into the disentangled representation and the entangled representation. In particular, the former method aims to learn disentangled latent representations by separating the style information from the content, while the latter method learns latent representations that entangle the style with the content. Disentangled representations are often interpretable and consequently most of the current work adopts this method (Hu et al., 2017; Yang et al., 2018; Zhao et al., 2018; John et al., 2019; Bao et al., 2019). However, learning disentangled representations is often challenging; and multiple attribute-specific decoders are commonly required for text generation, which is undesirable especially when transferring multiple attributes. The entangled representations, on the other hand, has been shown to achieve promising performance on the content preservation and to produce fluent sentences with a much less complicated architecture (Lample et al., 2019; Wang et al., 2019; Liu et al., 2020).

Although existing models achieve adequate performance on text style transfer, most of them are designed specifically for style transfer (Hu et al., 2017; Shen et al., 2017; Yang et al., 2018; Lample et al., 2019; John et al., 2019; Bao et al., 2019; Wang et al., 2019), and meanwhile lack of explicit modeling of the latent space. We argue that the quality of latent representations is crucial for text generation. In this study, we focus on building a generative model that supports both text style transfer and text generation with regularized entangled latent representations.

Our contributions can be summarized as follows: (1) We extend the framework of adversarial auto-encoder by including a classifier for both the regularization of the latent space and text style transfer. We show that the classifier can divide sentences with different attributes into different regions in the latent space and thus greatly improve the performance of style transfer. (2) We provide algorithms for both single-attribute and multi-attribute style transfer. We empirically compare with sev-

Proceedings of the 6th Workshop on Representation Learning for NLP (RepL4NLP-2021), pages 72–82
Bangkok, Thailand (Online), August 6, 2021. ©2021 Association for Computational Linguistics

eral state-of-the-art baselines and show that our proposed method achieves promising results.

2 Related Work

In this section, we first introduce several Generative Adversarial Network (GAN)-regularized autoencoders, which have been successfully used for text manipulation. Then we review some recent methods for text style transfer focusing on the latent representation.

2.1 Probabilistic Generative Autoencoders

GANs (Goodfellow et al., 2014) are popular generative models consisting of two basic components: a generator for generating new samples and a discriminator for distinguishing real samples from generated samples. Makhzani et al. (2015) introduce adversarial autoencoders (AAEs), which turn basic autoencoders into probabilistic models. The encoder $\mathcal{E}_\phi$ maps the input $\boldsymbol{x}$ to a latent representation $\boldsymbol{z}$, $\boldsymbol{z} = \mathcal{E}_\phi(\boldsymbol{x})$. The decoder $\mathcal{D}_\theta$ reconstructs the input from $\boldsymbol{z}$ as $\hat{\boldsymbol{x}} = \mathcal{D}_\theta(\boldsymbol{z})$. The discriminator $\mathcal{D}_w$ is introduced to distinguish between $\boldsymbol{z}$ and samples from a prior distribution $\mathrm{P}_{\boldsymbol{z}}$. The objective of AAEs is formulated below:

$$\begin{aligned}
&\min_{\phi,\theta} \max_{w} \mathcal{L}_{rec}(\phi,\theta) - \lambda \mathcal{L}_{adv}(\phi, w),\\
&\mathcal{L}_{rec}(\phi,\theta) = \mathrm{E}_{\boldsymbol{x}\sim \mathrm{P}_{\boldsymbol{x}}}[-\mathrm{log} p_\theta(\boldsymbol{x}|\mathcal{E}_\phi(\boldsymbol{x}))],\\
&\mathcal{L}_{adv}(\phi, w) = \mathrm{E}_{\boldsymbol{z}\sim \mathrm{P}_{\boldsymbol{z}}}[-\mathrm{log}\mathcal{D}_w(\boldsymbol{z})]\\
&\qquad + \mathrm{E}_{\boldsymbol{x}\sim \mathrm{P}_{\boldsymbol{x}}}[-\mathrm{log}(1-\mathcal{D}_w(\mathcal{E}_\phi(\boldsymbol{x})))].
\end{aligned}$$

Shen et al. (2020) adopt AAEs and introduce denoising adversarial autoencoders (DAAEs) with a smoother structure of latent space. Based on the Wasserstein autoencoders (WAEs) (Tolstikhin et al., 2018; Zhao et al., 2018) propose adversarially regularized autoencoders (ARAE) by extending AAEs for discrete sequences. Unlike AAEs which use a fixed prior distribution, Zhao et al. (2018) adopt a learnable prior parameterized by the generator of a GAN . Particularly, the discriminator and the generator are first learned by using the latent representation from the encoder. The discriminator is then used to adversarially train the encoder by minimizing the discrepancy between the posterior and the prior.

2.2 Methods for Text Style Transfer

Disentangled latent representation Most work on text style transfer is based on learning disentangled latent representations (Hu et al., 2017; Shen et al., 2017; Yang et al., 2018; John et al., 2019; Bao et al., 2019), where the attributes are separated from the content. For example, to generate a sentence with desired attributes, the decoder in (Hu et al., 2017) takes the style-independent latent representation and the desired style as the input. Shen et al. (2017) adopts adversarial training by using a binary CNN-based discriminator to determine whether a generated sentence is successfully transferred or not. Yang et al. (2018) use a target domain language model instead of a conventional binary classifier as the discriminator.

Entangled latent representation On the contrary, some recent work proposes to learn latent representations that entangle the style with the content. Although the learning of disentangled latent representations is unnecessary, other mechanisms are needed to guide the style transfer. For example, Lample et al. (2019) apply the back-translation mechanism (referred to as BTDAE) and the algorithm achieves the state-of-the-art performance on the content preservation. Wang et al. (2019) transfer text style by updating the latent representation (referred to as TAE) based on the Fast Gradient Sign Method (FGSM) (Goodfellow et al., 2015). Liu et al. (2020) also use a gradient-based optimization to update the latent representation.

Style classifier A classifier is commonly used in a style discriminator to enforce the desired style (Hu et al., 2017; Yang et al., 2018; Tian et al., 2018). For example, ARAE (Zhao et al., 2018) imposes a style classifier on the latent representation of a sentence to ensure the transferred sentence containing the target attribute.

The main differences between our method and ARAE (Zhao et al., 2018) can be summarized as follows: 1) Representation structure: the latent representation of ARAE can be considered as disentangled while ours is entangled. 2) Style classifier: the style classifier we adopt helps the clustering of latent representations based on attributes while the classifier in ARAE only enforces the target contribute on transferred sentences. 3) To realize style transfer, ARAE uses the classifier to train the encoder net adversarially, such that the latent representation of the given text could contain the information of the target attribute. However, in our method, the style transfer is realized by directly modifying the latent representation. 4) Due to the adversarial training process ARAE requires multiple decoders to perform style transfer, while our method can use only one decoder.

3 Our Method

We first briefly explain text style transfer as follows. Generally, a source or an input sentence includes both the content and the attribute. In Figure 1, we use (x, y) to include both the input x and the attribute y. As a concrete example, a sentence "this place is a great place to live !" has two types of attribute: the positive sentiment and the present tense. The positive sentiment is reflected by the word "great" and the present tense is reflected by the word "is". All remaining words in this sentence are considered as the content. For single-attribute style transfer, only one attribute (e.g. sentiment) will be transferred, and the other attributes and the content will be kept the same. In the above example with the sentiment style transfer, the sentence will be converted into a negative sentence: "this place is a terrible place to live !" by flipping the sentiment label y from positive to negative. In contrast, for multi-attribute style transfer, two or more attributes will be transferred simultaneously while the rest will be preserved. Again, in the above example the sentence will be converted into "this place was a terrible place to live !" by transferring both the sentiment and the tense.

3.1 Network Architecture

We propose a generative model that can be used for both text style transfer and text generation. The network architecture of our method is illustrated in Figure 1, where the top one is for training and the bottom one is for style transfer. The network for training includes three parts: an autoencoder, a GAN, and a style classifier. Specifically, the autoencoder is learned to reconstruct the input sentences. The discriminator of the GAN is to distinguish the aggregated posterior of the encoder from the prior, which is modeled by the generator of the GAN. The style classifier uses the latent representation as the input, and classifies latent representations based on their attributes. The classifier can also be used in style transfer, which will be explained later.

3.2 Objective Function for Training

The overall objective function for training includes three parts: the reconstruction loss, the adversarial loss induced by the GAN, and the classification loss. Similar to ARAE (Zhao et al., 2018), we use the Wasserstein distance to measure the discrepancy between two distributions. Denote the parameters of the encoder, the decoder, the discriminator, the generator, and the classifier as ϕ, θ, w, ψ, and ϕ_c, respectively. The overall objective function is defined as follows.

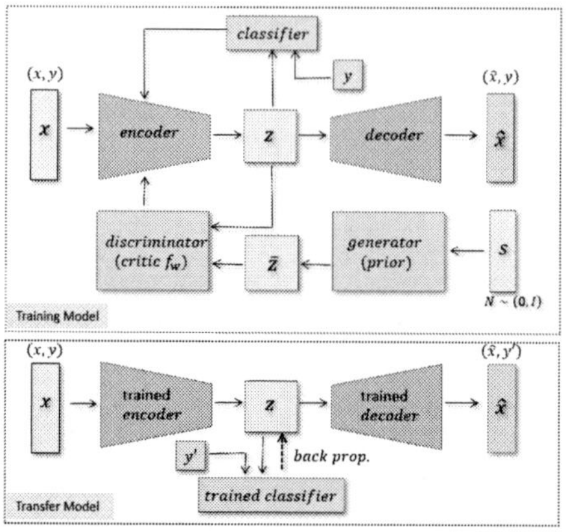

Figure 1: Network architecture: training (top) and text style transfer (bottom).

$$\mathcal{L}(\phi, \theta, \phi_c) = \mathcal{L}_{rec}(\phi, \theta) + \lambda_w \mathcal{L}_{crit}(\phi) + \lambda_c \mathcal{L}_{clas}(\phi, \phi_c),$$

where

$$\mathcal{L}_{rec}(\phi, \theta) = \mathrm{E}_{\boldsymbol{x} \sim \mathrm{P}_{\boldsymbol{x}}}[-\mathrm{log} p_\theta(\boldsymbol{x}|\mathcal{E}_\phi(\boldsymbol{x}))],$$
$$\mathcal{L}_{crit}(\phi) = \mathrm{E}_{\tilde{\boldsymbol{z}} \sim \mathrm{P}_{\boldsymbol{z}}}[f_w(\tilde{\boldsymbol{z}})] - \mathrm{E}_{\boldsymbol{x} \sim \mathrm{P}_{\boldsymbol{x}}}[f_w(\mathcal{E}_\phi(\boldsymbol{x}))],$$
$$\mathcal{L}_{clas}(\phi, \phi_c) = \mathrm{E}_{\boldsymbol{x} \sim \mathrm{P}_{\boldsymbol{x}}}[-\mathrm{log} p_{\phi_c}(y|\mathcal{E}_\phi(\boldsymbol{x}))].$$

In the above expressions, the variable $\tilde{\boldsymbol{z}}$ is the output of the generator $\mathcal{G}_\psi(\boldsymbol{s})$, where the noise $\boldsymbol{s} \in \mathcal{N}(0, \boldsymbol{I})$; y is the label of the source attribute; and the critic function f_w of the discriminator is obtained by a min-max optimization:

$$\min_{\psi} \max_{w} \mathcal{L}_{crit}(\psi, w) = \mathrm{E}_{\boldsymbol{x} \sim \mathrm{P}_{\boldsymbol{x}}}[f_w(\mathcal{E}_\phi(\boldsymbol{x}))] - \mathrm{E}_{\tilde{\boldsymbol{z}} \sim \mathrm{P}_{\boldsymbol{z}}}[f_w(\tilde{\boldsymbol{z}})].$$

We summarize the training algorithm in Algorithm 1. First, the autoencoder is trained by minimizing the reconstruction loss, *i.e.*, $\min_{\phi,\theta} \mathcal{L}_{rec}(\phi, \theta)$. Next, based on the latent representation from the encoder, the encoder and the style classifier are jointly trained by minimizing the classification loss, *i.e.*, $\min_{\phi,\phi_c} \mathcal{L}_{clas}(\phi, \phi_c)$. Meanwhile, the critic function f_w and the generator of the GAN are learned via the min-max optimization $\min_{\psi} \max_{w} \mathcal{L}_{crit}(\psi, w)$. Finally, the critic function f_w is utilized to adversarially train the encoder, *i.e.*, $\min_\phi \mathcal{L}_{crit}(\phi)$. We emphasize that we do not explicitly disentangle the attributes from the content in the latent representation. Therefore, to implement style transfer, the style classifier is crucial, which guides the clustering of the entangled latent representations based on their attributes.

Algorithm 1: Training Algorithm.

```
Inputs: P_x input distribution; E_φ encoder; G_ψ
        generator; f_w discriminator/critic function
for each training iteration do
    // Train the encoder and decoder
       for reconstruction(φ,θ).
    Sample {x^(i)}_{i=1}^m ~ P_x and compute
      z^(i) = E_φ(x^(i)) ;
    Backprop loss:
      L_rec(φ,θ) = -1/m Σ_{i=1}^m logp_θ(x^(i)|z^(i)) ;

    // Train the attribute
       classifier(φ_c) and optimize
       the encoder using the
       classifier regularisation(φ).
    Sample {x^(i)}_{i=1}^m ~ P_x and save attribute y^(i);
    Backprop loss:
      L_clas(φ_c,φ) =
      -1/m Σ_{i=1}^m logp_{φ_c}(y^(i)|E_φ(x^(i)));

    // Train the
       discriminator/critic
       function(w).
    Sample {x^(i)}_{i=1}^m ~ P_x and
      {s^(i)}_{i=1}^m ~ N(0,I) ;
    Compute z^(i) = E_φ(x^(i));
    Backprop loss:
      min_ψ max_w L_crit(w,ψ) =
      1/m Σ_{i=1}^m f_w(z^(i)) - 1/m Σ_{i=1}^m f_w(G_ψ(s^(i))) ;

    // Train the encoder
       adversarially(φ).
    Sample {x^(i)}_{i=1}^m ~ P_x ;
    compute z̃^(i) = G_ψ(s^(i)) ;
    Backprop loss:
      L_crit(φ) =
      1/m Σ_{i=1}^m f_w(E_φ(x^(i))) - 1/m Σ_{i=1}^m f_w(z̃^(i)) ;
end
```

3.3 Style Transfer

After training the network, we can implement text style transfer (as shown at the bottom of Figure 1). We summarize the algorithm for style transfer in Algorithm 2, which works for both single-attribute and multi-attribute style transfer. Normally for multi-attribute style transfer, multiple style classifiers are required: each corresponding to an attribute. To make the network scalable, we instead use a single style classifier by combining the labels of attributes. In this case, each attribute label corresponds to an attribute-combination (such as present-positive, past-positive, present-negative, and past-negative with both the tense and the sentiment as the attributes for transferring).

Algorithm 2: Transfer Algorithm.

```
Inputs: input distribution P_x; encoder E_φ;
        well-trained classifier C_{φ_c}; the initial weights
        w = {w_j}; decay coefficient λ; target
        attribute y'; threshold t; maximal iterations I;
        attribute vector v; the weight of attribute
        vector k.
Result: A target latent representation ẑ_f^(i) or ẑ_v^(i).
Sample {x^(i)}_{i=1}^m ~ P_x and compute
  z^(i) = E_φ(x^(i)) ;
// Method 1: based on Fast
   Gradient Sign Method.
for each w_j ∈ w do
    ẑ^(i) = z^(i) - w ∇_z *L_clas(C_{φ_c}(z^(i)), y'^(i)) ;
    for |C_{φ_c}(z^(i)) - y'^(i)| > t do
        it++ ;
        w_j = λw_j ;
        ẑ_f^(i) =
          z^(i) - w ∇_z *L_clas(C_{φ_c}(z^(i)), y'^(i)) ;
        if it > I then
            break ;
        end
    end
end

// Method 2: based on vector
   arithmetic. x_s^(i) are the samples
   with source attribute and x_t^(i)
   are the samples with target
   attribute.
Sample {x_s^(i)}_{i=1}^n ~ P_x and {x_t^(i)}_{i=1}^n ~ P_x ;
compute z_s^(i) = E_φ(x_s^(i)) and compute
  z_t^(i) = E_φ(x_t^(i)) ;
Calculate the attribute vector
  v = 1/n Σ_{i=1}^n z_s^(i) - 1/n Σ_{i=1}^n z_t^(i);
ẑ_v^(i) = z^(i) ± k * v
```

To perform style transfer, given an input sentence, we first get its latent representation as the output of the encoder. With the entangled latent representation, the key of style transfer is how to update the latent representation of the source sentence. To achieve that, we adopt two different but commonly used updates: the fast gradient based and the vector arithmetic based. To obtain the target sentence with the desired attribute, we then feed the updated latent representation to the decoder.

Fast gradient based: FGSM is employed by Wang et al. (2019) to update the latent representation for style transfer. Concretely, the latent representation is updated along the gradient of the classification loss with the step size w. A set $\boldsymbol{w}$ contains a few step sizes with an increasing order. We sequentially test these step sizes until obtaining the desired latent representation. This is to maximally preserve the content of the sentence and also to prevent the modification of the latent presentation from falling into a local optimum. In each iteration, the updated latent representation $\hat{z}_f$ is given as follows:

$$\hat{z}_f = z - w \nabla_z * \mathcal{L}_{clas}(\mathcal{C}_{\phi_c}(z), y'),$$

where $\mathcal{L}_{clas}$ represents a style classifier loss, $\mathcal{C}_{\phi_c}$ is a well-trained classifier, and y' represents the target label. The detailed algorithm is displayed in Method 1 of Algorithm 2.

Vector arithmetic based: In several studies *e.g.*, Zhao et al. (2018); Shen et al. (2020), the latent vector arithmetic based method is employed in text style transfer or text interpolation. Specifically, the latent representation z of the source sentence is modified by an attribute vector "v". For example, assume that the source attribute is positive. When transferring the attribute from positive to negative we can update z by $z - v$; and when transferring from negative to positive we can update z by $z + v$. The same as Shen et al. (2020), the attribute vector "v" uses the mean of the latent representations of 100 samples with the source attribute and 100 samples with the target attribute from the validation set. For multi-attribute transfer, the attribute vector v is computed in the same way. The only difference is that the label of the source attribute and the target attribute corresponds to an attribute-combination as explained before. The updated latent representation $\hat{z}_v$ can be formulated as follows:

$$\hat{z}_v = z \pm k * v,$$

where k is a hyperparameter denoting the weight associated with the attribute vector.

4 Experiments

In this section, we first visualize the latent representation of our method, and then compare our method with several baselines, namely, TAE (Wang et al., 2019), ARAE (Zhao et al., 2018), and DAAE (Shen et al., 2020) for single-attribute and multiple-attribute text style transfer. We then evaluate our model on text generation and compare it with ARAE.

4.1 Datasets

We use Yelp and Amazon datasets for evaluation.

Yelp: This dataset consists of Yelp restaurant and business reviews (Li et al., 2018), which includes $444K$ training samples, $4K$ validation samples, and $1K$ test samples.

Amazon: This dataset includes product reviews from Amazon (He and McAuley, 2016), which includes $555K$ training samples, $2K$ validation samples, and $1K$ test samples.

On both Yelp and Amazon datasets, reviews with a rating score above three are considered as positive samples, otherwise are considered as negative samples.

4.2 Experimental setups

In our experiment, similar to ARAE (Zhao et al., 2018), we use one layer LSTM with 200 hidden units for both the encoder and the decoder. Both the generator and the discriminator in the GAN use simple MLP networks. The style classifier is built by a shallow MLP network with two hidden layers, as our experiment indicates that too many layers can degrade the performance of the classifier.

The weighting parameters λ_w and λ_c are set to 0.1 on Yelp and 1 on Amazon. In the fast gradient method, the set of the initial weights w is set to $\{0.005, 0.006, 0.007, 0.008, 0.009, 0.01\}$, where the weights are ordered increasingly.

4.3 Evaluation

Following previous studies, for both automatic and human evaluations, we assess the performance of style transfer from three perspectives: transfer control, content preservation, and fluency. In automatic evaluation, three commonly used metrics are adopted: the transfer rate, the BLEU score, and the Perplexity (PPL) score.

Transfer control: It evaluates whether the style of the source sentences is correctly flipped. The transfer rate is the percentage of the corrected transferred sentences, and we use a *fastText* classifier (Joulin et al., 2017) to determine that.

Content preservation: It evaluates how the content is preserved in the transferred sentences. We use n-gram statistics (4-gram) of the BLEU score (Papineni et al., 2002) to quantify the content preservation against the references (Li et al., 2018).

Fluency: It evaluates the grammatical structure and the naturalness of the generated (or transferred) text sentences. We use a language model KenLM (Heafield, 2011) to calculate the PPL score of text sentences for evaluating fluency.

4.4 Evaluation on Latent Representation

4.4.1 Visualization

We show the projected latent representation of both the source and the target sentences and compare it with TAE (Wang et al., 2019). To better show the structure of the latent representation, we use the visualization tool t-SNE (van der Maaten and Hinton, 2008) in 2-dimension. Figure 2(a) shows the latent representations of 1000 source samples with positive and negative labels. Figure 2(b) and Figure 2(c) show the latent representations of six target samples, which are updated by FGSM. $w[i]$ in these two figures denotes the i-th step size in the set $\boldsymbol{w}$, and a larger value of i indicates a larger value of $w[i]$.

In our framework, both the GAN and the style classifier help the regularization of the latent representation. Figure 2(a) indicates that in our method, the latent representations tend to form two clusters. Specifically, the positive samples tend to locate at the bottom while the negative samples tend to locate on the top. In contrast, the positive and the negative samples in TAE are generally mixed together. In Figure 2(c), as the value of the step size w increases in our method, the latent representation of the positive samples tends to move towards the bottom, which corresponds to the position of the positive cluster. In contrast, the latent representation of the negative samples tends to move towards the top, which corresponds to the position of the negative cluster. This observation clearly shows the guidance of the style classifier on clustering the latent representations. In comparison, in Figure 2(b), without the GAN and the style classifier in TAE, the latent representation of each target sample needs to be updated along different directions.

4.4.2 Evaluation of Latent Representation via K-nearest-neighbours

It is desirable that close latent representations lead to semantically similar sentences after feeding latent representations to the decoder. Such property indicates the smoothness of the latent space. In this experiment, we find $k = 9$ nearest neighbours of the latent representation of a sentence "*service is terrible and won't return.*", and then generate sentences by feeding these latent representations to the decoder. It is expected that the generated sentences are close to the source sentence in terms of the sentiment attribute and the content. For comparison, we consider four differ network architectures and

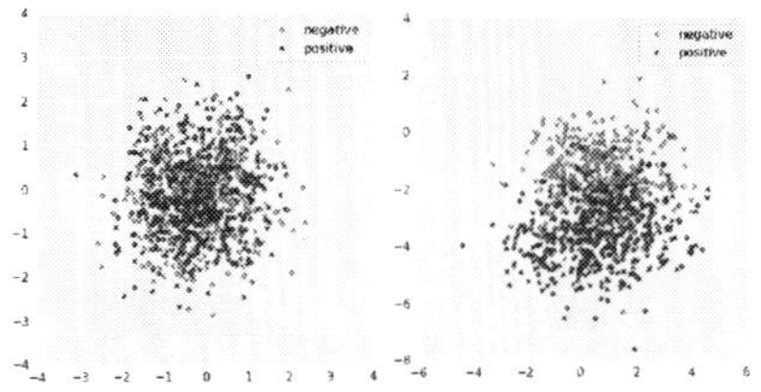

(a) Projected latent representations in TAE (left) and in our method (right).

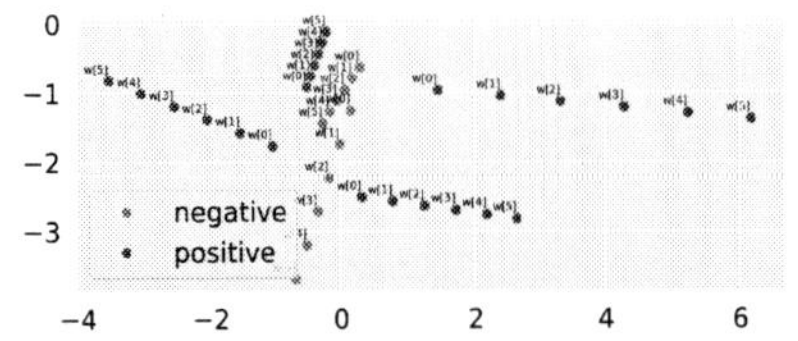

(b) Projected target latent representations with FGSM update in TAE.

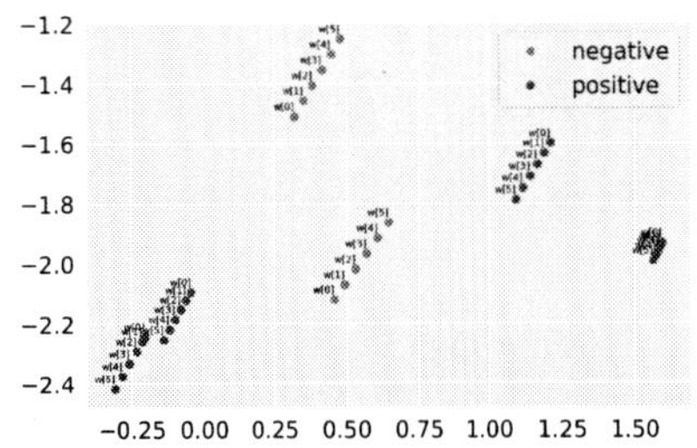

(c) Projected target latent representations with FGSM update in our method.

Figure 2: Comparison between our method and TAE on projected latent representations.

show the generated sentences in Table 1.

- **TAE**: The generated sentences contain both the positive and the negative samples. Moreover, many of them have different contents that are related to "place" or "location" instead of the source content "service" or "return".

- **TAE+GAN**: We regularize the latent representation in TAE by a GAN. Although all sentences are related to the source content "service" their sentiment attributes are largely different.

- **TAE + classifier**: We add a style classifier in TAE. Different from **TAE+GAN**, the generated sentences have the same negative attribute but some sentences deviate from the source content "service" or "return".

- **Our method**: Our network architecture includes both the GAN and a style classifier.

All generated sentences have the same negative attribute and are related to the source content "service" or "return".

Table 1: Evaluation of the smoothness of the latent space via k-nearest-neighbours. The source sentence is "*service is terrible and won't return* ".

TAE	**TAE + GAN**
service was terrible .	service is great and friendly .
their service is terrible .	service isn't that great either .
service is great and friendly .	service is mediocre and slow .
this *place* is terrible !	service is slow and horrible .
service is slow and horrible .	service is lacking and food is mediocre .
this *location* is terrible .	the service is friendly and fast .
service is always good .	prices are good and the service is great .
service was bad .	service is quick and friendly .
everything was great and i will return !	the service is always friendly and good .
TAE + classifier guidance	**Our method**
service was terrible .	service is n't that great either .
their service is terrible .	i wo n't be back .
food was terrible .	the service is n't frequent enough .
this *place* is terrible .	will not return to this place .
service is slow and horrible .	needless to say we wo n't be back !
the *waiter* was terrible .	service was n't too bad - nice people .
i wo n't be back .	the service was not that professional !
service is mediocre and slow .	the service did n't get any better .
terrible service .	service is n't too bad , but could be better .

4.5 Evaluation of Style Transfer

4.5.1 Single-Attribute Style Transfer

We compare our method with TAE by using FGSM to update the latent representation since TAE is only designed with FGSM (Table 2). TAE has a very low transfer rate in experiments. This however leads to high BLEU scores and low PPL scores as most target sentences are the same as the source sentences. By contrast, our method can successfully transfer most sentences, and leads to decent BLEU and PPL scores.

Table 2: Comparison between our method and TAE for sentiment transfer on Yelp.

Methods	Transfer ↑	BLEU ↑	PPL ↓
TAE			
$w = 2$	0.24	**37.98**	**42.08**
$w = 4$	0.25	35.70	48.73
$w = 6$	0.25	33.33	56.50
Our method:			
$w = 0.005$	0.76	25.74	**70.16**
$w = 0.007$	0.80	25.16	72.70
$w = 0.01$	**0.87**	23.90	75.46

We also compare the performance of our methods with ARAE and DAAE using the vector arithmetic based update on latent representations for style transfer. As mentioned before, the vector arithmetic based update can be used to evaluate the smoothness of the latent space. In Table 3, we compare with two baselines on both Yelp and Amazon and display the results that achieve the best trade-off among the three evaluation metrics. The hyperparameter k of vector arithmetic method is chosen based on the performance in the validation set. Our method achieves the highest transfer rate and a comparable BLEU score with ARAE on Yelp, while ARAE achieves the lowest PPL score. On Amazon, our method obtains the best performance on the transfer rate and the BLEU score with a slightly higher PPL score than ARAE. By contrast, DAAE does not perform well on both datasets especially on Amazon.

Table 3: Evaluation results of style transfer based on the vector arithmetic based update on Yelp and Amazon.

	Methods	Transfer ↑	BLEU ↑	PPL ↓
Yelp	**ARAE** $\pm 1.5v$	0.536	**20.08**	**64.75**
	DAAE $\pm 2.0v$	0.461	18.55	114.59
	Our method $\pm 1.5v$	**0.792**	19.90	78.63
Amazon	**ARAE** $\pm 2.5v$	0.513	14.71	**31.37**
	DAAE $\pm 1.0v$	0.473	3.50	–
	Our method $\pm 2.0v$	**0.884**	**14.73**	33.86

FGSM and vector arithmetic method for style transfer have their pros and cons. Table 4 shows the evaluation results of both FGSM based and vector arithmetic based methods on Yelp data. Generally, for both methods, as the step size $\boldsymbol{w}$ or $\boldsymbol{v}$ increases, the transfer rate is improving, while the performance of BLEU and PPL are decreasing. In the case of the FGSM based method, the best trade-off is when w is set as 0.007, while the vector arithmetic based method has the best trade-off when v is set as 1.5. With $w = 0.007$ and $v = 1.5$, FGSM based method achieves better transfer rate and BLEU score but the lower performance of PPL than vector arithmetic based method. From our experiment, we also observe that FGSM based style transfer needs much longer updating time in testing than the vector arithmetic based method.

Table 4: Comparison results between FGSM based and vector arithmetic based style transfer on Yelp.

Methods	w/v	Transfer ↑	BLEU ↑	PPL ↓
FGSM based	$w = 0.005$	0.76	25.74	70.16
	$w = 0.007$	*0.80*	*25.16*	*72.70*
	$w = 0.01$	0.87	23.90	75.46
Vector arithmetic based	$\pm 1.0v$	0.49	**30.00**	**49.42**
	$\pm 1.5v$	*0.79*	*19.90*	*78.63*
	$\pm 2.0v$	**0.94**	11.38	113.52

Although the automatic evaluation metrics *e.g.*, the BLEU score, are widely used, they sometimes do not well align with the human judgement (Ma et al., 2018). Therefore, to fully evaluate the performance we also carried out the human evaluation on sentiment transfer and compare it with ARAE on Yelp. We use the vector arithmetic based update of the latent representation on the first 200 positive and 200 negative sentences in the test set. Three annotators were recruited and provided scores in the range of 1∼5 regarding the transfer control, the content preservation and the fluency. The Kappa statistic of the agreement between raters in the human evaluation is 0.657. The average scores over three annotators are shown in Table 5, and our method generally outperforms ARAE.

Table 5: Human evaluation results of sentiment transfer on Yelp.

Methods	Transfer ↑ Control	Content ↑ Preservation	Fluency ↑
ARAE	3.388	2.671	3.439
Our method	**3.468**	**3.018**	**3.612**

4.5.2 Multi-Attribute Style Transfer

We also evaluate our model for multi-attribute transfer and compare with ARAE on Yelp. The goal of multi-attribute style transfer is to transform multiple attributes in a sentence at once while preserving the main content of the sentence. Using the same example sentence "this place is a great place to live !" with positive sentiment and present tense, multi-attribute transfer converts it into a sentence with the negative sentiment and the past tense "this place was a terrible place to live !".

In the training phase, the style classifier uses both the latent vector of a given sentence and the original attribute label as the inputs; while in style transfer, the style classifier uses both the latent vector and the desired attribute label as the inputs. In pre-processing of single-attribute style transfer, the attribute is labelled as either "0" or "1". In multi-attribute style transfer (e.g. tense and sentiment), each attribute combination will be defined as an individual class (e.g. present-positive: "0", past-positive: "1", present-negative: "2", and past-negative: "3").

In particular, we use the Stanford Parser to extract the main verb of a sentence from Yelp and then determine the tense of a sentence based on its part-of-speech tag (POS tags) (Klein and Manning, 2003). Table 6 shows the evaluation results of style transfer for two attributes: sentiment and tense transfer. In our model, we test on two network variants, one consisting of two style classifiers each corresponding to one attribute, and the other consists of only one style classifier that combines both attributes into one label as described before. The results show that our method is superior to ARAE even with one style classifier. When using two classifiers to realize multiple attributes transfer, for example, tense and sentiment transfer, each classifier is responsible for transferring one attribute. Specifically, after the sentiment-classifier transferred sentiment attribute, the transferred sentences will be the inputs of the tense-classifier for transferring tense attribute. As using two classifiers, each classifier only needs to transfer one attribute, having less pressure of transferring two attributes together, it achieves higher accuracy than one classifier case. However, since it requires two steps transfer, the self BLEU score decreases slightly.

Table 6: Results of multiple attributes (sentiment and tense) transfer on Yelp.

Methods	Transfer ↑	Self BLEU ↑	PPL ↓
ARAE ($\pm 2.0v$)	0.663	11.57	86.99
Our method:			
2 classifiers; $\pm 1.5v$	**0.750**	13.86	85.47
1 classifier; $\pm 1.5v$	0.733	**14.34**	**85.41**

4.6 Evaluation of Text Generation

Unlike most of the current models for style transfer, our model can also be used to generate new text sentences owing to the introduction of the latent prior distribution. To generate a new sentence, we first take the noise s as the input to the generator of the GAN and get a latent representation. Then we feed the latent representation to the decoder and obtain the new sentence.

In previous work, both LSTM (Zhao et al., 2018; Lample et al., 2019; Shen et al., 2020) and transformer (Wang et al., 2019) have been used as the base network in the encoder and decoder architecture. Hence, we further evaluate the performance of our method based on these two networks on Yelp and show the results in Table 7. Experimental results indicate that both the transformer-based networks and the LSTM-based networks in our method achieve a similar trade-off among the three evaluation metrics. The transformer-based method achieves higher BLEU scores but lower transfer rates and higher PPL scores, while the LSTM-based method leads to a better performance on the transfer rate and the PPL score, but a worse performance on the BLEU score.

Table 7: Comparison of sentiment transfer between the transformer-based autoencoder and the LSTM-based autoencoder in our method on Yelp.

Methods	Transfer ↑	BLEU ↑	PPL ↓
Transformer-based:			
w=0.7	0.73	**31.14**	71.58
w=0.8	0.79	27.42	84.13
w=0.9	0.82	24.48	92.65
w=1.0	0.85	21.40	97.21
LSTM-based:			
w=0.005	0.76	25.74	**70.16**
w=0.007	0.80	25.16	72.70
w=0.009	0.84	24.50	74.32
w=0.01	**0.87**	23.90	75.46

We evaluate the quality of the text generation using the LSTM-based network in our method by comparing $10,000$ generated sentences with sentences generated by ARAE on Yelp. The experimental results in Table 8 show that our method achieves a better degree of fluency. In particular, the PPL score of our method is lower than that of ARAE by around 10% (the PPL score of our method and ARAE is 76.83 and 86.98, respectively).

Table 8: Generated sentences of our method and ARAE.

Our method
the woman who could give up the store says you are very picky .
the wait staff is great but overall i did n't like the customer.
i will not recommend this place to any women in future .
the man was always great and the service was really helpful .
do not waste a star from the older man this place is overpriced .
the store experience is awesome the salesman it was very nice.
oh ok and the man in the service looked nice .
kind of really nice man 's walking the restaurant that they 're very delish .
ARAE
the gentleman i left inside the kitchen was a rather nice follow up .
this woman has gotten me .
the woman in a little job of perfect !
the man was not that amazing if i tried to order it .
this woman has a cake must me in the burgh .
all was excellent by the salesman we had to do .
there is a friendly man and the crowd of bacon in your face .
their woman was under staffed as very polite and how talented .

Text samples of ARAE are from Zhao et al. (2018).

4.7 Style Classifier in Other Models

Through the above experiments, we have illustrated the effect of the style classifier in our method on clustering the latent representations based on the attributes. We also perform an ablation study regarding the style classifier on two other advanced models: DAAE and BTDAE (Lample et al., 2019). In DAAE, we implement style transfer by the vector arithmetic based update, and in BTDAE the back-translation algorithm is used for style transfer. From Table 9, we observe that with the inclusion of a style classifier in DAAE the performance on all evaluation metrics is improved. For BTDAE, with a style classifier the BLEU and the PPL scores are improved. These results again demonstrate the effectiveness of a style classifier on style transfer.

Table 9: Comparison between the models and the models with a style classifier on Yelp.

Methods	Transfer ↑	BLEU ↑	PPL ↓
DAAE ($\pm 2.0v$)	0.461	18.55	114.59
DAAE + Class.($\pm 1.5v$)	**0.646**	**22.02**	**112.50**
BTDAE	**0.87**	38.41	36.42
BTDAE + Class.	0.86	**39.87**	**34.39**

As the official code of BTDAE is unavailable, we implemented the algorithm based on the description in Lample et al. (2019).

5 Conclusion and Future Work

In this paper, we proposed a new approach for text style transfer with entangled latent representations. We added a classifier to regularize the distribution of latent sentences in a probabilistic autoencoder. Extensive experiments show that this regularized latent structure significantly improves the downstream text manipulation tasks. Compared with benchmarks our method achieves impressive results on both single-attribute and multi-attribute text style transfer. Moreover, both approaches of fast gradient and vector arithmetic style transfer outperform baselines on style transfer tasks. In addition, we demonstrated that the classifier regularization also improves other style transfer models.

In the future, we would like to explore other methods to regularize latent representation in controllable text generation. Moreover, text generation models have a wide range of applications in NLP tasks. Besides style transfer, we will apply our model to other tasks such as text simplification and examine the latent structure in these applications.

References

Rafael E. Banchs and Haizhou Li. 2012. IRIS: a chat-oriented dialogue system based on the vector space model. In *Proceedings of the ACL 2012 System Demonstrations*, pages 37–42, Jeju Island, Korea. Association for Computational Linguistics.

Yu Bao, Hao Zhou, Shujian Huang, Lei Li, Lili Mou,

Olga Vechtomova, Xin-yu Dai, and Jiajun Chen. 2019. Generating sentences from disentangled syntactic and semantic spaces. In *Proceedings of the 57th Annual Meeting of the Association for Computational Linguistics*, pages 6008–6019, Florence, Italy. Association for Computational Linguistics.

Yixin Cao, Ruihao Shui, Liangming Pan, Min-Yen Kan, Zhiyuan Liu, and Tat-Seng Chua. 2020. Expertise style transfer: A new task towards better communication between experts and laymen. In *Proceedings of the 58th Annual Meeting of the Association for Computational Linguistics*, Online. Association for Computational Linguistics.

I. J. Goodfellow, J. Pouget-Abadie, M. Mirza, B. Xu, D. Warde-Farley, S. Ozair, A. Courville, and Y. Bengio. 2014. Generative adversarial networks. In *Advances in Neural Information Processing Systems*, pages 2672–2680.

Ian J. Goodfellow, Jonathon Shlens, and Christian Szegedy. 2015. Explaining and harnessing adversarial examples.

Mengqiao Han, Ou Wu, and Zhendong Niu. 2017. Unsupervised automatic text style transfer using LSTM. In *NLPCC*.

Ruining He and Julian McAuley. 2016. Ups and downs: Modeling the visual evolution of fashion trends with one-class collaborative filtering. WWW '16, page 507–517, Republic and Canton of Geneva, CHE. International World Wide Web Conferences Steering Committee.

Kenneth Heafield. 2011. KenLM: Faster and smaller language model queries. In *Proceedings of the sixth workshop on statistical machine translation*, pages 187–197.

Zhiting Hu, Zichao Yang, Xiaodan Liang, Ruslan Salakhutdinov, and Eric P. Xing. 2017. Toward controlled generation of text. In *Proceedings of the 34th International Conference on Machine Learning*, volume 70, pages 1587–1596, International Convention Centre, Sydney, Australia. PMLR.

Vineet John, Lili Mou, Hareesh Bahuleyan, and Olga Vechtomova. 2019. Disentangled representation learning for non-parallel text style transfer. In *Proceedings of the 57th Annual Meeting of the Association for Computational Linguistics*, Florence, Italy. Association for Computational Linguistics.

Armand Joulin, Edouard Grave, Piotr Bojanowski, and Tomas Mikolov. 2017. Bag of tricks for efficient text classification. *arXiv:1607.01759*.

Seokhwan Kim, Cheongjae Lee, Sangkeun Jung, and Gary Geunbae Lee. 2007. A spoken dialogue system for electronic program guide information access. In *IEEE*.

Dan Klein and Christopher D Manning. 2003. Fast exact inference with a factored model for natural language parsing. In *Advances in neural information processing systems*, pages 3–10.

Guillaume Lample, Sandeep Subramanian, Eric Smith, Ludovic Denoyer, Marc'Aurelio Ranzato, and Y-Lan Boureau. 2019. Multiple-attribute text rewriting. In *International Conference on Learning Representations*.

Juncen Li, Robin Jia, He He, and Percy Liang. 2018. Delete, retrieve, generate: a simple approach to sentiment and style transfer. In *Proceedings of the 2018 Conference of the North American Chapter of the Association for Computational Linguistics: Human Language Technologies*.

Dayiheng Liu, Jie Fu, Yidan Zhang, Chris Pal, and Jiancheng Lv. 2020. Revision in continuous space: Fine-grained control of text style transfer.

Linqing Liu, Yao Lu, Min Yang, Qiang Qu, Jia Zhu, and Hongyan Li. 2018. Generative adversarial network for abstractive text summarization.

Qingsong Ma, Ondřej Bojar, and Yvette Graham. 2018. Results of the wmt18 metrics shared task: Both characters and embeddings achieve good performance. In *Proceedings of the third conference on machine translation: shared task papers*, pages 671–688.

Laurens van der Maaten and Geoffrey Hinton. 2008. Viualizing data using t-SNE. *Journal of Machine Learning Research*, 9:2579–2605.

Alireza Makhzani, Jonathon Shlens, Navdeep Jaitly, Ian Goodfellow, and Brendan Frey. 2015. Adversarial autoencoders. *arXiv:1511.05644*.

Makbule Ozsoy, Ferda Alpaslan, and Ilyas Cicekli. 2011. Text summarization using latent semantic analysis. *J. Information Science*, 37:405–417.

Kishore Papineni, S. Roukos, T. Ward, and Wei-Jing Zhu. 2002. BLEU: a method for automatic evaluation of machine translation. In *ACL*.

Sudha Rao and Joel Tetreault. 2018. Dear sir or madam, may I introduce the GYAFC dataset: Corpus, benchmarks and metrics for formality style transfer. In *Proceedings of the 2018 Conference of the North American Chapter of the Association for Computational Linguistics: Human Language Technologies, Volume 1 (Long Papers)*, pages 129–140, New Orleans, Louisiana. Association for Computational Linguistics.

Tianxiao Shen, Tao Lei, Regina Barzilay, and Tommi Jaakkola. 2017. Style transfer from non-parallel text by cross-alignment. In *Advances in neural information processing systems*, pages 6830–6841.

Tianxiao Shen, Jonas Mueller, Regina Barzilay, and Tommi S. Jaakkola. 2020. Educating text autoencoders: Latent representation guidance via denoising.

Youzhi Tian, Zhiting Hu, and Zhou Yu. 2018. Structured content preservation for unsupervised text style transfer. *arXiv*, arXiv:1810.06526.

Ilya Tolstikhin, Olivier Bousquet, Sylvain Gelly, and Bernhard Schoelkopf. 2018. Wasserstein auto-encoders. In *ICLR 2018*.

Ke Wang, Hang Hua, and Xiaojun Wan. 2019. Controllable unsupervised text attribute transfer via editing entangled latent representation. In *Advances in Neural Information Processing Systems*, pages 11036–11046.

Zichao Yang, Zhiting Hu, Chris Dyer, Eric P Xing, and Taylor Berg-Kirkpatrick. 2018. Unsupervised text style transfer using language models as discriminators. In *Advances in Neural Information Processing Systems*, pages 7287–7298.

Junbo Zhao, Yoon Kim, Kelly Zhang, Alexander Rush, and Yann LeCun. 2018. Adversarially regularized autoencoders. In *Proceedings of the 35th International Conference on Machine Learning*, volume 80, pages 5902–5911. PMLR.

Inductively Representing Out-of-Knowledge-Graph Entities by Optimal Estimation Under Translational Assumptions

Damai Dai[1]*, Hua Zheng[1]*, Fuli Luo[1], Pengcheng Yang[1], Baobao Chang[1,2], Zhifang Sui[1,2]†
[1]Key Lab of Computational Linguistics (MOE), Peking University
[2]Peng Cheng Laboratory, China
{daidamai,zhenghua,luofuli,yang_pc,chbb,szf}@pku.edu.cn

Abstract

Conventional Knowledge Graph Completion (KGC) assumes that all test entities appear during training. However, in real-world scenarios, Knowledge Graphs (KG) evolve fast with out-of-knowledge-graph (OOKG) entities added frequently, and we need to efficiently represent these entities. Most existing Knowledge Graph Embedding (KGE) methods cannot represent OOKG entities without costly retraining on the whole KG. To enhance efficiency, we propose a simple and effective method that inductively represents OOKG entities by their optimal estimation under translational assumptions. Moreover, given pretrained embeddings of the in-knowledge-graph (IKG) entities, our method even needs no additional learning. Experimental results on two KGC tasks with OOKG entities show that our method outperforms the previous methods by a large margin with higher efficiency.[1]

1 Introduction

Knowledge Graphs (KG) play a pivotal role in various NLP tasks, but generally suffer from incompleteness. To address this problem, Knowledge Graph Completion (KGC) aims to predict missing relations in a KG based on Knowledge Graph Embeddings (KGE). Transductive KGE methods, such as TransE (Bordes et al., 2013) and RotatE (Sun et al., 2019), achieve success in conventional KGC, which assumes that all test entities appear during training. However, in real-world scenarios, KGs evolve fast with out-of-knowledge-graph (OOKG) entities added frequently. To represent these emerging OOKG entities, transductive KGE methods need to retrain on the whole KG frequently, which

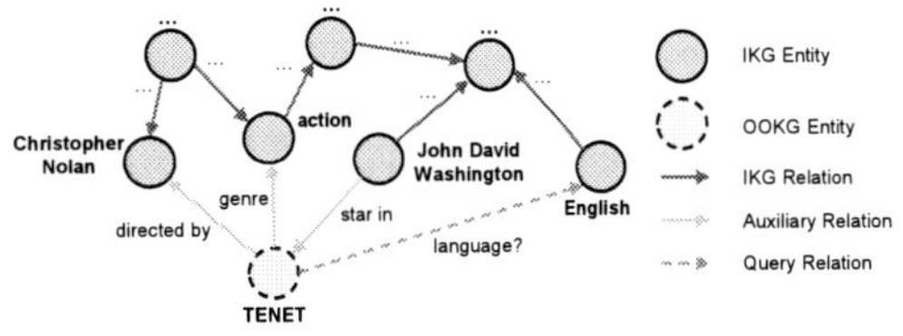

Figure 1: An example of KGC with OOKG entities. When an OOKG entity "**TENET**" is added, we can represent it efficiently via information of its IKG neighbors to predict its missing relations with other entities.

is extremely time-consuming. Faced with this problem, we are in urgent need of an efficient method to tackle KGC with OOKG entities.

Figure 1 shows an example of KGC with OOKG entities. Based on an existing KG, a new movie "**TENET**" is added as an OOKG entity with some auxiliary relations that connect it with some in-knowledge-graph (IKG) entities. To predict the missing relations between "**TENET**" and other entities, we need to obtain its embedding first. Being aware that "**TENET**" is directed by "**Christopher Nolan**", is an "**action**" movie, and is starred by "**John David Washington**", we can combine these clues to profile "**TENET**" and estimate its embedding. This embedding can then be used to predict whether its relation with "**English**" is "language".

In recent years, some inductive methods have been proposed for OOKG entities without retraining. Hamaguchi et al. (2017); Wang et al. (2019); Bi et al. (2020); Zhao et al. (2020) adopt Graph Neural Networks (GNN) to aggregate the IKG neighbors to represent the OOKG entities. These methods are effective but require relatively complex calculations, which could be simplified for higher efficiency. Xie et al. (2016, 2017); Shi and Weninger (2018) utilize external resources such as entity descriptions or images to enrich the OOKG entity embedding, thus avoiding retraining. How-

*Equal contribution.
†Corresponding author.
[1]The code is available at https://github.com/Hunter-DDM/InvTransE-and-InvRotatE.

Proceedings of the 6th Workshop on Representation Learning for NLP (RepL4NLP-2021), pages 83–89
Bangkok, Thailand (Online), August 6, 2021. ©2021 Association for Computational Linguistics

ever, high-quality external resources are expensive to acquire, which may limit the feasibility.

In this paper, we propose an inductive method that derives formulas from translational assumptions to estimate OOKG entity embeddings. Compared to existing methods for KGC with OOKG entities, our method has simpler calculations and does not need external resources. For a triplet (h, r, t), translational assumptions of translational distance KGE models suppose that embedding $\mathbf{h}$ can establish a connection with $\mathbf{t}$ via an $\mathbf{r}$-specific operation. Assuming that h is an OOKG entity and t is an IKG entity, we show that if a translational assumption can derive a specific formula to compute $\mathbf{h}$ via pretrained $\mathbf{t}$ and $\mathbf{r}$, then there will be no other candidate for $\mathbf{h}$ that better fits this translational assumption. Therefore, the computed $\mathbf{h}$ is the optimal estimation of the OOKG entity under this translational assumption. Among existing typical KGE models, we discover that translational assumptions of TransE and RotatE can derive these specific estimation formulas. Therefore, based on them, we design two instances of our method called **InvTransE** and **InvRotatE**, respectively. Note that our estimation formulas have no trainable parameters, so our method needs no additional learning when given pretrained IKG embeddings.

Our contributions are summarized as follows: (1) We propose a simple and effective method to inductively represent OOKG entities by their optimal estimation under translational assumptions. (2) Our method needs no external resources. Given pretrained IKG embeddings, our method even needs no additional learning. (3) We evaluate our method on two KGC tasks with OOKG entities. Experimental results show that our method outperforms the state-of-the-art methods by a large margin with higher efficiency, and maintains a robust performance even with higher OOKG entity ratios.

2 Methodology

2.1 Notations and problem formulation

Let $\mathcal{E}$ denote the IKG entity set and $\mathcal{R}$ denote the relation set. $\mathcal{K}_{\text{train}}$ is the training set where all entities are IKG. $\mathcal{K}_{\text{aux}}$ is the auxiliary set connecting OOKG and IKG entities during inference, where each triplet contains an OOKG and an IKG entity. We define the $\mathcal{K}$-neighbor set of an entity e as all its neighbor entities and relations in $\mathcal{K}$: $\mathcal{N}_{\mathcal{K}}(e) = \{(r,t)|(e,r,t) \in \mathcal{K}\} \cup \{(h,r)|(h,r,e) \in \mathcal{K}\}$.

Using notations above, we formulate our problem as follows: Given $\mathcal{K}_{\text{aux}}$ and IKG embeddings pretrained on $\mathcal{K}_{\text{train}}$, we need to represent an OOKG entity $e \notin \mathcal{E}$ as an embedding. This embedding can then be used to tackle KGC with OOKG entities.

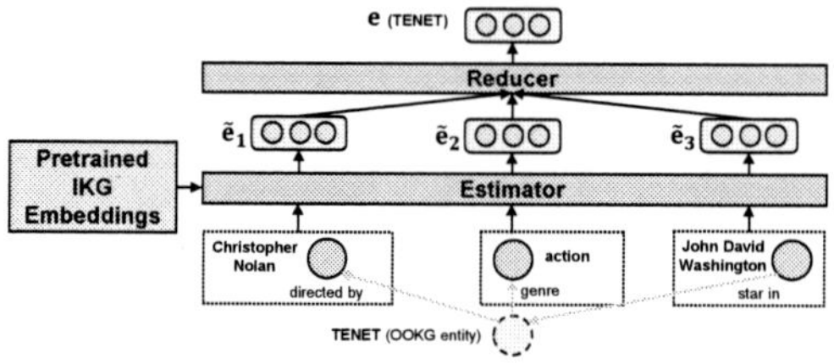

Figure 2: An illustration of our method, which consists of an estimator and a reducer.

2.2 Proposed method

As shown in Figure 2, our proposed method is composed of an estimator and a reducer. The estimator aims to compute a set of candidate embeddings for an OOKG entity via its IKG neighbor information. The reducer aims to reduce these candidates to the final embedding of the OOKG entity.

2.2.1 Estimator

For an OOKG entity e, given its IKG neighbors $\mathcal{N}_{\mathcal{K}_{\text{aux}}}(e)$ with pretrained embeddings, the estimator aims to compute a set of candidate embeddings. Except TransE and RotatE, other typical KGE models have relatively complex calculations in their translational assumptions. These complex calculations prevent their translational assumptions from deriving specific estimation formulas for OOKG entities.[2] Therefore, we design two sets of estimation formulas based on TransE and RotatE, respectively. To be specific, if e is the head entity, we can obtain its optimal estimation $\widetilde{\mathbf{e}}$ by the following formulas:

$$\widetilde{\mathbf{e}} = \begin{cases} \mathbf{t} - \mathbf{r}, & \text{for } \textbf{InvTransE}, \\ \mathbf{t} \circ \mathbf{r}^{-1}, & \text{for } \textbf{InvRotatE}, \end{cases}$$

where $\circ$ denotes the element-wise product, $\mathbf{r}^{-1}$ denotes the element-wise inversion.

Otherwise, if e is the tail entity, we can obtain its optimal estimation $\widetilde{\mathbf{e}}$ by the following formulas:

$$\widetilde{\mathbf{e}} = \begin{cases} \mathbf{h} + \mathbf{r}, & \text{for } \textbf{InvTransE}, \\ \mathbf{h} \circ \mathbf{r}, & \text{for } \textbf{InvRotatE}. \end{cases}$$

2.2.2 Reducer

After the estimator computes $|\mathcal{N}_{\mathcal{K}_{\text{aux}}}(e)|$ candidate embeddings, the reducer aims to reduce them to the

[2] Detailed proof is included in Appendix A.

final embedding of the OOKG entity by weighted average. We design two weighting functions.

Correlation-based weights are query-aware. Inspired by Wang et al. (2019), we first use the conditional probability to model the correlation between two relations:

$$P(r_2|r_1) = \frac{\sum_{e \in \mathcal{E}} \mathbb{1}\left(r_1, r_2 \in \mathcal{N}_{\mathcal{K}_{\text{train}}}(e)\right)}{\sum_{e \in \mathcal{E}} \mathbb{1}\left(r_1 \in \mathcal{N}_{\mathcal{K}_{\text{train}}}(e)\right)}.$$

When the query relation r_q is specified, we assign more weight to the candidate that is computed via a more relevant relation to r_q:

$$w_{\text{corr}}(\widetilde{\mathbf{e}}) = \frac{\left(P\left(r_{\widetilde{\mathbf{e}}}|r_q\right) + P\left(r_q|r_{\widetilde{\mathbf{e}}}\right)\right)^s}{Z_{\text{corr}}},$$

where Z_{corr} is the normalization factor, $r_{\widetilde{\mathbf{e}}}$ is the neighbor relation via which $\widetilde{\mathbf{e}}$ is computed, s is a hyper-parameter set to 4.0.

Degree-based weights focus more on the entity with higher degree in the training set:

$$w_{\text{deg}}(\widetilde{\mathbf{e}}) = \frac{\log\left(d_{\widetilde{\mathbf{e}}} + \delta\right)}{Z_{\text{deg}}},$$

where Z_{deg} is the normalization factor, $d_{\widetilde{\mathbf{e}}}$ is the degree of the neighbor entity via which $\widetilde{\mathbf{e}}$ is computed, δ is a smoothing factor set to 0.1.

Based on these weighting functions, the final embedding of the OOKG entity $\mathbf{e}$ is computed by

$$\mathbf{e} = \sum_{\widetilde{\mathbf{e}} \in C} \widetilde{\mathbf{e}} \cdot w_{\text{corr/deg}}(\widetilde{\mathbf{e}}),$$

where C denotes the candidate embedding set.

3 Experiments

3.1 Tasks and datasets

We conduct experiments on two KGC tasks with OOKG entities: link prediction and triplet classification. For link prediction, we use two datasets released by Wang et al. (2019) built based on FB15k (Bordes et al., 2013): FB15k-Head-10 and FB15k-Tail-10. For triplet classification, we use nine datasets released by Hamaguchi et al. (2017) built based on WN11 (Socher et al., 2013): WN11-Head-1000, WN11-Head-3000, WN11-Head-5000, WN11-Tail-1000, WN11-Tail-3000, WN11-Tail-5000, WN11-Both-1000, WN11-Both-3000, and WN11-Both-5000. Each of the datasets mentioned above is composed of four sets: a training set, an auxiliary set, a validation set, and a test set. Each triplet in the training and validation sets contains only IKG entities. Each triplet in the auxiliary set contains an OOKG entity and an IKG entity. Each triplet in the test set contains at least one OOKG entity. The dataset statistics are shown in Table 1.

3.2 Experimental settings

We tune pretraining hyper-parameters on the validation set. We use Adam (Kingma and Ba, 2015) with an initial learning rate of 10^{-3} as the optimizer and a batch size of 1,024. For link prediction, we use 1,000-dimensional embeddings and the correlation-based weights. For triplet classification, we use 300-dimensional embeddings and the degree-based weights. Details are included in Appendix B.

3.3 Baselines

For link prediction, we compare our method with three strong GNN-based baselines. **GNN-MEAN** (Hamaguchi et al., 2017) uses a mean function to aggregate neighbors. **GNN-LSTM** adopts LSTM for aggregation. **LAN** (Wang et al., 2019) adopts both rule- and network-based attention mechanisms for aggregation. For triplet classification, we compare with two more competitive GNN-based baselines. **ConvLayer** (Bi et al., 2020) uses convolutional layers as the transition function. **FCLEntity** (Zhao et al., 2020) uses fully-connected networks as the transition function with an attention-based aggregation.

3.4 Evaluation metrics

For link prediction, we use Mean Reciprocal Rank (MRR) and the proportion of ground truth entities ranked in top-k (Hits@k, $k \in \{1, 10\}$). All the metrics are filtered versions that exclude false negative candidates. For triplet classification, we use Accuracy. We determine relation-specific thresholds δ_r by maximizing the accuracy on the validation set.

3.5 Main results

Evaluation results of **link prediction** are shown in Table 2. From the table, we observe that: (1) With the optimal estimation under translational assumptions, both instances of our method significantly outperform all baselines. (2) Neighbors are unordered, so order-insensitive methods like ours or LAN perform better, while GNN-LSTM that captures ordered information performs worse. For **triplet classification**, we show the results in Table 3. The table shows that our method achieves the best performance, consistent with the link pre-

Dataset	$\lvert\mathcal{K}_{\text{train}}\rvert$	$\lvert\mathcal{K}_{\text{valid}}\rvert$	$\lvert\mathcal{K}_{\text{aux}}\rvert$	$\lvert\mathcal{K}_{\text{test}}\rvert$	$\lvert\mathcal{R}\rvert$	$\lvert\mathcal{E}\rvert$	$\lvert\mathcal{E}'\rvert$
FB15k-Head-10	108,854	11,339	249,798	2,811	1,170	10,336	2,082
FB15k-Tail-10	99,783	10,190	261,341	2,987	1,126	10,603	1,934
WN11-Head-1000	108,197	4,561	1,938	955	11	37,700	340
WN11-Head-3000	99,963	4,068	5,311	2,686	11	36,646	985
WN11-Head-5000	92,309	3,688	8,048	4,252	11	35,560	1,638
WN11-Tail-1000	96,968	3,864	6,674	852	11	36,771	811
WN11-Tail-3000	78,812	2,851	12,824	2,061	11	33,800	1,874
WN11-Tail-5000	68,040	2,258	15,414	2,968	11	31,311	2,589
WN11-Both-1000	93,683	3,625	7,875	873	11	36,277	1,136
WN11-Both-3000	71,618	2,436	14,453	2,242	11	32,254	2,805
WN11-Both-5000	58,923	1,788	16,660	3,218	11	28,979	3,934

Table 1: Statistics of datasets with OOKG entities. These datasets are built based on FB15k or WN11 and named in the form of "Base-Pos-Num". Base denotes the based datasets. Pos denotes the position of OOKG entities in test triplets. Num distinguishes different numbers of OOKG entities represented by $\lvert\mathcal{E}'\rvert$.

Method	FB15k-Head-10			FB15k-Tail-10		
	MRR	H@10	H@1	MRR	H@10	H@1
GNN-LSTM	0.254	42.9	16.2	0.219	37.3	14.3
GNN-MEAN	0.310	48.0	22.2	0.251	41.0	17.1
LAN	0.394	56.6	30.2	0.314	48.2	22.7
InvTransE	**0.462**	**60.4**	**38.5**	0.357	48.7	29.0
InvRotatE	0.453	**60.4**	36.9	**0.362**	**49.1**	**29.3**

Table 2: Evaluation results (MRR, Hits@k) of link prediction. **Bold** is the best. Underline is the second best.

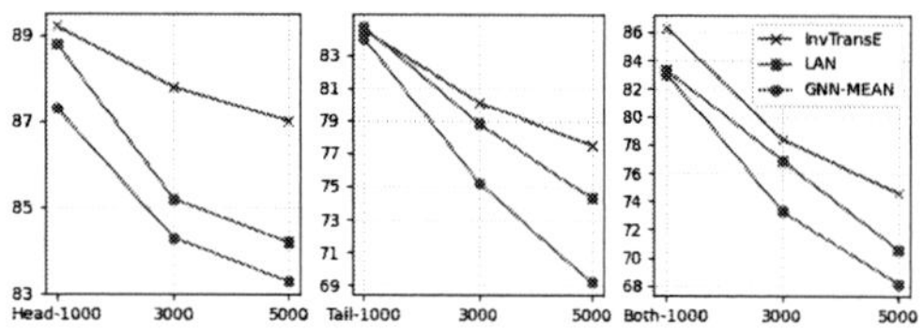

Figure 3: Results with increasing OOKG entity ratios.

diction results. This again validates the effect of our method.

3.6 Analysis

How does our method perform with increasing OOKG entity ratios? We compare the triplet classification results of InvTransE, LAN, and GNN-MEAN with increasing OOKG entity ratios in Figure 3. We find that, when the OOKG entity ratio increases, the performance of our method drops the slowest. This suggests that our method is more robust to increasing OOKG entity ratios.

How efficient is our method? We compare LAN and InvTransE to analyze our efficiency. Considering the time complexity, LAN needs $\mathcal{O}(md^2)$ to represent an entity, where m is the number of neighbors and d is the embedding dimension. By contrast, InvTransE needs only $\mathcal{O}(d)$ and $\mathcal{O}(md)$ to represent an IKG and OOKG entity, respectively. Empirically, taking triplet classification as an example, InvTransE is nearly 15 times faster than LAN under similar configurations. Moreover, when given IKG embeddings pretrained by TransE, InvTransE does not even need training. This suggests that our method is highly efficient.

Do our weighting functions matter? We attempt to reduce candidates with uniform weights. As shown in Table 4, the performance without our weighting functions drops dramatically. This verifies the effectiveness of our weighting functions.

How does the number of neighbors impact the performance? We randomly select up to $k \in \{32, 8, 1\}$ IKG neighbors to use. As shown in Table 4, as the number of used neighbors decreases, the performance drops. This suggests that using more neighbors can lead to better performance. Moreover, we find that InvTransE can outperform previous methods using only up to 32 neighbors.

4 Related Work

Transductive KGE methods map entities and relations to embeddings, and then use score functions to measure the triplet salience. TransE (Bordes et al., 2013) pioneers translational distance methods and is widely-used. It derives a series of methods, such as TransH (Wang et al., 2014), TransR (Lin et al., 2015), and RotatE (Sun et al., 2019). Besides, semantic matching methods form another mainstream (Nickel et al., 2011; Yang et al., 2015; Trouillon et al., 2016; Nickel et al., 2016; Balazevic et al., 2019). These transductive KGE methods achieve success in conventional KGC, but

Method	WN11-Head			WN11-Tail			WN11-Both		
	1000	3000	5000	1000	3000	5000	1000	3000	5000
ConvLayer	-	-	-	-	-	-	74.9	-	64.6
FCLEntity	-	82.6	-	-	72.1	-	-	68.6	-
GNN-LSTM	87.0	83.5	81.8	82.9	71.4	63.1	78.5	71.6	65.8
GNN-MEAN	87.3	84.3	83.3	84.0	75.2	69.2	83.0	73.3	68.2
LAN	88.8	85.2	84.2	**84.7**	78.8	74.3	83.3	76.9	70.6
InvTransE	**89.2**	**87.8**	**87.0**	84.5	**80.1**	**77.5**	**86.3**	**78.4**	**74.6**
InvRotatE	88.6	86.9	86.5	**84.7**	**80.1**	75.8	84.2	75.0	70.6

Table 3: Evaluation results (Accuracy) of triplet classification. **Bold** is the best. Underline is the second best. The results of all five baselines are taken from their original papers.

Method	MRR	H@10	H@1
InvTransE (Full)	0.462	60.4	38.5
Uniform Weights	0.361	52.0	28.1
Up to 32 Neighbors	0.447	59.2	37.2
Up to 8 Neighbors	0.386	52.0	31.3
Only 1 Neighbor	0.246	37.9	18.1

Table 4: Ablation experiment results for InvTransE on the FB15k-Head-10 dataset of link prediction.

fail to directly represent OOKG entities efficiently.

To improve efficiency, some inductive methods adopt GNN to aggregate IKG neighbors to produce embeddings for OOKG entities (Hamaguchi et al., 2017; Wang et al., 2019; Bi et al., 2020; Zhao et al., 2020). These methods are effective but need relatively complex calculations. Other inductive methods incorporate external resources to enrich embeddings and represent OOKG entities via only external resources (Xie et al., 2016; Shi and Weninger, 2018; Xie et al., 2017). However, high-quality external resources are hard and expensive to acquire, which may limit the feasibility.

5 Conclusion

This paper aims to efficiently represent OOKG entities. We propose a simple and effective method that inductively represents OOKG entities by their optimal estimation under translational assumptions. Moreover, given pretrained IKG embeddings, our method needs no additional learning. Evaluations on two KGC tasks show that our method outperforms the state-of-the-art methods by a large margin with higher efficiency, and maintains a robust performance with higher OOKG entity ratios.

Acknowledgments

This paper is supported by the National Key Research and Development Program of China (2020AAA0106700) and NSFC project (U19A2065).

References

Ivana Balazevic, Carl Allen, and Timothy M. Hospedales. 2019. TuckER: Tensor factorization for knowledge graph completion. In *EMNLP-IJCNLP 2019*, pages 5184–5193.

Zhongqin Bi, Tianchen Zhang, Ping Zhou, and Yongbin Li. 2020. Knowledge transfer for out-of-knowledge-base entities: Improving graph-neural-network-based embedding using convolutional layers. *IEEE Access*, 8:159039–159049.

Antoine Bordes, Nicolas Usunier, Alberto Garcia-Duran, Jason Weston, and Oksana Yakhnenko. 2013. Translating embeddings for modeling multi-relational data. In *NeurIPS 2013*, pages 2787–2795.

Takuo Hamaguchi, Hidekazu Oiwa, Masashi Shimbo, and Yuji Matsumoto. 2017. Knowledge transfer for out-of-knowledge-base entities: A graph neural network approach. In *IJCAI 2017*, pages 1802–1808.

Diederik P Kingma and Jimmy Ba. 2015. Adam: A method for stochastic optimization. In *ICLR 2015*.

Yankai Lin, Zhiyuan Liu, Maosong Sun, Yang Liu, and Xuan Zhu. 2015. Learning entity and relation embeddings for knowledge graph completion. In *AAAI 2015*, pages 2181–2187.

Maximilian Nickel, Lorenzo Rosasco, and Tomaso A. Poggio. 2016. Holographic embeddings of knowledge graphs. In *AAAI 2016*, pages 1955–1961.

Maximilian Nickel, Volker Tresp, and Hans-Peter Kriegel. 2011. A three-way model for collective learning on multi-relational data. In *ICML 2011*, pages 809–816.

Baoxu Shi and Tim Weninger. 2018. Open-world knowledge graph completion. In *AAAI 2018*, pages 1957–1964.

Richard Socher, Danqi Chen, Christopher D Manning, and Andrew Ng. 2013. Reasoning with neural tensor networks for knowledge base completion. In *NeurIPS 2013*, pages 926–934.

Zhiqing Sun, Zhi-Hong Deng, Jian-Yun Nie, and Jian Tang. 2019. RotatE: Knowledge graph embedding by relational rotation in complex space. In *ICLR 2019*.

Théo Trouillon, Johannes Welbl, Sebastian Riedel, Éric Gaussier, and Guillaume Bouchard. 2016. ComplEx embeddings for simple link prediction. In *ICML 2016*, pages 2071–2080.

Peifeng Wang, Jialong Han, Chenliang Li, and Rong Pan. 2019. Logic attention based neighborhood aggregation for inductive knowledge graph embedding. In *AAAI 2019*, pages 7152–7159.

Zhen Wang, Jianwen Zhang, Jianlin Feng, and Zheng Chen. 2014. Knowledge graph embedding by translating on hyperplanes. In *AAAI 2014*, pages 1112–1119.

Ruobing Xie, Zhiyuan Liu, Jia Jia, Huanbo Luan, and Maosong Sun. 2016. Representation learning of knowledge graphs with entity descriptions. In *AAAI 2016*, pages 2659–2665.

Ruobing Xie, Zhiyuan Liu, Huanbo Luan, and Maosong Sun. 2017. Image-embodied knowledge representation learning. In *IJCAI 2017*, pages 3140–3146.

Bishan Yang, Wen-tau Yih, Xiaodong He, Jianfeng Gao, and Li Deng. 2015. Embedding entities and relations for learning and inference in knowledge bases. In *ICLR 2015*.

Ming Zhao, Weijia Jia, and Yusheng Huang. 2020. Attention-based aggregation graph networks for knowledge graph information transfer. In *PAKDD 2020*, pages 542–554.

Appendices

A Which Translational Assumptions Can Derive Specific Estimation Formulas for OOKG Entities?

For a triplet (h, r, t), translational assumptions of KGE models suppose that $\mathbf{h}$ can establish a connection with $\mathbf{t}$ via an $\mathbf{r}$-specific operation, which can be formulated by the following equation:

$$\mathcal{F}_{\mathbf{r}}(\mathbf{h}, \mathbf{t}) = 0, \tag{1}$$

where $\mathcal{F}_{\mathbf{r}}(\cdot)$ is an $\mathbf{r}$-specific function that is determined by the specific KGE model. Without loss of generality, we may assume that h is an OOKG entity and t is an IKG entity. Under a translational assumption, we can obtain a specific estimation formula for $\mathbf{h}$ if and only if (1) we regard $\mathbf{h}$ as unknown, and its solution in Equation 1 exists, (2) the solution is unique. If the above two conditions hold, the unique solution of $\mathbf{h}$ is the optimal estimation under the translational assumption, since no other candidate for $\mathbf{h}$ can better fit Equation 1. In the following parts, we analyze translational assumptions of four KGE models (TransE, RotatE, TransH, TransR) as examples.

A.1 TransE

For TransE, its translational assumption is formulated by

$$\mathcal{F}_{\mathbf{r}}(\mathbf{h}, \mathbf{t}) = ||\mathbf{h} + \mathbf{r} - \mathbf{t}||_{1/2} = 0. \tag{2}$$

In this case, we can obtain a unique solution of $\mathbf{h}$ by the following steps:

$$||\mathbf{h} + \mathbf{r} - \mathbf{t}||_{1/2} = 0, \tag{3}$$
$$\Longrightarrow \mathbf{h} + \mathbf{r} - \mathbf{t} = \mathbf{0}, \tag{4}$$
$$\Longrightarrow \mathbf{h} = \mathbf{t} - \mathbf{r}. \tag{5}$$

This computed $\mathbf{h}$ is the optimal estimation under the translational assumption.

A.2 RotatE

For RotatE, its translational assumption is formulated by

$$\mathcal{F}_{\mathbf{r}}(\mathbf{h}, \mathbf{t}) = ||\mathbf{h} \circ \mathbf{r} - \mathbf{t}||_{1/2} = 0. \tag{6}$$

In this case, we can obtain a unique solution of $\mathbf{h}$ by the following steps:

$$||\mathbf{h} \circ \mathbf{r} - \mathbf{t}||_{1/2} = 0, \tag{7}$$
$$\Longrightarrow \mathbf{h} \circ \mathbf{r} - \mathbf{t} = \mathbf{0}, \tag{8}$$
$$\Longrightarrow \mathbf{h} = \mathbf{t} \circ \mathbf{r}^{-1}. \tag{9}$$

This computed $\mathbf{h}$ is the optimal estimation under the translational assumption.

A.3 TransH

For TransH, its translational assumption is formulated by

$$\mathcal{F}_{\mathbf{r}}(\mathbf{h}, \mathbf{t}) = \left\|(\mathbf{h} - \mathbf{w}_r^{\top}\mathbf{h}\mathbf{w}_r) + \mathbf{r} - (\mathbf{t} - \mathbf{w}_r^{\top}\mathbf{t}\mathbf{w}_r)\right\|_{1/2} = 0, \tag{10}$$

where $\mathbf{w}_r$ is the unit normal vector of the plane P that $\mathbf{r}$ lies on. From the translational assumption, we can derive the following equations:

$$\left\|(\mathbf{h} - \mathbf{w}_r^{\top}\mathbf{h}\mathbf{w}_r) + \mathbf{r} - (\mathbf{t} - \mathbf{w}_r^{\top}\mathbf{t}\mathbf{w}_r)\right\|_{1/2} = 0, \tag{11}$$
$$\Longrightarrow (\mathbf{h} - \mathbf{w}_r^{\top}\mathbf{h}\mathbf{w}_r) + \mathbf{r} - (\mathbf{t} - \mathbf{w}_r^{\top}\mathbf{t}\mathbf{w}_r) = \mathbf{0}, \tag{12}$$
$$\Longrightarrow (\mathbf{h} - \mathbf{w}_r^{\top}\mathbf{h}\mathbf{w}_r) = (\mathbf{t} - \mathbf{w}_r^{\top}\mathbf{t}\mathbf{w}_r) - \mathbf{r} \triangleq \mathbf{v}. \tag{13}$$

Datasets	d	γ	α	n	L2	Training Steps
FB15k-based	1,000	24.0	1.0	256	N/A	100,000
WN11-based	300	0.5	1.0	128	10^{-5}	20,000

Table 5: Hyper-parameters for two categories of datasets. We use the same hyper-parameters for two FB15k-based datasets and the same hyper-parameters for nine WN11-based datasets. On each dataset, we use the same hyper-parameters for two pretrained models. d denotes the embedding dimension. γ denotes the margin. α denotes the sampling temperature. n denotes the negative sampling size. L2 denotes the parameter of L2 regularization, where N/A means no regularization.

From a geometric perspective, $\mathbf{h} - \mathbf{w}_r^\top \mathbf{h}\mathbf{w}_r$ is the projection of $\mathbf{h}$ on the plane P. From the translational assumption, we can only deduce that the projection of $\mathbf{h}$ is equal to $\mathbf{v}$. However, there exist infinitely many possible $\mathbf{h}$ that can satisfy this condition. Therefore, the solution of $\mathbf{h}$ is not unique, and we cannot obtain a specific estimation formula from the translational assumption of TransH.

A.4 TransR

For TransR, its translational assumption is formulated by

$$\mathcal{F}_{\mathbf{r}}(\mathbf{h}, \mathbf{t}) = ||\mathbf{M}_r\mathbf{h} + \mathbf{r} - \mathbf{M}_r\mathbf{t}||_{1/2} = 0, \quad (14)$$

where $\mathbf{M}_r$ is an r-specific matrix. From the translational assumption, we can derive the following equations:

$$||\mathbf{M}_r\mathbf{h} + \mathbf{r} - \mathbf{M}_r\mathbf{t}||_{1/2} = 0, \quad (15)$$

$$\Longrightarrow \mathbf{M}_r\mathbf{h} + \mathbf{r} - \mathbf{M}_r\mathbf{t} = \mathbf{0}, \quad (16)$$

$$\Longrightarrow \mathbf{M}_r\mathbf{h} = \mathbf{M}_r\mathbf{t} - \mathbf{r} \triangleq \mathbf{v}. \quad (17)$$

In this case, we derive a system of linear equations from the translational assumption. In this system, there exists a unique solution for $\mathbf{h}$ if and only if the rank of the coefficient matrix $\mathbf{M}_r$ is equal to the rank of the augmented matrix $[\mathbf{M}_r; \mathbf{v}]$. However, $\mathbf{M}_r$ is automatically learned by TransR without this restriction. Therefore, we cannot guarantee that there exists a unique solution for $\mathbf{h}$, and we cannot obtain a specific estimation formula from the translational assumption of TransR.

B Details of Experimental Settings

To pretrain the TransE and RotatE models, we adopt the self-adversarial negative sampling loss proposed by Sun et al. (2019) in consideration of its good performance on training TransE and RotatE. The self-adversarial negative sampling loss L is formulated as:

$$\begin{aligned} L = & -\log \sigma (\gamma - \mathcal{D}(\mathbf{h}, \mathbf{r}, \mathbf{t})) \\ & - \sum_{i=1}^{n} p(h'_i, r, t'_i) \log \sigma (\mathcal{D}(\mathbf{h}'_i, \mathbf{r}, \mathbf{t}'_i) - \gamma), \end{aligned} \quad (18)$$

where σ is the sigmoid function, γ is the margin, n is the negative sampling size and (h'_i, r, t'_i) is the i-th negative sample triplet. $\mathcal{D}(\cdot)$ is the distance function. $\mathcal{D}(\mathbf{h}, \mathbf{r}, \mathbf{t})$ is equal to $||\mathbf{h} + \mathbf{r} - \mathbf{t}||_{1/2}$ for TransE and is equal to $||\mathbf{h} \circ \mathbf{r} - \mathbf{t}||_{1/2}$ for RotatE. p is the self-adversarial weight function which gives more weight to the high-scored negative samples:

$$p(h'_i, r, t'_i) \propto \exp(\alpha \cdot \mathcal{F}(\mathbf{h}'_i, \mathbf{r}, \mathbf{t}'_i)), \quad (19)$$

where α is a hyper-parameter called sampling temperature to be tuned. $\mathcal{F}(\cdot)$ is the score function that is equal to $-\mathcal{D}(\cdot)$.

We conduct each experiment on a single Nvidia Geforce GTX-1080Ti GPU and tune hyper-parameters on the validation set. Generally, we set the batch size to 1,024 and use Adam (Kingma and Ba, 2015) with an initial learning rate of 10^{-3} as the optimizer. We choose the correlation-based weights for link prediction and choose the degree-based weights with a smoothing factor of 0.1 for triplet classification. Other hyper-parameters are shown in Table 5.

Revisiting Pretraining with Adapters

Seungwon Kim, Alex Shum, Nathan Susanj, Jonathan Hilgart
Georgia Institute of Technology
{skim3222, ashum7, nsusanj3, jhilgart3}@gatech.edu

Abstract

Pretrained language models have served as the backbone for many state-of-the-art NLP results. These models are large and expensive to train. Recent work suggests that continued pretraining on task-specific data is worth the effort as pretraining leads to improved performance on downstream tasks. We explore alternatives to full-scale task-specific pretraining of language models through the use of adapter modules, a parameter-efficient approach to transfer learning. We find that adapter-based pretraining is able to achieve comparable results to task-specific pretraining while using a fraction of the overall trainable parameters. We further explore direct use of adapters without pretraining and find that the direct fine-tuning performs mostly on par with pretrained adapter models, contradicting previously proposed benefits of continual pretraining in full pretraining fine-tuning strategies. Lastly, we perform an ablation study on task-adaptive pretraining to investigate how different hyperparameter settings can change the effectiveness of the pretraining.

1 Introduction

Pretrained Language Models (PLM) are predominant in tackling current Natural Language Processing (NLP) tasks. Most PLMs based on the Transformer architecture (Vaswani et al., 2017) are first trained on massive text corpora with the self-supervised objective to learn word representations (Devlin et al., 2019; Liu et al., 2019), and then are fine-tuned for a specific target task. The pretraining and fine-tuning of PLMs achieves state-of-the-art (SOTA) performance in many NLP tasks. Inspired by the benefits of pretraining, there have been studies demonstrate the effects of continued pretraining on the domain of a target task or the target task dataset (Mitra et al., 2020; Han and Eisenstein, 2019; Gururangan et al., 2020). Gururangan et al., 2020 adapt PLMs on the target task by further pretraining RoBERTa (Liu et al., 2019) on the target text corpus before it is fine-tuned for the corresponding task and showed that this task adaptation consistently improves the performance for text classification tasks.

However, this full process of pretraining and then fine-tuning can be parameter inefficient for recent PLMs that have millions or billions of parameters (Devlin et al., 2019; Radford et al., 2018). This parameter inefficiency becomes even worse when one continues pre-training all the parameters of PLMs on the task-specific corpus. Furthermore, recent PLMs need more than 100s of MB to store all the weights (Liu et al., 2019; Radford et al., 2018), making it difficult to download and share the pre-trained models on the fly.

Recently, adapters have been proposed as an alternative approach to decrease the substantial number of parameters of PLMs in the fine-tuning stage (Houlsby et al., 2019). Finetuning with adapters mostly matches the performance of those with the full fine-tuning strategy on many NLP tasks including GLUE benchmark (Wang et al., 2018) and reduces the size of the model from 100s of MB to the order of MB (Pfeiffer et al., 2020b). As such, a natural question arises from the successes of the adapter approach: can the adapter alone adapt PLMs to the target task when it is used in the second phase of the pretraining stage and thus lead to the improvement of the performance on the corresponding task?

In this paper, we explore task-adaptive pretraining, termed TAPT (Gururangan et al., 2020), with adapters to address this question and overcome the limitations of the conventional full pretraining and fine-tuning. We only train the adapter modules in the second phase of pretraining as well as the fine-tuning stage to achieve both parameter efficiency and the benefits of continual pretraining and compare those with the adapter-based model without pretraining. Surprisingly, we find that directly

Proceedings of the 6th Workshop on Representation Learning for NLP (RepL4NLP-2021), pages 90–99
Bangkok, Thailand (Online), August 6, 2021.

fine-tuning adapters performs mostly on par with the pre-trained adapter model and outperforms the full TAPT, contradicting the previously proposed benefits of continual pretraining in the full pretraining fine-tuning scheme. As directly fine-tuning adapters skips the second phase of pretraining and the training steps of adapters are faster than those of the full model, it substantially reduces the training time. We further investigate different hyperparameter settings that affect the effectiveness of pretraining.

2 Pretraining and Adapters

Pre-trained language model We use RoBERTa (Liu et al., 2019), a Transformer-based language model that is pre-trained on a massive text corpus, following Gururangan et al., 2020. RoBERTa is an extension of BERT (Devlin et al., 2019) with optimized hyperparameters and a modification of the pretraining objective, which excludes next sentence prediction and only uses the randomly masked tokens in the input sentence. To evaluate the performance of RoBERTa on a certain task, a classification layer is appended on top of the language model after the pretraining and all the parameters in RoBERTa are trained in a supervised way using the label of the dataset. In this paper, training word representations using RoBERTa on a masked language modeling task will be referred to as pretraining. Further, taking this pretrained model and adding a classification layer with additional updates to the language model parameters will be referred to as fine-tuning.

Task-adaptive pretraining (TAPT) Although RoBERTa achieves strong performance by simply fine-tuning the PLMs on a target task, there can be a distributional mismatch between the pretraining and target corpora. To address this issue, pretraining on the target task or the domain of the target task can be usefully employed to adapt the language models to the target task and it further improves the performance of the PLMs. Such methods can be referred to as Domain-Adaptive Pretraining (DAPT) or Task Adaptive-Pretraining (TAPT) (Gururangan et al., 2020). In this paper, we limit the scope of our works to TAPT as domain text corpus is not always available for each task, whereas TAPT can be easily applied by directly using the dataset of the target task while its performance often matches with DAPT (Gururangan et al., 2020). In TAPT, the second phase of pretraining is performed with RoBERTa using the unlabeled text corpus of the target task, and then it is fine-tuned on the target task.

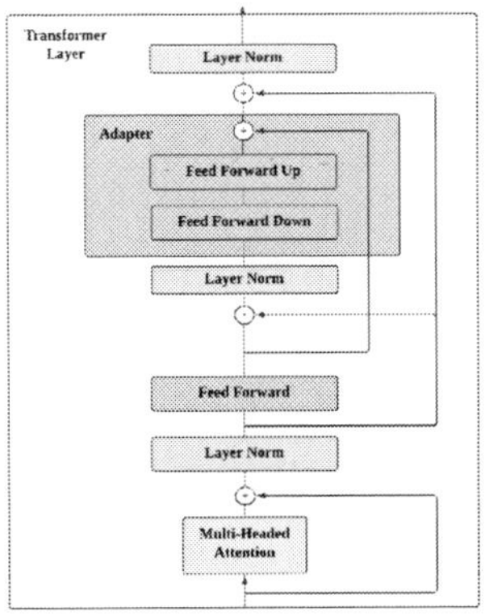

Figure 1: The adapter achitecture in the Transformer layer (Pfeiffer et al., 2020a)

Adapter Adapter modules have been employed as a feature extractor in computer vision (Rebuffi et al., 2017) and have been recently adopted in the NLP literature as an alternative approach to fully fine-tuning PLMs. Adapters are sets of new weights that are typically embedded in each transformer layer of PLMs and consist of feed-forward layers with normalizations, residual connections, and projection layers. The architectures of adapters vary with respect to the different configuration settings. We use the configuration proposed by Pfeiffer et al., 2020a in Figure 1, which turned out to be effective on diverse NLP tasks, and add the adapter layer to each transformer layer.

Pfeiffer et al., 2020c use two types of adapter: language-specific adapters and task-specific adapters for cross-lingual transfer. These two types of adapter modules have similar architecture as in Figure 1. However, the language adapters involve invertible adapters after the embedding layer to capture token-level language representation when those are trained via masked language modeling in the pretraining stage, whereas the task adapters are simply embedded in each transformer layer and trained in the fine-tuning stage to learn the task representation. Following Pfeiffer et al., 2020c, we employ language adapter modules with invertible adapter layers to perform pretraining adapters on the unlabeled target dataset. However, we perform fine-tuning pre-trained parameters of the language adapter modules for evaluation to align with

Domain	Task	Label type	Number of inst (Train/Dev/Test)	Classes
Biomedical	CHEMPROT	Relationship classification	4169 / 2427 / 3469	13
Biomedical	RCT	Abstract sentence roles	18040 / 30212 / 30135	5
Computer Science	ACL-ARC	Citation intent	1688 / 114 / 139	6
Computer Science	SCIERC	Relation classification	3219 / 455 / 974	7
News	HYPERPARTISAN	Partisanship	515 / 65 / 65	2
News	AGNEWS	Topic	115000 / 5000 / 7600	4
Reviews	HELPFULNESS	Review helpfulness	115251 / 5000 / 25000	2
Reviews	IMDB	Review sentiment	20000 / 5000 / 25000	2

Table 1: Datasets used for experimentation. Datasets include both high-resource (RCT (Dernoncourt and Lee, 2017), AGNEWS (Zhang et al., 2015), HELPFULNESS (McAuley et al., 2015), IMDB (Maas et al., 2011)) and low-resource (CHEMPROT (Kringelum et al., 2016), ACL-ARC (Jurgens et al., 2018), SCIERC (Luan et al., 2018), HYPERPARTISAN (Kiesel et al., 2019) settings.

TAPT, whereas Pfeiffer et al., 2020c employ both the language and the task adapters by stacking task adapters on top of the language adapters.

3 Experiments

We now propose an adapter-based approach that is a parameter efficient variant of Task-Adaptive Pretraining (TAPT) and measure the margin of the performance between the pre-trained adapter model and the adapter model without pretraining. For pretraining adapters, we added the adapter module in each transformer layer of RoBERTa using adapter-transformer (Pfeiffer et al., 2020b)[1] and continued pretraining all the weights in adapter layers on target text corpus while keeping the original parameters in RoBERTa fixed. After finishing the second phase of pretraining, we performed fine-tuning of RoBERTa by training the weights in the adapters and the final classification layers while keeping all of the parameters in RoBERTa frozen.

3.1 Dataset

Following Gururangan et al., 2020 [2], we consider 8 classification tasks from 4 different domains. The specification of each task is shown in Table 1. We covered news and review texts that are similar to the pretraining corpus of RoBERTa as well as scientific domains in which text corpora can have largely different distributions from those of RoBERTa. Furthermore, the pretraining corpora of the target tasks include both large and small cases to determine whether the adapter-based approach can be applicable in both low and high-resource settings.

[1]https://github.com/Adapter-Hub/adapter-transformers

[2]Downloadble link for task dataset: https://github.com/allenai/dont-stop-pretraining

3.2 Implementation Details

Our implementation is based on HuggingFace since we found AllenNLP (Gardner et al., 2018) used in Gururangan et al., 2020 is incompatible with adapter-transformer (Pfeiffer et al., 2020b). We follow the hyperparameters setting in Gururangan et al., 2020, and each model in the pretraining and fine-tuning stage is trained on a single GPU (NVIDIA RTX 3090). Details of hyperparameters are described in Appendix A. Note that for the pretraining step, we use a batch size of 8 and accumulate the gradient for every 32 steps to be consistent with the hyperparameter setting in Gururangan et al., 2020.

We perform pretraining with the self-supervised objectives, which are randomly masked tokens, with a probability of 15% for each epoch and we do not apply validation to pretraining and save the model at the end of the training from a single seed. For TAPT, we train the entire parameters of the RoBERTa via masked language modeling (MLM) on the target dataset, whereas for the adapter-based model, we embed the language adapters in each transformer layer and add invertible adapters after the embedding layers to perform MLM while freezing the original parameters of RoBERTa, following Pfeiffer et al., 2020c. Fine-tuning step is straightforward. We perform fine-tuning parameters that are pretrained via MLM for both TAPT and the adapter model. Validation is performed after each epoch and the best checkpoint is loaded at the end of the training to evaluate the performance on the test set.

3.3 Experimental setup

Experiments cover four different models. First, we reproduce the performance of RoBERTa and TAPT in Gururangan et al., 2020 as presented in Appendix C. Then we proceed to the adapter-based approach.

Dataset	Baseline RoBERTa	TAPT	Adapter w/o PT	Adapter w/ PT
CHEMPROT	81.9 $_{1.0}$	82.6 $_{0.4}$	82.69 $_{0.4}$	**82.71** $_{0.4}$
RCT	87.2 $_{0.1}$	**87.7** $_{0.1}$	87.35 $_{0.04}$	87.4 $_{0.1}$
ACL-ARC	63.0 $_{5.8}$	67.4 $_{1.8}$	**69.47** $_{2.4}$	69.25 $_{2.5}$
SCIERC	77.3 $_{1.9}$	79.3 $_{1.5}$	81.5 $_{0.9}$	**82.37** $_{1.0}$
HYPERPARTISAN	86.6 $_{0.9}$	90.4 $_{5.2}$	**93.01** $_{4.7}$	84.97 $_{6.4}$
AGNEWS	93.9 $_{0.2}$	**94.5** $_{0.1}$	94.00 $_{0.1}$	93.94 $_{0.1}$
HELPFULNESS	65.1 $_{3.4}$	68.5 $_{1.9}$	**70.96** $_{0.6}$	70.83 $_{0.8}$
IMDB	95.0 $_{0.2}$	95.5 $_{0.1}$	95.51 $_{0.1}$	**95.57** $_{0.1}$
Average F_1	81.3	83.24	**84.31**	83.38
Trainable params per task (PT/FT)	-/124.64M	163.35M/124.64M	**-/1.78M**	2.18M/2.08M
Ratio to total params (PT/FT)	-/100%	100% /100%	**-/1.42%**	1.32%/1.65%
Relative training speed (PT/FT)	-/1.0	1.0/1.0	**-/1.29**	1.14/1.24
Relative inference speed (PT/FT)	**-/1.0**	**1.0/1.0**	-/0.98	0.88/0.98

Table 2: Average F_1 score with standard deviation on test set. Each score is averaged over 5 random seeds. Evaluation metric is macro-F_1 scores on test set for each task except for CHMEPROT and RCT which use micro-F_1. We report the results of baseline RoBERTa and TAPT from Gururangan et al., 2020. Following Rücklé et al., 2020, we measure the average relative speed for the training and the inference time across all tasks except for the the inference speed in fine-tuning stage, which excludes low-resource tasks. PT and FT indicate pretraining and fine-tuning respectively.

To investigate the benefits of task-adaptive pretraining with adapters, we compare the performance of the pre-trained adapter model with the model without pretraining, i.e., directly fine-tuning adapters in RoBERTa on the target task.

For the adapter-based approach, we compare the adapter-based model with the second phase of pretraining and the model without the pretraining. Since the weights of the adapters are randomly initialized, we empirically found that a larger learning rate worked well compared to the full fine-tuning experiments. We sweep the learning rates in {2e-5, 1e-4, 3e-4, 6e-4} and the number of epochs in {10, 20} on the validation set and report the test score that performs the best on the validation set.

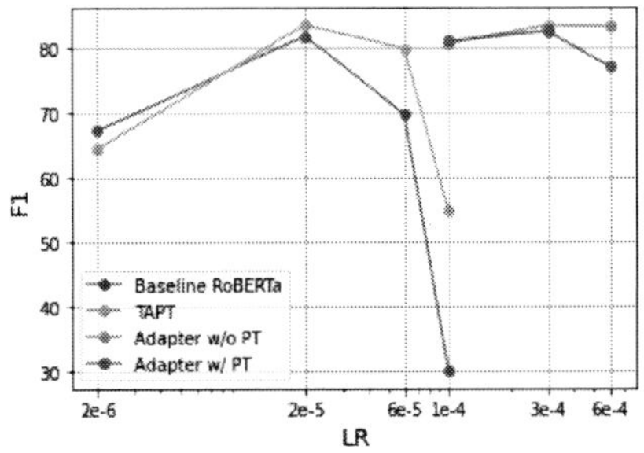

Figure 2: F_1 score as a function of learning rate on test set with log scale on x-axis. F_1 score is averaged over 5 random seeds for low-resource tasks (CHEMPROT, ACL-ARC, SCIERC, HYPER) due to the high variance. For high-resource tasks (RCT, AGNEWS, HELPFULNESS, IMDB), we report the F_1 score from a single random seed for each task. For RoBERTa and TAPT, we follow the hyper-parameter settings in Gururangan et al., 2020 except for the learning rate.

3.4 Results

The results are summarized in Table 2. Surprisingly, for the average F_1 score, the adapter-based model without task-adaptive pretraining performs best, followed by the other adapter with the pretraining model, TAPT, and the baseline RoBERTa. Except for Hyperpartisan news, the adapter model without pretraining performs mostly on par with the counterpart adapter model that involves pretraining on target text corpus, suggesting that the benefits of additional task-adaptive pretraining diminish when we use the adapter-based approach. Furthermore, directly fine-tuned adapter model only trains 1.42% of the entire parameters which leads to the 30% faster-training step than the full model and skips the pretraining stage that typically expensive to train than the fine-tuning, substantially reducing the training time while the relative speed for the inference only decreases by 2% to the full model.

3.5 Analysis

We analyze how the adapter alone can surpass or perform on par with both the full model and adapter model with task-adaptive pretraining. Since we sweep the learning rates and the number of epochs in the range that includes larger figures compared to those in the full model when fine-tuning adapters and kept the other hyper-parameters the same as in Gururangan et al., 2020, we hypothesize that

Dataset	Baseline RoBERTa	TAPT
CHEMPROT	**82.8** $_{0.9}$	82.62 $_{0.5}$
RCT	86.89 $_{0.1}$	**87.4** $_{0.2}$
ACL-ARC	69.24 $_{2.6}$	**70.08** $_{2.3}$
SCIERC	80.59 $_{0.9}$	**81.28** $_{1.2}$
HYPER	**94.53** $_{2.0}$	86.17 $_{1.3}$
AGNEWS	93.9 $_{0.2}$	**94.05** $_{0.1}$
HELPFUL	69.63 $_{0.6}$	**71.28** $_{0.8}$
IMDB	94.93 $_{0.1}$	**95.33** $_{0.1}$
Average F_1	**84.06**	83.52

Table 3: Best performance of baseline RoBERTa and TAPT (Gururangan et al., 2020) on our implementation. Each score is averaged over 5 random seeds. Best configuration settings for each task is described in Appendix Table 8.

the larger learning rate zeroes out the benefits of pretraining. Figure 2. shows the average F_1 score across all tasks as a function of learning rate.

The adapter model without a second phase of pretraining consistently outperforms or performs on par with the adapter model with pretraining from 1e-4 to 6e-4, demonstrating that the additional pretraining turns out to be ineffective. In contrast, TAPT outperforms baseline RoBERTa from 2e-5, where both TAPT and baseline RoBERTa perform best. The results show that different learning rates used in the fine-tuning stage can affect the effectiveness of pretraining and demonstrate that directly fine-tuning a fraction of parameters can provide comparable performance to the full-model as well as the adapter model with pretraining while substantially reducing the training time.

Inspired by the results of the adapter models, we perform the same experiments for the full model (baseline RoBERTa and TAPT) on our implementation by sweeping the learning rates and the number of epochs. We hypothesize that proper hyper-parameter settings such as a larger learning rate or increasing the number of training steps in the fine-tuning stage can improve the performance of baseline RoBERTa, making pretraining on the unlabeled target task less effective. We sweep the learning rates in $\{$1e-5, 2e-5, 3e-5$\}$ and the number of epochs in $\{10, 20\}$ on the validation set and report the test score that performs the best on the validation set. Table 3 shows the best performance of the full models for each task among different hyper-parameter settings. The average F_1 score of baseline RoBERTa greatly increases and surprisingly, it surpasses the performance of TAPT in some tasks. The results ensure that although pretraining PLMs on the target task results in better performance, one can achieve comparable performance by simply using a larger learning rate or increasing training steps in the fine-tuning stage while skipping the pretraining step that is computationally demanding compared to the fine-tuning.

4 Conclusion

Our work demonstrates that adapters provide a competitive alternative to large-scale task-adaptive pretraining for NLP classification tasks. We show that it is possible to achieve similar performance to TAPT with pretraining training just 1.32% of the parameters through pretraining with adapters. However, the most computationally efficient option is to skip pretraining and only perform fine-tuning with adapters. We found that skipping pretraining altogether and just fine-tuning with adapters outperforms or performs mostly on par with TAPT and the adapter model with pretraining across our tasks while substantially reducing the training time.

Acknowledgments

We would like to thank Zsolt Kira, Mandeep Baines, Shruti Bhosale, and Siddharth Goyal for helpful feedback and suggestions. We also would like to thank anonymous reviewers for their insightful comments on the earlier version of the paper.

References

Franck Dernoncourt and Ji Young Lee. 2017. PubMed 200k RCT: a dataset for sequential sentence classification in medical abstracts. In *Proceedings of the Eighth International Joint Conference on Natural Language Processing (Volume 2: Short Papers)*, pages 308–313, Taipei, Taiwan. Asian Federation of Natural Language Processing.

Jacob Devlin, Ming-Wei Chang, Kenton Lee, and Kristina Toutanova. 2019. BERT: Pre-training of deep bidirectional transformers for language understanding. In *Proceedings of the 2019 Conference of the North American Chapter of the Association for Computational Linguistics: Human Language Technologies, Volume 1 (Long and Short Papers)*, pages 4171–4186, Minneapolis, Minnesota. Association for Computational Linguistics.

Matt Gardner, Joel Grus, Mark Neumann, Oyvind Tafjord, Pradeep Dasigi, Nelson F. Liu, Matthew Peters, Michael Schmitz, and Luke Zettlemoyer. 2018. AllenNLP: A deep semantic natural language processing platform. In *Proceedings of Workshop for NLP Open Source Software (NLP-OSS)*, pages 1–6, Melbourne, Australia. Association for Computational Linguistics.

Suchin Gururangan, Ana Marasović, Swabha Swayamdipta, Kyle Lo, Iz Beltagy, Doug Downey, and Noah A. Smith. 2020. Don't stop pretraining: Adapt language models to domains and tasks. In *Proceedings of the 58th Annual Meeting of the Association for Computational Linguistics*, pages 8342–8360, Online. Association for Computational Linguistics.

Xiaochuang Han and Jacob Eisenstein. 2019. Unsupervised domain adaptation of contextualized embeddings for sequence labeling. In *EMNLP*.

Neil Houlsby, Andrei Giurgiu, Stanislaw Jastrzebski, Bruna Morrone, Quentin De Laroussilhe, Andrea Gesmundo, Mona Attariyan, and Sylvain Gelly. 2019. Parameter-efficient transfer learning for NLP. In *Proceedings of the 36th International Conference on Machine Learning*, volume 97 of *Proceedings of Machine Learning Research*, pages 2790–2799. PMLR.

David Jurgens, Srijan Kumar, Raine Hoover, Dan McFarland, and Dan Jurafsky. 2018. Measuring the evolution of a scientific field through citation frames. *Transactions of the Association for Computational Linguistics*, 6:391–406.

Johannes Kiesel, Maria Mestre, Rishabh Shukla, Emmanuel Vincent, Payam Adineh, David Corney, Benno Stein, and Martin Potthast. 2019. SemEval-2019 task 4: Hyperpartisan news detection. In *Proceedings of the 13th International Workshop on Semantic Evaluation*, pages 829–839, Minneapolis, Minnesota, USA. Association for Computational Linguistics.

Jens Kringelum, Sonny Kim Kjaerulff, Søren Brunak, Ole Lund, Tudor I Oprea, and Olivier Taboureau. 2016. Chemprot-3.0: a global chemical biology diseases mapping. *Database*, 2016.

Yinhan Liu, Myle Ott, Naman Goyal, Jingfei Du, Mandar Joshi, Danqi Chen, Omer Levy, Mike Lewis, Luke Zettlemoyer, and Veselin Stoyanov. 2019. Roberta: A robustly optimized bert pretraining approach. *arXiv preprint arXiv:1907.11692*.

Yi Luan, Luheng He, Mari Ostendorf, and Hannaneh Hajishirzi. 2018. Multi-task identification of entities, relations, and coreference for scientific knowledge graph construction. In *Proceedings of the 2018 Conference on Empirical Methods in Natural Language Processing*, pages 3219–3232, Brussels, Belgium. Association for Computational Linguistics.

Andrew L. Maas, Raymond E. Daly, Peter T. Pham, Dan Huang, Andrew Y. Ng, and Christopher Potts. 2011. Learning word vectors for sentiment analysis. In *Proceedings of the 49th Annual Meeting of the Association for Computational Linguistics: Human Language Technologies*, pages 142–150, Portland, Oregon, USA. Association for Computational Linguistics.

Julian McAuley, Christopher Targett, Qinfeng Shi, and Anton Van Den Hengel. 2015. Image-based recommendations on styles and substitutes. In *Proceedings of the 38th international ACM SIGIR conference on research and development in information retrieval*, pages 43–52.

Arindam Mitra, Pratyay Banerjee, Kuntal Kumar Pal, Swaroop Ranjan Mishra, and Chitta Baral. 2020. Exploring ways to incorporate additional knowledge to improve natural language commonsense question answering. arXiv:1909.08855v3.

Jonas Pfeiffer, Aishwarya Kamath, Andreas Rücklé, Kyunghyun Cho, and Iryna Gurevych. 2020a. Adapterfusion: Non-destructive task composition for transfer learning. *arXiv preprint arXiv:2005.00247*.

Jonas Pfeiffer, Andreas Rücklé, Clifton Poth, Aishwarya Kamath, Ivan Vulić, Sebastian Ruder, Kyunghyun Cho, and Iryna Gurevych. 2020b. AdapterHub: A framework for adapting transformers. In *Proceedings of the 2020 Conference on Empirical Methods in Natural Language Processing: System Demonstrations*, pages 46–54, Online. Association for Computational Linguistics.

Jonas Pfeiffer, Ivan Vulić, Iryna Gurevych, and Sebastian Ruder. 2020c. MAD-X: An Adapter-Based Framework for Multi-Task Cross-Lingual Transfer. In *Proceedings of the 2020 Conference on Empirical Methods in Natural Language Processing (EMNLP)*, pages 7654–7673, Online. Association for Computational Linguistics.

Alec Radford, Karthik Narasimhan, Tim Salimans, and Ilya Sutskever. 2018. Improving language understanding by generative pre-training.

Sylvestre-Alvise Rebuffi, Hakan Bilen, and Andrea Vedaldi. 2017. Learning multiple visual domains with residual adapters. In *Advances in Neural Information Processing Systems*, volume 30, pages 506–516. Curran Associates, Inc.

Andreas Rücklé, Gregor Geigle, Max Glockner, Tilman Beck, Jonas Pfeiffer, Nils Reimers, and Iryna Gurevych. 2020. Adapterdrop: On the efficiency of adapters in transformers. *arXiv preprint arXiv:2010.11918*.

Ashish Vaswani, Noam Shazeer, Niki Parmar, Jakob Uszkoreit, Llion Jones, Aidan N Gomez, Ł ukasz Kaiser, and Illia Polosukhin. 2017. Attention is all you need. In *Advances in Neural Information Processing Systems*, volume 30, pages 5998–6008. Curran Associates, Inc.

Alex Wang, Amanpreet Singh, Julian Michael, Felix Hill, Omer Levy, and Samuel Bowman. 2018. GLUE: A multi-task benchmark and analysis platform for natural language understanding. In *Proceedings of the 2018 EMNLP Workshop BlackboxNLP: Analyzing and Interpreting Neural Networks for NLP*, pages 353–355, Brussels, Belgium. Association for Computational Linguistics.

Xiang Zhang, Junbo Zhao, and Yann LeCun. 2015. Character-level convolutional networks for text classification. In *Advances in Neural Information Processing Systems*, volume 28, pages 649–657. Curran Associates, Inc.

A Hyperparameter Details

Details of hyperparameter setting including the learning rates for the best performing results are provided in Table 4, 5, and 6.

B Validation Results

We present validation performance in Table 7 and Figure 3 and 8.

C Replication results

We provide replication results of Gururangan et al., 2020 in Table 9.

Hyper-parameter	Value
Optimizer	Adam
Adam epsilon	1e-8, 0.999
Learning rate	1e-4
Batch size	8
Gradient accumulation step	32
Epochs	40 or 100
Adapter reduction factor	12
Maximum sequence length	512

Table 4: Details of hyperparameters used in pretraining experiments. We used 40 number of epochs for HELPFULNESS and 100 for the other tasks.

Hyper-parameter	Value
Optimizer	Adam
Adam epsilon	1e-8, 0.999
Batch size	16
Gradient accumulation step	1
Epochs	10 or 20
Patience	3 or 5
Adapter reduction factor	12
Dropout	0.1
Feedforward layer	1
Feedforward nonlinearity	tanh
Classification layer	1
Learning rate	see Table 6
Learning rate decay	linear
Warmup proportion	0.06
Maximum sequence length	512

Table 5: Details of hyperparameters used in fine-tuning experiments. For baseline RoBERTa and TAPT, we used 10 number of epochs with patience of 3 and the learning rate of 2e-5. For adapter experiments, see Table 6.

Dataset	Adapter w/o PT (LR, Epochs, Patience)	Adapter w/ PT (LR, Epochs, Patience)
CHEMPROT	3e-4, 20, 5	6e-4, 20, 5
RCT	1e-4, 10, 3	1e-4, 10, 3
ACL-ARC	6e-4, 10, 3	6e-4, 20, 5
SCIERC	3e-4, 20, 5	6e-4, 20, 5
HYPER	3e-4, 20, 5	1e-4, 20, 5
AGNEWS	1e-4, 10, 3	1e-4, 10, 3
HELPFUL	3e-4, 20, 5	1e-4, 20, 5
IMDB	1e-4, 10, 3	1e-4, 10, 3

Table 6: Learning rate, the nubmer of epochs and patience for best-performing models. For adapter experiments, we sweep the learning rates in {1e-4, 3e-4, 6e-4}, the number of epochs in {10, 20}, and patience factor in {3, 5} on validation set.

Dataset	Adapter w/o pretraining	Adapter w/ pretraining
CHEMPROT	83.77 $_{0.5}$	84.02 $_{0.7}$
RCT	88.16 $_{0.1}$	88.13 $_{0.1}$
ACL-ARC	72.41 $_{2.2}$	77.31 $_{2.9}$
SCIERC	86.86 $_{0.5}$	87.87 $_{0.3}$
HYPER	86.33 $_{1.4}$	86.00 $_{3.5}$
AGNEWS	94.28 $_{0.1}$	94.57 $_{0.1}$
HELPFUL	70.83 $_{1.2}$	70.8 $_{0.7}$
IMDB	95.52 $_{0.1}$	95.6 $_{0.1}$
Average F_1	84.77	85.54

Table 7: Validation performance of adapter experiments. Each score is averaged over 5 random seeds. Evaluation metric is macro-F_1 scores for each task except for CHMEPROT and RCT which use micro-F_1.

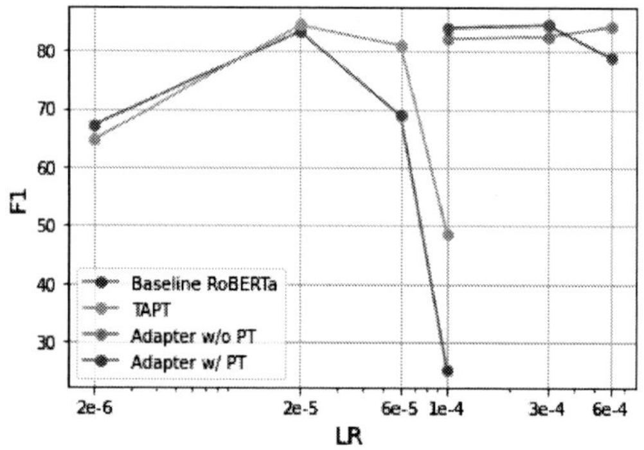

Figure 3: F_1 score as a function of learning rate on development setwith log scale on x-axis. F_1 score is averaged over 5 random seeds for low-resource tasks (CHEMPROT, ACL-ARC, SCIERC, HYPER) due to the high variance. For high-resource tasks (RCT, AGNEWS, HELPFULNESS, IMDB), we report the F_1 score from a single random seed for each task. Here we sweep the learning rates in {1e-4, 3e-4, 6e-4}, the number of epochs in {10, 20}, and the patience factor in {3, 5}.

Dataset	Baseline RoBERTa	TAPT	Hyper-parameters (LR, Epochs, Patience)
CHEMPROT	**82.8** $_{0.9}$	82.62 $_{0.5}$	3e-5, 20, 5
RCT	86.89 $_{0.1}$	**87.4** $_{0.2}$	2e-5, 10, 3
ACL-ARC	69.24 $_{2.6}$	**70.08** $_{2.3}$	3e-5, 20, 5
SCIERC	80.59 $_{0.9}$	**81.28** $_{1.2}$	2e-5, 20, 5
HYPER	**94.53** $_{2.0}$	86.17$_{1.3}$	3e-5, 10, 3
AGNEWS	93.9 $_{0.2}$	**94.05**$_{0.1}$	2e-5, 10, 3
HELPFUL	69.63 $_{0.6}$	**71.28**$_{0.8}$	2e-5, 20, 5
IMDB	94.93 $_{0.1}$	**95.33**$_{0.1}$	2e-5, 20, 5
Average F_1	**84.06**	83.52	

Table 8: Validation performance of Baseline RoBERTa and TAPT experiments that corresponds to Table 3. Each score is averaged over 5 random seeds.

Dataset	Original Results Baseline RoBERTa	Original Results TAPT	Our Results Baseline RoBERTa	Our Results TAPT
CHEMPROT	81.9 $_{1.0}$	82.6 $_{0.4}$	81.64 $_{0.8}$	82.58 $_{0.5}$
RCT	87.2 $_{0.1}$	87.7 $_{0.1}$	86.89 $_{0.1}$	87.4 $_{0.2}$
ACL-ARC	63.0 $_{5.8}$	67.4 $_{1.8}$	64.12 $_{5.5}$	66.11 $_{4.6}$
SCIERC	77.3 $_{1.9}$	79.3 $_{1.5}$	78.89 $_{2.7}$	79.94 $_{0.7}$
HYPER	86.6 $_{0.9}$	90.4 $_{5.2}$	85.03 $_{6.0}$	91.56 $_{2.5}$
AGNEWS	93.9 $_{0.2}$	94.5 $_{0.1}$	93.72 $_{0.2}$	94.05 $_{0.1}$
HELPFULNESS	65.1 $_{3.4}$	68.5 $_{1.9}$	69.2 $_{1.4}$	71.24 $_{0.7}$
IMDB	95.0 $_{0.2}$	95.5 $_{0.1}$	95.15 $_{0.1}$	95.33 $_{0.1}$
Average F_1	81.3	83.24	81.83	83.53

Table 9: Reproducing Baseline RoBERTa and TAPT Results, average F_1 Scores with standard deviation. F_1 score is averaged over 5 random seeds. We use the same hyper-parameters in Gururangan et al., 2020.

Knodle: Modular Weakly Supervised Learning with PyTorch

Anastasiia Sedova
University of Vienna
Vienna, Austria
anastasiia.sedova@univie.ac.at

Andreas Stephan
University of Vienna
Vienna, Austria
andreas.stephan@univie.ac.at

Marina Speranskaya
Ludwig Maximilian University of Munich
Munich, Germany
speranskaya@cis.lmu.de

Benjamin Roth
University of Vienna
Vienna, Austria
benjamin.roth@univie.ac.at

Abstract

Strategies for improving the training and prediction quality of weakly supervised machine learning models vary in how much they are tailored to a specific task or integrated with a specific model architecture. In this work, we introduce *Knodle*, a software framework that treats weak data annotations, deep learning models, and methods for improving weakly supervised training as separate, modular components. This modularization gives the training process access to fine-grained information such as data set characteristics, matches of heuristic rules, or elements of the deep learning model ultimately used for prediction. Hence, our framework can encompass a wide range of training methods for improving weak supervision, ranging from methods that only look at correlations of rules and output classes (independently of the machine learning model trained with the resulting labels), to those that harness the interplay of neural networks and weakly labeled data. We illustrate the benchmarking potential of the framework with a performance comparison of several reference implementations on a selection of datasets that are already available in *Knodle*.

1 Introduction

Most of today's machine learning success stories are built on top of huge labeled data sets. Creating and maintaining such data sources manually is a time-consuming, complicated and thus an expensive and error-prone process. Various research directions address the hunger for bigger and better datasets.

One of the most popular approaches that has recently gained traction is *weak supervision*. The learning algorithm is confronted with labels which are easy to obtain but are not guaranteed to be correct, and as such often demand denoising. Such weak labels are created, for example, with the use of regular expressions, keyword lists or external databases. Typically, methods for improving weakly supervised learning (and their respective implementations) are tailored towards domain-specific tasks or integrated with a specific model architecture. Examples include the attention-over-instances architecture introduced for relation extraction (Lin et al., 2016), an EM-based algorithm used for event extraction (Keith et al., 2017) or models of systematic label flips for named entity recognition (Hedderich et al., 2021). Such diversity and specificity of approaches makes it difficult to compare or transfer them across tasks without extensive adjustments dictated by the implementation, the task or the data set.

We introduce *Knodle*: a framework for *Know*ledge-supervised *D*eep *Le*arning, i.e weak supervision with neural networks. The framework provides a simple tensor-driven abstraction based on PyTorch allowing researchers to efficiently develop methods for improving weakly supervised machine learning models and try them interchangeably to find the one that works the best for a given task. Within this work, we refer to a denoising method as any method that helps to improve weakly supervised learning regardless the type of noise or bias and the exact level of denoising (weak labels, weak rules etc).

The following points summarize *Knodle*'s main design goals:

- **Data abstraction.** A tensor-driven data abstraction subsumes a large number of input variants and is applicable to a diverse range of tasks.
- **Method independence.** A decoupled implementation of weak supervision denoising methods and prediction models enables comparability and accounts for domain-specific inductive biases.

Proceedings of the 6th Workshop on Representation Learning for NLP (RepL4NLP-2021), pages 100–111
Bangkok, Thailand (Online), August 6, 2021.

- **Accessibility.** A high-level interface makes it easy to test existing methods, incorporate new ones and benchmark them against each other.

Several denoising algorithms are already included in *Knodle*. We also propose a new denoising algorithm, *WSCrossWeigh*, which extends *CrossWeigh* (Wang et al., 2019), a method for detecting mistakes in crowd-sourced annotation, to the weak supervision setting. The experiments demonstrate that it outperforms other existing methods on the majority of dataset s.

All implemented methods are tested on several datasets, also included in the *Knodle* ecosystem, and we discuss their performance. Each dataset exhibits different characteristics, such as the amount or the precision-recall balance of the used rules. Moreover, depending on the weakly labeled data set, methods for improving weak labels need to remove spurious matches in some cases, or generalize from them in others.

It is clear that such a diverse problem space should be paired with a rich pool of methods so that the most appropriate denoising method can be found for any task or dataset. *Knodle* allows to easily explore the spaces of weakly supervised learning settings and label improvement algorithms, and hopefully will facilitate a better understanding of the phenomena that are inherent to weakly supervised learning.

The framework is published as an open-source Python package `knodle` and available at `https://github.com/knodle/knodle`.

2 Related work

Many strategies have been introduced to reduce the need for large amounts of manually labeled data. Among these are *active learning* (Sun and Grishman, 2012), where automatically selected instances are manually annotated by experts, and *semi-supervised learning* (Agichtein and Gravano, 2000; Kozareva et al., 2008), where a small annotated dataset is combined with a large unlabeled one. Fine-tuning pretrained language models such as BERT (**?**) shows good results if moderate to small amounts of annotations are available.

2.1 Weak supervision

In weak supervision, tedious expert work is replaced with easy to obtain, but potentially error-prone labels, that are usually derived from a set of heuristic rules. One of the most popular strategies of weakly supervised learning is *distant supervision*, which uses knowledge from existing data sources to annotate unlabeled data. The technique is used extensively for relation extraction (Craven and Kumlien, 1999; Mintz et al., 2009; **?**; Riedel et al., 2013; Lin et al., 2016), where various knowledge databases, such as WordNet (Snow et al., 2004), Wikipedia (Wu and Weld, 2007) and Freebase (Mintz et al., 2009), are used as annotation sources.

When using heuristic rules, it is not uncommon that one sample turns out to be annotated by multiple rules. The most straightforward approach to resolve such cases is majority voting, which is used in early weak supervision algorithms (Thomas et al., 2011) as well as in more recent experiments (Krasakis et al., 2019; Boland and Krüger, 2019). However, majority voting does not deal with the different types of noise introduced by weak supervision, and more noise-specific algorithms are necessary. For example, the noise produced by *incomplete labels*, which stems from the incompleteness of weak supervision sources and often leads to an increased amount of false negatives, is commonly reduced by data manipulations, e.g. enhancing the knowledge base (Xu et al., 2013), a thorough construction of negative examples to balance the positive ones (Riedel et al., 2013), or explicitly modelling missing knowledge base information with latent variables (Ritter et al., 2013). The problem of *noisy features*, i.e. an increased amount of false positive labels stemming from overgeneralization, is often approached by using a relaxed distant supervision assumption (Riedel et al., 2010; Hoffmann et al., 2011), by active learning with additional manual expertise (Sterckx et al., 2014), with help of topic models (Yao et al., 2011; Roth and Klakow, 2013), as well as by using a combination of multiple methods (Roth, 2014).

Apart from that, methods treat the identified potentially noisy samples differently. They are either kept for further training with reduced weights (Jat et al., 2018; He et al., 2020), corrected (Shang, 2019) or eliminated (Qin et al., 2018). Thus, denoising methods vary significantly depending on the data and task, what makes the creation of a platform for comparison crucial.

2.2 Structure Learning

Structure learning assumes multiple weak labels per instance where each label is created by a so called *labeling function*. The goal is to learn a dependency structure within these labeling functions which motivates the term structure learning. Most labeling functions are generated by human intuitions, motivating correlation and dependence between labeling functions. The first algorithm was implemented in the software package *Snorkel* (Ratner et al., 2017), which also implemented the data programming paradigm, allowing to programmatically create labeling functions. Subsequently improvements were made (Bach et al., 2017; Varma et al., 2019) and variations, such as semi-supdervised learning (Chatterjee et al., 2019; Maheshwari et al., 2020) were introduced.

2.3 Noise-aware learning

A common idea to mitigate single noisy labels is to build an architecture which accounts for noisy data. There are different approaches that model noise-robustness by adapting the loss function (Patrini et al., 2017). Examples include a generalization of cross-entropy and the mean absolute error (Zhang and Sabuncu, 2018) or the addition of a special noise layer to a neural network (Sukhbaatar et al., 2015). Many approaches are based on noise assumptions, such as on the assumption of symmetric label noise (van Rooyen et al., 2015). Another approach aims at finding and removing wrongly labeled samples from the training procedure. An example in this domain is given by the confidence learning framework *CleanLab*, which is based on the intuition that low-confidence predictions in cross-validation are more likely to be labeled wrongly (Northcutt et al., 2021). Note that most of these methods were built with the assumption that there is one label corresponding to each instance, while *Knodle* makes use of several weak signals per instance.

2.4 Crowdsourcing annotations

Another solution to reduce the cost of manual data supervision by experts is **crowdsourcing**. In order to increase the supervision accuracy for a task, most crowdsourcing experiments rely on annotations by multiple people, and the final label is defined by majority voting (Kosinski et al., 2012) or measuring the inter-annotator agreement (Tratz and Hovy, 2010). More sophisticated denoising strategies include anomaly detection (Eskin, 2000), annotator's reliability modelling (Dawid and Skene, 1979), Bayesian approaches (Raykar and Yu, 2012) and generative models (Hovy et al., 2013). Some mistakes can be identified by such methods. For example, mistakes consistently made by careful but biased people (Ipeirotis et al., 2010), or errors introduced by *spammers* (Raykar and Yu, 2012).

As both, automatically and human labeled data, are subject to noise and structural errors, many algorithms can be used for both domains. For example, the MACE algorithm (Hovy et al., 2013), initially proposed for improving noisy annotations from human annotators, was adapted to the setting of denoising automatically labeled data for named entity recognition (Rehbein and Ruppenhofer, 2017). With the same motivation, we introduce *WSCrossWeigh* (see Section 4 for more details). We demonstrate the usefulness of the *Knodle* framework to transfer algorithms for improving crowd-sourced annotations to weak supervision problems.

2.5 Frameworks

Knodle is based upon the ideas of several software frameworks. On a low level, *Knodle* is built on top of PyTorch (Paszke et al., 2017). As for design decisions, we followed several other high-level libraries that aim to ease the training and prediction experience. Namely, we drew inspiration from PyTorch lightning (Falcon, 2019), which in essence tries to remove the burdens of writing your own train loop, and Huggingface's Transformers library (Wolf et al., 2020), which gives easy access to various transformer-based architectures in a fixed manner, so that they can be effortlessly interchanged in code.

3 Weakly supervised learning with *Knodle*

The *Knodle* architecture provides a layer of abstraction that allows integrated label improvement and model training with weakly supervised learning signals in PyTorch. On the one hand, since *Knodle* has access to the information which rules matched for each sample, it is not restricted to methods that denoise only weak labels, such as Cleanlab (Northcutt et al., 2021). On the other hand, the *Knodle* abstraction also provides access to input and learned representations, and thus does not restrict denoising methods to rely on rule match correlations alone (as Snorkel (Ratner et al., 2017)). Moreover, access to the deep learning model enables the integration of denoising methods that use or manipulate the prediction model itself.

To the best of our knowledge, *Knodle* is the first framework to provide a modular architecture for interchangable application of a wide spectrum of denoising algorithms. For that reason we believe that it can become a testbed where different algorithms for improving the weakly supervised data are implemented and compared with each other to find the most fruitful task-to-denoising-method combination or to use it as a foundation for further studies.

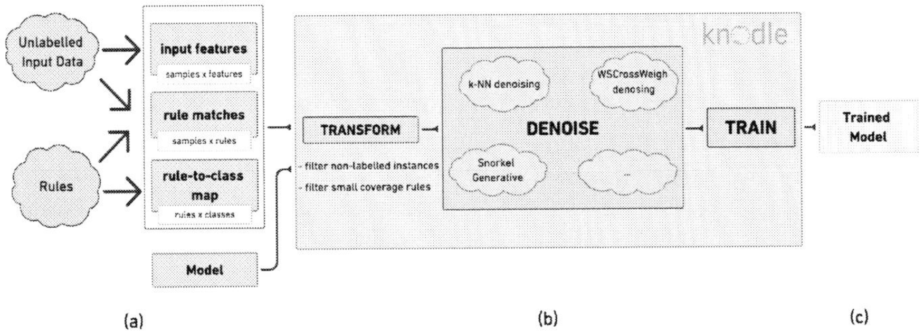

Figure 1: The figure gives an overview of our system. (a) represents the preprocessed input, given as tensors.(b) resembles the internals of *Knodle*. The `Trainer` classes introduced in Section 3.2 handle transformation, denoising and model training. Note that these three steps could be performed subsequently or subsumed in a single training step. Then, (c) shows the output, a trained PyTorch model.

The framework follows two main design principles, outlined below:

1. Tensor-based representations of input data and weak label matches

Similar to Pytorch models, where the data (input, labels) is already expected to be in tensor format, and the specific pre-processing that led to the tensor representation of the data is outside the scope of the deep learning model implementation, we choose to exclude the process of weak label generation from *Knodle*. Rather, we encode the information about weak labels in two tensors. One tensor contains information about which rules matched for each data instance, while another tensor describes the relationship between rules and output classes.

Formally, assume we have n samples, r rules and k classes. Rule matches are gathered in a binary matrix $Z \in \{0,1\}^{n \times r}$, where $Z_{ij} = 1$ if rule j matches sample i. The initial mapping from rules to the corresponding classes is given by another binary matrix $T \in \{0,1\}^{r \times k}$, $T_{jk} = 1$ if rule j is indicative of class k.

This separation between one tensor that contains rule matches and another tensor that translates them to labels allows *Knodle* to access this fine-grained information during training for certain denoising algorithms. This is in contrast to other approaches that treat weak supervision as learning from a noisy heuristic label matrix $Y_{heur} = ZT$ without direct access to the individual rules.

2. Separation of the prediction model from the weak supervision aspects.

Knodle requires a standard PyTorch model for a given prediction task. It is defined independent of the weak supervision aspects, such as rule types or denoising method. Therefore the same PyTorch model definition can be used for direct or weakly supervised training, and the two settings can easily be compared. However, even though the prediction model is defined separately, the denoising methods may have access to it during training. For example, cross-validation schemes such as WSCrossWeigh (see Section 4) can use the PyTorch model definition for data reweighting or label correction. This is in contrast to approaches that modularize denoising and training by first adjusting label confidences by using correlations between rules only and then training a model with the adjusted labels (Takamatsu et al., 2012; Ratner et al., 2017). Furthermore, *Knodle*'s design is much more flexible compared to approaches where denoising is so tightly integrated into the underlying prediction model architecture that it could not be changed (Sukhbaatar et al., 2015).

3.1 Handling of negative instances

Different tasks need a different logic to handle data samples where no rule matched. These samples are traditionally called *negative instances*. Whether unlabeled instances should be used for training (as an additional OTHER class) depends on the task at hand and should be configurable. For example, in knowledge base population (Surdeanu, 2013) there is only a small number of relevant target relations, and it is important to confidently identify sentences that do not contain any of the target relations (requiring negative instances as examples for the OTHER class). However, in spam classification with only two classes (spam and not spam) there are rules covering both possible outcomes, and there is no need for unlabeled instances and filtering them out is reasonable. Current weak supervision frameworks provide only one of the two options: negative samples are either filtered out (Ratner et al., 2017) or included to the training dataset (Shu et al., 2020).

Knodle includes configurable functionality for handling such cases (allowing comparability of denoising methods across tasks with and without an OTHER class). From a technical point of view, there is a `filter_non_labeled` flag in a configuration file, which could be set to `False` if the negative instances should be filtered out. To make up for missing explicit annotations for negative samples, an additional `other_class` parameter is defined. Automatically all samples without a matching rule are set to belong to "other" class. Hence, the exact `other_class_id` could be either provided by the user or determined automatically by *Knodle*. These types of configurations are well encapsulated, allowing the specific model to deal with either input. The amount of negative instances that should included in the training set can be defined specifically for each denoising algorithm.

3.2 Implementation Details

Similar to the most popular deep learning frameworks, such as TensorFlow (Abadi et al., 2015) and PyTorch (Paszke et al., 2017), we realise learning as a mapping from input tensor(s) to output tensor(s) guided by a loss function that measures the quality of the learned mapping. However, while the most common solution is to represent the training data by a *design matrix* $X \in \mathbb{R}^{n \times d}$ (n instances represented by d feature dimensions) and a *label matrix* $Y \in \mathbb{R}^{n \times k}$ (k classes), input of *Knodle* are matrices X, Z and T described above. The heuristic labels themselves are calculated later during the weakly supervised learning using the information contained there. To ensure a seamless use, the weakly supervised algorithms need to be tightly integrated with automatic differentiation and optimization supported by PyTorch.

The denoising and training procedures are realised within `Trainer` classes. During initialization, they receive data, a possibly pre-initialized or pre-trained model, and a method-specific configuration, inheriting from `Config` containing information such as model training parameters, criterion, validation method, class weights, various options to handle cases where no rule matches discussed in 3.1 and others. The level of integration between denoising and training is different for each `Trainer`. Sometimes these procedures can be completely disentangled. For instance, the `SnorkelTrainer` firstly denoises the input rules with Snorkel and, secondly, trains the classification model on the purified labels. Other methods highly integrate denoising and training with each other. An example is given by the `WSCrossWeighTrainer`, where several models are trained in oder to calculate sample weights as part of the denoising procedure before the final classifier is trained.

While in standard deep learning frameworks training can be executed by calling `model.train(X,Y)`, in *Knodle* the same functionality would be invoked with the following command (illustrates the Trainer with k-NN search, which we describe in Section 4):

```
kNNAggregationTrainer(model, X, Z,
        T, config).train()
```

The following code snippet shows an end-to-end process, starting from data loading, training and evaluation:

```
import torch
from knodle.trainer.knn_aggregation import \
    kNNAggregationTrainer, kNNConfig

# load data in Knodle format
X_train, Z, T, X_test, Y_test = load_data()

# define custom config (or use default)
config = kNNConfig(epochs=2, k=3)

# initialize trainer
trainer = kNNAggregationTrainer(
    model, X_train, Z, T, config
)

# train
trainer.train()

# evaluate
eval_dict = trainer.test(X_test, Y_test)
```

More detailed information about `kNNAggregationTrainer` as well as about other `Trainers` included to *Knodle* is provided in the next section.

4 Trainers

Knodle currently provides several out-of-the-box baselines and trainers, which we outline in the following section. All `Trainer` classes are compatible with any PyTorch model. As examples for PyTorch classifiers, *Knodle* provides code using logistic regression and HuggingFace's `transformers` (Wolf et al., 2020).

Majority Voting Baseline. As a simple baseline, the rules are directly applied to the test data without any additional model training. If several rules match, the prediction is done based on the majority; ties are broken randomly. As was already mentioned in Section 2, it is one of the most basic approaches to denoise the data labeled by two or more rules or human annotators.

Trainer without Denoising. The simplest trained model is the `NoDenoisingTrainer`. The majority vote is computed on the training data and used to train the given model. This is the most direct use of the rule matches for training a classifier. To cover cases where several rules match, this trainer can be configured to either use a one-hot encoding of the winning label from the majority vote or a distribution over labels (relative to the number of matching rules).

Trainer with kNN Denoising. This `kNNAggregationTrainer` includes the label denoising method with a simple geometric interpretation. The intuition behind it is that similar samples should be activated by the same rules which is allowed by a smoothness assumption on the target space. The trainer looks at the k most similar samples sorted by, for example, TF-IDF features combined with L_2 distance, and activates the rules matching the neighbors to create a denoised $\hat{Z}$. Importantly, *Knodle* allows separate features for the model training and the neighborhood activation. This method also provides a way to activate rules for initially unmatched samples.

Trainer with Snorkel Denoising. *Knodle* provides a wrapper of the Snorkel system (Ratner et al., 2017) `SnorkelTrainer` which incorporates both generative and discriminative Snorkel steps. The generative step constitutes a denoising method in *Knodle*'s terminology, while the discriminative step corresponds to a prediction model. The structure within labels and rules, in our notation $P(Y,Z,T)$, is learned in an unsupervised fashion by the generative model. Afterwards, the final discriminative model, i.e. the prediction model, is trained with weak labels provided by the generative model, following the general *Knodle* design. Both steps are conveniently provided in a single method call.

Trainer with Weak Supervision CrossWeigh Denoising. Finally, we implemented our own algorithm for noise correction in weakly supervised data. It is based on the CrossWeight method (Wang et al., 2019) and included to *Knodle* as `WSCrossWeighTrainer`. While the original CrossWeigh method was proposed for mistakes identification in crowdworkers annotations, we extend it for denoising the weakly supervised data as well. In WSCrossWeigh we adopted the same logic for estimating the reliability of weakly annotated data, but made some necessarily corrections specific to weakly supervised learning.

The main intuition behind WSCrossWeigh is the following: if a labeling rule corresponds to a wrong class and, therefore, annotates many samples in the training set with a wrong label, a machine learning model is likely to learn the incorrect pattern and to make similar mistakes when labeling the test samples. However, if we take a sufficiently big portion of data with samples *not* labeled by this rule, train the model on it, and then classify the samples matched by the rule, the predictions will contradict the initial *wrong* labels, and help us to trace the misclassified samples and reduce their importance in final classifier training.

As in the original CrossWeigh, the basic idea is similar to the k-fold cross-validation, where input data is split into k folds, each of which becomes, in turn, a test set, while the model is trained on the other folds. In WSCrossWeigh, however, the splitting is performed not randomly, but based on which rules match for the samples. Firstly, the rules are randomly split into ***K*** folds $\{r_1,...,r_k\}$ and, iteratively, each $fold_l$ is chosen to form a test set that is built from all samples matched this fold's rules. Other samples constitute a training set that is used for training the classification model. During the testing of the trained model on the hold-out fold samples, the predicted label $\hat{y_i}$ for each test sample x_i is compared to the label y_i originally assigned to x_i by weak supervision. If $\hat{y_i} \neq y_i$, this is taken as an indication that the sample x_i is likely to be potentially mislabeled, and its weights w_{x_i} is reduced by a value of an empirically estimated parameter ϵ. This procedure is repeated several times with different splits to detect misclassified samples more accurately.

The final classifier is trained on the whole reweighed training dataset. As a result, the more times the original y_i label of data sample x_i was suspected to be wrong, the smaller is its weight w_{x_i}, and, therefore, the smaller part it will play in the classifier training.

Along with other denoising algorithms, WSCrossWeigh was tested on the datasets described in Section 5 and showed quite promising results: it outperforms all other algorithms on three out of four datasets (for more details please see Section 6).

5 Datasets

Apart from denoising methods, *Knodle* includes a few datasets from previous works in the *Knodle*-specific tensor format in order to demonstrate the abilities of the framework. All datasets are rather simple, but have

dataset	classes	train / test samples	rules	avg. rule hits	class ratio
Spam	2	1586 / 250	10	1.63	0.47
Spouse	2	22254 / 2701	9	0.34	0.08
IMDb	2	40000 / 5000	6786	33.97	0.50
TAC-based RE	41	1937211 / 18660	182292	0.51	-

Table 1: Summary of data statistics. The average rule hits are computed on the train set. Class ratio describes the amount of positive samples in the test set for binary classification datasets, i.e. data skewedness.

their own peculiarities with respect to the respective Z and T matrices, that are worth investigating. The overview of dataset statistics is provided in Table 1.

Spam Dataset. The first task uses the YouTube comments dataset (Alberto et al., 2015). Here, the task is to classify whether a text is relevant to the video or holds spam, such as advertisement. The dataset has a small size of both train and test sets. Thus, a single wrongly labeled instance might have quite a big impact on the learning algorithm. We use the preprocessed version by the Snorkel team (Snorkel, 2020b). Among others, the rules were created based on keywords and regular expressions.

Spouse Dataset. This relation extraction dataset is based on the Signal Media One-Million News Articles Dataset (Corney et al., 2016). The task is to decide whether a sentence holds a spouse relation or not. Again, the preprocessed version by the Snorkel team is used (Snorkel, 2020a), so the results can be related to previous studies (Ratner et al., 2017). The rules are created via a set of known spouse relationships from DBPedia (Lehmann et al., 2014) as well as keywords and encoded language patterns. The difficulty of the Spouse dataset is its skewness: over 90% of samples in the test set hold a no-spouse relation.

IMDb Dataset. The third dataset is based on the well-known IMDb dataset (**?**), which consists of short movie reviews. The task is to determine whether a review holds a positive or negative sentiment. Despite the training set has labels, we do not use them in our experiments, but handle this data in an unsupervised fashion. To create the Z and T matrices, we use positive and negative keyword lists (Hu and Liu, 2004), with a total of 6800 keywords.

TAC-based Relation Extraction Dataset. Lastly, given the importance of distant supervision for relation extraction, we add a larger dataset with more relations (than just spouse). For development and test purposes the TACRED corpus annotated via crowdsourcing and human labeling from KBP (Zhang et al., 2017) is used. As human labels are not allowed in weak training, the training is performed not on the TACRED dataset, but on a weakly-supervised noisy corpus built on TAC KBP corpora (Surdeanu, 2013; Roth, 2014), which was annotated with entity pairs extracted from Freebase (Google, 2014) with corresponding relations mapped to the 41 TAC relations. The amount of entity pairs per relation is limited to 10.000 and each entity pair is allowed to be mentioned in no more than 500 sentences. An important difference of this dataset to the other three is the presence of negative instances added to the dataset in equal proportion to the positive ones.

6 Experiments

The aim of *Knodle* is not to find the best denoising method in general. Rather, the goal is to find the method that improves weak labels most for a given task or dataset and its specific properties. Thus, *Knodle* supports experimentation to get a better understanding in which settings a certain method works well and when it does not.

6.1 Experimental Details

In all experiments, the DistilBert uncased model for English language (Sanh et al., 2019) provided by the HuggingFace [1] (Wolf et al., 2020) library is used as the prediction model. The optimization is performed with the AdamW optimizer (Loshchilov and Hutter, 2019) and a learning rate of $1e{-}4$. We employ a cross-entropy loss accepting a probability distribution over all labels as reference input whenever the output of a denoising algorithm is a distribution over weak labels (e.g. `kNNAggregationTrainer`, `SnorkelTrainer`). Reducing this representation to a single label (i.e. log-likelihood) would lead to a loss of weak signals, whereas a label distribution allows to exploit the information from Z and T to the fullest. Each model was trained for 2 epochs (unless stated otherwise), which was enough to receive a stable result.

[1] https://huggingface.co/

	Spam	Spouse			IMDb	TAC-based RE		
Mode	Acc	P	R	F1	Acc	P	R	F1
Majority vote	0.81	0.12	0.79	0.22	0.65	0.09	0.001	0.001
Majority + DistilBert	0.87	0.09	0.90	0.17	0.67	0.20	0.19	0.19
k-NN + DistilBert	**0.94**	0.12	0.86	0.21	0.50	0.10†	0.11†	0.10†
WSCrossWeigh + DistilBert	**0.94**	0.09	0.69	0.16	**0.73**	0.25	0.27	**0.26**
Snorkel + DistilBert	0.88	0.13	0.70	**0.23**	0.50	-	-	-

Table 2: Results of the classifier training with different denoising methods on the test sets of datasets included in *Knodle*. †The neighbors were searched with Approximate Nearest Neighbors (Bernhardsson, 2015) because of computation complexity of *k*-NN search.

For the *k*-NN algorithm, nearest neighbors were found using the cosine similarity of TF-IDF features based on a dictionary of 3000 words, and the number of k neighbors is treated as a hyper-parameter. In our experiments, we used $k = 2$ except where otherwise noted. Hyperparameters for the WSCrossWeigh denoising algorithm are the number of folds the data is be split into, the number of partitions (that is, how many times the splitting for mistake estimation is done) and a weight-reducing rate (the value, by which the initial sample weights are reduced to each time the sample is predicted wrongly). These parameters are tuned for each dataset individually. The following best parameter values were found empirically: ($folds = 3$, $partitions = 10$ and $\epsilon = 0.3$) for the Spam dataset, (3, 2 and 0.3) for the Spouse dataset and (2, 25, 0.7) for the IMDb dataset. Apart from that, *Knodle* provides the opportunity to train the cross-validated sample weights with a model different from the final classifier. In our experiments, the weights were calculated using a Bidirectional LSTM with GloVe Embeddings (Pennington et al., 2014), while the final training was performed with DistilBert using the same settings as in the experiments with other denoising methods. The only difference is the number of epochs on the TAC-based dataset: the best results were obtained with 1 DistilBert epoch.

6.2 Results

An overview of the results is given in Table 2. In the Spam dataset, all denoising methods show an improvement over the simple majority vote baseline. The data-adaptive *k*-NN and WSCrossWeigh methods perform best in this setting. Snorkel and standard majority voting followed by DistilBert fine-tuning overfit to the noisy majority votes. This becomes obvious with the observation that Snorkel achieves a score of 0.93 with a simple logistic regression discriminative model. Interestingly, *k*-NN performs well which can serve as a proof for the reliability of neighboring labels.

Compared to the Spam dataset, the Spouse dataset is much larger. As the task is to find sentences holding spouse relations, we relate all metrics to the *is-spouse* relation. Note that the *non-spouse* relation remains in this case completely disregarded. Furthermore, the class ratio equals 0.08 shows that *is-spouse* is the complicated class of interest. On average, 0.34 rules hit per instance, meaning that almost 70% of the data match no rule. In these cases, majority vote uses a random vote which oversamples the *is-spouse* relation, rendering a high recall but low precision. We found that the rule matches overrepresent the *is-spouse* class as they are closer to a class ratio of 0.5 than to the true class ratio of 0.9. Thus, the additional model training magnifies overfitting towards the *is-spouse* class which, again, is expressed by increased recall and lower precision. The only denoising system that generalizes is Snorkel. One possible explanation could be that it is the only method that provides explicit rule denoising.

For IMDb, the majority vote shows that the rules have rather low quality on their own, but an additional trained model on top manages to generalize beyond the given labels. In contrast, denoising with the *k*-NN algorithm only aggravates the problems inherent to labels as the classifier's performance drops down to a random vote (50% accuracy). This behaviour can be explained by the high density of rule hits: on average, no less than 33 keywords match for each sentence, which means that already for $k = 1$ many neighbors are added and that the propagation of imprecise labelings overrules the expected benefits of *k*-NN. In general, there are cues that *k*-NN might useful in cases where the weak labels are already rather reliable but fail in cases where weak labels are too noisy. The Snorkel based denoising does not perform well on

IMDb dataset as well, which can be explained by the lack of dependencies between the rules that the Snorkel system relies on. However, WSCrossWeigh appears to be very robust to these data characteristics, the large amount of rules seems to help tease out and mutually reinforce the data characteristics associated with a specific label in cross-validation.

The distantly supervised TAC-based RE dataset turns out to be the most complicated dataset among all because of a larger size of samples n and a larger number of rules r. Due to its specificity, there are almost no rule matches (entity pairs from the seed KB) on the test set, implying that the simple majority baseline has scores close to 0. Training with DistilBert improves the result, however the performance remains considerably worse than for the data sets discussed above. On the contrary the WSCrossWeigh method that not directly denoise the rules, but downweigh the mislabeled data samples is still able to improve the results. Snorkel denoising could not be performed on this dataset on a machine with CPU frequency of 2.2GHz with 40 cores due to the immense amount of rules without the data manipulations we want to avoid (such as significantly reducing the number of rules). The computation of distances between almost 2 millions instances, which are necessary to determine the nearest neighbors, also turned out to be extremely memory- and time-consuming, explaining why k-NN algorithm was also not performed. Instead, we work around this by applying an *approximated* k-NN algorithm. In our experiments we used the Annoy library (Bernhardsson, 2015) and $k = 3$ parameter. The poor performance of approximated k-NN could be explained by a small average of rule hits in the TAC-based RE data set; the possible approximation losses are also not to be neglected. In contrast, the WSCrossWeigh method performs quite well. Our explanation is that WSCrossWeigh does not directly denoise the rules, but down-weighs samples it is less confident about. This makes this approach more robust in cases where the rules are very noisy.

7 Conclusion

This work introduces the Knowledge-supervised Deep Learning framework *Knodle*. *Knodle* provides a unified interface to work with multiple weak labeling sources, so that they can be seamlessly integrated with the training of deep neural networks. This is achieved by a tensor-based input format and a intuitive separation of weak supervision aspects and model training. The framework facilitates experimentation that helps researchers to gain better insights into the correspondence between characteristics of weak supervision problems, and the effectiveness of methods for improving weakly supervised learning. From a practical perspective, *Knodle* can be used to compare different denoising methods and select the one that gives the best result for a specific task.

Knodle's modular approach makes it easy to add new data sets and denoising algorithms. Adding functionality to *Knodle* is straightforward, and we do hope that it will encourage researchers to create their own algorithms to improve learning with weakly annotated data, and incorporate them into the *Knodle* framework.

Acknowledgments

This research was funded by the WWTF through the project "Knowledge-infused Deep Learning for Natural Language Processing" (WWTF Vienna Research Group VRG19-008), by the Deutsche Forschungsgemeinschaft (DFG, German Research Foundation) - RO 5127/2-1, and supported by a gift from Diffbot [2].

References

Martín Abadi, Ashish Agarwal, Paul Barham, Eugene Brevdo, Zhifeng Chen, Craig Citro, Greg S. Corrado, Andy Davis, Jeffrey Dean, Matthieu Devin, Sanjay Ghemawat, Ian Goodfellow, Andrew Harp, Geoffrey Irving, Michael Isard, Yangqing Jia, Rafal Jozefowicz, Lukasz Kaiser, Manjunath Kudlur, Josh Levenberg, Dandelion Mané, Rajat Monga, Sherry Moore, Derek Murray, Chris Olah, Mike Schuster, Jonathon Shlens, Benoit Steiner, Ilya Sutskever, Kunal Talwar, Paul Tucker, Vincent Vanhoucke, Vijay Vasudevan, Fernanda Viégas, Oriol Vinyals, Pete Warden, Martin Wattenberg, Martin Wicke, Yuan Yu, and Xiaoqiang Zheng. 2015. TensorFlow: Large-scale machine learning on heterogeneous systems. Software available from tensorflow.org.

Eugene Agichtein and Luis Gravano. 2000. Snowball: Extracting relations from large plain-text collections. In *Proceedings of the Fifth ACM Conference on Digital Libraries*, DL '00, page 85–94, New York, NY, USA. Association for Computing Machinery.

T C Alberto, J V Lochter, and T A Almeida. 2015. TubeSpam: Comment Spam Filtering on YouTube. In *2015 IEEE 14th International Conference on Machine Learning and Applications (ICMLA)*, pages 138–143.

Stephen H Bach, Bryan Dawei He, Alexander Ratner, and Christopher Ré. 2017. Learning the Structure of Generative Models without Labeled Data. *CoRR*, abs/1703.0.

E. Bernhardsson. 2015. Annoy on github. Last accessed 23 April 2021.

[2]https://www.diffbot.com/

K. Boland and F. Krüger. 2019. Distant supervision for silver label generation of software mentions in social scientific publications. In *BIRNDL@SIGIR*.

Oishik Chatterjee, Ganesh Ramakrishnan, and Sunita Sarawagi. 2019. Data Programming using Continuous and Quality-Guided Labeling Functions. *CoRR*, abs/1911.0.

D. Corney, M. Albakour, Miguel Martinez-Alvarez, and Samir Moussa. 2016. What do a million news articles look like? In *NewsIR@ECIR*.

Mark Craven and Johan Kumlien. 1999. Constructing biological knowledge bases by extracting information from text sources. In *Proceedings of the Seventh International Conference on Intelligent Systems for Molecular Biology*, page 77–86. AAAI Press.

A. P. Dawid and A. M. Skene. 1979. Maximum likelihood estimation of observer error-rates using the em algorithm. *Journal of the Royal Statistical Society. Series C (Applied Statistics)*, 28(1):20–28.

Eleazar Eskin. 2000. Detecting errors within a corpus using anomaly detection. In *1st Meeting of the North American Chapter of the Association for Computational Linguistics*.

WA Falcon. 2019. Pytorch lightning. *GitHub. Note: https://github.com/PyTorchLightning/pytorch-lightning Cited by*, 3.

Google. 2014. Freebase data dumps. `https://developers.google.com/freebase/data`.

Zhengqiu He, Wenliang Chen, Yuyi Wang, Wei Zhang, Guanchun Wang, and Min Zhang. 2020. Improving neural relation extraction with positive and unlabeled learning. *Proceedings of the AAAI Conference on Artificial Intelligence*, 34:7927–7934.

Michael A. Hedderich, Dawei Zhu, and Dietrich Klakow. 2021. Analysing the noise model error for realistic noisy label data.

Raphael Hoffmann, Congle Zhang, Xiao Ling, Luke Zettlemoyer, and Daniel S. Weld. 2011. Knowledge-based weak supervision for information extraction of overlapping relations. In *Proceedings of the 49th Annual Meeting of the Association for Computational Linguistics: Human Language Technologies*, pages 541–550, Portland, Oregon, USA. Association for Computational Linguistics.

Dirk Hovy, Taylor Berg-Kirkpatrick, Ashish Vaswani, and Eduard Hovy. 2013. Learning whom to trust with MACE. In *Proceedings of the 2013 Conference of the North American Chapter of the Association for Computational Linguistics: Human Language Technologies*, pages 1120–1130, Atlanta, Georgia. Association for Computational Linguistics.

Minqing Hu and Bing Liu. 2004. Mining and Summarizing Customer Reviews. In *Proceedings of the Tenth ACM SIGKDD International Conference on Knowledge Discovery and Data Mining*, KDD '04, pages 168–177, New York, NY, USA. Association for Computing Machinery.

Panos Ipeirotis, Foster Provost, and Jing Wang. 2010. Quality management on amazon mechanical turk. *In:Proceedings of the ACM SIGKDD Workshop on Human Computation.*

Sharmistha Jat, Siddhesh Khandelwal, and Partha Talukdar. 2018. Improving distantly supervised relation extraction using word and entity based attention.

Katherine A. Keith, Abram Handler, Michael Pinkham, Cara Magliozzi, Joshua McDuffie, and Brendan O'Connor. 2017. Identifying civilians killed by police with distantly supervised entity-event extraction. *CoRR*, abs/1707.07086.

Michal Kosinski, Yoram Bachrach, Gjergji Kasneci, Jurgen Van-Gael, and Thore Graepel. 2012. Crowd iq: Measuring the intelligence of crowdsourcing platforms. *Proceedings of the 3rd Annual ACM Web Science Conference, WebSci'12.*

Zornitsa Kozareva, Ellen Riloff, and Eduard Hovy. 2008. Semantic class learning from the web with hyponym pattern linkage graphs. In *Proceedings of ACL-08: HLT*, pages 1048–1056, Columbus, Ohio. Association for Computational Linguistics.

Antonios Minas Krasakis, E. Kanoulas, and G. Tsatsaronis. 2019. Semi-supervised ensemble learning with weak supervision for biomedical relationship extraction. In *AKBC*.

Jens Lehmann, Robert Isele, Max Jakob, Anja Jentzsch, Dimitris Kontokostas, Pablo Mendes, Sebastian Hellmann, Mohamed Morsey, Patrick Van Kleef, Sören Auer, and Christian Bizer. 2014. Dbpedia - a large-scale, multilingual knowledge base extracted from wikipedia. *Semantic Web Journal*, 6.

Yankai Lin, Shiqi Shen, Zhiyuan Liu, Huanbo Luan, and Maosong Sun. 2016. Neural relation extraction with selective attention over instances. In *Proceedings of the 54th Annual Meeting of the Association for Computational Linguistics (Volume 1: Long Papers)*, pages 2124–2133, Berlin, Germany. Association for Computational Linguistics.

Ilya Loshchilov and Frank Hutter. 2019. Decoupled Weight Decay Regularization.

Ayush Maheshwari, Oishik Chatterjee, KrishnaTeja Killamsetty, Rishabh Iyer, and Ganesh Ramakrishnan. 2020. Data Programming using Semi-Supervision and Subset Selection.

Mike Mintz, Steven Bills, Rion Snow, and Daniel Jurafsky. 2009. Distant supervision for relation extraction without labeled data. In *Proceedings of the Joint Conference of the 47th Annual Meeting of the ACL and the 4th International Joint Conference on Natural Language Processing of the AFNLP*, pages 1003–1011, Suntec, Singapore. Association for Computational Linguistics.

Curtis G Northcutt, Lu Jiang, and Isaac L Chuang. 2021. Confident Learning: Estimating Uncertainty in Dataset Labels.

Adam Paszke, Sam Gross, Soumith Chintala, Gregory Chanan, Edward Yang, Zachary DeVito, Zeming Lin, Alban Desmaison, Luca Antiga, and Adam Lerer. 2017. Automatic differentiation in pytorch. *NIPS Workshop*.

Giorgio Patrini, Alessandro Rozza, Aditya Menon, Richard Nock, and Lizhen Qu. 2017. Making Deep Neural Networks Robust to Label Noise: a Loss Correction Approach.

Jeffrey Pennington, Richard Socher, and Christopher D. Manning. 2014. Glove: Global vectors for word representation. In *Empirical Methods in Natural Language Processing (EMNLP)*, pages 1532–1543.

Pengda Qin, Weiran Xu, and William Yang Wang. 2018. Robust distant supervision relation extraction via deep reinforcement learning. In *Proceedings of the 56th Annual Meeting of the Association for Computational Linguistics (Volume 1: Long Papers)*, pages 2137–2147, Melbourne, Australia. Association for Computational Linguistics.

Alexander Ratner, Stephen H Bach, Henry R Ehrenberg, Jason Alan Fries, Sen Wu, and Christopher R é. 2017. Snorkel: Rapid Training Data Creation with Weak Supervision. *CoRR*, abs/1711.1.

Vikas C. Raykar and Shipeng Yu. 2012. Eliminating spammers and ranking annotators for crowdsourced labeling tasks. *Journal of Machine Learning Research*, 13(16):491–518.

Ines Rehbein and Josef Ruppenhofer. 2017. Detecting annotation noise in automatically labelled data. In *Proceedings of the 55th Annual Meeting of the Association for Computational Linguistics (Volume 1: Long Papers)*, pages 1160–1170, Vancouver, Canada. Association for Computational Linguistics.

Sebastian Riedel, Limin Yao, and Andrew McCallum. 2010. Modeling relations and their mentions without labeled text. In *Proceedings of the 2010 European Conference on Machine Learning and Knowledge Discovery in Databases: Part III*, ECML PKDD'10, page 148–163, Berlin, Heidelberg. Springer-Verlag.

Sebastian Riedel, Limin Yao, Andrew McCallum, and Benjamin M. Marlin. 2013. Relation extraction with matrix factorization and universal schemas. In *Proceedings of the 2013 Conference of the North American Chapter of the Association for Computational Linguistics: Human Language Technologies*, pages 74–84, Atlanta, Georgia. Association for Computational Linguistics.

Alan Ritter, Luke Zettlemoyer, Mausam, and Oren Etzioni. 2013. Modeling missing data in distant supervision for information extraction. *Transactions of the Association for Computational Linguistics*, 1:367–378.

Brendan van Rooyen, Aditya Krishna Menon, and Robert C Williamson. 2015. Learning with Symmetric Label Noise: The Importance of Being Unhinged.

Benjamin Roth. 2014. *Effective distant supervision for end-to-end knowledge base population systems*. Ph.D. thesis, Saarland University.

Benjamin Roth and Dietrich Klakow. 2013. Feature-based models for improving the quality of noisy training data for relation extraction. In *Proceedings of the 22nd ACM International Conference on Information and Knowledge Management*, CIKM '13, page 1181–1184, New York, NY, USA. Association for Computing Machinery.

Victor Sanh, Lysandre Debut, Julien Chaumond, and Thomas Wolf. 2019. Distilbert, a distilled version of bert: smaller, faster, cheaper and lighter. *ArXiv*, abs/1910.01108.

Yuming Shang. 2019. Are noisy sentences useless for distant supervised relation extraction?

Kai Shu, Subhabrata Mukherjee, Guoqing Zheng, Ahmed Hassan, Milad Shokouhi, and Susan Dumais. 2020. Learning with weak supervision for email intent detection. pages 1051–1060.

Snorkel. 2020a. Detecting spouse mentions in sentences. Last accessed 25 February 2021.

Snorkel. 2020b. Snorkel intro tutorial: Data labeling. Last accessed 25 February 2021.

Rion Snow, Daniel Jurafsky, and Andrew Ng. 2004. Learning syntactic patterns for automatic hypernym discovery. In *NIPS*, volume 17.

Lucas Sterckx, Thomas Demeester, Johannes Deleu, and Chris Develder. 2014. Using active learning and semantic clustering for noise reduction in distant supervision. In *NIPS 2014*.

Sainbayar Sukhbaatar, Joan Bruna, Manohar Paluri, Lubomir Bourdev, and Rob Fergus. 2015. Training Convolutional Networks with Noisy Labels.

Ang Sun and Ralph Grishman. 2012. Active learning for relation type extension with local and global data views. In *Proceedings of the 21st ACM International Conference on Information and Knowledge Management*, CIKM '12, page 1105–1112, New York, NY, USA. Association for Computing Machinery.

M. Surdeanu. 2013. Overview of the tac2013 knowledge base population evaluation: English slot filling and temporal slot filling. *Theory and Applications of Categories*.

Shingo Takamatsu, Issei Sato, and Hiroshi Nakagawa. 2012. Reducing wrong labels in distant supervision for relation extraction. In *Proceedings of the 50th Annual Meeting of the Association for Computational Linguistics (Volume 1: Long Papers)*, pages 721–729, Jeju Island, Korea. Association for Computational Linguistics.

Philippe Thomas, Illés Solt, Roman Klinger, and Ulf Leser. 2011. Learning protein–protein interaction extraction using distant supervision. In *Proceedings of Workshop on Robust Unsupervised and Semisupervised Methods in Natural Language Processing*, pages 25–32, Hissar, Bulgaria. Association for Computational Linguistics.

Stephen Tratz and Eduard Hovy. 2010. A taxonomy, dataset, and classifier for automatic noun compound interpretation. In *Proceedings of the 48th Annual Meeting of the Association for Computational Linguistics*, pages 678–687.

Paroma Varma, Frederic Sala, Ann He, Alexander Ratner, and Christopher Ré. 2019. Learning Dependency Structures for Weak Supervision Models.

Zihan Wang, Jingbo Shang, Liyuan Liu, Lihao Lu, Jiacheng Liu, and Jiawei Han. 2019. CrossWeigh: Training named entity tagger from imperfect annotations. In *Proceedings of the 2019 Conference on Empirical Methods in Natural Language Processing and the 9th International Joint Conference on Natural Language Processing (EMNLP-IJCNLP)*, pages 5154–5163, Hong Kong, China. Association for Computational Linguistics.

Thomas Wolf, Lysandre Debut, Victor Sanh, Julien Chaumond, Clement Delangue, Anthony Moi, Pierric Cistac, Tim Rault, Rémi Louf, Morgan Funtowicz, Joe Davison, Sam Shleifer, Patrick von Platen, Clara Ma, Yacine Jernite, Julien Plu, Canwen Xu, Teven Le Scao, Sylvain Gugger, Mariama Drame, Quentin Lhoest, and Alexander M Rush. 2020. HuggingFace's Transformers: State-of-the-art Natural Language Processing.

Fei Wu and Daniel S. Weld. 2007. Autonomously semantifying wikipedia. In *CIKM*, page 41– 50. ACM.

Wei Xu, Raphael Hoffmann, Le Zhao, and Ralph Grishman. 2013. Filling knowledge base gaps for distant supervision of relation extraction. In *Proceedings of the 51st Annual Meeting of the Association for Computational Linguistics (Volume 2: Short Papers)*, pages 665–670, Sofia, Bulgaria. Association for Computational Linguistics.

Limin Yao, Aria Haghighi, Sebastian Riedel, and Andrew McCallum. 2011. Structured relation discovery using generative models. In *Proceedings of the 2011 Conference on Empirical Methods in Natural Language Processing*, pages 1456–1466, Edinburgh, Scotland, UK. Association for Computational Linguistics.

Yuhao Zhang, Victor Zhong, Danqi Chen, Gabor Angeli, and Christopher D. Manning. 2017. Position-aware attention and supervised data improve slot filling. In *Proceedings of the 2017 Conference on Empirical Methods in Natural Language Processing (EMNLP 2017)*, pages 35–45.

Zhilu Zhang and Mert R Sabuncu. 2018. Generalized Cross Entropy Loss for Training Deep Neural Networks with Noisy Labels.

X2Parser: Cross-Lingual and Cross-Domain Framework for Task-Oriented Compositional Semantic Parsing

Zihan Liu, Genta Indra Winata, Peng Xu, Pascale Fung
Center for Artificial Intelligence Research (CAiRE)
Department of Electronic and Computer Engineering
The Hong Kong University of Science and Technology, Clear Water Bay, Hong Kong
zihan.liu@connect.ust.hk, pascale@ece.ust.hk

Abstract

Task-oriented compositional semantic parsing (TCSP) handles complex nested user queries and serves as an essential component of virtual assistants. Current TCSP models rely on numerous training data to achieve decent performance but fail to generalize to low-resource target languages or domains. In this paper, we present **X2Parser**, a transferable **Cross**-lingual and **Cross**-domain **Parser** for TCSP. Unlike previous models that learn to generate the hierarchical representations for nested intents and slots, we propose to predict flattened intents and slots representations separately and cast both prediction tasks into sequence labeling problems. After that, we further propose a fertility-based slot predictor that first learns to dynamically detect the number of labels for each token, and then predicts the slot types. Experimental results illustrate that our model can significantly outperform existing strong baselines in cross-lingual and cross-domain settings, and our model can also achieve a good generalization ability on target languages of target domains. Furthermore, our model tackles the problem in an efficient non-autoregressive way that reduces the latency by up to 66% compared to the generative model.[1]

1 Introduction

Virtual assistants can perform a wide variety of tasks for users, such as setting reminders, searching for events, and sending messages. Task-oriented compositional semantic parsing (TCSP) which comprehends users' intents and detects the key information (slots) in the utterance is one of the core components in virtual assistants. Existing TCSP models highly rely on large amounts of training data that usually only exist in high-resource domains and languages (e.g., English), and they

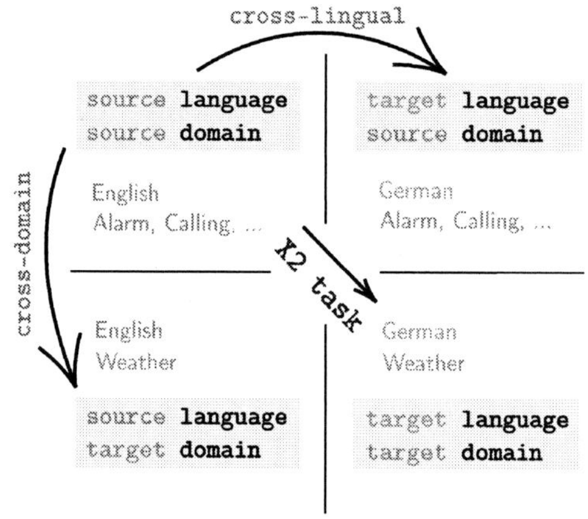

Figure 1: Illustration of the cross-lingual task, cross-domain task, and the combination of both (X2 task).

generally fail to generalize well in a low-resource scenario. Given that collecting enormous training data is expensive and time-consuming, we aim to develop a transferable model that can quickly adapt to low-resource target languages and domains.

The traditional semantic parsing can be treated as a simple joint intent detection and slot filling task (Liu and Lane, 2016; Goo et al., 2018; Zhang et al., 2019), while compositional semantic parsing has to cope with complex nested queries, which requires more sophisticated models. Current state-of-the-art TCSP models (Rongali et al., 2020; Li et al., 2020a) are generation-based models that learn to directly generate the hierarchical representations which contain nested intent and slot labels.[2] We argue that the hierarchical representations are relatively complex, and the models need to learn when to generate the starting intent or slot label, when to copy tokens from the input, and when to generate the end of the label. Hence, large quantities of train-

[1] The code will be released in https://github.com/zliucr/X2Parser.

[2] An example of hierarchical representations is illustrated at the bottom of Figure 2.

Proceedings of the 6th Workshop on Representation Learning for NLP (RepL4NLP-2021), pages 112–127
Bangkok, Thailand (Online), August 6, 2021. ©2021 Association for Computational Linguistics

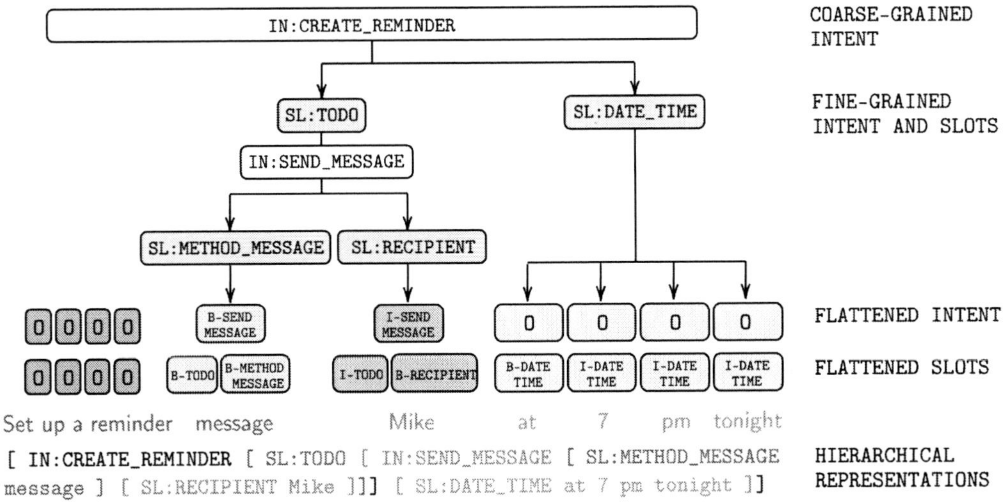

Figure 2: One data example with the illustration of our proposed flattened intents and slots representations, as well as the hierarchical representations used in Li et al. (2020a).

ing data are necessary for the models to learn these complicated skills (Rongali et al., 2020), while they cannot generalize well when large datasets are absent (Li et al., 2020a). Moreover, the inference speed of generation-based models will be greatly limited by the output length.

In this paper, we propose a transferable cross-lingual and cross-domain parser (X2Parser) for TCSP. Instead of generating hierarchical representations, we convert the nested annotations into flattened intent and slot representations (as shown in Figure 2) so that the model can learn to predict the intents and slots separately. We cast the nested slot prediction problem into a special sequence labeling task where each token can have multiple slot labels. To tackle this task, our model first learns to predict the number of slot labels, which helps it capture the hierarchical slot information in user queries. Then, it copies the corresponding hidden state for each token and uses those hidden states to predict the slot labels. For the nested intent prediction, we cast the problem into a normal sequence labeling problem where each token only has one intent label since the nested cases for intents are simpler than those for slots. Compared to generation-based models (Li et al., 2020a), X2Parser simplifies the problem by flattening the hierarchical representations and tackles the task in a non-autoregressive way, which strengthen its adaptation ability in low-resource scenarios and greatly reduce the latency.

As shown in Figure 1, we conduct experiments on three low-resource settings: cross-lingual, cross-domain, and a combination of both. Results show that our model can remarkably surpass existing strong baselines in all the low-resource scenarios by more than 10% exact match accuracy, and can reduce the latency by up to 66% compared to generation-based models. We summarize the main contributions of this paper as follows:

- We provide a new perspective to tackle the TCSP task, which is to flatten the hierarchical representations and cast the problem into several sequence labeling tasks.
- X2Parser can significantly outperform existing strong baselines in different low-resource settings and notably reduce the latency compared to the generation-based model.
- We conduct extensive experiments in different few-shot settings and explore the combination of cross-lingual and cross-domain scenarios.

2 Related Work

2.1 Task-Oriented Semantic Parsing

The majority of works on task-oriented semantic parsing focused on non-compositional user queries (Mesnil et al., 2013; Liu and Lane, 2016; Goo et al., 2018; Zhang et al., 2019), which turns the parsing task into a combination of intent detection and slot filling. Recently, Gupta et al. (2018)

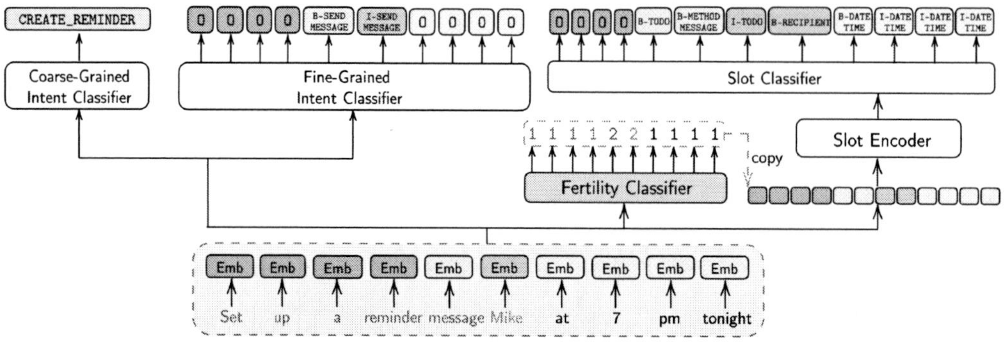

Figure 3: The architecture of X2Parser. We consider the TCSP task as a combination of the coarse-grained intent classification, fine-grained intent prediction, and slot filling tasks.

introduced a new dataset, called TOP, annotated with complex nested intents and slots and proposed to use the hierarchical representations to model the task. After that, Rongali et al. (2020) showed that leveraging a sequence-to-sequence model based on a copy mechanism (See et al., 2017) to directly generate the hierarchical representations was effective at parsing the nested queries. Taking this further, Chen et al. (2020) and Li et al. (2020a) extended the TOP dataset into multiple domains and multiple languages, and Li et al. (2020a) conducted zero-shot cross-lingual experiments using the combination of the multilingual pre-trained models (Conneau et al., 2020; Tran et al., 2020) and the copy mechanism method proposed in Rongali et al. (2020). Lately, Babu et al. (2021) and Shrivastava et al. (2021), which are concurrent works of X2Parser, proposed to tackled the TCSP task in a non-autoregressive way. Different from them, we propose to flatten the hierarchical representations and cast the problem into several sequence labeling tasks.

2.2 Language and Domain Adaptation

Recently, cross-lingual and cross-domain models that aim to tackle low-resource issues have been applied to natural language understanding (Conneau et al., 2018; Huang et al., 2019; Conneau et al., 2020; Gururangan et al., 2020), sentiment analysis (Zhou et al., 2016; Ziser and Reichart, 2017), task-oriented semantic parsing (Chen et al., 2018; Schuster et al., 2019; Liu et al., 2019; Wu et al., 2019; Liu et al., 2020a; Chen et al., 2020; Liu et al., 2020b), named entity recognition (Ni et al., 2017; Xie et al., 2018; Jia et al., 2019; Liu et al., 2020c), speech recognition (Mimura et al., 2017; Winata et al., 2020), abstractive summarization (Zhu et al., 2019; Ouyang et al., 2019; Yu et al., 2021), etc. Despite numerous studies related to the cross-lingual and cross-domain areas, only a few of them have explored how to effectively adapt models to the target languages in target domains, and the investigated tasks are limited to sentiment analysis (Fernández et al., 2016; Li et al., 2020b), abusive language detection (Pamungkas and Patti, 2019), and machine reading comprehension (Charlet et al., 2020). To the best of our knowledge, we are the first to study the combination of cross-lingual and cross-domain adaptations in the TCSP task.

3 Task Decomposition

In this section, we first introduce the intuition of decomposing the compositional semantic parsing into intent predictions and slot filling. Then, we describe how we construct intent and slot labels.

3.1 Intuition of Task Decomposition

We argue that hierarchical representations containing nested annotations for intents and slots are relatively complex. We need large enough training data to train a good model based on such representations, and the model's performance will be greatly limited in low-resource scenarios. Therefore, instead of incorporating intents and slots into one representation, we propose to predict them separately so that we can simplify the parsing problem and enable the model to easily learn the skills for each decomposed task, and finally, our model can achieve a better adaptation ability in low-resource scenarios. As illustrated in Figure 2, we obtain the coarse-grained intent, flattened fine-grained intents and flattened slot labels from the hierarchical representations, and train the model based on these three categories in a multi-task fashion. Note that we can always reconstruct the hierarchical representations based on the labels in these three categories, which means that the decomposed labels and the hierarchical labels are equivalent.

3.2 Label Constructions

Slot Labels We extract nested slot labels from the hierarchical representations and assign the labels to corresponding tokens based on the BIO (begin-inside-outside) structure. As we can see from Figure 2, there could exist multiple slot labels for one token, and we consider the order of the labels so as to reconstruct the hierarchical representations. Specifically, we put the more fine-grained slot label at the later position. For example, "message" (in Figure 2) has `B-TODO` and `B-METHOD-MESSAGE` labels, and `B-METHOD-MESSAGE` comes after `B-TODO` since it is a more fine-grained slot label.

Intent Labels Each data sample has one intent label for the whole user utterance, and we extract it as an individual coarse-grained intent label. For the intents expressed by partial tokens (i.e., fine-grained intents), we use the BIO structure to label the corresponding tokens. We notice that we only need to assign one intent label to each token since the nested cases for intents are relatively simple.[3] Therefore, the fine-grained intent classification becomes a sequence labeling task.

4 X2Parser

The model architecture of our X2Parser is illustrated in Figure 3. To enable the cross-lingual ability of our model, we leverage the multilingual pre-trained model XLM-R (Conneau et al., 2020) as the sequence encoder. Let us define $X = \{x_1, x_2, ..., x_n\}$ as the user utterance and $H = \{h_1, h_2, ..., h_n\}$ as the hidden states (denoted as Emb in Figure 3) from XLM-R.

4.1 Slot Predictor

The slot predictor consists of a fertility classifier, a slot encoder, and a slot classifier. Inspired by Gu et al. (2018), the fertility classifier learns to predict the number of slot labels for each token, and then it copies the corresponding number of hidden states. Finally, the slot classifier is trained to conduct the sequence labeling based on the slot labels we constructed. The fertility classifier not only helps the model identify the number of labels for each token but also guides the model to implicitly learn the nested slot information in user queries. It relieves the burden of the slot classifier, which needs to predict multiple slot entities for certain tokens.

Fertility Classifier (FC) We add a linear layer (FC) on top of the hidden states from XLM-R to predict the number of labels (fertility), which we formulate as follows:

$$F = \{f_1, f_2, ..., f_n\} = \text{FC}(\{h_1, h_2, ..., h_n\}), \quad (1)$$

where FC is an n-way classifier (n is the maximum label number) and $f_i (i \in [1, n])$ is a positive integer representing the number of labels for x_i.

Slot Filling After obtaining the fertility predictions, we copy the corresponding number of hidden states from XLM-R:

$$H' = \text{CopyHiddens}(H, F). \quad (2)$$

Then, we add a transformer encoder (Vaswani et al., 2017) (slot encoder (SE)) on top of H' to incorporate the sequential information into the hidden states, followed by adding a linear layer (slot classifier (SC)) to predict the slots, which we formulate as follows:

$$P_{\text{slot}} = \text{SC}(\text{SE}(H')), \quad (3)$$

where P_{slot} is a sequence of slots that has the same length as the sum of the fertility numbers.

4.2 Intent Predictor

Coarse-Grained Intent The coarse-grained intent is predicted based on the hidden state of the "`[CLS]`" token from XLM-R since it can be the representation for the whole sequence, and then we add a linear layer (coarse-grained intent classifier (CGIC)) on top of the hidden state to predict the coarse-grained intent:

$$p_{\text{cg}} = \text{CGIC}(h_{\text{cls}}), \quad (4)$$

where p_{cg} is a single intent prediction.

Fine-Grained Intent We add a linear layer (fine-grained intent classifier (FGIC)) on top of the hidden states H to produce the fine-grained intents:

$$P_{\text{fg}} = \text{FGIC}(\{h_1, h_2, ..., h_n\}), \quad (5)$$

where P_{fg} is a sequence of intent labels that has the same length as the input sequence.

[3]We place more details about how we construct labels for fine-grained nested intents in the Appendix A.

Model	en	es	fr	de	hi	th	Avg.
Seq2Seq w/ CRISS (Li et al., 2020a)	**84.20**	48.60	46.60	36.10	31.20	0.00	32.50
Seq2Seq w/ XLM-R (Li et al., 2020a)	83.90	50.30	43.90	42.30	30.90	26.70	38.82
Neural Layered Model (NLM)	82.40	59.99	58.16	54.91	29.31	28.78	46.23
X2Parser	83.39	**60.30**	**58.34**	**56.16**	**37.06**	**29.35**	**48.24**

Table 1: Exact match accuracies for the zero-shot **cross-lingual setting**. "Avg." denotes the averaged performance over all target languages (English excluded). The results of X2Parser and NLM are averaged over five runs.

Model	Alarm	Call.	Event	Msg.	Music	News	People	Recipe	Remind	Timer	Weather	Avg.
Seq2Seq	67.94	64.25	61.93	50.11	32.20	43.20	52.54	34.21	46.32	44.83	73.58	51.92
NLM	76.32	70.02	73.60	70.58	**56.52**	58.01	67.33	50.01	57.28	64.37	80.15	65.83
X2Parser	**76.72**	**73.16**	**77.33**	**71.45**	55.19	**64.43**	**69.77**	**51.78**	**58.86**	**65.98**	**81.17**	**67.80**

Table 2: Exact match accuracies (averaged over three runs) for the **cross-domain setting** in English. The scores represent the performance for the corresponding target domains. We use 10% of training samples in the target domain. **"Seq2Seq" denotes the "Seq2Seq w/ XLM-R" baseline** (same for the following tables and figures).

5 Experiments

5.1 Experimental Setup

Dataset We conduct the experiments on the MTOP dataset proposed by Li et al. (2020a), which contains six languages: English (en), German (de), French (fr), Spanish (es), and Thai (th), and 11 domains: alarm, calling, event, messaging, music, news, people, recipes, reminder, timer, and weather. The data statistics are reported in the Appendix B.

Cross-Lingual Setting In the cross-lingual setting, we use English as the source language and the other languages as target languages. In addition, we consider a zero-shot scenario where we only use English data for training.

Cross-Domain Setting In the cross-domain setting, we only consider training and evaluation in English. We choose ten domains as source domains and the other domain as the target domain. Different from the cross-lingual setting, we consider a few-shot scenario where we first train the model using the data from the ten source domains, and then we fine-tune the model using a few data samples (e.g., 10% of the data) from the target domain. We consider the few-shot scenario because zero-shot adapting the model to the target domain is extremely difficult due to the unseen intent and slot types, while zero-shot to target languages is easier using multilingual pre-trained models.

Cross-Lingual Cross-Domain Setting This setting combines the cross-lingual and cross-domain settings. Specifically, we first train the model on the English data from the ten source domains, and then fine-tune it on a few English data samples from the other (target) domain. Finally, we conduct the zero-shot evaluation on all the target languages of the target domain.

5.2 Baselines

Seq2Seq w/ XLM-R Rongali et al. (2020) proposed a sequence-to-sequence (Seq2Seq) model using a pointer-generator network (See et al., 2017) to handle nested queries, and achieved new state-of-the-art results in English. Li et al. (2020a) adopted this architecture for zero-shot cross-lingual adaptation. They replaced the encoder with the XLM-R (Conneau et al., 2020) and used a customized decoder to learn to generate intent and label types and copy tokens from the inputs.[4]

Seq2Seq w/ CRISS It is the same architecture as *Seq2Seq w/ XLM-R*, except that Li et al. (2020a) replaced XLM-R with the multilingual pre-trained model, CRISS (Tran et al., 2020), as the encoder for the zero-shot cross-lingual adaptation.

Neural Layered Model (NLM) This baseline conducts the multi-task training based on the same task decomposition as X2Parser, but it replaces the slot predictor module in X2Parser with a neural

[4] In order to compare the performance in the cross-domain and cross-lingual cross-domain settings, we follow Li et al. (2020a) to reimplement this baseline since the source code is not publicly available.

Model	Alarm	Call.	Event	Msg.	Music	News	People	Recipe	Remind	Timer	Weather	Avg.
Seq2Seq	34.29	47.00	41.81	25.86	19.21	25.39	22.13	16.12	9.80	20.01	36.90	22.25
NLM	48.53	43.30	44.62	43.32	36.25	28.60	43.29	28.54	20.50	34.16	59.57	39.15
X2Parser	**48.72**	**51.30**	**53.22**	**43.99**	**37.25**	**34.85**	**45.97**	**32.99**	**27.87**	**36.61**	**60.05**	**42.98**

Table 3: Exact match accuracies (averaged over three runs) for the **cross-lingual cross-domain setting**. The result for each domain is the averaged performance over all target languages. We use 10% of training samples in the English target domain, and do not use any data in the target languages.

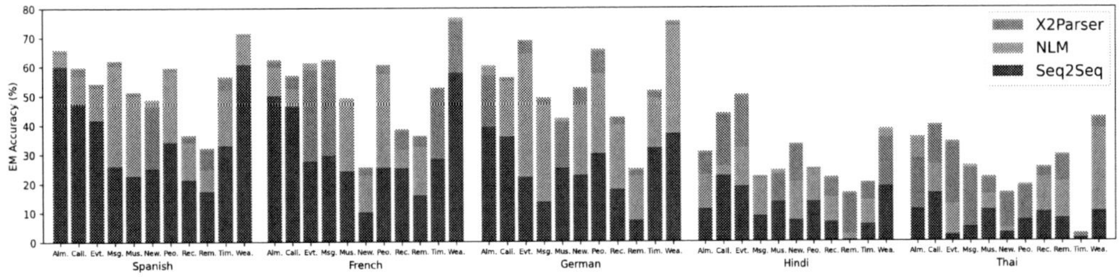

Figure 4: Full **cross-lingual cross-domain** results (across all target languages of target domains) for Table 3.

layered model (Ju et al., 2018),[5] while keeping the other modules the same. Unlike our fertility-based slot predictor, NLM uses several stacked layers to predict entities of different levels. We use this baseline to verify the effectiveness of our fertility-based slot predictor.

5.3 Training Details

We use XLM-R Large (Conneau et al., 2020) as the sequence encoder. For a word (in an utterance) with multiple subword tokens, we take the representations from the first subword token to predict the labels for this word. The transformer encoder (slot encoder) has one layer with a head number of 4, a hidden dimension of 400, and a filter size of 64. We set the fertility classifier as a 3-way classifier since the maximum label number for each token in the dataset is 3. We train X2Parser using the Adam optimizer (Kingma and Ba, 2015) with a learning rate of 2e-5 and a batch size of 32. We follow Li et al. (2020a) and use the exact match accuracy to evaluate the models. For our model, the prediction is considered correct only when the predictions for the coarse-grained intent, fine-grained intents, and the slots are all correct. To ensure a fair comparison, we use the same three random seeds to run each model and calculate the averaged score for each target language and domain.

[5]This model was originally proposed to tackle the nested named entity recognition task

6 Results & Discussion

6.1 Main Results

Cross-Lingual Setting As we can see from Table 1, X2Parser achieves similar performance in English compared to Seq2Seq-based models, while it significantly outperforms them in the zero-shot cross-lingual setting, with $\sim$10% accuracy improvement on average. In the English training process, the Seq2Seq-based models can well learn the specific scope of tokens that need to be copied and assigned to a specific label type based on numerous training data. However, these models will easily lose effectiveness when the input sequences are in target languages due to the inherent variances across languages and the difficulty of generating hierarchical representations. X2Parser separates the TCSP task into predicting intents and slots individually, which lowers the task difficulty and boosts its zero-shot adaptation ability to target languages. Interestingly, we find that compared to *Seq2Seq w/ XLM-R*, X2Parser greatly boosts the performance on target languages that are topologically close to English (e.g., French (fr)) with more than 10% scores, while the improvements for languages that are topologically distant from English (e.g., Thai (th) and Hindi (hi)) are relatively limited. We argue that the large discrepancies between English and Thai make the representation alignment quality between English and Thai (Hindi) in XLM-R relatively low, and their different language patterns lead to unstable slot and intent predictions. These

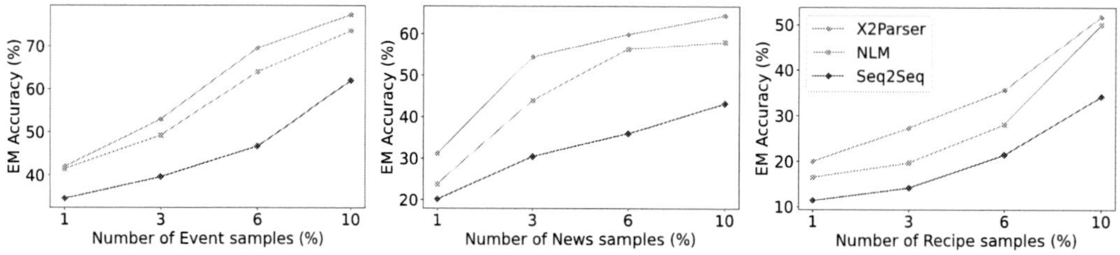

Figure 5: Few-shot exact match results on the **cross-domain setting** for Event, News and Recipe target domains.

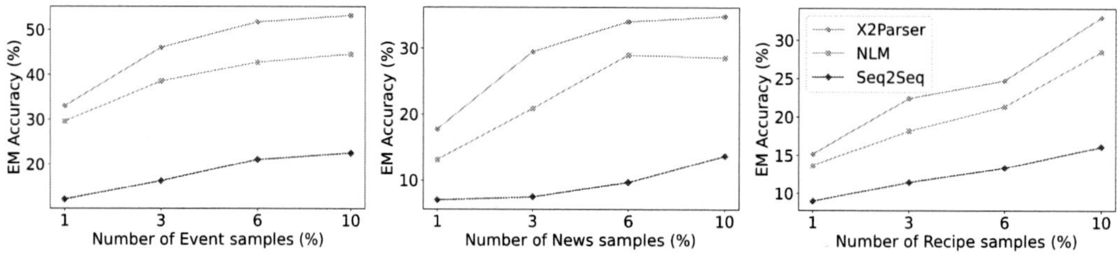

Figure 6: Few-shot exact match results on the **cross-lingual cross-domain setting** for Event, News and Recipe target domains. The results are averaged over all target languages.

factors limit the improvement for X2Parser on the adaptation to topologically distant languages.

From Table 1, although NLM achieves marginally lower performance in English compared to *Seq2Seq w/ XLM-R*, it produces significant improvements in target languages. This can be attributed to the fact that NLM leverages the same task decomposition as X2Parser, which further indicates the effectiveness of decomposing the TCSP task into intent and slot predictions for low-resource scenarios. Additionally, X2Parser surpasses NLM by $\sim$2% exact match accuracy on average in target languages. We conjecture that the stacked layers in NLM could make the model confused about which layer needs to generate which entity types, and this confusion is aggravated in the zero-shot cross-lingual setting where no training data are available. However, our fertility-based method helps the model implicitly learn the structure of hierarchical slots by predicting the number of labels for each token, which allows the slot classifier to predict the slot types more easily in the cross-lingual setting.

Cross-Domain Setting As shown in Table 2, X2Parser and NLM notably surpass the Seq2Seq model, with $\sim$15% improvements on the averaged scores. This can be largely attributed to the effectiveness of our proposed task decomposition for low-resource scenarios. Seq2Seq models need to learn when to generate the label, when to copy tokens from the inputs, and when to produce the end of the label to generate hierarchical representations. This generation process requires a relatively large number of data samples to learn, which leads to the weak few-shot cross-domain performance for the Seq2Seq model. Furthermore, X2Parser outperforms NLM, with a $\sim$2% averaged score. We conjecture that our fertility classifier guides the model to learn the inherent hierarchical information from the user queries, making it easier for the slot classifier to predict slot types for each token. However, the NLM's slot classifier, which consists of multiple stacked layers, needs to capture the hierarchical information and correctly assign slot labels of different levels to the corresponding stacked layer, which requires relatively larger data to learn.

Cross-Lingual Cross-Domain Setting From Table 3 and Figure 4, we can further observe the effectiveness of our proposed task decomposition and X2Parser in the cross-lingual cross-domain setting. X2Parser and NLM consistently outperform the Seq2Seq model in all target languages of the target domains and boost the averaged exact match accuracy by $\sim$20%. Additionally, from Table 3, X2Parser also consistently outperforms NLM on all 11 domains and surpasses it by 3.84% accuracy on average. From Figure 4, X2Parser greatly improves on NLM in topologically distant languages (i.e., Hindi and Thai). It illustrates the powerful transferability and robustness of the fertility-based

Model	Spanish		French		German		Hindi		Thai		Average	
	NN	Nested	NN	Nested	NN	Nested	NN	Nested	NN	Nested	NN	Nested
Seq2Seq	56.21	29.38	48.11	32.83	46.02	20.25	37.84	22.30	33.27	13.56	44.29	23.66
NLM	65.65	**41.95**	61.02	42.91	56.90	37.94	36.48	24.36	34.15	15.70	50.84	32.57
X2Parser	**66.69**	39.19	**63.45**	**44.28**	**58.43**	**39.71**	**42.64**	**28.55**	**35.96**	**16.67**	**53.43**	**33.68**

Table 4: Zero-shot cross-lingual exact match accuracies for nested and non-nested (NN) cases.

slot prediction that enables X2Parser to have a good zero-shot cross-lingual performance after it is fine-tuned to the target domain.

6.2 Few-shot Analysis

We conduct few-shot experiments using different sample sizes from the target domain for the cross-domain and cross-lingual cross-domain settings. The few-shot results on the Event, News, and Recipe target domains for both settings[6] are shown in Figure 5 and Figure 6. We find that the performance of the Seq2Seq model is generally poor in both settings, especially when only 1% of data samples are available. With the help of the task decomposition, NLM and X2Parser remarkably outperform the Seq2Seq model in various target domains for both the cross-domain and cross-lingual cross-domain settings across different few-shot scenarios (from 1% to 10%). Moreover, X2Parser consistently surpasses NLM for both the cross-domain and cross-lingual cross-domain settings in different few-shot scenarios, which further verifies the strong adaptation ability of our model.

Interestingly, we observe that the improvement of X2Parser over Seq2Seq grows as the number of training samples increases. For example, in the cross-lingual cross-domain setting of the event domain, the improvement goes from 20% to 30% as the training data increases from 1% to 10%. We hypothesize that in the low-resource scenario, the effectiveness of X2Parser will be greatly boosted when a relatively large number of data samples are available, while the Seq2Seq model needs much larger training data to achieve good performance.

6.3 Analysis on Nested & Non-Nested Data

To further understand how our model improves the performance, we split the test data in the MTOP dataset (Li et al., 2020a) into nested and non-nested samples. We consider the user utterances that do not have fine-grained intents and nested slots as the non-nested data sample and the rest of the data as the nested data sample. As we can see from Table 4, X2Parser significantly outperforms the Seq2Seq model on both nested and non-nested user queries with an average of ∼10% accuracy improvement in both cases. In addition, X2Parser also consistently surpasses NLM on all target languages in both the nested and non-nested scenarios, except for the Spanish nested case, which further illustrates the stable and robust adaptation ability of X2Parser.

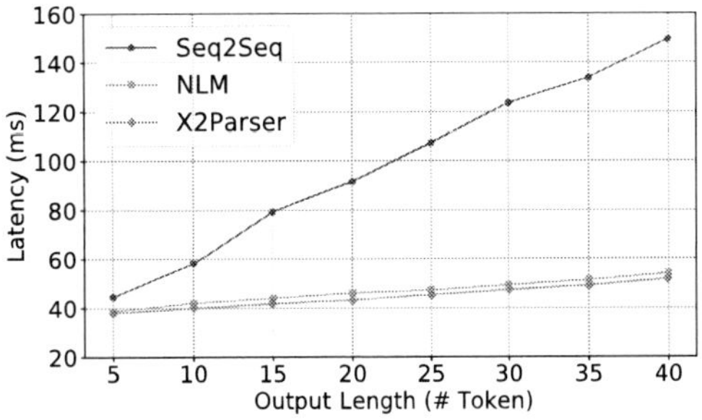

Figure 7: Averaged latencies for our model and baselines on different output lengths of the MTOP dataset.

6.4 Latency Analysis

We can see from Figure 7 that, as the output length increases, the latency discrepancy between the Seq2Seq-based model (Seq2Seq) and sequence labeling-based models (NLM and X2Parser) becomes larger, and when the output length reaches 40 tokens (around the maximum length in MTOP), X2Parser can achieve an up to 66% reduction in latency compared to the Seq2Seq model. This can be attributed to the fact that the Seq2Seq model has to generate the outputs token by token, while X2Parser and NLM can directly generate all the outputs. In addition, the inference speed of X2Parser is slightly faster than that of NLM. This is because NLM uses several stacked layers to predict slot entities of different levels, and the higher-level layer has to wait for the predictions from the lower-level layer, which slightly decreases the inference speed.

[6]We only report three domains due to the page limit, and place the full results for all 11 target domains in the Appendix C and Appendix D.

7 Conclusion

In this paper, we develop a transferable and non-autoregressive model (X2Parser) for the TCSP task that can better adapt to target languages and domains with a faster inference speed. Unlike previous TCSP models that learn to generate hierarchical representations, we propose to decompose the task into intent and slot predictions so as to lower the difficulty of the task, and then we cast both prediction tasks into sequence labeling problems. After that, we further propose a fertility-based method to cope with the slot prediction task where each token could have multiple labels. Results illustrate that X2Parser significantly outperforms strong baselines in all low-resource settings. Furthermore, our model is able to reduce the latency by up to 66% compared to the generation-based model.

Acknowledgement

We want to say thanks to the anonymous reviewers for the insightful reviews and constructive feedback. This work is partially funded by ITF/319/16FP and MRP/055/18 of the Innovation Technology Commission, the Hong Kong SAR Government.

References

Arun Babu, Akshat Shrivastava, Armen Aghajanyan, Ahmed Aly, Angela Fan, and Marjan Ghazvininejad. 2021. Non-autoregressive semantic parsing for compositional task-oriented dialog. In *Proceedings of the 2021 Conference of the North American Chapter of the Association for Computational Linguistics: Human Language Technologies*, pages 2969–2978.

Delphine Charlet, Géraldine Damnati, Frédéric Béchet, Johannes Heinecke, et al. 2020. Cross-lingual and cross-domain evaluation of machine reading comprehension with squad and calor-quest corpora. In *Proceedings of The 12th Language Resources and Evaluation Conference*, pages 5491–5497.

Wenhu Chen, Jianshu Chen, Yu Su, Xin Wang, Dong Yu, Xifeng Yan, and William Yang Wang. 2018. Xl-nbt: A cross-lingual neural belief tracking framework. In *Proceedings of the 2018 Conference on Empirical Methods in Natural Language Processing*, pages 414–424.

Xilun Chen, Asish Ghoshal, Yashar Mehdad, Luke Zettlemoyer, and Sonal Gupta. 2020. Low-resource domain adaptation for compositional task-oriented semantic parsing. In *Proceedings of the 2020 Conference on Empirical Methods in Natural Language Processing (EMNLP)*, pages 5090–5100.

Alexis Conneau, Kartikay Khandelwal, Naman Goyal, Vishrav Chaudhary, Guillaume Wenzek, Francisco Guzmán, Édouard Grave, Myle Ott, Luke Zettlemoyer, and Veselin Stoyanov. 2020. Unsupervised cross-lingual representation learning at scale. In *Proceedings of the 58th Annual Meeting of the Association for Computational Linguistics*, pages 8440–8451.

Alexis Conneau, Ruty Rinott, Guillaume Lample, Adina Williams, Samuel Bowman, Holger Schwenk, and Veselin Stoyanov. 2018. Xnli: Evaluating cross-lingual sentence representations. In *Proceedings of the 2018 Conference on Empirical Methods in Natural Language Processing*, pages 2475–2485.

Alejandro Moreo Fernández, Andrea Esuli, and Fabrizio Sebastiani. 2016. Distributional correspondence indexing for cross-lingual and cross-domain sentiment classification. *Journal of artificial intelligence research*, 55:131–163.

Chih-Wen Goo, Guang Gao, Yun-Kai Hsu, Chih-Li Huo, Tsung-Chieh Chen, Keng-Wei Hsu, and Yun-Nung Chen. 2018. Slot-gated modeling for joint slot filling and intent prediction. In *Proceedings of the 2018 Conference of the North American Chapter of the Association for Computational Linguistics: Human Language Technologies, Volume 2 (Short Papers)*, pages 753–757.

Jiatao Gu, James Bradbury, Caiming Xiong, Victor O.K. Li, and Richard Socher. 2018. Non-autoregressive neural machine translation. In *International Conference on Learning Representations*.

Sonal Gupta, Rushin Shah, Mrinal Mohit, Anuj Kumar, and Mike Lewis. 2018. Semantic parsing for task oriented dialog using hierarchical representations. In *Proceedings of the 2018 Conference on Empirical Methods in Natural Language Processing*, pages 2787–2792.

Suchin Gururangan, Ana Marasović, Swabha Swayamdipta, Kyle Lo, Iz Beltagy, Doug Downey, and Noah A Smith. 2020. Don't stop pretraining: Adapt language models to domains and tasks. In *Proceedings of the 58th Annual Meeting of the Association for Computational Linguistics*, pages 8342–8360.

Haoyang Huang, Yaobo Liang, Nan Duan, Ming Gong, Linjun Shou, Daxin Jiang, and Ming Zhou. 2019. Unicoder: A universal language encoder by pre-training with multiple cross-lingual tasks. In *Proceedings of the 2019 Conference on Empirical Methods in Natural Language Processing and the 9th International Joint Conference on Natural Language Processing (EMNLP-IJCNLP)*, pages 2485–2494.

Chen Jia, Xiaobo Liang, and Yue Zhang. 2019. Cross-domain ner using cross-domain language modeling. In *Proceedings of the 57th Annual Meeting of the Association for Computational Linguistics*, pages 2464–2474.

Meizhi Ju, Makoto Miwa, and Sophia Ananiadou. 2018. A neural layered model for nested named entity recognition. In *Proceedings of the 2018 Conference of the North American Chapter of the Association for Computational Linguistics: Human Language Technologies, Volume 1 (Long Papers)*, pages 1446–1459.

Diederik P Kingma and Jimmy Ba. 2015. Adam: A method for stochastic optimization. In *ICLR (Poster)*.

Haoran Li, Abhinav Arora, Shuohui Chen, Anchit Gupta, Sonal Gupta, and Yashar Mehdad. 2020a. Mtop: A comprehensive multilingual task-oriented semantic parsing benchmark. *arXiv preprint arXiv:2008.09335*.

Juntao Li, Ruidan He, Hai Ye, Hwee Tou Ng, Lidong Bing, and Rui Yan. 2020b. Unsupervised domain adaptation of a pretrained cross-lingual language model. In *IJCAI*.

Bing Liu and Ian Lane. 2016. Attention-based recurrent neural network models for joint intent detection and slot filling. *Interspeech 2016*, pages 685–689.

Zihan Liu, Jamin Shin, Yan Xu, Genta Indra Winata, Peng Xu, Andrea Madotto, and Pascale Fung. 2019. Zero-shot cross-lingual dialogue systems with transferable latent variables. In *Proceedings of the 2019 Conference on Empirical Methods in Natural Language Processing and the 9th International Joint Conference on Natural Language Processing (EMNLP-IJCNLP)*, pages 1297–1303.

Zihan Liu, Genta Indra Winata, Zhaojiang Lin, Peng Xu, and Pascale Fung. 2020a. Attention-informed mixed-language training for zero-shot cross-lingual task-oriented dialogue systems. In *Proceedings of the AAAI Conference on Artificial Intelligence*, volume 34, pages 8433–8440.

Zihan Liu, Genta Indra Winata, Peng Xu, and Pascale Fung. 2020b. Coach: A coarse-to-fine approach for cross-domain slot filling. In *Proceedings of the 58th Annual Meeting of the Association for Computational Linguistics*, pages 19–25.

Zihan Liu, Yan Xu, Tiezheng Yu, Wenliang Dai, Ziwei Ji, Samuel Cahyawijaya, Andrea Madotto, and Pascale Fung. 2020c. Crossner: Evaluating cross-domain named entity recognition. *arXiv preprint arXiv:2012.04373*.

Grégoire Mesnil, Xiaodong He, Li Deng, and Yoshua Bengio. 2013. Investigation of recurrent-neural-network architectures and learning methods for spoken language understanding. In *Interspeech*, pages 3771–3775.

Masato Mimura, Shinsuke Sakai, and Tatsuya Kawahara. 2017. Cross-domain speech recognition using nonparallel corpora with cycle-consistent adversarial networks. In *2017 IEEE Automatic Speech Recognition and Understanding Workshop (ASRU)*, pages 134–140. IEEE.

Jian Ni, Georgiana Dinu, and Radu Florian. 2017. Weakly supervised cross-lingual named entity recognition via effective annotation and representation projection. In *Proceedings of the 55th Annual Meeting of the Association for Computational Linguistics (Volume 1: Long Papers)*, pages 1470–1480.

Jessica Ouyang, Boya Song, and Kathleen McKeown. 2019. A robust abstractive system for cross-lingual summarization. In *Proceedings of the 2019 Conference of the North American Chapter of the Association for Computational Linguistics: Human Language Technologies, Volume 1 (Long and Short Papers)*, pages 2025–2031.

Endang Wahyu Pamungkas and Viviana Patti. 2019. Cross-domain and cross-lingual abusive language detection: A hybrid approach with deep learning and a multilingual lexicon. In *Proceedings of the 57th annual meeting of the association for computational linguistics: Student research workshop*, pages 363–370.

Subendhu Rongali, Luca Soldaini, Emilio Monti, and Wael Hamza. 2020. Don't parse, generate! a sequence to sequence architecture for task-oriented semantic parsing. In *Proceedings of The Web Conference 2020*, pages 2962–2968.

Sebastian Schuster, Sonal Gupta, Rushin Shah, and Mike Lewis. 2019. Cross-lingual transfer learning for multilingual task oriented dialog. In *Proceedings of the 2019 Conference of the North American Chapter of the Association for Computational Linguistics: Human Language Technologies, Volume 1 (Long and Short Papers)*, pages 3795–3805.

Abigail See, Peter J Liu, and Christopher D Manning. 2017. Get to the point: Summarization with pointer-generator networks. In *Proceedings of the 55th Annual Meeting of the Association for Computational Linguistics (Volume 1: Long Papers)*, pages 1073–1083.

Akshat Shrivastava, Pierce Chuang, Arun Babu, Shrey Desai, Abhinav Arora, Alexander Zotov, and Ahmed Aly. 2021. Span pointer networks for non-autoregressive task-oriented semantic parsing. *arXiv preprint arXiv:2104.07275*.

Chau Tran, Yuqing Tang, Xian Li, and Jiatao Gu. 2020. Cross-lingual retrieval for iterative self-supervised training. In *Advances in Neural Information Processing Systems*, volume 33, pages 2207–2219. Curran Associates, Inc.

Ashish Vaswani, Noam Shazeer, Niki Parmar, Jakob Uszkoreit, Llion Jones, Aidan N Gomez, Lukasz Kaiser, and Illia Polosukhin. 2017. Attention is all you need. In *NIPS*.

Genta Indra Winata, Samuel Cahyawijaya, Zihan Liu, Zhaojiang Lin, Andrea Madotto, Peng Xu, and Pascale Fung. 2020. Learning fast adaptation on cross-accented speech recognition. *Proc. Interspeech 2020*, pages 1276–1280.

Chien-Sheng Wu, Andrea Madotto, Ehsan Hosseini-Asl, Caiming Xiong, Richard Socher, and Pascale Fung. 2019. Transferable multi-domain state generator for task-oriented dialogue systems. In *Proceedings of the 57th Annual Meeting of the Association for Computational Linguistics*, pages 808–819.

Jiateng Xie, Zhilin Yang, Graham Neubig, Noah A Smith, and Jaime G Carbonell. 2018. Neural cross-lingual named entity recognition with minimal resources. In *Proceedings of the 2018 Conference on Empirical Methods in Natural Language Processing*, pages 369–379.

Tiezheng Yu, Zihan Liu, and Pascale Fung. 2021. Adaptsum: Towards low-resource domain adaptation for abstractive summarization. In *Proceedings of the 2021 Conference of the North American Chapter of the Association for Computational Linguistics: Human Language Technologies*, pages 5892–5904.

Chenwei Zhang, Yaliang Li, Nan Du, Wei Fan, and S Yu Philip. 2019. Joint slot filling and intent detection via capsule neural networks. In *Proceedings of the 57th Annual Meeting of the Association for Computational Linguistics*, pages 5259–5267.

Xinjie Zhou, Xiaojun Wan, and Jianguo Xiao. 2016. Attention-based lstm network for cross-lingual sentiment classification. In *Proceedings of the 2016 conference on empirical methods in natural language processing*, pages 247–256.

Junnan Zhu, Qian Wang, Yining Wang, Yu Zhou, Jiajun Zhang, Shaonan Wang, and Chengqing Zong. 2019. Ncls: Neural cross-lingual summarization. In *Proceedings of the 2019 Conference on Empirical Methods in Natural Language Processing and the 9th International Joint Conference on Natural Language Processing (EMNLP-IJCNLP)*, pages 3045–3055.

Yftah Ziser and Roi Reichart. 2017. Neural structural correspondence learning for domain adaptation. In *Proceedings of the 21st Conference on Computational Natural Language Learning (CoNLL 2017)*, pages 400–410.

A Intent Label Construction

In this section, we further describe how we convert the fine-grained intent prediction into a sequence labeling task (each token has only one label). We use a few examples to illustrate our intent label construction method.

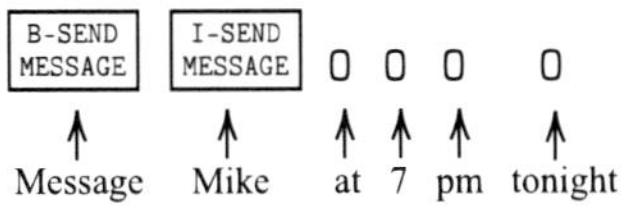

Figure 8: A labeling example for non-nested intent.

As illustrated in Figure 8, when there are no nested intents in the input utterance, we follow the BIO structure to give intent labels.

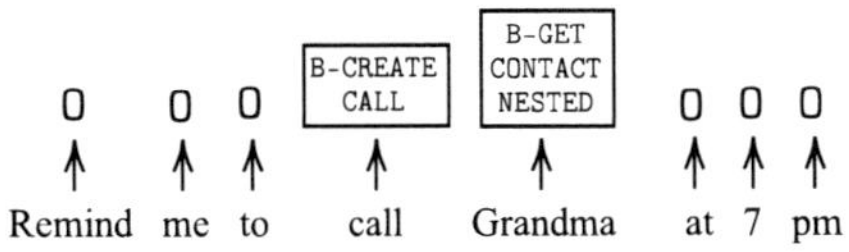

Figure 9: A labeling example for nested intent.

We can see from Figure 9 that "call Grandma" is a `CREATE-CALL` intent and "Grandma" is a `GET-CONTACT` intent. Hence, the `GET-CONTACT` intent is nested in the `CREATE-CALL` intent. We use a special intent label (with "NESTED") for the "`GET-CONTACT`" intent (`B-GET-CONTACT-NESTED`) to represent that this intent is nested in another intent, and hence, the scope of the `CREATE-CALL` intent is automatically expanded from "call" to "call Grandma". [7]

Note that we cannot apply this labeling method to the slot prediction since one token in the user utterance could be the starting token for more than one slot entity. If that is the case, we have to use more than one slot label for this token to denote the starting position for each slot entity. Given that in the MTOP dataset, one token will not be the starting token of more than one intent, we can apply this method for the intent label construction. In the future, when more complex and sophisticated datasets are collected for the task-oriented compositional semantic parsing task, where there could exist more than one intent label for each token, we can always use the fertility-based method (currently applied for the slot prediction) for the intent prediction.

[7]We notice that if two intents have overlaps, one intent either fully covers the other intent or is fully covered by the other intent.

B Data Statistics

The data statistics for MTOP are shown in Table 5.

C Few-shot Cross-Domain Results

Full few-shot cross-domain results across all 11 target domains are shown in Figure 10 and Table 6.

D Few-shot Cross-Lingual Cross-Domain Results

Full few-shot cross-lingual cross-domain results across all 11 target domains are shown in Figure 11 and Tables 7, 8, 9, 10, and 11.

Domain	Number of Utterances						Intent	Slot
	English	German	French	Spanish	Hindi	Thai	Types	Types
Alarm	1,783	1,581	1,706	1,377	1,510	1,783	6	5
Calling	2,872	2,797	2,057	2,515	2,490	2,872	19	14
Event	1,081	1,051	1,115	911	988	1,081	12	12
Messaging	1,053	1,239	1,335	1,164	1,082	1,053	7	15
Music	1,648	1,499	1,312	1,509	1,418	1,648	27	12
News	1,393	905	1,052	1,130	930	1,393	3	6
People	1,449	1,392	763	1,408	1,168	1,449	17	16
Recipes	1,586	1,002	762	1,382	929	1,586	3	18
Reminder	2,439	2,321	2,202	1,811	1,833	2,439	19	17
Timer	1,358	1,014	1,165	1,159	1,047	1,358	9	5
Weather	2,126	1,785	1,990	1,816	1,800	2,126	4	4
Total	18,788	16,585	15,459	16,182	15,195	18,788	117	78

Table 5: Data statistics of the MTOP dataset. The data are roughly divided into a 70:10:20 percent split for train, eval and test

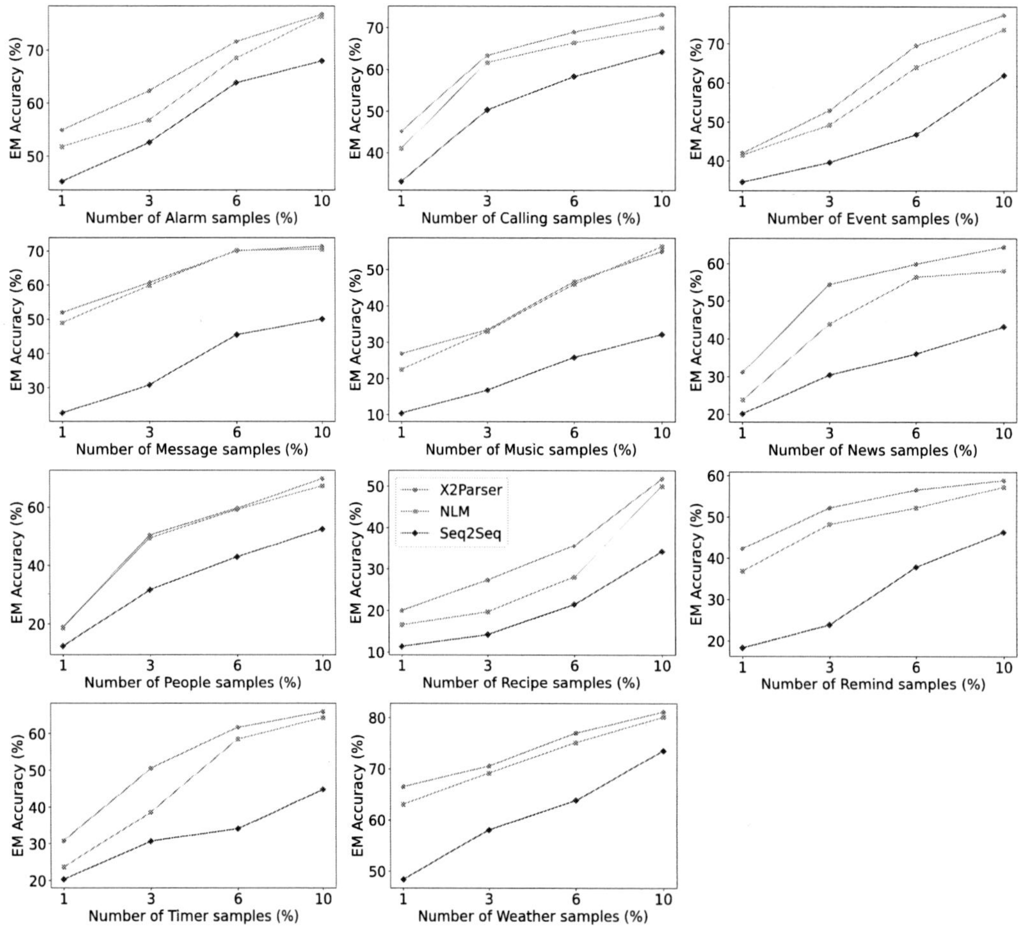

Figure 10: Few-shot exact match accuracies for the **cross-domain setting** across all 11 target domains.

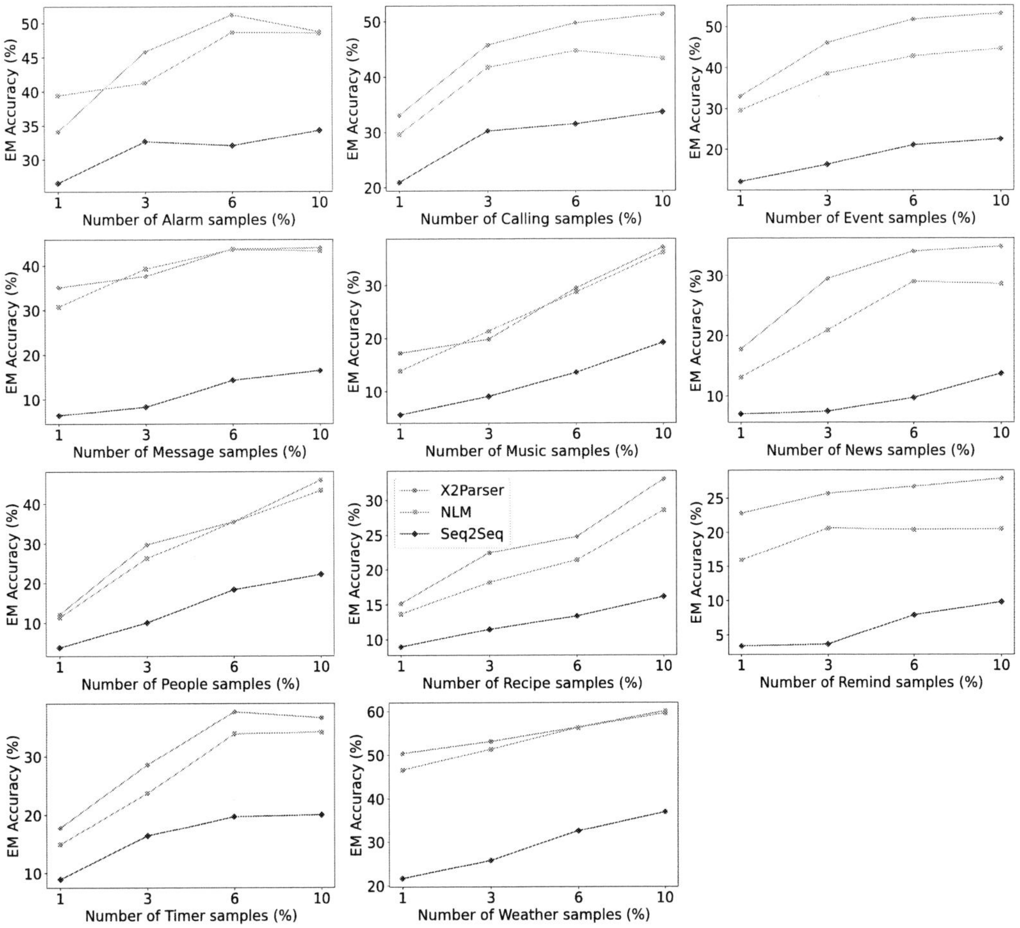

Figure 11: Few-shot Exact match accuracies for the **cross-lingual cross-domain setting** across all 11 target domains. The results are averaged over all target languages.

# Sample	Model	Alarm	Call.	Event	Msg.	Music	News	People	Recipe	Remind	Timer	Weather	Avg
	Seq2Seq	45.22	33.07	34.52	22.58	10.38	20.14	12.43	11.39	18.33	20.34	48.36	25.16
1%	NLM	51.75	41.00	41.46	48.97	22.49	23.84	18.65	16.52	36.84	23.67	63.11	35.30
	X2Parser	**54.94**	**45.20**	**41.96**	**51.91**	**26.83**	**31.19**	**18.83**	**20.00**	**42.31**	**30.80**	**66.53**	**39.14**
	Seq2Seq	52.55	50.33	39.59	30.87	16.82	30.45	31.64	14.20	23.90	30.69	58.06	34.46
3%	NLM	56.86	61.68	49.24	59.86	33.06	43.95	49.43	19.71	48.23	38.62	69.20	48.17
	X2Parser	**62.36**	**63.37**	**52.97**	**60.70**	**33.42**	**54.38**	**50.47**	**27.34**	**52.21**	**50.58**	**70.57**	**52.58**
	Seq2Seq	63.88	58.32	46.70	45.48	25.87	36.03	42.94	21.45	37.81	34.14	63.86	43.32
6%	NLM	68.53	66.42	63.96	**70.28**	45.98	56.33	59.23	28.12	52.21	58.51	75.16	58.61
	X2Parser	**71.61**	**68.97**	**69.54**	70.09	**46.70**	**59.87**	**59.70**	**35.65**	**56.57**	**61.70**	**77.00**	**61.58**
	Seq2Seq	67.94	64.25	61.93	50.11	32.20	43.20	52.54	34.21	46.32	44.83	73.58	51.92
10%	NLM	76.32	70.02	73.60	70.58	**56.52**	58.01	67.33	50.01	57.28	64.37	80.15	65.83
	X2Parser	**76.72**	**73.16**	**77.33**	**71.45**	55.19	**64.43**	**69.77**	**51.78**	**58.86**	**65.98**	**81.17**	**67.80**

Table 6: Complete results of the **cross-domain setting**.

# Sample	Model	Alarm	Call.	Event	Msg.	Music	News	People	Recipe	Remind	Timer	Weather	Avg
1%	Seq2Seq	33.81	28.00	24.29	9.89	8.22	13.59	4.49	15.87	7.87	14.29	38.86	18.11
	NLM	44.41	31.75	36.53	41.95	14.36	16.34	12.82	**23.28**	21.76	24.67	57.92	29.62
	X2Parser	**51.51**	**36.67**	**36.72**	**51.84**	**20.86**	**19.90**	**15.60**	19.05	**26.16**	**30.74**	**59.65**	**33.52**
3%	Seq2Seq	48.58	41.75	30.51	14.07	12.35	10.68	17.31	19.84	6.94	28.57	42.82	24.86
	NLM	53.41	50.33	43.31	**54.37**	**26.10**	29.45	34.19	**24.61**	25.46	38.96	**64.03**	40.38
	X2Parser	**56.06**	**54.75**	**46.14**	53.23	24.25	**33.82**	**34.61**	23.54	**30.79**	**44.73**	63.61	**42.32**
6%	Seq2Seq	51.70	43.50	36.16	25.48	16.91	18.45	27.56	23.02	12.50	33.33	51.49	30.92
	NLM	60.32	52.83	48.02	60.84	**41.46**	**47.25**	**46.58**	26.19	27.70	53.10	67.41	48.34
	X2Parser	**66.10**	**61.67**	**53.30**	**61.85**	40.24	44.82	44.01	**27.78**	**31.48**	**53.97**	**68.81**	**50.37**
10%	Seq2Seq	59.94	47.00	41.81	25.86	22.85	25.39	34.21	21.25	17.59	32.90	60.69	35.41
	NLM	64.57	57.08	53.11	60.08	49.86	**48.84**	58.12	34.13	24.61	51.95	70.30	52.06
	X2Parser	**65.81**	**59.75**	**54.24**	**61.98**	**51.36**	46.12	**59.62**	**36.51**	**32.10**	**56.57**	**71.45**	**54.14**

Table 7: Complete results of the **cross-lingual cross-domain setting** in Spanish.

# Sample	Model	Alarm	Call.	Event	Msg.	Music	News	People	Recipe	Remind	Timer	Weather	Avg
1%	Seq2Seq	43.94	30.77	15.72	11.55	8.07	5.66	8.09	12.15	5.87	13.16	35.67	17.33
	NLM	53.13	35.04	**41.51**	46.75	16.07	7.55	15.32	18.78	26.01	23.51	59.74	31.22
	X2Parser	**54.65**	**37.48**	**41.51**	**49.40**	**21.67**	**10.27**	**18.01**	**20.44**	**29.28**	**26.67**	**65.07**	**34.04**
3%	Seq2Seq	51.21	42.91	16.98	10.76	9.07	8.81	8.09	14.92	5.22	22.11	43.54	21.24
	NLM	55.66	49.58	51.57	**54.98**	**25.32**	17.82	33.34	23.94	30.73	34.91	65.73	40.33
	X2Parser	**59.70**	**52.87**	**54.72**	52.99	24.40	**18.03**	**38.60**	**27.81**	**31.74**	**40.18**	**65.92**	**42.45**
6%	Seq2Seq	49.70	45.24	25.79	19.92	17.86	5.66	19.85	19.89	14.78	31.05	55.62	27.76
	NLM	64.08	50.00	57.86	**63.88**	36.67	23.27	**48.41**	28.73	28.48	50.18	**74.72**	47.84
	X2Parser	**66.77**	**59.22**	**58.49**	59.49	**38.45**	**25.16**	46.81	**29.84**	**35.29**	**55.62**	71.82	**49.72**
10%	Seq2Seq	50.00	46.34	27.67	29.48	24.29	10.18	25.43	25.10	16.09	28.42	57.81	30.98
	NLM	59.64	52.68	**61.22**	**62.29**	48.93	22.59	57.35	31.49	32.75	**52.81**	**76.69**	50.77
	X2Parser	**62.32**	**56.84**	58.70	61.89	**49.17**	**25.58**	**60.54**	**38.49**	**36.31**	52.28	75.37	**52.50**

Table 8: Complete results of the **cross-lingual cross-domain setting** in French.

# Sample	Model	Alarm	Call.	Event	Msg.	Music	News	People	Recipe	Remind	Timer	Weather	Avg
1%	Seq2Seq	35.13	21.61	7.36	8.81	7.98	11.74	3.58	6.90	0.89	17.19	24.15	13.21
	NLM	46.27	37.43	44.58	27.81	18.95	24.50	14.70	11.84	16.03	22.00	57.86	29.27
	X2Parser	**52.03**	**39.32**	**45.40**	**34.72**	**21.68**	**33.97**	**15.17**	**15.29**	**19.98**	**27.09**	**60.52**	**33.20**
3%	Seq2Seq	38.81	35.45	15.34	8.81	13.89	13.26	15.41	11.03	2.46	28.12	23.69	18.75
	NLM	52.50	48.44	57.87	38.86	**28.94**	38.38	38.35	16.32	21.55	36.98	64.84	40.28
	X2Parser	**52.69**	**50.18**	**58.28**	**39.90**	25.82	**48.36**	**45.04**	**24.71**	**23.64**	**39.32**	**65.83**	**43.07**
6%	Seq2Seq	37.68	38.10	20.25	17.62	15.80	18.18	25.81	13.10	6.49	30.47	36.67	23.65
	NLM	54.77	50.00	62.78	42.14	34.75	47.35	50.54	21.72	21.92	47.27	70.31	45.78
	X2Parser	**59.39**	**55.31**	**69.32**	**48.70**	**35.08**	**51.77**	**53.53**	**28.74**	**25.28**	**50.00**	**73.20**	**50.03**
10%	Seq2Seq	39.38	35.90	22.09	13.47	25.17	22.83	30.24	17.83	7.38	32.03	36.89	25.75
	NLM	**60.13**	54.76	64.01	46.98	**42.16**	46.84	57.35	40.12	22.30	49.22	73.88	50.70
	X2Parser	56.75	**56.23**	**68.92**	**49.05**	40.96	**52.65**	**65.59**	**42.64**	**24.91**	**51.56**	**75.47**	**53.16**

Table 9: Complete results of the **cross-lingual cross-domain setting** in German.

# Sample	Model	Alarm	Call.	Event	Msg.	Music	News	People	Recipe	Remind	Timer	Weather	Avg
	Seq2Seq	11.99	13.30	9.85	1.46	1.65	3.23	1.91	3.08	0.00	0.00	6.89	4.85
1%	NLM	**16.10**	17.67	15.15	20.39	9.92	12.73	**9.54**	5.73	1.27	**3.25**	30.44	12.92
	X2Parser	**16.10**	**25.04**	**25.00**	**20.55**	**10.60**	**15.59**	7.76	**7.64**	**12.88**	**3.25**	**31.63**	**16.00**
	Seq2Seq	11.61	18.00	14.39	6.80	4.83	3.76	5.73	3.96	0.38	2.56	14.07	7.83
3%	NLM	14.23	28.62	23.49	**24.27**	13.54	14.87	16.29	9.25	3.28	5.47	**34.33**	17.06
	X2Parser	**25.59**	**34.76**	**40.91**	21.85	**14.46**	**34.77**	**19.08**	**17.03**	**15.66**	**16.93**	32.64	**24.88**
	Seq2Seq	14.61	13.73	18.18	6.31	10.26	4.84	11.83	5.29	0.38	2.56	12.87	9.17
6%	NLM	**29.63**	**35.29**	29.80	22.17	**20.11**	21.33	20.74	9.84	2.15	16.07	**38.42**	22.32
	X2Parser	27.97	34.05	**47.47**	**23.62**	17.36	**36.74**	**21.88**	**16.59**	**16.54**	**26.84**	33.34	**27.49**
	Seq2Seq	11.24	22.53	18.94	8.74	13.31	7.23	13.54	6.52	0.38	5.64	19.07	11.56
10%	NLM	22.58	25.61	32.07	21.36	**24.38**	20.25	24.30	15.13	2.40	14.19	**38.61**	21.90
	X2Parser	**30.71**	**43.92**	**50.25**	**22.33**	22.73	**33.33**	**25.06**	**22.02**	**16.54**	**20.17**	35.53	**29.33**

Table 10: Complete results of the **cross-lingual cross-domain setting** in Hindi.

# Sample	Model	Alarm	Call.	Event	Msg.	Music	News	People	Recipe	Remind	Timer	Weather	Avg
	Seq2Seq	7.82	10.81	3.40	0.00	1.82	0.64	0.94	6.90	2.31	0.00	2.59	3.38
1%	NLM	**37.08**	26.27	10.20	16.92	9.93	4.46	**4.40**	8.74	14.65	1.06	26.82	14.59
	X2Parser	34.12	**26.77**	**16.33**	**18.95**	**11.29**	**8.92**	4.25	**13.33**	**25.76**	**1.24**	**34.87**	**17.80**
	Seq2Seq	12.93	12.96	4.08	1.02	5.08	0.64	3.77	7.59	3.20	0.53	4.60	5.13
3%	NLM	30.61	31.54	16.49	**24.03**	**12.75**	3.82	8.96	16.78	22.02	**2.29**	27.59	17.90
	X2Parser	**35.03**	**36.09**	**30.16**	20.14	10.07	**12.32**	**11.32**	**19.08**	**26.55**	1.77	**37.36**	**21.81**
	Seq2Seq	6.46	16.95	4.76	2.03	6.86	1.27	6.60	5.52	5.32	1.06	6.03	5.71
6%	NLM	34.39	35.31	15.42	**29.10**	10.48	5.73	10.85	20.46	21.73	**2.65**	30.36	19.68
	X2Parser	**35.83**	**38.21**	**30.16**	25.21	**16.19**	**11.68**	**11.16**	**20.92**	**24.87**	1.77	**34.36**	**22.76**
	Seq2Seq	10.88	16.53	2.04	4.57	10.45	2.91	7.25	9.90	7.56	1.06	10.02	7.56
10%	NLM	**35.75**	26.34	12.70	**25.89**	15.92	4.46	**19.34**	21.84	20.45	**2.65**	38.39	20.34
	X2Parser	28.00	**39.75**	**34.01**	24.70	**22.04**	**16.56**	19.02	**25.29**	**29.50**	2.47	**42.43**	**25.80**

Table 11: Complete results of the **cross-lingual cross-domain setting** in Thai.

Unsupervised Representation Disentanglement of Text: An Evaluation on Synthetic Datasets

Lan Zhang[♠] **Victor Prokhorov**[♣] **Ehsan Shareghi**[♠♣]
[♠] Department of Data Science & AI, Monash University
[♣] Language Technology Lab, University of Cambridge
lan.zhang@monash.edu vp361@cam.ac.uk
ehsan.shareghi@monash.edu

Abstract

To highlight the challenges of achieving representation disentanglement for text domain in an unsupervised setting, in this paper we select a representative set of successfully applied models from the image domain. We evaluate these models on 6 disentanglement metrics, as well as on downstream classification tasks and homotopy. To facilitate the evaluation, we propose two synthetic datasets with known generative factors. Our experiments highlight the existing gap in the text domain and illustrate that certain elements such as representation sparsity (as an inductive bias), or representation coupling with the decoder could impact disentanglement. To the best of our knowledge, our work is the first attempt on the intersection of unsupervised representation disentanglement and text, and provides the experimental framework and datasets for examining future developments in this direction.[1]

1 Introduction

Learning task-agnostic unsupervised representations of data has been the center of attention across various areas of Machine Learning and more specifically NLP. However, little is known about the way these continuous representations organise information about data. In recent years, the NLP community has focused on the question of design and selection of suitable linguistic tasks to probe the presence of syntactic or semantic phenomena in representations as a whole (Bosc and Vincent, 2020; Voita and Titov, 2020; Torroba Hennigen et al., 2020; Pimentel et al., 2020; Hewitt and Liang, 2019; Ettinger et al., 2018; Marvin and Linzen, 2018; Conneau et al., 2018). Nonetheless, a fine-grain understanding of information organisation in coordinates of a continuous representation is yet to be achieved.

Arguably, a necessity to move in this direction is agreeing on the cognitive process behind language generation (fusing semantic, syntactic, and lexical components), which can then be reflected in the design of representation learning frameworks. However, this still remains generally as an area of debate and perhaps less pertinent in the era of self-supervised masked language models and the resulting surge of new state-of-the-art results.

Even in the presence of such an agreement, learning to disentangle the surface realization of the underlying factors of data (e.g., semantics, syntactic, lexical) in the representation space is a non-trivial task. Additionally, there is no established study for evaluating such models in NLP. A handful of recent works have looked into disentanglement for text by splitting the representation space into *predefined* disentangled subspaces such as style and content (Cheng et al., 2020; John et al., 2019), or syntax and semantics (Balasubramanian et al., 2021; Bao et al., 2019; Chen et al., 2019), and rely on *supervision* during training. However, a generalizable and realistic approach needs to be *unsupervised* and capable of identifying the underlying factors solely via the regularities presented in data.

In areas such as image processing, the same question has been receiving a lot of attention and inspired a wave of methods for learning and evaluating unsupervised representation disentanglement (Ross and Doshi-Velez, 2021; Mathieu et al., 2019; Kim and Mnih, 2018; Burgess et al., 2018; Higgins et al., 2018, 2017) and creation of large scale datasets (Dittadi et al., 2021). It has been argued that disentanglement is the means towards representation interpretability (Mathieu et al., 2019), generalization (Montero et al., 2021), and robustness (Bengio et al., 2013; Bengio, 2013). However, these benefits are yet to be realized and evaluated in text domain.

[1]Code and datasets are available at https://github.com/lanzhang128/disentanglement

Proceedings of the 6th Workshop on Representation Learning for NLP (RepL4NLP-2021), pages 128–140
Bangkok, Thailand (Online), August 6, 2021.

In this work we take a representative set of *unsupervised* disentanglement learning frameworks widely used in image domain (§2.1) and apply them to two artificially created corpora with known underlying generative factors (§3). Having known generative factors (while being ignored during the training phase) allows us to evaluate the performance of these models on imposing representation disentanglement via 6 disentanglement metrics (§2.2; §4.1). Additionally, taking the highest scoring models and corresponding representations, we investigate the impact of representation disentanglement on two downstream text classification tasks (§4.3), and dimension-wise homotopy (§4.4).

We show that existing disentanglement models, when evaluated on a wide range of metrics, are inconsistent and highly sensitive to model initialisation. However, where disentanglement is achieved, it shows its positive impact on improving downstream task performance. Our work highlights the potential and existing challenges of disentanglement on text. We hope our proposed datasets, accessible description of disentanglement metrics and models, and experimental framework will set the path for developments of models specific to for text.

2 Disentanglement Models and Metrics

Let $\mathbf{x}$ denote data points and $\mathbf{z}$ denote latent variables in the latent representation space, and assume data points are generated by the combination of two random process: The first random process samples a point $\mathbf{z}^{(i)}$ from the latent space with prior distribution of $\mathbf{z}$, denoted by $p(\mathbf{z})$. The second random process generates a point $\mathbf{x}^{(i)}$ from the data space, denoted by $p(\mathbf{x}|\mathbf{z}^{(i)})$.

We consider $\mathbf{z}$ as a disentangled representation for $\mathbf{x}$, if the changes in single latent dimensions of $\mathbf{z}$ are sensitive to changes in single generative factors of $\mathbf{x}$ while being relatively invariant to changes in other factors (Bengio et al., 2013). Several probabilistic models are designed to reveal this process, here we look at some of the most widely used ones.

2.1 Disentanglement Models

A prominent approach for learning disentangled representations is through adjusting Variational Auto-Encoders (VAEs) (Kingma and Welling, 2014) objective function, which decompose the representation space into independently learned coordinates. We start by introducing vanilla VAE, and then cover some of its widely used extensions that encourage disentanglement:

VAE uses a combination of a probabilistic encoder $q_\phi(\mathbf{z}|\mathbf{x})$ and decoder $p_\theta(\mathbf{x}|\mathbf{z})$, parameterised by ϕ and θ, to learn this statistical relationship between $\mathbf{x}$ and $\mathbf{z}$. The VAEs are trained by maximizing the lower bound of the logarithmic data distribution $\log p(\mathbf{x})$, called evidence lower bound,

$$\mathbb{E}_{q_\phi(\mathbf{z}|\mathbf{x})}\big[\log p_\theta(\mathbf{x}|\mathbf{z})\big] - \mathbb{D}_{KL}(q_\phi(\mathbf{z}|\mathbf{x}), p(\mathbf{z}))$$

The first term of is the expectation of the logarithm of data likelihood under the posterior distribution of z. The second term is KL-divergence, measuring the distance between the posterior distribution $q_\phi(\mathbf{z}|\mathbf{x})$ and the prior distribution $p(\mathbf{z})$ and can be seen as a regularisation.

β-VAE (Higgins et al., 2017) adds a hyperparameter β to control the regularisation from the KL-term via the following objective function:

$$\mathbb{E}_{q_\phi(\mathbf{z}|\mathbf{x})}\big[\log p_\theta(\mathbf{x}|\mathbf{z})\big] - \beta\mathbb{D}_{KL}(q_\phi(\mathbf{z}|\mathbf{x}), p(\mathbf{z}))$$

Reconstructing under β-VAE (with the right value of β) framework encourages encoding data points on a set of representational axes on which nearby points along those dimensions are also close in original data space (Burgess et al., 2018).

CCI-VAE (Burgess et al., 2018) extends β-VAE via constraint optimisation:

$$\mathbb{E}_{q_\phi(\mathbf{z}|\mathbf{x})}\big[\log p_\theta(\mathbf{x}|\mathbf{z})\big] - \beta\,|\mathbb{D}_{KL}(q_\phi(\mathbf{z}|\mathbf{x}), p(\mathbf{z})) - C|$$

where C is a positive real value which represents the target KL-divergence term value. This has an information-theoretic interpretation, where the placed constraint C on the KL term is seen as the amount of information transmitted from a sender (encoder) to a receiver (decoder) via the message ($\mathbf{z}$) (Alemi et al., 2018), and impacts the sharpness of the posterior distribution (Prokhorov et al., 2019). This constraint allows the model to prioritize underlying factors of data according to the availability of channel capacity and their contributions to the reconstruction loss improvement.

MAT-VAE (Mathieu et al., 2019) introduces an additional term to β-VAE, $\mathbb{D}_{MMD}(q_\phi(\mathbf{z}), p_\theta(\mathbf{z}))$,

$$\mathbb{E}_{q_\phi(\mathbf{z}|\mathbf{x})}[\log p_\theta(\mathbf{x}|\mathbf{z})] - \beta\mathbb{D}_{KL}(q_\phi(\mathbf{z}|\mathbf{x}), p(\mathbf{z})) \\ -\lambda\mathbb{D}_{MMD}(q_\phi(\mathbf{z}), p(\mathbf{z}))$$

where $\mathbb{D}_{MMD}$ is computed using maximum mean discrepancy (Gretton et al. (2012), MMD) and λ is the scalar weight. This term regularises the aggregated posterior $q_\phi(\mathbf{z})$ with a factorised spike-and-slab prior (Mitchell and Beauchamp, 1988), which aims for disentanglement via clustering and sparsifying the representations of $\mathbf{z}$.

2.1.1 Issue of KL-Collapse

In text modelling, the presence of powerful auto-regressive decoders poses a common optimisation challenge for training VAEs called posterior collapse, where the learned posterior distribution $q_\phi(\mathbf{z}|\mathbf{x})$, collapses to the prior $p(\mathbf{z})$. Posterior collapse results in the latent variables $\mathbf{z}$ being ignored by the decoder. Several strategies have been proposed to alleviate this problem from different angles such as choice of decoders (Yang et al., 2017; Bowman et al., 2016), adding more dependency between encoder and decoder (Dieng et al., 2019), adjusting the training process (Bowman et al., 2016; He et al., 2019), imposing direct constraints to the KL term (Pelsmaeker and Aziz, 2020; Razavi et al., 2019; Burgess et al., 2018; Higgins et al., 2017). In this work, both β-VAE (with $\beta < 1$) and CCI-VAE are effective methods to avoid KL-collpase.

2.2 Disentanglement Metrics

In this section we provide a short overview of six widely used disentanglement metrics, highlighting their key differences and commonalities, and refer the readers to the corresponding papers for exact details of computations.

Eastwood and Williams (2018) define three criteria for disentangled representations: *disentanglement*, which measures the degree of one dimension only encoding information about no more than one generative factor; *completeness*, which measures whether a generative factor is only captured by one latent variable; *informativeness*, which measures the degree by which representations capture exact values of the generative factors.[2] They design a series of classification tasks to predict the value of a generative factor based on the latent code, and extract the relative importance of each latent code for each task to calculate disentanglement and completeness scores. Informativeness score is measured by the accuracy of the classifier directly. Other existing metrics reflect at least one of these three criteria, as summarised in Table 1.

[2]These criteria are referred to modularity, compactness and explicitness by Ridgeway and Mozer (2018).

Metric	Dis.	Com.	Info.	Ex.1↑	Ex.2↑
Higgins et al. (2017)	Yes	No	No	100	100
Ridgeway and Mozer (2018)	Yes	No	No	100	100
Kim and Mnih (2018)	Yes	Yes	No	100	100
Chen et al. (2018)	No	Yes	No	81.05	5.73
Eastwood and Williams (2018)	Yes	Yes	Yes	66.47	63.45
Kumar et al. (2018)	No	Yes	Yes	4.68	3.98

Table 1: The disentanglement (Dis.), completeness (Com.), and informativeness (Info.) criteria reflected in six metrics. The Ex.1 and Ex.2 columns are corresponding metrics' scores (%) on two ideally disentangled representations.

Higgins et al. (2017) focus on disentanglement and propose to use the absolute difference of two groups of representations with the same value on one generative factor to predict this generative factor. For perfectly disentangled representations, latent dimensions not encoding information about this generative factor would have zero difference. Hence, even simple linear classifiers could easily identify the generative factors based on the changes of values. Kim and Mnih (2018) consider both disentanglement and completeness by first finding the dimension which has the largest variance when fixing the value on one generative factor, and then using the found dimension to predict that generative factor. Kumar et al. (2018) propose a series of classification tasks each of which uses a single latent variable to predict the value of a generative factor and treat the average of the difference between the top two accuracy scores for each generative factor as the final disentanglement score.

Apart from designing classification tasks for disentanglement evaluation, another method is based on estimating the mutual information (MI) between a single dimension of the latent variable and a single generative factor. Chen et al. (2018) propose to use the average of the gap (difference) between the largest normalised MI (by the information entropy of the generative factor) and the second largest normalised MI over all generative factors as the disentanglement score, whereas the modularity metric of Ridgeway and Mozer (2018) measures whether a single latent variable has the highest MI with only one generative factor and none with others.

The algorithmic details for computing the above metrics are provided in Appendix A.

Empirical Difference. To highlight the empirical difference between these metrics, we use a toy set built by permuting four letters: A B C D. Each letter representing a generative factor with 20 choices of assignments (i.e, $X = \{X1, \ldots, X20\}$

where $X \in \{A, B, C, D\}$). We consider two settings where each generative factor is embedded in a single dimension (denoted by Ex.1), or two dimensions (denoted by Ex.2). In each setting we uniformly sample 20 values from -1 to 1 to represent 20 assignments per factor and use them to allocate the assignments into distinctive bins per each corresponding dimension. By concatenating dimensions for each generative factor, we construct two ideal disentangled representations for data points in this toy dataset, amounting to 4 and 8 dimensional representations, respectively. Using these representations (skipping the encoding step), we measured the above metrics. Table 1 (Ex.1 and Ex.2 columns) summarises the results, illustrating that out of the 6 metrics, Higgins et al. (2017); Ridgeway and Mozer (2018); Kim and Mnih (2018) are the only ones that reach the potential maximum (i.e., 100), while Chen et al. (2018) exhibits its sensitivity towards *completeness* when we allocate two dimensions per factors.

Data Requirement. Measuring the mentioned disentanglement metrics requires a dataset satisfying the following attributes:

1. A set $\mathbb{F}$ where each of its elements is a generative factor which should be disentangled through representations;
2. For each element $f_i \in \mathbb{F}$, a value space $\mathbb{V}_i$ which is the domain of f_i;
3. For each value $v_{ij} \in \mathbb{V}_i$, a sample space $\mathbb{S}_{ij}$ which contains observations who has value v_{ij} on generative factor f_i while everything else is arbitrary.

We present two synthetic datasets (§3) that meet these criteria and use them in our experiments (§4).

3 Generative Synthetic Datasets

The use of synthetic datasets is the common practice for evaluating disentanglement in image domain (Dittadi et al., 2021; Higgins et al., 2017; Kim and Mnih, 2018). Generative simplistic datasets in image domain define independent generative factors (e.g. shape, color) behind the data generation. However, a comparable resource is missing in text domain. We develop two synthetic generative datasets with varying degrees of difficulty to analyse and measure disentanglement: The YNOC dataset (§3.1) which has only three structures and generative factors appearing in every sentence, and the POS dataset (§3.2) which has more structures while some generative factors are not guaranteed to appear in every sentence. The YNOC dataset offers a simpler setting for disentanglement.

Simple Sentence Structures	# of Sentences
n. v. n. end-punc.	200
n. v. adj. n. end-punc.	1,000
n. adv. v. n. end-punc.	1,000
n. adv. v. adj. n. end-punc.	5,000
n. v. prep. n. end-punc.	1,000
n. v. prep. adj. n. end-punc.	5,000
n. adv. v. prep. n. end-punc.	5,000
n. adv. v. prep. adj. n. end-punc.	25,000
adj. n. v. n. end-punc.	1,000
adj. n. v. adj. n. end-punc.	4,000
adj. n. adv. v. n. end-punc.	5,000
adj. n. adv. v. adj. n. end-punc.	20,000
adj. n. v. prep. n. end-punc.	5,000
adj. n. v. prep. adj. n. end-punc.	20,000
adj. n. adv. v. prep. n. end-punc.	25,000
adj. n. adv. v. prep. adj. n. end-punc.	100,000

n. [dogs cats foxes horses tigers]
v. [want need have get require]
adv. [really recently gradually frequently eventually]
adj. [happy big small beautiful fantastic]
prep. [on in for to of]
conj1. [although because when where whereas]
conj2. [and or]
comma [,]
end-punc. [. !]

Table 2: Simple sentence structures and the vocabulary used for each POS tag in our synthetic dataset.

3.1 YNOC Dataset

Sentences in YNOC are generated by 4 generative factors: Year (Y), Name (N), Occupation (O), and City (C), describing the occupation of a person. Since we often use different means to express the same message, we considered three templates to generate YNOC sentences:

Template I. *in Y, N was a/an O in C.*
Template II. *in Y's C, N was a/an O.*
Template III. *N was a/an O in C in Y.*

The templates were then converted into real sentences using 10 years, 40 names, 20 occupations, and 30 cities. This amounted to a total of 720K sentences, split as (60%,20%,20%) into training, validation, and test sets.

3.2 POS Dataset

We use part-of-speech (POS) tags to simulate the structure of sentences and define a base grammar as *"n. v. n. end-punc."*, where 'n.' denotes noun, 'v.' denotes verb and 'end-punc.' denotes the punctuation which appears at the end of sentences. Then we define simple sentence structures as *"(adj.) n.*

(adv.) v. (prep.) (adj.) n. end-punc.", where 'adj.' denotes adjective, 'adv.' denotes adverb, 'prep.' denotes preposition, and '()' marks the arbitrary inclusion/removal of the corresponding POS tag. We populate the structures with $2^4 = 16$ simple structures presented in Table 2.

Next, we define complex sentence structures as combinations of two simple sentence structures by applying one of the following three rules:

Rule I. *conj1. S1 comma S2 end-punc.*
Rule II. *S1 conj1. S2 end-punc.*
Rule III. *S1 comma conj2. S2 end-punc.*

where 'conj1.' and 'conj2.' denote two different kinds of conjunction, 'comma' denotes ',' and 'S1' and 'S2' are two simple sentence structures without 'end-punc.' We limit the number of POS tags that appear in 'S1' and 'S2' to 9 to control the complexity of generating sentences and obtain 279 complex structures in total. A maximum of 5 words is chosen for each POS to construct our sentences.

The frequency of appearance for each word in a sentence is limited to one. Although this construction does not focus on sentences being "realistic", it simulate natural text in terms of the presence of an underlying grammar and rules over POS tags.[3] We deliberately ignore semantics, since isolating semantics in terms of generative factors potentially involves analysis over multiple dimensions (combinatorial space) and quantifying grouped disentanglement requires suitable disentanglement metrics to be developed. We leave further exploration of this to our future work.

We split the dataset into training, validation and test sets with proportion 60%, 20%, 20%. This proportion is used for every structure to ensure they have representative sentences in each portion of the data splits. The final size of (training, validation, test) sets are (1723680, 574560, 574560). All three sets are unbiased on word selection for each POS tag: e.g., all 5 noun POS vocabs from Table 2 have equal frequency (i.e., 20%). Exactly the same proportions are preserved for validation and test sets.

Through the process of the generation, we can define each POS tag as one ground truth generative factor for sentences.[4] Because the choices of words for different POS tags are independent, these generative factors are independent. However, for the same POS, the choices of words are dependent and POS tags are dependent on the structures as well. It is noteworthy that in contrast to the image domain where all generative factors are always present in the data, in POS dataset this cannot be guaranteed, making it a more challenging setting.

4 Experiments and Analysis

In this section, we examine the introduced disentanglement models on text. We measure the disentanglement scores of each model on our two synthetic datasets and quantify how well-correlated these metrics are with reconstruction loss, active units, and KL (§4.1). We then look at various strategies for coupling the latent code during decoding and highlight their impacts on training and disentanglement behaviors (§4.2). We continue our analysis by showing how the representation learned by the highest scoring model (on disentanglement metrics) performs compared to vanilla VAE in two text classification tasks (§4.3), and finish our analysis by looking at these models' generative behaviors (§4.4).

Training Configuration. We adopt the VAE architecture from (Bowman et al., 2016), using a LSTM encoder-decoder. Unless stated otherwise, (word embedding, LSTM, representation embedding) dimensionalities for YNOC and POS datasets are (4D, 32D, 4D) and (4D, 64D, 8D), respectively, and we use the latent code to initialize the hidden state of the LSTM decoder. We use greedy decoding. All models are trained from multiple random starts using Adam (Kingma and Ba, 2015) with learning rate 0.001 for 10 epochs. We set batch size to 256 and 512 for YNOC and POS, respectively.

4.1 Disentanglement Metrics

Taking the models (§2.1) and also an Autoencoder (AE) as a baseline we use the YNOC and POS datasets to report average KL-divergence (KL), reconstruction loss (Rec.), and number of active units (AU)[5] in Table 3, and illustrate disentanglement metrics' scores in Figure 1.

As demonstrated in Table 3, different models pose various behaviors, noteworthy of those are:

[3] For structures which can produce more than 10k sentences (e.g. longer structures), we randomly choose 10k.

[4] While we consider POS tags as the generative factors in this paper, further sub-categorisation of POS tags based on position (e.g., first-noun and second-noun, etc) or grammatical roles (e.g., subject-noun and object-noun, etc) is a possibility for future investigation.

[5] i is active if $\text{Covariance}_{\mathbf{x}}(\mathbb{E}_{i\sim q(i|\mathbf{x})}[i]) > 0.01$.

Model	YNOC				POS			
	KL	Rec.↓	AU↑	Top-3↑	KL	Rec.↓	AU↑	Top-3↑
AE	-	$8.87_{\pm 0.66}$	$4.0_{\pm 0.0}$	1	-	$4.91_{\pm 1.83}$	$8.0_{\pm 0.0}$	3
Vanilla-VAE	$0.02_{\pm 0.02}$	$13.48_{\pm 0.02}$	$0.4_{\pm 0.5}$	0	$0.01_{\pm 0.00}$	$19.57_{\pm 0.00}$	$0.2_{\pm 0.4}$	3
β-VAE ($\beta = 0.2$)	$4.25_{\pm 0.31}$	$9.72_{\pm 0.25}$	$1.0_{\pm 0.0}$	3	$11.19_{\pm 2.88}$	$12.03_{\pm 2.04}$	$2.8_{\pm 0.7}$	3
β-VAE ($\beta = 0.4$)	$3.44_{\pm 0.23}$	$10.32_{\pm 0.23}$	$1.2_{\pm 0.4}$	1	$7.75_{\pm 0.69}$	$13.87_{\pm 0.85}$	$2.6_{\pm 0.5}$	3
β-VAE ($\beta = 0.8$)	$1.39_{\pm 0.41}$	$12.14_{\pm 0.40}$	$1.0_{\pm 0.0}$	1	$5.61_{\pm 0.78}$	$14.26_{\pm 0.72}$	$1.8_{\pm 0.4}$	1
CCI-VAE ($C = 5$)	$5.00_{\pm 0.00}$	$9.51_{\pm 0.30}$	$1.8_{\pm 1.0}$	1	$5.04_{\pm 0.03}$	$15.01_{\pm 0.30}$	$2.2_{\pm 0.4}$	0
CCI-VAE ($C = 10$)	$10.00_{\pm 0.00}$	$9.48_{\pm 0.49}$	$3.4_{\pm 0.5}$	2	$10.01_{\pm 0.01}$	$12.76_{\pm 1.18}$	$4.0_{\pm 1.3}$	1
MAT-VAE ($\beta = 0.1, \lambda = 0.1$)	$6.11_{\pm 0.39}$	$9.49_{\pm 0.17}$	$1.0_{\pm 0.0}$	2	$22.14_{\pm 2.92}$	$8.47_{\pm 2.28}$	$3.0_{\pm 0.0}$	3
MAT-VAE ($\beta = 0.01, \lambda = 0.1$)	$15.38_{\pm 1.86}$	$7.12_{\pm 0.32}$	$3.2_{\pm 0.7}$	7	$45.48_{\pm 1.65}$	$3.47_{\pm 0.99}$	$8.0_{\pm 0.0}$	1

Table 3: Results are calculated on the test set. We report mean value and standard deviation across 5 runs.

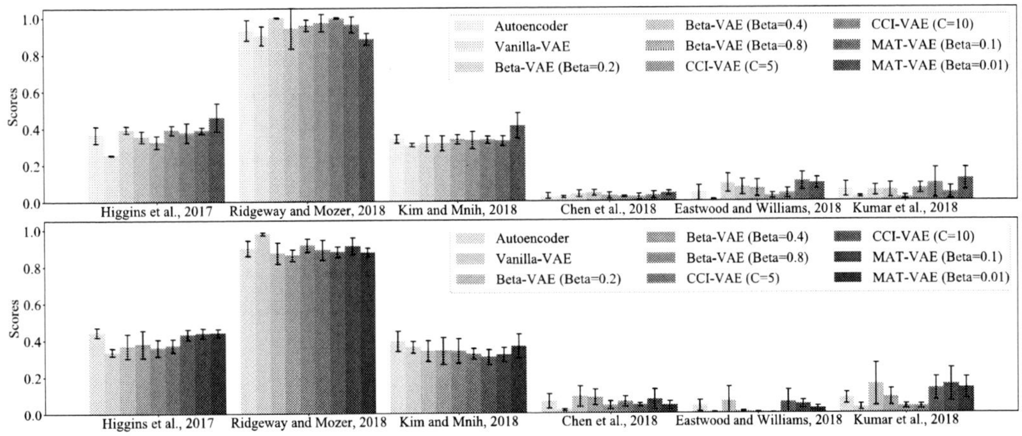

Figure 1: Disentanglement scores across six metrics on **top:** YNOC dataset and **bottom:** POS dataset. For better illustration, we multiply the scores of Eastwood and Williams (2018) and Kumar et al. (2018) by 10.

(1) the positive correlation of C with AU which intuitively means the increase of channel capacity demands more dimensions of the representation to carry information which then translates into having a better reconstruction of data, (2) the negative correlation between the increase of β and decrease of reconstruction loss, (3) the best Rec. and AU are achieved by AE and MAT-VAE whereas the worst one is achieved by the (collapsed) vanilla-VAE, (4) the MAT-VAE ($\beta = 0.01, \lambda = 0.1$) model which induces more sparse representations [6] performs the best on both datasets, indicating the positive impact of representation sparsity as an inductive bias.

As illustrated in Figure 1, the difference between means of each disentanglement score on various models is relatively small, and due to large standard deviation on metrics, it is difficult to single out a superior model. This verifies findings of Locatello et al. (2019) on image domain. In Table 3 (Top-3 column) we report the number of appearances of a model among the top 3 highest scoring models on at least one disentanglement metric. The ranking suggests that β-VAE with smaller β values reach better disentangled representations, and MAT-VAE performing superior on YNOC and poorly on POS, highlighting its more challenging nature. For MAT-VAE we also observe an interesting correlation between sparsity and disentanglement: for instance on YNOC, MAT-VAE ($\beta = 0.01, \lambda = 0.1$) achieves the highest Hoyer (See Table 4) and occurs 7 times among Top-3 (see Table 3). Interestingly, the success of MAT-VAE does not translate to POS dataset, where it underperforms AE. These two observations suggest that sparsity could be a facilitator for disentanglement, but achieving a stable level of sparsity remains as a challenge. The more recent development in the direction of sparsity, HSVAE (Prokhorov et al., 2020), addresses the stability issue of MAT-VAE but we leave its exploration to future work.

To further analyse the inconsistency between different metrics we calculate the Pearson product-

[6] Sparsity is measured using Hoyer (Hurley and Rickard, 2009). In this paper we report this as the average Hoyer over data points' posterior means. Hoyer for data point x_i with posterior mean μ_i is calculated as $\frac{\sqrt{d} - ||\bar{\mu}_i||_1 / ||\bar{\mu}_i||_2}{\sqrt{d} - 1}$, where d is the dimensionality of the representations and $\bar{\mu}_i = \mu_i / \sigma(\mu)$, where $\mu = \{\mu_1, ..., \mu_n\}$, and $\sigma(.)$ is the standard deviation.

	AE	VAE	β-VAE			CCI-VAE		MAT-VAE	
			$\beta = 0.2$	$\beta = 0.4$	$\beta = 0.8$	$C = 5$	$C = 10$	$\beta = 0.1, \lambda = 0.1$	$\beta = 0.01, \lambda = 0.1$
YNOC	$0.22_{\pm 0.03}$	$0.03_{\pm 0.02}$	$0.30_{\pm 0.03}$	$0.30_{\pm 0.02}$	$0.30_{\pm 0.05}$	$0.32_{\pm 0.04}$	$0.30_{\pm 0.01}$	$0.36_{\pm 0.03}$	$0.43_{\pm 0.09}$
POS	$0.30_{\pm 0.05}$	$0.21_{\pm 0.03}$	$0.25_{\pm 0.00}$	$0.27_{\pm 0.01}$	$0.29_{\pm 0.04}$	$0.29_{\pm 0.05}$	$0.28_{\pm 0.01}$	$0.29_{\pm 0.00}$	$0.28_{\pm 0.01}$

Table 4: Hoyer scores are calculated on the test set. We report mean value and standard deviation across 5 runs.

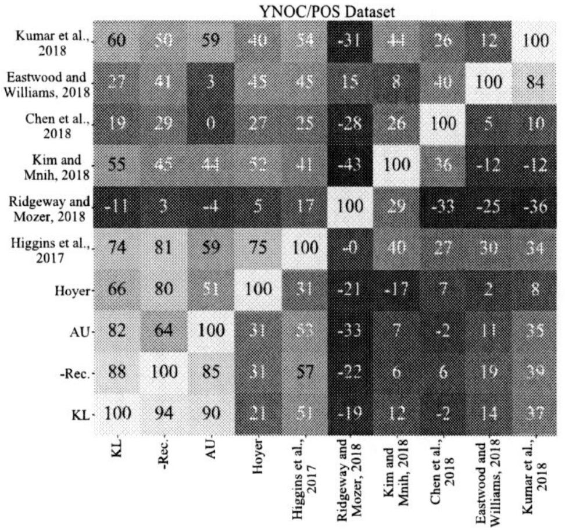

Figure 2: Correlation coefficients between six disentanglement metrics, Hoyer, AU, Rec, and KL on **Upper Triangle:** YNOC dataset and **Lower Triangle:** POS dataset.

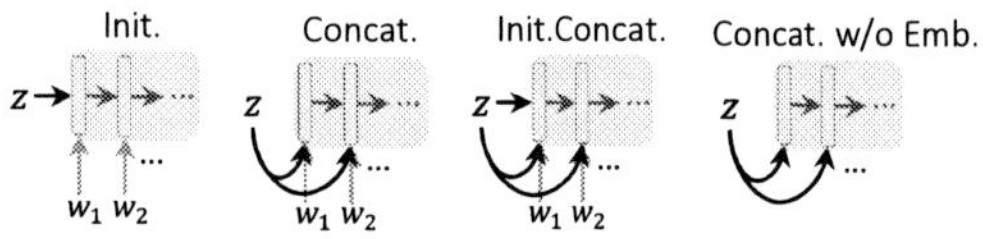

(a) Different coupling strategies for the latent code and decoder (§4.2). Gray box denotes decoder.

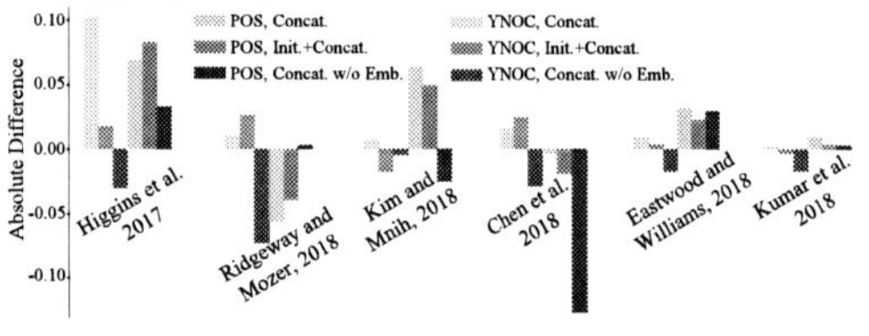

(b) Absolute differences between disentanglement metrics' scores of Init. coupling and others (§4.2).

Figure 3: Different coupling strategies for the latent code and decoder and their impacts on disentanglement on POS and YNOC.

		Coupling Methods			
		Init.	Concat.	Init.Concat.	Concat. w/o Emb.
YNOC	KL	1.51±0.01	1.52±0.01	1.52±0.01	1.62±0.04
	Rec.↓	12.04±0.04	12.06±0.03	12.01±0.02	12.29±0.16
	AU↑	1.2±0.4	2.0±0.0	1.0±0.0	1.2±0.4
POS	KL	5.54±0.02	5.53±0.02	5.51±0.00	5.69±0.03
	Rec.↓	14.54±0.33	15.89±0.26	15.98±0.05	16.48±0.09
	AU↑	2.2±0.4	4.0±0.0	3.2±0.4	3.6±0.5

Table 5: Test set KL, Reconstruction loss, Active Units using 4 coupling methods (§4.2).

moment correlation coefficient between them and KL, -Rec, AU, Hoyer on POS and YNOC datasets. See the heatmap in Figure 2. While text-specific metrics are yet to be developed, our experiment suggests Higgins et al. (2017) is a good candidate to try first for text domain as it seems to be the one with strong correlation with Hoyer, AU, -Rec, and KL and has the highest level of agreement (overall) with other metrics.

4.2 Coupling Latent Code and Decoder

In VAEs, we typically feed the decoder with the latent code as well as word embeddings during training. The method to couple the latent code with decoder could have some effects on disentanglement for text. To highlight this, we train with 4 different coupling strategies: *Init*, *Concat*, *Init Concat*, *Concat w/o Emb*. See Figure 3a for an accessible visualisation. To analyse the impact of coupling, we opt for CCI-VAE which allows the comparisons to be made for the same value of KL.

We first use *Concat w/o Emb* to find an optimal KL in vanilla VAEs, which is then used as the C to train CCI-VAEs using the other coupling metrics on YNOC and POS datasets. For YNOC, $C = 1.5$, and for POS, $C = 5.5$. This is to keep KL-divergence and reconstruction loss at the same level for fair comparison across different strategies. We report results in Table 5. Among the investigated coupling methods, the key distinguishing factor for disentanglement is their impacts on AU which is the highest for *Concat*.

Next, using *Init* as the baseline, we measure the absolute difference between disentanglement scores of different coupling methods in Figure 3b. In general, using concatenation can bring a large improvement in disentanglement. Using both initialization and concatenation do not lead to a better result. Despite our expectation, not feeding word embeddings into decoder during training does not encourage disentanglement due to the added reliance on the latent code.

A confounding factor which could pollute this analysis is the role of strong auto-regressive decoding of VAEs and the type of information captured

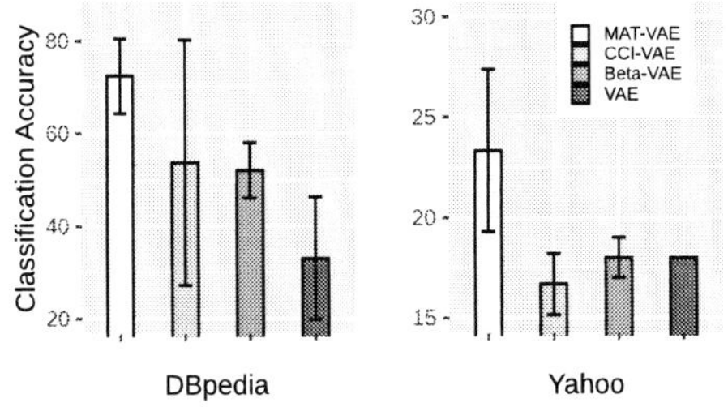

Figure 4: Classification accuracy on DBpedia and Yahoo Question using different VAE models. Results are reported as mean and std across 3 randomly initialised runs.

by the decoder in such scenario. While a preliminary analysis has been provided recently (Bosc and Vincent, 2020), this has been vastly underexplored and requires more explicit attempts. We leave deeper investigation of this to future work.

4.3 Disentanglement and Classification

To examine the performance of these models on real-world downstream task setting, we consider the classification task. For our classification datasets, we use DBpedia (14 classes) and Yahoo Question (10 classes) (Zhang et al., 2015). Each **class** of these two datasets has (10k, 1k, 1k) randomly chosen sentences in (train, dev, test) sets. We train Vanilla-VAE, β-VAE ($\beta = 0.2$), CCI-VAE ($C = 10$), and MAT-VAE ($\beta = 0.01, \lambda = 0.1$) from Table 3 on DBpedia and Yahoo (without the labels), then freeze the trained encoders and place a classifier on top to use the mean vector representations from the encoder as a feature to train a classifier.

We set the dimensionality of word embedding, LSTM, and the latent space to 128, 512, 32, respectively. The VAE models are trained using a batch size of 64, for 6 epochs with Adam (learning rate 0.001). For the classifier, we use a single linear layer with 1024 neurons, followed by a Softmax and train it for 15 epochs, using Adam (learning rate 0.001) and batch size 512. We illustrate the mean and standard deviation across 3 runs of models in Figure 4.

We observe that the ranking of classification accuracy among the models on DBpedia is consistent with their Top-3 performance in Table 3, with MAT-VAE outperforming the other three variants. We see roughly the same trend for Yahoo, with MAT-VAE being the dominating model. This indicates

START	z_1	$[\mathbf{z_{1,1}}, \mathbf{z_{1,2}}, \mathbf{z_{1,3}}]$		
$i = 1$	$z'_{1,1}$	$\boxed{z_{1,1}}, z_{1,2}, z_{1,3}$	$\rightarrow$	$\boxed{z_{2,1}}, z_{1,2}, z_{1,3}$
$i = 2$	$z'_{1,2}$	$z_{2,1}, \boxed{z_{1,2}}, z_{1,3}$	$\rightarrow$	$z_{2,1}, \boxed{z_{2,2}}, z_{1,3}$
$i = 3$	$z'_{1,3}$	$z_{2,1}, z_{2,2}, \boxed{z_{1,3}}$	$\rightarrow$	$z_{2,1}, z_{2,2}, \boxed{z_{2,3}}$
END	z_2			$[\mathbf{z_{2,1}}, \mathbf{z_{2,2}}, \mathbf{z_{2,3}}]$

Table 6: An example of a 3D latent code transformation in the dimension-wise homotopy. In row i, $\rightarrow$ denotes the start and end points of interpolation, solid box denotes the two dimensions being interpolated, and dashed box denotes the updated dimensions from $i - 1$.

that disentangled representations are likely to be easier to discriminate, although the role of sparsely learned representations could contribute to MAT-VAE's success as well (Prokhorov et al., 2020).

4.4 Disentanglement and Generation

To observe the effect of disentanglement in homotopy (Bowman et al., 2016), we use the exactly same toy dataset introduced in §2.1 and assess the homotopy behaviour of the highest scoring VAE vs. an ideal representation. To conduct homotopy, we interpolate between two sampled sequences' representations and pass the intermediate representations to decoder to generate the output. We use 4D word embedding, 16D LSTM, 4D latent space. We report the results for the VAEs scoring the highest on disentanglement (w.r.t. Higgins et al. (2017) denoted as VAE-Higg) and completeness (w.r.t. Chen et al. (2018) denoted as VAE-Chen). The VAE-Higg and VAE-Chen are β-VAE with $\beta = 0.4$ and MAT-VAE with $\beta = 0.01, \lambda = 0.1$, respectively.

Additionally, to highlight the role of generative factor in generation, we conduct a dimension-wise homotopy, transitioning from the first to the last sentence by interpolating between the dimensions one-by-one. This is implemented as follows: (i) using prior distribution[7] we sample two latent codes denoted by $\mathbf{z}_1 = (z_{1,1}, z_{1,2}, \dots, z_{1,n})$, $\mathbf{z}_2 = (z_{2,1}, z_{2,2}, \dots, z_{2,n})$; (ii) for i-th dimension, using $\mathbf{z}'_{1,i} = (z_{2,1}, \dots, z_{2,i-1}, z_{1,i}, \dots, z_{1,n})$ as the start, we interpolate along the i-th dimension towards $\mathbf{z}'_{2,i} = (z_{2,1}, \dots, z_{2,i}, z_{1,i+1}, \dots, z_{1,n})$. Table 6 illustrates this for a 3D latent code example.

Results: Table 7 reports the outputs for standard homotopy (top block) and dimension-wise homotopy. The results for standard homotopy demon-

[7] Instead of prior, we sample two sentences from test set and use their representations. This is to avoid the situation where samples are not in the well-estimated region of the posterior.

	Ideal	VAE-Higg	VAE-Chen
$\mathbf{z}_1$	**A9 B17 C13 D3**	**A12 B14 C14 D12**	**A9 B4 C10 D15**
Homotopy	A20 B17 C1 D3	A12 B14 C14 D12	A7 B4 C10 D15
	A4 B17 C12 D6	A8 B14 C14 D12	A14 B4 C10 D15
	A3 B1 C6 D6	A20 B14 C14 D12	A20 B19 C10 D15
	A13 B1 C6 D20	A15 B14 C14 D12	A8 B19 C10 D15
$\mathbf{z}_2$	**A15 B2 C8 D10**	**A4 B14 C14 D12**	**A12 B19 C10 D15**
$\mathbf{z}_1$	**A9 B17 C13 D3**	**A12 B14 C14 D12**	**A9 B4 C10 D15**
Dim 1	A20 B17 C13 D3	A12 B14 C14 D12	A7 B4 C10 D15
	A4 B17 C13 D3	A8 B14 C14 D12	A4 B19 C10 D15
	A3 B17 C13 D3	A20 B14 C14 D12	A8 B19 C10 D15
	A13 B17 C13 D3	A18 B14 C14 D12	A12 B19 C10 D15
$\mathbf{z}'_{1,2}$	**A15** B17 C13 D3	**A4** B14 C14 D12	**A12** B19 C10 D15
Dim 2	A15 B17 C13 D3	A4 B14 C14 D12	A12 B19 C10 D15
	A15 B17 C13 D3	A4 B14 C14 D12	A12 B19 C10 D15
	A15 B17 C13 D3	A4 B14 C14 D12	A12 B19 C10 D15
	A15 B1 C13 D3	A4 B14 C14 D12	A12 B19 C10 D15
$\mathbf{z}'_{1,3}$	A15 **B2** C13 D3	A4 **B14** C14 D12	A12 **B19** C10 D15
Dim 3	A15 B2 C1 D3	A4 B14 C14 D12	A12 B19 C10 D15
	A15 B2 C12 D3	A4 B14 C14 D12	A12 B19 C10 D15
	A15 B2 C6 D3	A4 B14 C14 D12	A12 B19 C10 D15
	A15 B2 C6 D3	A4 B14 C14 D12	A12 B19 C10 D15
$\mathbf{z}'_{1,4}$	A15 B2 **C8** D3	A4 B14 **C14** D12	A12 B19 **C10** D15
Dim 4	A15 B2 C8 D3	A4 B14 C14 D12	A12 B19 C10 D15
	A15 B2 C8 D6	A4 B14 C14 D12	A12 B19 C10 D15
	A15 B2 C8 D6	A4 B14 C14 D12	A12 B19 C10 D15
	A15 B2 C8 D20	A4 B14 C14 D12	A12 B19 C10 D15
$\mathbf{z}_2$	**A15 B2 C8 D10**	**A4 B14 C14 D12**	**A12 B19 C10 D15**

Table 7: The homotopy experiments, comparing an ideal generator and the best disentangled VAEs according to Higgins et al. (2017) (VAE-Higg) and Chen et al. (2018) (VAE-Chen).

strate that the presence of ideally disentangled representation translates into disentangled generation in general. However, both VAE-Higg and VAE-Chen seem to mainly be producing variations of the letter in the first position (letter **A**) during the interpolation. The same observation holds in the dimension-wise experiments. VAE-Chen also produces variations of the letter in the second position (letter **B**) along with the variation of letter **A**, which suggests the lesser importance of completeness for disentangled representations.

This indicates that despite the relative superior performance of certain models on the metrics and classification tasks, the amount of disentanglement present in the representation is not sufficient enough to be reflected by the generative behavior of these models. As a future work, we would look into the role of auto-regressive decoding and teacher-forcing as confounding factors that can potentially affect the disentanglement process.

5 Conclusion and Future Directions

We evaluated a set of recent *unsupervised* disentanglement learning frameworks widely used in image domain on two artificially created corpora with known underlying generative factors. Our experiments highlight the existing gaps in text domain, the daunting tasks state-of-the-art models from image domain face on text, and the confounding elements that pose further challenges towards representation disentanglement in text domain. Motivated by our findings, in future, we will explore the role of inductive biases such as representation sparsity in achieving representation disentanglement. Additionally, we will look into alternative forms of decoding and training which may compromise reconstruction quality but increase the reliance of decoding on the representation, hence allowing for a more controlled analysis and evaluation.

Our synthetic datasets and experimental framework provide a set of quantitative and qualitative measures to facilitate and future research in developing new models, datasets, and evaluation metrics specific for text.

References

Alexander Alemi, Ben Poole, Ian Fischer, Joshua Dillon, Rif A Saurous, and Kevin Murphy. 2018. Fixing a broken elbo. In *International Conference on Machine Learning*, pages 159–168. PMLR.

Vikash Balasubramanian, Ivan Kobyzev, Hareesh Bahuleyan, Ilya Shapiro, and Olga Vechtomova. 2021. Polarized-VAE: Proximity based disentangled representation learning for text generation. In *Proceedings of the 16th Conference of the European Chapter of the Association for Computational Linguistics: Main Volume*, pages 416–423, Online. Association for Computational Linguistics.

Yu Bao, Hao Zhou, Shujian Huang, Lei Li, Lili Mou, Olga Vechtomova, Xin-yu Dai, and Jiajun Chen. 2019. Generating sentences from disentangled syntactic and semantic spaces. In *Proceedings of the 57th Annual Meeting of the Association for Computational Linguistics*, pages 6008–6019, Florence, Italy. Association for Computational Linguistics.

Y. Bengio, A. Courville, and P. Vincent. 2013. Representation learning: A review and new perspectives. *IEEE Transactions on Pattern Analysis and Machine Intelligence*, 35(8):1798–1828.

Yoshua Bengio. 2013. Deep learning of representations: Looking forward. In *Statistical Language and Speech Processing - First International Conference, SLSP 2013, Tarragona, Spain, July 29-31, 2013. Proceedings*, volume 7978 of *Lecture Notes in Computer Science*, pages 1–37. Springer.

Tom Bosc and Pascal Vincent. 2020. Do sequence-to-sequence VAEs learn global features of sentences? In *Proceedings of the 2020 Conference on Empirical Methods in Natural Language Processing (EMNLP)*, pages 4296–4318, Online. Association for Computational Linguistics.

Samuel R. Bowman, Luke Vilnis, Oriol Vinyals, Andrew M. Dai, Rafal Józefowicz, and Samy Bengio. 2016. Generating sentences from a continuous space. In *Proceedings of the 20th SIGNLL Conference on Computational Natural Language Learning, CoNLL 2016*, pages 10–21, Berlin, Germany. ACL.

Christopher P. Burgess, Irina Higgins, Arka Pal, Loïc Matthey, Nick Watters, Guillaume Desjardins, and Alexander Lerchner. 2018. Understanding disentangling in β-vae. *CoRR*, abs/1804.03599.

Mingda Chen, Qingming Tang, Sam Wiseman, and Kevin Gimpel. 2019. A multi-task approach for disentangling syntax and semantics in sentence representations. In *Proceedings of the 2019 Conference of the North American Chapter of the Association for Computational Linguistics: Human Language Technologies, Volume 1 (Long and Short Papers)*, pages 2453–2464, Minneapolis, Minnesota. Association for Computational Linguistics.

Ricky T. Q. Chen, Xuechen Li, Roger B Grosse, and David K Duvenaud. 2018. Isolating sources of disentanglement in variational autoencoders. In *Advances in Neural Information Processing Systems*, volume 31, pages 2610–2620. Curran Associates, Inc.

Pengyu Cheng, Martin Renqiang Min, Dinghan Shen, Christopher Malon, Yizhe Zhang, Yitong Li, and Lawrence Carin. 2020. Improving disentangled text representation learning with information-theoretic guidance. In *Proceedings of the 58th Annual Meeting of the Association for Computational Linguistics*, pages 7530–7541, Online. Association for Computational Linguistics.

Alexis Conneau, German Kruszewski, Guillaume Lample, Loïc Barrault, and Marco Baroni. 2018. What you can cram into a single $&!#* vector: Probing sentence embeddings for linguistic properties. In *Proceedings of the 56th Annual Meeting of the Association for Computational Linguistics (Volume 1: Long Papers)*, pages 2126–2136, Melbourne, Australia. Association for Computational Linguistics.

Adji B. Dieng, Yoon Kim, Alexander M. Rush, and David M. Blei. 2019. Avoiding latent variable collapse with generative skip models. In *The 22nd International Conference on Artificial Intelligence and Statistics, AISTATS 2019*, volume 89 of *Proceedings of Machine Learning Research*, pages 2397–2405, Naha, Okinawa, Japan. PMLR.

Andrea Dittadi, Frederik Träuble, Francesco Locatello, Manuel Wuthrich, Vaibhav Agrawal, Ole Winther, Stefan Bauer, and Bernhard Schölkopf. 2021. On the transfer of disentangled representations in realistic settings. In *International Conference on Learning Representations*.

Cian Eastwood and Christopher K. I. Williams. 2018. A framework for the quantitative evaluation of disentangled representations. In *International Conference on Learning Representations*.

Allyson Ettinger, Ahmed Elgohary, Colin Phillips, and Philip Resnik. 2018. Assessing composition in sentence vector representations. In *Proceedings of the 27th International Conference on Computational Linguistics*, pages 1790–1801, Santa Fe, New Mexico, USA. Association for Computational Linguistics.

Arthur Gretton, Karsten M. Borgwardt, Malte J. Rasch, Bernhard Schölkopf, and Alexander Smola. 2012. A kernel two-sample test. *Journal of Machine Learning Research*, 13(25):723–773.

Junxian He, Daniel Spokoyny, Graham Neubig, and Taylor Berg-Kirkpatrick. 2019. Lagging inference networks and posterior collapse in variational autoencoders. In *7th International Conference on Learning Representations, ICLR 2019*, New Orleans, LA, USA.

John Hewitt and Percy Liang. 2019. Designing and interpreting probes with control tasks. In *Proceedings of the 2019 Conference on Empirical Methods in Natural Language Processing and the 9th International Joint Conference on Natural Language Processing (EMNLP-IJCNLP)*, pages 2733–2743, Hong Kong, China. Association for Computational Linguistics.

Irina Higgins, David Amos, David Pfau, Sébastien Racanière, Loïc Matthey, Danilo J. Rezende, and Alexander Lerchner. 2018. Towards a definition of disentangled representations. *CoRR*, abs/1812.02230.

Irina Higgins, Loïc Matthey, Arka Pal, Christopher Burgess, Xavier Glorot, Matthew Botvinick, Shakir Mohamed, and Alexander Lerchner. 2017. beta-vae: Learning basic visual concepts with a constrained variational framework. In *5th International Conference on Learning Representations, ICLR 2017, Conference Track Proceedings*, Toulon, France.

N. Hurley and S. Rickard. 2009. Comparing measures of sparsity. *IEEE Transactions on Information Theory*, 55(10):4723–4741.

Vineet John, Lili Mou, Hareesh Bahuleyan, and Olga Vechtomova. 2019. Disentangled representation learning for non-parallel text style transfer. In *Proceedings of the 57th Annual Meeting of the Association for Computational Linguistics*, pages 424–434, Florence, Italy. Association for Computational Linguistics.

Hyunjik Kim and Andriy Mnih. 2018. Disentangling by factorising. In *Proceedings of the 35th International Conference on Machine Learning, ICML 2018*, volume 80 of *Proceedings of Machine Learning Research*, pages 2649–2658, Stockholmsmässan, Stockholm Sweden. PMLR.

Diederik P. Kingma and Jimmy Ba. 2015. Adam: A method for stochastic optimization. In *3rd International Conference on Learning Representations,*

ICLR 2015, Conference Track Proceedings, San Diego, CA, USA.

Diederik P. Kingma and Max Welling. 2014. Auto-encoding variational bayes. In *2nd International Conference on Learning Representations, ICLR 2014, Banff, AB, Canada, April 14-16, 2014, Conference Track Proceedings*.

Abhishek Kumar, Prasanna Sattigeri, and Avinash Balakrishnan. 2018. VARIATIONAL INFERENCE OF DISENTANGLED LATENT CONCEPTS FROM UNLABELED OBSERVATIONS. In *International Conference on Learning Representations*.

Francesco Locatello, Stefan Bauer, Mario Lucic, Gunnar Raetsch, Sylvain Gelly, Bernhard Schölkopf, and Olivier Bachem. 2019. Challenging common assumptions in the unsupervised learning of disentangled representations. In *Proceedings of the 36th International Conference on Machine Learning, ICML 2019*, volume 97 of *Proceedings of Machine Learning Research*, pages 4114–4124, Long Beach, California, USA. PMLR.

Rebecca Marvin and Tal Linzen. 2018. Targeted syntactic evaluation of language models. In *Proceedings of the 2018 Conference on Empirical Methods in Natural Language Processing*, pages 1192–1202, Brussels, Belgium. Association for Computational Linguistics.

Emile Mathieu, Tom Rainforth, N Siddharth, and Yee Whye Teh. 2019. Disentangling disentanglement in variational autoencoders. In *Proceedings of the 36th International Conference on Machine Learning*, volume 97 of *Proceedings of Machine Learning Research*, pages 4402–4412. PMLR.

T. J. Mitchell and J. J. Beauchamp. 1988. Bayesian variable selection in linear regression. *Journal of the American Statistical Association*, 83(404):1023–1032.

Milton Llera Montero, Casimir JH Ludwig, Rui Ponte Costa, Gaurav Malhotra, and Jeffrey Bowers. 2021. The role of disentanglement in generalisation. In *International Conference on Learning Representations*.

Tom Pelsmaeker and Wilker Aziz. 2020. Effective estimation of deep generative language models. In *Proceedings of the 58th Annual Meeting of the Association for Computational Linguistics*, pages 7220–7236, Online. Association for Computational Linguistics.

Tiago Pimentel, Josef Valvoda, Rowan Hall Maudslay, Ran Zmigrod, Adina Williams, and Ryan Cotterell. 2020. Information-theoretic probing for linguistic structure. In *Proceedings of the 58th Annual Meeting of the Association for Computational Linguistics*, pages 4609–4622, Online. Association for Computational Linguistics.

Victor Prokhorov, Yingzhen Li, Ehsan Shareghi, and Nigel Collier. 2020. Hierarchical sparse variational autoencoder for text encoding. *arXiv preprint arXiv:2009.12421*.

Victor Prokhorov, Ehsan Shareghi, Yingzhen Li, Mohammad Taher Pilehvar, and Nigel Collier. 2019. On the importance of the Kullback-Leibler divergence term in variational autoencoders for text generation. In *Proceedings of the 3rd Workshop on Neural Generation and Translation*, pages 118–127, Hong Kong. Association for Computational Linguistics.

Ali Razavi, Aäron van den Oord, Ben Poole, and Oriol Vinyals. 2019. Preventing posterior collapse with delta-vaes. In *7th International Conference on Learning Representations, ICLR 2019*, New Orleans, LA, USA.

Karl Ridgeway and Michael C Mozer. 2018. Learning deep disentangled embeddings with the f-statistic loss. In *Advances in Neural Information Processing Systems*, volume 31, pages 185–194. Curran Associates, Inc.

Andrew Slavin Ross and Finale Doshi-Velez. 2021. Benchmarks, algorithms, and metrics for hierarchical disentanglement. *CoRR*, abs/2102.05185.

Lucas Torroba Hennigen, Adina Williams, and Ryan Cotterell. 2020. Intrinsic probing through dimension selection. In *Proceedings of the 2020 Conference on Empirical Methods in Natural Language Processing (EMNLP)*, pages 197–216, Online. Association for Computational Linguistics.

Elena Voita and Ivan Titov. 2020. Information-theoretic probing with minimum description length. In *Proceedings of the 2020 Conference on Empirical Methods in Natural Language Processing (EMNLP)*, pages 183–196, Online. Association for Computational Linguistics.

Zichao Yang, Zhiting Hu, Ruslan Salakhutdinov, and Taylor Berg-Kirkpatrick. 2017. Improved variational autoencoders for text modeling using dilated convolutions. In *Proceedings of the 34th International Conference on Machine Learning, ICML 2017*, volume 70 of *Proceedings of Machine Learning Research*, pages 3881–3890, Sydney, NSW, Australia. PMLR.

Xiang Zhang, Junbo Zhao, and Yann LeCun. 2015. Character-level convolutional networks for text classification. In *Proceedings of the 28th International Conference on Neural Information Processing Systems - Volume 1*, NIPS'15, page 649–657, Cambridge, MA, USA. MIT Press.

A Disentanglement Metrics Algorithms

To evaluate representations learned by a model on a dataset having the attributes of **Data Requirement**, we further require a series of representation space $\mathbb{R}_{ij}$, who has a bijection mapping with $\mathbb{S}_{ij}$. Hence, when sampling representations which have the same value on one generative factor, we only need to sample in one $\mathbb{R}_{ij}$.

Under these notations, we write the pseudo code of metrics in Algorithm 1-6. For Algorithm 5 and 6, although we only use one criterion in the main paper, we still provide the details for other criteria. We set $N = 1000$ and $L = 64$ for Algorithm 1 and 2, and $N = 10000$ for Algorithm 3, 4, 5, and 6.

Algorithm 1 Metric of Higgins et al. (2017)

$\mathbb{D} = \varnothing$
for $f_i \in \mathbb{F}$ **do**
  for $n = 1, 2, \ldots, N$ **do**
    Sample s_n from $\bigcup_j \mathbb{S}_{ij}$
    Find the value v_{ij} on f_i for s_n
    Sample $(\mathbf{z}_1^{(1)}, \ldots, \mathbf{z}_L^{(1)})$ from $\mathbb{R}_{ij}$
    Sample $(\mathbf{z}_1^{(2)}, \ldots, \mathbf{z}_L^{(2)})$ from $\mathbb{R}_{ij}$
    $\mathbf{z}_n = \frac{1}{L}\sum_{l=1}^{L} |\mathbf{z}_l^{(1)} - \mathbf{z}_l^{(2)}|$
    $\mathbb{D} = \{(\mathbf{z}_n, f_i)\} \bigcup \mathbb{D}$
Split $\mathbb{D}$ into training set $\mathbb{TR}$ and test set $\mathbb{TE}$ with proportion (80%, 20%)
Train 10 MLPs with only input and output layer on $\mathbb{TR}$
Calculate the accuracy on $\mathbb{TE}$ for 10 models
Calculate the mean and variance of accuracy

Algorithm 2 Metric of Kim and Mnih (2018)

$\mathbb{D} = \varnothing$
for $d = 1, 2, \ldots, dim_z$ **do**
  Calculate the standard deviation σ_d of dimension d
for $f_i \in \mathbb{F}$ **do**
  for $n = 1, 2, \ldots, N$ **do**
    Sample s_n from $\bigcup_j \mathbb{S}_{ij}$
    Find the value v_{ij} on f_i for s_n
    Sample $(\mathbf{z}_1, \ldots, \mathbf{z}_L)$ from $\mathbb{R}_{ij}$
    $d_n^* = \arg\max_d var(\frac{z_{1,d}}{\sigma_d}, \ldots, \frac{z_{L,d}}{\sigma_d})$
    $\mathbb{D} = \{(d_n^*, f_i)\} \bigcup \mathbb{D}$
Split $\mathbb{D}$ into training set $\mathbb{TR}$ and test set $\mathbb{TE}$ with proportion (80%, 20%)
Train 10 majority vote classifiers on $\mathbb{TR}$
Calculate the accuracy on $\mathbb{TE}$ for 10 models
Calculate the mean and variance of accuracy

Algorithm 3 Metric of Kumar et al. (2018)

for $f_i \in \mathbb{F}$ **do**
  for $v_{ij} \in \mathbb{V}_i$ **do**
    $p(v_{ij}) = \frac{Count(\mathbb{S}_{ij})}{\sum_j Count(\mathbb{S}_{ij})}$
    Sample $N_j = N \times p(v_{ij})$ representations $\mathbf{z}^j$ from $\mathbb{R}_{ij}$
  for $d = 1, 2, \ldots, dim_z$ **do**
    $\mathbb{D}_d = \varnothing$
    for $v_{ij} \in \mathbb{V}_i$ **do**
      for $n = 1, 2, \ldots, N_j$ **do**
        $\mathbb{D}_{id} = \{(z_{n,d}^j, v_{ij})\} \bigcup \mathbb{D}_{id}$
    Split $\mathbb{D}_d$ into training set $\mathbb{TR}_d$ and test set $\mathbb{TE}_d$ with proportion (80%, 20%)
    Train a linear SVM classifier on $\mathbb{TR}_d$
    Record the accuracy acc_d on $\mathbb{TE}_{id}$
  $d^* = \arg\max_d acc_d$
  $SAP_i = acc_{d^*} - \max_{d \neq d^*} acc_d$
$score = avg(SAP_i)$

Algorithm 4 Metric of Chen et al. (2018)

for $d = 1, 2, \ldots, dim_z$ **do**
  Divide values on dimension d into 20 uniform bins $\mathbb{B}_d$
  for $n = 1, 2, \ldots, 20$ **do**
    $p(z_d \in \mathbb{B}_d^n) = \frac{Count(\{z_d \in \mathbb{B}_d^n\})}{\sum_{n=1}^{20} Count(\{z_d \in \mathbb{B}_d^n\})}$
  $H(z_d) = -\sum_{n=1}^{20} p(z_d \in \mathbb{B}_d^n) \log p(z_d \in \mathbb{B}_d^n)$
for $f_i \in \mathbb{F}$ **do**
  for $v_{ij} \in \mathbb{V}_i$ **do**
    $p(v_{ij}) = \frac{Count(\mathbb{S}_{ij})}{\sum_j Count(\mathbb{S}_{ij})}$
    Sample $N_j = N \times p(v_{ij})$ representations $\mathbf{r}^j$ from $\mathbb{R}_{ij}$
  $H(f_i) = -\sum_j p(v_{ij}) \log p(v_{ij})$
  for $d = 1, 2, \ldots, dim_z$ **do**
    for $v_{ij} \in \mathbb{V}_i$ **do**
      for $n = 1, 2, \ldots, 20$ **do**
        $p(z_d \in \mathbb{B}_d^n | v_{ij}) = \frac{Count(\{r_d^j \in \mathbb{B}_d^n\})}{\sum_{n=1}^{20} Count(\{r_d^j \in \mathbb{B}_d^n\})}$
    $H(z_d|f_i) = -\sum_j p(v_{ij}) \sum_{n=1}^{20} p(z_d \in \mathbb{B}_d^n | v_{ij}) \log p(z_d \in \mathbb{B}_d^n | v_{ij})$
    $I(z_d, f_i) = H(z_d) - H(z_d|f_i)$
  $d^* = \arg\max_d \frac{I(z_d, f_i)}{H(f_i)}$
  $MIG_i = \frac{I(z_{d^*}, f_i)}{H(f_i)} - \max_{d \neq d^*} \frac{I(z_d, f_i)}{H(f_i)}$
$score = avg(MIG_i)$

Algorithm 5 Metric of Ridgeway and Mozer (2018)

Modularity:

Same steps as Algorithm 4 without step 17, 18 and 19
for $d = 1, 2, \dots, dim_z$ **do**
  $i^* = \arg\max_i I(z_d, f_i)$
  $\theta_d = I(z_d, f_{i^*})$
  for $f_i \in \mathbb{F}$ **do**
    if $i = i^*$ **then**
      $t_i = \theta_d$
    else
      $t_i = 0$
  $\delta_d = \frac{\sum_i (I(z_d, f_i) - t_i)^2}{\theta_d^2 (Count(\mathbb{F}) - 1)}$
$score = avg(1 - \delta_d)$

Explicitness:

for $f_i \in \mathbb{F}$ **do**
  $\mathbb{D}_i = \varnothing$
  for $v_{ij} \in \mathbb{V}_i$ **do**
    $p(v_{ij}) = \frac{Count(\mathbb{S}_{ij})}{\sum_j Count(\mathbb{S}_{ij})}$
    Sample $N_j = N \times p(v_{ij})$ representations $\mathbf{r}^j$ from $\mathbb{R}_{ij}$
    for $n = 1, 2, \dots, N_j$ **do**
      $\mathbb{D}_i = \{(\mathbf{r}_n^j, v_{ij})\} \bigcup \mathbb{D}$
  Split $\mathbb{D}_i$ into training set $\mathbb{TR}_i$ and test set $\mathbb{TE}_i$ with proportion (80%, 20%)
  Train an one-versus-rest logistic regress classifier on $\mathbb{TR}_i$
  Record the ROC area-under-the-curve (AUC) auc_{ij} on $\mathbb{TR}_i$ for every v_{ij}
$score = avg(auc_{ij})$

Algorithm 6 Metric of Eastwood and Williams (2018)

for $f_i \in \mathbb{F}$ **do**
  $\mathbb{D}_i = \varnothing$
  for $v_{ij} \in \mathbb{V}_i$ **do**
    $p(v_{ij}) = \frac{Count(\mathbb{S}_{ij})}{\sum_j Count(\mathbb{S}_{ij})}$
    Sample $N_j = N \times p(v_{ij})$ representations $\mathbf{z}^j$ from $\mathbb{R}_{ij}$
    for $n = 1, 2, \dots, N_j$ **do**
      $\mathbb{D}_i = \{(\mathbf{z}_n^j, v_{ij})\} \bigcup \mathbb{D}$
  Split $\mathbb{D}_i$ into training set $\mathbb{TR}_i$ and test set $\mathbb{TE}_i$ with proportion (80%, 20%)
  Train a random forest classifier on $\mathbb{TR}_i$
  Informativeness score inf_i is the accuracy on $\mathbb{TE}_i$
  r_{id} is the relative importance of dimension d in predicting v_{ij}, obtained from the random forest
  for $d = 1, 2, \dots, dim_z$ **do**
    $P_d = \frac{r_{id}}{\sum_d r_{id}}$
  $H = -\sum_d P_d \log_{dim_z} P_d$
  $dis_i = 1 - H$
$score_{disentanglement} = avg(dis_i)$
$score_{informativeness} = avg(inf_i)$
for $d = 1, 2, \dots, dim_z$ **do**
  for $f_i \in \mathbb{F}$ **do**
    $Q_i = \frac{r_{id}}{\sum_i r_{id}}$
  $H = -\sum_i Q_i \log_{Count(\mathbb{F})} Q_i$
  Completeness score $com_d = 1 - H$
$score_{completeness} = avg(com_d)$

Learn The Big Picture: Representation Learning for Clustering

Sumanta Kashyapi
Department of Computer Science
University of New Hampshire
sk1105@wildcats.unh.edu

Laura Dietz
Department of Computer Science
University of New Hampshire
dietz@cs.unh.edu

Abstract

Existing supervised models for text clustering find it difficult to directly optimize for clustering results. This is because clustering is a discrete process and it is difficult to estimate meaningful gradient of any discrete function that can drive gradient based optimization algorithms. So, existing supervised clustering algorithms indirectly optimize for some continuous function that approximates the clustering process. We propose a scalable training strategy that directly optimizes for a discrete clustering metric. We train a BERT-based embedding model using our method and evaluate it on two publicly available datasets. We show that our method outperforms another BERT-based embedding model employing Triplet loss and other unsupervised baselines. This suggests that optimizing directly for the clustering outcome indeed yields better representations suitable for clustering.

1 Introduction

Text clustering is a well-studied problem which finds its application in a wide range of tasks: organizing documents in cluster-based information retrieval (Cutting et al., 2017; Mei and Chen, 2014), representation of search results (Scaiella et al., 2012; Navigli and Crisafulli, 2010), analyzing different opinions about a subject (Tsirakis et al., 2017) among many others. Each of these applications may focus on text contents of different granularities (e.g. words, sentences, passages, articles) but all of them follow a common high-level approach to clustering: represent the documents in form of vectors and then cluster them based on vector similarities. Although clustering is typically employed in an unsupervised setting, many semi-supervised deep learning models have been proposed recently. Many of these approaches formulate this as a representation space learning problem (Yang et al., 2017) that projects initial document vectors into a latent vector space which is more suitable for the clustering task and generate clusters similar to some ground truth. However, most of these algorithms do not directly optimize for a clustering evaluation metric during training. Instead, they optimize for a different criterion that approximates the global clustering error. Semi-supervised clustering approaches (Basu et al., 2002) cast the clustering problem into binary classification by learning pairwise constraints extracted from the available training examples: *must-links* for sample pairs sharing the same cluster and *cannot-links* for different clusters. However, clustering problems with numerous small clusters produce only a few *must-links* among all possible links, leading to highly unbalanced training data. Consequently, the trained model is biased towards predicitng *cannot-links*. Learning triplet-based constraints (Dor et al., 2018) that combine a positive and a negative sample in a single triplet, mitigate such bias towards negative samples. However, the sample complexity (Bartlett, 1998) (number of samples required to cover all interactions in a dataset) grows more rapidly compared to paired samples. Also, such approximation of the original clustering problem may lead to unsatisfactory results because the optimization criterion does not always correspond with the clustering quality. These observations motivate us to hypothesize the following:

1. Instead of learning to solve some approximation of the original clustering problem, we need to directly optimize for a clustering evaluation metric in order to train a model specialized for clustering.

2. Instead of sample-pairs in case of pairwise constraints or triplets in case of Triplet-loss, we can make efficient and scalable use of the available training data by presenting all inter-

Proceedings of the 6th Workshop on Representation Learning for NLP (RepL4NLP-2021), pages 141–151
Bangkok, Thailand (Online), August 6, 2021. ©2021 Association for Computational Linguistics

actions between a set of data points as a single clustering sample. This way the training approach neither suffers from unbalanced data nor from sample complexity.

To test our hypotheses, we propose an alternative training strategy that directly draws its supervision signal from an evaluation metric that measures clustering quality to train a representation model for text documents. During training, it consumes a complete clustering example of a set of data points as a single training sample in form of an interaction matrix. Due to this, we experiment with clustering datasets containing numerous small clustering examples instead of a single instance of a large clustering problem.

It is challenging to derive training signals directly from the clustering ground truth or a clustering evaluation metric because the clustering process is discrete. In other words, a function that estimates the clustering quality of a random partition of the input data is not continuous and hence non-differentiable. As most supervised algorithms rely on gradient-based optimization algorithms, it is difficult for them to orchestrate a useful training process without proper gradient. So far some continuous approximation of the clustering problem is used as discussed earlier to bypass the core optimization issue. Recently a novel gradient approximation method, *blackbox backpropagation* (Vlastelica et al., 2019) is proposed for combinatorial problems that finds solution in a discrete space. We leverage their findings by molding the clustering problem into a combinatorial problem. This allows us to derive meaningful gradients out of the clustering process and to train a representation model by directly optimizing for a clustering evaluation metric.

Our contribution: We make the following contributions through this work.

1. We develop a new training strategy for supervised clustering that directly obtains its supervision signal from optimizing a clustering metric.[1] We utilize recently proposed *blackbox backpropagation* technique to derive gradients from discrete clustering results that drives the training process.

2. We use our training strategy to train a BERT-based (Devlin et al., 2018) representation model suitable for topical clustering. To support the training mechanism, we design a loss function that effectively optimizes a clustering evaluation metric.

3. We empirically show that our method is more efficient in terms of training time and utilizing available training examples when compared to existing supervised clustering methods. The resulting representation model achieves better clustering results than other strong baseline models.

2 Related Work

Traditionally, text clustering is achieved by employing a distance-based clustering algorithm (e.g. KMeans) on vector representations of documents such as TF-IDF (Jones, 1972). Recent works focus on learning text representaions suitable for clustering (Chen, 2017; Xu et al., 2017; Hadifar et al., 2019). Alternatively, they explore different similarity metrics between the vectors that govern the clustering algorithm through pairwise binary constraints (Basu et al., 2002; Kulis et al., 2009). In this work, we focus on the former – representation learning of documents, suitable for text clustering.

Deep clustering (Min et al., 2018) is an active field of research that utilizes recent advancements of deep learning techniques to improve supervised clustering. The primary focus is to learn a suitable representation space that optimizes some clustering criterion (e.g. cluster assignment loss) along with a representation criterion (e.g. reconstruction loss) (Xie et al., 2016; Li et al., 2018; Ghasedi Dizaji et al., 2017; Jiang et al., 2016). It has also been shown that clustering criterions alone are sufficient to train such representation space (Yang et al., 2016). However, none of these approaches attempt to receive direct supervision from a clustering evaluation metric. Motivated by earlier works that learn a representation model under pairwise binary constraints, Chang et al. (2017) envisions the clustering task as a binary classification task of paired data samples and achieves state-of-the-art results on multiple image clustering datasets. Reimers and Gurevych (2019) propose Sentence-BERT which trains a BERT-based sentence embedding model by employing Triplet loss (Dor et al., 2018) that uses triples of sentences as training samples where exactly two of them are from the same section of Wikipedia. Although both

[1]The source code is available at `https://github.com/nihilistsumo/Blackbox_clustering`

of these approaches are supervised, each training sample only consists of a fraction of the whole clustering instance. Hence, during training, these methods mostly ignore the overall relationships between multiple data samples and how they form clusters.

The main hindrance of drawing a supervision signal directly from a clustering evaluation metric is the combinatorial nature of the clustering problem. Some research introduce differentiable building blocks for special cases of combinatorial algorithms such as satisfiability (SAT) problems (Wang et al., 2019). Wilder et al. (2019) use a differentiable variant of the K-means algorithm to approximate a harder combinatorial problem (e.g. graph optimization). Such relaxations of the original combinatorial problem may lead to sub-optimal results. Recently, Vlastelica et al. (2019) proposed a novel technique of differentiating combinatorial solvers as a blackbox without any relaxation that allows us to use an optimal combinatorial algorithm as a component of a deep representation learning model and optimize it end-to-end. We give a brief background of their approach in the following section.

Blackbox backpropagation. In their approach to optimize for a combinatorial function Vlastelica et al. (2019) formalize combinatorial solvers as a mapping function between continuous input, $w \in W \subseteq \mathbb{R}^N$ and discrete output, $\hat{y} \in Y$ as $w \mapsto \hat{y}$ such that the output $\hat{y} = \arg\min_{y \in Y} c(w, y)$ where c is the cost that the solver tries to minimize. Here W is the N-dimensional continuous input space and Y is a finite set of all possible solutions. For a linear cost function c, a continuous interpolation of the original cost function is constructed and the gradient of this interpolation is used during backpropagation. The closeness of the interpolation to the original function is controlled by a single hyperparameter, λ. In our work, we extend this approach for clustering framework to draw the supervision signals directly from the clustering results and learn our model parameters.

3 Methodology

Our text clustering method works in two steps: 1. Train a text representation model directly from example clusters of text snippets, 2. Cluster the trained embedding vectors using hierarchical agglomerative clustering (HAC). Our primary contribution lies in the training strategy of step 1 which we refer here as **C**lustering **O**ptimization as **B**lackbox (**COB**). We describe COB in the following sections.

3.1 Overall Approach

Supervised text clustering is a combinatorial problem. Let $\mathcal{P}$ be a set of N documents and Y be the set of all possible k-partitions of set $\mathcal{P}$. Also let V_ϕ be a representation model with trainable parameters ϕ. We obtain the set of representation vectors $V_\phi(\mathcal{P})$ for each of the documents in set $\mathcal{P}$ using the model, V_ϕ. Based on the Euclidean distances between representation vectors in $V_\phi(\mathcal{P})$, a clustering algorithm chooses a particular k-partition $\hat{y} \in Y$ that minimizes some linear cost function $c(V_\phi(\mathcal{P}), y)$ e.g. intra-cluster distances for HAC. Hence the clustering process can be expressed as the following mapping:

$$V_\phi(\mathcal{P}) \mapsto \hat{y} \quad \text{such that} \quad \hat{y} = \arg\min_{y \in Y} c(V_\phi(\mathcal{P}), y)$$

The clustering ground truth $y^* \in Y$ is the correct k-partition of set $\mathcal{P}$. The training process of COB is governed by a loss function $\mathcal{L}(y^*, \hat{y})$ that optimizes a clustering evaluation metric.

However, we want to emphasize here that the minimization of the cost function $c(V_\phi(\mathcal{P}), y)$ takes place inside the clustering algorithm and remains opaque for our supervised model. As a result, COB is not dependent on the exact clustering algorithm we choose. In this work however, we choose to use HAC as our clustering algorithm. We optimize for RAND index in this work but our method can be applied to optimize for other clustering evaluation metrics as well (e.g. purity).

3.2 Optimizing for RAND index

Our goal is to train the representation model, V_ϕ, such that the resulting clusters maximize a clustering evaluation metric of our choice. In this work, we focus on optimizing for RAND index, a widely used clustering metric, which measures the similarity between the generated clusters and the clustering ground truth. If $y^* \in Y$ be the ground truth partition or the ideal clustering of $\mathcal{P}$, then the clustering quality of a candidate cluster $\hat{y}$ is expressed in terms of RAND index (RI):

$$RI = \frac{\text{No. of unordered data pairs that agrees between } y^* \text{ and } \hat{y}}{\binom{n}{2}}$$

where $n =$ total number of data samples.

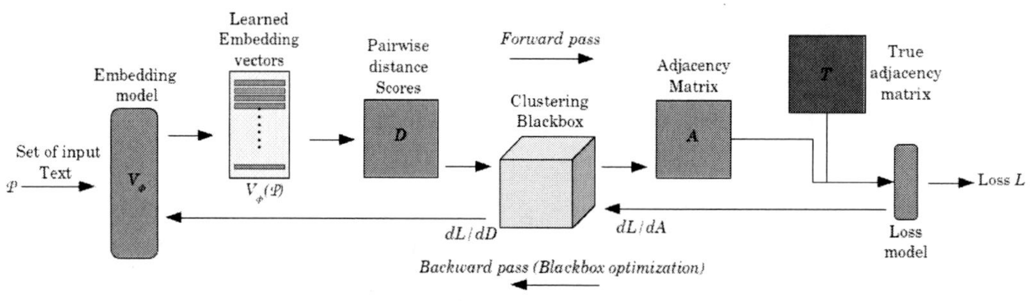

Figure 1: Training loop of our proposed supervised clustering approach.

Table 1: Description of variables used in Figure 1.

Variable	Description
$\mathcal{P}$	Set of documents to be clustered
V_ϕ	Embedding model with trainable parameters ϕ
$V_\phi(\mathcal{P})$	Representation vectors of $\mathcal{P}$ obtained using V_ϕ
D	Pairwise distance matrix of vectors in $V_\phi(\mathcal{P})$
A	Adjacency matrix denoting clustering result
T	Adjacency matrix denoting ground truth clusters

3.3 COB Training Loop

Figure 1 and Table 1 presents the overall training approach. The focus of the training loop is to train the representation model V_ϕ. First, the set of representation vectors $V_\phi(\mathcal{P})$ is obtained for all documents in set $\mathcal{P}$. Then we encode the input to the clustering algorithm as a square symmetric matrix D with pairwise Euclidean distance scores between vectors in $V_\phi(\mathcal{P})$.

$$D_{ij} = ||V_\phi(p_i) - V_\phi(p_j)||_2 \quad \text{where} \quad p_i, p_j \in \mathcal{P}$$

The solution to the clustering problem is expressed in form of an adjacency matrix A such that

$$A_{ij} = 1 \text{ if } i, j \text{ share same cluster and 0 otherwise}$$

We denote the adjacency matrix of the clustering ground truth as T. Now, we can express RI using the following form:

$$RI = 1 - \frac{\sum_{ij} |A_{ij} - T_{ij}|}{2\binom{n}{2}} \quad \text{see Appendix}$$

It is clear from the above equation that if we want to maximize RI, we need to minimize the difference between A and T. Intuitively, if we are able to produce ideal clustering results, then A and T would be identical, meaning $A - T$ is a zero matrix. Hence, we define our loss function $\mathcal{L}$ as the sum of $A - T$. Formally:

$$\mathcal{L} = \sum_{ij} |A_{ij} - T_{ij}|$$

The backward pass of this training loop involves estimating the gradient of the loss $\mathcal{L}$ with respect to the distance matrix D, the input to the clustering algorithm. This is achieved using blackbox backpropagation technique and the resulting gradient is used to drive a gradient descent algorithm for training the representation model V_ϕ.

3.4 Regularization

The purpose of any clustering algorithm is to identify groups of similar data points. By optimizing for a clustering metric such as RI, we learn a notion of similarity that most likely yields the ground truth clusters when used in HAC. However, we want to encourage a large margin between similar and dissimilar data points. This is achieved when the loss function encourages *inter-cluster* distances to increase and *intra-cluster* distances to decrease. While this is part of the optimization process within the clustering algorithm, it is opaque during neural network training, due to the blackbox optimization technique. The clustering evaluation metric does not encourage a margin that is larger than necessary. Hence we incorporate a measure of intra versus inter-cluster distance as a regularizer in our optimization criterion as described below.

$$\begin{aligned}\mathcal{L}_r &= \mathcal{L} + r \cdot [\text{mean intra-cluster distance} \\ &\quad - \text{mean inter-cluster distance}] \\ &= \mathcal{L} + r \cdot \left[\underbrace{\frac{\sum_{ij} D_{ij}T_{ij}}{\sum_{ij} T_{ij}}}_{\text{intra-cluster}} - \underbrace{\frac{\sum_{ij} D_{ij}(1 - T_{ij})}{\sum_{ij}(1 - T_{ij})}}_{\text{inter-cluster}} \right]\end{aligned}$$

where r is the regularization constant

The regularization constant r controls how much emphasis is placed on increasing the margin between similar and dissimilar data points versus optimizing the clustering evaluation metric.

Table 2: Dataset statistics: N = total no. of documents, C = total no. of clustering instances, n = average number of documents per clustering instance, k = average number of clusters per clustering instance.

Dataset	N	C	n	k	
20NG train	11314	226	50	18	
20NG test	7532	150	50	18	
				k(coarse)	k(fine)
CAR train	6.8M	597K	11	3.84	5.04
CAR test	6K	126	47	7.78	17.16

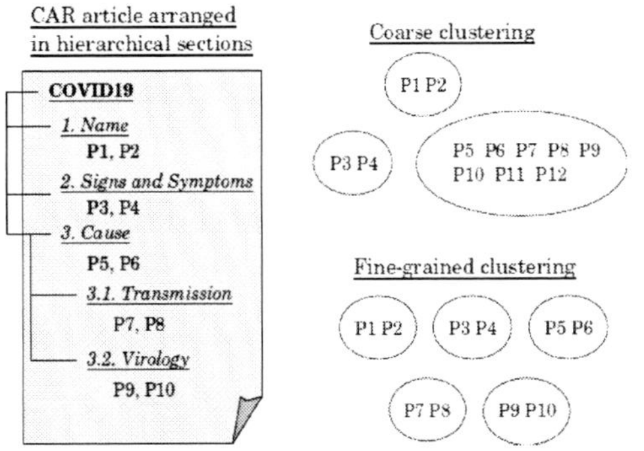

Figure 2: Coarse and fine-grained clustering benchmarks from CAR dataset.

4 Experimental Results

In this section, we describe the datasets used for our experiments, discuss our evaluation paradigm and present experimental results that demonstrate efficacy of the representation model trained using our proposed training strategy over our baseline models.

4.1 Datasets

To evaluate our proposed approach, we use two publicly available datasets: 20 newsgroups (20NG[2]) and TREC Complex Answer Retrieval (CAR[3]). As discussed earlier, for our proposed method, each training example consists of the ideal clustering of a set of documents. To produce enough such training samples, we choose to train and evaluate on multiple smaller clustering instances instead of a single but large clustering instance. We note that it will not make any difference in the way our baseline model is trained because they consume the training data in form of triples (SBERT Triplet), as long as we ensure that all models are trained on the same set of clustering examples. We take the following approach to construct such clustering benchmarks from the datasets (detailed statistics are presented in Table 2):

20NG dataset is a widely used public collection of 18846 documents, each categorized into any one of twenty topics. To convert this to a clustering benchmark, both train and test split of 20NG dataset is randomly grouped into sets of 50 documents along with their topic labels, resulting in 226 and 150 clustering instances respectively. Each set of 50 documents represents a single instance of clustering problem.

CAR dataset (version 2.0 year 1) is a large collection of Wikipedia articles. Each article consists of text passages about a topic, segmented into hierarchical subtopics using sections. From the CAR dataset, we use `train.v2.0` as train split (CAR train) and `benchmarkY1test` as test split (CAR test). This dataset is originally designed for a passage retrieval task where passages in CAR articles are relevant for different sections under the overarching topic of the article. This relevance information is part of the dataset in form of the ground truth. We assume that all relevant passages for an article are already retrieved and our focus is to cluster these passages. So each article is a separate clustering problem where our task is to cluster all the passages of the article such that passages from same sections in the original article share the same cluster. We treat the section label under which a passage appears as the clustering label of the passage.

Section labels in CAR dataset are hierarchical. This provides an opportunity to evaluate our clustering models under different levels of granularity. As depicted in Figure 2, passages p_6 and p_7 in article *COVID 19* belong to the sections *Cause* and *Cause/Transmission* respectively. For a coarse-grained view of the clustering, we consider p_6, p_7 under the same topic cluster *Cause*. However, for fine-grained clustering we have to consider p_6, p_7 under separate subtopic clusters. The CAR dataset provides both in form of *top-level* (coarse) and *hierarchical* (fine-grained) benchmarks. We train and evaluate our models on both flavors of the dataset.

4.2 Evaluation Paradigm

Our primary focus is to evaluate the efficacy of our proposed training strategy for supervised clustering and compare it with other training methods while ensuring the fairness of our evaluation. Hence, we train the same text embedding model with the same training data differing only in the training strate-

[2]Part of scikit-learn datasets Pedregosa et al. (2011)
[3]`http://trec-car.cs.unh.edu/`

gies. For the embedding model, we use Sentence-BERT (Reimers and Gurevych, 2019), a recent BERT-based embedding model. Finally, macro-average performance on all clustering instances on the test sets are reported with statistical significance testing. We use three clustering evaluation metrics, RAND index (RI), Adjusted RAND index (ARI) and Normalized Mutual Information (NMI).

Compared methods. In this section we discuss all the methods which are compared in our experiments. All methods are trained until no significant improvement is observed on the validation set. For each method, models are saved on regular interval and we use the best model found during training in terms of validation ARI score to evaluate on the test set.

SBERT COB. We train Sentence-BERT with our proposed training strategy and refer the obtained model as **SBERT COB**.

SBERT Triplet. To compare our approach with a strong supervised baseline, we train Sentence-BERT with Triplet loss function (Dor et al., 2018). It is designed to generate document representations that capture topical similarities. Here, each training example consists of two similar (d, d^+) and one dissimilar (d^-) documents. Triplet loss trains the document representation model V_{trip} so that the Euclidean distance between the similar pair of representations $||V_{trip}(d) - V_{trip}(d^+)||_2$ is less than the negative pair $||V_{trip}(d) - V_{trip}(d^-)||_2$ by at least a margin ϵ.

$$\mathcal{L}_{triplet} = \max(0, ||V_{trip}(d) - V_{trip}(d^+)||_2 - ||V_{trip}(d) - V_{trip}(d^-)||_2 + \epsilon)$$

Unsupervised baselines. To compare the performances of unsupervised clustering approaches for our use cases, we also include:

1. *SBERT raw*, the pre-trained Sentence-BERT model without any finetuning and

2. *TFIDF* with cosine similarity as a more canonical approach.

4.3 Hyperparameter Optimization

The interpolation parameter λ (Section 2) and regularization constant r (Section 3.4) are two hyperparameters we have to tune in SBERT COB. We use Optuna (Akiba et al., 2019), a recently proposed hyperparameter optimization framework, to search for optimum λ, r pair in terms of validation performance for each dataset. Table 3 presents the optimum hyperparameter values used for our experiments.

Table 3: Optimum values for interpolation parameter λ and regularization constant r found using Optuna.

Dataset	λ	r
NG20	90.0	1.0
CAR coarse	47.0	3.8
CAR fine-grained	103.0	0.3

Table 4: Clustering performance on NG20 dataset in terms of mean RAND index (RI), its corrected for chance version Adjusted RAND Index (ARI) and mean Normalized Mutual Information (NMI). Paired t-test ($\alpha = 0.05$) is carried out with respect to SBERT Triplet (denoted with *) and ▲ and ▼ denotes significantly higher or lower performance.

Method	RI	ARI	NMI
SBERT COB	**0.925**	**0.233▲**	**0.725▲**
SBERT Triplet*	0.924	0.223	0.721
SBERT raw	0.754▼	0.041▼	0.582▼
TFIDF	0.624▼	0.008▼	0.506▼

4.4 Clustering Evaluation

Here we present details of all the experiments carried out and discuss the results. All experiments are executed on a single NVIDIA Titan XP GPU with 12GB memory. For all the SBERT models, we use uncased DistilBERT (Sanh et al., 2019) as the underlying BERT embedding model.

4.4.1 Experiment 1: 20NG

We train SBERT COB and other supervised methods using 80% of the train split of 20NG dataset and the remainder is held out for validation. Table 4 presents the performance on the test set evaluated using mean RI, ARI and NMI.

We observe that our proposed method SBERT COB outperforms all other baselines in terms of RI, ARI and NMI. For ARI and NMI, the improvement is statistically significant in terms of paired t-test with $\alpha = 0.05$ carried out with respect to the best performing baseline, SBERT Triplet. Both TFIDF and SBERT raw fail to obtain meaningful clusters, demonstrating the efficacy of supervised representation models in clustering context.

4.4.2 Experiment 2: CAR

Due to large size of the CAR training split (`train.v2.0`), it is impractical to train SBERT Triplet with all possible triplets in the training set.

Table 5: Dataset statistics: N, C, n, k denotes the same as Table 2, t denotes the total number of available triples to train SBERT Triplet method.

Subset	N	C	k(coarse)	k(fine)	t(coarse)	t(fine)
n=30	71K	2.4K	5.97	10.64	8.6M	5.8M
n=35	56K	1.6K	6.27	12.17	9.3M	5.9M
n=40	50K	1.2K	6.73	13.62	10.8M	6.5M

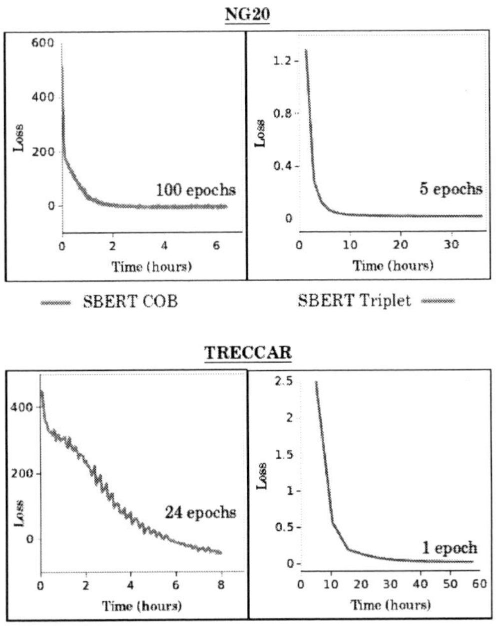

Figure 3: Comparison between SBERT COB and SBERT Triplet in terms of total training time.

Instead, we compare the supervised models trained on three smaller subsets of the training dataset. Each subset contains articles with exactly n passages where $n = 30, 35$ and 40. However, they are always evaluated on the same CAR test set. These values of n are chosen so that we obtain reasonable numbers of training samples while their statistics remain close to the CAR test set on which we are evaluating. Table 5 presents statistics about these three training subsets.

We report the coarse and fine-grained clustering performance in Table 6 and Table 7 respectively. For both coarse and fine-grained clustering, we observe that for each of the training splits ($n = 30, 35, 40$), our proposed method SBERT COB consistently performs better than the best performing baseline, SBERT Triplet ($n = 30$) in terms of both ARI and NMI. As expected, clustering performance in terms of RI score mostly correlates with ARI score. The only exception is SBERT

Table 6: Coarse-level clustering performance on CAR dataset using top-level benchmarks. Supervised models are trained with set of clustering examples each containing n passages. Paired t-test ($\alpha = 0.05$) is carried out with respect to SBERT Triplet ($n = 30$) and marked with *.

Method	RI	ARI	NMI
Trained on n=30 subset			
SBERT COB	0.742	0.230	0.502
SBERT Triplet*	0.738	0.214	0.494
Trained on n=35 subset			
SBERT COB	**0.744**	**0.236**	0.512▲
SBERT Triplet	0.715▼	0.167▼	0.460▼
Trained on n=40 subset			
SBERT COB	0.726	0.231	**0.514▲**
SBERT Triplet	0.704▼	0.145▼	0.438▼
Unsupervised			
SBERT raw	0.563▼	0.101▼	0.406▼
TFIDF	0.544▼	0.072▼	0.375▼

Table 7: Fine-grained clustering performance on CAR dataset using hierarchical benchmarks. Notations used are same as in Table 6.

Method	RI	ARI	NMI
Trained on n=30 subset			
SBERT COB	0.849	**0.178**	**0.682**
SBERT Triplet*	0.848	0.173	0.678
Trained on n=35 subset			
SBERT COB	0.837▼	0.163	0.672
SBERT Triplet	0.830▼	0.152▼	0.665▼
Trained on n=40 subset			
SBERT COB	0.832▼	0.154	0.666▼
SBERT Triplet	**0.860▲**	0.138▼	0.662▼
Unsupervised			
SBERT raw	0.796▼	0.130▼	0.646▼
TFIDF	0.788▼	0.110▼	0.631▼

Triplet trained on $n = 40$ for fine-grained clustering. However, we also observe overall decrease in ARI scores for all methods in case of fine-grained clustering. This is expected as fine-grained clustering is a harder problem largely due to fewer passage pairs sharing a cluster. Note that RI and NMI measures are only comparable within table because unlike ARI, it is not adjusted for chance.

4.4.3 Experiment 3: Training Convergence

Existing methods for learning clustering representation spaces, focus solely on classifying individual pairs as similar or different, and hence ignore to which extent other data points already form clusters. The key difference in our work is that we learn the representation space to directly optimize for the clustering evaluation metric, which is based on the clustering results of HAC when used with pairwise Euclidean distances. This allows the model to reach convergence much faster, leading to reduced overall training time, when compared to other methods

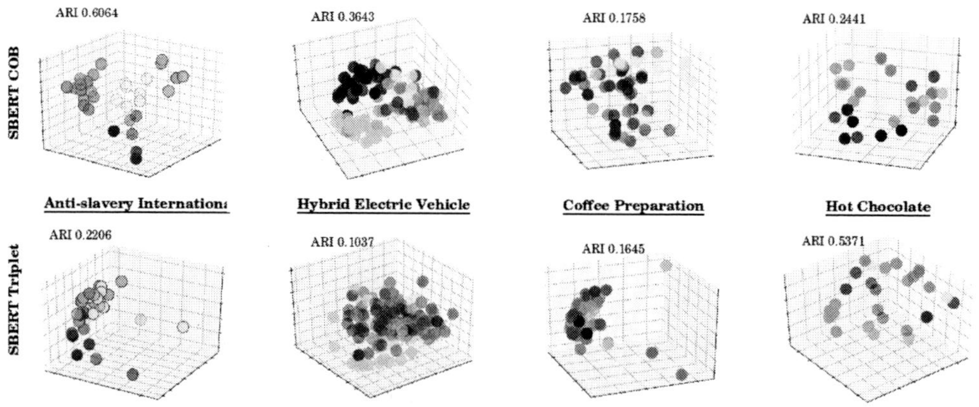

Figure 4: Visual comparison of clustering results between SBERT COB and SBERT Triplet ($n = 35$). Each dot denotes a passage from an article projected into the representation space after applying PCA. Different color denotes different subtopics. Clear separation of different colored blobs indicates good clustering quality.

that uses only a sub-sample of each clustering example (e.g. Triplets). This is particularly helpful in scenarios when we want to regularly update our model to incorporate new training examples.

To demonstrate this we present Figure 5 that compares the time taken to reach convergence during training of SBERT Triplet and SBERT COB on 20NG dataset and CAR dataset (coarse $n = 35$) respectively. For both the datasets, SBERT COB is able to converge at least five times sooner than SBERT Triplet, leading to much faster overall training time. Moreover, for NG20 dataset each epoch of SBERT COB is about 100 times faster than SBERT Triplet. This leads to decrease in overall training time even though SBERT COB takes many more epochs to converge than SBERT Triplet. We observe similar training behaviour for CAR dataset.

4.5 Qualitative Evaluation

Here, we demonstrate efficacy of SBERT COB over SBERT Triplet ($n = 35$) through visual comparison of clustering results from the CAR dataset. Principle Component Analysis (PCA) is used to transform the representation vectors into 3D vectors which are then visualized as points in 3D vector space. Figure 4 compares the results obtained for four articles from CAR test split.

For articles *Anti-slavery International* and *Hybrid Electric Vehicle*, SBERT COB is able to clearly identify clusters of different topics and projects them in different regions of the embedding space. On the contrary, it is difficult to find any clear cluster boundaries in the SBERT Triplet representation space which is also reflected in the ARI scores obtained by the methods. For the article *Coffee Preparation*, both the methods perform poorly in terms of ARI scores. But in case of SBERT COB we see a tendency to separate dissimilar passages. SBERT Triplet projects almost all the passages in a dense region except for a few outlier passages. For the article *Hot Chocolate*, SBERT Triplet obtains numerous small clusters of similar passages. As ARI metric is based on sample-pairs, SBERT Triplet obtains better ARI score even though it does not achieve clear groupings of similar elements.

It is clear from the examples that SBERT COB provides better global clustering quality than SBERT Triplet. This is expected because unlike SBERT Triplet, SBERT COB observes the relationships between all passages in a clustering instance at once to directly optimize for RAND index. Hence, SBERT COB is able to make better global clustering decisions than other pair-based methods.

4.6 Quadratic Scaling of SBERT COB

As SBERT COB learns from all possible interactions of data points in a clustering instance at once, it requires all the adjacency matrices in a batch of clustering samples to fit in memory. Thus the space complexity increases quadratically with the size of each clustering instance. Hence, the batch size is kept small to allow training with a limited GPU memory. However, even with batch size of 1, SBERT COB is observed to obtain superior results in terms of training speed and clustering performance as reported earlier.

5 Conclusion

In this work, we propose an alternative training strategy to train a representation model, for clustering. Our training strategy, COB (Clustering Optimization as Blackbox), directly optimizes the RAND index, a clustering evaluation metric. Using our method, we train SBERT COB, a BERT-based text representation model. We empirically show that SBERT COB significantly outperforms other supervised and unsupervised text embedding model on two separate datasets in terms of RI, ARI and NMI, indicating better cluster quality. Visual representations of the resulting vectors also confirm that SBERT COB learns to holistically distinguish clusters of different topics. Moreover, each epoch in SBERT COB training loop is about 100 times faster when compared to SBERT Triplet, our best performing baseline method. This leads to a significant decrease in overall training time even though SBERT COB requires more iterations to converge than SBERT Triplet. This makes SBERT COB suitable for applications that require clustering models to be updated on a regular basis as new training samples become available. Lastly, although we have conducted experiments with a specific clustering algorithm (HAC) and a clustering metric to optimize (RAND index), our model is independent of the particular choice of algorithm or the metric.

References

Takuya Akiba, Shotaro Sano, Toshihiko Yanase, Takeru Ohta, and Masanori Koyama. 2019. Optuna: A next-generation hyperparameter optimization framework. In *Proceedings of the 25rd ACM SIGKDD International Conference on Knowledge Discovery and Data Mining*.

Peter L Bartlett. 1998. The sample complexity of pattern classification with neural networks: the size of the weights is more important than the size of the network. *IEEE transactions on Information Theory*, 44(2):525–536.

Sugato Basu, Arindam Banerjee, and Raymond Mooney. 2002. Semi-supervised clustering by seeding. In *In Proceedings of 19th International Conference on Machine Learning (ICML-2002*. Citeseer.

Jianlong Chang, Lingfeng Wang, Gaofeng Meng, Shiming Xiang, and Chunhong Pan. 2017. Deep adaptive image clustering. In *Proceedings of the IEEE international conference on computer vision*, pages 5879–5887.

Chien-Hsing Chen. 2017. Improved tfidf in big news retrieval: An empirical study. *Pattern Recognition Letters*, 93:113–122.

Douglass R Cutting, David R Karger, Jan O Pedersen, and John W Tukey. 2017. Scatter/gather: A cluster-based approach to browsing large document collections. In *ACM SIGIR Forum*, volume 51, pages 148–159. ACM New York, NY, USA.

Jacob Devlin, Ming-Wei Chang, Kenton Lee, and Kristina Toutanova. 2018. Bert: Pre-training of deep bidirectional transformers for language understanding. *arXiv preprint arXiv:1810.04805*.

Liat Ein Dor, Yosi Mass, Alon Halfon, Elad Venezian, Ilya Shnayderman, Ranit Aharonov, and Noam Slonim. 2018. Learning thematic similarity metric from article sections using triplet networks. In *Proceedings of the 56th Annual Meeting of the Association for Computational Linguistics (Volume 2: Short Papers)*, pages 49–54.

Kamran Ghasedi Dizaji, Amirhossein Herandi, Cheng Deng, Weidong Cai, and Heng Huang. 2017. Deep clustering via joint convolutional autoencoder embedding and relative entropy minimization. In *Proceedings of the IEEE international conference on computer vision*, pages 5736–5745.

Amir Hadifar, Lucas Sterckx, Thomas Demeester, and Chris Develder. 2019. A self-training approach for short text clustering. In *Proceedings of the 4th Workshop on Representation Learning for NLP (RepL4NLP-2019)*, pages 194–199.

Zhuxi Jiang, Yin Zheng, Huachun Tan, Bangsheng Tang, and Hanning Zhou. 2016. Variational deep embedding: An unsupervised and generative approach to clustering. *arXiv preprint arXiv:1611.05148*.

Karen Sparck Jones. 1972. A statistical interpretation of term specificity and its application in retrieval. *Journal of documentation*.

Brian Kulis, Sugato Basu, Inderjit Dhillon, and Raymond Mooney. 2009. Semi-supervised graph clustering: a kernel approach. *Machine learning*, 74(1):1–22.

Fengfu Li, Hong Qiao, and Bo Zhang. 2018. Discriminatively boosted image clustering with fully convolutional auto-encoders. *Pattern Recognition*, 83:161–173.

Jian Ping Mei and Lihui Chen. 2014. Proximity based k-partitions clustering with ranking for document categorization and analysis. *Expert systems with applications*, 41(16):7095–7105.

Erxue Min, Xifeng Guo, Qiang Liu, Gen Zhang, Jianjing Cui, and Jun Long. 2018. A survey of clustering with deep learning: From the perspective of network architecture. *IEEE Access*, 6:39501–39514.

Roberto Navigli and Giuseppe Crisafulli. 2010. Inducing word senses to improve web search result clustering. In *Proceedings of the 2010 conference on empirical methods in natural language processing*, pages 116–126.

F. Pedregosa, G. Varoquaux, A. Gramfort, V. Michel, B. Thirion, O. Grisel, M. Blondel, P. Prettenhofer, R. Weiss, V. Dubourg, J. Vanderplas, A. Passos, D. Cournapeau, M. Brucher, M. Perrot, and E. Duchesnay. 2011. Scikit-learn: Machine learning in Python. *Journal of Machine Learning Research*, 12:2825–2830.

Nils Reimers and Iryna Gurevych. 2019. Sentence-bert: Sentence embeddings using siamese bert-networks. *arXiv preprint arXiv:1908.10084*.

Victor Sanh, Lysandre Debut, Julien Chaumond, and Thomas Wolf. 2019. Distilbert, a distilled version of bert: smaller, faster, cheaper and lighter. *arXiv preprint arXiv:1910.01108*.

Ugo Scaiella, Paolo Ferragina, Andrea Marino, and Massimiliano Ciaramita. 2012. Topical clustering of search results. In *Proceedings of the fifth ACM international conference on Web search and data mining*, pages 223–232, New York, NY, USA.

Nikos Tsirakis, Vasilis Poulopoulos, Panagiotis Tsantilas, and Iraklis Varlamis. 2017. Large scale opinion mining for social, news and blog data. *Journal of Systems and Software*, 127:237–248.

Marin Vlastelica, Anselm Paulus, Vít Musil, Georg Martius, and Michal Rolínek. 2019. Differentiation of blackbox combinatorial solvers. *arXiv preprint arXiv:1912.02175*.

Po-Wei Wang, Priya Donti, Bryan Wilder, and Zico Kolter. 2019. Satnet: Bridging deep learning and logical reasoning using a differentiable satisfiability solver. In *International Conference on Machine Learning*, pages 6545–6554. PMLR.

Bryan Wilder, Eric Ewing, Bistra Dilkina, and Milind Tambe. 2019. End to end learning and optimization on graphs. *arXiv preprint arXiv:1905.13732*.

Junyuan Xie, Ross Girshick, and Ali Farhadi. 2016. Unsupervised deep embedding for clustering analysis. In *International conference on machine learning*, pages 478–487. PMLR.

Jiaming Xu, Bo Xu, Peng Wang, Suncong Zheng, Guanhua Tian, and Jun Zhao. 2017. Self-taught convolutional neural networks for short text clustering. *Neural Networks*, 88:22–31.

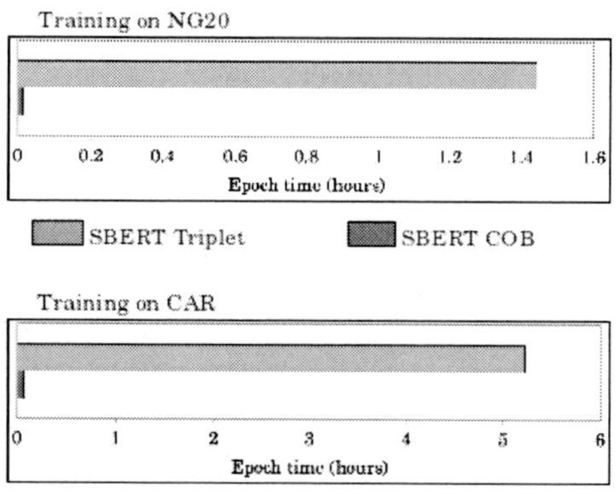

Figure 5: Comparison between SBERT COB and SBERT Triplet in terms of epoch time.

Bo Yang, Xiao Fu, Nicholas D Sidiropoulos, and Mingyi Hong. 2017. Towards k-means-friendly spaces: Simultaneous deep learning and clustering. In *international conference on machine learning*, pages 3861–3870. PMLR.

Jianwei Yang, Devi Parikh, and Dhruv Batra. 2016. Joint unsupervised learning of deep representations and image clusters. In *Proceedings of the IEEE conference on computer vision and pattern recognition*, pages 5147–5156.

A Relation between RAND index and Adjacency matrix

Given a set of n data points $\mathcal{P}$, let us compare two clustering results of $\mathcal{P}$, C_T and C_A, in terms of RAND index. We know that RAND index is expressed as:

$$RI = \frac{a+b}{\binom{n}{2}}$$

$$\text{where } a = \text{number of pairs that share the same cluster both in } C_T \text{ and } C_A$$

$$\text{where } b = \text{number of pairs that are from different clusters both in } C_T \text{ and } C_A$$

Now we can express any clustering result C_M in form of an adjacency matrix M where $M_{ij} = 1$ if the i, j-th data points in $\mathcal{P}$ share the same cluster in C_M and $M_{ij} = 0$ otherwise. We represent the clustering results C_T and C_A with such adjacency matrices T and A respectively. Also, the difference matrix of A, T denoted as $|A - T|$ indicates the ordered pairs that do not agree between A, T. In other words, $|A_{ij} - T_{ij}| = 1$ denotes that the i, j-th data points do not agree between A and T. Now, we can express RAND index in terms of A and T as follows:

$$
\begin{aligned}
RI &= \frac{a+b}{\binom{n}{2}} \\
&= \frac{\text{No. of agreements between } C_T, C_A}{\binom{n}{2}} \\
&= \frac{\text{No. of unordered pairs in } \mathcal{P} \text{ that agrees between } C_T, C_A}{\binom{n}{2}} \\
&= \frac{\text{No. of ordered pairs in } \mathcal{P} \text{ that agrees between } C_T, C_A}{2\binom{n}{2}} \\
&= \frac{\text{Total ordered pairs in } \mathcal{P} - \sum_{ij} |A_{ij} - T_{ij}|}{2\binom{n}{2}} \\
&= \frac{2\binom{n}{2} - \sum_{ij} |A_{ij} - T_{ij}|}{2\binom{n}{2}} \\
&= 1 - \frac{\sum_{ij} |A_{ij} - T_{ij}|}{2\binom{n}{2}}
\end{aligned}
$$

B Comparison of Epoch Time

Figure 5 shows the mean epoch time of SBERT Triplet and SBERT COB on 20NG dataset and CAR dataset (coarse n = 35) respectively.

Probing Cross-Modal Representations in Multi-Step Relational Reasoning

Iuliia Parfenova*, **Desmond Elliott**[†], **Raquel Fernández**[‡], **Sandro Pezzelle**[‡]
*Department of Computer Science, Vrije Universiteit Amsterdam
[†]Department of Computer Science, University of Copenhagen
[‡]Institute for Logic, Language and Computation, University of Amsterdam
research@julia.jig-san.me, de@di.ku.dk,
{raquel.fernandez | s.pezzelle}@uva.nl

Abstract

We investigate the representations learned by vision and language models in tasks that require relational reasoning. Focusing on the problem of assessing the relative size of objects in abstract visual contexts, we analyse both one-step and two-step reasoning. For the latter, we construct a new dataset of three-image scenes and define a task that requires reasoning at the level of the individual images and across images in a scene. We probe the learned model representations using diagnostic classifiers. Our experiments show that pretrained multimodal transformer-based architectures can perform higher-level relational reasoning, and are able to learn representations for novel tasks and data that are very different from what was seen in pretraining.

1 Introduction

Intelligence is classically described as "*the ability to see the similarities among dissimilar things and the dissimilarities among similar things*" (Thomas Acquinas, 1225-1274, reported by Ruiz, 2011). Developing systems that can reason over objects and their relations is indeed a long-standing goal of artificial intelligence research, as argued by Johnson et al. (2017). In recent years, huge progress toward this goal has been made in the language and vision community. Starting from Malinowski and Fritz (2014) and Antol et al. (2015), a wealth of studies have focused on language-driven visual reasoning, namely the problem of reasoning about an image given some linguistic input.

Generally speaking, there are two main types of problems in visual reasoning datasets (see Santoro et al., 2017): *non-relational*, requiring models to focus only on a given object (e.g., answering the question "*What material is the cube made of?*"), and *relational*, requiring models to pay attention to several or even all the objects in the image (e.g., indicating whether the statement "*There are four cubes that are red*" is true or false). Relational problems call for higher-level abilities, such as counting or directly comparing objects, both of which involve recognising the (dis)similarities among things.

In this paper, we focus on an important but understudied, relational reasoning task: assessing the relative size of objects in visual contexts, that is, determining whether an object counts as 'big' or 'small' in an image. We define a *multi-step* relational reasoning problem formulated as a sentence verification task. We construct a dataset of three-image scenes where a given target object, e.g., a blue triangle, is present in each image: two images have target objects with the same contextually-defined size and one image stands out in this regard. The task requires verifying whether a simple natural language statement standing for a first-order logical form describes a scene, e.g., "*There is exactly one blue triangle that is small in its image in this scene*" (Figure 1). Such multi-step relational reasoning is at play in many real-life situations: e.g., the same exact pan may count as 'big' in all contexts except a restaurant kitchen.

We experiment with two types of models to solve this task: a modular neural network (Hu et al., 2017) and LXMERT, a pre-trained multimodal transformer (Tan and Bansal, 2019). We probe the learned representations of LXMERT to assess whether, and to what extent, it has learned the underlying structure of the data. By means of two experiments with probing classifiers (Alain and Bengio, 2017; Hupkes et al., 2018; Belinkov and Glass, 2019), we first verify that it is able to perform the task at the image level (i.e., to compute the relative size of the target object at the image level); then, we test its ability to reason at the multi-image level and detect the image that stands out.

The experiments show that LXMERT is able to solve the multi-step relational reasoning task

Proceedings of the 6th Workshop on Representation Learning for NLP (RepL4NLP-2021), pages 152–162
Bangkok, Thailand (Online), August 6, 2021.

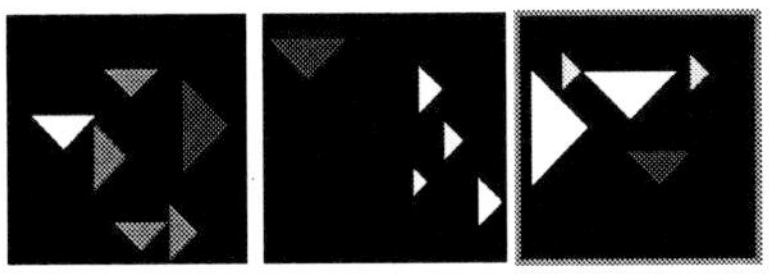

Figure 1: One sample scene from our dataset and the four statements it can be paired with, including corresponding truth values assigned as explained in Section 4.1. For clarity, the odd-one-out image (holding the *odd* size) is framed in red. Best viewed in color.

with an accuracy of 88.8%, and that the majority of errors occur when the relative size of the target object is difficult to determine. Our analyses show that (i) in most cases, different attention heads in LXMERT specialise to localising the smallest and biggest objects in the images, (ii) that the cross-modal representations learned appear encode a threshold function that controls whether an object is 'big' or 'small' in an image, and (iii) that a simple diagnostic classifier successfully identifies the instance that stands out in a three-image scene. Taken together, these findings lend further support to the advanced reasoning abilities of pre-trained transformer-based architectures, showing that they can perform higher-level relational reasoning and are able to deal with novel tasks and novel data, including synthetic data not available during pre-training.[1]

2 Problem Formulation

We investigate multi-step relational reasoning by formulating the problem as a visually grounded sentence verification task (see Figure 1). Given a pair ⟨`scene`, `statement`⟩ consisting of a visual scene and a statement about such scene, the task consists in classifying the statement as either `true` or `false`. In our setup, a `scene` consists of 3 images: $\langle \texttt{img}_1, \texttt{img}_2, \texttt{img}_3 \rangle$, each including an instance of the target object (e.g., a blue triangle) together with other geometrical shapes of the same type (e.g., triangles of other colours). A `statement` paired with a scene is of the following form: "*there is exactly one blue triangle that is small in its image in this scene*" or "*there are exactly two blue triangles that are big in their images in this scene*". As we will explain in detail in Sec. 4.1, the dataset is created such that the target object counts as either 'big' or 'small' *in only one* of the three images in a scene.

Arguably, solving the task requires the following two steps of relational reasoning: (1) identifying whether the target object counts as either 'big' or 'small' in each image, and (2) counting how many images include a big/small target. However, in our setup there is no direct supervision for any of these steps. In other words, the training data does not indicate which images contain an object that counts as big/small nor explicitly how many images contain a big/small target.

3 Related Work

3.1 Visual Reasoning

To evaluate *reasoning* abilities of multimodal models, several datasets of synthetic scenes and questions, such as CLEVR (Johnson et al., 2017), ShapeWorld (Kuhnle and Copestake, 2017), and MALeViC (Pezzelle and Fernández, 2019) have been proposed in recent years. Our work directly builds on them, and particularly on approaches adopting a multi-image setting, such as NLVR (Suhr et al., 2017) and NLVR2 (which, however, contains pairs of natural scenes; Suhr et al., 2019). In NLVR, in particular, a crowdsourced statement is coupled with a synthetic scene including 3 independent images, and models must verify whether the statement is true or false with respect to the entire visual input. This involves handling phenomena such as counting, negation or comparisons, that require perform *relational* reasoning over the entire scene, e.g.: *There is a black item in every box*, *There is a tower with yellow base*, etc. However, most ⟨*scene*, *statement*⟩ pairs do not challenge models to do the same at the level of the single image (or *box*), where a low-level understanding of the object(s) of interest (shape, color, etc.) often suffices. Our approach is novel since it requires two steps of *relational* reasoning: at the level of both the single image and the multi-image context.

3.2 Multi-Image Approaches

Our approach is also related to other work in language and vision involving multiple images. One is the *spot-the-difference* task: in Jhamtani and Berg-Kirkpatrick (2018), models are fed with pairs of video-surveillance images that only differ in one detail, and asked to generate text which de-

[1]The code to generate the data, and to train and evaluate the models, is available at `https://github.com/jig-san/multi-step-size-reasoning`.

scribes such difference. The same task—with different real-scene datasets—is explored by Forbes et al. (2019) and Su et al. (2017); others experiment with pairs of similar images drawn from CLEVR (Johnson et al., 2017) or similar synthetic 3D datasets (Park et al., 2019; Qiu et al., 2020). This task is akin to ours since it requires a higher-level reasoning step: systems must *reason* over the two independent representations to describe what is different. However, in practice, it does not always require semantic understanding (Jhamtani and Berg-Kirkpatrick, 2018); when it does, the changes often involve one object's *fixed* attribute (color, shape, material, etc.) rather than a *contextually-defined* property whose applicability depends on the other objects in the image.[2]

A similar, partially overlapping task is *discriminative captioning*: systems are fed with a set of similar images and asked to provide a description that unequivocally refers to a target one. Many approaches have been proposed focusing on synthetic (Andreas and Klein, 2016; Achlioptas et al., 2019) or natural scenes (Vedantam et al., 2017; Cohn-Gordon et al., 2018; Vered et al., 2019), very often embedding pragmatic components based on the Rational Speech Acts framework (RSA; Goodman and Frank, 2016). Also in this case, however, differences among images mainly involve *intrinsic* attributes of the objects rather than relational properties defined at the level of the image.

4 Method

4.1 3POS1 Dataset

Our dataset is based on the POS1 dataset from MALeViC (Pezzelle and Fernández, 2019), in which images contain 4 to 9 same-shape objects, e.g., squares. Each object is labeled with a ground-truth relative size, indicating whether the object counts as either *big* or *small* in that particular context. The label is determined by the following threshold function motivated by cognitive science studies on how humans interpret relative gradable adjectives (Schmidt et al., 2009):

$$T = \text{Max} - k(\text{Max} - \text{Min}) \tag{1}$$

where Max and Min represent the areas of the biggest and smallest objects in the image, and k is a positive value < 0.5.[3] Thus, an object with a certain area can count as *big* in one image and as *small* in another one. In total, the POS1 dataset contains 20K $\langle image, statement \rangle$ datapoints (16K train, 2K val, 2K test), where statements are about the size of a *target* object based on its unique color: e.g., *"the blue triangle is a small triangle"*.

The dataset for the present experiments, which we name 3POS1, is constructed as follows: For each image in each split of POS1, we randomly sample two images from that split with the same target object (e.g., a blue triangle) but the opposite ground-truth size (e.g., *big*). We obtain 20K sets of three images where one size is *prevalent*, i.e., present in two images, and one is *odd*, i.e., held by only one image.[4] The sizes *big* and *small* are the prevalent ones in 10K cases each, thus the dataset is balanced. Then, for each three-image `scene`, we generate four logic-based templated statements, two of which are *true* and two *false* for the given `scene`.[5] The only variation in the statements is the target object. The four types of statement are (alongside examples with respect to Figure 1):

(i) one $\langle shape, color \rangle$ small:
"There is exactly one blue triangle that is small in its image in this scene" → `True`

(ii) one $\langle shape, color \rangle$ big:
"There is exactly one blue triangle that is big in its image in this scene" → `False`

(iii) two $\langle shapes, color \rangle$ small:
"There are exactly two blue triangles that are small in their images in this scene" → `False`

(iv) two $\langle shapes, color \rangle$ big:
"There are exactly two blue triangles that are big in their images in this scene" → `True`

4.2 Models

To tackle the visually grounded sentence verification task, we use two models that achieve state of the art results on the NLVR (Suhr et al., 2017) and NLVR2 (Suhr et al., 2019) tasks, respectively: N2NMN (Hu et al., 2017) and LXMERT (Tan and Bansal, 2019). The End-to-End Module Network

[2] One notable exception is position (Park et al., 2019; Qiu et al., 2020), which can involve spatial relations of objects.

[3] To account for gradable adjectives' *vagueness*, for each image k was randomly sampled from the normal distribution centered on 0.29, the best-predictive value in Schmidt et al. (2009). See Pezzelle and Fernández (2019) for further details.

[4] On average, each target image appears 2 times as a distractor in the dataset (min: 0, max: 10). The position of the odd-one-out image in the scene is assigned randomly.

[5] The odd-one-out is the same for all statements; see Fig. 1.

(N2NMN), belongs to the family of *modular* networks, which treat a sentence as a collection of predefined subproblems (e.g., counting, localization, conjunction, etc.), each handled by a dedicated *module*. Compared to its direct predecessor NMN (Andreas et al., 2016), in particular, N2NMN does not require any external supervision (e.g., a parser) to process the sentence into its components. The latter, Learning Cross-Modality Encoder Representations from Transformers (LXMERT), is a transformer-based multimodal architecture pre-trained on several language-and-vision tasks; as such, it is claimed to be *universal*, that is, capable of solving virtually any visual reasoning problem. LXMERT uses BERT (Devlin et al., 2019) to encode the language input; as for the image, it considers the sequence of N salient regions output by Faster R-CNN (Ren et al., 2015).

To assess the suitability of these models for the 3POS1 task, we first evaluate them on the original POS1 task where statements are evaluated against a single image. For N2NMN, we use a public implementation,[6] specifically, the code developed for training and an evaluating the model on the CLEVR dataset (Johnson et al., 2017). For LXMERT, we use a snapshot pre-trained on several multi-modal tasks,[7] that we fine-tune using the training set of POS1. The ceiling performance for this task is 97% accuracy (using a fixed interpretation of the threshold parameter $k = 0.29$). LXMERT achieves 93.4% accuracy, which outperforms both N2NMN (78.1%) and the models tested by Pezzelle and Fernández (2019). This shows the overall advantage of transformer-based architectures over competing methods, in line with previous findings (Devlin et al., 2019). Moreover, it indicates the capability of LXMERT—which is pre-trained on natural images and language—to deal with synthetic data after fine-tuning (crucially, when not fine-tuned it yields an accuracy of 50%, i.e., random). Based on its performance, we focus on LXMERT in the main experiments and analyses in this paper.

4.3 Experimental Setup

We fine-tune LXMERT on the 3POS1 dataset by adapting the method applied by Suhr et al. (2019) for the two-image scenes of NLVR2 to our three-image scenes. More concretely, each datum in 3POS1 is composed of 3 images

[6]https://github.com/ronghanghu/n2nmn.

[7]Downloaded from http://nlp1.cs.unc.edu/data/model_LXRT.pth

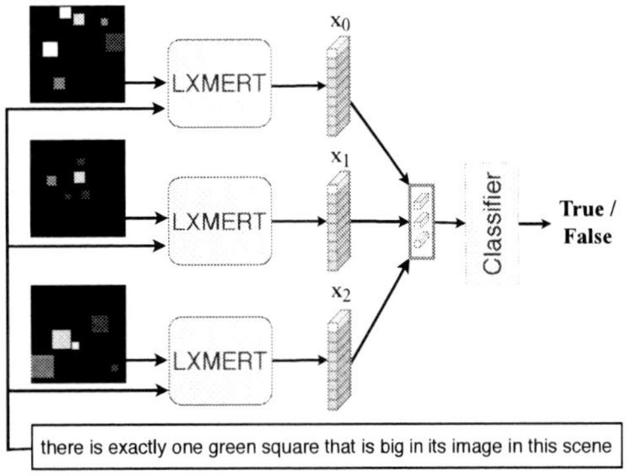

Figure 2: Overview of our visually-grounded sentence verification model. Given a three-image scene and a statement, LXMERT encodes each image–statement pair separately, from which a single cross-modal representation is extracted from the special [CLS] token (shown in yellow). These [CLS] representations are concatenated and propagated through a non-linear classifier to predict whether the statement accurately describes the scene.

$\langle \mathtt{img}_0, \mathtt{img}_1, \mathtt{img}_2 \rangle$, a statement $\mathtt{stat}$, and a ground truth label $\mathtt{True}$ or $\mathtt{False}$. Recall, that the visually grounded sentence verification task is to predict a label (True or False), given a representation of the images and the statement. An overview of how this is achieved with LXMERT is shown in Figure 2. First, visual features are extracted separately for each image with Faster R-CNN (Ren et al., 2015). Then cross-modal representations $\mathbf{x_i}$ are extracted from the [CLS] from the LXMERT encoder for each image in a scene:

$$\begin{aligned} \mathbf{x_0} &= \text{lxmert\_encoder}(\mathtt{img}_0, \mathtt{stat}) \\ \mathbf{x_1} &= \text{lxmert\_encoder}(\mathtt{img}_1, \mathtt{stat}) \\ \mathbf{x_2} &= \text{lxmert\_encoder}(\mathtt{img}_2, \mathtt{stat}) \end{aligned} \quad (2)$$

For label prediction, we train a classifier on the concatenation of the three image–statement representations (Eqn. 3), followed by a linear layer with learned parameters $\mathbf{W}$ and a bias vector $\mathbf{b}$ (Eqn. 4), followed by layer normalization (Ba et al., 2016) and a GeLU activation (Hendrycks and Gimpel, 2016) (Eqn. 5), and finally, a sigmoid activation function over a linear layer with learned parameters

	test accuracy	
statement type	*true*	*false*
one ⟨*shape*, *color*⟩ big	0.868	0.876
two ⟨*shapes*, *color*⟩ big	0.880	0.908
one ⟨*shape*, *color*⟩ small	0.872	0.900
two ⟨*shapes*, *color*⟩ small	0.876	0.924
overall	0.888	

Table 1: LXMERT results on the test set of 3POS1 by the best model's run, split by statement type.

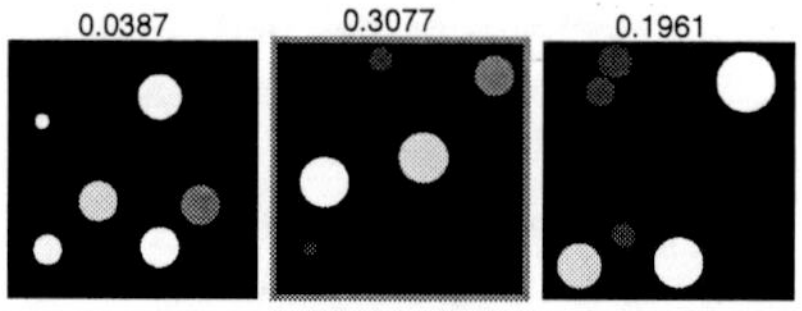

Figure 3: A sample from the test split of 3POS1, for which LXMERT predicts the incorrect label (*True*, instead of *False*). The numbers above the images are the distances of the target object (*green circle*) from the image-specific threshold. Here, the target object in the leftmost image is very close to that image's threshold value, so it is challenging for the model to detect whether it is *big* or *small*. The odd-one-out image is framed in red. Best viewed in color.

$\mathbf{W_1}$ and a bias vector $\mathbf{b_1}$ (Eqn. 6):[8]

$$\mathbf{c} = [\mathbf{x_0}; \mathbf{x_1}; \mathbf{x_2}] \quad (3)$$

$$\mathbf{z} = \mathbf{W}\mathbf{c} + \mathbf{b} \quad (4)$$

$$\mathbf{z_1} = \text{LayerNorm}(\text{GeLU}(\mathbf{z})) \quad (5)$$

$$\mathbf{y} = \sigma(\mathbf{W_1}\mathbf{z_1} + \mathbf{b_1}) \quad (6)$$

The LXMERT encoder and the classifier are fine-tuned for 12 epochs to prevent overfitting with a batch size 64. The learning rate of the Adam optimizer (Kingma and Ba, 2014) is 5e-5. The fine-tuning is performed for 5 random seeds.

5 Results

Overall, LXMERT achieves a very high accuracy on the task, averaged across 5 runs: 0.8909 ± 0.004 in validation set, 0.8864 ± 0.005 in test set. Moreover, its performance turns out to be fairly stable across various statement types, with the best model run's accuracy (see Table 1) ranging from 0.868 (one $\langle shape, color \rangle$ big, $true$) to 0.924 (two $\langle shapes, color \rangle$ small, $false$). Interestingly, for all four statement types, the model experiences a slight advantage with *false* over *true* statements, even though the dataset was carefully balanced. Taken together, these results indicate that the model, which is pre-trained on natural images, can deal with the synthetic scenes in our dataset after fine-tuning. This is in line with the claim that off-the-shelf transformer-based models can be applied to a wide range of different learning problems and data. At the same time, the model yields random accuracy when not fine-tuned, which reveals that our new dataset is challenging and involves a type of reasoning not captured during pre-training.

In Pezzelle and Fernández (2019), models were shown to make more errors when the area of the queried object is closer to the threshold (see Eq. 1). We check if this is the case also for LXMERT on our 3POS1 task. To do so, we consider the cases where the model gives a wrong prediction. Among the 3 images in a scene, we take the one with the lowest distance from the threshold. We then check whether the model makes more errors when such distance is lower, i.e., when there is at least one image in the scene with a *borderline* size. As reported in Table 2, this is indeed the case: 75% of incorrect predictions involve cases where (at least) in one image the target object is close to the threshold (< 0.1) (see Figure 3 , where the leftmost image is *borderline*). In contrast, only around 3% of the errors involve clear-cut cases, i.e., images where the target object's distance from threshold is ≥ 0.2. As observed by Pezzelle and Fernández (2019), this may suggest that the model is genuinely learning to compute the threshold function based on the areas of the relevant objects in the scene. Further support for this is given by the performance of the model on the 15 cases in the test set where the target object has the same area in the three-image scene. These cases could be expected to act as a confound for the model,[9] but LXMERT succeeds in 14/15 cases. Consistently with the error pattern reported above, the missed case contains low-distance objects (the lowest distance is equal to 0.1). In the next section, we more extensively explore this issue.

6 Analysis at the Individual Image Level

Our results show that LXMERT achieves a high level of accuracy on our visually-grounded sentence verification task on the three-image 3POS1

[8] This is identical to the approach followed by Tan and Bansal (2019) to finetune LXMERT for NLVR2 classification.

[9] The target objects have exactly the same area in pixels but each target object has its own context-defined size.

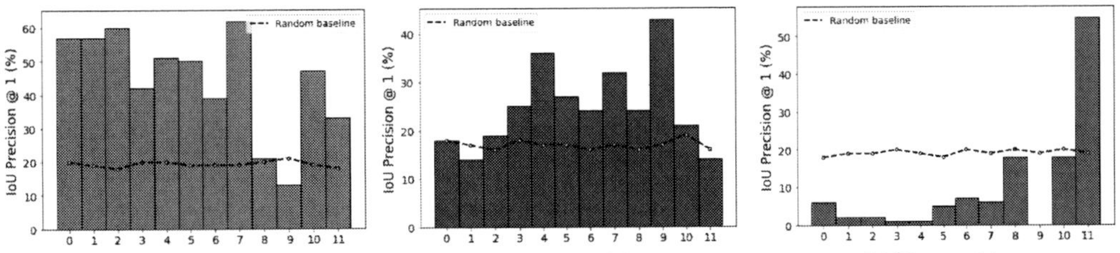

(a) Target object (b) Smallest object (c) Biggest object

Figure 4: Intersection over Union Precision at K=1, per attention head (in the x-axis), for the target object in an image (a), the smallest object in an image (b), and the largest object in an image (c).

threshold distance	< 0.1	< 0.15	< 0.2	≥ 0.2	total
% of errors	75.89	13.84	7.14	3.13	100
number of cases	170	31	16	7	224

Table 2: Analysis of LXMERT's errors with respect to target object's distance from the threshold. Threshold distance refers to the lowest value in the visual scene.

dataset. In this section, we investigate how the model may be solving the task. Specifically, we explore what visual information the model attends to within each image and whether the representations learned by the model encode information about the context-dependent threshold that determines what counts as *big* or *small* in a given image.

6.1 Visual Attention over Key Object Types

Recall that the ground truth labels in our dataset are assigned based on the function in Eqn. 1, which was shown to fit well with human judgements about relative gradable adjectives (Schmidt et al., 2009). This function computes a threshold value taking into account the biggest and smallest objects in the context of an image. Thus, a possible strategy adopted by the model at the level of individual images could be to identify the target object and reason about the context by focusing on the biggest and smallest objects. We test this hypothesis by checking whether the model pays particular attention to these object types (target, biggest, smallest) or whether its attention is rather uniformly distributed over all regions detected by Faster R-CNN (Ren et al., 2015).

To compute which objects are the most attended, we use the Intersection over Union (IoU) metric (Russakovsky et al., 2015). We take the attention weights provided by the `[CLS]` token representation, extracted from the final layer of the best fine-tuned model with frozen parameters. We then use IoU Precision @ K to find the percentage of the labels correctly predicted by the model using the following steps:

1. **Extract top-K object proposals:** For each correctly predicted label, separately for each of the three images in a scene, we take the object proposals of the image regions detected by Faster R-CNN with K-highest scores in the `[CLS]` token. We perform the procedure for each attention head of the representation, extracted from the cross-modality encoder for the corresponding visual-language input. We ignore the object proposals related to the background areas of the image, which we identify based on the labels provided by Faster R-CNN.[10]
2. **Extract ground-truth bounding boxes:** We take the ground-truth bounding boxes of the biggest/the smallest/target objects from all three images in the input scene.[11]
3. **Calculate Pairwise IoU:** We calculate the pairwise IoU between the top-K object proposals and the ground truth bounding boxes, obtained in Steps 1 and 2. We take the highest IoU value calculated for all these pairs.
4. **Calculate IoU Precision@K:** The IoU precision @ K is the percentage of all the IoU values obtained in Step 3 that are > 0.5.

We also compute a random baseline for all three categories with the same steps, except in Step 1 we randomly select K objects from the 36 detected by Faster R-CNN, instead of using the ones with the highest attention scores.

We use the smallest possible value for K = 1, as the most illustrative case in which the metric only

[10]The attributes predicted for the regions corresponding to the black background in our scenes could be *black* or *dark*.

[11]We calculate the coordinates of the boxes using objects position and radius provided in the annotation of the POS1 dataset by Pezzelle and Fernández (2019).

Figure 5: Example of object proposals most attended to by the 9th head of the last layer of the cross-modality encoder. In each image, the model attends to all of the objects except the biggest ones. Simultaneously, in the leftmost image, it also focuses on the *green circle*, which is the target object in this scene.

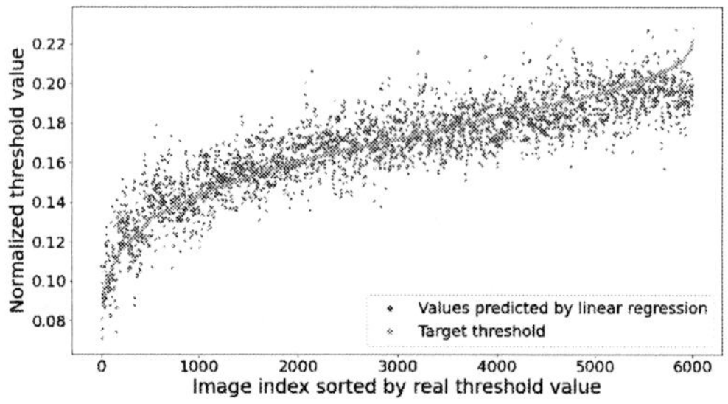

Figure 6: Comparison of threshold values predicted by the linear regression model (blue dots) with the actual threshold for each of the 6000 test images (orange dots). Here, the real target values are sorted in ascending order, and the predicted values are sorted with respect to the corresponding targets' indices. The thresholds are normalized by the area of the one image, with the square root transformation. Best viewed in color.

looks at the single object in each image to which the model attends the most.

Figure 4 shows the results of the IoU Precision @ K for the 12 attention heads in LXMERT. In particular, Figure 4a shows that many of the attention heads attend to the target object that is queried directly in the input sentence. Figures 4b and 4c demonstrate that the model also looks at the surrounding visual context, which is needed to perform relational reasoning. A comparison of behaviour across the Figures reveals that different attention heads *appear* to specialise on different object types: attention head 9 learns to attend to the smallest objects while it pays no attention to the biggest objects and less than random attention to the target objects. We also highlight the observed behaviour of attention head 11, which is the only head that reliably attends to the biggest objects.

Figure 5 shows an example of the objects attended to by attention head 9 in one sample scene. Here, we can see that the model is primarily attending to the smallest objects in the scene.

6.2 Implicit Knowledge of the Threshold

The analysis above showed that the model, besides the target object, also pays attention to key contextual information, particularly to the smallest and biggest objects in an image. These objects are critical to compute the threshold to determine if a target object is *big* or *small* relative to the context of an image. To test whether the representations learned by the model implicitly encode information about the context-dependent threshold, we use a diagnostic classifier (Alain and Bengio, 2017; Hupkes et al., 2018; Belinkov and Glass, 2019). Probing or diagnostic tests are useful tools to better understand the inner workings of deep models. Given a hypothesis about information that may be encoded by a trained model, a probe checks whether such information is accessible by a relatively simple classifier.

Concretely, in this experiment we use a linear regression classifier[12] to predict the threshold values for each of the three images in a scene given the cross-modality features learned by the LXMERT encoder (x_0, x_1, x_2 in Eqn. 2). The classifier uses the same train/val/test splits of the 3POS1 dataset. The predicted and actual values are displayed in Figure 6, which shows that a simple linear classifier can predict the threshold values for each image in a scene remarkably accurately (mean squared error on the test set is $6.64e-05$). This confirms that the cross-modality representations learned by the model are representing the threshold in each image.

7 Analysis at the Multi-Image Level

In the previous section, we analysed the model representations at the level of the independent images. Here, we probe the representations with respect to the entire three-image scene. First, we investigate whether the representations encode information on the overall configuration of the scene (Sec. 7.1). Second, we probe their effectiveness in identifying the odd-one-out image in the scene (Sec. 7.2). In both analyses, we use diagnostic classifiers,[13] that take as input the concatenation of the three image-statement cross-modal representations (Eqn. 3).

[12]Least squares linear regression from the `sklearn`.

[13]Trained on the same splits as the main experiments.

		sentence verification (LXMERT full model) ✓	sentence verification (LXMERT full model) ✗
scene configuration classification (linear diagnostic)	✓	85.70	2.45
	✗	3.10	8.75

Table 3: Confusion matrix with % of scenes in the test set that are (in)correctly classified by the full LXMERT model for the original sentence verification task and by the linear SVM for the scene configuration task.

7.1 Scene Configuration Classification

We first investigate whether the representations learned by the model encode the *configuration* of the scene, that is, whether they are effective to distinguish between scenes where 1 target object counts as small and 2 as big (hence, *1small2big*), and vice versa (*1big2small*). In principle, this counting step is necessary to solve the sentence-verification task (see Sec. 2), and this probe determines whether the model is reasoning at the level of the scene or exploiting other strategies, such as capturing random correlations in the data.

We use an SVM classifier with linear kernel (Boser et al., 1992)[14] to probe the representations learned by the model, and find that they are indeed useful for predicting the configurations. Accuracy on the test set is 88.15%, which is well above chance level (50%). As reported in Table 3, in the large majority of cases (85.7%) a correct prediction in the sentence verification task corresponds to a correct assessment by the diagnostic classifier. This confirms that LXMERT learns representations that encode the configuration of the scene.

7.2 Odd-One-Out Image Identification

Our results so far show that the model is able to perform the multi-step sentence verification task with high accuracy and that the representations encode information about different configurations of scenes. However, there is yet no guarantee that the model is able to identify the odd-one-out image (i.e., the image that is not prevalent; see Sec. 4.1). We test this by means of another diagnostic classifier: given a scene representation, the task is to predict the position of the odd-one-out image (hence, OOO), namely image 0, 1, or 2.

We initially experiment with the same type of diagnostic classifier used in the previous analysis: an SVM with a linear kernel. However, this linear classifier was only able to accurately classify the position of odd-one-out images associated with `image-scene` instances labelled `True`, suggesting that the prediction of the position of the odd-one-out cannot be solved by a linear classifier. Therefore, we use a non-linear MLP and also report the results of a control task, where the labels are randomly assigned to the instances (Hewitt and Liang, 2019). The MLP is a two-layer neural network with 128 units in each layer followed by a ReLU activation function, and finally a learned projection into 3 output units, followed by a softmax normalisation. We train the MLP with a cross-entropy objective function for four epochs using the Adam optimiser with the default learning rate.

	train	valid	test
OOO	0.8767	0.8771	0.8659
control	0.3385	0.3386	0.3359

Table 4: Accuracy of the MLP diagnostic classifier on the train/val/test splits of the data on both the OOO and the control setting. Chance level is 0.33 for all splits.

Table 4 reports the results of the non-linear diagnostic classifier in both the OOO and *control* settings. As can be seen, while the MLP does not exceed chance level in the control setting, in the OOO it achieves a striking 87.67% accuracy, a similar performance as the one reported in Sec. 7.1. On the one hand, this indicates that the model cannot fit the data when the assigned labels are not related to the actual OOO image positions. On the other hand, these results show that the representations learned by LXMERT do encode information regarding the odd-one-out object in the scene.

Taken together, these analyses demonstrate that LXMERT reasons over the multi-image scene to perform the sentence-verification task. In particular, it is able to compute the contextually-defined size of the objects in the scene and perform higher-level reasoning over these representations.

8 Conclusion

We performed an in-depth analysis of the representations learned by the pretrained multimodal transformer LXMERT when performing relational reasoning. We proposed a multimodal reasoning task that requires multi-step relational reasoning and showed that LXMERT can perform the task with high accuracy. Our analysis reveals that the

[14]Implemented in linear support vector machine classification (`LinearSVC`) from the `sklearn`.

majority of the errors arise from target objects with contextually-defined sizes close to the threshold, and that LXMERT solves the task by (i) encoding information regarding the size of objects and by (ii) reasoning over that size. Most of its errors concern *borderline* cases for which the first, image-level reasoning step was shown to be challenging. Overall, our results show that transformer-based architectures pretrained on natural images can generalise to synthetic datasets. We leave to future work an extensive exploration of the extent to which our findings apply to similar tasks and models, for example other vision and langauge transformers (Bugliarello et al., 2021), as well as to natural multimodal data.

Acknowledgments

The authors would like to thank Elia Bruni for providing feedback on a preliminary version of this work and Dieuwke Hupkes for her advice on probing methods. The work has received funding from the European Research Council (ERC) under the European Union's Horizon 2020 research and innovation programme (grant agreement No. 819455).

References

Panos Achlioptas, Judy Fan, Robert Hawkins, Noah Goodman, and Leonidas J Guibas. 2019. Shapeglot: Learning language for shape differentiation. In *Proceedings of the IEEE International Conference on Computer Vision*, pages 8938–8947.

Guillaume Alain and Yoshua Bengio. 2017. Understanding intermediate layers using linear classifier probes. In *International Conference on Learning Representations (ICLR) – Workshop Track.*

Jacob Andreas and Dan Klein. 2016. Reasoning about pragmatics with neural listeners and speakers. In *Proceedings of the 2016 Conference on Empirical Methods in Natural Language Processing*, pages 1173–1182.

Jacob Andreas, Marcus Rohrbach, Trevor Darrell, and Dan Klein. 2016. Neural module networks. In *Proceedings of the IEEE Conference on Computer Vision and Pattern Recognition*, pages 39–48.

Stanislaw Antol, Aishwarya Agrawal, Jiasen Lu, Margaret Mitchell, Dhruv Batra, C Lawrence Zitnick, and Devi Parikh. 2015. VQA: Visual question answering. In *Proceedings of the IEEE International Conference on Computer Vision*, pages 2425–2433.

Jimmy Lei Ba, Jamie Ryan Kiros, and Geoffrey E Hinton. 2016. Layer normalization. *arXiv preprint arXiv:1607.06450.*

Yonatan Belinkov and James Glass. 2019. Analysis methods in neural language processing: A survey. *Transactions of the Association for Computational Linguistics*, 7:49–72.

Bernhard E Boser, Isabelle M Guyon, and Vladimir N Vapnik. 1992. A training algorithm for optimal margin classifiers. In *Proceedings of the fifth annual workshop on Computational learning theory*, pages 144–152.

Emanuele Bugliarello, Ryan Cotterell, Naoaki Okazaki, and Desmond Elliott. 2021. Multimodal pretraining unmasked: A meta-analysis and a unified framework of vision-and-language BERTs. *Transactions of the Association for Computational Linguistics.*

Reuben Cohn-Gordon, Noah Goodman, and Christopher Potts. 2018. Pragmatically informative image captioning with character-level inference. In *Proceedings of the 2018 Conference of the North American Chapter of the Association for Computational Linguistics: Human Language Technologies, Volume 2 (Short Papers)*, pages 439–443.

Jacob Devlin, Ming-Wei Chang, Kenton Lee, and Kristina Toutanova. 2019. BERT: Pre-training of deep bidirectional transformers for language understanding. In *Proceedings of the 2019 Conference of the North American Chapter of the Association for Computational Linguistics: Human Language Technologies, Volume 1 (Long and Short Papers)*, pages 4171–4186.

Maxwell Forbes, Christine Kaeser-Chen, Piyush Sharma, and Serge Belongie. 2019. Neural naturalist: Generating fine-grained image comparisons. In *Proceedings of the 2019 Conference on Empirical Methods in Natural Language Processing and the 9th International Joint Conference on Natural Language Processing (EMNLP-IJCNLP)*, pages 708–717.

Noah D Goodman and Michael C Frank. 2016. Pragmatic language interpretation as probabilistic inference. *Trends in cognitive sciences*, 20(11):818–829.

Dan Hendrycks and Kevin Gimpel. 2016. Gaussian error linear units (gelus). *arXiv preprint arXiv:1606.08415.*

John Hewitt and Percy Liang. 2019. Designing and interpreting probes with control tasks. In *Proceedings of the 2019 Conference on Empirical Methods in Natural Language Processing and the 9th International Joint Conference on Natural Language Processing (EMNLP-IJCNLP)*, pages 2733–2743, Hong Kong, China. Association for Computational Linguistics.

Ronghang Hu, Jacob Andreas, Marcus Rohrbach, Trevor Darrell, and Kate Saenko. 2017. Learning to reason: End-to-end module networks for visual question answering. In *Proceedings of the IEEE International Conference on Computer Vision*, pages 804–813.

Dieuwke Hupkes, Sara Veldhoen, and Willem Zuidema. 2018. Visualisation and 'diagnostic classifiers' reveal how recurrent and recursive neural networks process hierarchical structure. *Journal of Artificial Intelligence Research*, 61:907–926.

Harsh Jhamtani and Taylor Berg-Kirkpatrick. 2018. Learning to describe differences between pairs of similar images. In *Proceedings of the 2018 Conference on Empirical Methods in Natural Language Processing*, pages 4024–4034.

Justin Johnson, Bharath Hariharan, Laurens van der Maaten, Li Fei-Fei, C Lawrence Zitnick, and Ross Girshick. 2017. Clevr: A diagnostic dataset for compositional language and elementary visual reasoning. In *Proceedings of the IEEE Conference on Computer Vision and Pattern Recognition*, pages 2901–2910.

Diederik P Kingma and Jimmy Ba. 2014. Adam: A method for stochastic optimization. *arXiv preprint arXiv:1412.6980*.

Alexander Kuhnle and Ann Copestake. 2017. Shape-World: A new test methodology for multimodal language understanding. *arXiv preprint arXiv:1704.04517*.

Mateusz Malinowski and Mario Fritz. 2014. A multi-world approach to question answering about real-world scenes based on uncertain input. In *Advances in neural information processing systems*, pages 1682–1690.

Dong Huk Park, Trevor Darrell, and Anna Rohrbach. 2019. Robust change captioning. In *Proceedings of the IEEE International Conference on Computer Vision*, pages 4624–4633.

Sandro Pezzelle and Raquel Fernández. 2019. Is the red square big? MALeViC: Modeling adjectives leveraging visual contexts. In *Proceedings of the 2019 Conference on Empirical Methods in Natural Language Processing and the 9th International Joint Conference on Natural Language Processing (EMNLP-IJCNLP)*, pages 2858–2869.

Yue Qiu, Yutaka Satoh, Ryota Suzuki, Kenji Iwata, and Hirokatsu Kataoka. 2020. 3d-aware scene change captioning from multiview images. *IEEE Robotics and Automation Letters*, 5(3):4743–4750.

Shaoqing Ren, Kaiming He, Ross Girshick, and Jian Sun. 2015. Faster r-cnn: Towards real-time object detection with region proposal networks. In *Advances in neural information processing systems*, pages 91–99.

Philippe E Ruiz. 2011. Building and solving odd-one-out classification problems: A systematic approach. *Intelligence*, 39(5):342–350.

Olga Russakovsky, Jia Deng, Hao Su, Jonathan Krause, Sanjeev Satheesh, Sean Ma, Zhiheng Huang, Andrej Karpathy, Aditya Khosla, Michael Bernstein, et al. 2015. Imagenet large scale visual recognition challenge. *International Journal of Computer Vision*, 115(3):211–252.

Adam Santoro, David Raposo, David G Barrett, Mateusz Malinowski, Razvan Pascanu, Peter Battaglia, and Timothy Lillicrap. 2017. A simple neural network module for relational reasoning. In *Advances in neural information processing systems*, pages 4967–4976.

Lauren A Schmidt, Noah D Goodman, David Barner, and Joshua B Tenenbaum. 2009. How tall is tall? Compositionality, statistics, and gradable adjectives. In *Proceedings of the 31st annual conference of the cognitive science society*, pages 2759–2764. Citeseer.

Jong-Chyi Su, Chenyun Wu, Huaizu Jiang, and Subhransu Maji. 2017. Reasoning about fine-grained attribute phrases using reference games. In *Proceedings of the IEEE International Conference on Computer Vision*, pages 418–427.

Alane Suhr, Mike Lewis, James Yeh, and Yoav Artzi. 2017. A corpus of natural language for visual reasoning. In *Proceedings of the 55th Annual Meeting of the Association for Computational Linguistics (Volume 2: Short Papers)*, pages 217–223.

Alane Suhr, Stephanie Zhou, Ally Zhang, Iris Zhang, Huajun Bai, and Yoav Artzi. 2019. A corpus for reasoning about natural language grounded in photographs. In *Proceedings of the 57th Annual Meeting of the Association for Computational Linguistics*, pages 6418–6428.

Hao Tan and Mohit Bansal. 2019. LXMERT: Learning cross-modality encoder representations from transformers. In *Proceedings of the 2019 Conference on Empirical Methods in Natural Language Processing and the 9th International Joint Conference on Natural Language Processing (EMNLP-IJCNLP)*, pages 5103–5114.

Ramakrishna Vedantam, Samy Bengio, Kevin Murphy, Devi Parikh, and Gal Chechik. 2017. Context-aware captions from context-agnostic supervision. In *Proceedings of the IEEE Conference on Computer Vision and Pattern Recognition*, pages 251–260.

Gilad Vered, Gal Oren, Yuval Atzmon, and Gal Chechik. 2019. Joint optimization for cooperative image captioning. In *Proceedings of the IEEE International Conference on Computer Vision*, pages 8898–8907.

A Computing infrastructures

We ran all the experiments with LXMERT using Python 3.7 on a computer with Ubuntu 18.04.5

LTS, single GPU Tesla V100-SXM2, and NVIDIA driver 455.38, CUDA 10.1, and 24GB RAM.

For N2NMN, we used a computer cluster with Debian 10, a single GPU GeForce 1080Ti, 11GB GDDR5X, NVIDIA driver 450.80.02, CUDA 11.0, 260GB RAM, and Python 3.6.

B Hyperparameters and training for N2NMN

We performed a parameter search to determine the best values for training N2NMN[15] on the training split of the POS1 dataset[16] for 3000 iterations of batch size 64 for each combination. We experimented with the following parameters: encoder dropout (0, 0.5, 0.8), decoder dropout (0, 0.5, 0.8), weight decay (5e-5, 5e-4), baseline decay (0.8, 0.99), lambda entropy (0.1, 0.01, 0.001). Their best values (corresponding to the best validation accuracy) are shown in Table 5. We trained the final model using these parameters for 14,000 iterations with batch size 64. The training took approximately 4 hours.

encoder dropout	**decoder dropout**	**weight decay**	**baseline decay**	**lambda entropy**
0.8	0.8	5e-5	0.99	0.01

Table 5: Best parameters for N2NMN model, found with a grid search.

C Hyperparameters and fine-tuning for LXMERT

For the fine-tuning of LXMERT, the pre-trained model with standard hyperparameters was used[17], with only the learning rate changed from 1e-5 to 5e-5, since even with these out-of-the-box parameters, it was able to achieve high performance on the given task. We fine-tuned this model with the POS1 training split using early stopping after 12 epochs, with the parameter number of epochs of BertADAM optimizer set to 150, learning rate 1e-5, and batch size 32 (the only difference in the used hyperparameters during the fine-tuning with 3POS1 was in the batch size 64). We validated the model after each epoch, then the best model was selected, which showed the highest validation accuracy during the 12 epochs, and further evaluated on the test split.

The running time of each fine-tuning epoch for the POS1 dataset was 3 minutes, while each epoch of fine-tuning with 3POS1 took around 6 minutes.

[15] `https://github.com/ronghanghu/n2nmn`

[16] `https://github.com/sandropezzelle/malevic`

[17] `https://github.com/airsplay/lxmert.git`

In-Batch Negatives for Knowledge Distillation with Tightly-Coupled Teachers for Dense Retrieval

Sheng-Chieh Lin*, Jheng-Hong Yang* and Jimmy Lin

David R. Cheriton School of Computer Science
University of Waterloo

Abstract

We present an efficient training approach to text retrieval with dense representations that applies knowledge distillation using the ColBERT late-interaction ranking model. Specifically, we propose to transfer the knowledge from a bi-encoder teacher to a student by distilling knowledge from ColBERT's expressive MaxSim operator into a simple dot product. The advantage of the bi-encoder teacher–student setup is that we can efficiently add in-batch negatives during knowledge distillation, enabling richer interactions between teacher and student models. In addition, using ColBERT as the teacher reduces training cost compared to a full cross-encoder. Experiments on the MS MARCO passage and document ranking tasks and data from the TREC 2019 Deep Learning Track demonstrate that our approach helps models learn robust representations for dense retrieval effectively and efficiently.

1 Introduction

For well over half a century, solutions to the *ad hoc* retrieval problem—where the system's task is return a list of top k texts from an arbitrarily large corpus $\mathcal{D}$ that maximizes some metric of quality such as average precision or NDCG—has been dominated by *sparse* vector representations, for example, bag-of-words BM25. Even in modern multi-stage ranking architectures, which take advantage of large pretrained transformers such as BERT (Devlin et al., 2019), the models are deployed as *rerankers* over initial candidates retrieved based on sparse vector representations; this is sometimes called "first-stage retrieval". One well-known example of this design is the BERT-based reranker of Nogueira and Cho (2019); see Lin et al. (2020) for a recent survey.

The standard reranker architecture, while effective, exhibits high query latency, on the order of seconds per query (Hofstätter and Hanbury, 2019; Khattab and Zaharia, 2020) because expensive neural inference must be applied at query time on query–passage pairs. This design is known as a cross-encoder (Humeau et al., 2020), which exploits query–passage attention interactions across all transformer layers. As an alternative, a bi-encoder design provides an approach to ranking with dense representations that is far more efficient than cross-encoders (Lee et al., 2019; Reimers and Gurevych, 2019; Khattab and Zaharia, 2020; Karpukhin et al., 2020; Luan et al., 2021; Xiong et al., 2021; Qu et al., 2020; Hofstätter et al., 2021). Prior to retrieval, the vector representations can be precomputed for each of the texts in a corpus. When retrieving texts in response to a given query, computationally expensive transformer inference is replaced by much faster approximate nearest neighbor (ANN) search (Liu et al., 2004; Malkov and Yashunin, 2020).

Recently, researchers have proposed bi-encoders that produce multiple vectors to represent a query (or a passage) (Humeau et al., 2020; Luan et al., 2021; Khattab and Zaharia, 2020), which have proven to be effective both theoretically and empirically. However, the main disadvantage of these designs is their high storage requirements. For example, ColBERT (Khattab and Zaharia, 2020) requires storing all the WordPiece token vectors of each text (passage) in the corpus. On the MS MARCO passage corpus comprising 8.8M passages, for example, this requires 154 GiB.

Of course, a common alternative is to produce single vectors for queries and passages (Reimers and Gurevych, 2019). Although this design is less storage-demanding, it sacrifices ranking effectiveness since its structure breaks rich interactions between queries and passages compared to

*Contributed equally.

Proceedings of the 6th Workshop on Representation Learning for NLP (RepL4NLP-2021), pages 163–173
Bangkok, Thailand (Online), August 6, 2021.

multi-vector bi-encoders or cross-encoders. Hence, improving the effectiveness of single-vector bi-encoders represents an important problem.

One approach to improving the effectiveness of single-vector bi-encoders is hard negative mining, by training with carefully selected negative examples that emphasize discrimination between relevant and non-relevant texts. There are several approaches to accomplish this. Karpukhin et al. (2020) and Qu et al. (2020) leverage large in-batch negatives to enrich training signals. Guu et al. (2020) and Xiong et al. (2021) propose to mine hard negatives using the trained bi-encoder itself. By searching for global negative samples from an asynchronously updated ANN index, the bi-encoder can learn information not present in the training data produced by sparse representations (Xiong et al., 2021). However, both large in-batch negative sampling and asynchronous ANN index updates are computationally demanding. The later is especially impractical for large corpora since it requires periodic inference over *all* texts in the corpus to ensure that the best negative examples are retrieved.

There is also work that explores knowledge distillation (KD) (Hinton et al., 2015) to enhance retrieval effectiveness and efficiency. Most related to our study is Hofstätter et al. (2020), who demonstrate that KD using a cross-encoder teacher significantly improves the effectiveness of bi-encoders for dense retrieval. Similarly, Barkan et al. (2020) investigate the effectiveness of distilling a trained cross-encoder into a bi-encoder for sentence similarity tasks. Gao et al. (2020a) explore KD combinations of different objectives such as language modeling and ranking. However, the above papers use computationally expensive cross-encoder teacher models; thus, combining them for KD with more advanced negative sampling techniques can be impractical.

In light of existing work on hard negative mining and knowledge distillation, we propose to improve the effectiveness of single-vector bi-encoders with a more efficient KD approach: in-batch KD using a bi-encoder teacher. The advantage of our design is that, during distillation, it enables the efficient exploitation of all possible query–passage pairs within a minibatch, which we call *tight coupling* (illustrated in Figure 1). This is a key difference between our KD approach and previous methods for dense retrieval, where only the scores of given query–passage triplets (not all combinations) are computed due to the computational costs of cross-encoders (Hofstätter et al., 2020; Gao et al., 2020a; Barkan et al., 2020).

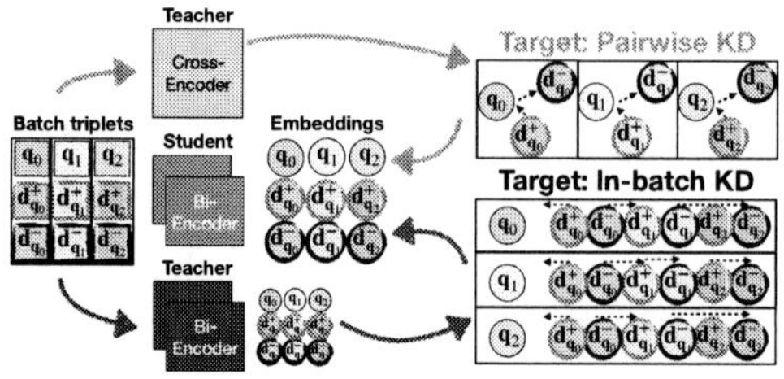

Figure 1: Illustration of the differences between pairwise knowledge distillation and our proposed in-batch knowledge distillation.

The contribution of this work is a simple technique for efficiently adding in-batch negative samples during knowledge distillation when training a single-vector bi-encoder. For the remainder of this paper, we refer to this technique as "in-batch KD" for convenience. We empirically show that our model, even trained with BM25 negatives, can be more effective than cross-encoder teachers. With hard negatives, our method approaches the state of the art in dense retrieval. Our in-batch KD technique is able to incorporate hard negatives in a computationally efficient manner, without requiring large amounts of GPU memory for large batch sizes or expensive periodic index refreshes.

2 Background

We focus on improving the training efficiency and retrieval effectiveness of dense retrieval and begin by formalizing it as a dense representation learning problem. To be more specific, we propose to use knowledge distillation to enrich training signals and stabilize the representation learning procedure of bi-encoder models in the context of the well-known Noise-Contrastive Estimation (NCE) framework.

2.1 Dense Retrieval with Bi-encoders

The bi-encoder design has been widely adopted for dense retrieval (Lee et al., 2019; Chang et al., 2020; Guu et al., 2020; Karpukhin et al., 2020; Luan et al., 2021; Qu et al., 2020; Xiong et al., 2021), where queries and passages are encoded in a low-dimensional space. It aims to learn low-dimensional representations that pull queries and relevant passages together and push queries and non-relevant passages apart.

Following the work of Mnih and Kavukcuoglu

(2013), we formulate a common objective for dense representation learning for passage retrieval. Given a query q and a parameterized scoring function ϕ_θ that computes the relevance between a query and a candidate passage p, we define a probability distribution over documents in a corpus $\mathcal{D}$ with respect to relevance, as follows:

$$P_\theta^q(p, \mathcal{D}) = \frac{\exp(\phi_\theta(q, p))}{\sum_{p' \in \mathcal{D}} \exp(\phi_\theta(q, p'))} = \frac{\exp(\mathbf{h}_q \cdot \mathbf{h}_p)}{\sum_{p' \in \mathcal{D}} \exp(\mathbf{h}_q \cdot \mathbf{h}_{p'})}, \quad (1)$$

where $\mathbf{h}_q$ ($\mathbf{h}_p$) $\in \mathbb{R}^d$ denotes the query (passage) representation produced by the bi-encoder. A typical bi-encoder uses a simple scoring function for ϕ_θ, for example, the inner product of two vectors, as shown above.

The main challenge of evaluating and computing gradients of Eq. (1) is the prohibitively expensive computation cost given the number of passages in the corpus $\mathcal{D}$, typically millions (or even more). This is already setting aside the cost of using pretrained transformers such as BERT as the encoder to compute $\mathbf{h}_q$ and $\mathbf{h}_p$.

Thus, previous work approximates Eq. (1) by NCE, which samples $p \in \mathcal{D}^+$ from training data and $p' \in \mathcal{D}' = \{\mathcal{D}^+ \cup \mathcal{D}^-\}$, where $\mathcal{D}^-$ is from a noisy distribution such as candidates retrieved by BM25 (Nogueira and Cho, 2019), filtered by fine-tuned transformers (Qu et al., 2020), or retrieved by an asynchronously updated bi-encoder model itself (Xiong et al., 2021). Another simple yet effective approach is in-batch negative sampling, as used by Karpukhin et al. (2020), which takes p and p' of other queries within a minibatch as negative examples in NCE.

2.2 Knowledge Distillation

Other than designing sophisticated sampling methods for p', training bi-encoder models using knowledge distillation (KD) with effective teacher models is another promising approach (Hofstätter et al., 2020). In this case, we aim to make the bi-encoder model mimic the teacher model's probability distribution as follows:

$$P_{\theta;\text{student}}^q(p, \mathcal{D}') = \frac{\exp(\mathbf{h}_q \cdot \mathbf{h}_p)}{\sum_{p' \in \mathcal{D}'} \exp(\mathbf{h}_q \cdot \mathbf{h}_{p'})} \approx \frac{\exp(\phi_{\hat{\theta}}(q, p)/\tau)}{\sum_{p' \in \mathcal{D}'} \exp(\phi_{\hat{\theta}}(q, p')/\tau)} = P_{\hat{\theta};\text{teacher}}^q(p, \mathcal{D}'), \quad (2)$$

where $\phi_{\hat{\theta}}$ denotes the relevance score estimated by a pretrained model parameterized by $\hat{\theta}$ and τ, the temperature hyperparameter used in the KD framework. To improve retrieval effectiveness, one can leverage pre-computed scores from pretrained models such as cross-encoders, e.g., BERT, bi-encoders, e.g., ColBERT, or ensembled scores from multiple models $\phi_{\hat{\theta}} = \sum_j \phi_{\hat{\theta};j}$.

3 Our Approach

3.1 In-batch Knowledge Distillation

Using KD in Eq. (2) provides soft labels for bi-encoder training, and can be integrated with the previously mentioned NCE framework. In this work, we propose to enhance teacher–student interactions by adding in-batch negatives to our knowledge distillation. Specifically, we estimate ϕ_θ on in-batch examples from a minibatch $\mathcal{B}$ guided by an auxiliary teacher model $\phi_{\hat{\theta}}$ through the minimization of Kullback–Leibler (KL) divergence of the two distributions:

$$\arg\min_\theta \sum_{q \in \mathcal{Q}_\mathcal{B}} \sum_{p \in \mathcal{D}'_\mathcal{B}} \mathcal{L}_{\phi_\theta, \phi_{\hat{\theta}}}, \quad (3)$$

where $\mathcal{L}_{\phi_\theta, \phi_{\hat{\theta}}}$ is:

$$P_{\hat{\theta};\text{teacher}}^q(p, \mathcal{D}'_\mathcal{B}) \log \frac{P_{\hat{\theta};\text{teacher}}^q(p, \mathcal{D}'_\mathcal{B})}{P_{\theta;\text{student}}^q(p, \mathcal{D}'_\mathcal{B})}. \quad (4)$$

Note that here we consider all pairwise relationship between queries and passages within a minibatch that contains a query set $\mathcal{Q}_\mathcal{B}$ and a passage set $\mathcal{D}'_\mathcal{B}$.

3.2 Teacher Model Choice

A **cross-encoder** has been shown to be an effective teacher (Hofstätter et al., 2020; Gao et al., 2020a) since it allows rich interactions between the intermediate transformer representations of a query q and a passage p. For example, a "vanilla" cross-encoder design using BERT can be denoted as:

$$\phi_{\hat{\theta};\text{Cat}} \triangleq W f(\mathbf{h}_{q \oplus p}), \quad (5)$$

where the ranking score is first computed by the hidden representation of the concatenation $q \oplus p$ from BERT (along with the standard special tokens) and then mapped to a scalar by a pooling operation f and a mapping matrix W.

Although effective, due to BERT's quadratic complexity with respect to input sequence length, this design makes exhaustive combinations between a query and possible candidates impractical, since this requires evaluating cross-encoders $|\mathcal{B}|^2$ times to compute Eq. (3) using Eq. (5). Thus, an alternative is to conduct *pairwise* KD by computing the KL divergence of only two probabilities of a positive pair (q, p) and a negative pair (q, p') for each query q. However, this might not yield a good approximation of Eq. (2).

A **bi-encoder** can also be leveraged as a teacher model, which has the advantage that it is more feasible to perform exhaustive comparisons between queries and passages since they are passed through the encoder independently. Among bi-encoder designs, ColBERT is a representative model that uses late interactions of multiple vectors $(\{\mathbf{h}_q^1, \ldots, \mathbf{h}_q^i\}, \{\mathbf{h}_p^1, \ldots, \mathbf{h}_p^j\})$ to improve the robustness of dense retrieval, as compared to inner products of pairs of single vectors $(\mathbf{h}_q, \mathbf{h}_p)$. Specifically, Khattab and Zaharia (2020) propose the following fine-grained scoring function:

$$\phi_{\hat{\theta};\text{MaxSim}} \triangleq \sum_{i \in |\mathbf{h}_q|} \max_{j \in |\mathbf{h}_p|} \mathbf{h}_q^i \cdot \mathbf{h}_p^j, \qquad (6)$$

where i and j are the indices of token representations of a query q and a passage p of ColBERT (Khattab and Zaharia, 2020).

The contribution of our work is in-batch knowledge distillation with a tightly-coupled teacher. The computation of $\phi_{\hat{\theta};\text{MaxSim}}$ enables exhaustive inference over all query–passage combinations in the minibatch $\mathcal{B}$ with only $2 \cdot |\mathcal{B}|$ computation cost, enabling enriched interactions between teacher and student. We call this design **T**ightly-**C**oupled **T**eacher ColBERT (TCT-ColBERT). Table 1 provides a training cost comparison between different teachers. When training with pairwise KD, cross-encoders exhibit the highest training cost. On the other hand, ColBERT enables in-batch KD at a modest training cost compared to pairwise KD.

TCT-ColBERT provides a flexible design for bi-encoders, as long as the encoders produce query and passage representations independently. For simplicity, our student model adopts shared encoder weights for both the query and the passage, just like the teacher model ColBERT. Following Khattab and Zaharia (2020), for each query (passage), we prepend the `[CLS]` token and another special `[Q]` (`[D]`) token in the input sequence for both our teacher and student models. The student encoder outputs single-vector dense representations $(\mathbf{h}_q, \mathbf{h}_p)$ by performing average pooling over the token embeddings from the final layer.

Table 1: Training cost comparison. We report the training time per batch against the baseline (without a teacher model) on a single TPU-v2. Our backbone model is BERT-base, with batch size 96. The in-batch cross-encoder training time is not available because it exceeds the memory limit.

Teacher / KD strategy	Pairwise	In-batch
Cross-encoder ($\phi_{\hat{\theta};\text{Cat}}$)	+48.1%	OOM
ColBERT ($\phi_{\hat{\theta};\text{MaxSim}}$)	+32.7%	+33.5%

3.3 Hard Negative Sampling

Given that in-batch negative sampling is an efficient way to add more information into knowledge distillation, we wonder whether our tightly-coupled teacher design works well when applied to more sophisticated sampling methods. Following the work of Xiong et al. (2021), we use our pretrained bi-encoder model, namely TCT-ColBERT, to encode the corpus and sample "hard" negatives for each query to create new training triplets by using the negatives $\mathcal{D}^-$ of the bi-encoder instead of BM25. Specifically, we explore three different training strategies:

1. **HN**: we train the bi-encoder using in-batch hard negatives without the guide of ColBERT.
2. **TCT HN**: we train the bi-encoder with TCT-ColBERT;
3. **TCT HN+**: we first fine-tune our ColBERT teacher with augmented training data containing hard negatives and then distill its knowledge into the bi-encoder student through TCT-ColBERT.

We empirically explore the effectiveness of these strategies for both passage and document retrieval.

4 Experiments

In this section, we conduct experiments on the MS MARCO passage and document corpora. For passage ranking, we first train models on BM25 negatives as warm-up and compare different KD methods. We then further train models on the hard negatives retrieved by the BM25 warmed-up checkpoint. For document ranking, following previous work (Xiong et al., 2021; Zhan et al., 2020; Lu et al., 2021), we start with our BM25 warmed-up checkpoint for passage ranking and conduct additional hard negative training.

Table 2: Passage retrieval results with BM25 negative training. For knowledge distillation (KD) methods, the effectiveness of teacher (T) models is also reported. All our implemented models are labeled with a number and superscripts represent significant improvements over the labeled model (paired t-test, $p < 0.05$).

Strategy	Model	# params of Teacher	MARCO Dev		TREC-DL '19	
			MRR@10 (T/S)	R@1K	NDCG@10 (T/S)	R@1K
-	(1) Baseline	-	- / .310	.945	- / .626	.658
Pairwise KD	KD-T1 (Hofstätter et al., 2020)	110M	.376 / .304	.931	.730 / .631	.702
	KD-T2 (Hofstätter et al., 2020)	467M	.399 / .315	.947	.743 / .668	.737
	(2) KD-T2 (Ours)	467M	.399 / .341^{1}	.964^{1}	.743 / .659^{1}	.708^{1}
	(3) KD-ColBERT	110M	.350 / .339^{1}	.962^{1}	.730 / .670^{1}	.710^{1}
In-batch KD	(4) TCT-ColBERT	110M	.350 / **.344**^{1,3}	**.967**^{1,3}	.730 / **.685**^{1}	**.745**^{1,2,3}

4.1 Passage Retrieval

We perform *ad hoc* passage retrieval on the MS MARCO passage ranking dataset (Bajaj et al., 2016), which consists of a collection of 8.8M passages from web pages and a set of ~0.5M relevant (query, passage) pairs as training data. We evaluate model effectiveness on two test sets of queries:

1. MARCO Dev: the development set of MS MARCO comprises 6980 queries, with an average of one relevant passage per query.
2. TREC-DL '19 (Craswell et al., 2019): the organizers of the Deep Learning Track at the 2019 Text REtrieval Conference (TREC) released 43 queries with multi-graded (0–3) relevance labels on 9K (query, passage) pairs.

To evaluate output quality, we report MRR@10 (NDCG@10) for MARCO Dev (TREC-DL '19) and Recall@1K, denoted as R@1K. To compare with current state-of-the-art models, we evaluate our design, TCT-ColBERT, under two approaches for negative sampling: (1) BM25 and (2) hard negatives retrieved by the bi-encoder itself.

4.1.1 Training with BM25 Negatives

In this setting, models are trained using the official public data `triples.train.small`, where negative samples are produced by BM25. We compare different bi-encoder models using BERT-base as the backbone, which uses single 768-dim vectors to represent each query and passage:

1. **Baseline**: a single-vector bi-encoder trained with in-batch negatives, as discussed in Section 2.1, which is similar to Karpukhin et al. (2020) but with a smaller batch size.
2. **Pairwise KD**: the approach of Hofstätter et al. (2020), who improve ranking effectiveness using cross-encoders with pairwise KD.

We also compare against two models, KD-T1 and KD-T2, which use BERT-base bi-encoders as student models. In the former, the student is distilled from a BERT-base cross-encoder, while the latter is distilled from ensembled cross-encoders comprising BERT-base, BERT-large, and ALBERT-large. These figures reported in Table 2 are copied from Hofstätter et al. (2020). For a fair comparison with our models based on KL-divergence KD, we also implement our KD-T2 using the precomputed pairwise softmax probabilities provided by Hofstätter et al. (2020) (who use MSE margin loss for KD). In addition, we adopt *pairwise* softmax probabilities from fine-tuned ColBERT to train KD-ColBERT for comparison.

All our models are fine-tuned with batch size 96 and learning rate 7×10^{-6} for 500K steps on a single TPU-V2. For TCT-ColBERT, there are two steps in our training procedure: (1) fine-tune $\phi_{\hat{\theta};\text{MaxSim}}$ as our teacher model, (2) freeze $\phi_{\hat{\theta};\text{MaxSim}}$ and distill knowledge into our student model ϕ_{θ}. We keep all the hyperparameter settings the same but adjust temperature $\tau = 0.25$ for KD at the second step. For all our models, including the baseline, we initialize the student model using the fine-tuned weights of the teacher model in the first step. We limit the input tokens to 32 (150) for queries (passages). To evaluate effectiveness, we encode all passages in the corpus and conduct brute force search over the vector representations.

Our main results, including paired t-test for significance testing, are shown in Table 2. In addition to the effectiveness of the student models, we also show the effectiveness of the teacher models for the KD methods.[1]

First, we see that pairwise KD methods show significant improvements over the baseline, indicat-

[1]We report our trained ColBERT's accuracy by reranking the top-1000 candidates provided officially.

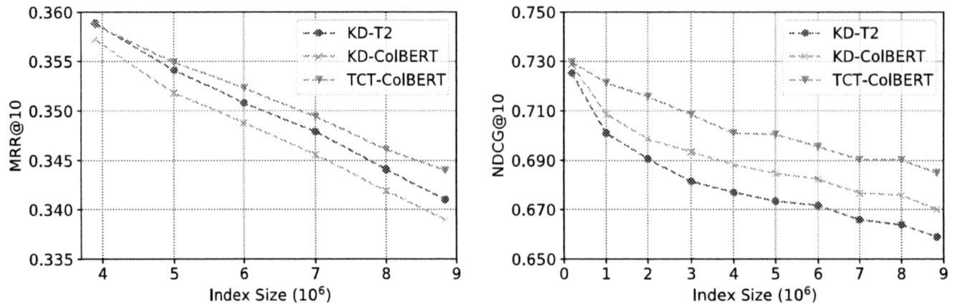

(a) MARCO Dev

(b) TREC-DL '19

Figure 2: Passage retrieval effectiveness on a synthetic corpus comprising relevant passages and BM25 results as additional "distractors" randomly sampled from the corpus are added.

ing that information from BM25 negatives cannot be fully exploited without teacher models. Second, although KD-T2 improves the bi-encoder's effectiveness over KD-T1, it is not consistently better than KD-ColBERT in terms of students' effectiveness. We suspect that they have comparable capabilities to discriminate most paired passages (BM25 negative vs. positive samples), i.e., ColBERT is good enough to guide bi-encoder student models to discriminate them. On the other hand, our TCT-ColBERT model, which uses only one teacher model and adds only 33% more training time over the baseline, yields the best effectiveness, demonstrating the advantages of our proposed in-batch KD — exhaustive exploitation of all query–document combinations in a minibatch.

To understand why TCT-ColBERT yields better results, we study the models' retrieval effectiveness against carefully selected distractors. We start with a small synthetic corpus composed of the relevant passages and the top-1000 BM25 candidates of the 6980 (43) queries from MARCO Dev (TREC-DL '19). To increase the corpus size, we gradually add passages uniformly sampled from the corpus without replacement. From Figure 2, we see that the three KD models exhibit nearly the same effectiveness when the corpus only contains BM25 candidates. This shows that the bi-encoders learn to discriminate relevant passages from the BM25 negative samples well. However, as the index size increases, TCT-ColBERT demonstrates better ranking effectiveness than the other pairwise KD methods, indicating that the learned representations are more robust. We attribute this robustness against "distractors" to the enriched information from in-batch KD, where we are able to exploit all in-batch query–document combinations.

4.1.2 Training with Hard Negatives

In this subsection, we evaluate TCT-ColBERT when training with hard negatives (HNs). We compare our model to four competitive approaches:

1. **ANCE** (Xiong et al., 2021) is the most representative work, which proposes asynchronous index refreshes to mine hard negatives. The model is trained for 600K steps with index refreshes every 10K steps. ANCE uses RoBERTa-base as its backbone.
2. **LTRe** (Zhan et al., 2020) further improves from an ANCE checkpoint by adding more training steps with the same hard negative mining approach; thus, the computation cost of index refreshes from ANCE cannot be neglected. LTRe also use RoBERTa-base as its backbone.
3. **SEED-Encoder** (Lu et al., 2021) leverages a pretraining strategy to enhance the capability of the bi-encoder, which is further fine-tuned with HNs using asynchronous index refreshes.
4. **RocketQA** (Qu et al., 2020) trains a bi-encoder model using hard negatives denoised by a cross-encoder, ERNIE-2.0-Large (Sun et al., 2019). It further demonstrates that training bi-encoders with many in-batch negatives (batch size up to 4096) significantly improves ranking effectiveness; however, this approach is computationally expensive (the authors report using 8×V100 GPUs for training). To the best of our knowledge, RocketQA represents the state of the art in single-vector bi-encoders for dense retrieval. For a more fair comparison, we also report the ranking effectiveness of their model trained with a smaller batch size of 128.

For all the approaches above, we directly copy the reported effectiveness from the original papers.

Table 3: Passage retrieval results with hard negative training. All our implemented models are labeled with a number and superscripts represent significant improvements over the labeled model (paired t-test, $p < 0.05$).

Model	# Index Refresh	Batch Size	MARCO Dev		TREC-DL '19	
			MRR@10	R@1K	NDCG@10	R@1K
ANCE (Xiong et al., 2021)	60	32	.330	.959	.648	-
LTRe (Zhan et al., 2020)	60	32	.341	.962	.675	-
SEED-Encoder (Lu et al., 2021)	≥10 (est.)	-	.339	.961	-	-
RocketQA (Qu et al., 2020)	1	128	.310	-	-	-
RocketQA (Qu et al., 2020)	1	4096	**.364**	-	-	-
(1) TCT-ColBERT	0	96	.344	.967	.685	.745
(2) w/ HN	1	96	.237	.929	.543	.674
(3) w/ TCT HN	1	96	$.354^{1,2}$	$\mathbf{.971}^{1,2}$	$.705^{2}$	$\mathbf{.765}^{1,2}$
(4) w/ TCT HN+	1	96	$.359^{1,2}$	$.970^{1}$	$\mathbf{.719}^{1,2}$	$.760^{1}$

For our TCT-ColBERT model, following the settings of the above approaches, we first use our TCT-ColBERT model trained on BM25 negatives as a warm-up starting point and index all 8.8M MARCO passages. Using the warmed-up index, we retrieve top-200 passages for each training query and randomly sample (with replacement) hard negatives from the 200 candidates to form our training data. Note that due to resource limitations we do not conduct experiments with asynchronous index refreshes since multiple V100 GPUs are required for such a model training scheme.[2] In this experiment, all the hyperparameter settings are the same as the ones in the BM25 negative training, except for training steps, which is set to 100K for both student and teacher training.

Table 3 reports the results of our experiments with hard negative training. First, we observe that our TCT-ColBERT model trained with BM25 negatives marginally outperforms the other models trained with HNs, except for RocketQA. Comparing the different training strategies discussed in Section 3.3 (second main block of the table), we see that the ranking effectiveness of TCT-ColBERT (HN) degrades when training on hard negatives without the guide of a teacher. This is consistent with the findings of Qu et al. (2020) that hard negatives contain noisy information (i.e., some hard negatives may actually be relevant). Also, Xiong et al. (2021) show that training bi-encoders with hard negatives can be unstable: hard negatives benefit ranking effectiveness only under certain hyperparameter settings.

In contrast, hard negative training using ColBERT's in-batch KD further boosts ranking effectiveness, especially when our teacher (ColBERT) is trained with the same hard negative samples beforehand. It is also worth noting that our TCT-ColBERT (w/ TCT HN+) with batch size 96 yields competitive ranking effectiveness compared to RocketQA (the current state of the art), which uses batch size 4096. These results demonstrate the advantages of our TCT design: our approach effectively exploits hard negatives in a computationally efficient manner (i.e., without the need for large batch sizes or periodic index refreshes).

4.2 Document Retrieval

To validate the effectiveness and generality of our training strategy, we conduct further experiments on document retrieval using the MS MARCO document ranking dataset. This dataset contains 3.2M web pages gathered from passages in the MS MARCO passage ranking dataset. Similar to the passage condition, we evaluate model effectiveness on two test sets of queries:

1. MARCO Dev: the development set contains 5193 queries, each with exactly one relevant document.
2. TREC-DL '19: graded relevance judgments are available from the TREC 2019 Deep Learning Track, but on only 43 queries.

Per official guidelines, we report different metrics for the two query sets: MRR@100 for MARCO Dev and NDCG@10 for TREC-DL '19.

Following the FirstP setting for document retrieval described in Xiong et al. (2021), we feed the first 512 tokens of each document for encoding, and start with the warmed-up checkpoint for our encoder's parameters trained for passage retrieval (using BM25 negatives, as described in Section 4.1.1). The settings for fine-tuning our warmed-up encoder

[2]Re-encoding the entire corpus takes ~10 hours on one GPU.

Table 4: Document retrieval results using the FirstP approach. All our implemented models are labeled with a number and superscripts represent significant improvements over the labeled model (paired t-test, $p < 0.05$).

Model	MARCO Dev	TREC-DL '19
	MRR@100	NDCG@10
ANCE (Xiong et al., 2021)	.368	.614
LTRe (Zhan et al., 2020)	-	.634
SEED-Encoder (Lu et al., 2021)	.394	-
(1) TCT-ColBERT	.339	.573
(2) w/ TCT HN+	.392^{1}	.613
(3) w/ 2× TCT HN+	**.418**^{1,2}	**.650**^{1,2}

(e.g., learning rate, training steps, top-200 negative sampling) are the same as passage retrieval except for batch size, which is set to 64.

Ranking effectiveness is reported in Table 4. First, we observe that TCT-ColBERT (our warmed-up checkpoint) performs far worse than other approaches to document retrieval using the FirstP method. This may be due to the fact that FirstP document retrieval is very different from passage retrieval, making zero-shot transfer ineffective. After applying HN training on both teacher and student models (condition 2), the ranking effectiveness increases significantly. In addition, we find that another iteration of training with an index refresh (condition 3) further improves ranking effectiveness. To sum up, in the document ranking task, TCT-ColBERT yields competitive effectiveness with a one-time index refresh and outperforms other computationally expensive methods with one additional index refresh.

4.3 Dense–Sparse Hybrids

In our final set of experiments, we show that dense retrieval with single-vector representations can be integrated with results from sparse retrieval to further increase effectiveness. We illustrate the end-to-end tradeoffs in terms of quality, time, and space of different dense–sparse hybrid combinations on the passage retrieval tasks.

Many papers (Luan et al., 2021; Gao et al., 2020b; Ma et al., 2021; Lin et al., 2021) have demonstrated that sparse retrieval can complement dense retrieval via a simple linear combination of their scores. In our implementation, for each query q, we use sparse and dense techniques to retrieve the top-1000 passages, $\mathcal{D}_{sp}$ and $\mathcal{D}_{ds}$, with their relevance scores, $\phi_{sp}(q, p \in \mathcal{D}_{sp})$ and $\phi_{ds}(q, p \in \mathcal{D}_{ds})$, respectively. Then, we compute the final relevance score for each retrieved passage $\phi(q, p)$, where $p \in \mathcal{D}_{sp} \cup \mathcal{D}_{ds}$, as follows:

$$\begin{cases} \alpha \cdot \phi_{sp}(q,p) + \min\limits_{p \in \mathcal{D}_{ds}} \phi_{ds}(q,p), & \text{if } p \notin D_{ds} \\ \alpha \cdot \min\limits_{p \in \mathcal{D}_{sp}} \phi_{sp}(q,p) + \phi_{ds}(q,p), & \text{if } p \notin D_{sp} \\ \alpha \cdot \phi_{sp}(q,p) + \phi_{ds}(q,p), & \text{otherwise.} \end{cases}$$

This technique is an approximation of a linear combination of sparse and dense retrieval scores. Specifically, if $p \notin \mathcal{D}_{sp}$(or $\mathcal{D}_{ds}$), we instead use the minimum score of $\phi_{sp}(q, p \in \mathcal{D}_{sp})$, or $\phi_{ds}(q, p \in \mathcal{D}_{ds})$ as a substitute.

For the sparse and dense retrieval combinations, we tune the hyperparameter α on 6000 randomly sampled queries from the MS MARCO training set. We conduct dense–sparse hybrid experiments with sparse retrieval (BM25 ranking) on the original passages (denoted BM25) and on passages with docTTTTTquery document expansion (Nogueira and Lin, 2019) (denoted doc2query-T5). To characterize end-to-end effectiveness and efficiency, we perform sparse retrieval with the Pyserini toolkit (Lin et al., 2021) and dense retrieval with Faiss (Johnson et al., 2017), but implement the score combination in separate custom code.

Table 5 shows passage retrieval results in terms of ranking effectiveness, query latency, and storage requirements (i.e., index size) for each model and Table 6 reports the component latencies of our TCT-ColBERT dense–sparse hybrid.[3] The cross-encoder reranker of Nogueira and Cho (2019) provides a point of reference for multi-stage reranking designs, which is effective but slow.

Generally, dense retrieval methods (whether single-vector or multi-vector) are more effective but slower than sparse retrieval methods, which rely on bag-of-words querying using inverted indexes. Single-vector dense models also require more space than sparse retrieval methods. Moving

[3]Here we assume running dense and sparse retrieval in parallel.

Table 5: End-to-end comparisons of output quality, query latency, and storage requirements for passage retrieval.

	Ranking effectiveness		Latency	Storage
	MARCO Dev	TREC-DL '19	ms/q	GiB
Sparse retrieval				
BM25 with Anserini (Yang et al., 2018)	.184	.506	55	4
DeepCT (Dai and Callan, 2020)	.243	.551	55	4
doc2query-T5 (Nogueira and Lin, 2019)	.277	.551	64	14
Dense retrieval: single-vector				
TAS-B (Hofstätter et al., 2021)	.343	.722	64	13
RocketQA (Qu et al., 2020)	.370	-	107[b]	13[a]
TCT-ColBERT	.344	.685	107	13
TCT-ColBERT (w/ TCT HN+)	.359	.719	107	13
Dense retrieval: multi-vector				
ME-BERT (Luan et al., 2021)	.334	.687	-	96
ColBERT (Khattab and Zaharia, 2020)	.360	-	458	154
Hybrid dense + sparse				
CLEAR (Gao et al., 2020b)	.338	.699	-	17[a]
ME-HYBRID-E (Luan et al., 2021)	.343	.706	-	100
TAS-B + doc2query-T5 (Hofstätter et al., 2021)	.360	.753	67	27[a]
TCT-ColBERT + BM25	.356	.720	110	17
TCT-ColBERT + doc2query-T5	.366	.734	110	27
TCT-ColBERT (w/ TCT HN+) + BM25	.369	.730	110	17
TCT-ColBERT (w/ TCT HN+) + doc2query-T5	.375	.741	110	27
Multi-stage reranking				
BM25 + BERT-large (Nogueira and Cho, 2019)	.365	.736	3500	4
TAS-B + doc2query-T5 + Mono-Duo-T5 (Hofstätter et al., 2021)	.421	.759	12800	27[a]
RocketQA with reranking (Qu et al., 2020)	.439	-	-	13[a]

[a] We estimate dense index size using 16-bit floats; for hybrid, we add the sizes of sparse and dense indexes.
[b] We assume latency comparable to our settings.

Table 6: Component latencies per query of our model.

Stage	latency (ms)	device
BERT query encoder	7	GPU
Dot product search	100	GPU
Score combination	3	CPU

from single-vector to multi-vector dense models, we see that ColBERT exhibits higher effectiveness but is slower and requires much more storage.

Finally, when integrated with sparse retrieval methods, TCT-ColBERT is able to beat a basic multi-stage reranking design (BM25 + BERT-large), but with much lower query latency, although at the cost of increased storage. Hybrid TCT-ColBERT (w/ TCT HN+) + doc2query-T5 compares favorably with a recent advanced model, TAS-B + doc2query-T5 (Hofstätter et al., 2021), which introduces topic-aware sampling and dual teachers, incorporating part of our TCT-ColBERT work. Nevertheless, even the best hybrid variant of TCT-ColBERT alone, without further reranking, remains quite some distance from RocketQA, the current state of the art (with reranking using cross-encoders). This suggests that there remain relevance signals that require full attention interactions to exploit.

5 Conclusions

Improving the effectiveness of single-vector bi-encoders is an important research direction in dense retrieval because of lower latency and storage requirements compared to multi-vector approaches. We propose a teacher–student knowledge distillation approach using tightly coupled bi-encoders that enables exhaustive use of query–passage combinations in each minibatch. More importantly, a bi-encoder teacher requires less computation than a cross-encoder teacher. Finally, our approach leads to robust learned representations.

Overall, our hard negative sampling strategy leads to an effective *and* efficient dense retrieval technique, which can be further combined with sparse retrieval techniques in dense–sparse hybrids. Together, these designs provide a promising solution for end-to-end text retrieval that balances quality, query latency, and storage requirements.

Acknowledgements

This research was supported in part by the Canada First Research Excellence Fund and the Natural Sciences and Engineering Research Council (NSERC) of Canada.

References

Payal Bajaj, Daniel Campos, Nick Craswell, Li Deng, Jianfeng Gao, Xiaodong Liu, Rangan Majumder, Andrew McNamara, Bhaskar Mitra, Tri Nguyen, et al. 2016. MS MARCO: A human generated machine reading comprehension dataset. *arXiv:1611.09268.*

Oren Barkan, Noam Razin, Itzik Malkiel, Ori Katz, Avi Caciularu, and Noam Koenigstein. 2020. Scalable attentive sentence-pair modeling via distilled sentence embedding. In *Proc. AAAI.*

Wei-Cheng Chang, Felix X. Yu, Yin-Wen Chang, Yiming Yang, and Sanjiv Kumar. 2020. Pre-training tasks for embedding-based large-scale retrieval. In *Proc. ICLR.*

Nick Craswell, Bhaskar Mitra, and Daniel Campos. 2019. Overview of the TREC 2019 deep learning track. In *Proc. TREC.*

Zhuyun Dai and Jamie Callan. 2020. Context-aware term weighting for first stage passage retrieval. In *Proc. SIGIR*, page 1533–1536.

Jacob Devlin, Ming-Wei Chang, Kenton Lee, and Kristina Toutanova. 2019. BERT: Pre-training of deep bidirectional transformers for language understanding. In *Proc. NAACL*, pages 4171–4186.

Luyu Gao, Zhuyun Dai, and Jamie Callan. 2020a. Understanding BERT rankers under distillation. In *Proc. ICTIR*, pages 149–152.

Luyu Gao, Zhuyun Dai, Zhen Fan, and Jamie Callan. 2020b. Complementing lexical retrieval with semantic residual embedding. *arXiv:2004.13969.*

Kelvin Guu, Kenton Lee, Zora Tung, Panupong Pasupat, and Ming-Wei Chang. 2020. REALM: Retrieval-augmented language model pre-training. *arXiv:2002.08909.*

Geoffrey Hinton, Oriol Vinyals, and Jeffrey Dean. 2015. Distilling the knowledge in a neural network. In *Proc. NeurIPS: Deep Learning and Representation Learning Workshop.*

Sebastian Hofstätter, Sophia Althammer, Michael Schröder, Mete Sertkan, and Allan Hanbury. 2020. Improving efficient neural ranking models with cross-architecture knowledge distillation. *arXiv:2010.02666v2.*

Sebastian Hofstätter and Allan Hanbury. 2019. Let's measure run time! Extending the IR replicability infrastructure to include performance aspects. In *Proc. OSIRRC: CEUR Workshop*, pages 12–16.

Sebastian Hofstätter, Sheng-Chieh Lin, Jheng-Hong Yang, Jimmy Lin, and Allan Hanbury. 2021. Efficiently teaching an effective dense retriever with balanced topic aware sampling. In *Proc. SIGIR.*

Samuel Humeau, Kurt Shuster, Marie-Anne Lachaux, and Jason Weston. 2020. Poly-encoders: Architectures and pre-training strategies for fast and accurate multi-sentence scoring. In *Proc. ICLR.*

Jeff Johnson, Matthijs Douze, and Hervé Jégou. 2017. Billion-scale similarity search with GPUs. *arXiv:1702.08734.*

Vladimir Karpukhin, Barlas Oğuz, Sewon Min, Ledell Wu, Sergey Edunov, Danqi Chen, and Wen-tau Yih. 2020. Dense passage retrieval for open-domain question answering. In *Proc. EMNLP*, pages 6769–6781.

Omar Khattab and Matei Zaharia. 2020. ColBERT: Efficient and effective passage search via contextualized late interaction over BERT. In *Proc. SIGIR*, page 39–48.

Kenton Lee, Ming-Wei Chang, and Kristina Toutanova. 2019. Latent retrieval for weakly supervised open domain question answering. In *Proc. ACL*, pages 6086–6096.

Jimmy Lin, Xueguang Ma, Sheng-Chieh Lin, Jheng-Hong Yang, Ronak Pradeep, and Rodrigo Nogueira. 2021. Pyserini: A Python toolkit for reproducible information retrieval research with sparse and dense representations. In *Proc. SIGIR.*

Jimmy Lin, Rodrigo Nogueira, and Andrew Yates. 2020. Pretrained transformers for text ranking: BERT and beyond. *arXiv:2010.06467.*

Ting Liu, Andrew W. Moore, Alexander Gray, and Ke Yang. 2004. An investigation of practical approximate nearest neighbor algorithms. In *Proc. NeurIPS*, page 825–832.

Shuqi Lu, Chenyan Xiong, Di He, Guolin Ke, Waleed Malik, Zhicheng Dou, Paul Bennett, Tieyan Liu, and Arnold Overwijk. 2021. Less is more: Pretraining a strong siamese encoder using a weak decoder. *arXiv:2102.09206.*

Yi Luan, Jacob Eisenstein, Kristina Toutanova, and Michael Collins. 2021. Sparse, dense, and attentional representations for text retrieval. *Transactions of the Association for Computational Linguistics*, 9:329–345.

Xueguang Ma, Kai Sun, Ronak Pradeep, and Jimmy Lin. 2021. A replication study of dense passage retriever. *arXiv:2104.05740.*

Yu A. Malkov and D. A. Yashunin. 2020. Efficient and robust approximate nearest neighbor search using hierarchical navigable small world graphs. *Transactions on Pattern Analysis and Machine Intelligence*, 42(4):824–836.

Andriy Mnih and Koray Kavukcuoglu. 2013. Learning word embeddings efficiently with noise-contrastive estimation. In *Proc. NIPS*, pages 2265–2273.

Rodrigo Nogueira and Kyunghyun Cho. 2019. Passage re-ranking with BERT. *arXiv:1901.04085*.

Rodrigo Nogueira and Jimmy Lin. 2019. From doc2query to docTTTTTquery.

Yingqi Qu, Yuchen Ding, Jing Liu, Kai Liu, Ruiyang Ren, Wayne Xin Zhao, Daxiang Dong, Hua Wu, and Haifeng Wang. 2020. RocketQA: An optimized training approach to dense passage retrieval for open-domain question answering. *arxiv:2010.08191v1*.

Nils Reimers and Iryna Gurevych. 2019. Sentence-BERT: Sentence embeddings using Siamese BERT-networks. In *Proc. EMNLP*, pages 3982–3992.

Yu Sun, Shuohuan Wang, Yukun Li, Shikun Feng, Hao Tian, Hua Wu, and Haifeng Wang. 2019. ERNIE 2.0: A continual pre-training framework for language understanding. *arXiv:1907.12412*.

Lee Xiong, Chenyan Xiong, Ye Li, Kwok-Fung Tang, Jialin Liu, Paul Bennett, Junaid Ahmed, and Arnold Overwijk. 2021. Approximate nearest neighbor negative contrastive learning for dense text retrieval. In *Proc. ICLR*.

Peilin Yang, Hui Fang, and Jimmy Lin. 2018. Anserini: Reproducible ranking baselines using Lucene. *Journal of Data and Information Quality*, 10(4):Article 16.

Jingtao Zhan, Jiaxin Mao, Yiqun Liu, Min Zhang, and Shaoping Ma. 2020. Learning to retrieve: How to train a dense retrieval model effectively and efficiently. *arXiv:2010.10469*.

NPVec1: Word Embeddings for Nepali - Construction and Evaluation

Pravesh Koirala
Institute of Engineering, Pulchowk Campus
Lalitpur, Nepal
praveshkoirala@gmail.com

Nobal B. Niraula
Nowa Lab
Madison, Alabama, USA
nobal@nowalab.com

Abstract

Word Embedding maps words to vectors of real numbers. It is derived from a large corpus and is known to capture semantic knowledge from the corpus. Word Embedding is a critical component of many state-of-the-art Deep Learning techniques. However, generating good Word Embeddings is a special challenge for low-resource languages such as Nepali due to the unavailability of large text corpus. In this paper, we present *NPVec1* which consists of 25 state-of-art Word Embeddings for Nepali that we have derived from a large corpus using GloVe, Word2Vec, fastText, and BERT. We further provide intrinsic and extrinsic evaluations of these Embeddings using well established metrics and methods. These models are trained using 279 million word tokens and are the largest Embeddings ever trained for Nepali language. Furthermore, we have made these Embeddings publicly available to accelerate the development of Natural Language Processing (NLP) applications in Nepali.

1 Introduction

Recent Deep Learning (DL) techniques provide state-of-the-art performances in almost all Natural Language Processing (NLP) tasks such as Text Classification (Conneau et al., 2016; Yao et al., 2019; Zhou et al., 2015), Question Answering (Peters et al., 2018; Devlin et al., 2018), Named Entity Recognition (Huang et al., 2015; Lample et al., 2016) and Sentiment Analysis (Zhang et al., 2018; Severyn and Moschitti, 2015). DL techniques are attractive due to their capacity of learning complex and intricate features automatically from the raw data (Li et al., 2020). This significantly reduces the required time and effort for feature engineering, a costly step in traditional feature-based approaches which further requires considerable amount of engineering and domain expertise. Thus, DL techniques are very useful for low-resource languages such as Nepali.

Many Deep Learning techniques require Word Embeddings to represent each word by a vector of real numbers. Word Embeddings learn a meaningful representation of words directly from a large unlabeled corpus using co-occurrence statistics (Bojanowski et al., 2017). The closer the word representations to actual meanings, the better the performance. Consequently, Word Embeddings have received special attention from the research community and are predominantly used in current NLP researches.

Word Embeddings can generally be divided into two categories: Context-Independent embeddings such as GloVe (Pennington et al., 2014), Word2Vec (Mikolov et al., 2013), and fastText (Bojanowski et al., 2017), and Context-Dependent embeddings such as BERT (Bidirectional Encoder Representations from Transformers) (Devlin et al., 2018) and ELMo (Embeddings from Language Models) (Peters et al., 2018). Context-dependent word embedding is generated for a word as a function of the sentence it occurs in. Thus, it can learn multiple representations for polysemous words (Peters et al., 2018). To learn these deep contextualized representations, BERT uses a transformer based architecture pretrained on Masked Language Modelling and Next Sentence Prediction tasks, whereas, ELMo uses a Bidirectional LSTM architecture for combining both forward and backward language models.

In this paper, we present *NPVec1*, a suite of Word Embedding resources for Nepali, a low-resource language, which is the official language and de-facto lingua franca of Nepal. It is spoken by more than 20 million people mainly in Nepal and many other places in the world including Bhutan, India, and Myanmar (Niraula et al., 2020). Even though Word Embeddings can be directly learned from raw texts in an unsupervised fashion, gathering a large amount of data for its training remains a huge challenge in itself for a low-resource lan-

Proceedings of the 6th Workshop on Representation Learning for NLP (RepL4NLP-2021), pages 174–184
Bangkok, Thailand (Online), August 6, 2021.

guage such as Nepali. In addition, Nepali is a morphologically rich language which has multiple agglutinative suffixes as well as affix inflections and thus proves challenges during its preprocessing i.e. tokenization, normalization and stemming.

We have collected data over many years and combined it with multiple other publicly available data sets to generate a suite of Word Embeddings, i.e. *NPVec1*, using GloVe, Word2Vec, fastText and BERT. It consists of 25 Word Embeddings corresponding to different preprocessing schemes. In addition, we perform the intrinsic and extrinsic evaluations of the generated Word Embeddings using well established methods and metrics. Our pre-trained Embedding models and resources are made publicly available[1] for the acceleration and development of NLP research and application in Nepali language.

The novel contributions of this study are:

- First formal analyses of different Word Embeddings in Nepali language using intrinsic and extrinsic methods.
- First study of effects of preprocessing such as normalization, tokenization and stemming in different Word Embeddings in Nepali language.
- First contextualized word embedding (BERT) generation and evaluation in Nepali language.
- The largest Word2Vec, GloVe, fastText and BERT based Word Embeddings ever trained and made available for Nepali language to date.

The rest of this paper is organized as follows. We review related works in Section 2. We describe the data collection and corpus construction in Section 3. We describe our experiments to develop Word Embedding methods in Section 4. We present model evaluations in Section 5 and conclusion and future directions in Section 6.

2 Related Works

Word Embeddings provide continuous word representations and are the building blocks of many NLP applications. They capture distributional information of words from a large corpora. This information helps the generalization of machine learning models especially when the data set is limited (Mikolov et al., 2017). Word Embedding tools, technologies and pre-trained models are widely available for resource rich languages such as English (Mikolov et al., 2013; Pennington et al., 2014; Bojanowski et al., 2017) and Chinese (Li et al., 2018; Chen et al., 2015). Due to the wide use of Word Embeddings, pre-trained models are increasingly available for resource poor languages such as Portuguese(Hartmann et al., 2017), Arabic (Elrazzaz et al., 2017; Soliman et al., 2017), and Bengali (Ahmad and Amin, 2016).

Most Word Embedding algorithms are unsupervised. Which means that they can be trained for any language as long as the corpus data is available. One such effort is by Grave et al. (2018) who generated and made available word vectors for 157 languages, including Nepali, using Wikipedia and Common Crawl data. The pre-trained models for Skip-gram and CBOW are available at `https://fasttext.cc`. Another useful resource is `http://vectors.nlpl.eu/repository` which is a community repository for Word Embeddings maintained by Language Technology Group at the University of Oslo (Kutuzov et al., 2017). It currently hosts 209 pre-trained word Embeddings for most languages but not Nepali.

Word Embeddings for Nepali are derived in small scale by Grave et al. (2018) using fastText and by Lamsal (2019) using Word2Vec. Both of these efforts have major limitations. First, they have limited diversity in the corpus. Grave et al. use Wikipedia and Common Crawl data while Lamsal uses news corpus. Second, their corpus is very small compared to ours (Section 3). Third, they do not provide any evaluation of the generated models. Fourth, they have done limited or no prepossessing on the data. We show later in Section 3.3 that tokenization and text normalization are critical for processing morphologically rich Nepali text. In contrast, we have conducted a large scale study of Word Embeddings in more diverse and large data sets using GloVe, fastText, and Word2Vec. Our corpus is nearly four times bigger than the corpus used by aforementioned approaches (see Section 3). We have constructed 8 inputs for each combination of binary variables: Tokenization, Normalization and Stemming which has resulted in 24 pre-trained Embeddings for GloVe, Word2Vec, and fastText combined. Additionally, we have trained BERT for one of these preprocess-

[1] `https://github.com/nowalab/nepali-word-embeddings`

ing schemes and performed intrinsic and extrinsic evaluations for each of these 25 models.

3 Corpus Preparation

In this Section, we present our data sources and preprocessing techniques for the corpus. To help readers understand the Nepali words used in this paper, we have provided a gloss in Section 8 with their transliterations and English translations.

3.1 The Corpus

Our corpus consists of a mixture of news, Wikipedia articles, and OSCAR (Ortiz Suárez et al., 2019) corpus. We summarize the data sets in Table 1.

3.1.1 News Corpus

We crawled Nepali online news media over a year and collected more than 700,000 unique news articles ($\sim$ 3GB). As expected, the news articles cover diverse topics including politics, sports, technology, society, and so on. We obtained another news data set from IEEE DataPort (Lamsal, 2020) (1.7GB).

3.1.2 OSCAR Nepali Corpus

We obtained the shuffled data in deduplicated form (1.2GB) for Nepali language from OSCAR (Open Super-large Crawled ALMAnaCH coRpus) (Ortiz Suárez et al., 2019).[2] It is a large multilingual corpus obtained by language classification and filtering of the Common Crawl corpus. Common Crawl[3] is a non-profit organization which collects data through web crawling and makes it publicly available.

3.1.3 Nepali Wikipedia Corpus

We obtained Nepali Wikipedia corpus from Kaggle (Gaurav, 2020). It consists of 39k Wikipedia articles for Nepali (83MB).

3.2 Deduplication

We collected data from multiple sources which might have crawled the same data. Furthermore, there were some boilerplate text in the data. Thus, it was important to remove duplicate texts from the corpus. To remove these duplicates, we followed an approach similar to Grave et al. (2018). With this approach, we computed hash for each sentence and collected the sentence only if the hash was not known before. We were able to remove $\sim$ 22% duplicated sentences from our corpus.

3.3 Preprocessing

After removing duplicates, we discarded sentences with less than 10 characters as they provide little context to learn Word Embeddings. We also removed punctuations and replaced numbers with a special *NN* token. We then applied following *Normalization*, *Tokenization* and *Stemming* preprocessing techniques to derive corpus for the study.

3.3.1 Normalization

Analogous to how there are different cases (lower/upper) in English with no phonetic differences, there are different written vowels sounds in Nepali which, when spoken, are indistinguishable from each other. For example: the two different words नेपाली (Nepali) and नेपालि are spoken the same way even though their written representations differ. Thus, people often mistakenly use multiple written version of the same words which introduces noise in the data set. Normalization, in the context of this study, is identification of all these nuances and mapping them to a same word.

3.3.2 Tokenization

Nepali language has multiple post-positional and agglutinative suffixes like ले, मा, बाट, देखि etc., which can be compounded together with nouns and pronouns to produce new words. For example, the word नेपाली (Nepalese) can be compounded as नेपालीले (Nepalese did), नेपालीहरु (Nepalese+plural), नेपालीको (Of Nepalese), so on and so forth. Thus, these different words can be tokenized as नेपाली + ले , नेपाली + हरु, नेपाली + को which serves to drastically reduce the vocabulary size without the loss of any linguistic functionality. Tokenization, in this context, means the same.

3.3.3 Stemming

In addition, there are also other case markers and bound suffixes that primarily inflect verbs to produce new words. For example, from the same root word खा (eat), words such as खायो (ate), खाँदै (eating), खाएको (had eaten), खाएर (after eating), etc can be constructed. Stemming, in this context, means the reduction of all such inflected words to their base forms.

For the purpose of this study, we have improved upon the preprocessing techniques developed by Koirala and Shakya (2018) for preprocessing (normalizing, tokenizing and stemming) our

[2] `https://oscar-corpus.com`

[3] `https://commoncrawl.org/`

Corpus	Tokens	Types	Genre	Description
Our News Corpus	216M	3.3M	News	Online news
Lamsal (Lamsal, 2020)	58.8M	1.2M	News	Online news
OSCAR (Ortiz Suárez et al., 2019)	71.8M	2.2M	Mixed	Mixed Genre
Wikipedia (Gaurav, 2020)	5.1M	0.3M	Mixed	Mixed Genre

Table 1: Corpus Description

Preprocessing Scheme	Code	#Tokens	#Types
Base	(B)	279M	**3.14M**
Base+Normalized	(BN)	279M	2.6M
Base+Normalized+Tokenized	(BNT)	**360M**	1.4M
Base+Normalized+Stemmed	(BNS)	279M	2.04M
Base+Normalized+Tokenized+Stemmed	(BNTS)	359M	**1.09M**
Base+Tokenized	(BT)	357M	1.8M
Base+Tokenized+Stemmed	(BTS)	357M	1.4M
Base+Stemmed	(BS)	279M	2.5M

Table 2: Eight Corpus of NepVec1. Base refers to the raw text.

corpus. Specifically, we generated eight corpus corresponding to different combination of these three preprocessing techniques. The final eight corpus are listed in Table 2.

4 Embedding Methods

4.1 Context-independent Word Embeddings

We chose three state-of-the-art methods for obtaining context-independent Word Embeddings, namely Word2vec, fastText and GloVe. Word embeddings from these methods were learned with the same parameters for fair comparison. We fixed vector dimension to 300 and set minimum word frequency, window size, and the negative sampling size to 5 respectively. Word2vec and fastText models were trained via the Gensim (Řehůřek and Sojka, 2010) implementation using skip-gram method. Whereas, GloVe embeddings were trained via the tool provided by StanfordNLP [4].

4.2 Context-dependent Word Embeddings

We chose BERT to learn context-dependent embeddings. We trained a BERT model using the Huggingface's transformers library (Wolf et al., 2019). BERT model, unlike the other word embedding models, was only trained in one pre-processing scheme i.e. base+normalized+tokenized (BNT)[5] due to resource constraints. Due to the same reason, we reduced both the number of hidden layers and the attention heads to 6 and the hidden dimensions to 300 unlike the original implementation of 12 hidden layers and attention heads and 768 hidden dimensions. The maximum sequence size was chosen to be 512 whereas maximum vocabulary size for the BERT's wordpiece tokenizer was set to 30,000. Our implementation of BERT has 22.5M parameters (in contrast to the 110M parameters of the original implementation i.e. BERT-base) and unlike BERT's original implementation, where it is pre-trained on the task of Masked Language Modelling (MLM) and Next Sentence Prediction, we only pre-trained it for the MLM objective for just a single epoch due to limited computing resources.

5 Evaluation

5.1 Intrinsic Evaluation

Intrinsic evaluation of word embedding models is commonly performed in tasks such as analogies (Grave et al., 2018). There is, however, no such data set available for Nepali language. Thus, we followed the clustering approach suggested in

[4] `https://github.com/stanfordnlp/GloVe`

[5] Our motivation for training BERT in this scheme was the superior performance of context-independent word embeddings in our intrinsic evaluation task for this particular scheme as per section 5.1

Relatedness Set		Sentiment Set	
Kitchen	Nature	Positive	Negative
रोटि, तरकारी, चिनि, नुन, मसला, अदुवा, लसुन, तेल, मरिच, दाल, थाल, कराइ, भाडो, खोर्सानि, चामल, पिठो, डाडु, पुन्यु, चुल्हो, कचौरा, ग्लास	हिमाल, पहाड, हाइकिङ्ग, ट्रेकिङ्ग, फोटो, जङ्गल, गन्तव्य, खोला, नाला, झरना, गोरेटो, बाटो, घुम्ती, चौतारा, यात्रा, हिउ, हरियाली, देउराली, ताल, उकाली	राम्रो, सस्तो, जाँगरिलो, ठूलो, अग्लो, सफा, हलुको, कोमल, उज्यालो, बुद्धिमान, साँचो, लाभ, निशुल्क, छिटो, सफल, अर्थ, न्याय, सक्षम, धनी	नराम्रो, महगो, पातलो, सानो, होचो, फोहोर, भारी, कठोर, अँध्यारो, अल्छे, मुर्ख, झुठो, हानि, ससुल्क, ढिलो, असफल, अनर्थ, अन्याय, असक्षम, गरिब

Table 3: Data Set for Intrinsic Evaluation of Word Embeddings

(Soliman et al., 2017) which requires a manually constructed data set of terms in different themes (clusters). The goal then is to recover these themes (clusters) using the learned word representations. We constructed following two data sets for the evaluation purposes.

5.1.1 Relatedness Set

This set consisted of twenty one word examples each from two different topics i.e. kitchen and nature. The kitchen topic included words such as चिनि (sugar) नुन (salt) भाडो (pot) etc. whereas, the nature topic included words such as हिमाल (mountain), पहाड (hill), खोला (river) etc. The Relatedness data set is presented in Table 3.

5.1.2 Sentiment Set

This set consisted of nineteen examples each of positive and negative sentiments. The positive sentiment set included words such as राम्रो (good), ठूलो (big), न्याय(justice), etc. whereas the negative sentiment set included their antonyms such as नराम्रो (bad), सानो(small), अन्याय(injustice) etc. The Sentiment data set is presented in Table 3.

Ideally word embeddings should capture both word relatedness and word similarity properties of a word. These two terms are related but are not the same (Niraula et al., 2015; Banjade et al., 2015). For example, chicken and egg are less similar (living vs non-living) but are highly related as they often appear together. Relatedness and Sentiment sets were developed to evaluate the models in these these two aspects.

For each of these cases (sentiment and relatedness), K-Means clustering was applied to the constituent words to generate two clusters (i.e. K=2). The obtained clusters were evaluated using the purity metric which is further elaborated in Section 5.1.3. Since Word2Vec and GloVe cannot handle out-of-vocabulary (OOV) words, unlike fastText and BERT, the average of all corresponding word vectors were used to represent the OOV words.

While Word2Vec, fastText and GloVe models provide a simple word to vector mapping, BERT's learned representations are a bit different and thus, need to be extracted accordingly. For the sake of simplicity, we have averaged the hidden state of the last two hidden layers to get the embeddings for each word token. The words were run without any context.

5.1.3 Purity

The purity metric is an extrinsic cluster evaluation technique (Manning et al., 2008) which requires a gold standard data set. It measures the extent to which a cluster contains homogeneous elements. The purity metric ranges from 0 (bad clustering) to 1 (perfect clustering). Thus, the higher the purity score, the better the results.

5.1.4 Results for Intrinsic Evaluation

The results for the intrinsic evaluations are listed in Table 4. All models performed better in recovering original clusters in the Relatedness Set compared to that of the Sentiment Set i.e. they have higher purity scores in the Relatedness Set than the Sentiment Set. This is expected as semantically opposite words often appear in a very similar context (e.g. This is a *new* model vs. This is an *old* model). Relying on neighboring terms alone would provide little context to capture the semantic meaning of a word. Of all three models, however, GloVe performed the best in the sentiment set by an average of 10% (except in the BNTS scheme). This seem to make it more suitable for tasks such as Sentiment Analyses. Interestingly, BERT model did not perform well compared to other models in the Relatedness set. It, however, provided very competitive score in the Sentiment Set.

Models in the BNT scheme scored highest in

Scheme	Model	Intrinsic		Extrinsic		
		Purity (Sen)	Purity (Rel)	Precision	Recall	F_1
B	Baseline			0.76	0.68	0.69
	Word2Vec	0.54	0.98	0.80	0.79	0.79
	fastText	0.51	1	0.79	0.78	0.78
	GloVe	0.67	0.95	0.78	0.77	0.77
BN	Baseline			0.77	0.72	0.72
	Word2Vec	0.56	1	0.79	0.78	0.78
	fastText	0.51	1	0.79	0.78	0.78
	GloVe	0.62	0.98	0.78	0.77	0.77
BT	Baseline			0.77	0.72	0.72
	Word2Vec	0.51	0.98	0.78	0.77	0.77
	fastText	0.54	0.98	0.78	0.76	0.76
	GloVe	0.67	1	0.79	0.77	0.77
BS	Baseline			0.76	0.70	0.70
	Word2Vec	0.51	0.93	0.79	0.77	0.77
	fastText	0.54	0.93	0.79	0.78	0.78
	GloVe	0.59	0.93	0.78	0.77	0.77
BNT	Baseline			0.77	0.73	0.73
	Word2Vec	0.54	1	0.76	0.74	0.74
	fastText	0.51	1	0.78	0.76	0.76
	GloVe	0.69	1	0.77	0.76	0.75
	BERT	0.59	0.83	0.77	0.76	0.76
BNS	Baseline			0.77	0.71	0.72
	Word2Vec	0.51	0.95	0.79	0.77	0.77
	fastText	0.51	0.95	0.79	0.78	0.78
	GloVe	0.64	0.95	0.79	0.77	0.77
BTS	Baseline			0.76	0.73	0.74
	Word2Vec	0.51	0.95	0.78	0.76	0.75
	fastText	0.51	0.95	0.78	0.77	0.76
	GloVe	0.62	0.95	0.76	0.73	0.73
BNTS	Baseline			0.76	0.73	0.74
	Word2Vec	0.51	0.95	0.76	0.74	0.74
	fastText	0.54	0.95	0.78	0.76	0.76
	GloVe	0.51	0.95	0.78	0.77	0.77

Table 4: Intrinsic and Extrinsic Results. Sen and Rel refer to Sentiment and Relatedness respectively. Similarly, B=Base i.e. Raw Text, N=Normalized, T=Tokenized, and S=Stemmed.

both of the intrinsic data sets. Purity for relatedness task for all of the three models in this scheme was 1 whereas GloVe model obtained the global best score of 0.69 in the sentiment set in this scheme. In general, it seems that applying the Normalization scheme has a positive effect on model's capacity to learn the representation which makes sense because Normalization reduces differently spelled versions of the same word to a single representation. Purity dropped significantly for all tasks in all schemes that included Stemming. This may be attributed to the possible over-stemming of the words (under-stemming doesn't seem to be a problem because the model is performing well in the Base scheme).

5.2 Extrinsic Evaluation

The primary objective of extrinsic evaluation for this study was to compare how the word embeddings helped generalize the training of other supervised models with very few data labels. For this purpose, a feed-forward neural network architecture was used for a classification objective in a multi-class classification setup.

5.2.1 Data

The data set for classification was derived from a publicly available Github repository i.e. Nepali News Dataset [6]. It consists of Nepali news articles in 10 different categories. Each category has 1000 articles. As mentioned, the goal of extrinsic evaluation here is to see how the learned word representations help the generalization of machine learning model for text classification task when limited training data set is available, a practical scenario for low resource language. If we use large training examples, virtually any classifier would learn to perform better even if the word representations are poor. For this reason, we extracted 3000 samples from the dataset with uniform representation from each categories (i.e. 300 examples each) and further split them randomly into chunks of sizes 10%, 10%, and 80% each. This yielded us examples of sizes 313, 326, and 2361 respectively which were subsequently used for training, validation and testing purposes. Training set had at least 21 examples per class whereas the testing set had at least 227 examples per class. The test set was deliberately chosen to be larger to better estimate the generalization of the classification model across different embedding schemes.

5.2.2 Architecture

We implemented a very simple text classification model using Keras[7]. For each example (news article), we only used the first five hundred tokens and obtained their embedding vectors from the word embedding model under the study. These vectors were then fed to a Keras model where they were first pooled together by a one-dimensional averaging layer and then passed to a hidden layer with 64 units with the ReLU activation and then to the output layer of 10 units with Sigmoid activation. Binary crossentropy function was used to calculate the loss and the model was trained using the Adam Optimizer (Kingma and Ba, 2014) for 60 epochs each. In case of BERT, we averaged the hidden states from the last two hidden layers to get the embeddings, whereas, for getting the baseline results, instead of using any pre-trained word vectors, a trainable Keras embedding layer was used in front of the architecture mentioned above which automatically learns the word embeddings by only using the provided training examples.

5.2.3 Results for Extrinsic Evaluation

Macro Precision, Recall and F_1 metrics were used for the evaluation of the classification model. On average, the F_1 scores for word embedding models exceeded the baseline scores by a margin of 5 percent. This suggests that the use of pre-trained word embeddings helps to generalize classification models better than simply using the embeddings learned from the training set. Interestingly, the global maximum F_1 score was obtained in the Base scheme i.e. with no preprocessing applied, and Normalization seemed to make no difference to the score. This can be attributed to the fact that our data set came from highly reputed newspapers i.e. all word spellings were grammatically correct. We foresee significant increase due to Normalization in data sets such as tweets, social media posts and blogs where grammatical errors are more frequent.

Similarly, Tokenization schemes seemed to drop the classification scores for embedding models but increase the scores for the baseline models in general. This leads us to believe that the representations of the post-positions and agglunitative suffixes, which are the most frequently occurring words in Nepali language, learned by the Word Embedding models may be partial to particular top-

[6] https://github.com/kamalacharya2044/NepaliNewsDataset

[7] https://keras.io

ics. We suggest the omission of post-positions and other frequently occurring words from the data set before using these embeddings in a classification setting.

The standard deviation in the F-scores of Word2Vec model, fastText and GloVe model across the different pre-processing schemes are 2.4%, 1% and 1.4% respectively, which suggests that fastText might be more resilient to problems like over-stemming. We thus recommend the usage of fastText models in applications where it is desirable to stem words.

Interestingly, BERT model, while produced competitive results, did not exceed our expectations on the classification task. We expect a raise in performance of this model if trained in the architecture proposed in its original implementation i.e. 12 attention heads and 12 hidden layers unlike our slimmed down version of 6 attention heads and 6 hidden layers trained for only one epoch. Training on more data and with more epochs are potential future directions to this end.

6 Conclusion and Future Work

In this paper, we trained 25 Word Embedding models for Nepali language with multiple preprocessing schemes and made them publicly available for accelerating NLP research in low-resource language Nepali[8]. This, to our knowledge, is the first formal and large scale study of Word Embeddings in Nepali. We compared the performances of these models using intrinsic and extrinsic evaluation tasks. Our findings clearly indicate that these word embedding models perform exceptionally well in identifying related words compared to discovering semantically similar words. We also suggest that further comparisons be made with an improved stemmer, which has fewer over-stemming error rates than what we've used, to study the effects of over-stemming in word embeddings. Performance of these Word Embeddings in clustering of related words also suggest us that these models will obtain good results in tasks such as Named Entity Recognition and POS Tagging. This is something that we would like to explore in future.

As far as our study with BERT goes, we obviously recommend training the original BERT architecture, rather than what we have used, with more data. For comparison, the original BERT model was trained on a total of 3.3 billion words whereas we've trained our model in just 360 million words. Unfortunately, for a resource poor language like Nepali, this is not a trivial task. Similarly, it would be most interesting to see performances of other context-dependent embedding models such as ELMo, GPT2 (Radford et al., 2019), XLNet (Yang et al., 2019) and RoBERTa (Liu et al., 2019) in case of Nepali language.

[8]https://github.com/nowalab/nepali-word-embeddings

7 Acknowledgments

We would like acknowledge Mr. Ganesh Pandey for his valuable contribution in providing the hardware setup for our experiments. Similarly, we thank Ms. Samiksha Bhattarai and Dr. Diwa Koirala for their continued support and encouragement.

8 Glossary

Original	Transliteration	Meaning
नेपाली	Nepali	Nepalese
रोटि	Roti	Flatbread
तरकारी	Tarkari	Vegetable
चिनि	Cheeni	Sugar
नुन	Noon	Salt
मसला	Masala	Spices
अदुवा	Aduwa	Ginger
लसुन	Lasun	Garlic
तेल	Tel	Oil
मरिच	Marich	Pepper
दाल	Daal	Lentils
थाल	Thaal	Plate
कराइ	Karai	Cooking Pot
भाडो	Bhaado	Utensils
खोर्सानि	Khorsani	Chili
चामल	Chaamal	Rice
पिठो	Peetho	Wheat
डाडु	Daadu	Ladle
पुन्यु	Punyu	Spatula
चुल्हो	Chulho	Stove
कचौरा	Kachaura	Bowl
ग्लास	Glass	Glass
हिमाल	Himal	Mountain
पहाड	Pahad	Hill
हाइकिङ्ग	Hiking	Hiking
ट्रेकिङ्ग	Trekking	Trekking
फोटो	Photo	Photo
जङ्गल	Jungle	Jungle
गन्तव्य	Gantabya	Destination
खोला	Khola	River

Original	Transliteration	Meaning
नाला	Naala	Rivulets
झरना	Jharana	Waterfall
गोरटो	Goreto	Trail
बाटो	Baato	Road
घम्ती	Ghumti	Bend
चौतारा	Chautara	Rest area
यात्रा	Yatra	Travel
हिउ	Hiu	Snow
हरियाली	Hariyali	Greenery
दउराली	Deurali	Hilltop
ताल	Taal	Lake
उकाली	Ukali	Uphill
राम्रो	Ramro	Good
सस्तो	Sasto	Inexpensive
जागरिलो	Jagarilo	Energetic
ठलो	Thulo	Big
अंग्लो	Aglo	Tall
सुफा	Safaa	Clean
हलको	Haluko	Lightweight
कोमल	Komal	Soft
उज्यालो	Ujyalo	Bright
बद्धिमान	Buddhiman	Wise
साचो	Sacho	Truth
लाभ	Laabh	Gain
निशंल्क	Nisulka	Free
छिटो	Cheeto	Fast
सफुल	Safal	Successful
अथ	Aartha	Meaning
न्याय	Nyaya	Justice
सक्षम	Sakchyam	Capable
धनी	Dhani	Rich
नराम्रो	Naramro	Bad
महगो	Mahango	Expensive
पातलो	Patalo	Skinny
सानो	Saano	Small
होचो	Hocho	Short
फोहोर	Fohor	Waste
भारी	Bhaari	Heavy
कठोर	Kathor	Hard
अँध्यारो	Adhyaro	Dark
अल्छ	Alche	Lazy
मख	Murkha	Fool
झठौ	Jhutho	Lies
हुानि	Haani	Damage
ससुल्क	Sasulka	Not-Free
ढिलो	Dhilo	Late
असुफल	Asafal	Failure
अनथ	Anartha	Meaningless
अन्याय	Anyaya	Injustice
असक्षम	Asakchyam	Incompetent
गरिब	Gareeb	Poor

References

Adnan Ahmad and Mohammad Ruhul Amin. 2016. Bengali word embeddings and it's application in solving document classification problem. In *2016 19th International Conference on Computer and Information Technology (ICCIT)*. IEEE, 425–430.

Rajendra Banjade, Nabin Maharjan, Nobal B Niraula, Vasile Rus, and Dipesh Gautam. 2015. Lemon and tea are not similar: Measuring word-to-word similarity by combining different methods. In *International conference on intelligent text processing and computational linguistics*. Springer, 335–346.

Piotr Bojanowski, Edouard Grave, Armand Joulin, and Tomas Mikolov. 2017. Enriching word vectors with subword information. *Transactions of the Association for Computational Linguistics* 5 (2017), 135–146.

Xinxiong Chen, Lei Xu, Zhiyuan Liu, Maosong Sun, and Huanbo Luan. 2015. Joint learning of character and word embeddings. In *Twenty-Fourth International Joint Conference on Artificial Intelligence*.

Alexis Conneau, Holger Schwenk, Loïc Barrault, and Yann Lecun. 2016. Very deep convolutional networks for text classification. *arXiv preprint arXiv:1606.01781* (2016).

Jacob Devlin, Ming-Wei Chang, Kenton Lee, and Kristina Toutanova. 2018. Bert: Pre-training of deep bidirectional transformers for language understanding. *arXiv preprint arXiv:1810.04805* (2018).

Mohammed Elrazzaz, Shady Elbassuoni, Khaled Shaban, and Chadi Helwe. 2017. Methodical evaluation of Arabic word embeddings. In *Proceedings of the 55th Annual Meeting of the Association for Computational Linguistics (Volume 2: Short Papers)*. 454–458.

Gaurav. 2020. Nepali Wikipedia Corpus. `https://www.kaggle.com/disisbig/nepali-wikipedia-articles`

Edouard Grave, Piotr Bojanowski, Prakhar Gupta, Armand Joulin, and Tomas Mikolov. 2018. Learning Word Vectors for 157 Languages. In *Proceedings of the International Conference on Language Resources and Evaluation (LREC 2018)*.

Nathan Hartmann, Erick Fonseca, Christopher Shulby, Marcos Treviso, Jessica Rodrigues, and Sandra Aluisio. 2017. Portuguese word embeddings: Evaluating on word analogies and natural language tasks. *arXiv preprint arXiv:1708.06025* (2017).

Zhiheng Huang, Wei Xu, and Kai Yu. 2015. Bidirectional LSTM-CRF models for sequence tagging. *arXiv preprint arXiv:1508.01991* (2015).

Diederik P Kingma and Jimmy Ba. 2014. Adam: A method for stochastic optimization. *arXiv preprint arXiv:1412.6980* (2014).

Pravesh Koirala and Aman Shakya. 2018. A Nepali Rule Based Stemmer and its performance on different NLP applications. In *Proceedings of the 4th International IT Conference on ICT with Smart Computing and 9th National Students' Conference on Information Technology, (NaSCoIT 2018)*. 16–20.

Andrei Kutuzov, Murhaf Fares, Stephan Oepen, and Erik Velldal. 2017. Word vectors, reuse, and replicability: Towards a community repository of large-text resources. In *Proceedings of the 58th Conference on Simulation and Modelling*. Linköping University Electronic Press, 271–276.

Guillaume Lample, Miguel Ballesteros, Sandeep Subramanian, Kazuya Kawakami, and Chris Dyer. 2016. Neural architectures for named entity recognition. *arXiv preprint arXiv:1603.01360* (2016).

Rabindra Lamsal. 2019. 300-Dimensional Word Embeddings for Nepali Language. https://doi.org/10.21227/dz6s-my90

Rabindra Lamsal. 2020. A large scale Nepali text corpus. https://doi.org/10.21227/jxrd-d245

Jing Li, Aixin Sun, Jianglei Han, and Chenliang Li. 2020. A survey on deep learning for named entity recognition. *IEEE Transactions on Knowledge and Data Engineering* (2020).

Shen Li, Zhe Zhao, Renfen Hu, Wensi Li, Tao Liu, and Xiaoyong Du. 2018. Analogical Reasoning on Chinese Morphological and Semantic Relations. In *Proceedings of the 56th Annual Meeting of the Association for Computational Linguistics (Volume 2: Short Papers)*. Association for Computational Linguistics, 138–143. http://aclweb.org/anthology/P18-2023

Yinhan Liu, Myle Ott, Naman Goyal, Jingfei Du, Mandar Joshi, Danqi Chen, Omer Levy, Mike Lewis, Luke Zettlemoyer, and Veselin Stoyanov. 2019. Roberta: A robustly optimized bert pretraining approach. *arXiv preprint arXiv:1907.11692* (2019).

Christopher D. Manning, Prabhakar Raghavan, and Hinrich Schütze. 2008. *Introduction to Information Retrieval*. Cambridge University Press. ISBN 978-0-521-86571-5.

Tomas Mikolov, Edouard Grave, Piotr Bojanowski, Christian Puhrsch, and Armand Joulin. 2017. Advances in pre-training distributed word representations. *arXiv preprint arXiv:1712.09405* (2017).

Tomas Mikolov, Ilya Sutskever, Kai Chen, Greg S Corrado, and Jeff Dean. 2013. Distributed representations of words and phrases and their compositionality. In *Advances in neural information processing systems*. 3111–3119.

Nobal B Niraula, Saurab Dulal, and Diwa Koirala. 2020. Linguistic Taboos and Euphemisms in Nepali. *arXiv preprint arXiv:2007.13798* (2020).

Nobal Bikram Niraula, Dipesh Gautam, Rajendra Banjade, Nabin Maharjan, and Vasile Rus. 2015. Combining word representations for measuring word relatedness and similarity. In *The twenty-eighth international flairs conference*.

Pedro Javier Ortiz Suárez, Benoît Sagot, and Laurent Romary. 2019. Asynchronous Pipeline for Processing Huge Corpora on Medium to Low Resource Infrastructures. In *7th Workshop on the Challenges in the Management of Large Corpora (CMLC-7)*, Piotr Bański, Adrien Barbaresi, Hanno Biber, Evelyn Breiteneder, Simon Clematide, Marc Kupietz, Harald Lüngen, and Caroline Iliadi (Eds.). Leibniz-Institut für Deutsche Sprache, Cardiff, United Kingdom. https://doi.org/10.14618/IDS-PUB-9021

Jeffrey Pennington, Richard Socher, and Christopher D. Manning. 2014. GloVe: Global vectors for word representation. In *Proceedings of the 2014 conference on empirical methods in natural language processing (EMNLP)*. 1532–1543.

Matthew E Peters, Mark Neumann, Mohit Iyyer, Matt Gardner, Christopher Clark, Kenton Lee, and Luke Zettlemoyer. 2018. Deep contextualized word representations. *arXiv preprint arXiv:1802.05365* (2018).

Alec Radford, Jeffrey Wu, Rewon Child, David Luan, Dario Amodei, and Ilya Sutskever. 2019. Language models are unsupervised multitask learners. *OpenAI Blog* 1, 8 (2019), 9.

Radim Řehůřek and Petr Sojka. 2010. Software Framework for Topic Modelling with Large Corpora. In *Proceedings of the LREC 2010 Workshop on New Challenges for NLP Frameworks*. ELRA, Valletta, Malta, 45–50. http://is.muni.cz/publication/884893/en.

Aliaksei Severyn and Alessandro Moschitti. 2015. Twitter sentiment analysis with deep convolutional neural networks. In *Proceedings of the 38th International ACM SIGIR Conference on Research and Development in Information Retrieval*. 959–962.

Abu Bakr Soliman, Kareem Eissa, and Samhaa R El-Beltagy. 2017. Aravec: A set of arabic word embedding models for use in arabic nlp. *Procedia Computer Science* 117 (2017), 256–265.

Thomas Wolf, Lysandre Debut, Victor Sanh, Julien Chaumond, Clement Delangue, Anthony Moi, Pierric Cistac, Tim Rault, Rémi Louf, Morgan Funtowicz, Joe Davison, Sam Shleifer, Patrick von Platen, Clara Ma, Yacine Jernite, Julien Plu, Canwen Xu, Teven Le Scao, Sylvain Gugger, Mariama Drame, Quentin Lhoest, and Alexander M. Rush. 2019. HuggingFace's Transformers: State-of-the-art Natural Language Processing. *ArXiv* abs/1910.03771 (2019).

Zhilin Yang, Zihang Dai, Yiming Yang, Jaime Carbonell, Russ R Salakhutdinov, and Quoc V Le. 2019.

Xlnet: Generalized autoregressive pretraining for language understanding. In *Advances in neural information processing systems*. 5753–5763.

Liang Yao, Chengsheng Mao, and Yuan Luo. 2019. Graph convolutional networks for text classification. In *Proceedings of the AAAI Conference on Artificial Intelligence*, Vol. 33. 7370–7377.

Lei Zhang, Shuai Wang, and Bing Liu. 2018. Deep learning for sentiment analysis: A survey. *Wiley Interdisciplinary Reviews: Data Mining and Knowledge Discovery* 8, 4 (2018), e1253.

Chunting Zhou, Chonglin Sun, Zhiyuan Liu, and Francis Lau. 2015. A C-LSTM neural network for text classification. *arXiv preprint arXiv:1511.08630* (2015).

Deriving Word Vectors from Contextualized Language Models using Topic-Aware Mention Selection

Yixiao Wang[1], **Zied Bouraoui**[2], **Luis Espinosa Anke**[1] and **Steven Schockaert**[1]
[1]School of Computer Science & Informatics, Cardiff University, UK
[2] CRIL-CNRS, Université d'Artois, France
{wangy306,espinosa-ankel,schockaerts1}@cardiff.ac.uk, zied.bouraoui@cril.fr

Abstract

One of the long-standing challenges in lexical semantics consists in learning representations of words which reflect their semantic properties. The remarkable success of word embeddings for this purpose suggests that high-quality representations can be obtained by summarizing the sentence contexts of word mentions. In this paper, we propose a method for learning word representations that follows this basic strategy, but differs from standard word embeddings in two important ways. First, we take advantage of contextualized language models (CLMs) rather than bags of word vectors to encode contexts. Second, rather than learning a word vector directly, we use a topic model to partition the contexts in which words appear, and then learn different topic-specific vectors for each word. Finally, we use a task-specific supervision signal to make a soft selection of the resulting vectors. We show that this simple strategy leads to high-quality word vectors, which are more predictive of semantic properties than word embeddings and existing CLM-based strategies.

1 Introduction

In the last few years, contextualized language models (CLMs) such as BERT (Devlin et al., 2019) have largely replaced the use of static (i.e. non-contextualized) word vectors in many Natural Language Processing (NLP) tasks. However, static word vectors remain important in applications where word meaning has to be modelled in the absence of (sentence) context. For instance, static word vectors are needed for zero-shot image classification (Socher et al., 2013) and zero-shot entity typing (Ma et al., 2016), for ontology alignment (Kolyvakis et al., 2018) and completion (Li et al., 2019), taxonomy learning (Bordea et al., 2015, 2016), or for representing query terms in information retrieval systems (Nikolaev and Kotov, 2020). Moreover, Liu et al. (2020) recently found that static word vectors can complement CLMs, by serving as anchors for contextualized vectors, while Alghanmi et al. (2020) found that incorporating static word vectors could improve the performance of BERT for social media classification.

Given the impressive performance of CLMs across many NLP tasks, a natural question is whether such models can be used to learn high-quality static word vectors, and whether the resulting vectors have any advantages compared to those from standard word embedding models (Mikolov et al., 2013; Pennington et al., 2014). A number of recent works have begun to explore this question (Ethayarajh, 2019; Bommasani et al., 2020; Vulic et al., 2020). Broadly speaking, the idea is to construct a static word vector for a word w by randomly selecting sentences in which this word occurs, and then averaging the contextualized representations of w across these sentences.

Since it is not usually computationally feasible to run the CLM on all sentences mentioning w, a sample of such sentences has to be selected. This begs the question: how should these sentences be chosen? In the aforementioned works, sentences are selected at random, but this may not be optimal. If we want to use the resulting word vectors in downstream tasks such as zero-shot learning or ontology completion, we need vectors that capture the salient semantic properties of words. Intuitively, we should thus favor sentences that best reflect these properties. For instance, many of the mentions of the word *banana* on Wikipedia are about the cultivation and export of bananas, and about the specifics of particular banana cultivars. By learning a static word vector from such sentences, we may end up with a vector that does not reflect our commonsense understanding of bananas, e.g. the fact that they are curved, yellow and sweet.

The main aim of this paper is to analyze to what

Proceedings of the 6th Workshop on Representation Learning for NLP (RepL4NLP-2021), pages 185–194
Bangkok, Thailand (Online), August 6, 2021.

extent topic models such as Latent Dirichlet Allocation (Blei et al., 2003) can be used to address this issue. Continuing the previous example, we may find that the word *banana* occurs in Wikipedia articles on the following topics: economics, biology, food or popular culture. While most mentions might be in articles on economics and biology, it is the latter two topics that are most relevant for modelling the commonsense properties of bananas. Note that the optimal selection of topics is task-dependent, e.g. in an NLP system for analyzing financial news, the economics topic would clearly be more relevant. For this reason, we propose to learn a word vector for each topic separately. Since the optimal choice of topics is task-dependent, we then rely on a task-specific supervision signal to make a soft selection of these topic-specific vectors.

Another important question is how CLMs should be used to obtain contextualized word vectors. Given a sentence mentioning w, a model such as BERT-base constructs 12 vector representations of w, i.e. one for each layer of the transformer stack. Previous work has suggested to use the average of particular subsets of these vectors. In particular, Vulic et al. (2020) found that lexical semantics is most prevalent in the representations from the early layers, and that averaging vectors from the first few layers seems to give good results on many benchmarks. On the other hand, these early layers are least affected by the sentence context (Ethayarajh, 2019), hence such strategies might not be suitable for learning topic-specific vectors. We therefore also explore a different strategy, which is to mask the target word in the given sentence, i.e. to replace the entire word by a single [MASK] token, and to use the vector representation of this token at the final layer. The resulting vector representations thus specifically encode what the given sentence reveals about the target word, making this a natural strategy for learning topic-specific vectors.

Note that there is a clear relationship between this latter strategy and CBOW (Mikolov et al., 2013): where in CBOW the vector representation of w is obtained by averaging the vector representations of the context words that co-occur with w, we similarly represent words by averaging context representations. The main advantage compared to CBOW thus comes from the higher-quality context encodings that can be obtained using CLMs. The main challenge, as already mentioned, is that we cannot consider all the mentions of w, whereas this is typically feasible for CBOW (and other standard word embedding models). Our contributions can be summarized as follows[1]:

- We analyze different strategies for deriving word vectors from CLMs, which rely on sampling mentions of the target word from a text collection.
- We propose the use of topic models to improve how these mentions are sampled. In particular, rather than learning a single vector representation for the target word, we learn one vector for each sufficiently relevant topic.
- We propose to construct the final representation of a word w as a weighted average of different vectors. This allows us to combine multiple vectors without increasing the dimensionality of the final representations. We use this approach for combining different topic-specific vectors and for combining vectors from different transformer layers.

2 Related Work

A few recent works have already proposed strategies for computing static word vectors from CLMs. While Ethayarajh (2019) relied on principal components of individual transformer layers for this purpose, most approaches rely on averaging the contextualised representations of randomly selected mentions of the target word (Bommasani et al., 2020; Vulic et al., 2020). Several authors have pointed out that the representations obtained from early layers tend to perform better in lexical semantics probing tasks. However, Bommasani et al. (2020) found that the optimal layer depends on the number of sampled mentions, with later layers performing better when a large number of mentions is used. Rather than fixing a single layer, Vulic et al. (2020) advocated averaging representations from several layers. Note that none of the aforementioned methods uses masking when computing contextualized vectors. This means that the final representations may have to be obtained by pooling different word-piece vectors, usually by averaging them.

[1] All code and data to replicate our experiments is available at `https://github.com/Activeyixiao/topic-specific-vector/`.

As an alternative to using topic models, Chronis and Erk (2020) cluster the contextual word vectors, obtained from mentions of the same word. The resulting multi-prototype representation is then used to compute word similarity in an adaptive way. Along similar lines, Amrami and Goldberg (2019) cluster contextual word vectors for word sense induction. Thompson and Mimno (2020) showed that clustering the contextual representations of a given set of words can produce clusters of semantically related words, which were found to be similar in spirit to LDA topics. The idea of learning topic-specific representations of words has been extensively studied in the context of standard word embeddings (Liu et al., 2015; Li et al., 2016; Shi et al., 2017; Zhu et al., 2020). To the best of our knowledge, learning topic-specific word representations using CLMs has not yet been studied. More broadly, however, some recent methods have combined CLMs with topic models. For instance, Peinelt et al. (2020) use such a combination for predicting semantic similarity. In particular they use the LDA or GSDMM topic distribution of two sentences to supplement their BERT encoding. Finally, Bianchi et al. (2020) suggested using sentence embeddings from SBERT (Reimers and Gurevych, 2019) as input to a neural topic model, with the aim of learning more coherent topics.

3 Constructing Word Vectors

In Section 3.1, we first describe different strategies for deriving static word vectors from CLMs. Section 3.2 subsequently describes how we choose the most relevant topics for each word, and how we sample topic-specific word mentions. Finally, in Section 3.3 we explain how the resulting topic-specific representations are combined to obtain task-specific word vectors.

3.1 Obtaining Contextualized Word Vectors

We first briefly recall the basics of the BERT contextualised language model. BERT represents a sentence s as a sequence of word-pieces $w_1 ..., w_n$. Frequent words will typically be represented as a single word-piece, but in general, word-pieces may correspond to sub-word tokens. Each of these word-pieces w is represented as an input vector, which is constructed from a static word-piece embedding $\mathbf{w}_0$ (together with vectors that encode at which position in the sentence the word appears, and in which sentence). The resulting sequence of word-piece vectors is then fed to a stack of 12 (for BERT-base) or 24 (for BERT-large) transformer layers. Let us write $\mathbf{w}_i^s$ for the representation of word-piece w in the ith transformer layer. We will refer to the representation in the last layer, i.e. $\mathbf{w}_{12}^s$ for BERT-base and $\mathbf{w}_{24}^s$ for BERT-large, as the output vector. When BERT is trained, some of the word-pieces are replaced by a special [MASK] token. The corresponding output vector then encodes a prediction of the masked word-piece.

Given a sentence s in which the word w is mentioned, there are several ways in which BERT and related models can be used to obtain a vector representation of w. If w consists of a single word-piece, a natural strategy is to feed the sentence s as input and use the output vector as the representation of w. However, several authors have found that it can be beneficial to also take into account some or all of the earlier transformer layers, where fine-grained word senses are mostly captured in the later layers (Reif et al., 2019) but word-level lexical semantic features are primarily found in the earlier layers (Vulic et al., 2020). For this reason, we will also experiment with models in which the vectors $\mathbf{w}_1^s, ..., \mathbf{w}_{12}^s$ (or $\mathbf{w}_1^s, ..., \mathbf{w}_{24}^s$ in the case of BERT-large) are all used. In particular, our model will construct a weighted average of these vectors, where the weights will be learned from training data (see Section 3.3). For words that consist of multiple word-pieces, following common practice, we compute the representation of w as the average of its word-piece vectors. For instance, this strategy was found to outperform other aggregation strategies in Bommasani et al. (2020).

We will also experiment with a strategy that relies on masking. In this case, the word w is replaced by a single [MASK] token (even if w would normally be tokenized into more than one word-piece). Let us write $\mathbf{m}_w^s$ for the output vector corresponding to this [MASK] token. Since this vector corresponds to BERT's prediction of what word is missing, this vector should intuitively capture the properties of w that are asserted in the given sentence. We can thus expect that these vectors $\mathbf{m}_w^s$ will be more sensitive to how the sentences mentioning w are chosen. Note that in this case, we only use the output layer, as the earlier layers are less likely to be informative.

To obtain a static representation of w, we first select a set of sentences $s_1, ..., s_n$ in which w is mentioned. Then we compute vector representations

$\mathbf{w}^{s_1}, ..., \mathbf{w}^{s_n}$ of w from each of these sentences, using any of the aforementioned strategies. Our final representation $\mathbf{w}$ is then obtained by averaging these sentence-specific representations, i.e.:

$$\mathbf{w} = \frac{\sum_{i=1}^{n} \mathbf{w}^{s_i}}{\| \sum_{i=1}^{n} \mathbf{w}^{s_i} \|}$$

3.2 Selecting Topic-Specific Mentions

To construct a vector representation of $\mathbf{w}$, we need to select some sentences $s_1, ..., s_n$ mentioning w. While these sentences are normally selected randomly, our hypothesis in this paper is that purely random strategies may not be optimal. Intuitively, this is because the contexts in which a given word w is most frequently mentioned might not be the most informative ones, i.e. they may not be the contexts which best characterize the properties of w that matter for a given task. To test this hypothesis, we experiment with a strategy based on topic models. Our strategy relies on the following steps:

1. Identify the topics which are most relevant for the target word w;
2. For each of the selected topics t, select sentences $s_1^t, ..., s_n^t$ mentioning w from documents that are closely related to this topic.

For each of the selected topics t, we can then use the sentences $s_1^t, ..., s_n^t$ to construct a topic-specific vector $\mathbf{w}^t$, using any of the strategies from Section 3.1. The final representation of w will be computed as a weighted average of these topic-specific vectors, as will be explained in Section 3.3.

We now explain these two steps in more detail. First, we use Latent Dirichlet Allocation (LDA) (Blei et al., 2003) to obtain a representation of each document d in the considered corpus as a multinomial distribution over m topics. Let us write $\tau_i(d)$ for the weight of topic i in the representation of document d, where $\sum_{i=1}^{m} \tau_i(d) = 1$. Suppose that the word w is mentioned N_w times in the corpus, and let d_j^w be the document in which the jth mention of w occurs. Then we define the importance of topic i for word w as follows:

$$\tau_i(w) = \frac{1}{N_w} \sum_{j=1}^{N_w} \tau_i(d_j^w) \tag{1}$$

In other words, the importance of topic i for word w is defined as the average importance of topic i for the documents in which w occurs. To select the set of topics $\mathcal{T}_w$ that are relevant to w, we rank the topics from most to least important and then select the smallest set of topics whose cumulative importance is at least 60%, i.e. $\mathcal{T}_w$ is the smallest set of topics such that $\sum_{t_i \in \mathcal{T}_w} \tau_i(w) \geq 0.6$.

For each of the topics t_i in $\mathcal{T}_w$ we select the corresponding sentences $s_1^t, ..., s_n^t$ as follows. We rank all the documents in which w is mentioned according to $\tau_i(d)$. Then, starting with the document with the highest score (i.e. the document for which topic i is most important), we iterate over the ranked list of documents, selecting all sentences from these documents in which w is mentioned, until we have obtained a total of n sentences.

3.3 Combining Word Representations

Section 3.1 highlighted a number of strategies that could be used to construct a vector representation of a target word w. As mentioned before, it can be beneficial to combine vector representations from different transformer layers. To this end, we propose to learn a weighted average of the different input vectors, using a task specific supervision signal. In particular, let $\mathbf{w}_1, ..., \mathbf{w}_k$ be the different vector representations we have available for word w (e.g. the vectors from different transformer layers). To combine these vectors, we compute a weighted average as follows:

$$\lambda_i = \frac{\exp(a_i)}{\sum_{j=1}^{k} \exp(a_i)} \tag{2}$$

$$\mathbf{w} = \frac{\sum_i \lambda_i \mathbf{w}_i}{\| \sum_i \lambda_i \mathbf{w}_i \|} \tag{3}$$

where the scalar parameters $a_1, ... a_k \in \mathbb{R}$ are jointly learned with the model in which $\mathbf{w}$ is used. Another possibility would be to concatenate the input vectors $\mathbf{w}_1, ..., \mathbf{w}_k$. However, this significantly increases the dimensionality of the word representations, which can be challenging in downstream applications. In initial experiments, we also confirmed that this concatenation strategy indeed under-performs the use of weighted averages.

If topic-specific vectors are used, we also want to compute a weighted average of the available vectors. However, (2)–(3) cannot be used in this case, because the set of topics for which topic-specific vectors are available differs from word to word. Let us write $\mathbf{w}_{topic}^i$ for the representation of word w that was obtained for topic t_i, where we assume $\mathbf{w}^i_{topic} = \mathbf{0}$ if $t_i \notin \mathcal{T}_w$. We then define:

$$\mu_i^w = \frac{\exp(b_i) \cdot \mathbb{1}[t_i \in \mathcal{T}_w]}{\sum_{j=1}^k \exp(b_i) \cdot \mathbb{1}[t_j \in \mathcal{T}_w]} \tag{4}$$

$$\mathbf{w}_{topic} = \frac{\sum_i \mu_i^w \mathbf{w}^i_{topic}}{\| \sum_i \mu_i^w \mathbf{w}^i_{topic} \|} \tag{5}$$

where $\mathbb{1}[t_i \in \mathcal{T}_w] = 1$ if topic t_i is considered to be relevant for word w (i.e. $t_i \in \mathcal{T}_w$), and $\mathbb{1}[t_i \in \mathcal{T}_w] = 0$ otherwise. Note that the softmax function in (4) relies on the scalar parameters $b_1, ..., b_k \in \mathbb{R}$, which are independent of w. However, the softmax is selectively applied to those topics that are relevant to w, which is why the resulting weight μ_i^w is dependent on w, or more precisely, on the set of topics $\mathcal{T}_w$.

4 Evaluation

We compare the proposed strategy with standard word embeddings and existing CLM-based strategies. In Section 4.1 we first describe our experimental setup. Section 4.2 then provides an overview of the datasets we used for the experiments, where we focus on lexical classification benchmarks. These benchmarks in particular allow us to assess how well various semantic properties can be predicted from the word vectors. The experimental results are discussed in Section 4.3 and a qualitative analysis is presented in Section 4.4.

4.1 Experimental Setup

We experiment with a number of different strategies for obtaining word vectors:

$\mathbf{C_{last}}$ We take the vector representation of w from the last transformer layer (i.e. $\mathbf{w}^s_{12}$ or $\mathbf{w}^s_{24}$).

$\mathbf{C_{input}}$ We take the input embedding of w (i.e. $\mathbf{w}_0$).

$\mathbf{C_{avg}}$ We take the average of $\mathbf{w}_0, \mathbf{w}^s_1, ..., \mathbf{w}^s_{12}$ for the *base* models and $\mathbf{w}_0, \mathbf{w}^s_1, ..., \mathbf{w}^s_{24}$ for the *large* models.

$\mathbf{C_{all}}$ We use all of $\mathbf{w}_0, \mathbf{w}^s_1, ..., \mathbf{w}^s_{12}$ as input for the *base* models, and all of $\mathbf{w}_0, \mathbf{w}^s_1, ..., \mathbf{w}^s_{24}$ for the *large* models. These vectors are then aggregated using (2)–(3), i.e. we use a learned soft selection of the transformer layers.

$\mathbf{C_{mask}}$ We replace the target word by [MASK] and use the corresponding output vector.

For words consisting of more than one word-piece, we average the corresponding vectors in all cases, except for $\mathbf{C_{mask}}$ where we always end up with a single vector (i.e. we replace the entire word by a single [MASK] token). We also consider three variants that rely on topic-specific vectors:

$\mathbf{T_{last}}$ We learn topic-specific vectors using the last transformer layers. These vectors are then used as input to (4)–(5).

$\mathbf{T_{avg}}$ Similar to the previous case but using the average of all transformer layers.

$\mathbf{T_{mask}}$ Similar to the previous cases but using the output vector of the masked word mention.

Furthermore, we consider variants of $\mathbf{T_{last}}$, $\mathbf{T_{avg}}$ and $\mathbf{T_{mask}}$ in which a standard (i.e. unweighted) average of the available topic-specific vectors is computed, instead of relying on (4)–(5). We will refer to these averaging-based variants as $\mathbf{A_{last}}$, $\mathbf{A_{avg}}$ and $\mathbf{A_{mask}}$. As baselines, we also consider the two Word2vec models (Mikolov et al., 2013):

SG 300-dimensional Skip-gram vectors trained on a May 2016 dump of the English Wikipedia, using a window size of 5 tokens, and minimum frequency threshold of 10.

CBOW 300-dimensional Continuous Bag-of-Words vectors trained on the same corpus and with the same hyperparameters as **SG**.

We show results for four pre-trained CLMs (Devlin et al., 2019; Liu et al., 2019): BERT-base-uncased, BERT-large-uncased, RoBERTa-base-uncased, RoBERTa-large-uncased[2]. As the corpus for sampling word mentions, we used the same Wikipedia dump as for training the word embeddings models. For $\mathbf{C_{mask}}$, $\mathbf{C_{last}}$, $\mathbf{C_{avg}}$ and $\mathbf{C_{all}}$ we selected 500 mentions. For the topic-specific strategies ($\mathbf{T_{last}}$, $\mathbf{T_{avg}}$ and $\mathbf{T_{mask}}$) we selected 100 mentions per topic. To obtain the topic assignments, we used Latent Dirichlet Allocation (Blei et al., 2003) with 25 topics. We set $\alpha = 0.0001$ to restrict the total number of topics attributed to a document, and use default values for the other hyper-parameters[3]. To select the relevant topics for a given word w, we find the smallest set of topics whose cumulative importance score $\tau_i(w)$ is at least 60%, with

[2]We used the implementations from `https://github.com/huggingface/transformers`.

[3]We used the implementation from `https://radimrehurek.com/gensim/wiki.html`.

a maximum of 6 topics. In the experiments, we restrict the vocabulary to those words with at least 100 occurrences in Wikipedia.

4.2 Datasets

For the experiments, we focus on a number of lexical classification tasks, where categories of individual words need to be predicted. In particular, we used two datasets which are focused on commonsense properties (e.g. *dangerous*): the extension of the McRae feature norms dataset (McRae et al., 2005) that was introduced by Forbes et al. (2019)[4] and the CSLB Concept Property Norms[5]. We furthermore used the WordNet supersenses dataset[6], which groups nouns into broad categories (e.g. *human*). Finally, we also used the BabelNet domains dataset[7] (Camacho-Collados and Navigli, 2017), which assigns lexical entities to thematic domains (e.g. *music*).

In our experiments, we have only considered properties/classes for which sufficient positive examples are available, i.e. at least 10 for McRae, 30 for CSLB, and 100 for WordNet supersenses and BabelNet domains. For the McRae dataset, we used the standard training-validation-test split. For the other datasets, we used random splits of 60% for training, 20% for tuning and 20% for testing. An overview of the datasets is shown in Table 2.

For all datasets, we consider a separate binary classification problem for each property and we report the (unweighted) average of the F1 scores for the different properties. To classify words, we feed their word vector directly to a sigmoid classification layer. We optimise the network using AdamW with a cross-entropy loss. The batch size and learning rate were tuned, with possible values chosen from 4,8,16 and 0.01, 0.005, 0.001, 0.0001 respectively. Note that for $\mathbf{C}_{\mathbf{all}}$ and the topic-specific variants, the classification network jointly learns the parameters of the classification layer and the attention weights in (2) and (4) for combining the input vectors.

4.3 Results

The results are shown in Table 1. We consistently see that the topic-specific variants outperform the different **C**-variants, often by a substantial margin. This confirms our main hypothesis, namely that using topic models to determine how context sentences are selected has a material effect on the quality of the resulting word representations. Among the **C**-variants, the best results are obtained by $\mathbf{C}_{\mathbf{mask}}$ and $\mathbf{C}_{\mathbf{last}}$. None of the three **T**-variants consistently outperforms the others. Surprisingly, the **A**-variants outperform the corresponding **T**-variants in several cases. This suggests that the outperformance of the topic-specific vectors primarily comes from the fact that the context sentences for each word were sampled in a more balanced way (i.e. from documents covering a broader range of topics), rather than from the ability to adapt the topic weights based on the task. This is a clear benefit for applications, as the **A**-variants allow us to simply represent each word as a static word vector.

The performance of SG and CBOW is also surprisingly strong. In particular, these traditional word embedding models outperform all of the **C**-variants, as well as the **T** and **A** variants in some cases, especially for BERT-base and RoBERTa-base. This seems to be related, at least in part, to the lower dimensionality of these vectors. The classification network has to be learned from a rather small number of examples, especially for McRae and CSLB. Having 768 or 1024 dimensional input vectors can be problematic in such cases. To analyse this effect, we used Principal Component Analysis (PCA) to reduce the dimensionality of the CLM-derived vectors to 300. For this experiment, we focused in particular on $\mathbf{C}_{\mathbf{mask}}$ and $\mathbf{T}_{\mathbf{mask}}$. The results are also shown in Table 1 as $\mathbf{C}_{\mathbf{mask}}$**-PCA** and $\mathbf{T}_{\mathbf{mask}}$**-PCA**. As can be seen, this dimensionality reduction step has a clearly beneficial effect, with $\mathbf{T}_{\mathbf{mask}}$**-PCA** outperforming all baselines, except for the BabelNet domains benchmark. The latter benchmark is focused on thematic similarity rather than semantic properties, which the CLM-based representations seem to struggle with.

4.4 Qualitative analysis

Topic-specific vectors can be expected to focus on different properties, depending on the chosen topic. In this section, we present a qualitative analysis in support of this view. In Table 3 we list, for a sample of words from the WordNet supersenses dataset, the top 5 nearest neighbours per topic in terms of cosine similarity. For this analysis, we used the BERT-base masked embeddings. We can

[4]https://github.com/mbforbes/physical-commonsense

[5]https://cslb.psychol.cam.ac.uk/propnorms

[6]https://wordnet.princeton.edu/download

[7]http://lcl.uniroma1.it/babeldomains/

	BERT-base				BERT-large				RoBERTa-base				RoBERTa-large			
	MC	**CS**	**SS**	**BD**	**MC**	**CS**	**SS**	**BD**	**MC**	**CS**	**SS**	**BD**	**MC**	**CS**	**SS**	**BD**
SG	59.6	54.5	55.6	**49.1**	59.6	54.5	55.6	**49.1**	59.6	54.5	55.6	**49.1**	59.6	54.5	55.6	**49.1**
CBOW	61.1	50.6	48.4	45.0	61.1	50.6	48.4	45.0	61.1	50.6	48.4	45.0	61.1	50.6	48.4	45.0
$\mathbf{C_{mask}}$	54.6	44.0	48.8	38.9	52.0	43.0	48.7	38.7	56.0	43.4	47.1	42.1	55.8	42.3	47.0	38.1
$\mathbf{C_{last}}$	52.9	45.1	46.7	38.4	54.3	46.2	48.2	39.6	56.5	42.2	46.1	37.3	56.3	43.8	46.5	37.8
$\mathbf{C_{input}}$	48.9	32.2	41.1	34.8	53.1	33.0	39.0	34.5	42.1	25.6	35.2	31.8	51.3	31.4	28.6	36.0
$\mathbf{C_{avg}}$	45.9	32.8	44.1	36.4	50.0	37.1	42.7	36.7	39.4	21.6	30.8	28.7	43.7	22.9	30.1	28.2
$\mathbf{C_{all}}$	45.9	31.0	41.3	35.4	45.0	33.7	43.4	24.6	32.8	19.0	25.9	24.7	37.5	21.2	30.4	28.6
$\mathbf{T_{mask}}$	58.6	54.1	60.1	45.8	62.8	54.6	**61.4**	46.2	56.4	49.4	56.7	42.1	59.6	50.4	57.2	42.1
$\mathbf{T_{last}}$	**63.6**	51.8	59.5	47.3	60.5	54.8	61.2	49.2	52.8	40.1	54.6	41.2	60.2	48.5	59.5	45.2
$\mathbf{T_{avg}}$	61.0	52.7	59.6	42.3	65.2	52.4	60.7	48.4	54.2	39.9	55.9	41.5	59.5	46.8	60.0	45.2
$\mathbf{A_{mask}}$	61.6	53.5	59.6	41.5	63.0	56.4	60.6	41.5	61.2	55.3	59.6	40.6	63.4	**57.1**	61.2	42.3
$\mathbf{A_{last}}$	60.8	49.6	57.9	44.4	61.4	55.5	60.3	46.7	50.3	36.8	56.5	39. 7	59.5	47.3	58.0	41.2
$\mathbf{A_{avg}}$	60.7	49.7	57.9	44.4	63.9	52.0	59.4	44.0	55.6	40.6	56.4	39.8	59.4	47.3	58.0	41.2
$\mathbf{C_{mask}}$**-PCA**	56.8	46.4	49.2	38.8	56.6	43.5	48.4	39.2	58.8	51.6	50.4	39.2	58.3	49.8	49.3	39.3
$\mathbf{T_{mask}}$**-PCA**	63.3	**56.2**	**62.6**	46.9	**64.4**	**57.3**	60.6	48.0	**61.6**	**55.8**	**62.5**	46.0	**65.4**	56.3	**64.1**	46.4

Table 1: Results of lexical feature classification experiments for the extended McRae feature norms (MC), CSLB norms (CS), WordNet Supersenses (SS) and BabelNet domains (BD). Results are reported in terms of F1 (%).

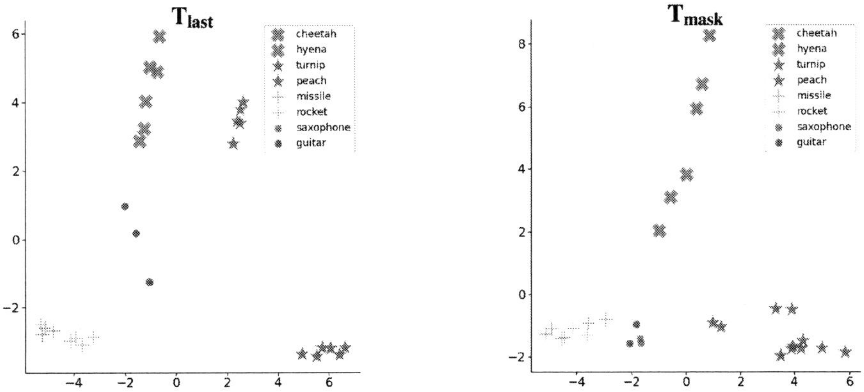

Figure 1: BERT-base topic-specific vectors when using the output vectors without using masking (left) and with masking (right). Words have been selected from the McRae dataset.

Dataset	**Type**	**Words**	**Properties**
McRae	Commonsense	475	49
CSLB	Commonsense	570	54
WN supersenses	Taxonomic	24,324	24
BN domains	Topical	43,319	34

Table 2: Overview of the considered datasets.

see that for the word *'partner'*, its topic-specific embeddings correspond to its usage in the context of 'finance', 'stock market' and 'fiction'. These three embeddings roughly correspond to three different senses of the word[8]. This de-conflation or implicit disambiguation is also found for words such as *'cell'*, *'port'*, *'bulb'* or *'mail'*, which shows a striking relevance of the role of mail in the election topic, being semantically similar in the corresponding vector space to words such as 'telemarketing', 'spam' or 'wiretap'. In the case of *'fingerprint'*, we can also see some implicit disambiguation (distinguishing between fingerprinting in computer science, as a form of hashing, and the more traditional sense). However, we also see a more topical distinction, revealing differences between the role played by fingerprints in fictional works and forensic research. This tendency of capturing different contexts is more evidently shown in the last four examples. First, for *'sky'* and *'strength'*, the topic-

[8]In fact, we can directly pinpoint these vectors to the following WordNet (Miller, 1995) senses: `partner.n.03`, `collaborator.n.03` and `spouse.n.01`.

WORD	TOPIC	NEAREST NEIGHBOURS
partner	{research, professor, science, education, institute}	beneficiary, creditor, investor, employer, stockholder
	{football, republican, coach, senate, representatives}	lobbyist, bookkeeper, cashier, stockbroker, clerk
	{game, book, novel, story, reception}	nanny, spouse, lover, friend, secretary
cell	{protein, disease, medical, cancer, cells}	lymphocyte, macrophage, axon, astrocyte, organelle
	{food, plant, water, gas, power, oil}	electrode, electrolyte, cathode, anode, substrate
	{physics, mathematics, space, ngc, theory}	surface, torus, mesh, grid, cone
port	{station, building, railway, historic, church}	harbor, seaport, dock, waterfront, city
	{radio, station, fm, software, data, forewings}	link, gateway, router, line, socket
	{game, book, novel, story, reception}	version, remake, compilation, patch, modification
bulb	{station, building, railway, historic, church}	lamp, transformer, dynamo, projector, lighting
	{protein, disease, medical, cancer, cells}	epithelium, ganglion, nucleus, gland, cortex
	{species, genus, described, description, flowers}	rootstock, fern, vine, tuber, clover
mail	{station, building, railway, historic, church}	cargo, grain, baggage, coal, livestock
	{game, book, novel, story, reception}	paper, jewelry, telephone, telegraph, typewriter
	{party, election, minister, elected, elections}	telemarketing, spam, wiretap, internet, money
fingerprint	{radio, station, fm, software, data, forewings}	signature, checksum, bitmap, texture, text
	{game, book, novel, story, reception}	cadaver, skull, wiretap, body, tooth
	{party, election, minister, elected, elections}	wiretap, forensics, postmortem, polygraph, check
sky	{greek, ancient, castle, king, roman}	underworld, sun, afterlife, zodiac, moon
	{river, lake, mountain, island, village}	horizon, ocean, earth, sun, globe
	{physics, mathematics, space, ngc, theory}	ionosphere, sun, globe, earth, heliosphere
strength	{food, plant, water, gas, power}	stiffness, ductility, hardness, permeability, viscosity
	{game, book, novel, story, reception}	intelligence, agility, charisma, power, telepathy
	{army, regiment, navy, ship, air}	morale, firepower, resistance, force, garrison
noon	{physics, mathematics, space, ngc, theory}	declination, night, equinox, perihelion, latitude
	{army, regiment, navy, ship, air}	dawn, sunset, night, morning, shore
galaxy	{physics, mathematics, space, ngc, theory}	nebula, quasar, pulsar, nova, star
	{game, book, novel, story, reception}	globe, future, world, planet, nation

Table 3: Nearest neighbours of topic-specific embeddings for a sample of words from the WordNet SuperSenses dataset, using BERT-base embeddings. The top 6 selected samples illustrate clear topic distributions per word sense, and the bottom 4 also show topical properties within the same sense. The most relevant words for each topic are shown under the **TOPIC** column.

wise embeddings do *not represent different senses of these words*, but rather indicate different types of usage (possibly related to cultural or commonsense properties). Specifically, we see that the same sense of *'sky'* is used in mythological, landscaping and geological contexts. Likewise, *'strength'* is clustered into different mentions, but while this word also preserves the same sense, it is clearly used in different contexts: physical, as a human feature, and in military contexts. Finally, *'noon'* and *'galaxy'* (which only occur in two topics), also show this topicality. In both cases, we have representations that reflect their physics and everyday usages, for the same senses of these words.

As a final analysis, In Figure 1 we plot a two-dimensional PCA-reduced visualization of selected words from the McRae dataset, using two versions of the topic-specific vectors: $\mathbf{T_{mask}}$ and $\mathbf{T_{last}}$. In both cases, BERT-base was used to obtain the vectors. We select four pairs of concepts which are topically related, which we plot with the same datapoint marker (animals, plants, weapons and musical instruments). For $\mathbf{T_{last}}$, we can see that the different topic-specific representations of the same word are clustered together, which is in accordance with the findings from Ethayarajh (2019). For $\mathbf{T_{mask}}$, we can see that the representations of words with similar properties (e.g. *cheetah* and *hyena*) become more similar, suggesting that $\mathbf{T_{mask}}$ is more tailored towards modelling the semantic properties of words, perhaps at the expense of a reduced ability to differentiate between closely related words. The case of *turnip* and *peach* is particularly striking, as the vectors are clearly separated in the $\mathbf{T_{last}}$ plot, while being clustered together in the $\mathbf{T_{mask}}$ plot.

5 Conclusions

We have proposed a strategy for learning static word vectors, in which topic models are used to help select diverse mentions of a given target word and a contextualized language model is subsequently used to infer vector representations from the selected mentions. We found that selecting an equal number of mentions per topic substantially outperforms purely random selection strategies. We also considered the possibility of learning a weighted average of topic-specific vector representations, which in principle should allow us to "tune" word representations to different tasks, by learning task-specific topic importance weights. However, in practice we found that a standard average of the topic specific vectors leads to a comparable performance, suggesting that the outperformance of our vectors comes from the fact that they are obtained from a more diverse set of contexts.

Acknowledgments

This work was performed using the computational facilities of the Advanced Research Computing @ Cardiff (ARCCA) Division, Cardiff University and using HPC resources from GENCI-IDRIS (Grant 2021-[AD011012273]).

References

Israa Alghanmi, Luis Espinosa Anke, and Steven Schockaert. 2020. Combining bert with static word embeddings for categorizing social media. In *Proceedings of the Sixth Workshop on Noisy User-generated Text*, pages 28–33.

Asaf Amrami and Yoav Goldberg. 2019. Towards better substitution-based word sense induction. *arXiv:1905.12598*.

Federico Bianchi, Silvia Terragni, and Dirk Hovy. 2020. Pre-training is a hot topic: Contextualized document embeddings improve topic coherence. *CoRR*, abs/2004.03974.

David M. Blei, Andrew Y. Ng, and Michael I. Jordan. 2003. Latent dirichlet allocation. *J. Mach. Learn. Res.*, 3:993–1022.

Rishi Bommasani, Kelly Davis, and Claire Cardie. 2020. Interpreting pretrained contextualized representations via reductions to static embeddings. In *Proceedings ACL*, pages 4758–4781.

Georgeta Bordea, Paul Buitelaar, Stefano Faralli, and Roberto Navigli. 2015. SemEval-2015 task 17: Taxonomy extraction evaluation (TExEval). In *Proceedings SemEval*, pages 902–910.

Georgeta Bordea, Els Lefever, and Paul Buitelaar. 2016. Semeval-2016 task 13: Taxonomy extraction evaluation (texeval-2). In *Proceedings SemEval*, pages 1081–1091.

Jose Camacho-Collados and Roberto Navigli. 2017. BabelDomains: Large-scale domain labeling of lexical resources. In *Proceedings EACL*, pages 223–228.

Gabriella Chronis and Katrin Erk. 2020. When is a bishop not like a rook? when it's like a rabbi! multi-prototype BERT embeddings for estimating semantic relationships. In *Proceedings CoNLL*, pages 227–244.

Jacob Devlin, Ming-Wei Chang, Kenton Lee, and Kristina Toutanova. 2019. BERT: pre-training of deep bidirectional transformers for language understanding. In *Proceedings NAACL-HLT*.

Kawin Ethayarajh. 2019. How contextual are contextualized word representations? comparing the geometry of BERT, ELMo, and GPT-2 embeddings. In *Proceedings EMNLP*, pages 55–65.

Maxwell Forbes, Ari Holtzman, and Yejin Choi. 2019. Do neural language representations learn physical commonsense? *Proceedings CogSci*.

Prodromos Kolyvakis, Alexandros Kalousis, and Dimitris Kiritsis. 2018. Deepalignment: Unsupervised ontology matching with refined word vectors. In *Proceedings NAACL-HLT*, pages 787–798.

Na Li, Zied Bouraoui, and Steven Schockaert. 2019. Ontology completion using graph convolutional networks. In *Proceedings ISWC*, pages 435–452.

Shaohua Li, Tat-Seng Chua, Jun Zhu, and Chunyan Miao. 2016. Generative topic embedding: a continuous representation of documents. In *Proceedings ACL*.

Qianchu Liu, Diana McCarthy, and Anna Korhonen. 2020. Towards better context-aware lexical semantics: Adjusting contextualized representations through static anchors. In *Proceedings EMNLP*, pages 4066–4075.

Yang Liu, Zhiyuan Liu, Tat-Seng Chua, and Maosong Sun. 2015. Topical word embeddings. In *Proceedings AAAI*, pages 2418–2424.

Yinhan Liu, Myle Ott, Naman Goyal, Jingfei Du, Mandar Joshi, Danqi Chen, Omer Levy, Mike Lewis, Luke Zettlemoyer, and Veselin Stoyanov. 2019. Roberta: A robustly optimized BERT pretraining approach. *CoRR*, abs/1907.11692.

Yukun Ma, Erik Cambria, and Sa Gao. 2016. Label embedding for zero-shot fine-grained named entity typing. In *Proceedings COLING*, pages 171–180.

Ken McRae et al. 2005. Semantic feature production norms for a large set of living and nonliving things. *Behavior research methods*, 37:547–559.

Tomas Mikolov, Kai Chen, Greg Corrado, and Jeffrey Dean. 2013. Efficient estimation of word representations in vector space. In *Proceedings ICLR*.

George A Miller. 1995. Wordnet: a lexical database for English. *Communications of the ACM*, 38(11):39–41.

Fedor Nikolaev and Alexander Kotov. 2020. Joint word and entity embeddings for entity retrieval from a knowledge graph. In *Proceedings ECIR*, pages 141–155.

Nicole Peinelt, Dong Nguyen, and Maria Liakata. 2020. tBERT: Topic models and BERT joining forces for semantic similarity detection. In *Proceedings ACL*, pages 7047–7055.

Jeffrey Pennington, Richard Socher, and Christopher D. Manning. 2014. GloVe: Global vectors for word representation. In *Proceedings EMNLP*, pages 1532–1543.

Emily Reif, Ann Yuan, Martin Wattenberg, Fernanda B. Viégas, Andy Coenen, Adam Pearce, and Been Kim. 2019. Visualizing and measuring the geometry of BERT. In *Proceedings NeurIPS*, pages 8592–8600.

Nils Reimers and Iryna Gurevych. 2019. Sentence-BERT: Sentence embeddings using Siamese BERT-networks. In *Proceedings EMNLP*, pages 3982–3992.

Bei Shi, Wai Lam, Shoaib Jameel, Steven Schockaert, and Kwun Ping Lai. 2017. Jointly learning word embeddings and latent topics. In *Proceedings SIGIR*, pages 375–384.

Richard Socher, Milind Ganjoo, Christopher D Manning, and Andrew Ng. 2013. Zero-shot learning through cross-modal transfer. In *Proceedings NIPS*, pages 935–943.

Laure Thompson and David Mimno. 2020. Topic modeling with contextualized word representation clusters. *CoRR*, abs/2010.12626.

Ivan Vulic, Edoardo Maria Ponti, Robert Litschko, Goran Glavas, and Anna Korhonen. 2020. Probing pretrained language models for lexical semantics. In *Proceedings EMNLP*, pages 7222–7240.

Lixing Zhu, Deyu Zhou, and Yulan He. 2020. A neural generative model for joint learning topics and topic-specific word embeddings. *Trans. Assoc. Comput. Linguistics*, 8:471–485.

Zero-shot Sequence Labeling for Transformer-based Sentence Classifiers

Kamil Bujel
Department of Computing
Imperial College London
United Kingdom
kdb19@imperial.ac.uk

Helen Yannakoudakis
Department of Informatics
King's College London
United Kingdom
helen.yannakoudakis@kcl.ac.uk

Marek Rei
Department of Computing
Imperial College London
United Kingdom
marek.rei@imperial.ac.uk

Abstract

We investigate how sentence-level transformers can be modified into effective sequence labelers at the token level without any direct supervision. Existing approaches to zero-shot sequence labeling do not perform well when applied on transformer-based architectures. As transformers contain multiple layers of multi-head self-attention, information in the sentence gets distributed between many tokens, negatively affecting zero-shot token-level performance. We find that a soft attention module which explicitly encourages sharpness of attention weights can significantly outperform existing methods.

1 Introduction

Sequence labeling and sentence classification can represent facets of the same task at different granularities; for example, detecting grammar errors and predicting the grammaticality of sentences. Transformer-based architectures such as BERT (Devlin et al., 2019) and RoBERTa (Liu et al., 2019) have been shown to achieve state-of-the-art results on both sequence labeling (Bell et al., 2019) and sentence classification (Sun et al., 2019) problems. However, such tasks are typically treated in isolation rather than within a unified approach.

In this paper, we investigate methods for inferring token-level predictions from transformer models trained only on sentence-level annotations. The ability to classify individual tokens without direct supervision opens possibilities for training sequence labeling models on tasks and datasets where only sentence-level or document-level annotation is available. In addition, attention-based architectures allow us to directly investigate what the model is learning and to quantitatively measure whether its *rationales* (supporting evidence) for particular input sentences match human expectations. While evaluating the *faithfulness* (Herman, 2017) of a model's rationale is still an open research question and up for debate (Jain and Wallace, 2019; Wiegreffe and Pinter, 2019; DeYoung et al., 2020; Jacovi and Goldberg, 2020; Atanasova et al., 2020), the methods explored here allow for measuring the *plausibility* (agreeability to human annotators; DeYoung et al. (2020)) of transformer-based models using existing sequence labeling datasets.

We evaluate and compare different methods for adapting pre-trained transformer models into zero-shot sequence labelers, trained using only gold sentence-level signal. Our experiments show that applying existing approaches (Rei and Søgaard, 2018) to transformer architectures is not straightforward – transformers already contain several layers of multi-head attention, distributing sentence-level information across many tokens, whereas the existing methods rely on all the information going through one central attention module. Approaches such as LIME (Ribeiro et al., 2016) for scoring word importance also struggle to infer correct token-level annotations in a zero-shot manner (e.g., it achieves only 2% F-score on one of our datasets). We find that a modified attention function is needed to allow transformers to better focus on individual important tokens and achieve a new state-of-the-art on zero-shot sequence labeling.

The contributions of this paper are fourfold:

- We present the first experiments utilizing (pre-trained) sentence-level transformers as zero-shot sequence labelers;
- We perform a systematic comparison of alternative methods for zero-shot sequence labeling on different datasets;
- We propose a novel modification of the attention function that significantly improves zero-shot sequence-labeling performance of transformers over the previous state of the art,

Proceedings of the 6th Workshop on Representation Learning for NLP (RepL4NLP-2021), pages 195–205
Bangkok, Thailand (Online), August 6, 2021.

while achieving on-par or better results on sentence classification;

- We make our source code and models publicly available to facilitate further research in the field.[1]

2 Methods

We evaluate four different methods for turning sentence-level transformer models into zero-shot sequence labelers.

2.1 LIME

LIME (Ribeiro et al., 2016) generates local word-level importance scores through a meta-model that is trained on perturbed data generated by randomly masking out words in the input sentence. It was originally investigated in the context of Support Vector Machine (Hearst et al., 1998) text classifiers with unigram features.

We apply LIME to a RoBERTa model supervised as a sentence classifier and investigate whether its scores can be used for sequence labeling. We use RoBERTa's MASK token to mask out individual words and allow LIME to generate 5000 masked samples per sentence. The resulting explanation weights are then used as classification scores for each word, with the decision threshold fine-tuned based on the development set performance.

Thorne et al. (2019) found LIME to outperform attention-based approaches on the task of explaining NLI models. LIME was used to probe a LSTM-based sentence-pair classifier (Lan and Xu, 2018) by removing tokens from the premise and hypothesis sentences separately. The generated scores were used to perform binary classification of tokens, with the threshold based on F_1 performance on the development set. The token-level predictions were evaluated against human explanations of the entailment relation using the e-SNLI dataset (Camburu et al., 2018). LIME was found to outperform other methods, however, it was also $1000\times$ slower than attention-based methods at generating these explanations.

2.2 Attention heads

The attention heads in a trained transformer model are designed to identify and combine useful information for a particular task. Clark et al. (2019) found that specific heads can specialize on different linguistic properties such as syntax and coreference. However, transformer models contain many layers with multiple attention heads, distributing the text representation and making it more difficult to identify token importance for the overall task.

Given a particular head, we can obtain an importance score for each token by averaging the attention scores from all the tokens that attend to it. In order to investigate the best possible setting, we report results for the attention head that achieves the highest token-level Mean Average Precision score on the development set.

2.3 Soft attention

Rei and Søgaard (2018) described a method for predicting token-level labels based on a bidirectional LSTM (Hochreiter and Schmidhuber, 1997) architecture supervised at the sentence-level only. A dedicated attention module was integrated for building sentence representations, with its attention weights also acting as token-level importance scores. The architecture was found to outperform a gradient-based approach on the tasks of zero-shot sequence labeling for error detection, uncertainty detection, and sentiment analysis.

In order to obtain a single raw attention value $\widetilde{e}_i$ for each token, biLSTM output vectors were passed through a feedforward layer:

$$e_i = tanh(W_e h_i + b_e) \quad \widetilde{e}_i = W_{\widetilde{e}} e_i + b_{\widetilde{e}} \quad (1)$$

where e_i is the attention vector for token t_i; h_i is the biLSTM output for t_i; and $\widetilde{e}_i$ is the single raw attention value. W_e, b_e, $W_{\widetilde{e}}$, $b_{\widetilde{e}}$ are trainable parameters.

Instead of softmax or sparsemax (Martins and Astudillo, 2016), which would restrict the distribution of the scores, a soft attention based on sigmoid activation was used to obtain importance scores:

$$\widetilde{a}_i = \sigma(\widetilde{e}_i) \qquad a_i = \frac{\widetilde{a}_i}{\sum_{k=1}^{N} \widetilde{a}_k} \quad (2)$$

where N is the number of tokens and σ is the logistic function. $\widetilde{a}_i$ shows the importance of a particular token and is in the range $0 \leq \widetilde{a}_i \leq 1$, independent of any other scores in the sentence; therefore, it can be directly used for sequence labeling with a natural threshold of 0.5. a_i contains the same information but is normalized to sum up to 1 over the whole sentence, making it suitable for attention weights when building the sentence representation.

[1] `https://github.com/bujol12/bert-seq-interpretability`

As a_i and $\widetilde{a}_i$ are directly tied, training the former through the sentence classification objective will also train the latter for the sequence labeling task.

The attention values were then used to obtain the sentence representation c by acting as weights for the biLSTM token outputs:

$$c = \sum_{i=0}^{N} a_i h_i \tag{3}$$

Finally, the sentence representation c was passed through the final feedforward layer, followed by a sigmoid to obtain the predicted score y for the sentence:

$$d = tanh(W_d c + b_d) \qquad y = \sigma(W_y d + b_y) \tag{4}$$

where d is the sentence vector, c is the sentence representation, and y is the sentence prediction score. W_d, b_d, W_y, b_y are all trainable parameters.

We adapt this approach to the transformer models by attaching a separate soft attention module on top of the token-level output representations. This effectively ignores the CLS token, which is commonly used for sentence classification, and instead builds a new sentence representation from the token representations, which replace the previously used biLSTM outputs:

$$e_i = tanh(W_e T_i + b_e) \quad c = \sum_{i=0}^{N} a_i T_i \tag{5}$$

where T_i is the contextualized embedding for token t_i. A diagram of the model architecture is included in Appendix F.

Commonly used tokenizers for transformer models split words into subwords, while sequence labeling datasets are annotated at the word level. We find that taking the maximum attention value over all the subwords as the word-level importance score produces good results on the development sets. For a word w_i split into tokens $[t_j, ..., t_m]$, where $j, m \in [1, N]$, the resulting final word importance score r_i is then given by:

$$r_i = max(\{\widetilde{a}_j, \widetilde{a}_{j+1}, ..., \widetilde{a}_m\}) \tag{6}$$

During training, we optimize sentence-level binary cross-entropy as the main objective function:

$$L_1 = \frac{\sum_j CrossEntropy(y^{(j)}, \widetilde{y}^{(j)})}{|y|} \tag{7}$$

where $y^{(j)}$ and $\widetilde{y}^{(j)}$ are the predicted sentence classification logits and the gold label for the jth sentence respectively. We also adopt the additional loss functions from Rei and Søgaard (2018), which encourage the attention weights to behave more like token-level classifiers:

$$L_2 = \frac{\sum_j (min_j(\widetilde{a}_i) - 0)^2}{|y|} \tag{8}$$

$$L_3 = \frac{\sum_j (max_j(\widetilde{a}_i) - \widetilde{y}^{(j)})^2}{|y|} \tag{9}$$

Eq. 8 optimizes the minimum unnormalized attention to be 0 and therefore incentivizes the model to only focus on some, but not all words; Eq. 9 ensures that some attention weights are close to 1 if the overall sentence is classified as positive. We then jointly optimize these three loss functions using a hyperparameter γ: $L = L_1 + \gamma(L_2 + L_3)$.

2.4 Weighted soft attention

Our experiments show that, when combined with transformer-based models, the soft attention method tends to spread out the attention too widely. Instead of focusing on specific important words, the model broadly attends to the whole sentence. Figures 3 and 4 in Appendix A present examples demonstrating such behaviour. As transformers contain several layers of attention, with multiple heads in each layer, the information in the sentence gets distributed across all tokens before it reaches the soft attention module at the top.

To improve this behaviour and incentivize the model to direct information through a smaller and more focused set of tokens, we experiment with a weighted soft attention:

$$a_i = \frac{\widetilde{a}_i^{\beta}}{\sum_{k=1}^{N} \widetilde{a}_k^{\beta}} \tag{10}$$

where β is a hyperparamete and where values $\beta > 1$ make the weight distribution sharper, allowing the model to focus on a smaller number of tokens. We experiment with values of $\beta \in \{1, 2, 3, 4\}$ on the development sets and find $\beta = 2$ to significantly improve token labeling performance without negatively affecting sentence classification results.

3 Datasets

We investigate the performance of these methods as zero-shot sequence labelers using three different datasets. Gold token-level annotation in these

	FCE			BEA 2019			CoNLL 2010		
	Sent F_1	F_1	MAP	Sent F_1	F_1	MAP	Sent F_1	F_1	MAP
Random baseline	-	23.19	33.95	-	16.73	27.01	-	1.63	14.15
RoBERTa	84.51	-	-	83.66	-	-	86.66	-	-
Rei and Søgaard (2018)	84.75	28.73	48.56	81.27	18.53	31.69	84.16	**72.42**	87.82
LIME	84.51	24.60	37.90	83.66	2.09	31.41	86.66	57.14	78.44
Attention heads	84.51	24.34	48.04	83.66	19.69	40.55	86.66	25.64	79.82
Soft attention	**85.62**	32.16	48.90	83.41	22.92	35.79	86.25	8.45	20.04
Weighted soft attention	**85.62**	**33.31**	**53.91**	**83.68**	**24.35**	**41.07**	**87.20**	67.28	**91.18**

Table 1: Results on FCE, BEA 2019 and CoNLL 2010. *Sent* F_1 refers to F-measure on the sentence classification task; F_1 refers to token-level classification performance; *MAP* is the token-level Mean Average Precision.

datasets is used for evaluation; however, the models are trained using sentence-level labels only.

The **CoNLL 2010** shared task (Farkas et al., 2010)[2] focuses on the detection of uncertainty cues in natural language text. The dataset contains 19,542 examples with both sentence-level uncertainty labels and annotated keywords indicating uncertainty. We use the train/test data from the task and randomly choose 10% of the training set for development.

We also evaluate on the task of grammatical error detection (GED) – identifying which sentences are grammatically incorrect (i.e., contain at least one grammatical error). The First Certificate in English dataset **FCE** (Yannakoudakis et al., 2011) consists of essays written by non-native learners of English, annotated for grammatical errors. We use the train/dev/test splits released by Rei and Yannakoudakis (2016) for sequence labeling, with a total of 33,673 sentences.

In addition, we evaluate on the Write & Improve (Yannakoudakis et al., 2018) and LOCNESS (Granger, 1998) GED dataset[3] (38,692 sentences) released as part of the **BEA 2019** shared task (Bryant et al., 2019). It contains English essays written in response to varied topics and by English learners from different proficiency levels, as well as native English speakers. As the gold test set labels are not publicly available, we evaluate on the released development set and use 10% of the training data for tuning[4]. For both GED datasets, we train the model to detect grammatically incorrect sentences and evaluate how well the methods can identify individual tokens that have been annotated as errors.

[2]https://rgai.sed.hu/node/118

[3]https://www.cl.cam.ac.uk/research/nl/bea2019st/

[4]https://github.com/bujol12/bert-seq-interpretability/blob/master/dev_indices_train_ABC.txt

4 Experimental setup

We use the pre-trained RoBERTa-base (Liu et al., 2019) model, made available by HuggingFace (Wolf et al., 2020), as our transformer architecture. Following Mosbach et al. (2021), transformer models are fine-tuned for 20 epochs, and the best performing checkpoint is then chosen based on sentence-level performance on the development set. Each experiment is repeated with 5 different random seeds and the averaged results are reported. The average duration of training on Nvidia GeForce RTX 2080Ti was 1 hour. Significance testing is performed with a two-tailed paired t-test and $a = 0.05$. Hyperparameteres are tuned on the development set and presented in Appendices B and C.

The LIME and attention head methods provide only a score without a natural decision boundary for classification. Therefore, we choose their thresholds based on the token-level F_1-score on the development set. In contrast, the soft attention and weighted soft attention methods do not require such additional tuning that uses token-level labels.

5 Results

The results are presented in Table 1. Each model is trained as a sentence classifier and then evaluated as a token labeler. The challenge of the zero-shot sequence-labeling setting lies in the fact that the models are trained without utilizing any gold token-level signal; nevertheless, some methods perform considerably better than others. For reference, we also include a random baseline, which samples token-level scores from the standard uniform distribution; a RoBERTa model supervised as a sentence classifier only; and the model from Rei and Søgaard (2018) based on BiLSTMs.

We report the F_1-measure on the token level along with Mean Average Precision (MAP) for returning positive tokens. The MAP metric views the task as a ranking problem and therefore removes

	HEAD	LIME	SA	W-SA
Th17	0.00	0.01	0.99	0.01
cell	0.00	0.01	0.99	0.01
may	0.17	0.54	0.99	0.99
not	0.01	0.09	0.99	0.94
be	0.00	0.06	0.99	0.07
correct	0.01	0.05	0.99	0.03
,	0.01	0.02	0.99	0.02
as	0.02	0.00	0.99	0.03
there	0.00	0.00	0.99	0.02
seems	0.37	0.12	0.99	0.99
to	0.03	0.15	0.99	0.15
be	0.00	0.06	0.99	0.03
further	0.01	0.00	0.99	0.02
complexity	0.01	0.01	0.99	0.02

Figure 1: Example word-level importance scores r_i (Eq. 6) of different methods applied to an excerpt from the CoNLL10 dataset. *HEAD* corresponds to attention heads; *SA* to soft attention; and *W-SA* to weighted soft attention. We can observe how *W-SA* is the only method that correctly assigns substantially higher weights to the 'may' and 'seems' uncertainty cues.

the dependence on specific classification thresholds. In addition, we report the F_1-measure on the main sentence-level task to ensure the proposed methods do not have adverse effects on sentence classification performance. Precision and recall values are included in Appendix E.

LIME has relatively low performance on FCE and BEA 2019, while it achieves somewhat higher results on CoNLL 2010. Comparing the MAP scores, the attention head method performs substantially better, especially considering that it is much more lightweight and requires no additional computation. Nevertheless, both of these methods rely on using some annotated examples to tune their classification threshold, which precludes their application in a truly zero-shot setting.

Combining the soft attention mechanism with the transformer architecture provides some improvements over the previous methods, while also improving over Rei and Søgaard (2018). A notable exception is the CoNLL 2010 dataset where this method achieves only 8% F_1 and 20% MAP. Error analysis revealed that this is due to the transformer representations spreading attention scores evenly between a large number of tokens, as observed in Figure 1. Uncertainty cues in CoNLL 2010 can span across whole sentences (e.g., *'Either ... or ...'*), with such examples encouraging the model to distribute information even further.

The weighted soft attention modification addresses this issue and considerably improves performance across all metrics on all datasets. Compared to the non-weighted version of the soft attention method, applying the extra weights leads to a significant improvement in terms of MAP, with a minimum of 5.01% absolute gain on FCE. The improvements are also statistically significant compared to the current state of the art (Rei and Søgaard, 2018): 5.35% absolute improvement on FCE; 9.38% on BEA 2019; and 3.36% on CoNLL 2010. While the F_1 on CoNLL 2010 is slightly lower, the MAP score is higher, indicating that the model has difficulty finding an optimal decision boundary, but nevertheless provides a better ranking. In future work, the weighted soft attention method for transformers could potentially be combined with token supervision in order to train robust multi-level models (Barrett et al., 2018; Rei and Søgaard, 2019).

6 Conclusion

We investigated methods for inferring token-level predictions from transformer models trained only on sentence-level annotations. Experiments showed that previous approaches designed for LSTM architectures do not perform as well when applied to transformers. As transformer models already contain multiple layers of multi-head attention, the input representations get distributed between many tokens, making it more difficult to identify the importance of each individual token. LIME was not able to accurately identify target tokens, while the soft attention method primarily assigned equal attention scores across most words in a sentence. Directly using the scores from the existing attention heads performed better than expected, but required some annotated data for tuning the decision threshold. Modifying the soft attention module with an explicit sharpness constraint on the weights was found to encourage more distinct predictions, significantly improving token-level results.

Acknowledgments

We would like to thank James Thorne for his assistance in setting up the LIME experiments. Kamil Bujel was funded by the Undergraduate Research Opportunities Programme Bursary from the Department of Computing at Imperial College London.

References

Pepa Atanasova, Jakob Grue Simonsen, Christina Lioma, and Isabelle Augenstein. 2020. A diagnostic study of explainability techniques for text classification. In *Proceedings of the 2020 Conference on Empirical Methods in Natural Language Processing (EMNLP)*, pages 3256–3274, Online. Association for Computational Linguistics.

Maria Barrett, Joachim Bingel, Nora Hollenstein, Marek Rei, and Anders Søgaard. 2018. Sequence classification with human attention. In *Proceedings of the 22nd Conference on Computational Natural Language Learning*, pages 302–312, Brussels, Belgium. Association for Computational Linguistics.

Samuel Bell, Helen Yannakoudakis, and Marek Rei. 2019. Context is key: Grammatical error detection with contextual word representations. In *Proceedings of the Fourteenth Workshop on Innovative Use of NLP for Building Educational Applications*, pages 103–115, Florence, Italy. Association for Computational Linguistics.

Christopher Bryant, Mariano Felice, Øistein E. Andersen, and Ted Briscoe. 2019. The BEA-2019 shared task on grammatical error correction. In *Proceedings of the Fourteenth Workshop on Innovative Use of NLP for Building Educational Applications*, pages 52–75, Florence, Italy. Association for Computational Linguistics.

Oana-Maria Camburu, Tim Rocktäschel, Thomas Lukasiewicz, and Phil Blunsom. 2018. e-snli: Natural language inference with natural language explanations. In *NeurIPS*, pages 9560–9572.

Kevin Clark, Urvashi Khandelwal, Omer Levy, and Christopher D. Manning. 2019. What does BERT look at? an analysis of BERT's attention. In *Proceedings of the 2019 ACL Workshop BlackboxNLP: Analyzing and Interpreting Neural Networks for NLP*, pages 276–286, Florence, Italy. Association for Computational Linguistics.

Jacob Devlin, Ming-Wei Chang, Kenton Lee, and Kristina Toutanova. 2019. BERT: Pre-training of deep bidirectional transformers for language understanding. In *Proceedings of the 2019 Conference of the North American Chapter of the Association for Computational Linguistics: Human Language Technologies, Volume 1 (Long and Short Papers)*, pages 4171–4186, Minneapolis, Minnesota. Association for Computational Linguistics.

Jay DeYoung, Sarthak Jain, Nazneen Fatema Rajani, Eric Lehman, Caiming Xiong, Richard Socher, and Byron C. Wallace. 2020. ERASER: A benchmark to evaluate rationalized NLP models. In *Proceedings of the 58th Annual Meeting of the Association for Computational Linguistics*, pages 4443–4458, Online. Association for Computational Linguistics.

Richárd Farkas, Veronika Vincze, György Móra, János Csirik, and György Szarvas. 2010. The CoNLL-2010 shared task: Learning to detect hedges and their scope in natural language text. In *Proceedings of the Fourteenth Conference on Computational Natural Language Learning – Shared Task*, pages 1–12, Uppsala, Sweden. Association for Computational Linguistics.

Sylviane Granger. 1998. *The computer learner corpus: A versatile new source of data for SLA research*. Longman.

Marti A. Hearst, Susan T Dumais, Edgar Osuna, John Platt, and Bernhard Scholkopf. 1998. Support vector machines. *IEEE Intelligent Systems and their applications*, 13(4):18–28.

Bernease Herman. 2017. The promise and peril of human evaluation for model interpretability. *arXiv preprint arXiv:1711.07414*.

Sepp Hochreiter and Jürgen Schmidhuber. 1997. Long short-term memory. *Neural computation*, 9(8):1735–1780.

Alon Jacovi and Yoav Goldberg. 2020. Towards faithfully interpretable NLP systems: How should we define and evaluate faithfulness? In *Proceedings of the 58th Annual Meeting of the Association for Computational Linguistics*, pages 4198–4205, Online. Association for Computational Linguistics.

Sarthak Jain and Byron C. Wallace. 2019. Attention is not Explanation. In *Proceedings of the 2019 Conference of the North American Chapter of the Association for Computational Linguistics: Human Language Technologies, Volume 1 (Long and Short Papers)*, pages 3543–3556, Minneapolis, Minnesota. Association for Computational Linguistics.

Wuwei Lan and Wei Xu. 2018. Neural network models for paraphrase identification, semantic textual similarity, natural language inference, and question answering. In *Proceedings of the 27th International Conference on Computational Linguistics*, pages 3890–3902, Santa Fe, New Mexico, USA. Association for Computational Linguistics.

Yinhan Liu, Myle Ott, Naman Goyal, Jingfei Du, Mandar Joshi, Danqi Chen, Omer Levy, Mike Lewis, Luke Zettlemoyer, and Veselin Stoyanov. 2019. Roberta: A robustly optimized bert pretraining approach. *arXiv preprint arXiv:1907.11692*.

Andre Martins and Ramon Astudillo. 2016. From softmax to sparsemax: A sparse model of attention and multi-label classification. In *International Conference on Machine Learning*, pages 1614–1623. PMLR.

Marius Mosbach, Maksym Andriushchenko, and Dietrich Klakow. 2021. On the stability of fine-tuning {bert}: Misconceptions, explanations, and strong baselines. In *International Conference on Learning Representations*.

Marek Rei and Anders Søgaard. 2018. Zero-shot sequence labeling: Transferring knowledge from sentences to tokens. In *Proceedings of the 2018 Conference of the North American Chapter of the Association for Computational Linguistics: Human Language Technologies, Volume 1 (Long Papers)*, pages 293–302, New Orleans, Louisiana. Association for Computational Linguistics.

Marek Rei and Anders Søgaard. 2019. Jointly learning to label sentences and tokens. In *Proceedings of the AAAI Conference on Artificial Intelligence*, volume 33, pages 6916–6923.

Marek Rei and Helen Yannakoudakis. 2016. Compositional sequence labeling models for error detection in learner writing. In *Proceedings of the 54th Annual Meeting of the Association for Computational Linguistics (Volume 1: Long Papers)*, pages 1181–1191, Berlin, Germany. Association for Computational Linguistics.

Marco Ribeiro, Sameer Singh, and Carlos Guestrin. 2016. "Why Should I Trust You?": Explaining the Predictions of Any Classifier. In *Proceedings of the 2016 Conference of the North American Chapter of the Association for Computational Linguistics: Demonstrations*, pages 97–101, San Diego, California. Association for Computational Linguistics.

Chi Sun, Xipeng Qiu, Yige Xu, and Xuanjing Huang. 2019. How to fine-tune bert for text classification? In *China National Conference on Chinese Computational Linguistics*, pages 194–206. Springer.

James Thorne, Andreas Vlachos, Christos Christodoulopoulos, and Arpit Mittal. 2019. Generating token-level explanations for natural language inference. In *Proceedings of the 2019 Conference of the North American Chapter of the Association for Computational Linguistics: Human Language Technologies, Volume 1 (Long and Short Papers)*, pages 963–969, Minneapolis, Minnesota. Association for Computational Linguistics.

Sarah Wiegreffe and Yuval Pinter. 2019. Attention is not not explanation. In *Proceedings of the 2019 Conference on Empirical Methods in Natural Language Processing and the 9th International Joint Conference on Natural Language Processing (EMNLP-IJCNLP)*, pages 11–20, Hong Kong, China. Association for Computational Linguistics.

Thomas Wolf, Lysandre Debut, Victor Sanh, Julien Chaumond, Clement Delangue, Anthony Moi, Pierric Cistac, Tim Rault, Remi Louf, Morgan Funtowicz, Joe Davison, Sam Shleifer, Patrick von Platen, Clara Ma, Yacine Jernite, Julien Plu, Canwen Xu, Teven Le Scao, Sylvain Gugger, Mariama Drame, Quentin Lhoest, and Alexander Rush. 2020. Transformers: State-of-the-art natural language processing. In *Proceedings of the 2020 Conference on Empirical Methods in Natural Language Processing: System Demonstrations*, pages 38–45, Online. Association for Computational Linguistics.

Helen Yannakoudakis, Øistein E Andersen, Ardeshir Geranpayeh, Ted Briscoe, and Diane Nicholls. 2018. Developing an automated writing placement system for esl learners. *Applied Measurement in Education*, 31(3):251–267.

Helen Yannakoudakis, Ted Briscoe, and Ben Medlock. 2011. A new dataset and method for automatically grading ESOL texts. In *Proceedings of the 49th Annual Meeting of the Association for Computational Linguistics: Human Language Technologies*, pages 180–189, Portland, Oregon, USA. Association for Computational Linguistics.

A Example word-level predictions

We present samples of word-level predictions (word-level importance scores r_i, Eq. 6) to illustrate differences between methods. In the figures that follow, *HEAD* refers to attention heads, SA to soft attention, and *W-SA* to weighted soft attention.

	HEAD	LIME	SA	W-SA
In	0.00	0.00	0.00	0.01
addition	0.00	0.00	0.00	0.01
,	0.00	0.00	0.00	0.01
Th2	0.00	0.00	0.00	0.01
cells	0.00	0.00	0.00	0.01
have	0.00	0.00	0.00	0.01
been	0.03	0.00	0.00	0.01
shown	0.67	0.00	0.00	0.01
to	0.01	0.00	0.00	0.01
mediate	0.00	0.00	0.00	0.01
allergic	0.02	0.00	0.00	0.01
diseases	0.00	0.00	0.00	0.01
such	0.00	0.00	0.00	0.01
as	0.00	0.00	0.00	0.01
asthma	0.00	0.00	0.00	0.01
,	0.00	0.00	0.00	0.01
rhinitis	0.01	0.00	0.00	0.01
,	0.00	0.00	0.00	0.01
and	0.00	0.00	0.00	0.01
atopic	0.02	0.00	0.00	0.01
dermatitis	0.00	0.00	0.00	0.01
(	0.00	0.00	0.00	0.01
11	0.00	0.00	0.00	0.01
)	0.00	0.00	0.00	0.01
.	0.10	0.00	0.00	0.00

Figure 2: CoNLL 2010 negative sentence (without uncertainty cues). We can clearly see that most methods correctly put weights close to 0 for all words, except from HEAD, which focuses on 'shown' and '.'. We surmise this is due to the fact that, for HEAD, weights over the whole sentence have to sum up to 1.

	HEAD	LIME	SA	W-SA
It	0.01	0.00	0.99	0.01
is	0.01	0.05	0.99	0.02
also	0.02	0.00	0.99	0.02
clear	0.02	0.02	0.99	0.19
that	0.01	0.04	0.99	0.21
the	0.00	0.06	0.99	0.01
notion	0.00	0.00	0.99	0.01
of	0.00	0.00	0.99	0.01
a	0.00	0.03	0.99	0.01
single	0.00	0.00	0.99	0.01
type	0.00	0.02	0.99	0.02
of	0.00	0.02	0.99	0.01
Th17	0.00	0.01	0.99	0.01
cell	0.00	0.01	0.99	0.01
may	0.17	0.54	0.99	0.99
not	0.01	0.09	0.99	0.94
be	0.00	0.06	0.99	0.07
correct	0.01	0.05	0.99	0.03
,	0.01	0.02	0.99	0.02
as	0.02	0.00	0.99	0.03
there	0.00	0.00	0.99	0.02
seems	0.37	0.12	0.99	0.99
to	0.03	0.15	0.99	0.15
be	0.00	0.06	0.99	0.03
further	0.01	0.00	0.99	0.02
complexity	0.01	0.01	0.99	0.02
in	0.00	0.01	0.99	0.01
terms	0.00	0.00	0.99	0.01
of	0.00	0.02	0.99	0.01
the	0.00	0.06	0.99	0.01
cytokines	0.00	0.00	0.99	0.01
produced	0.00	0.01	0.99	0.01
by	0.00	0.00	0.99	0.01
these	0.00	0.01	0.99	0.01
cells	0.00	0.01	0.99	0.01
.	0.06	0.03	0.00	0.01

Figure 3: CoNLL 2010 positive sentence (with uncertainty cues). We can observe that HEAD correctly identifies both of the uncertainty cues: 'may' and 'seems'; however the weight for 'may' is quite low. Similarly, LIME identifies both tokens, but the weight for 'seems' is particularly low (lower than for 'to'). SA simply assigns high weights to all words. W-SA focuses primarily on the two uncertainty cue words; however, it also incorrectly focuses on 'not'.

	HEAD	LIME	SA	W-SA
Secondly	0.03	0.00	0.80	0.00
the	0.01	0.00	0.95	0.24
best	0.00	0.00	0.94	0.12
way	0.01	0.00	0.94	0.28
to	0.01	0.00	0.95	0.32
go	0.02	0.00	0.93	0.23
from	0.00	0.00	0.92	0.20
the	0.00	0.00	0.92	0.31
hotel	0.00	0.00	0.80	0.13
to	0.01	0.00	0.91	0.35
the	0.00	0.00	0.91	0.56
conference	0.00	0.00	0.52	0.13
center	0.00	0.00	0.88	0.58
is	0.01	0.00	0.95	0.05
to	0.01	0.00	0.95	0.10
use	0.02	0.00	0.95	0.59
one	0.01	0.00	0.96	0.62
of	0.00	0.00	0.97	0.83
the	0.01	0.00	0.97	0.84
shutel	0.01	0.00	0.96	0.88
buses	0.01	0.00	0.96	0.79
we	0.01	0.00	0.97	0.75
provide	0.29	0.00	0.97	0.88
at	0.03	0.00	0.97	0.91
this	0.10	0.00	0.97	0.92
efect.	0.05	0.00	0.98	0.95
they	0.01	0.00	0.97	0.91
are	0.00	0.00	0.97	0.90
going	0.01	0.00	0.97	0.81
to	0.01	0.00	0.97	0.82
leave	0.02	0.00	0.96	0.83
at	0.01	0.00	0.96	0.74
9.00	0.01	0.00	0.95	0.44
o'clock	0.01	0.00	0.95	0.32
.	0.07	0.00	0.00	0.81

Figure 4: FCE positive sentence (contains grammatical errors). We can see that both LIME and HEAD struggle to assign informative and/or useful weights to the words. All SA weights are relatively high, with small variations in value. We can see that squaring (W-SA) leads to more well-defined weights over the whole sentence, with high weights mainly observed in the second part of the sentence, which is the one that contains incorrect words. However, on this dataset, even W-SA struggles to correctly identify which words precisely are incorrect.

B Hyperparameters

Name	Value
γ	0.1
max seq length	128
per device train batch size	16
per device eval batch size	64
warmup ratio	0.1
learning rate	2e-5
weight decay	0.1
adam epsilon	1e-7
hidden layer dropout	0.1
soft attention layer size	100
soft attention hidden size	300
initializer	glorot

Table 2: Model hyperparameters.

C Word-level prediction thresholds

Dataset	Method	Threshold
CoNLL 2010	LIME	0.200
	Random baseline	0.500
	Attention heads	0.320
	Rei and Søgaard (2018)	0.500
	Soft attention	0.500
	Weighted soft attention	0.500
FCE	LIME	0.001
	Random baseline	0.500
	Attention heads	0.080
	Rei and Søgaard (2018)	0.500
	Soft attention	0.500
	Weighted soft attention	0.500
BEA 2019	LIME	0.010
	Random baseline	0.500
	Attention heads	0.080
	Rei and Søgaard (2018)	0.500
	Soft attention	0.500
	Weighted soft attention	0.500

Table 3: Word-level thresholds above which a word is classified as positive.

D Validation set results

Dataset	Method	Sent F_1
CoNLL 2010	LIME	91.77
	RoBERTa	91.77
	Attention heads	91.77
	Soft attention	92.12
	Weighted soft attention	91.82
FCE	LIME	84.49
	RoBERTa	84.49
	Attention heads	84.49
	Soft attention	84.82
	Weighted soft attention	85.56
BEA 2019	LIME	83.65
	RoBERTa	83.65
	Attention heads	83.65
	Soft attention	83.47
	Weighted soft attention	83.64

Table 4: Mean sentence-level F_1 score on the development set, averaged over 5 runs.

E Full test set results

	FCE		
	Sent F_1	Sent P	Sent R
Random baseline	-	-	-
RoBERTa	84.51	84.25	**84.93**
Rei and Søgaard (2018)	84.75	-	-
LIME	84.51	84.25	**84.93**
Attention heads	84.51	84.25	**84.93**
Soft attention	**85.62**	**86.92**	84.42
Weighted soft attention	**85.62**	86.88	84.45

Table 5: Sentence-level results: *P*, *R* and F_1 refer to Precision, Recall and F-measure respectively on the positive class.

	BEA 2019		
	Sent F_1	Sent P	Sent R
Random baseline	-	-	-
RoBERTa	83.66	**82.29**	85.15
Rei and Søgaard (2018)	81.27		
LIME	83.66	**82.29**	85.15
Attention heads	83.66	**82.29**	85.15
Soft attention	83.41	81.47	85.54
Weighted soft attention	**83.68**	79.95	**87.91**

Table 6: Sentence-level results: *P*, *R* and F_1 refer to Precision, Recall and F-measure respectively on the positive class.

	CoNLL 2010		
	Sent F_1	Sent P	Sent R
Random baseline	-	-	-
RoBERTa	86.66	84.90	**88.63**
Rei and Søgaard (2018)	84.16	-	-
LIME	86.66	84.90	**88.63**
Attention heads	86.66	84.90	**88.63**
Soft attention	86.25	85.75	86.89
Weighted soft attention	**87.20**	**89.17**	85.37

Table 7: Sentence-level results: *P*, *R* and F_1 refer to Precision, Recall and F-measure respectively on the positive class.

	FCE			
	P	R	F_1	MAP
Random baseline	15.11	49.81	23.19	33.95
RoBERTa	-	-	-	-
Rei and Søgaard (2018)	**29.16**	29.04	28.73	48.56
LIME	19.06	34.70	24.60	37.90
Attention heads	26.67	22.38	24.34	48.04
Soft attention	19.84	**85.38**	32.16	48.90
Weighted soft attention	20.76	85.36	**33.31**	**53.91**

Table 8: Token-level results: *P*, *R* and F_1 refer to Precision, Recall and F-measure respectively on the positive class. *MAP* is the Mean Average Precision at the token-level.

	BEA 2019			
	P	R	F_1	MAP
Random baseline	10.05	50.00	16.73	27.01
RoBERTa	-	-	-	-
Rei and Søgaard (2018)	10.93	61.63	18.53	31.69
LIME	13.49	1.13	2.09	31.41
Attention heads	**18.48**	21.07	19.69	40.55
Soft attention	13.20	**87.19**	22.92	35.79
Weighted soft attention	14.20	85.49	**24.35**	**41.07**

Table 9: Token-level results: *P*, *R* and F_1 refer to Precision, Recall and F-measure respectively on the positive class. *MAP* is the Mean Average Precision at the token-level.

	CoNLL 2010			
	P	R	F_1	MAP
Random baseline	0.83	49.70	1.63	14.15
RoBERTa	-	-	-	-
Rei and Søgaard (2018)	**78.99**	67.06	**72.42**	87.82
LIME	63.25	52.11	57.14	78.44
Attention heads	22.33	30.11	25.64	79.82
Soft attention	4.48	**86.14**	8.45	20.04
Weighted soft attention	58.80	78.89	67.28	**91.18**

Table 10: Token-level results: *P*, *R* and F_1 refer to Precision, Recall and F-measure respectively on the positive class. *MAP* is the Mean Average Precision at the token-level.

F Weighted soft attention architecture

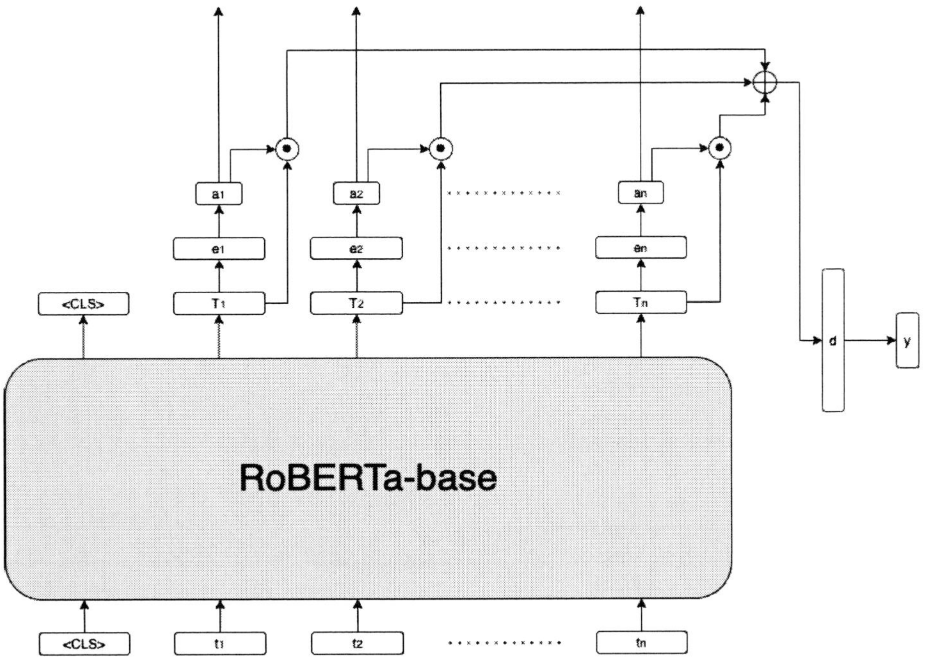

Figure 5: Architecture of our proposed weighted soft attention model. $[t_1, t_2, ..., t_n]$ represent the tokenized input sentence, while $[T_1, T_2, ..., T_n]$ are the resulting contextual embeddings. $[e_1, e_2, ..., e_n]$ are attention vectors, and $[a_1, a_2, ..., a_n]$ are normalized attention weights. d represents the output vector and y the final output logits.

Predicting the Success of Domain Adaptation in Text Similarity

Nicolai Pogrebnyakov[*†] **Shohreh Shaghaghian**[*]
[*] Thomson Reuters Labs, Canada [†]Copenhagen Business School, Denmark
Emails: firstname.lastname@thomsonreuters.com

Abstract

Transfer learning methods, and in particular domain adaptation, help exploit labeled data in one domain to improve the performance of a certain task in another domain. However, it is still not clear what factors affect the success of domain adaptation. This paper models adaptation success and selection of the most suitable source domains among several candidates in text similarity. We use descriptive domain information and cross-domain similarity metrics as predictive features. While mostly positive, the results also point to some domains where adaptation success was difficult to predict.

1 Introduction

Since the data-hungry deep learning models have beaten state-of-the-art performances in different natural language processing (NLP) tasks, many efforts have been made to deal with the scarcity of labeled data (Wang et al., 2020; Settles, 2010; Kouw and Loog, 2019). One of the main avenues taken by researchers of this field is investigating the portability of models between different data distributions, often referred to as different domains (Luo et al., 2019; Gururangan et al., 2020). While multiple approaches have been proposed to make this portability feasible and efficient, it is still unclear how to predict the adaptability of two domains in advance. It is particularly important to address this gap because almost all domain adaptation approaches adjust a model to a new domain at the expense of more computational resources. Therefore, in practice it is neither desirable nor scalable to try all possible dataset candidates.

Most relevant existing work seeks to identify key factors that can be used to justify why transfer learning between two domains work (Asch and Daelemans, 2010; Dai et al., 2019; Kashyap et al., 2021; Mou et al., 2016; Shah et al., 2018). In practice, however, one needs to be able to quantitatively select a set of existing datasets that can best be adapted to a certain domain for a certain task.

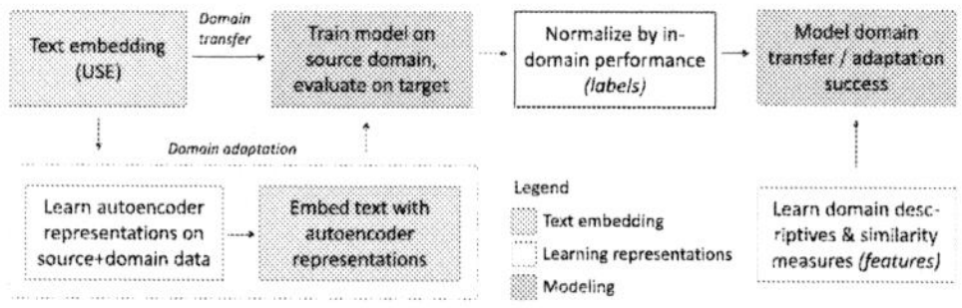

Figure 1: The process of modeling the success of domain transfer & adaptation.

We propose a simple yet effective approach to predict the success of transfer or adaptation, with the hope of drawing the research community's attention to this gap. We use the term *domain transfer* (DT) when a model trained on one domain is simply used for inference in another domain. *Domain adaptation* (DA) is used for approaches that bridge the source and target domain representations (e.g., by mapping or aligning feature spaces of the two domains) so that a model trained on labeled source data (and unlabeled target data) performs well in the target domain. While for the experiments in this paper we focus on the task of text similarity and autoencoder approaches to DA, the proposed process, shown in Figure 1, can be easily applied to other NLP tasks and other unsupervised DA approaches.

Domain Adaptation. The need for domain adaptation arises when a model trained using labeled data from one (source) domain needs to be applied to another (target) domain with a different data distribution (Miller, 2019). We focus specifically on unsupervised domain adaptation, which learns using unlabeled data in both source and target domains. Model-based approaches to unsupervised DA have been classified into modifying the feature space and augmenting the

Proceedings of the 6th Workshop on Representation Learning for NLP (RepL4NLP-2021), pages 206–212
Bangkok, Thailand (Online), August 6, 2021.

loss function (see Ramponi and Plank (2020) for a comprehensive review).

Domain Similarity. Extant studies have proposed a variety of measures to quantitatively express similarity between a pair of domains. Dai et al. (2019) define three main metrics to measure different aspects of similarity between source and target datasets and investigate how these measures correlate with the effectiveness of named entity recognition tasks. Target vocabulary coverage, language model perplexity, and word vector variance are used as these similarity measures. Asch and Daelemans (2010) show a correlation between six similarity metrics based on word frequency, and the performance of some part-of-speech tagging tasks.

Autoencoders for Domain Adaptation. Stacked denoising autoencoders (SDA) learn latent representations that align feature spaces of the source and target domains (Ramponi and Plank, 2020; Vincent et al., 2010). SDA first add noise to input, such as dropout or Gaussian noise, and then aim to reconstruct the uncorrupted input (Gondara, 2016).

A further development of this approach is marginalized SDA, which marginalizes the reconstruction loss. The solution to the loss has a closed form, which lowers computational cost and improves scalability compared to the original SDA (Ramponi and Plank, 2020; Chen et al., 2012).

Inspired by another approach to DA, domain adversarial (Ganin et al., 2016), Clinchant et al. (2016) add a regularization term based on a domain classifier to the reconstruction loss. We refer to this approach as marginalized SDA with domain regularization (mSDAR). There also exists a closed-form solution to that loss, and that approach was shown to outperform marginalized SDA.

2 Data

We use 11 publicly available semantic text similarity datasets. Seven of them were obtained from StackExchange forums, with data from 2015 to November 2020: Apple, AskUbuntu, Math, StackOverflow, Stats, SuperUser and Unix[1]. We also use Quora Question Pairs, Microsoft Research Paraphrase Corpus (MRPC) (Dolan and Brockett, 2005), Paraphrase Adversaries from Word Scrambling (PAWS) (Zhang et al., 2019) and Sentences Involving Compositional Knowledge—Relatedness (SICK) (SemEval, 2014). All datasets contain binary labels indicating whether the text pair is similar or not. The exception is SICK, where we convert the original relevance score of 1—5 into a binary score of 0 (not semantically similar) if the relevance score is below 4, and 1 otherwise. Each of the 11 datasets is considered a separate domain.

3 Modeling Domain Transfer and Adaptation

Figure 1 shows the process we use to implement DT and DA and train a model that can best identify a proper source domain for a particular target domain. We start with embedding text in each of the 11 domains with the Universal Sentence Encoder (USE) (Cer et al., 2018). For DT, USE representations are used directly to train models in a source domain S and evaluate the performance in the target domain T. For DA, we implement both SDA and mSDAR. A three-layer SDA is trained on each source-target domain pair. Text from the source and target domains is embedded with USE and corrupted with Gaussian noise, whose parameters are estimated from the hidden representation of the previous layer. In mSDAR, the hyperparameters we use are 5 layers, the target regularization parameter $\lambda = 1$, dropout probability 0.6 and the regularization objective $\mathbf{R} = \mathbf{1}$. These parameters have the same meaning as in Clinchant et al. (2016). Both SDA and mSDAR encoders are then used to embed the USE representations of the text in the source and target domains. Figure 2 shows the original and mSDAR representations for StackOverflow and SuperUser domains, demonstrating the effect of mSDAR on aligning the feature spaces of the two domains.

The representations described above are used to train a dense 3-layer neural network in the source domain and evaluate its performance in the target domain by reporting the F1-score. (We train three such models for each domain pair and average their performance.) We denote this cross-domain performance by $F1_{ST}$. In order to make the DT and DA results robust to the relative difficulty of learning in different domains, we normalize $F1_{ST}$ by the in-domain F1-score, $F1_{TT}$, which denotes the performance of the fully supervised model trained and evaluated in the same domain. The normalized F1-score, averaged over all domain

[1] Obtained from https://data.stackexchange.com

pairs, is 0.775 for DT, 0.799 for SDA and 0.817 for mSDAR. This is in line with previous work showing better performance of mSDAR over SDA (Clinchant et al., 2016).

4 Domain Similarity Measures

Considering a source domain S and a target domain T with unigram sets U_S and U_T , we define a set of features $F^{ST} = \{f_1^{ST}, \ldots, f_{10}^{ST}\}$ as follows.

Unigram Coverage. The simplest metric to evaluate the similarity of two domains is the percentage of their common unigrams. We use the ratio of common unigrams in the source $f_1^{ST} = \frac{|U_S \cap U_T|}{|U_S|}$ and target $f_2^{ST} = \frac{|U_S \cap U_T|}{|U_T|}$ domains as two features for the classifiers.

Dataset Size. The number of labeled data points in source (f_3^{ST}) and target (f_4^{ST}) domains as well as the average number of tokens per example for the source and target domains (f_5^{ST} and f_6^{ST}) are additional features we use for the classifiers.

Distribution Similarity. In order to measure the similarity of how tokens have been distributed in the two domains, we add Rényi divergence (f_7^{ST}) (Asch and Daelemans, 2010) and KL divergence (f_8^{ST}) (Plank and van Noord, 2011) to the set of features. We use $\alpha = 0.99$ as the value of the parameter in Rényi divergence.

Language Similarity. Similar to Dai et al. (2019), we train a trigram language model in each domain and evaluate its perplexity on other domains (f_9^{ST}). Since the target domain is expected to have many trigrams that are not seen in the source domain, we apply Kneser-Ney smoothing to account for those unseen trigrams (Kneser and Ney, 1995). We also use word vector variance between the source and target domains (f_{10}^{ST}) (Dai et al., 2019). This variance is calculated as $\frac{1}{|U_S \cap U_T| d} \Sigma_{v \in U_S \cap U_T} \Sigma_{j=1}^{d} \left| W_{Sv}^{j} - W_{Tv}^{j} \right|$, where W_{Sv}^{j} and W_{TV}^{j} are the jth element of the vector for word v respectively in the source and target domains. We use Word2vec Skipgram with vector length of 300.

5 Source Domain Selection

Success Prediction and Order Ranking. We evaluate two different approaches to select one or multiple source domains for a particular target domain. In the first approach, we train a classifier to predict if a domain can be a good candidate for transfer or adaptation to a specific target domain.

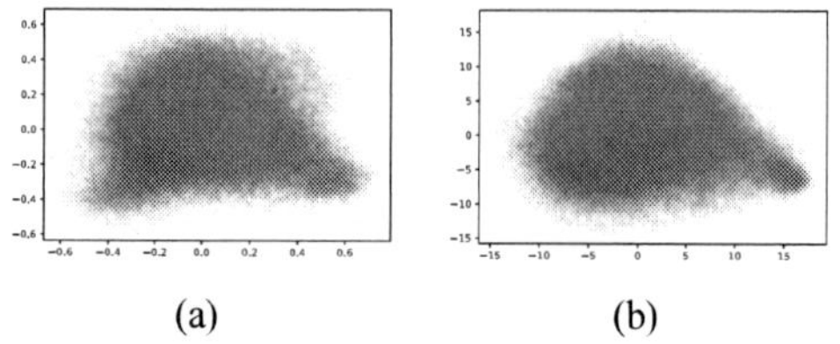

Figure 2. Original (a) and mSDAR (b) representations of text in the StackOverflow (red) and SuperUser (blue) domains (PCA projection).

We consider transfer or adaptation successful if the ratio $\frac{F1_{ST}}{F1_{TT}}$ is greater than 80% i.e., if it can achieve at least 80% of the performance of a fully supervised model on the target domain. We refer to the classifier trained in this approach as *Success Predictor*. In the second approach, irrespective of what percentage of a fully supervised model performance can be achieved, we order the existing source domains for each target domain. Therefore, we model the problem as a ranking problem and refer to the trained model as *Domain Ranker*. This ranking problem can be modeled as a binary classifier, in which a sample corresponds to the performance of two source domains S_1 and S_2 for a specific target domain T. The label is one if $F1_{S_1T} \geq F1_{S_2T}$ and zero otherwise.

Performance Evaluation. While the F1-scores and accuracies reflect how well the trained classifiers work, the original purpose of defining these two approaches was to find the *best candidates* for source domains. Hence, we also show the performance of the two approaches based on ordering-based metrics. To find the orderings for each target domain by Success Predictor, we order the source domains based on the predicted probability of the binary classifier. In Domain Ranker, we sort the source pairs using the pairwise preference predicted by the classifier. We handle the inconsistencies caused by incorrect predictions using the multi-sort algorithm proposed by Maystre and Grossglauser (2017).

To train the Success Predictor and Domain Ranker models, we use a set of features F^{ST} described in section 4. For both approaches, we train a binary XGBoost classifier with 5-fold cross-validation.

6 Results

Modeling Domain Adaptation

Ideally, the best way to evaluate the performance of the two approaches is to train the model on some

		DT						SDA						mSDAR					
	Target	**F1**	**Acc**	**CRP**	**Top1**	**Top3**	**Top5**	**F1**	**Acc**	**CRP**	**Top1**	**Top3**	**Top5**	**F1**	**Acc**	**CRP**	**Top1**	**Top3**	**Top5**
Success Predictor	Apple	1	1	0.4	1	0.67	1	0.89	0.9	0.3	0	0.67	1	0.89	0.9	0.4	1	1	1
	AskUbuntu	1	1	0.3	0	0.67	1	0.86	0.9	0	0	0.67	0.8	1	1	0.2	0	0.67	0.8
	MRPC	0.71	0.6	0.2	0	0.67	0.6	0.93	0.9	0.2	0	0.33	0.6	0.93	0.9	0.3	0	0.67	0.8
	Math	0.67	0.6	0.2	0	0.67	0.6	0.6	0.6	0	0	0.33	0.8	0.86	0.8	0.1	0	0.33	0.6
	PAWS	0	0	0.3	0	0.33	0.8	0.18	0.1	0.3	0	0.33	0.6	0.18	0.1	0	0	0.33	0.6
	Quora	0	0	0.3	0	0.67	1	0	0	0.3	1	0.67	0.8	0	0.1	0.3	1	0.33	0.8
	SICK	0.89	0.8	0.5	0	0.67	0.8	0.88	0.8	0.2	0	0	0.4	0.93	0.9	0.3	0	0.33	0.8
	StackOverflow	0.67	0.8	0.1	0	0.67	0.6	0	0.8	0.3	0	1	0.6	0.75	0.8	0.1	0	1	0.6
	Stats	0.67	0.8	0.2	1	0.33	0.8	0.67	0.9	0.5	1	0.67	0.6	0.4	0.7	0.4	1	0.67	0.8
	SuperUser	0.89	0.9	0.2	0	0.67	1	1	1	0.1	0	0.67	0.8	0.86	0.9	0.3	1	1	0.8
	Unix	1	1	0.3	1	0.67	1	1	1	0.7	1	1	1	0.86	0.9	0.5	1	1	1
	AVERAGE	**0.68**	**0.68**	**0.27**	**0.27**	**0.61**	**0.84**	**0.64**	**0.72**	**0.26**	**0.27**	**0.58**	**0.73**	**0.70**	**0.73**	**0.26**	**0.45**	**0.67**	**0.78**
Domain Ranker	Apple	0.86	0.89	0.8	1	1	1	0.97	0.98	0.8	1	1	1	0.89	0.91	0.5	1	0.67	1
	AskUbuntu	0.85	0.89	0.7	0	0.67	1	0.86	0.91	0.4	0	0.67	1	0.77	0.84	0.5	0	0.67	0.8
	MRPC	0.77	0.78	0.2	1	0.67	0.8	0.65	0.76	0.2	0	0.67	0.8	0.72	0.84	0.3	1	0.67	1
	Math	0.73	0.76	0.1	0	0.67	0.6	0.67	0.71	0.1	0	0.33	0.6	0.65	0.76	0.2	0	0.33	0.8
	PAWS	0.44	0.56	0.2	0	0.33	0.6	0.69	0.76	0.2	0	0.67	1	0.59	0.76	0.1	0	0.33	0.8
	Quora	0.86	0.84	0.4	0	0.67	1	0.87	0.87	0.3	0	0.67	1	0.76	0.82	0.2	0	0.67	0.8
	SICK	0.87	0.87	0.2	0	0.33	1	0.54	0.62	0.2	0	0.33	0.6	0.76	0.84	0.4	0	0.67	1
	StackOverflow	0.88	0.89	0.5	0	0.67	1	0.78	0.8	0.5	0	0.33	0.8	0.86	0.87	0.5	1	0.67	1
	Stats	0.91	0.91	0.7	1	0.67	0.8	0.86	0.87	0.4	1	0.67	0.8	0.83	0.87	0.4	1	0.67	0.8
	SuperUser	0.94	0.93	0.5	0	1	1	0.94	0.93	0.5	0	1	0.8	0.9	0.91	0.6	1	1	0.8
	Unix	0.92	0.91	0.4	0	0.67	1	0.89	0.89	0.3	1	0.67	0.8	0.93	0.93	0.5	0	1	0.8
	AVERAGE	**0.82**	**0.84**	**0.43**	**0.27**	**0.67**	**0.89**	**0.79**	**0.83**	**0.35**	**0.27**	**0.64**	**0.84**	**0.79**	**0.85**	**0.38**	**0.45**	**0.67**	**0.87**

Table 1: Performance of Success Predictor and Domain Ranker in identifying the most suitable target domains under domain transfer (DT) and two domain adaptation approaches (SDA and mSDAR).

set of domains and test it on orderings of an entirely different set of domains. However, since we only have 11 domains, to make the most use out of this small data, we train the classifier on multiple train-test splits and report the performance metrics of the trained binary classifier each time.

We can split the data into train and test sets randomly. However, to make sure that the target domain for which we want to select the best source domain has never been seen by the model as the target domain, each time we use one of the 11 domains as the target domain in the test data. Hence, we have 100 training and 10 test samples in each split. For Domain Ranker, we use $F^{S_1T} \cup F^{S_2T}$ as the feature set and use the same train-test split as for Success Predictor. This leaves us with 450 training and 45 test samples in each of the 11 splits.

Success Adaptation Prediction. Table 1 presents the performance metrics achieved for all target domains. Note that there is a wide variation in success prediction among the target domains. While the Success Predictor achieves good performance on Apple, AskUbuntu and Unix target domains, it performs poorly on PAWS and Quora datasets. This might be due to the difficulty of learning in these domains (Zhang et al., 2019), which is not captured by the descriptive and cross-domain metrics that we use.

Order Prediction. Rank correlation coefficients such as Kendall's τ are a common metric to measure the degree of similarity between two rankings. However, here we are more interested in finding out whether we have correctly identified the most relevant source domains. Hence, we report the percentages of top N domains we have identified correctly for $N = 1, 3, 5$. We also report a stricter metric, Correct Rank Percentage (CRP), which equals the percentage of the source domains that have been predicted with the same order as the true ordering. For example, for Stats as the target domain, the true ordering of other domains using SDA is [StackOverflow, AskUbuntu, Apple, Unix, MRPC, SuperUser, SICK, Math, PAWS, Quora]. The Success Predictor predicts the ordering of the source domains as [StackOverflow, Math, Apple, SuperUser, Unix, AskUbuntu, SICK, MRPC, PAWS, Quora]. In this case, CRP=0.5 since 5 out of the 10 domains have the same order in the predicted and true orderings. Also, Top1=1 since the domain with highest predicted order, StackOverflow, has also the highest order in the true ordering. Similarly, Top3=0.67 since only 2 out of the 3 highest ordered domains in true ordering exist in the top 3 of predicted ordering.

In-Domain and Cross-Domain Performance

Table 2 shows in-domain and cross-domain performance with DT and DA using absolute F1

Domain	In-domain average F1	Domain transfer		Domain adaptation (SDA)		Domain adaptation (mSDAR)	
		Average F1	# of transfer successes	Average F1	# of adaptation successes	Average F1	# of adaptation successes
Apple	0.87	0.55	5	0.55	4	0.56	4
AskUbuntu	0.91	0.53	4	0.55	4	0.57	4
Math	0.60	0.53	8	0.37	4	0.51	8
MRPC	0.76	0.51	5	0.66	8	0.65	7
PAWS	0.26	0.49	10	0.56	10	0.54	10
Quora	0.78	0.50	0	0.52	0	0.46	0
SICK	0.59	0.47	8	0.44	7	0.44	7
StackOverflow	0.94	0.49	3	0.55	2	0.57	3
Stats	0.82	0.43	2	0.49	2	0.53	4
SuperUser	0.91	0.57	5	0.56	4	0.58	3
Unix	0.88	0.56	4	0.55	4	0.59	4

Table 2. Average absolute F1 scores for in-domain and cross-domain performance with domain transfer (DT) and domain adaptation (DA). "In-domain" refers to a model trained and evaluated on the same domain, specified in the first column. DT and DA are results for a model *trained* on other domains (source) and *evaluated* on the domain in the first column (target). For DT and DA, "# of transfer/adaptation successes" is the number of source domains (out of 10) where a model evaluated on target performed at least at 80% of in-domain performance.

scores. Comparing columns "Average F1" with "In-domain average F1", DT and DA performance for most domains is lower than in-domain performance. The exception is PAWS, where DA delivers over twice the performance of in-domain training.

Additionally, for most domains DT and DA resulted in some successes and some failures (mostly between 3 and 8 successes for mSDAR). The exception was, again, PAWS, where all source domains succeeded in DT/DA, and Quora, where none succeeded.

7 Discussion

Adaptation Success Factors. Comparing CPR, Top1, Top3 and Top5 between Success Predictor and Domain Ranker for all DT and DA methods, we see that in general, Domain Ranker does a better job finding the orderings of candidate source domains. For Success Predictor, the features with highest importance are KL-divergence, f_8^{ST}, Target Ratio, f_2^{ST},and data size of the target domain f_4^{ST}. For Domain Ranker, average example lengths, $f_5^{S_1T}$, $f_5^{S_2T}$, Rényi divergences $f_7^{S_1T}$, $f_7^{S_2T}$ and perplexities $f_9^{S_1T}$, $f_9^{S_2T}$ in both source domains are the most informative features.

Adaptation Success by Dataset. While the Success Predictor performed reasonably well on most domains, its performance on PAWS and Quora datasets was miserable. We attribute this to the lack of domain similarity features that would reflect the complexities of these datasets, and note this for future work. The PAWS result can be explained by a representation and training we used (USE and dense neural network), which is different from bag-of-words and BERT used by PAWS authors (Zhang et al., 2019). For Quora, in-domain performance is in line with previous research (Wang et al., 2017, Tomar et al., 2017), and aggregate DT/DA results were similar to other datasets such as Stats.

8 Conclusion and Future Work

We studied the problem of selecting the most relevant labeled datasets from a pool of candidates to be used as a source domain in a transfer learning setup with a specific unlabeled target domain. The experiments focused on the text similarity task and autoencoder approaches to DA. Note that the proposed process can be extended to other NLP tasks and other unsupervised DA approaches as well. We used descriptive domain information and cross-domain similarity metrics as predictive features to model the success of DT and DA, and to rank source domains based on their relevancy.

In future work, we intend to study source selection in *multi-source* domain adaptation setup, using multiple source domains for DT/DA. Identifying additional adaptation success factors that could better predict the success of DT/DA for complex domains such as PAWS and Quora, and learning the success threshold (here, we fixed it at 80%) are other avenues to investigate. Other possibilities include experimenting with various text representations (such as bag-of-words) and models (e.g., Transformer-based).

References

Vincent Van Asch and Walter Daelemans. 2010. Using Domain Similarity for Performance Estimation. In *Proceedings of the 2010 Workshop on Domain Adaptation for Natural Language Processing*, pages 31–36, Uppsala, Sweden.

Daniel Cer, Yinfei Yang, Sheng-yi Kong, Nan Hua, Nicole Limtiaco, Rhomni St John, Noah Constant, Mario Guajardo-Cespedes, Steve Yuan, Chris Tar, Yun-Hsuan Sung, Brian Strope, and Ray Kurzweil. 2018. Universal Sentence Encoder for English. In *Proceedings of the 2018 Conference on Empirical Methods in Natural Language Processing: System Demonstrations*, pages 169-174, Brussels, Belgium.

Minmin Chen, Zhixiang Xu, Kilian Weinberger, and Fei Sha. 2012. Marginalized Denoising Autoencoders for Domain Adaptation. In *Proceedings of the 29th International Conference on Machine Learning*, Edinburgh, Scotland, UK, June. arXiv: 1206.4683.

Stephane Clinchant, Gabriela Csurka, and Boris Chidlovskii. 2016. A Domain Adaptation Regularization for Denoising Autoencoders. In *Proceedings of the 54th Annual Meeting of the Association for Computational Linguistics (Volume 2: Short Papers)*, pages 26–31, Berlin, Germany.

Xiang Dai, Sarvnaz Karimi, Ben Hachey, and Cecile Paris. 2019. Using Similarity Measures to Select Pretraining Data for NER. In *Proceedings of NAACL-HLT*, pages 1460–1470, Minneapolis, Minnesota.

William B Dolan and Chris Brockett. 2005. Automatically Constructing a Corpus of Sentential Paraphrases. In *Proceedings of the Third International Workshop on Paraphrasing (IWP2005)*, page 8.

Yaroslav Ganin, Evgeniya Ustinova, Hana Ajakan, Pascal Germain, Hugo Larochelle, François Laviolette, Mario Marchand, and Victor Lempitsky. 2016. Domain-Adversarial Training of Neural Networks. *Journal of Machine Learning Research*, 17(1), pages 1–35.

Lovedeep Gondara. 2016. Medical image denoising using convolutional denoising autoencoders. *2016.* In *Proceedings of the 16th International Conference on Data Mining Workshops (ICDMW)*. pages 241–246, Barcelona, Spain.

Suchin Gururangan, Ana Marasović, Swabha Swayamdipta, Kyle Lo, Iz Beltagy, Doug Downey, and Noah A. Smith. 2020. Don't Stop Pretraining: Adapt Language Models to Domains and Tasks. In *Proceedings of the 58th Annual Meeting of the Association for Computational Linguistics*, pages 8342–8360.

Abhinav Ramesh Kashyap, Devamanyu Hazarika, Min-Yen Kan, and Roger Zimmermann. 2021. Domain Divergences: a Survey and Empirical Analysis. *arXiv:2010.12198 [cs]*, April. arXiv: 2010.12198.

R. Kneser and H. Ney. 1995. Improved backing-off for M-gram language modeling. In *1995 International Conference on Acoustics, Speech, and Signal Processing*, volume 1, pages 181–184, Detroit, MI, USA.

Wouter M. Kouw and Marco Loog. 2019. An introduction to domain adaptation and transfer learning. Technical report, Delft University of Technology, January. arXiv: 1812.11806.

Yawei Luo, Liang Zheng, Tao Guan, Junqing Yu, and Yi Yang. 2019. Taking a Closer Look at Domain Shift: Category-Level Adversaries for Semantics Consistent Domain Adaptation. In *2019 IEEE/CVF Conference on Computer Vision and Pattern Recognition (CVPR)*, pages 2502–2511, Long Beach, CA, USA.

Lucas Maystre and Matthias Grossglauser. 2017. Just Sort It! A Simple and Effective Approach to Active Preference Learning. In *Proceedings of 34th International Conference on Machine Learning (PMLR), pages 2344-2353,* Sydney, Australia.

Timothy Miller. 2019. Simplified Neural Unsupervised Domain Adaptation. In *Proceedings of the 2019 Conference of the North American Chapter of the Association for Computational Linguistics: Human*

Language Technologies (NAACL-HLT), pages 414–419, Minneapolis, Minnesota.

Lili Mou, Zhao Meng, Rui Yan, Ge Li, Yan Xu, Lu Zhang, and Zhi Jin. 2016. How Transferable are Neural Networks in NLP Applications? In *Proceedings of the 2016 Conference on Empirical Methods in Natural Language Processing*, pages 479–489, Austin, Texas.

Barbara Plank and Gertjan van Noord. 2011. Effective Measures of Domain Similarity for Parsing. In *Proceedings of the 49th Annual Meeting of the Association for Computational Linguistics: Human Language Technologies*, pages 1566–1576, Portland, Oregon, USA.

Alan Ramponi and Barbara Plank. 2020. Neural Unsupervised Domain Adaptation in NLP-A Survey. In *Proceedings of the 28th International Conference on Computational Linguistics*, pages 6838–6855, Barcelona, Spain (Online).

Marco Marelli, Luisa Bentivogli, Marco Baroni, Raffaella Bernardi, Stefano Menini, Roberto Zamparelli, 2014. SemEval-2014 Task 1: Evaluation of compositional distributional semantic models on full sentences through semantic relatedness and textual entailment. In *Proceedings of the 8th International Workshop on Semantic Evaluation (SemEval 2014),* Dublin, Ireland.

Burr Settles. 2010. Active Learning Literature Survey. Technical Report Computer Sciences Technical Report 1648, University of Wisconsin-Madison.

Darsh Shah, Tao Lei, Alessandro Moschitti, Salvatore Romeo, and Preslav Nakov. 2018. Adversarial Domain Adaptation for Duplicate Question Detection. In *Proceedings of the 2018 Conference on Empirical Methods in Natural Language Processing (EMNLP)*, pages 1056–1063, Brussels, Belgium.

Gaurav Singh Tomar, Thyago Duque, Oscar Tackstrom, Jakob Uszkoreit, and Dipanjan Das. 2017. Neural Paraphrase Identification of Questions with Noisy Pretraining. In *Proceedings of the First Workshop on Subword and Character Level Models in NLP*, pages 142–147, Copenhagen, Denmark.

Pascal Vincent, Hugo Larochelle, Isabelle Lajoie, Yoshua Bengio, and Pierre-Antoine Manzagol. 2010. Stacked Denoising Autoencoders: Learning Useful Representations in a Deep Network with a Local Denoising Criterion. *Journal of Machine Learning Research,* 11(12), pages 3371–3408.

Yaqing Wang, Quanming Yao, James Kwok, and Lionel M. Ni. 2020. Generalizing from a Few Examples: A Survey on Few-Shot Learning. *ACM Computing Surveys (CSUR), 53(3),* pages 1-34.

Zhiguo Wang, Hamza Wael, and Florian Radu. 2017. Bilateral multi-perspective matching for natural language sentences, In *Proceedings of the 26th International Joint Conference on Artificial Intelligence (IJCAI),* pages 4144-4150.

Yuan Zhang, Jason Baldridge, and Luheng He. 2019. PAWS: Paraphrase Adversaries from Word Scrambling. In *Proceedings of the 2019 Conference of the North American Chapter of the Association for Computational Linguistics: Human Language Technologies (NAACL-HLT*, pages 1298–1308, Minneapolis, Minnesota.

Syntagmatic Word Embeddings for Unsupervised Learning of Selectional Preferences

Renjith P Ravindran, Akshay Badola and **Kavi Narayana Murthy**
School of Computer and Information Sciences
University of Hyderabad
{rpr,badola}@uohyd.ac.in
knmuh@yahoo.com

Abstract

Selectional Preference (SP) captures the tendency of a word to semantically select other words to be in direct syntactic relation with it, and thus informs us about syntactic word configurations that are meaningful. Therefore SP is a valuable resource for Natural Language Processing (NLP) systems and for semanticists. Learning SP has generally been seen as a supervised task, because it requires a parsed corpus as a source of syntactically related word pairs. In this paper we show that simple distributional analysis can learn a good amount of SP without the need for an annotated corpus. We extend the general word embedding technique with directional word context windows giving word representations that better capture syntagmatic relations. We test on the SP-10K dataset and demonstrate that syntagmatic embeddings outperform the paradigmatic embeddings. We also evaluate supervised version of these embeddings and show that unsupervised syntagmatic embeddings can be as good as supervised embeddings. We also make available the source code of our implementation[1].

1 Introduction

Selectional Preference (SP) (Wilks, 1975) encodes the syntagmatic relatedness between two words. Relations between words are either syntagmatic or paradigmatic (de Saussure, 1916). Two words are said to be paradigmatically related if one word can replace the other in a sentence. Words belonging to a narrow semantic class, such as 'cat', 'dog' can often be substituted with each other in a sentence. Syntagmatic relations are between syntactically related co-occurring words in a sentence. Such word relations encode both syntactic and semantic aspects of words. A *noun* may be modified by an *adjective*, but any particular instance of a noun tends to go more with some adjectives than others. For example *black dog* is more likely than *green dog*. SP deals with such semantic preferences between syntactically related word pairs. Common SP relations include 'adjective-noun', 'subject-verb', 'verb-object'. SP finds use in important NLP tasks like sense disambiguation (Resnik, 1997), semantic role classification (Zapirain et al., 2013), co-reference resolution (Hobbs, 1978; Zhang et al., 2019c), etc.

A computational method to induce SP from instances of syntactically related word pairs in a parsed corpus was introduced by Resnik (1996). In order to generalize to unseen data, this method made use of ontological classes obtained from WordNet (Miller, 1995). Rooth et al. (1999) showed that the dependence on external knowledge resources could be removed by learning the classes from the corpus itself using the EM algorithm. Erk (2007) showed that generalization is also possible via co-occurrence similarity between seen and unseen words. SP models are usually evaluated using the Pseudo-word Disambiguation task (Van de Cruys, 2014) which requires the identification of the more probable dependent word, from a less probable (random) word, given the head word and a syntactic relation. The dataset is generally created from the unseen part of a parsed corpus used for learning the model. Therefore this task measures only how well the model fits the corpus, which may be biased, and not how well it learns SP as perceived by humans. Recently, Zhang et al. (2019b) introduced SP-10K, a dataset for SP evaluation across 5 syntactic relations with a total of 10,000 items each with a human-annotated plausibility score. SP-10K measures the correlation between a model's SP score for a given word pair and the average human score. Therefore it is a better test for SP learning.

[1] https://github.com/renjithravindran/spvec

Proceedings of the 6th Workshop on Representation Learning for NLP (RepL4NLP-2021), pages 213–222
Bangkok, Thailand (Online), August 6, 2021.

The current state-of-the-art on SP-10K is reported by Multiplex Word Embeddings (MWE) (Zhang et al., 2019a). It is a negative sampling based word embedding model, trained on relation-specific word pairs from a parsed corpus. Compared to unsupervised embedding models such as Word2vec (Mikolov et al., 2013) and GloVe (Pennington et al., 2014), MWE provides a substantial boost in SP learning as it has access to syntactic relations. It also improves over D-embeddings (Levy and Goldberg, 2014a) which is a supervised embedding model. However, a dependency-parsed corpus is not readily available in many languages. Therefore the need for an effective unsupervised SP induction technique is palpable in the wider NLP community.

In this work we show that unsupervised word embeddings can easily be extended to get better at learning SP. We do this by taking directional (left/right) word context windows unlike symmetric windows of Word2vec, GloVe, etc. Having directional context windows gives two embeddings per word, one of its left context and other of its right context. This allows us to approximate syntactic relations with directions; all relations that happen to the left of a word are captured by the left embedding and those that happen to the right of a word are captured by the right embedding. Then the cosine similarity between the right embedding of a word and left embedding of another word indicates how likely the two are to be syntagmatically related.

In summary, our contributions are: 1) We provide a simple and effective method to capture selectional preference, called syntagmatic embeddings 2) Demonstrate that syntagmatic embeddings are superior to paradigmatic embeddings 3) We also show that our unsupervised syntagmatic representations can be as good as their supervised counterparts, therefore showing that a good range of SP information can be learned even without a dependency-parsed corpus.

2 Syntagmatic Representation

Symmetric and non-directional context windows in embedding techniques, such as GloVe, relate words that have similar (paradigmatic) contexts. Context words are other words that are in the immediate vicinity of a target word. A symmetric window considers equal number of words on the left and right as context words. Though syntagmatically related words may have similar contexts, a symmetric window tends to encode more of paradigmatic relations. But these paradigmatic embedding spaces do encode syntagmatic properties to a certain degree. For example, we may find that the cosine similarity between 'coffee' and 'cup' is generally greater than 'coffee' and 'car'. These embeddings are considered unsupervised as they are learned from a plain un-annotated corpus. Since their contexts are not dictated by syntactic relations they are generally inferior, at learning SP, compared to an embedding technique that has access to such information (Zhang et al., 2019a). Also, there is no direct way to extract syntagmatically related words. The nearest neighbours of a given word will largely be all paradigmatically related. Though it may include, given a larger context window, associated words ('coffee', 'cup') which have a syntagmatic nature.

2.1 Relations as Directions

Exact learning of SP requires word co-occurrence in a sentence to be defined as a pair of syntactically related words, which is available only in a dependency-parsed corpus. We can obtain a less exact representation for SP by replacing syntactic relations with directions, because in word-ordered languages, word-order or direction plays a major role in assigning syntactic relations. For example in an English sentence, the adjectival modifier of a noun is always found to its left. The nominal subject of a verb is found to its left and direct object to its right. The technique explored here exploits this fact to learn a substantial amount of selectional preference without the need for a large dependency-parsed corpus.

2.2 Unweighted Factorisation Model

Word embeddings are low-rank representations of row/column vectors in a word co-occurrence matrix (Levy and Goldberg, 2014b). Here, we consider unweighted factorisation of a word co-occurrence matrix using Truncated Singular Value Decomposition (SVD) (Kalman, 1996). Let M be the co-occurrence matrix of size $v \times v$, where v is the size of the vocabulary. Instead of a symmetric context window, we use non-symmetric and directional windows, directions being *left* and *right*. Let $M_{i,j}$ be the number of times word i co-occurred to the left of word j within a distance of k throughout the corpus, where k is the size of the co-occurrence window. Consequently, $M_{j,i}$ becomes the number

word	associations
car	**left:** vintage, second-hand, oncoming, luxury, buying, toy, saloon, buy, mercedes...
	right: collided, sped, exploded, maker, skidded, swerved, belonging, makers, roared...
eat	**left:** want, wants, going, wanting, let, tend, ought, let's, allowed, prefer, supposed, able...
	right: salad, beans, soup, cakes, pork, peas, bacon, pasta, fresh, pie, biscuits...
blue	**left:** wore, vivid, dull, wear, luminous, wears, dazzling, plain, dim, dressed, dyed...
	right: scarf, stripe, livery, robe, beret, overalls, blazer, slacks, gloves...
aggressive	**left:** increasingly, extremely, equally, become, very, highly, particularly, becoming...
	right: behaviour, attitude, manner, response, towards, tactics, stance, attack, actions...

Table 1: Examples of word associations from syntagmatic embeddings.

of times word i co-occurred to the right of word j. Thus the row i of matrix M gives the representation of word i using its left context words. And column j gives the representations of word j using its right context words. These two representations are different because our co-occurrence matrix is not symmetric. However, raw co-occurrence representation is very high-dimensional, highly sparse and noisy. A major component of word embedding techniques is dimensionality reduction, by approximating the original co-occurrence matrix with its low-rank representation $\hat{M}$. Dimensionality reduction is found to reduce noise in the data matrix by eliminating the low principle components of the data, thus increasing generalisation. We use Truncated SVD [2] to obtain rank d approximation. Equation 1 gives the factorisation of the matrix M.

$$M \sim \hat{M} = \hat{U}\hat{S}\hat{V}^{\intercal} \tag{1}$$

Where, $\hat{U}_{v\times d}$, $\hat{S}_{d\times d}$, $\hat{V}_{v\times d}$ are the factor matrices (singular vectors and singular values) obtained in SVD as, $M = USV^{\intercal}$, but truncated to keep only the top d principle components. $\hat{U}$ and $\hat{V}$ gives the left context and right context representations of words respectively, in terms of the leading d singular vectors. The singular values $\hat{S}$ gives the relative weightage of corresponding singular vectors, which may be used to scale the singular vectors appropriately. Our word representations are obtained by scaling the singular vectors by an exponential factor of their singular values. Thus, the final left embedding is given as $L = \hat{U}\hat{S}^p$ and the right embedding is $R = \hat{S}^p\hat{V}^{\intercal}$. Caron (2001) showed that the exponential weighting factor p allows for a softer rank selection such that $p > 0$ gives more weightage to the leading components and $p < 0$ gives weightage to the lower components, allowing the fine tuning of embeddings for different tasks. The number of components (dimension), exponential weighting factor, and co-occurrence window size are three important parameters that influence the performance of these embeddings. Our experiments include yet another parameter, the term-weight. So far we have assumed that M contains raw co-occurrence values, or the frequency count of two words to co-occur in the corpus. Various term-weighting schemes can be applied to transform the raw frequencies. We experiment with *log*, *PMI* (Point-wise Mutual Information) and *PPMI* (Positive Point-wise Mutual Information) term-weights along with the raw frequency counts.

[2] *randomized_svd* from *scikit-learn*

2.3 Weighted Factorisation Model

A factorisation model like the one presented in the previous section gives equal weightage to all errors in the low-rank approximation process. It has been shown that weighting errors from each co-occurrence term, by a function of their co-occurrence frequency yields better word embeddings (Levy and Goldberg, 2014b). Neural embedding techniques such as Word2vec do such weighting implicitly (Levy and Goldberg, 2014b), whereas techniques that makes use of co-occurrence matrix, such as GloVe, do this explicitly. For evaluating the performance of weighted factorisation on selectional preference, we minimally modify the GloVe model to get syntagmatic embeddings.

$$\mathbb{L} = \sum_{i,j=1,1}^{V,V} f(M_{i,j})(\mathbf{u}_{w_i}^{\intercal}\mathbf{v}_{w_j} + b_i + b_j - log\, M_{i,j})^2 \tag{2}$$

Equation 2 gives the loss function $\mathbb{L}$ for approximating the *log* co-occurrence with the dot product of the left embedding ($\mathbf{u}_w$) and the right embedding ($\mathbf{v}_w$). M here is the co-occurrence matrix and b_i, b_j are bias terms. With symmetric context, the final embeddings in the GloVe model are either just the left embeddings or the sum of left and right embeddings. But with asymmetric context, left and right embeddings are used distinctly. The weighting function (f) is given by equation 3.

$$f(x) = \begin{cases} (x/x_{max})^{\frac{3}{4}}, & \text{if } x < x_{max} \\ 1, & \text{otherwise} \end{cases} \quad (3)$$

x_{max} is generally taken as 100. GloVe's weighting function mainly reduces the influence of rarely co-occurring words which tend to be noisy.

2.4 Syntagmatic Association

Let $\overleftarrow{l_i}$ be the left embedding of word i , i.e. i^{th} row of L, and $\overrightarrow{r_j}$ be the right embedding of word j, i.e the jth column of R. Since $\overrightarrow{r_j}$ reflects the right context of word j and $\overleftarrow{l_i}$ reflects the left context of word i, similarity between $\overrightarrow{r_j}$ and $\overleftarrow{l_i}$ would reflect how often word j is found to the left of word i. Thus cosine similarity between $\overrightarrow{r}_j$ and $\overleftarrow{l_i}$ captures the association of word j to the left of word i, and the association of word i to the right of word j.

Table 1 gives few examples of left and right associations from syntagmatic embeddings. These examples have been filtered to remove words that tend to appear as both left and right associates. Let **l** and **r** be the set of left associates and right associates of a given word in the embedding space, then the examples given here are $\mathbf{l} - \mathbf{r}$ (left) and $\mathbf{r} - \mathbf{l}$ (right). We see that the left associates of a noun (car) tends to have adjectives (vintage) and verbs (buy) that take the noun as its direct object. Right associates of the noun are found to be verbs (collided) that take the noun as its subject. With a verb (eat) we see that its left associates are other verbs (want) to which the given verb is an open clausal component. The right associates are its direct objects (salad). With an adjective (blue) we see that its left associates are other adjectives (vivid) that act as intensifiers and verbs (wore) whose direct objects are modified by the given adjective. The right associates are nouns (scarf) that are modified by the adjective.

3 SP Evaluation

Examples of word association in the previous section gives a qualitative feel about the degree to which syntagmatic embeddings can capture selectional preference. In the next section we follow this up with detailed analysis using quantitative studies.

	head	dependent	human-score
amod	air	fresh	9.7
	number	medium	4.0
	wind	secret	0.7
dobj	eat	meal	10.0
	touch	food	5.5
	eat	mail	0.0
nsubj	sing	singer	10.0
	pray	woman	5.8
	eat	textbook	0.0

Table 2: Samples from SP-10K dataset.

3.1 Dataset

We use the SP-10K (Zhang et al., 2019b) dataset to quantify the correlation of between the SP information learned by our syntagmatic embeddings and that of human judgements. Other datasets with human scores for SP are McRae et al. (1998); Keller and Lapata (2003); Padó et al. (2006). But compared to SP-10K these are much smaller in size. SP-10K has 3 direct relations and 2 indirect relations. For our evaluation we only use the direct relations – **amod**, **nsubj** and **dobj**. In SP-10K there are 2000 evaluation instances under each relation class. Each instance is a triplet (*word1*, *word2*, *human-score*), where *word1* is the head and *word2* is a dependent, and *human-score* gives the plausibility of *word2* being dependent on *word1*, via the given relation, as judged by humans on a 0-10 scale. For **amod** relation, a noun is the head and an adjective is the dependent. For **nsubj** and **dobj** a verb is the head and a noun is the dependent. Table 2 gives some examples from the dataset. The model's capacity for SP is judged by the correlation (Spearman's) between the association score given by the model and the human-score. The model-score for a given head-dependent pair is the cosine similarity between the head and the dependent in the embedding space.

Since the syntagmatic embeddings relegate relations to left and right directions, the cosine similarity for each of the relations are computed as: **amod**: $\overrightarrow{r_d} \cdot \overleftarrow{l_h}$, **nsubj**: $\overrightarrow{r_d} \cdot \overleftarrow{l_h}$, **dobj**: $\overrightarrow{r_h} \cdot \overleftarrow{l_d}$, where subscript h and d denotes head and dependent words respectively, and symbol '$\cdot$' denotes cosine similarity.

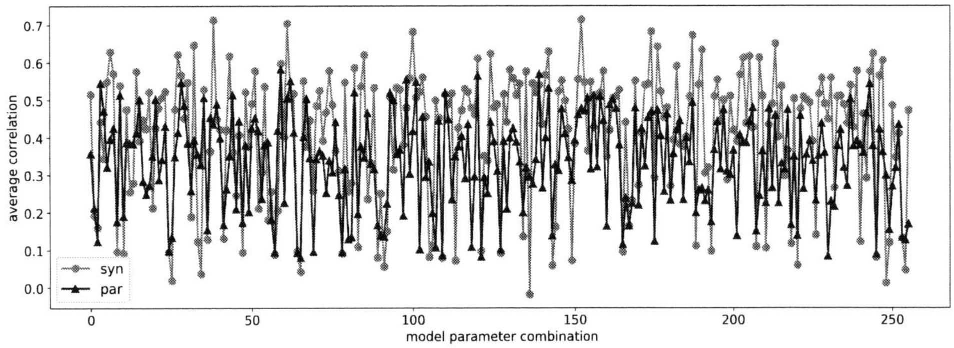

Figure 1: Average correlation of syntagmatic and paradigmatic models over various parameter combinations.

3.2 Baseline Models

We compare our syntagmatic model with 3 paradigmatic models: Word2vec (Mikolov et al., 2013), GloVe (Pennington et al., 2014) and DSG (Song et al., 2018). Both Word2vec (w2v) and GloVe (glove) are typical paradigmatic embeddings. DSG (Directional Skip-Gram) is a variant of Word2vec that claims to encode directional information by predicting the co-occurring words and also their directions. However, unlike syntagmatic embeddings DSG gives only one embedding per word. The best reported supervised model on SP-10K is Multiplex Word Embeddings (MWE). However, we could not use [3] the available implementation[4] for our experiments. Older supervised models for SP, that are not based on embeddings, have been previously evaluated on SP-10K (Zhang et al., 2019a), therefore we do not include those here.

3.3 Corpus

We use the British National Corpus (BNC-Consortium, 2007) as the source for word co-occurrences for the embeddings. Since BNC is sentence segmented, our co-occurrence counting never jumps across a sentence. The word casing is normalized to *small*, punctuations are removed, and the vocabulary is limited to words occurring at least 100 times in the corpus.

4 Experiments

In the following experiments, we compare our syntagmatic embeddings with its paradigmatic counterpart, identify its best parameters, distinguish weighted from unweighted factorisation, evaluate against baseline embeddings and test how our unsupervised SP learning method compares with a supervised model. The parameters involved in the factorisation of the word co-occurrence matrix are: 1) size of the co-occurrence window (**ws**), 2) term-weight or the co-occurrence weighting function (**tw**), 3) dimensionality of the embedding space or the number of principle components (**dim**), and 4) the exponential weight on singular values (**p**).

We experiment with the following parameter values: **ws**=[1, 2, 3, 4], **dim**=[20, 50, 100, 300], **p**=[-0.5, 0, 0.5, 1], **tw**=[*raw*, *log*, *pmi*, *ppmi*]. In term-weights *raw* denotes the co-occurrence frequency of the word as it is , *log* is the log_2 of the raw co-occurrence frequency, *pmi* is the point-wise mutual information given by equation 4 where subscript '*' stands for a summation across a particular axis, and *ppmi* is the positive-only variant of *pmi* as given by equation 5.

$$PMI_{i,j} = log\frac{M_{i,j}\, M_{*,*}}{M_{i,*}\, M_{*,j}} \quad (4)$$

$$PPMI_{i,j} = max(0, PMI_{i,j}) \quad (5)$$

4.1 Syntagmatic Vs Paradigmatic

In our first experiment we compare syntagmatic representation to paradigmatic representation. Here we consider only the unweighted factorisation model. The paradigmatic model is similar to the syntagmatic model described in section 2.2, but has a context window that is symmetric and non-directional. To get a more realistic picture of these methods, we compare a cohort of syntagmatic and paradigmatic models that have different parameter values. Each of the 4 parameters have 4 chosen parameter values. Since each parameter value combination gives us a different model, we get a total of 256 syntagmatic and 256 paradigmatic models.

[3]it runs only on a given prepackaged corpus, we found it difficult to replicate their packaging for our corpus

[4]https://github.com/HKUST-KnowComp/MWE

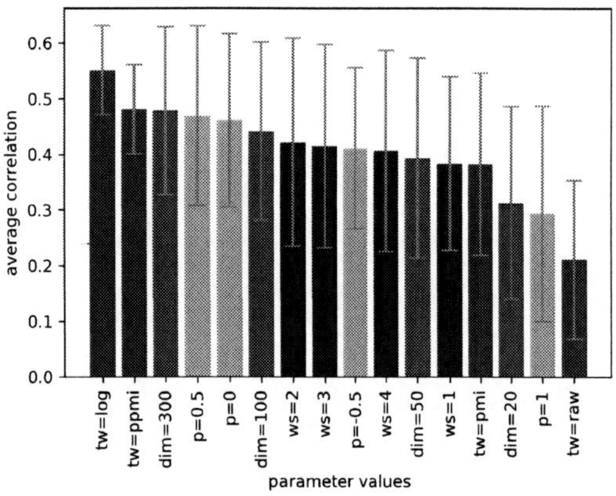

Figure 2: Average correlation (with standard deviation) in syntagmatic models that have the same parameter-value.

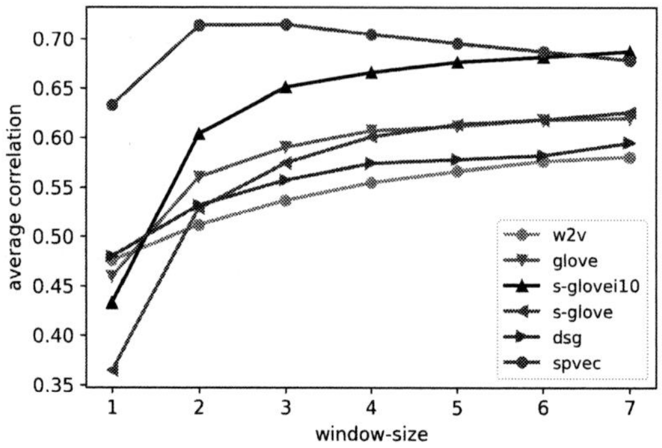

Figure 3: Average correlation of weighted and unweighted models with varying window sizes.

For each model (parameter-value combination) we compute the average correlation over the 3 SP relations. We see that in 69% of the total parameter instances the syntagmatic model is better than paradigmatic model. In those instances, on average the syntagmatic model improves the correlation by 0.14 points, which is an improvement of 54%. The maximum correlation obtained by a syntagmatic model is 0.71 and by the paradigmatic model is 0.58.

Figure 1 shows two line plots for the average correlation values of syntagmatic and paradigmatic embeddings. Each particular parameter-value combination is a value on the x-axis, for which the there are two correlation values on the y-axis; one of the syntagmatic model and the other of the paradigmatic model. Apart from showing that syntagmatic models are generally better than paradigmatic models, it shows that certain parameter combinations give syntagmatic models a much greater advantage. On the downside we see that for a good number of poorly performing paradigmatic models their, syntagmatic counterpart performed even worse. There are also certain pathological parameter combinations that substantially pull down syntagmatic representations compared to corresponding paradigmatic representation. But overall, this experiment shows that syntagmatic embeddings are substantially better at capturing SP.

4.2 Parameter Impact

In our second experiment we try to understand the relative importance of each parameter-value. For this we look at all 256 syntagmatic models and compute the mean and standard deviation of the correlation score among those models that have a particular parameter-value. For example we take the parameter-value **tw=***log* and look at all syntagmatic models with that particular parameter-value, and compute the mean and standard deviation of their correlation score. We do the same with all 16 parameter-values.

Figure 2 gives the results of this experiment. We see that term-weight is the most important parameter, and **tw=***log* the most significant parameter-value. No matter what the other parameters values are, using *log* as the term-weight gives on average a correlation score of 0.55 ± 0.07. Further, we see that the dimensionality of the embedding space is the next most significant parameter. Here we see that higher values are better, but this is only because we didn't consider even higher[5] values in this experiment (>300). It is well understood that there is an optimal dimension which is task and corpus dependent, below which a model does not have enough capacity, and above which the model tends to pick up noise (Yin and Shen, 2018). A more interesting aspect is the significance of the exponential weighting factor p. The SVD factorizes the co-occurrence matrix as $M = USV^\intercal$, which can be factored into left and right components as $M = [US^{\frac{1}{2}}][S^{\frac{1}{2}}V^\intercal]$. We see that **p=***0.5* is indeed the right[5] value for the exponential weight factor.

4.3 Influence of Weighted Factorisation

To understand the influence of weighted factorisation on syntagmatic embeddings, we compare the syntagmatic GloVe (**s-glove**) model, introduced in section 2.3 to our SVD based unweighted fac-

[5]See figure 5 in appendix

torisation model. We choose our best performing SVD based syntagmatic model (**tw**=*log*, **dim**=*300*, **p**=*0.5*) naming it **spvec**. We also test the SkipGram Word2vec (**w2v**) and GloVe (**glove**), for providing a comparison with popular paradigmatic models, and DSG to compare against a model with directional information. Embedding sizes in all models are 300, and window-sizes 1 to 7 are evaluated. Other parameters of **dsg**, **s-glove**, **glove**, **w2v** are kept to the default values in their respective implementations.

Figure 3 shows the results of the experiment. We find that our SVD based unweighted syntagmatic model outperforms all other models, including the weighted syntagmatic model based on GloVe. The **s-glove** model performed slightly worse than the paradigmatic glove (**glove**) model under low window-sizes. We tried increasing the number of iterations in the training process, from the default 5 to 10. The resulting model (**s-glovei10**) performed much better than than paradigmatic GloVe model. It is interesting to note that all weighted models behave similarly to increasing window-sizes. They perform better as window-sizes increase. Whereas, our SVD based unweighted model (**spvec**) gives a better performance at window-size 2 and 3 and gradually decreases in performance as window-size is further increased. The directional variant of Word2vec (**dsg**) performs better than Word2vec, but performs poorly compared to **spvec**. Comparing **s-glovei10** and **spvec**, we see that even at much higher window-size of 15 (not shown in figure 3), **s-glovei10** barely reaches an average correlation of 0.69. **spvec** on the other hand gets an average correlation 0.71 at a much smaller window-sizes (2 and 3).

4.4 Comparison to Supervised Models

Our syntagmatic word embedding model aims to provide an effective method to approach selectional preference in the absence of a parsed corpus. In this experiment we assess how deficient our unsupervised model is when compared to supervised models. Since we were not able to use the available implementation of MWE, we simply compare our unsupervised syntagmatic model (**spvec**) with supervised versions of itself. The supervised version of syntagmatic embeddings is obtained by defining word co-occurrence as a pair of words related by a dependency relation. For this we parse our corpus (BNC) using the Stanford dependency parser (Qi et al., 2020). In order to remain compatible with a syntagmatic model, we maintain word ordering of the co-occurrences. For example, the sentence 'big cat ate rat' gives three co-occurrences where the head and the dependent are ordered as they are found in the sentence: 'big cat', 'cat ate' and 'ate rat'. We test two supervised models 1) **spvec-s**: which uses all dependency related word pairs 2) **spvec-sr**: which uses only related word pairs in a particular dependency relation. **spvec-sr** thus has 3 distinct embedding pairs (left/right) per word, an embedding pair for each of the tested dependency relation: *amod*, *nsubj*, *dobj*. For comparison we also show the results of unsupervised paradigmatic models.

model	amod	nsubj	dobj	AVG
w2v	0.582	0.489	0.539	0.536
glove	0.694	0.489	0.587	0.590
dsg	0.625	0.490	0.556	0.557
s-glovei10	0.738	0.565	0.649	0.650
spvec	**0.750**	**0.654**	**0.738**	**0.714**
spvec-s	0.761	0.637	0.740	0.712
spvec-sr	0.757	0.653	0.741	0.717

Table 3: Spearman's correlation for supervised and unsupervised models on the SP-10K dataset.

Table 3 gives the results of this experiment. Surprisingly we see that our unsupervised model (**spvec**) is as good as its supervised counterparts (**spvec-s** and **spvec-sr**). The model trained on all dependency related word pairs scores lower than the fully unsupervised model. The model with relation specific embeddings improves on the fully unsupervised model only by a meager 0.4%. We clearly see that unsupervised syntagmatic embeddings are not deficient but may be as good as supervised models.

5 Related Work

There have been previous studies that explored Syntagmatic representations. Rapp (2002); Sahlgren (2006) viewed syntagmatic representations as first-order word co-occurrence statistics, and paradigmatic representations as second-order statistics. First-order models represent words using text units in which they appear. Text units are generally documents or large regions of text, like paragraphs. Thus, first order statistics come from a word-document co-occurrence matrix, whereas paradig-

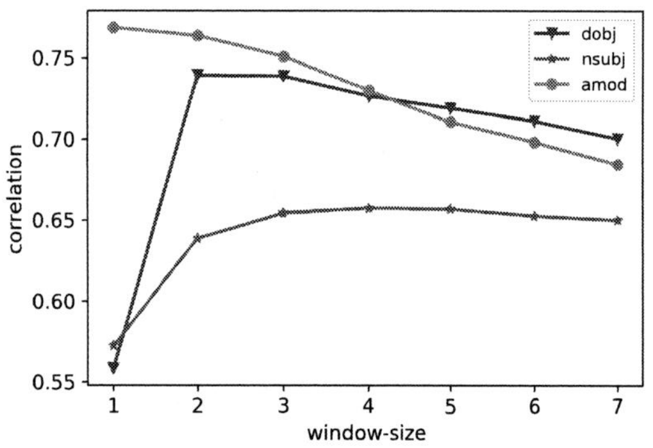

Figure 4: Window-size preferences of **spvec** for different relations.

matic representations come from word-word co-occurrence matrix and hence called second order. While their evaluation of paradigmatic representation as second-order statistics was appropriate, their claim of syntagmatic representation as first-order statistics is not well justified. This is because the evaluation datasets they used for first-order models were a mix of (mostly) paradigmatic and syntagmatic relations, and not purely syntagmatic. A large-scale study by Lapesa et al. (2014) showed that fine-tuned second-order statistics can capture both syntagmatic and paradigmatic relations. Different parametrisations, mainly window size and dimensionality reduction, were shown to adapt the second-order statistics to either relations accordingly.

The notion of syntagmatic representation explored in our work is adapted from Schütze and Pedersen (1993), in which the syntagmatic representation is introduced qualitatively without resorting to any quantitative studies. Our study on the other hand applies syntagmatic representation to the task of selectional preference, exploring various model parametrisations.

6 Discussion

Our experiments have shown that a weakly structured model can be as good as a strongly structured model. The **spvec** model, though unsupervised, incorporates a simple linguistically motivated bias/structure – directionality or word order. Such a weakly biased model, when coupled with low-rank embedding process, seems to pickup appropriate linguistic structure by effectively getting rid of noise. But why did the supervised models not have a bigger advantage when compared to the unsupervised model? We can hypothesize that words that are not directly related by a dependency relation but are in the vicinity of a target word make substantial contribution to the semantics of the word which may not be captured by a dependency-parsed model. It can also be because the low-rank embedding process is as good at removing noise as a dependency parse. A closer look at the results reveal that *amod* and *dobj* relations do benefit from supervision, although it is minor. The effect of window-size on each of the dependency relation, may help us to better understand this (figure 4). In the unsupervised model, *amod* relation is maximized with a window-size of 1, but the results reported in table 3 are of window-size 3. Certainly, the excess window-size will result in noise which may be mitigated by a dependency parse, as seen in the results of supervised models. Similarly, *dobj* relation which is maximized in the unsupervised model at window-size of 4 also benefits from the dependency parse. However, the case of *nsubj* relation does not fit this reasoning. *nsubj* is maximized in the unsupervised model at a window-size of 2, but even at window-size 3 it improves over the supervised model. Here we may have to consider the possibility that, words that are not directly related may contribute to the semantics, which is lost in a dependency-parsed model. We would also like to point out that parsing a large corpus can be resource intensive. Parsing the BNC consumed about 24 GPU[6] hours. However, our experiments show that the gains derived do not substantiate the compute incurred. The unsupervised **spvec** model performs the factorisation in less than 5 minutes on a 20-core CPU.

Weighted factorisation of word co-occurrences is generally found to produce high quality word embeddings. Previously such embeddings showed improvements in tasks such as word similarity and solving word analogies. But we have shown that, when it comes to selectional preference and syntagmatic embeddings, weighted factorisation may be detrimental.

We also observe that appropriate co-occurrence term-weights are crucial for the performance. *PPMI* has been shown to work well for tasks that test paradigmatic nature such as word similarity (Bullinaria and Levy, 2007). Pennington et al. (2014) remarked that *log* is better for solving word

[6]Nvidia RTX 2080 GPU

analogies than *PPMI*. Our experiments show that *log* is also valuable for learning selectional preference.

Here we have tested our syntagmatic embeddings only on English, but it should be directly applicable to other word-ordered languages also.

7 Conclusion

In this paper, we have introduced syntagmatic word embeddings, a simple and effective method, for learning selectional preference (SP). Our model is simple because it captures SP by direct factorisation of a word co-occurrence matrix. We have showed that by incorporating a weak linguistic bias of directionality as a proxy for syntactic relations, our model can be made as effective as a model with access to syntactic relations. This is important because SP has always been seen as a task that requires a dependency-parsed corpus, our work shows that it need not be the case.

We hope that syntagmatic embeddings will be a valuable source of selectional preference information for resource-poor as well as resource-rich languages. We also hope that the structural bias of directionality will be further explored in simple models for other NLP tasks, instead of relying on models that are complex and opaque to interpretation.

Acknowledgement

Renjith P Ravindran is funded by Department of Science and Technology (DST), Government of India, under the Inspire Fellowship Programme.

References

BNC-Consortium. 2007. The british national corpus, version 3 (bnc xml edition). Bodleian Libraries, University of Oxford. Http://www.natcorp.ox.ac.uk/.

John A. Bullinaria and Joseph P. Levy. 2007. Extracting semantic representations from word cooccurrence statistics: A computational study. *Behavior Research Methods*, pages 510–526.

John Caron. 2001. *Experiments with LSA Scoring: Optimal Rank and Basis*, page 157–169. Society for Industrial and Applied Mathematics, USA.

Tim Van de Cruys. 2014. A neural network approach to selectional preference acquisition. In *Proceedings of the 2014 Conference on Empirical Methods in Natural Language Processing (EMNLP)*, pages 26–35, Doha, Qatar. Association for Computational Linguistics.

Katrin Erk. 2007. A simple, similarity-based model for selectional preferences. In *Proceedings of the 45th Annual Meeting of the Association of Computational Linguistics*, pages 216–223, Prague, Czech Republic. Association for Computational Linguistics.

Jerry R. Hobbs. 1978. Resolving pronoun references. *Lingua*, 44(4):311–338.

Dan Kalman. 1996. A singularly valuable decomposition: The svd of a matrix. *The College Mathematics Journal*, 27(1):2–23.

Frank Keller and Mirella Lapata. 2003. Using the web to obtain frequencies for unseen bigrams. *Comput. Linguist.*, 29(3):459–484.

Gabriella Lapesa, Stefan Evert, and Sabine Schulte im Walde. 2014. Contrasting syntagmatic and paradigmatic relations: Insights from distributional semantic models. In *Proceedings of the Third Joint Conference on Lexical and Computational Semantics (*SEM 2014)*, pages 160–170, Dublin, Ireland. Association for Computational Linguistics and Dublin City University.

Omer Levy and Yoav Goldberg. 2014a. Dependency-based word embeddings. In *Proceedings of the 52nd Annual Meeting of the Association for Computational Linguistics (Volume 2: Short Papers)*, pages 302–308. Association for Computational Linguistics.

Omer Levy and Yoav Goldberg. 2014b. Neural word embedding as implicit matrix factorization. In *Proceedings of the 27th International Conference on Neural Information Processing Systems - Volume 2*, NIPS'14, pages 2177–2185, Cambridge, MA, USA. MIT Press.

Ken McRae, Michael J Spivey-Knowlton, and Michael K Tanenhaus. 1998. Modeling the influence of thematic fit (and other constraints) in on-line sentence comprehension. *Journal of Memory and Language*, 38(3):283–312.

Tomas Mikolov, Ilya Sutskever, Kai Chen, Greg S Corrado, and Jeff Dean. 2013. Distributed representations of words and phrases and their compositionality. In C. J. C. Burges, L. Bottou, M. Welling, Z. Ghahramani, and K. Q. Weinberger, editors, *Advances in Neural Information Processing Systems 26*, pages 3111–3119. Curran Associates, Inc.

George A. Miller. 1995. Wordnet: A lexical database for english. *Commun. ACM*, 38(11):39–41.

Ulrike Padó, Frank Keller, and Matthew W Crocker. 2006. Combining syntax and thematic fit in a probabilistic model of sentence processing. In *Proceedings of the 28th CogSci*, pages 657–662.

Jeffrey Pennington, Richard Socher, and Christopher Manning. 2014. Glove: Global vectors for word representation. In *Proceedings of the 2014 conference on empirical methods in natural language processing (EMNLP)*, pages 1532–1543.

Peng Qi, Yuhao Zhang, Yuhui Zhang, Jason Bolton, and Christopher D. Manning. 2020. Stanza: A Python natural language processing toolkit for many human languages. In *Proceedings of the 58th Annual Meeting of the Association for Computational Linguistics: System Demonstrations*.

Reinhard Rapp. 2002. The computation of word associations: Comparing syntagmatic and paradigmatic approaches. In *COLING 2002: The 19th International Conference on Computational Linguistics*.

Philip Resnik. 1996. Selectional constraints: An information-theoretic model and its computational realization. *Cognition*, 61(1-2):127–159.

Philip Resnik. 1997. Selectional preference and sense disambiguation. In *Tagging Text with Lexical Semantics: Why, What, and How?*

Mats Rooth, Stefan Riezler, Detlef Prescher, Glenn Carroll, and Franz Beil. 1999. Inducing a semantically annotated lexicon via em-based clustering. In *Proceedings of the 37th Annual Meeting of the Association for Computational Linguistics on Computational Linguistics*, ACL '99, page 104–111, USA. Association for Computational Linguistics.

Magnus Sahlgren. 2006. *The Word-Space Model: Using distributional analysis to represent syntagmatic and paradigmatic relations between words in high-dimensional vector spaces*. Ph.D. thesis, Institutionen för lingvistik, Stockholm University.

Ferdinand de Saussure. 1916. *Cours de linguistique générale*. Payot, Paris.

Hinrich Schütze and Jan Pedersen. 1993. A vector model for syntagmatic and paradigmatic relatedness. In *Making Sense of Words - Ninth Annual Conference of the UW Centre for the New OED and Text Re- search*, pages 104–113.

Yan Song, Shuming Shi, Jing Li, and Haisong Zhang. 2018. Directional skip-gram: Explicitly distinguishing left and right context for word embeddings. In *Proceedings of the 2018 Conference of the North American Chapter of the Association for Computational Linguistics: Human Language Technologies, Volume 2 (Short Papers)*, pages 175–180, New Orleans, Louisiana. Association for Computational Linguistics.

Y. Wilks. 1975. A preferential, pattern-seeking, semantics for natural language inference. *Artif. Intell.*, 6:53–74.

Zi Yin and Yuanyuan Shen. 2018. On the dimensionality of word embedding. In S. Bengio, H. Wallach, H. Larochelle, K. Grauman, N. Cesa-Bianchi, and R. Garnett, editors, *Advances in Neural Information Processing Systems 31*, pages 887–898. Curran Associates, Inc.

Beñat Zapirain, Eneko Agirre, Lluís Màrquez, and Mihai Surdeanu. 2013. Selectional preferences for semantic role classification. *Computational Linguistics*, 39(3):631–663.

Hongming Zhang, Jiaxin Bai, Yan Song, Kun Xu, Changlong Yu, Yangqiu Song, Wilfred Ng, and Dong Yu. 2019a. Multiplex word embeddings for selectional preference acquisition. In *Proceedings of the 2019 Conference on Empirical Methods in Natural Language Processing and the 9th International Joint Conference on Natural Language Processing (EMNLP-IJCNLP)*, pages 5247–5256, Hong Kong, China. Association for Computational Linguistics.

Hongming Zhang, Hantian Ding, and Yangqiu Song. 2019b. SP-10K: A large-scale evaluation set for selectional preference acquisition. In *Proceedings of the 57th Annual Meeting of the Association for Computational Linguistics*, pages 722–731, Florence, Italy. Association for Computational Linguistics.

Hongming Zhang, Yan Song, and Yangqiu Song. 2019c. Incorporating context and external knowledge for pronoun coreference resolution. In *Proceedings of the 2019 Conference of the North American Chapter of the Association for Computational Linguistics: Human Language Technologies, Volume 1 (Long and Short Papers)*, pages 872–881, Minneapolis, Minnesota. Association for Computational Linguistics.

A Detailed Parameter Study

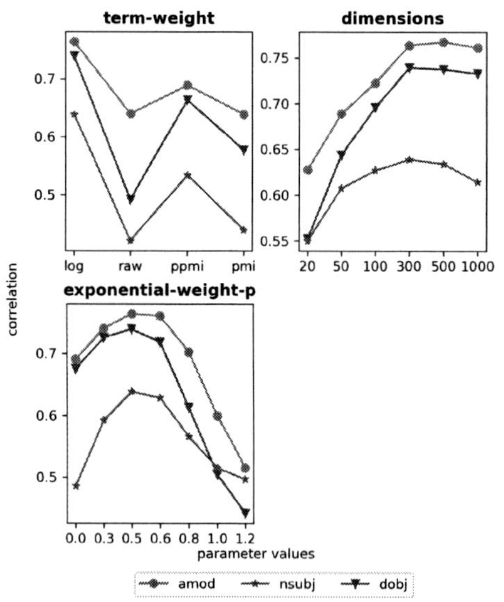

Figure 5: Variations in SP correlation of **spvec** on each relation with variations in parameter-values of term-weight, dimensions, and exponential-weight-p. Variations in window-size are shown in figure 4.

Bayesian Model-Agnostic Meta-Learning with Matrix-Valued Kernels for Quality Estimation

Abiola Obamuyide[1] **Marina Fomicheva**[1] **Lucia Specia**[1,2]
[1]Department of Computer Science, University of Sheffield
[2]Department of Computing, Imperial College London
United Kingdom
{a.obamuyide,m.fomicheva,l.specia}@sheffield.ac.uk

Abstract

Most current quality estimation (QE) models for machine translation are trained and evaluated in a fully supervised setting requiring significant quantities of labelled training data. However, obtaining labelled data can be both expensive and time-consuming. In addition, the test data that a deployed QE model would be exposed to may differ from its training data in significant ways. In particular, training samples are often labelled by one or a small set of annotators, whose perceptions of translation quality and needs may differ substantially from those of end-users, who will employ predictions in practice. Thus, it is desirable to be able to adapt QE models efficiently to new user data with limited supervision data. To address these challenges, we propose a Bayesian meta-learning approach for adapting QE models to the needs and preferences of each user with limited supervision. To enhance performance, we further propose an extension to a state-of-the-art Bayesian meta-learning approach which utilizes a matrix-valued kernel for Bayesian meta-learning of quality estimation. Experiments on data with varying number of users and language characteristics demonstrates that the proposed Bayesian meta-learning approach delivers improved predictive performance in both limited and full supervision settings.

1 Introduction

Quality Estimation (QE) models aim to evaluate the output of Machine Translation (MT) systems at run-time, when no reference translations are available (Blatz et al., 2004; Specia et al., 2009). QE models can be applied for instance to improve translation productivity by selecting high-quality translations amongst several candidates. A number of approaches have been proposed for this task (Specia et al., 2009, 2015; Kim et al., 2017; Kepler et al., 2019; Ranasinghe et al., 2020), and a shared task yearly benchmarks proposed approaches (Fonseca et al., 2019; Specia et al., 2020).

Different users of MT output have varying quality needs and standards, depending for instance on the downstream task at hand, or the level of their knowledge of the languages involved. Thus, the perception of the quality of MT output can be subjective, and therefore the quality estimates obtained from a model trained on data from one set of users may not serve the needs of a different set of users. In order to be able to make the most of these models, it is thus desirable to be able to efficiently adapt them to the needs and preferences of the end-user and with as little supervision as possible. However, most existing QE models are trained and evaluated in a fully supervised setting which assumes access to substantial quantities of labelled supervision data, which may not be available and can be expensive and time-consuming to obtain.

In order to endow QE models with the ability to learn to adapt efficiently with limited supervision data, this work proposes a Bayesian meta-learning framework for the training and evaluation of QE models that are able to adapt to the needs of end-users with limited supervision data. We further improve the performance of Bayesian meta-learning for the task of quality estimation by extending the state-of-the-art Bayesian Model-Agnostic Meta-Learning (BMAML) approach of Kim et al. (2018) to utilize Stein Variational Gradient Descent (Liu and Wang, 2016) with matrix-valued kernels (Wang et al., 2019), and demonstrate that this leads to enhanced predictive performance in both limited and full supervision settings.

2 Background

2.1 Model-Agnostic Meta-Learning

The goal of meta-learning, also known as learning to learn (Schmidhuber, 1987; Thrun and Pratt,

Proceedings of the 6th Workshop on Representation Learning for NLP (RepL4NLP-2021), pages 223–230
Bangkok, Thailand (Online), August 6, 2021.

1998), is to develop models that can learn more efficiently over time, by generalizing from knowledge of how to solve related tasks from a given distribution of tasks. Given a learner model $f_{\boldsymbol{w}}$, for instance a neural network parametrized by $\boldsymbol{w} \in \mathbb{R}^d$, and a distribution $p(\mathcal{T})$ over tasks $\mathcal{T}$, gradient-based model-agnostic meta-learning approaches such as *MAML* (Finn et al., 2017) seek to learn the parameters of the learner model which can be quickly adapted to new tasks sampled from the same distribution of tasks with limited supervision data.

In formal terms, these approaches seek parameters $\boldsymbol{w}$ that satisfy the meta-objective:

$$\min_{\boldsymbol{w}} \mathbb{E}_{\mathcal{T}\sim p(\mathcal{T})} \left[\mathcal{L}_{\mathcal{T}} \left(\mathcal{U}_k \left(\boldsymbol{w}; \mathcal{D}_{\mathcal{T}}\right)\right)\right], \tag{1}$$

where $\mathcal{L}_{\mathcal{T}}$ is the loss and $\mathcal{D}_{\mathcal{T}}$ is training data from task $\mathcal{T}$, and $\mathcal{U}_k$ denotes k steps of a gradient descent learning rule such as SGD.

Intuitively, the meta-objective explicitly encourages the model to learn model parameters that can be quickly adapted to achieve optimum predictive performance across all tasks using limited supervision data and with as few gradient descent steps as possible.

In order to account for uncertainty and improve robustness, Bayesian approaches to meta-learning have also been proposed (Kim et al., 2018; Finn et al., 2018; Ravi and Beatson, 2019; Wang et al., 2020; Nguyen et al., 2020). In contrast to their non-Bayesian counterparts which learn point estimates of the parameters, Bayesian meta-learning approaches learn a distribution over the parameters to further improve robustness in limited supervision settings.

2.2 Stein Variational Gradient Descent

Stein Variational Gradient Descent (SVGD)(Liu and Wang, 2016) is a Bayesian inference method which works by initializing a set of samples, also known as particles, from a simple distribution and iteratively updating the particles to match samples from a target distribution. Because its particle update rule is deterministic and differentiable, it can be used to perform Bayesian inference in the meta-learning inner loop, since the entire update process can still be differentiated through for gradient-based updates from the outer loop, for instance as was done in Kim et al. (2018).

In order to obtain N samples from a posterior $p(\boldsymbol{w})$, SVGD maintains N samples of model parameters, and iteratively transports the samples to match samples from the target distribution. Let the samples be represented by $W = \{\boldsymbol{w}^n\}_{n=1}^N$. At each successive iteration t, SVGD updates each sample with the following update rule:

$$\boldsymbol{w}_{t+1} \leftarrow \boldsymbol{w}_t + \alpha_t \phi\left(\boldsymbol{w}_t\right), \tag{2}$$

where $\phi\left(\boldsymbol{w}_t\right) =$

$$\frac{1}{N}\sum_{n=1}^{N}\left[k\left(\boldsymbol{w}_t^n, \boldsymbol{w}_t\right)\nabla_{\boldsymbol{w}_t^n}\log p\left(\boldsymbol{w}_t^n\right) + \nabla_{\boldsymbol{w}_t^n} k\left(\boldsymbol{w}_t^n, \boldsymbol{w}_t\right)\right], \tag{3}$$

α_t is a step-size parameter and $k : \mathbb{R}^d \times \mathbb{R}^d \to \mathbb{R}$ is a scalar-valued positive-definite kernel such as the Radial Basis Function (RBF) kernel. Intuitively, the first term in Equation 3 implies that a particle determines its update direction through a weighted aggregate of the gradients from the other particles, with the kernel distance between the particles serving as the weight. Thus, closer particles have more weight in the aggregate. The second term of the equation can be understood as a repulsive force that prevents the particles from collapsing to a single point. For the case when the number of particles is one, the SVGD update procedure reduces to standard gradient ascent on the objective $p(\boldsymbol{w})$ for any kernel with the property $\nabla_{\boldsymbol{w}} k\left(\boldsymbol{w}, \boldsymbol{w}\right) = 0$, such as the RBF kernel. SVGD has been applied in a wide range of settings, including reinforcement learning (Liu et al., 2017; Haarnoja et al., 2017), uncertainty quantification (Zhu and Zabaras, 2018), and online continual learning (Obamuyide et al., 2021).

2.3 Stein Variational Gradient Descent with Matrix-Valued Kernels

Let $\mathcal{H}_k$ denote a reproducing kernel Hilbert space (RKHS) $\mathcal{H}$ with kernel k. Wang et al. (2019) observed that the original SVGD as proposed in Liu and Wang (2016) searches for the optimal update direction ϕ in RKHS $\mathcal{H}_k^d = \mathcal{H}_k \times \cdots \times \mathcal{H}_k$, a product of d copies of RKHS of scalar-valued functions, which does not allow the encoding of any potential correlations between different co-ordinates of ϕ. Wang et al. (2019) proposed *Matrix-SVGD*, which addressed this limitation by replacing $\mathcal{H}_k^d$ with a more general RKHS of vector-valued functions (also known as vector-valued RKHS), which uses *matrix-valued* positive-definite kernels to specify rich correlation structures between the different co-ordinates. Concretely, Equation 3 as used in SVGD is replaced with Equation 4:

$$\phi(\boldsymbol{w}_t) = \frac{1}{N}\sum_{n=1}^{N}\left[\boldsymbol{K}(\boldsymbol{w}_t,\boldsymbol{w}_t^n)\nabla_{\boldsymbol{w}_t^n}\log p(\boldsymbol{w}_t^n) + \boldsymbol{K}(\boldsymbol{w}_t,\boldsymbol{w}_t^n)\nabla_{\boldsymbol{w}_t^n}\right], \tag{4}$$

where $\boldsymbol{K} : \mathbb{R}^d \times \mathbb{R}^d \rightarrow \mathbb{R}^{d\times d}$ is now a matrix-valued kernel, and $\boldsymbol{K}(\cdot,\boldsymbol{w})\nabla_{\boldsymbol{w}}$ is formally defined as the product of matrix $\boldsymbol{K}(\cdot,\boldsymbol{w})$ with vector $\nabla_{\boldsymbol{w}}$. The ℓ-th element of $\boldsymbol{K}(\cdot,\boldsymbol{w})\nabla_{\boldsymbol{w}}$ is computed as:

$$(\boldsymbol{K}(\cdot,\boldsymbol{w})\nabla_{\boldsymbol{w}})_\ell = \sum_{m=1}^{d}\nabla_{w^m}K_{\ell,m}(\cdot,\boldsymbol{w}), \tag{5}$$

where $K_{\ell,m}(\boldsymbol{w},\boldsymbol{w}')$ represents the (ℓ,m)-element of matrix $\boldsymbol{K}(\boldsymbol{w},\boldsymbol{w}')$ and w^m the m-element of $\boldsymbol{w}$.

Importantly, the advantage of *Matrix-SVGD* over the original SVGD algorithm is that it allows us to pre-condition SVGD by constructing a proper matrix kernel which incorporates the pre-conditioning information, in order to accelerate exploration and convergence.

2.4 Bayesian Model-Agnostic Meta-Learning

Kim et al. (2018) proposed a Bayesian Model-Agnostic Meta-Learning (BMAML) algorithm which learns a distribution over parameters which, when given data from a new task, can be adapted quickly to a task-specific distribution using SVGD updates as defined in Equation 3. Thus, BMAML as proposed in Kim et al. (2018) makes use of scalar-valued kernels for SVGD updates, which (as discussed earlier) does not allow the encoding of potential correlations between different parameter co-ordinates for effective optimization, a limitation which we next address.

3 Bayesian Model-Agnostic Meta-Learning with Matrix-SVGD

In this work we propose to improve the predictive performance of BMAML for quality estimation with the use of the Matrix-SVGD, which uses matrix-valued kernels for more effective parameter updates, in place of the original SVGD algorithm used in Kim et al. (2018). As pre-conditioning information, we use $\boldsymbol{P}$, the average of the Fisher information matrix of the particles:

$$\boldsymbol{P} = \frac{1}{N}\sum_{n=1}^{N}\boldsymbol{F}(w_n), \tag{6}$$

where $\boldsymbol{F}(\boldsymbol{w}_n)$ is the Fisher information matrix for particle $\boldsymbol{w}_n$. The matrix-valued kernel is then computed as:

$$\boldsymbol{K}_{\boldsymbol{P}}(\boldsymbol{w},\boldsymbol{w}') = \boldsymbol{P}^{-1}\exp\left(-\frac{1}{2h}\|\boldsymbol{w}-\boldsymbol{w}'\|_{\boldsymbol{P}}^2\right), \tag{7}$$

where $\|\boldsymbol{w}-\boldsymbol{w}'\|_{\boldsymbol{P}}^2 := (\boldsymbol{w}-\boldsymbol{w}')^\top \boldsymbol{P}(\boldsymbol{w}-\boldsymbol{w}')$ and h is a bandwidth parameter.

The full algorithm, which we refer to as *Matrix-BMAML*, is outlined in Algorithm 1. We use machine translation quality estimation as a case study in this work, and so assume access to a distribution of quality estimation tasks $p(T)$ (each QE task can be a QE user/annotator/post-editor with their corresponding data), and a quality estimation model f_W parameterized by W, though the approach can also be applied to other natural language processing or computer vision tasks.

Algorithm 1 Bayesian Model-Agnostic Meta-Learning with Matrix-SVGD

Require: Distribution of QE tasks $p(\mathcal{T})$
Require: QE model f_W, Number of update steps K
Require: Learning rates α, β
1: Initialize W
2: **while** not done **do**
3: Sample batch of QE tasks $\mathcal{T}_i \sim p(\mathcal{T})$
4: **for each** $\mathcal{T}_i$ **do**
5: Sample $\mathcal{D}_{\mathcal{T}_i}^{\text{train}}$ from $\mathcal{T}_i^{train}$
6: Sample $\mathcal{D}_{\mathcal{T}_i}^{\text{val}}$ from $\mathcal{T}_i^{val}$
7: $W_0^i \leftarrow W$
8: **for** k = 1,..K **do**
9: W_k^i = Matrix-SVGD$(W_{k-1}^i; \mathcal{D}_{\mathcal{T}_i}^{\text{train}}, \alpha)$
10: **end for**
11: **end for**
12: $W \leftarrow W - \beta\nabla_W \sum_{\mathcal{T}_i\sim p(\mathcal{T})}\mathcal{L}\left(f_{W_K^i}; \mathcal{D}_{\mathcal{T}_i}^{\text{val}}\right)$
13: **end while**

We first initialize the parameters of the quality estimation model (line 1). Then in each iteration, we sample a batch of QE tasks (line 3), and for each QE task, we sample instances from its training and validation sets (lines 4-6). Thereafter, task-specific parameters are initialized from the model's parameters (line 7), and then updated with K steps of Matrix-SVGD (using Equations (2) and (4) to (7)) (lines 8-10). At the end of each iteration, a meta-update is performed on the model's parameters W.

4 Experiments and Results

We conduct experiments in two settings: in a limited supervision setting, where we provide all models access to only a limited number of training instances per QE task; and in a full-supervision setting, where we provide the models with access to all available training instances for each QE task.

PE ID	Train	Dev	Test
PE1	1440	360	200
PE2	2160	540	300
PE3	1444	361	195
PE4	1834	459	244
PE5	4866	1217	617
PE6	1677	420	203
PE7	1567	392	241
Total	14988	3749	2000

(a) QT21 en-lv (nmt)

PE ID	Train	Dev	Test
PE1	9952	2488	559
PE2	3445	862	193
PE3	8770	2193	537
PE4	4579	1145	276
PE5	7651	1913	435
Total	34397	8601	2000

(b) QT21 en-cs (smt)

Table 1: Number of instances per QE Task/Post Editor (PE) for the QT21 dataset.

The QT21 Dataset We evaluate our approach with the publicly available **QT21** (Specia et al., 2017), a large-scale dataset containing translations from both statistical (smt) and neural (nmt) machine translation systems in multiple language directions [1]. This is the largest dataset with annotator information available. We make use of data from the English-Latvian (en-lv) and English-Czech (en-cs) language directions. The languages were chosen as they contain the largest number of annotators. Each instance in the dataset is a tuple of source sentence, its machine translation, the corresponding post-edited translation by a professional translator (post-editor), a reference translation and other information such as (anonymized) post-editor identifier. We construct a QE dataset from this corpus by computing the HTER (Snover et al., 2006) values between each source sentence and its post-edited translation. We thereafter split the data into train, dev and test splits for each post-editor, which constitutes a QE task. A breakdown of the number of train, dev and test instances per QE task/post-editor is available in Table 1.

5 QE Model

The quality estimation model used by all methods is based on multi-lingual DistilBERT (Sanh et al., 2019), a smaller version of multi-lingual BERT (Devlin et al., 2019) trained with knowledge distillation (Buciluă et al., 2006; Hinton et al., 2015). It accepts as input the source and machine translation outputs concatenated as a single text, separated by a '[SEP]' token and prepended with a '[CLS]' token. The representation of the '[CLS]' token is then passed to a linear layer to predict HTER (Snover et al., 2006) values as regression targets.

Benchmark Approaches We compare the proposed approach with the following: MTL-PRETRAIN is a baseline trained in classic multi-task fashion for multiple epochs using data from all QE tasks. It is thereafter fine-tuned using each QE task's training data before making predictions on its test set, in a similar fashion as the meta-learning approaches; REPTILE (Nichol and Schulman, 2018); Model-Agnostic Meta-Learning (MAML) (Finn et al., 2017); implicit Model-Agnostic Meta-Learning (iMAML) (Rajeswaran et al., 2019); Amortized Bayesian Meta-Learning (ABML) (Ravi and Beatson, 2019); and BMAML (Kim et al., 2018), a state-of-the-art Bayesian meta-learning method.

Evaluation We report Pearson's r correlation scores and Mean Absolute Error (MAE) between model output and gold labels, both standard evaluation metrics in QE.

Each experiment is repeated across five (5) different random seeds, and we report the average.

5.1 Limited Supervision Results

Results obtained in a setting where all approaches have access to only very limited training instances is presented in Figure 1. As expected, training with classic multi-task learning and then fine-tuning on the training data of each QE task (*MTL-PRETRAIN*) results in very poor performance on both datasets. This result is consistent with the results observed in Finn et al. (2017), since classic multi-task learning does not have any explicit objective that encourages the model to learn how to learn with limited supervision data. In contrast, all meta-learning approaches obtain consistent improvements over the *MTL-PRETRAIN* baseline. We find that in general, our approach (*Matrix-BMAML*) obtains marked performance improvements over the other Bayesian and non-Bayesian meta-learning approaches. This demonstrates the importance of incorporating pre-conditioning information through matrix-valued kernels for more ef-

[1] http://www.qt21.eu/resources/data/

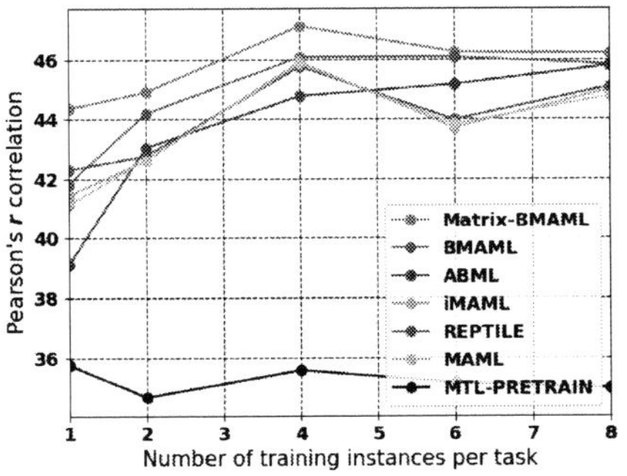

(a)

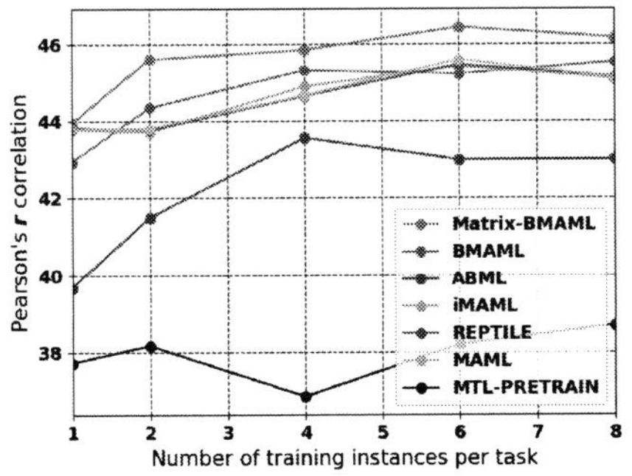

(b)

Figure 1: Results obtained using limited training instances for each task on the (a) *en-lv* and (b) *en-cs* quality estimation datasets.

fective SVGD updates in Bayesian model-agnostic meta-learning.

5.2 Full Supervision Results

Method	en-lv		en-cs	
	Pearson ↑	MAE ↓	Pearson ↑	MAE ↓
MTL-PRETRAIN	0.4505	0.1936	0.4473	0.1711
MAML	0.5239	0.1590	0.4894	0.1611
REPTILE	0.5237	0.1591	0.5037	0.1605
iMAML	0.5254	0.1588	0.5036	0.1605
ABML	0.5196	0.1600	0.4807	0.1620
BMAML	0.5295	**0.1585**	0.4963	0.1606
Matrix-BMAML	**0.5377**	0.1588	**0.5202**	**0.1566**

Table 2: Comparison with existing approaches.

Table 2 presents results obtained when the approaches are given access to all available training data for each QE task. We can observe that *Matrix-BMAML* obtained the best MAE on the *en-cs* dataset, and the best Pearson's correlation on both datasets, which again demonstrates the effectiveness of our approach in this setting.

6 Conclusions

We proposed a Bayesian meta-learning framework for adapting machine translation quality estimation models to the quality needs and preferences of each user with limited supervision data. We further extend a state-of-the-art Bayesian meta-learning method with the use of matrix-valued kernels, which enables the incorporation of preconditioning information for more effective SVGD updates. Using data from two language directions, we demonstrate improved predictive performance in both limited and full-supervision settings over recent state-of-the-art Bayesian and non-Bayesian meta-learning methods.

Acknowledgements

This work was supported by funding from the Bergamot project (EU H2020 grant no. 825303).

References

John Blatz, Erin Fitzgerald, George Foster, Simona Gandrabur, Cyril Goutte, Alex Kulesza, Alberto Sanchis, and Nicola Ueffing. 2004. Confidence estimation for machine translation. In *COLING 2004: Proceedings of the 20th International Conference on Computational Linguistics*, pages 315–321, Geneva, Switzerland.

Cristian Buciluă, Rich Caruana, and Alexandru Niculescu-Mizil. 2006. Model compression. In *Proceedings of the 12th ACM SIGKDD international conference on Knowledge discovery and data mining*, pages 535–541.

Jacob Devlin, Ming-Wei Chang, Kenton Lee, and Kristina Toutanova. 2019. BERT: pre-training of deep bidirectional transformers for language understanding. In *Proceedings of the 2019 Conference of the North American Chapter of the Association for Computational Linguistics: Human Language Technologies, NAACL-HLT 2019, Minneapolis, MN, USA, June 2-7, 2019, Volume 1 (Long and Short Papers)*, pages 4171–4186. Association for Computational Linguistics.

Chelsea Finn, Pieter Abbeel, and Sergey Levine. 2017. Model-agnostic meta-learning for fast adaptation of deep networks. In *Proceedings of the 34th International Conference on Machine Learning, ICML 2017, Sydney, NSW, Australia, 6-11 August 2017*, volume 70 of *Proceedings of Machine Learning Research*, pages 1126–1135. PMLR.

Chelsea Finn, Kelvin Xu, and S. Levine. 2018. Probabilistic model-agnostic meta-learning. In *Advances In Neural Information Processing Systems*.

Erick Fonseca, Lisa Yankovskaya, André F. T. Martins, Mark Fishel, and Christian Federmann. 2019. Findings of the WMT 2019 shared tasks on quality estimation. In *Proceedings of the Fourth Conference on Machine Translation (Volume 3: Shared Task Papers, Day 2)*, pages 1–10, Florence, Italy. Association for Computational Linguistics.

Tuomas Haarnoja, Haoran Tang, Pieter Abbeel, and Sergey Levine. 2017. Reinforcement learning with deep energy-based policies. In *Proceedings of the 34th International Conference on Machine Learning, ICML 2017, Sydney, NSW, Australia, 6-11 August 2017*, volume 70 of *Proceedings of Machine Learning Research*, pages 1352–1361. PMLR.

Geoffrey E. Hinton, Oriol Vinyals, and Jeffrey Dean. 2015. Distilling the knowledge in a neural network. *CoRR*, abs/1503.02531.

Fabio Kepler, Jonay Trénous, Marcos Treviso, Miguel Vera, and André F. T. Martins. 2019. OpenKiwi: An open source framework for quality estimation. In *Proceedings of the 57th Annual Meeting of the Association for Computational Linguistics: System Demonstrations*, pages 117–122, Florence, Italy. Association for Computational Linguistics.

Hyun Kim, Jong-Hyeok Lee, and Seung-Hoon Na. 2017. Predictor-estimator using multilevel task learning with stack propagation for neural quality estimation. In *Proceedings of the Second Conference on Machine Translation, WMT 2017, Copenhagen, Denmark, September 7-8, 2017*, pages 562–568. Association for Computational Linguistics.

Taesup Kim, Jaesik Yoon, O. Dia, S. Kim, Yoshua Bengio, and Sungjin Ahn. 2018. Bayesian model-agnostic meta-learning. In *Advances In Neural Information Processing Systems*.

Qiang Liu and Dilin Wang. 2016. Stein variational gradient descent: A general purpose bayesian inference algorithm. In *Advances in Neural Information Processing Systems 29*, pages 2378–2386. Curran Associates, Inc.

Yang Liu, Prajit Ramachandran, Qiang Liu, and Jian Peng. 2017. Stein variational policy gradient. In *Proceedings of the Thirty-Third Conference on Uncertainty in Artificial Intelligence, UAI 2017, Sydney, Australia, August 11-15, 2017*. AUAI Press.

Cuong Nguyen, Thanh-Toan Do, and Gustavo Carneiro. 2020. Uncertainty in model-agnostic meta-learning using variational inference. In *Proceedings of the IEEE/CVF Winter Conference on Applications of Computer Vision*, pages 3090–3100.

Alex Nichol and John Schulman. 2018. Reptile: a scalable metalearning algorithm. *arXiv preprint arXiv:1803.02999*, 2(2):1.

Abiola Obamuyide, Marina Fomicheva, and Lucia Specia. 2021. Continual quality estimation with online bayesian meta-learning. In *Proceedings of the Association for Computational Linguistics*.

Aravind Rajeswaran, Chelsea Finn, Sham M. Kakade, and Sergey Levine. 2019. Meta-learning with implicit gradients. In *Advances in Neural Information Processing Systems 32: Annual Conference on Neural Information Processing Systems 2019, NeurIPS 2019, December 8-14, 2019, Vancouver, BC, Canada*, pages 113–124.

Tharindu Ranasinghe, Constantin Orasan, and Ruslan Mitkov. 2020. Transquest at wmt2020: Sentence-level direct assessment. In *Proceedings of the Fifth Conference on Machine Translation*, pages 1049–1055, Online. Association for Computational Linguistics.

Sachin Ravi and Alex Beatson. 2019. Amortized bayesian meta-learning. In *7th International Conference on Learning Representations, ICLR 2019, New Orleans, LA, USA, May 6-9, 2019*. OpenReview.net.

Victor Sanh, Lysandre Debut, Julien Chaumond, and Thomas Wolf. 2019. Distilbert, a distilled version of bert: smaller, faster, cheaper and lighter. *ArXiv*, abs/1910.01108.

Jurgen Schmidhuber. 1987. Evolutionary principles in self-referential learning. *On learning how to learn: The meta-meta-... hook.) Diploma thesis, Institut f. Informatik, Tech. Univ. Munich.*

Matthew Snover, Bonnie Dorr, Richard Schwartz, Linnea Micciulla, and John Makhoul. 2006. A study of translation edit rate with targeted human annotation. In *Proceedings of the 7th Conference of the Association for Machine Translation in the Americas: Technical Papers*. Cambridge, MA.

Lucia Specia, Frédéric Blain, Marina Fomicheva, Erick Fonseca, Vishrav Chaudhary, Francisco Guzmán, and André F. T. Martins. 2020. Findings of the WMT 2020 shared task on quality estimation. In *Proceedings of the Fifth Conference on Machine Translation*, pages 743–764, Online. Association for Computational Linguistics.

Lucia Specia, Kim Harris, Aljoscha Burchardt, Marco Turchi, Matteo Negri, and Inguna Skadina. 2017. Translation quality and productivity: A study on rich morphology languages. In *Machine Translation Summit XVI*, pages 55–71.

Lucia Specia, Gustavo Paetzold, and Carolina Scarton. 2015. Multi-level translation quality prediction with quest++. In *Proceedings of the 53rd Annual Meeting of the Association for Computational Linguistics and the 7th International Joint Conference on Natural Language Processing of the Asian Federation of Natural Language Processing, ACL 2015, July 26-31, 2015, Beijing, China, System Demonstrations*, pages 115–120. The Association for Computer Linguistics.

Lucia Specia, Marco Turchi, Nicola Cancedda, Marc Dymetman, and Nello Cristianini. 2009. Estimating the sentence-level quality of machine translation systems. In *13th Conference of the European Association for Machine Translation*, pages 28–37.

Sebastian Thrun and Lorien Pratt. 1998. Learning to Learn: Introduction and Overview. In *Learning to Learn*, pages 3–17. Springer US, Boston, MA.

Dilin Wang, Ziyang Tang, C. Bajaj, and Qiang Liu. 2019. Stein variational gradient descent with matrix-valued kernels. *Advances in neural information processing systems*, 32:7834–7844.

Zhenyi Wang, Yang Zhao, Ping Yu, Ruiyi Zhang, and Changyou Chen. 2020. Bayesian meta sampling for fast uncertainty adaptation. In *8th International Conference on Learning Representations, ICLR 2020, Addis Ababa, Ethiopia, April 26-30, 2020*.

Yinhao Zhu and Nicholas Zabaras. 2018. Bayesian deep convolutional encoder-decoder networks for surrogate modeling and uncertainty quantification. *J. Comput. Phys.*, 366:415–447.

A Additional Experimental Details

Hyper-parameter	Value
Learning rate	3e-5
Mini-batch size	16
Max. sequence length	100

Table 3: Hyper-parameter values for all compared approaches

All compared approaches have a run time of about two hours on average. Each model was implemented as a linear layer on top of multilingual DistilBERT (Sanh et al., 2019), which has a total of 134M parameters. [2]

For the evaluation metrics, Pearson r correlation and MAE, we use open-source implementations available in SciPy [3] and scikit-learn [4] libraries respectively.

All models make use of the same values for hyper-parameters such as learning rate and batch size, selected by manual search in initial experiments. These are provided in Table 3.

[2] https://huggingface.co/distilbert-base-multilingual-cased

[3] https://www.scipy.org

[4] https://scikit-learn.org

Knowledge Informed Semantic Parsing for Conversational Question Answering

Raghuveer Thirukovalluru[1]*, **Mukund Sridhar**[2]*, **Dung Thai**[1]*, **Shruti Chanumolu**[1], **Nicholas Monath**[1], **Shankar Ananthakrishnan**[2], **Andrew McCallum**[1]

[1]UMass Amherst, [2]Amazon Alexa AI

{rthirukovall,dthai,schanumolu,nmonath,mccallum}@cs.umass.edu

{harakere,sanantha}@amazon.com

Abstract

Smart assistants are tasked to answer various questions regarding world knowledge. These questions range from retrieval of simple facts to retrieval of complex, multi-hops question followed by various operators (i.e., `filter`, `argmax`). Semantic parsing has emerged as the state-of-the-art for answering these kinds of questions by forming queries to extract information from knowledge bases (KBs). Specially, neural semantic parsers (NSPs) effectively translate natural questions to logical forms, which execute on KB and give desirable answers. Yet, NSPs suffer from non-executable logical forms for some instances in the generated logical forms might be missing due to the incompleteness of KBs. Intuitively, knowing the KB structure informs NSP with changes of the global logical forms structures with respect to changes in KB instances. In this work, we propose a novel knowledge-informed decoder variant of NSP. We consider the conversational question answering settings, where a natural language query, its context and its final answers are available at training. Experimental results show that our method outperformed strong baselines by 1.8 F1 points overall across 10 types of questions of the CSQA dataset. Especially for the "Logical Reasoning" category, our model improves by 7 F1 points. Furthermore, our results are achieved with 90.3% fewer parameters, allowing faster training for large-scale datasets.

1 Introduction

Knowledge base question answering (KBQA) has emerged as an important research topic over the past few years (Sun et al., 2018; Chakraborty et al., 2019; Sun et al., 2019; Shen et al., 2019) alongside with question answering over text corpora. In KBQA, world knowledge is given in the form of multi-relational graph databases (Vrandečić and Krötzsch, 2014; Lehmann et al., 2015) with millions of entities and interrelations between them. When a natural language question arrives, KBQA systems analyse relevant facts in the knowledge bases and derive the answers. In the presence of knowledge bases, question answering results are often time more interpretable and modifiable. For example, the question *"Who started his career at Manchester United in 1992?"* can be answered by fact triples such as (*"David Beckham"*, `member_of_sports_team`, *"Manchester United"*). This fact can be updated as the world knowledge changes while it might be non-trivial to achieve the same effect on text corpora. Likewise, KBQA systems face their own challenges (Chakraborty et al., 2019), especially in the real-world, conversational settings.

In real-world settings, KBQA systems need to perform multi-hop reasoning over chains of supporting facts and carry out various operations within the context of a conversation. For instance, answering the follow up question *"When did he win his first championship?"* might require identifying the player previously mentioned, all of his sport teams, the dates the sport teams won their championships. Then, `argmax` and `filter` operators are applied on the returned dates, yielding answers, i.e., *"1999"* for *"David Beckham"*. Semantic parsing provides a weak supervision framework to learn to perform all these reasoning steps from just the question answer pairs. Semantic parsers define a set of rules (or grammar) for generating logical forms from natural language questions. Candidate logical forms are executable queries on the knowledge bases that yield the corresponding answers. Neural semantic parsers (NSPs) (Liang et al., 2016; Guo et al., 2018; Shen et al., 2019; Guo et al., 2019) employ a neural network to translate natural language questions into logical forms. NSPs have shown good performance on KBQA tasks (Liang et al.,

* Equal contribution

Proceedings of the 6th Workshop on Representation Learning for NLP (RepL4NLP-2021), pages 231–240
Bangkok, Thailand (Online), August 6, 2021.

2016; Plepi et al., 2021) and further improved with reinforcement learning (Guo et al., 2018), multi-task learning (Shen et al., 2019), and most recently meta-learning (Hua et al., 2020). Most previous works place more emphasis on modeling the reasoning behavior given in the questions than on interactions with the KB. In this work, we propose a KB-aware NSP variant (KISP) to fill in this gap.

One of the main challenges in learning KBQA systems is to adapt to structural changes of the relevant sub-knowledge base. Different reasoning behaviors might apply to similar questions with respect to different sub-knowledge bases. For example, a similar question *"When did Tiger Woods win his first championship?"* would require a different reasoning chain since he didn't participate in a sports team. Structural changes of the sub-KB is a common phenomenon due to the incompleteness nature of knowledge bases. In such cases, knowing the attributes and relations would inform NSPs with changes in logical forms with respect to specific relevant KB entities. To address this problem, we propose a NSPs with a KB-informed decoder that utilizes local knowledge base structure encoded in pre-trained KB embeddings. Our model collects all relevant KB artifacts and integrates their embeddings into each decoding step, iteratively. We also introduce an attention layer on a set of associated KB random walks as an k-steps look ahead that prevents the decoder from going into KB regions where generated logical forms are not executable.

Pre-trained KB embeddings were shown to improve multi-hop KBQA where answers are entities and no operations are involved (Saxena et al., 2020). In this paper, we demonstrate our work on the full KBQA settings with 10 question categories with no constraints on the answers (Saha et al., 2018). While (Saxena et al., 2020) evaluates 2-hop questions (Yih et al., 2016) and 2 and 3-hop questions with limited relation types (Zhang et al., 2018). Our model is also the first NSP variant that utilizes pre-trained features for logical forms generation. CARTON (Plepi et al., 2021) uses an updated action grammar with stacked pointer networks. LASAGNE (Kacupaj et al., 2021) is an extension of CARTON which further includes a graph attention network to exploit correlations between entities, predicates. Empirical results showed that our model improves upon the MaSP model (Shen et al., 2019), a strong baseline for CSQA dataset, by an absolute 1.8 F1, 1.5% accuracy two sets of questions respectively.

Further, we find that by incorporating knowledge-graph information we can match the performance of much larger pre-trained encoder models while using 90.3% fewer parameters.

2 Background

We first formally describe our task and the Neural Semantic Parser (NSP) on which our work is based.

Knowledge Graph: Let $\mathcal{E} = \{e_0...e_N\}$ be a set of given entities, and let $\mathcal{R} = \{r_0...r_M\}$ be a set of relations. A knowledge graph $\mathcal{G}$ is a set of fact triples in $\mathcal{E} \times \mathcal{R} \times \mathcal{E}$. A triple is represented as (h, r, t) where $h, t \in \mathcal{E}$ and $r \in \mathcal{R}$. There is an extensive literature on representing the knowledge graph (Ji et al., 2020; Dai et al., 2020) that encode its semantics and structures. In this work, we use the pre-trained knowledge graph embeddings from Pytorch-BigGraph (Lerer et al., 2019).

Conversational Question Answering: In conversational question answering (CQA), the goal is to answer a question q within the context of the conversation history C. The question q and the history C are usually concatenated for handling ellipsis and coreference, forming the input $\mathbf{X}$ as $[C; q]$. At training time, a set of answering entities $\mathcal{A}$ is also given. The set $\mathcal{A}$ comprises entities that resolve to the answer depending on the answer's type. For example, answers of "Simple Question" are a list of entities, the answer of "Verification Question" is Yes/No, whether the set $\mathcal{A}$ is empty or not.

2.1 Neural Semantic Parser

Semantic parsing approach for CQA produces the answer set $\mathcal{A}$ by first generating a logical form $\mathbf{Y}$. Formally, a logical form $\mathbf{Y}$ is a sequence of actions $(y_1, y_2, ..., y_n)$ where the arguments of these actions can be constants (i.e., numbers, dates) or KG instances (i.e., entities, relations, types). The set of actions is defined by a grammar $\mathcal{S}$ (Shen et al., 2019). We consider the weak-supervision settings where the ground truth logical form $\mathbf{Y}$ is not available. Instead, we generate candidates for $\mathbf{Y}$ by performing BFS based on grammar $\mathcal{S}$ over the knowledge graph $\mathcal{G}$ and keeping the candidate logical forms that yield the answer set $\mathcal{A}$ (Guo et al., 2018). Given the input $\mathbf{X}$ and the labeled logical form $\mathbf{Y}$, we train an encoder-decoder neural network to generate logical forms given the question and its conversational context.

Encoder: The input $\mathbf{X}$ is formatted with BERT style. Then, it is fed into a Transformer-based encoder network $\texttt{ENC}$, producing a sequence of encoded states $\mathbf{H} = \texttt{ENC}(\mathbf{X}) = (h_{[CLS]}, h_0, ...)$.

Decoder: The decoder is a Transformer-based model with attention. It takes the input representation from the encoder $h_{[CLS]}$ and the previous decoding state s_{i-1} to produce the target action y_i.

$$Pr_{\mathbf{Y}\sim\mathcal{S}}(\mathbf{Y} \mid \mathbf{X}) = \prod_{y_i \in \mathcal{S}} Pr(y_i \mid s_{i-1}, \mathbf{H}) \qquad (1)$$
$$Pr(y_i \mid s_{i-1}, \mathbf{H}) = \text{softmax}(\text{ATTN}([s_{i-1}; h_{[CLS]}], \mathbf{H}))$$

Classifiers: The decoder is accompanied by a set of classifiers that predict the arguments for the decoder's actions at each decoding step. Our base NSP (Shen et al., 2019) employs FFNNs for relations and entity types classifiers; and pointer networks for entities and constants mentioned in the question. At each decoding step, these classifiers produce an entity e_i, an entity type t_i, a relation r_i, and a constant c_i. The logical form action at time step i is a tuple consists of y_i and its arguments within $\{e_i, t_i, r_i, c_i\}$ defined by the grammar $\mathcal{S}$.

3 Knowledge-Informed Decoder

In this section, we introduce a knowledge-informed decoder that utilizes KG information to generate logical forms. We propose a knowledge injection layer that incorporates KG embeddings into the decoder state at each decoding step. To further inform the decoder with information about the expected structure of the KG, we propose an attention layer on random, k-hops knowledge walks from entities we encounter at each decoding step.

3.1 Knowledge Injection Layer(KIL)

NSP decoders only look at the encoded question and the previous state of decoding to decide the next action. Information of the KB instances (i.e., entities, types, or relations) being considered so far could improve this decision making process. Therefore, at the decoding step i where the action involves a KB instance, we propose a **Knowledge Injection Layer (KIL)** to propagate KB information to the sub-sequence steps. KIL takes in the KB classifiers predictions, incorporates their embeddings into the current encoding state and forwards it to the next decoding step. Eq. 1 becomes

$$Pr_{\mathbf{Y}\sim\mathcal{S}}(\mathbf{Y} \mid \mathbf{X}) = \prod_{y_i \in \mathcal{S}} Pr(y_i \mid s^*_{i-1}, \mathbf{H}) \qquad (2)$$
$$s^*_{i-1} = \text{KIL}(s_{i-1}) = \text{FNN}([s_{i-1}; \text{EMBB}(v_{i-1})])$$

where v_{i-1} is the corresponding argument of y_{i-1} and $v_{i-1} \in \mathcal{E} \cup \mathcal{R}$, i.e., $v_i \in \{e_i, t_i, r_i, c_i\}$.

At step j where $j > i$, the decoder is informed of preceding KB instances, and is able to adapt to specific sub-KB structure. We find in cases where there multiple entities in context, having the right entity embedding at timestep j helps logical form in the upcoming steps. The entity embedding carries information about type of the entity, which our model is able to use more appropriate predicates for ambiguous mentions. We empirically show that KIL improves the exact match accuracy of the logical form attributes (logical form without KB).

3.2 Attention on KG Walks (AKW)

Now that the decoder is aware of the previous KB instances, it is also useful to peek at the possible reasoning chains coming out of the current decoding state. We do this to avoid reasoning paths that lead to an non-executable region where the logical form is invalid with respect to the KB. Therefore, we propose an attention look-ahead layer to inspect the upcoming KB structures before making the action prediction. We first generate a set of random walks on the KG from predicted entities and relations with the current decoding step. We then apply the attention look-ahead layer on these KG walks to obtain a representation of the expected KG structures. This representation is then fed back to the decoder to predict the action.

$$Pr_{\mathbf{Y}\sim\mathcal{S}}(\mathbf{Y} \mid \mathbf{X}) = \prod_{y_i \in \mathcal{S}} Pr(y_i \mid s^*_{i-1}, \mathbf{H}, \text{RANDWALK}(v))$$
$$\text{RANDWALK}(v) = \text{ATTN}(\{\text{EMBB}(p_j \sim \mathcal{G}(v))\}_{j=0..k})$$

where v is one among entities in the question and p_j is a random walk path on the KB starting from v, denoted as $\mathcal{G}(v)$. Here we use one hop random walks from predicates found in the input, though any type of random walk could be used.

With the two proposed layers, our NSP decoder is now fully informed with the past and the future KB structures. We demonstrate that our decoder variant achieves better performance on various question categories. Furthermore, we show that the pre-trained KG embeddings do a significant heavy lifting on representing KB information within the decoder states, resulting in less model parameters and required training data.

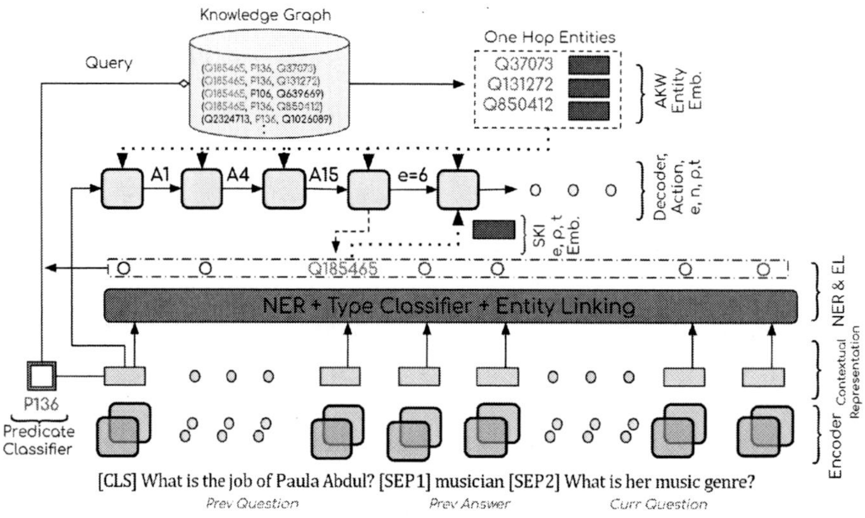

Figure 1: Overall Architecture and the different sources of knowledge used in KISP.

	Methods w\BERT	MaSP	CTN	KISP ♦	KISP ◇
	# train param	155M		157M	160M
F1	Overall	81.20	81.35	82.56	**83.01**
	Clarification	**80.10**	47.31	76.29	76.33
	Comparative	**68.19**	62.0	68.15	67.83
	Logical	76.40	80.80	87.41	**87.14**
	Quantitative	77.31	**80.62**	77.76	77.52
	Simple (Coref.)	78.33	**87.09**	78.78	79.66
	Simple (Direct)	86.57	85.92	87.03	**87.68**
	Simple (Ellipsis)	85.57	85.07	85.86	**86.06**
Acc.	Overall	44.73	**61.28**	46.22	46.22
	Compart.(Count)	28.71	**38.31**	27.65	27.32
	Quant.(Count)	50.07	**57.04**	50.82	50.92
	Verification(Bool)	65.00	**77.82**	72.29	72.72

Table 1: **CSQA w/ Large Models**. CARTON is CTN, KISP(KIL) is KISP♦, KISP(KIL+AKW) is KISP◇.

4 Experiments

Dataset and Evaluation We evaluate our approach on Complex Sequential Question Answering (CSQA) dataset. CSQA consists of 1.6M question answer pairs spread across 200K dialogues. Its has a 152K/16K/28K train, val, test split. More details on the dataset and evaluation metrics used are presented in Section A.1 of the Appendix.

4.1 Main Results

Our model[1] outperforms the MaSP model by 1.8 absolute points in F1-score for entity answer questions and 1.5 absolute points in accuracy for the boolean/counting categories. KISP shows significant improvements in Table 1 compared to MaSP. In more complex question types such 'Logical Reasoning', 'Verification' which require to reason over multiple tuples in the KG and questions that requiring operations like counting, our model outperforms the baseline by more than 10% points. Table 1 compares with MaSP (Shen et al., 2019). Appendix has additional analysis. Our model also beats CARTON (Plepi et al., 2021) in the entity answer questions despite them using an updated action grammar. For boolean, count type questions, the additional action vocabulary helps CARTON out perform our system. We will extend KISP to use this additional action vocabulary in the future.

[1]Code: https://github.com/raghavlite/kisp

4.2 Ablation Study

KG informed decoding with small models. A significant performance gain is expected in the smaller models by use of the knowledge graph information. We test this hypothesis by drastically reducing the size of the KISP encoder. This small version of KISP with only 9.7% of the baseline parameter slightly outperforms the baseline BERT model on overall F1-score. The gain comes from the fact that our models receive significant signal from KIL to make a more informed decision of valid actions/types in the next step even without a lot of knowledge from the encoder attention.

Low resource settings. A semantic parsing system as described above typically requires annotated

	Methods	MaSP (Small)	MaSP (BERT)	KISP◇ (Small)
	# of Parameters	15M	154.8M	15M
F1	Overall	78.91	81.20	**81.52**
	Clarification	75.05	80.10	**82.01**
	Comparative	66.85	68.19	**69.64**
	Logical	69.55	76.40	**84.54**
	Quantitative	74.29	**77.31**	73.9
	Simple (Coref.)	76.27	**78.33**	77.99
	Simple (Direct)	85.39	**86.57**	85.49
	Simple (Ellipsis)	83.04	**85.57**	83.60
Acc.	Overall	38.56	**44.73**	42.55
	Comparative(Count)	22.66	**28.71**	23.65
	Quantitative(Count)	42.73	**50.07**	45.65
	Verification	60.54	65.00	**71.63**

Table 2: Comparison of KISP◇=KISP(KIL+AKW)-Small with different sized baseline models.

golden logical forms for training. Logical form annotation is an resource intensive process (Berant et al., 2013; Liang et al., 2013; Zhong et al., 2017). It is also a difficult process to use brute force computation to find these logical forms; also this process often results in spurious logical forms Shen et al. (2019).

This calls for models which can work with very few training examples. Hence we evaluate the effectiveness of KISP in low resource settings where only a fraction of data is used for training. Table 3 shows that KISP is able to outperform MaSP in these data constrained cases. The gap between MaSP and KISP widens in these low resource settings further justifying our model.

Methods	10% Data		50% Data	
	F1	Acc.	F1	Acc.
MaSP++ (S)	72.99	35.61	79.31	40.27
KISP ♦ (S)	**75.45**	**37.70**	**80.93**	**42.53**

Table 3: Comparison of small KISP(KIL+AKW) and MaSP models. KISP♦=KISP(KIL+AKW)

Met.\Acc.	Sket.	Ent.	Pred.	Type	Num
MaSP (S)	80.55	87.39	97.11	90.62	96.30
KISP◇ (S)	82.32	95.30	98.83	**90.73**	100
KISP♦ (S)	**83.33**	**95.37**	98.83	90.66	100
MASP (B)	83.63	91.90	97.67	**93.11**	100
KISP◇ (B)	84.47	**96.25**	**99.40**	92.25	100
KISP♦ (B)	**85.92**	95.85	99.25	92.25	100

Table 4: Fine grained metrics. KISP◇=KISP(KIL), KISP♦=KISP(KIL+AKW). (S)-Small, (B)-Bert.

Impact of KIL and AKW To further understand how each classifier on the decoder is benefited from the knowledge graph, we look at the accuracies of these classifiers on the evaluation set. Table 4 displays accuracies of the five classifiers from Eq. 1 around logical form generation of different models.

KISP does as better job at predicting the overall skeleton of the logical form - (all the various non e_i, t_i, r_i, c_i) actions. We observe attending to knowledge graph improves the logical form skeleton up to 2.3 points. As shown in Example 3 and 4 of the Appendix, the $count, filter$ actions within the logical form are better predicted by KISP. KIL provides entity-embedding for the entity of interest at current timestep this helps the model pick the right predicates in the following steps in ambiguous cases. Cases requiring reasoning benefit from seeing random walks around entities in context - provided by AKW. These lead to better overall sketch accuracy.

KISP is also better at pointing to correct entity accuracy. Pointing to the right entity can has cascading effects on logical form prediction As shown by numbers in Table 4. KISP does a better job with entity pointer improving by almost 4 points. We attribute this to the KIL sytem of KISP which provides the KG embedding for entity of interest at given time step this helps the decoder's entity pointer mechanism.

Entity Linking Errors We follow Sheang (2019) in using a joint mention, type classifier followed by an inverse index entity linker on the input using the encoder representations. The entity pointer classifier described earlier sections looks at these entities in a sentence and points to one among them. We found that a large amount of errors had arisen from this inverse index. Recent work, (Kacupaj et al., 2021) also points this and uses a better entity linker. Improving this module should significantly add to final performance and hence is a very interesting direction for future work.

5 Conclusion

We introduced a neural semantic parsing decoder that uses additional knowledge graph information for Conversational QA. Results show that KISP can significantly boost performance in complex multi-hop question types like logical reasoning questions. Our method can help improve over strong baseline methods like MaSP. Finally we presented a smaller version of our model that is approx 10x smaller without any performance degradation compared to a system that doesn't use KG informed decoding.

References

Jonathan Berant, Andrew Chou, Roy Frostig, and Percy Liang. 2013. Semantic parsing on freebase from question-answer pairs. In *Proceedings of the 2013 conference on empirical methods in natural language processing*, pages 1533–1544.

Nilesh Chakraborty, Denis Lukovnikov, Gaurav Maheshwari, Priyansh Trivedi, Jens Lehmann, and Asja Fischer. 2019. Introduction to neural network based approaches for question answering over knowledge graphs. *arXiv preprint arXiv:1907.09361*.

Yuanfei Dai, Shiping Wang, Neal N Xiong, and Wenzhong Guo. 2020. A survey on knowledge graph embedding: Approaches, applications and benchmarks. *Electronics*, 9(5):750.

Daya Guo, Duyu Tang, Nan Duan, Ming Zhou, and Jian Yin. 2018. Dialog-to-action: Conversational question answering over a large-scale knowledge base. In *Advances in Neural Information Processing Systems*, pages 2942–2951.

Daya Guo, Duyu Tang, Nan Duan, Ming Zhou, and Jian Yin. 2019. Coupling retrieval and meta-learning for context-dependent semantic parsing. *ACL*.

Yuncheng Hua, Yuan-Fang Li, Gholamreza Haffari, Guilin Qi, and Wei Wu. 2020. Retrieve, program, repeat: Complex knowledge base question answering via alternate meta-learning. *arXiv preprint arXiv:2010.15875*.

Shaoxiong Ji, Shirui Pan, Erik Cambria, Pekka Marttinen, and Philip S Yu. 2020. A survey on knowledge graphs: Representation, acquisition and applications. *arXiv preprint arXiv:2002.00388*.

Endri Kacupaj, Joan Plepi, Kuldeep Singh, Harsh Thakkar, Jens Lehmann, and Maria Maleshkova. 2021. Conversational question answering over knowledge graphs with transformer and graph attention networks. *arXiv preprint arXiv:2104.01569*.

Jens Lehmann, Robert Isele, Max Jakob, Anja Jentzsch, Dimitris Kontokostas, Pablo N Mendes, Sebastian Hellmann, Mohamed Morsey, Patrick Van Kleef, Sören Auer, et al. 2015. Dbpedia–a large-scale, multilingual knowledge base extracted from wikipedia. *Semantic web*, 6(2):167–195.

Adam Lerer, Ledell Wu, Jiajun Shen, Timothee Lacroix, Luca Wehrstedt, Abhijit Bose, and Alex Peysakhovich. 2019. Pytorch-biggraph: A large-scale graph embedding system. *arXiv preprint arXiv:1903.12287*.

Chen Liang, Jonathan Berant, Quoc Le, Kenneth D Forbus, and Ni Lao. 2016. Neural symbolic machines: Learning semantic parsers on freebase with weak supervision. *arXiv preprint arXiv:1611.00020*.

Percy Liang, Michael I Jordan, and Dan Klein. 2013. Learning dependency-based compositional semantics. *Computational Linguistics*, 39(2):389–446.

Joan Plepi, Endri Kacupaj, Kuldeep Singh, Harsh Thakkar, and Jens Lehmann. 2021. Context transformer with stacked pointer networks for conversational question answering over knowledge graphs. *arXiv preprint arXiv:2103.07766*.

Amrita Saha, Vardaan Pahuja, Mitesh M Khapra, Karthik Sankaranarayanan, and Sarath Chandar. 2018. Complex sequential question answering: Towards learning to converse over linked question answer pairs with a knowledge graph. In *Thirty-Second AAAI Conference on Artificial Intelligence*.

Apoorv Saxena, Aditay Tripathi, and Partha Talukdar. 2020. Improving multi-hop question answering over knowledge graphs using knowledge base embeddings. In *Proceedings of the 58th Annual Meeting of the Association for Computational Linguistics*.

Kim Cheng Sheang. 2019. Multilingual complex word identification: Convolutional neural networks with morphological and linguistic features. In *Proceedings of the Student Research Workshop Associated with RANLP 2019*, pages 83–89, Varna, Bulgaria. INCOMA Ltd.

Tao Shen, Xiubo Geng, Tao Qin, Daya Guo, Duyu Tang, Nan Duan, Guodong Long, and Daxin Jiang. 2019. Multi-task learning for conversational question answering over a large-scale knowledge base. *EMNLP-IJCNLP*.

Haitian Sun, Tania Bedrax-Weiss, and William W Cohen. 2019. Pullnet: Open domain question answering with iterative retrieval on knowledge bases and text. *arXiv preprint arXiv:1904.09537*.

Haitian Sun, Bhuwan Dhingra, Manzil Zaheer, Kathryn Mazaitis, Ruslan Salakhutdinov, and William W Cohen. 2018. Open domain question answering using early fusion of knowledge bases and text. *arXiv preprint arXiv:1809.00782*.

Denny Vrandečić and Markus Krötzsch. 2014. Wikidata: a free collaborative knowledgebase. *Communications of the ACM*, 57(10):78–85.

Denny Vrandečić and Markus Krötzsch. 2014. Wikidata: A free collaborative knowledgebase. *Commun. ACM*, 57(10):78–85.

Wen-tau Yih, Matthew Richardson, Christopher Meek, Ming-Wei Chang, and Jina Suh. 2016. The value of semantic parse labeling for knowledge base question answering. In *Proceedings of the 54th Annual Meeting of the Association for Computational Linguistics (Volume 2: Short Papers)*, pages 201–206.

Yuyu Zhang, Hanjun Dai, Zornitsa Kozareva, Alexander Smola, and Le Song. 2018. Variational reasoning for question answering with knowledge graph. In *Proceedings of the AAAI Conference on Artificial Intelligence*, volume 32.

Victor Zhong, Caiming Xiong, and Richard Socher. 2017. Seq2sql: Generating structured queries from natural language using reinforcement learning. *arXiv preprint arXiv:1709.00103*.

A Appendices

A.1 Dataset and Evaluation

We evaluate our approach on Complex Sequential Question Answering (CSQA) dataset. CSQA consists of 1.6M question answer pairs spread across 200K dialogues. Its has a 152K/16K/28K train, val, test split. The dataset's knowledge graph is built on wikidata (Vrandečić and Krötzsch, 2014) and represented with triples. The KB consists of 21.2M triplets over 12.8M entities, 3054 distinct entity types, and 567 distinct predicates. There are 10 different question categories split into two groups. Answers to the first group of questions are a list of entities. Question categories of this group are evaluated by the macro F1 score between predicted entities and golden entities. Answers to question categories in the second group are either counts or boolean. This group is evaluated by accuracy. Overall scores for each group are the weighted averaged metrics of all the categories in the group. We refer the reader to Saha et al. (2018) for a more detailed understanding of different categories of questions. Following sections contain training/eval specifics.

A.2 Training details & Evaluation Metrics

We followed Shen et al (2019) to search for logical forms and create the training data. Exact hyperparameters used in the experiments are mentioned below. We followed Saha et al. (2018) for evaluation metrics. Macro Precision and Macro Recall were used when the answer was a list of entities. For questions with answer type boolean/number, we use accuracy.

A.3 Training time Analysis

Training times of different models are in Table.5

Model	Training Time (hrs)
MaSP++	6
KISP(SKI)	7.5
KISP(SKI+AKW)	8
MASP++ (BERT)	27.4
KISP(SKI) BERT	29.5
KISP(SKI + AKW) BERT	32
KISP(SKI + AKW) small	4.5
MASP++ small	3

Table 5: Running times of different models

There are some known in-efficiencies in the code, some from design and others conceptual. We intend to improve training time in future work by incorporating more e2e methods that will reduce GPU2CPU & CPU2GPU communication and also through some design changes in the short term.

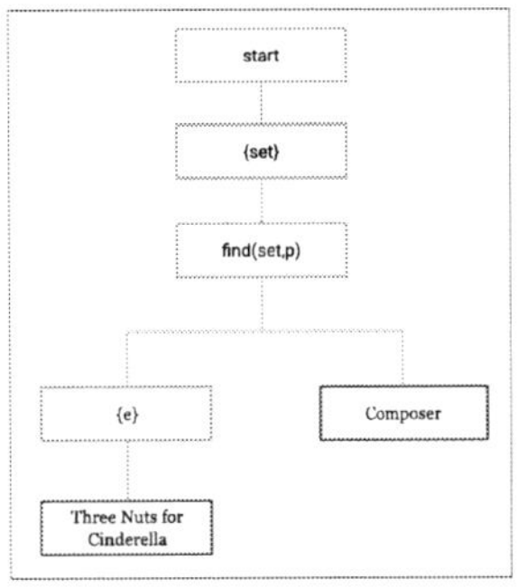

Figure 2: Example1 logical form KISP(SKI+AKW)BERT

A.4 Logical form Analysis

We identify examples to show performance improvement in KISP models, in predicting the correct answer and logical form. As shown in Table 6 below, KISP models for these examples do a better job at sketch, entity, num, type, predicate classification compared to MaSP. The coloured images in Figure 2- 6 show the differences between MaSP and KISP models. For each example we show the golden logical form tree(also predicted by one of the KISP models), MaSP's logical form and the mistakes made by the baseline in color red.

Example1

- **Utterance**

  Q: Which works of art stars Jiří Růžička as actor and originated in Germany ?

  A: Three Nuts for Cinderella

  Q: Who was that work of art composed by ?

  A: Karel Svoboda

- **Logical form**

  @ Gold
  find({Three Nuts for Cinderella}, Composer)

Example2

- **Utterance**

  Q: What is the job of Joe Falcon ?

  A: musician

  Q: What can be considered as category for Joe Falcon ?

Example	Curr_Question type	Predicted logical form = Gold logical form and Predicted answer = Gold answer			
		MaSP	KISP(SKI)	KISP(SKI+AKW)	KISP(SKI+AKW): BERT
Example1	Simple Question (Coreferenced)	Yes	Yes	Yes	Yes
Example2	Simple Question (Direct)	No	Yes	Yes	Yes
Example3	Quantitative Reasoning (Count) (All)	No	Yes	Yes	Yes
Example4	Quantitative Reasoning (Count) (All)	No	No	Yes	Yes
Example5	Logical Reasoning (All)	No	No	No	Yes

Table 6: Examples are based on the predicted logical form and answers in comparison to their gold counterpart

A: Cajun music

- **Logical form**

  @ Gold
  find({Joe Falcon}, genre)

  @ MaSP
  find({Joe Falcon}, Occupation)

Example3

- **Utterance**

  Q: How many administrative territories have atleast 4 administrative territories or french administrative divisions as their capital?

  A: 1

  Q: How many cities are associated to Albania as the capital?

  A: 1

- **Logical form**

  @ Gold
  count({*find*({Albania}, capital)})

  @ MaSP
  count({*filter*(city,{*union*({*find*({Albania },capital)},{Albania})})})

Example4

- **Utterance**

  Q: Is France the native country of Charles Boyer ?

  A: YES

  Q: How many works of art stars Charles Boyer as actor ?

  A: 68

- **Logical form**

  @ Gold
  count(*filter*(work of art,{*find*({Charles Boyer}, cast member)}))

  @ MaSP
  count({*union*({*filter*(work of art,{*find*({France},country of origin)})},{*find*({Charles Boyer},cast member)})})

  @ KISP(SKI)
  count({*diff*(*argmax*({*filter*(work of art, {Charles Boyer})},cast member),{*filter*(work of art,{Charles Boyer})})})

Example5

- **Utterance**

  Q: What is that person a member of ?

  A: Tunisia national football team

  Q: Which recurring events did Tunisia national football team and Alberto García Aspe participate in ?

  A: 2002 FIFA World Cup, 1998 FIFA World Cup

- **Logical form**

  @ Gold
  inter({*find*({Tunisia national football team}, participant)},{*find*({Alberto García Aspe}, participant)})

  @ MaSP
  inter(*find*({Alberto García Aspe}, participant),*find*({Alberto García Aspe}, participant))

  @ KISP(SKI)
  filter(recurring event,{*union*({*find*({Tunisia national football team}, participant)},{Alberto García })

  @ KISP(SKI+AKW)
  inter({*find*({Tunisia national football team }, participant)},{*find*({Tunisia national football team }, participant)})

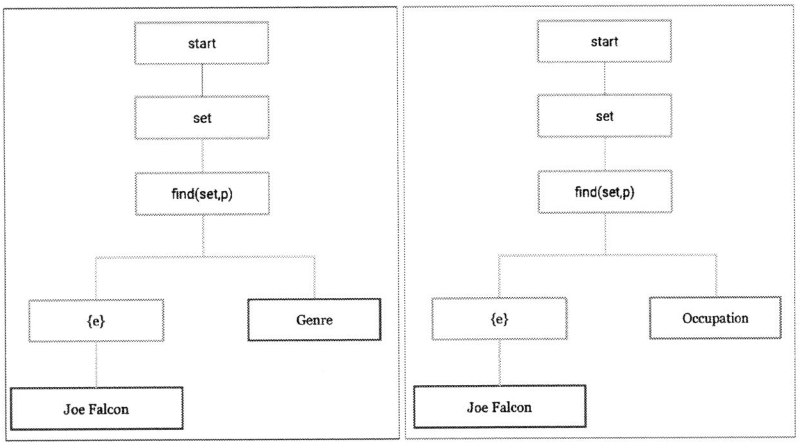

Figure 3: Example2 logical form KISP(SKI) vs MaSP

Example2 (Figure 3) and Example5 (Figure 6) show improvement in logical form entity and predicate instantiation compared to MaSP. We notice improvement in logical form skeleton for KISP(SKI+AKW)BERT model in Example4 (Figure 5). Example 3 (Figure 4) is a case where MaSP gets the right answer despite the incorrect logical form.

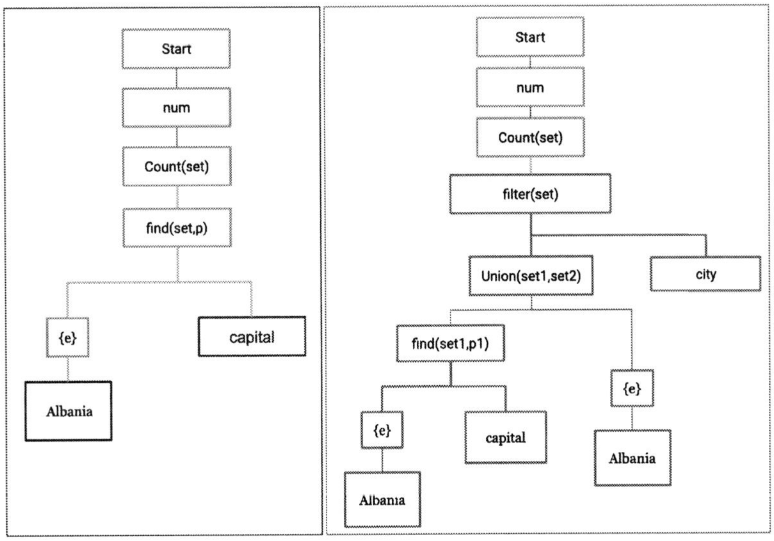

Figure 4: Example3 logical form KISP(SKI+AKW) vs MaSP

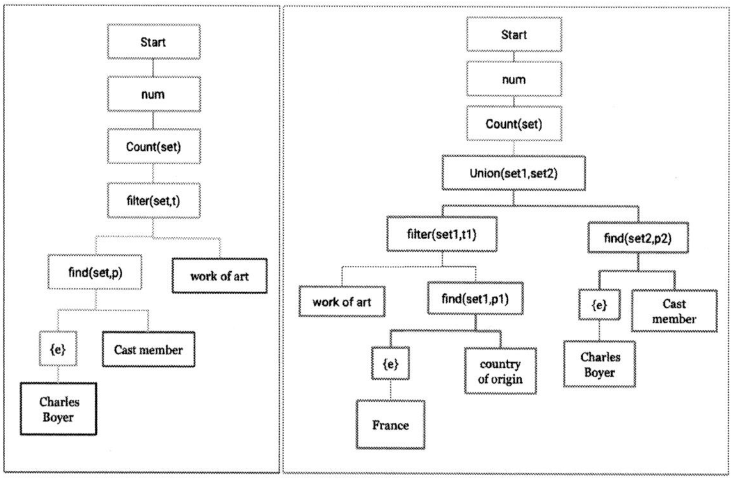

Figure 5: Example4 logical form KISP(SKI+AKW) vs MaSP

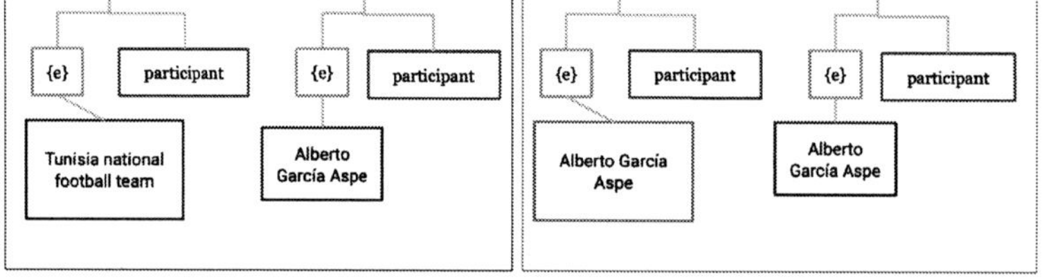

Figure 6: Example5 logical form KISP(SKI+AKW)BERT vs MaSP

Simultaneously Self-Attending to Text and Entities for Knowledge-Informed Text Representations

Dung Thai[1*], **Raghuveer Thirukovalluru**[1*], **Trapit Bansal**[1*], **Andrew McCallum**[1]
[1]UMass Amherst
{dthai, rthirukovall, tbansal, mccallum}@cs.umass.edu

Abstract

Pre-trained language models have emerged as highly successful methods for learning good text representations. However, the amount of structured knowledge retained in such models, and how (if at all) it can be extracted, remains an open question. In this work, we aim at directly learning text representations which leverage structured knowledge about entities mentioned in the text. This can be particularly beneficial for downstream tasks which are knowledge-intensive. Our approach utilizes self-attention between words in the text and knowledge graph (KG) entities mentioned in the text. While existing methods require entity-linked data for pre-training, we train using a mention-span masking objective and a candidate ranking objective – which doesn't require any entity-links and only assumes access to an alias table for retrieving candidates, enabling large-scale pre-training. We show that the proposed model learns knowledge-informed text representations that yield improvements on the downstream tasks over existing methods.

1 Introduction

Self-supervised representation learning on large text corpora using language modeling objectives has been shown to yield generalizable representations that improve performance for many downstream tasks. Examples of such approaches include BERT (Devlin et al., 2019), RoBERTa (Liu et al., 2019b), XLNET (Yang et al., 2019), GPT-2 (Radford et al., 2019), T5 (Raffel et al., 2019) etc. However, whether such models retain structured knowledge in their representation is still an open question (Petroni et al., 2019; Poerner et al., 2019; Logan et al., 2019; Roberts et al., 2020) which has led to active research on knowledge-informed representations (Zhang et al., 2019; Sun et al., 2019; Peters et al., 2019; Soares et al., 2019).

Models that learn knowledge-informed representations can be broadly classified into two categories. The first approach augments language model pre-training with the aim of storing structured knowledge in the model parameters. This is typically done by augmenting the pre-training task, for example by masking entity mentions (Sun et al., 2019) or enforcing representational similarity in sentences containing the same entities (Soares et al., 2019). While this makes minimal assumptions, it requires memorizing all facts encountered during training in the model parameters, necessitating larger models. The second approach directly conditions the representation on structured knowledge, for example fusing mention token representations with the mentioned entity's representation (Peters et al., 2019).

In this paper we consider the latter approach to learning knowledge-informed representations. Conditioning on relevant knowledge removes the burden on the model parameters to memorize all facts, and allows the model to encode novel facts not seen during training. However, existing methods typically assume access to entity-linked data for training (Zhang et al., 2019; Peters et al., 2019), which is scarce and expensive to annotate, preventing large scale pre-training. Moreover, these methods don't allow for bi-directional attention between both the text and the KG when representing text.

We propose a simple approach to incorporate structured knowledge into text representations. This is done using self-attention (Vaswani et al., 2017) to simultaneously attend to tokens in text and candidate KG entities mentioned in the text, in order to learn knowledge-informed representations after multiple layers of self-attention. The model is trained using a combination of a mention-masking objective and a weakly-supervised entity selection objective, which only requires access to an alias

* Equal Contribution

Proceedings of the 6th Workshop on Representation Learning for NLP (RepL4NLP-2021), pages 241–247
Bangkok, Thailand (Online), August 6, 2021.

table to generate candidate entities and doesn't assume any entity-linked data for training. We show that this objective allows the model to appropriately attend to relevant entities without explicit supervision for the linked entity and learn representations that perform competitively to models trained with entity-linked data.

We make the following contributions: (1) we propose KNowledge-Informed Transformers (KNIT), an approach to learn knowledge-informed text representations which does not require entity-linked data for training, (2) we train KNIT on a large corpora curated from the web with Wikidata as the knowledge graph, (3) we evaluate the approach on multiple tasks of entity typing and entity linking and show that it performs competitively or better than existing methods, yielding large improvements even while using $< 1\%$ of task-specific data for fine-tuning.

2 Related Works

BERT (Devlin et al., 2019) proposed a pre-training approach, called masked language modeling (MLM), which requires randomly replacing words in a sentence with a special [MASK] token and predicting the original masked tokens. RoBERTa (Liu et al., 2019b) trained a more robust BERT model on larger data. While MLM has been shown to learn general purpose representations, the amount of factual knowledge stored in such models is limited (Petroni et al., 2019; Poerner et al., 2019). Sun et al. (2019) propose a mention-masking objective which masks mentions of entities in a sentence, as opposed to random words, as a way of incorporating entity information into such models. Zhang et al. (2019) use entity-linked data and infuse representations of the linked entity in the final layer of the model to the representations of the corresponding entity mention. KnowBERT (Peters et al., 2019) learn an integrated entity linker that infuses entity representations into the word embedding input for the model and also relies on entity-linked data for training. K-Bert (Liu et al., 2019a) uses linked triples about entities in a sentence to inject knowledge. KGLM (Logan et al., 2019) proposed a fact-aware language model that selects and copies facts from KG for generation. Recently, Févry et al. (2020) introduced Entity-as-Experts (EAE), which is a masked language model coupled with an entity memory network. EAE learns to predict the entity spans, retrieves relevant entity memories and integrate them back to the Transformer layers. They also assume entity-linked data for training.

3 Knowledge-Informed Transformers (KNIT)

In this section, we describe the KNIT model as well as its training procedure. KNIT makes use of the mention-masking objective for training and conditions the encoder on both text as well as mentioned entities but does not assume any entity-linked data for training. Figure 1 shows the overall model.

3.1 Text and Entity Encoder

The input consists of a sentence along with *candidate* entities for the sentence. We first run a named entity extraction model on the sentence to extract mentions and then generate candidate entities based on cross-wikis (Ganea and Hofmann, 2017). We use a Wikipedia alias table for generating candidates, taken from Raiman and Raiman (2018). The start and end of mentions are demarcated using special tokens $\langle m \rangle$ and $\langle /m \rangle$. Given the text sequence $\{x_1, \ldots, x_n\}$ and the set of associated candidate entities for the sequence $\{e_1, \ldots, e_m\}$, we first embed the words and entities as vector embeddings. For entities, we use KG pre-trained embeddings (Lerer et al., 2019) and add a projection layer to upscale the entity embedding to the word embedding size. We will use Transformer self-attention (Vaswani et al., 2017) to encode both the text and the entities. Since self-attention has no notion of position in the sequence, it is common to concatenate a position embedding (Devlin et al., 2019) to the word embeddings. We follow this approach for the word embeddings. However, since the entities in the candidate set need to be encoded in a position-independent manner, we don't add any position embeddings to them. This entire sequence, position-dependent word embeddings and position-independent candidates, is passed through multiple layers of self-attention. The end result is contextualized token embeddings conditioned on the entities, $\{\tilde{x}_1, \ldots, \tilde{x}_n\}$, as well as candidate entity embeddings conditioned on the text $\{\tilde{e}_1, \ldots, \tilde{e}_m\}$.

3.2 Training

Mention-masking While the approach described above has the potential to learn knowledge-conditioned text representations, it needs a correct pre-training objective to learn to use the extra information from the entities. Since large

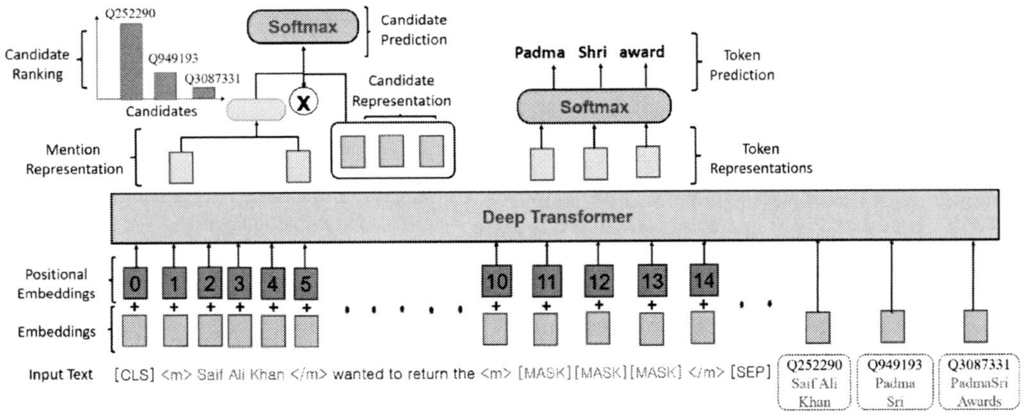

Figure 1: KNIT model with masked mention prediction and candidate ranking

	Random Tokens	Mention Tokens
RoBERTa	58.8	23.1
+ MM	61.6	25.7
KNIT	65.1	81.3

Table 1: Accuracy on predicting random tokens and entity mention tokens. While RoBERTa is highly accurate at predicting random words, it suffers when predicting mention tokens even when it is trained on a mention-masking (MM) objective.

Transformer models (Devlin et al., 2019) have a lot of parameters, they can be highly accurate at predicting random word tokens and thus directly using a MLM objective for training will not work as the model can ignore the entity embeddings. However, we find that, due to lack of factual knowledge, these models are not very good at predicting tokens of entity mentions. Table 1 shows this for RoBERTa (Liu et al., 2019b) model. Thus, mention-masking – predicting tokens of masked entity mentions, provides a better objective to learn to use the candidate entities and learn knowledge-informed representations. Note that in Table 1, even when RoBERTa is trained with mention-masking (+MM) it is unable to provide a high accuracy on predicting mention tokens. Thus including entity embeddings should provide enough context for the model to make correct predictions by using the entities, as reflected by the KNIT score in Table 1.

Candidate Ranking To further enable the model to use the correct entities for a mention, we use a weak entity linking objective that forces the model to rank one of the entities, from the candidate set of a mention, higher than all other entities for the sentence. Consider the i-th mention in a sentence with (m_{i1}, m_{i2}) as the start and end indices of the mention in the sentence, and a candidate set of entities C_i for this mention. We create a mention representation $\tilde{m}_i$ by concatenating $\tilde{x}_{m_{i1}}$ and $\tilde{x}_{m_{i2}}$. Now, given the representations, we score all entities for the mention i: $s_{ij} = W[\tilde{m}_i; \tilde{e}_j]$, where W is a learnable weight matrix. To enforce the model to select one entity from the mention's candidates, we find the highest scoring entity, $\hat{e}_i = \arg\max_{j \in C_i} s_{ij}$, and use that as a target in a cross-entropy loss:

$$\mathcal{L}^{cr} = \text{cross\_entropy}(\text{softmax}(s_{ij}), \mathbb{I}_{\hat{e}_i}) \quad (1)$$

where the softmax is over all entities (not just for mention i) in the sentence and $\mathbb{I}_{\hat{e}_i}$ is a one-hot vector with 1 for the entity $\hat{e}_i$ and 0 everywhere else. This objective enforces the model to rank one candidate higher than others candidates for the same mention as well as candidates of other entities. Similar objective has been explored for dealing with noise in entity typing models (Xu and Barbosa, 2018; Abhishek et al., 2017). The overall objective is a combination of bert-style MLM, mention-masking (MM) and candidate ranking:

$$\mathcal{L}^{mlm} + \alpha\mathcal{L}^{mm} + \beta\mathcal{L}^{cr} \quad (2)$$

4 Experiments

Implementation details are in Supplementary. Code of our models is available here[1].

[1] Source Code: https://github.com/dungtn/KNIT

Models evaluated: (1) RoBERTa (Liu et al., 2019b): the model uses the MLM objective for pre-training; (2) RoBERTa + MM: this model uses the mention-masking objective (Sun et al., 2019) in addition to the MLM objective; (3) KNIT: this is the proposed model which uses MLM, mention-masking and candidate ranking for pre-training. We use RoBERTa-base architecture for all models due to lack of computation resources. We compare our method with existing state-of-the-art in knowledge-informed representations: Ernie (Zhang et al., 2019), KnowBERT (Peters et al., 2019) and RELIC (Ling et al., 2020).

OpenEntity	**Precision**	**Recall**	**F1**
RoBERTa	76.91	73.84	75.34
RoBERTa+MM	74.67	74.63	74.65
Ernie	78.40	72.90	75.56
KnowBert	78.60	73.70	**76.10**
KNIT	76.48	75.76	**76.10**
FIGER	**Precision**	**Recall**	**F1**
RoBERTa	66.89	88.12	76.05
Ernie	57.19	76.51	73.39
KNIT	68.09	88.12	**76.80**

Table 2: Micro-averaged scores on entity typing tasks.

	OpenEnt (4%)	**FIGER** (0.5%)	**FIGER** (0.05%)
Roberta	$56.98_{\pm 4.71}$	$69.69_{\pm 0.38}$	$65.59_{\pm 1.65}$
+MM	$60.16_{\pm 2.44}$	$69.43_{\pm 0.62}$	$65.96_{\pm 1.38}$
KNIT	$\mathbf{63.97}_{\pm 1.59}$	$\mathbf{71.37}_{\pm 0.14}$	$\mathbf{67.40}_{\pm 0.41}$

Table 3: F1 score on entity typing when using only a fraction of the task-specific training data (0.05%−4%).

4.1 Results on Entity Typing

Entity typing is the task of identifying the semantic type of a given mention. We evaluate on two Entity typing datasets - OpenEntity (Choi et al., 2018) and FIGER (Ling et al., 2015). OpenEntity is a crowd-sourced dataset comprising 9 general types and 121 fine-grained types. We follow (Zhang et al., 2019) and evaluate on the nine general entity types. FIGER is a distant supervised dataset comprising over 2M examples and 113 entity types. Experimental results are shown in Table 2. KNIT outperforms RoBERTa(Liu et al., 2019b), Ernie(Zhang et al., 2019), and RoBERTa+MM(Sun et al., 2019) while being comparable to KnowBert (Peters et al., 2019). Note that KNIT performs comparably to the state-of-the-art without utilizing any entity-linked data for pre-training, unlike (Peters et al., 2019).

No Fine-tuning	
Wiki Alias Table	68.78
Our Top Candidate	70.66
RELIC	81.90
KNIT	82.71
KNIT +Wikilinks	**90.32**
Fine-tune (10% data)	
KNIT	92.04
Fine-tune (Full data)	
RELIC	94.90
Févry et al. (2020)	**96.70**
Raiman and Raiman (2018)	94.88
Radhakrishnan et al. (2018)	93.00
Le and Titov (2018)	93.07
Ganea and Hofmann (2017)	92.22
KNIT	92.87

Table 4: Entity linking accuracy under various fine-tuning scenarios.

To further evaluate the effectiveness of KNIT, we consider the scenario where only a fraction of the data is used for task-specific fine-tuning. For this, we sample equal number of examples per type to create the fine-tuning data. The models are fine-tuned using the sampled data but are evaluated on the entire test set. Table.3 shows that KNIT significantly outperforms RoBERTa(Liu et al., 2019b) and RoBERTa+MM in the data constrained cases.

4.2 Results on Entity Linking

We demonstrate that our pre-trained model can capture entity linking information. For this, we use the AIDA-CoNLL (Hoffart et al., 2011) dataset and evaluate the linking performance of the model *without any dataset-specific fine-tuning*. We also compare with a model that used wikipedia hyperlinks for supervision during pre-training (KNIT +Wikilinks). As shown in Table 4, KNIT improves upon the candidate ranking by 12.05% and 19.66% when partial entity linking supervision from Wiki linked-text data is available. Even without Wiki-linked data, it outperforms the best pre-trained model that considers mention context (RELIC) by 0.81%. To further explore the entity linking capacity of our model, we fine-tune the model and show that our model has competitive performance, even when using only 10% of the training data. When trained on the entire dataset, we find RELIC performs better, potentially due to the use of entity-linked data in its pre-training.

5 Conclusion

We propose a simple approach to learn knowledge-informed text representations using self-attention between text and mentioned entities. Our approach does not rely on any entity-linked data for training, enabling large-scale pre-training. We show that the method learns better representations than competing approaches and also learns entity-linking without explicit linking supervision. In the future, it will be interesting to explore how such methods can be used to condition the text encoder on structured KG facts about entities.

Acknowledgments

We thank members of UMass IESL and NLP groups for helpful discussion and feedback. We also thank DiffBot for their supports in collecting the linked-text data. This work is funded in part by the Center for Data Science and the Center for Intelligent Information Retrieval. The work reported here was performed in part using high performance computing equipment obtained under a grant from the Collaborative R&D Fund managed by the Massachusetts Technology Collaborative. Any opinions, findings and conclusions or recommendations expressed in this material are those of the authors and do not necessarily reflect those of the sponsor.

References

Abhishek Abhishek, Ashish Anand, and Amit Awekar. 2017. Fine-grained entity type classification by jointly learning representations and label embeddings. In *Proceedings of the 15th Conference of the European Chapter of the Association for Computational Linguistics: Volume 1, Long Papers*, pages 797–807.

Eunsol Choi, Omer Levy, Yejin Choi, and Luke Zettlemoyer. 2018. Ultra-fine entity typing. In *Proceedings of the 56th Annual Meeting of the Association for Computational Linguistics (Volume 1: Long Papers)*, pages 87–96, Melbourne, Australia. Association for Computational Linguistics.

Jacob Devlin, Ming-Wei Chang, Kenton Lee, and Kristina Toutanova. 2019. Bert: Pre-training of deep bidirectional transformers for language understanding. In *Proceedings of the 2019 Conference of the North American Chapter of the Association for Computational Linguistics: Human Language Technologies, Volume 1 (Long and Short Papers)*, pages 4171–4186.

Thibault Févry, Nicholas FitzGerald, Livio Baldini Soares, and Tom Kwiatkowski. 2020. Empirical evaluation of pretraining strategies for supervised entity linking. In *Automated Knowledge Base Construction*.

Thibault Févry, Livio Baldini Soares, Nicholas FitzGerald, Eunsol Choi, and Tom Kwiatkowski. 2020. Entities as experts: Sparse memory access with entity supervision. *arXiv*.

Octavian-Eugen Ganea and Thomas Hofmann. 2017. Deep joint entity disambiguation with local neural attention. In *Proceedings of the 2017 Conference on Empirical Methods in Natural Language Processing*, pages 2619–2629.

Johannes Hoffart, Mohamed Amir Yosef, Ilaria Bordino, Hagen Fürstenau, Manfred Pinkal, Marc Spaniol, Bilyana Taneva, Stefan Thater, and Gerhard Weikum. 2011. Robust disambiguation of named entities in text. In *Proceedings of the 2011 Conference on Empirical Methods in Natural Language Processing*, pages 782–792, Edinburgh, Scotland, UK. Association for Computational Linguistics.

Phong Le and Ivan Titov. 2018. Improving entity linking by modeling latent relations between mentions. In *Proceedings of the 56th Annual Meeting of the Association for Computational Linguistics (Volume 1: Long Papers)*, pages 1595–1604, Melbourne, Australia. Association for Computational Linguistics.

Adam Lerer, Ledell Wu, Jiajun Shen, Timothee Lacroix, Luca Wehrstedt, Abhijit Bose, and Alex Peysakhovich. 2019. PyTorch-BigGraph: A Large-scale Graph Embedding System. In *Proceedings of the 2nd SysML Conference*, Palo Alto, CA, USA.

Jeffrey Ling, Nicholas FitzGerald, Zifei Shan, Livio Baldini Soares, Thibault Févry, David Weiss, and Tom Kwiatkowski. 2020. Learning cross-context entity representations from text.

Xiao Ling, Sameer Singh, and Daniel S. Weld. 2015. Design challenges for entity linking. *Transactions of the Association for Computational Linguistics*, 3:315–328.

Weijie Liu, Peng Zhou, Zhe Zhao, Zhiruo Wang, Qi Ju, Haotang Deng, and Ping Wang. 2019a. K-bert: Enabling language representation with knowledge graph. *arXiv preprint arXiv:1909.07606*.

Yinhan Liu, Myle Ott, Naman Goyal, Jingfei Du, Mandar Joshi, Danqi Chen, Omer Levy, Mike Lewis, Luke Zettlemoyer, and Veselin Stoyanov. 2019b. Roberta: A robustly optimized bert pretraining approach. *arXiv preprint arXiv:1907.11692*.

Robert L. Logan, IV, Nelson F. Liu, Matthew E. Peters, Matt Gardner, and Sameer Singh. 2019. Barack's wife Hillary: Using knowledge graphs for fact-aware language modeling. In *Proceedings of the 57th Annual Meeting of the Association for Computational Linguistics (Volume 1: Long Papers)*, Florence, Italy. Association for Computational Linguistics.

Matthew E Peters, Mark Neumann, Robert Logan, Roy Schwartz, Vidur Joshi, Sameer Singh, and Noah A Smith. 2019. Knowledge enhanced contextual word representations. In *Proceedings of the 2019 Conference on Empirical Methods in Natural Language Processing and the 9th International Joint Conference on Natural Language Processing (EMNLP-IJCNLP)*, pages 43–54.

Fabio Petroni, Tim Rocktäschel, Sebastian Riedel, Patrick Lewis, Anton Bakhtin, Yuxiang Wu, and Alexander Miller. 2019. Language models as knowledge bases? In *Proceedings of the 2019 Conference on Empirical Methods in Natural Language Processing and the 9th International Joint Conference on Natural Language Processing (EMNLP-IJCNLP)*, pages 2463–2473.

Nina Poerner, Ulli Waltinger, and Hinrich Schütze. 2019. Bert is not a knowledge base (yet): Factual knowledge vs. name-based reasoning in unsupervised qa. *arXiv preprint arXiv:1911.03681*.

Alec Radford, Jeffrey Wu, Rewon Child, David Luan, Dario Amodei, and Ilya Sutskever. 2019. Language models are unsupervised multitask learners. *OpenAI Blog*, 1(8):9.

Priya Radhakrishnan, Partha Talukdar, and Vasudeva Varma. 2018. ELDEN: Improved entity linking using densified knowledge graphs. In *Proceedings of the 2018 Conference of the North American Chapter of the Association for Computational Linguistics: Human Language Technologies, Volume 1 (Long Papers)*, pages 1844–1853, New Orleans, Louisiana. Association for Computational Linguistics.

Colin Raffel, Noam Shazeer, Adam Roberts, Katherine Lee, Sharan Narang, Michael Matena, Yanqi Zhou, Wei Li, and Peter J Liu. 2019. Exploring the limits of transfer learning with a unified text-to-text transformer. *arXiv preprint arXiv:1910.10683*.

Jonathan Raiman and Olivier Raiman. 2018. Deeptype: multilingual entity linking by neural type system evolution. *arXiv preprint arXiv:1802.01021*.

Adam Roberts, Colin Raffel, and Noam Shazeer. 2020. How much knowledge can you pack into the parameters of a language model?

Livio Baldini Soares, Nicholas FitzGerald, Jeffrey Ling, and Tom Kwiatkowski. 2019. Matching the blanks: Distributional similarity for relation learning. *arXiv preprint arXiv:1906.03158*.

Yu Sun, Shuohuan Wang, Yukun Li, Shikun Feng, Xuyi Chen, Han Zhang, Xin Tian, Danxiang Zhu, Hao Tian, and Hua Wu. 2019. Ernie: Enhanced representation through knowledge integration. *arXiv preprint arXiv:1904.09223*.

Ashish Vaswani, Noam Shazeer, Niki Parmar, Jakob Uszkoreit, Llion Jones, Aidan N Gomez, Łukasz Kaiser, and Illia Polosukhin. 2017. Attention is all you need. In *Advances in neural information processing systems*, pages 5998–6008.

Peng Xu and Denilson Barbosa. 2018. Neural fine-grained entity type classification with hierarchy-aware loss. In *Proceedings of the 2018 Conference of the North American Chapter of the Association for Computational Linguistics: Human Language Technologies, Volume 1 (Long Papers)*, pages 16–25.

Zhilin Yang, Zihang Dai, Yiming Yang, Jaime Carbonell, Russ R Salakhutdinov, and Quoc V Le. 2019. Xlnet: Generalized autoregressive pretraining for language understanding. In *Advances in neural information processing systems*, pages 5753–5763.

Zhengyan Zhang, Xu Han, Zhiyuan Liu, Xin Jiang, Maosong Sun, and Qun Liu. 2019. Ernie: Enhanced language representation with informative entities. *arXiv preprint arXiv:1905.07129*.

A Appendices

A.1 Implementation Details(Pretraining)

To train KNIT, we collect 16M sentences from Wikipedia. We also collect 28M sentences from news articles and tag them using the DiffBot Entity Linker [2]. We further reduce the size of the entity vocabulary to 595K and remove examples that have no entity mentions. We limit each context sentence to 512 tokens and no more than 5 mentions per sentence with at least 2 and at most 10 candidate entities per mention span.

We use pre-trained entity embeddings with dimension $d = 200$ from (Lerer et al., 2019) and keep them fixed during the course of KNIT training. We use Adam optimizer with learning rate $1e^{-4}$, polynomial decay scheduler with warm-up, and clip norm 10. We also tune hyper-parameters in Equation (2) and choose $\alpha = 1$ and $\beta = 10$. The code will be made available on github[3].

A.2 Implementation Details(Entity Typing)

All results in Tables 2-3 are obtained by tuning a few hyperparameters - batch size, learning rate, dropout, attention dropout. Batch size was tuned in

[2] www.diffbot.com

[3] Code will be opensourced

Dataset	Train	Validation	Test
OpenEntity	1998	1,998	1,998
Figer	2,000,000	10,000	563
OpenEnt(4%)	82	1,998	1,998
Figer(0.5%)	11,300	10,000	563
Figer(0.05%)	1,130	10,000	563
AIDA-CoNLL	17,830	4,623	4,292

Table 5: Number of examples in Train, Validation and Test split of different datasets

range (16-64). Learning rate was tuned in (0.00001-0.0005). All dropouts were tuned sparsely in the range (0.1-0.3). During finetuning, we restrict the max number of candidates per mention to 10. Unlike pretraining, the entity embeddings were also finetuned during entity typing experiments and the best performing validation set checkpoint was used to generate test set results

Sample dataset creation for experiments of Table 3 were done using random seeds. Three different sample datasets were collected for each of OpenEnt(4%), Figer(0.5%) and Figer(0.05%). Each sample would comprise an equal number of examples per entity type but randomised across the three runs. Numbers reported in Table 3 correspond to mean and standard deviation values of the performance of the three sample dataset trained models on the test set.

A.2.1 Datasets

The sizes of sample and original datasets are shown in Table 5.

Deriving Contextualised Semantic Features from BERT (and Other Transformer Model) Embeddings

Jacob Turton
Department of Computer Science
UCL
j.turton@cs.ucl.ac.uk

David Vinson
Department of Psychology and Language Sciences
UCL
d.vinson@ucl.ac.uk

Robert Elliott Smith
Department of Computer Science
UCL
rob.smith@cs.ucl.ac.uk

Abstract

Models based on the transformer architecture, such as BERT, have marked a crucial step forward in the field of Natural Language Processing. Importantly, they allow the creation of word embeddings that capture important semantic information about words in context. However, as single entities, these embeddings are difficult to interpret and the models used to create them have been described as opaque. Binder and colleagues proposed an intuitive embedding space where each dimension is based on one of 65 core semantic features. Unfortunately, the space only exists for a small data-set of 535 words, limiting its uses. Previous work (Utsumi, 2018, 2020; Turton et al., 2020) has shown that Binder features can be derived from static embeddings and successfully extrapolated to a large new vocabulary. Taking the next step, this paper demonstrates that Binder features can be derived from the BERT embedding space. This provides two things; (1) semantic feature values derived from contextualised word embeddings and (2) insights into how semantic features are represented across the different layers of the BERT model.

1 Introduction

The last decade or so has seen a rapid progress in the field of Natural Language Processing (NLP) with a combination of new models and increasingly powerful hardware resulting in state of the art performances across a number of common tasks (Wang et al., 2020). One important area of improvement has been in the vector-space representation of words, known as word embeddings. Embedding models create word vectors within a vector space that captures important semantic and grammatical information (Boleda, 2020). Models such as Word2Vec (Mikolov et al., 2013) and GloVe (Pennington et al., 2014) were popular in the 2010s, but are static, meaning only one embedding is produced for each word. In reality words can have multiple meanings; 7% of common English word forms have homonyms and over 80% are polysemous (Rodd et al., 2002).

Deep learning language models such as ELMO: Embeddings from Language Models (Peters et al., 2018) addressed this issue, using deep neural-network language models to incorporate context and produce contextualised embeddings. Following this, the introduction of the transformer architecture and in particular its implementation in the Bidirectional Encoder Representations from Transformers (BERT) (Devlin et al., 2019) model, resulted in even better performing contextual embeddings.

Regardless of whether the embeddings mentioned are static or contextual, they all have the issue that, as individual objects, they are hard to interpret (Şenel et al., 2018). Whilst efforts have been made to produce more interpretable embeddings e.g. (Şenel et al., 2020; Panigrahi et al., 2019), the general approach has been to interpret them in relation to each-other. For example, the relative distance between word embeddings can indicate their semantic similarity (Schnabel et al., 2015). Alternatively, dimensionality reduction techniques can be used to visualise where the words sit within the embedding space (Liu et al., 2017). However, these methods may just show how the embeddings are related, rather than why, further feeding into the general criticism levelled at deep learning architectures; that they are opaque and difficult to interpret (Belinkov and Glass, 2019).

Binder et al. (2016) presented an alternative embedding space for words, based on 65 core semantic features, where each dimension relates to a feature. Unfortunately, the Binder dataset only contains 535 words, severely limiting its use for large scale text analysis. Previous research (Utsumi, 2018, 2020;

Proceedings of the 6th Workshop on Representation Learning for NLP (RepL4NLP-2021), pages 248–262
Bangkok, Thailand (Online), August 6, 2021.

Turton et al., 2020) has shown that the Binder feature values can be derived from static embeddings, such as Word2Vec, and successfully extrapolated to a large new vocabulary of words. The purpose of this research is to demonstrate that Binder features can be successfully derived from BERT embedding space allowing the features to be derived from contextual embeddings. Along the way, this also provided the opportunity to study how different types of semantic information are represented across the different layers of the BERT model.

2 Related Work

2.1 Probing Transformer Models

Whilst transformer models such as BERT have led to impressive improvements in NLP tasks, alongside other deep learning models they have been criticised as opaque "black boxes" that are difficult to interpret (Castelvecchi, 2016). To address this researchers have made efforts to better understand how they work. For example, Clark et al. (2019) were able to show that patterns of attention in BERT respond to certain syntactic relations between words. Other work has looked at how semantic information is represented in BERT. Researchers have shown that BERT can learn to represent semantic roles (Ettinger, 2020), entity types and semantic relations (Tenney et al., 2019). Reif et al. (2019) demonstrated clear 'clusters' for different senses of the same word, when visualising the spatial location of their BERT embeddings. Jawahar et al. (2019) demonstrated that embeddings from different layers of BERT performed better at different tasks, with semantic information tending to be better represented by the later layers. Whilst these studies provide important insights into the inner workings of transformer models, they do little to improve interpretability of individual word embeddings extracted from them.

2.2 Interpretable Word Embeddings

Research has also been done to produce more interpretable static word embeddings e.g. (Şenel et al., 2020; Panigrahi et al., 2019). For contextual embeddings, Aloui et al. (2020) produced embeddings with semantic super-senses as dimensions, but these are quite broad. The embedding space of Binder et al. (2016) offers a more fine-grained representation of semantics, but there are challenges in applying it to contextualised word embeddings.

2.3 Binder Semantic Features

Through a meta-analysis, Binder et al. (2016) identified 65 semantic features all believed to, and some demonstrated to, have neural correlates within the brain. They produced a 535 word data-set scored by participants across the 65 features. The features ranged from concrete object properties such as visual and auditory, to more abstract properties such as emotional aspects. This resulted in a 65-dimensional embedding for each word, where each dimension relates to a specific semantic feature.

This embedding space is useful as each dimension is easily interpretable and theoretically connected to a specific aspect of how people understand the meaning of words and concepts. Furthermore, representing words in this way makes it easy to understand how they are similar or different in terms of their semantic features. Figure 1 below demonstrates this by comparing the feature scores of the words *raspberry* and *mosquito*. It shows how the concepts differ across a range of dimensions. Also, since these features are derived from the psychological and neuroscience literature, it may mirror how people differentiate these concepts.

Unfortunately, the Binder dataset only exists for 535 words, which severely limits its uses. However, previous work (Utsumi, 2018, 2020) has shown that Binder feature values can be derived from static word embeddings such as Word2Vec and this can be used to extrapolate the feature space to a large

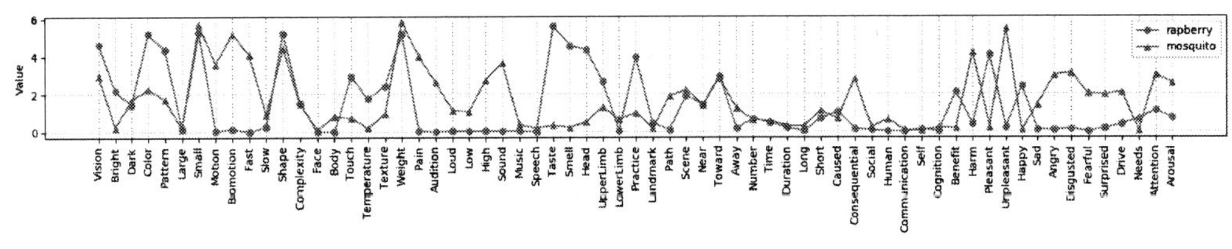

Figure 1: Binder feature values for *raspberry* and *mosquito*.

number of new words (Turton et al., 2020). Being able to do this using BERT embeddings would allow the features to be derived for words in context. Not only would this tackle the issues of polysemy and homonymy, but hopefully also mirror more subtle differences between words when used in context. Beyond this, the dataset also offers a powerful way to probe the semantic representation of words in models like BERT, by looking at: how well the different semantic features can be predicted overall, how the semantic representations build over the layers of the models and whether there are distinct patterns in how different types of semantic feature are represented across the layers.

3 Experiment 1a: Deriving Binder Embeddings from BERT and other Transformer Model Embeddings

3.1 Introduction

The aim of the first experiment was to derive Binder feature scores from the BERT embedding space. Words in the Binder dataset are presented out of context so the BERT embeddings were treated as *static* by taking an the average embedding over 250 randomly sampled sentences for each word. A selection of alternative transformer models were included for comparison: RoBERTa (Liu et al., 2019), XLNet (Yang et al., 2019) and GPT-2 (Radford et al.). Numberbatch embeddings (the best performing static embeddings from Turton et al. (2020)) (Speer et al., 2017) were used as a baseline comparison.

This experiment also offered the opportunity to investigate how different semantic features are represented across the different layers of BERT.

3.2 Materials

The Binder et al. (2016) data-set was used, providing scores across the 65 features for 535 words. For random sentences containing the Binder words, the One Billion Word Benchmark (BWB) (Chelba et al., 2014) was used. Author provided pre-trained versions of each transformer model were used. As far as possible, models of the same size were selected (see Appendix Table a for further details). Pre-trained Numberbatch embeddings were also used (Speer et al., 2017) as a benchmark. A simple 4 hidden-layer (300,200,100,50) neural network was used to predict semantic features from embeddings.

3.3 Method

The method here describes the process for the $\text{BERT}_{\text{BASE}}$ model, but was the same for all other models as well.

To produce static embeddings for each of the Binder words, 250 sentences containing each one were randomly sampled from the BWB dataset. Then using the pre-trained $\text{BERT}_{\text{BASE}}$ model the embeddings from all 12 layers (24 for large models) and the embedding layer were extracted for the target word for each of the sentences. A mean of the target word embedding across the 250 sentences was then taken. Additionally, for each model the best performing sub-word approach was used (see Table b and Figure a in Appendix for comparisons).

Semantic feature scores were predicted by feeding the extracted embeddings into a feed-forward neural network. 10-fold validation was used across the data-set and the final R-squared score averaged across the folds. Each of the 65 features was evaluated separately as was each of the layers. A Wilcoxon Ranks-sums test (Demšar, 2006) was used to compare performance of the different embedding models.

To investigate how the different semantic features are represented across the layers, each feature's R-squared score was re-scaled between 0-1 across the layers. A k-means clustering algorithm was then used to group the features according to similar patterns across the layers. The re-scaling ensured it was the pattern of behaviour across the layers rather than the absolute performance of each feature that was captured in the clustering. The membership of the clusters was compared to the categories of the features given in Binder data-set using the Adjusted Rand Index (Yeung and Ruzzo, 2001).

3.4 Results

Figure 2 below shows the mean R-squared scores across all semantic features for the different layers for the large and small models. The models showed slightly different performance across the layers with XLNet and RoBERTa peaking earlier than BERT. As per Table 1 row 2, BERT had the best performing single layer for both model sizes. Table 1 row 1 (combined) shows the performance of the models combining the best performing layer for each semantic feature. All models except GPT-2_{SMALL} significantly outperformed the Numberbatch baseline ($p<0.05$ for all). $\text{BERT}_{\text{BASE}}$

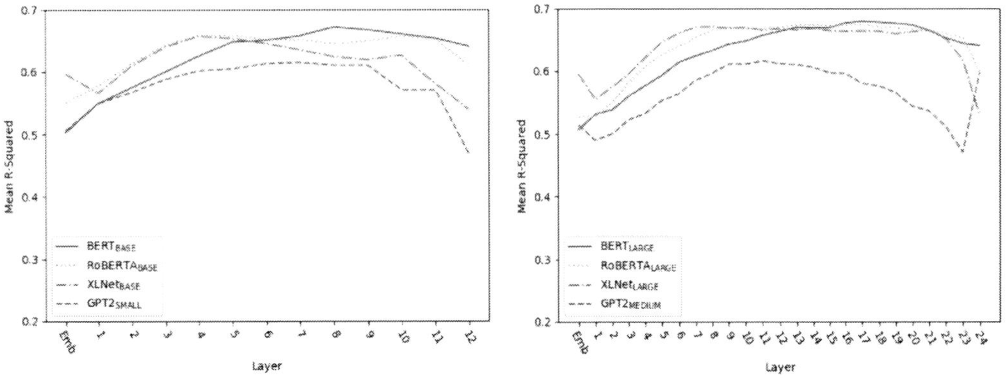

(a) (b)

Figure 2: Mean R-squared scores across all semantic features for layers of (a) small and (b) large models.

MEAN R-SQUARED	NumbrBatch	GPT-2		RoBERTa		XL-Net		BERT	
		Small	*Med.*	*Base*	*Large*	*Base*	*Large*	*Base*	*Large*
Combined	-	.631	.638	.673	**.692**	.665	.688	**.678**	.692
Best Layer	.646	.615	.616	.658	.674	.656	.670	**.667**	**.679**

Table 1: Best overall mean R-squared scores for the models across all 65 semantic features

also outperformed XLNet$_{BASE}$ ($p<0.05$) but not RoBERTa$_{BASE}$ ($p=0.17$).

There was variation in how well different features were predicted from the embeddings (some as low as 0.3 with others over 0.8) (See Figure b in the Appendix for full results). There was also general consistency between the models as to which features were well and poorly predicted with inter-feature variance (mean=0.011) larger than inter-model variance (mean=0.001). This indicates certain semantic features are difficult to predict regardless of the model.

For all models the larger version performed significantly better than the base version ($p<0.05$ for all). For the larger models there was no longer any significant difference between the BERT$_{LARGE}$, RoBERTa$_{LARGE}$ and XLNet$_{LARGE}$ models ($p>0.05$ for all), but all three did outperform GPT-2$_{MEDIUM}$ ($p>0.05$ for all).

The k-means clustering on the re-scaled BERT$_{BASE}$ R-squared scores indicated an optimal 3 clusters identified using an elbow plot. Figure 3 (a) below shows the memberships of the k-means clusters, along with their respective mean scores

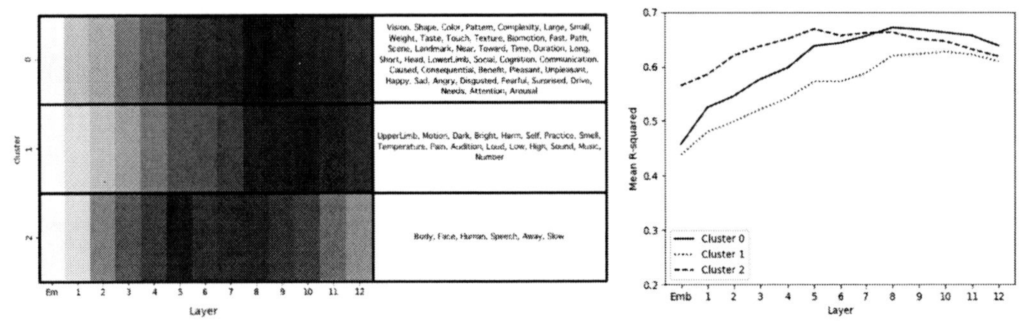

(a) (b)

Figure 3: (a) mean re-scaled R-squared scores for the three clusters with member features and (b) mean layer raw R-squared scores for the three clusters.

across each layer. Cluster 0 and 1 show a similar pattern showing a peak in the later layers. Cluster 2 shows a very different pattern with the peak much earlier in the mid-layers. Figure 3 (b) shows the mean raw R-squared layer scores for the different clusters. Clusters 0 2 achieve higher max scores than cluster 1. Whilst this does suggest different patterns of representation for the different features in the model, the clusters do not appear to match the categorisation of features given by Binder et al (2016) as the adjusted rand index was 0.02.

3.5 Discussion

The main purpose of this first experiment was to demonstrate that Binder style embeddings can successfully be derived from the BERT (and other similar model) embedding space. The secondary purpose was to explore how the representation of the semantic features varies across the different layers of a $\text{BERT}_{\text{BASE}}$ model. The results demonstrated that Binder features could be derived from BERT embeddings, outperforming static Numberbatch embeddings. This is interesting as Numberbatch embeddings make use of additional human provided information from a concept network, whereas BERT and the other models are purely trained on raw text. This hints towards the power of these bidirectional transformer models in capturing semantic information from word usage alone.

The poor performance of GPT-2 is not surprising due to its uni-directional attention architecture. GPT-2 has shown success when using very large models (up to 1.5B parameters, compared to $\text{BERT}_{\text{LARGE}}$'s 340M). These results highlight the power of the bidirectional architecture used by BERT, XLNet and RoBERTa

Perhaps most interesting results from this experiment are in relation to how the different semantic features are represented across the layers of BERT. In line with the findings of Jawahar et al. (2019), semantic features tended to be better represented by the later layers. However, a small subset of features were better represented by the middle layers. Clustering the features according to these behaviours did not match the Binder categories. However, the Binder categories are not the only way to group the features and there still are some similarities between the features in the different clusters. For example, Cluster 3 appears to capture a number of features (Human, Face, Speech, Body) relating to people and Cluster 2 captures 6 of the 7 features relating to audition.

Variation in how well different features were predicted by the models is more difficult to explain conclusively. On one hand, it may be that certain features are better represented by the transformer models than others. However, there is also variation in the underlying distributions of the different Binder features, with some more equally distributed across the score range than others. For certain features with very unbalanced distributions, this may have had a detrimental effect on their final R-squared score (see Appendix Figure f for residual plot examples).

Further improvements in predictive power may be possible by fine-tuning the transformer models directly on the Binder feature prediction task. For the purposes of this paper extracted embeddings rather than fine-tuning were used as (1) there were concerns over the small dataset size and (2) to keep the models as close as possible to their pre-trained state when comparing them.

4 Experiment 1b: Towards Contextualised Binder Features

4.1 Introduction

Experiment 1a demonstrated that Binder semantic features can be predicted from the BERT (and other model) embedding space, outperforming the best performing static embeddings (Numberbatch). However, the real power of the transformer architecture and its self-attention mechanism, is being able to represent a contextualised form of words (Reif et al., 2019). By treating the embeddings as "static" as in Experiment 1a, the embeddings were limited to an average of the word over many contexts. This may have added noise to the embeddings and consequently reduced performance by including word-senses not matching the sense suggested by the Binder features. Instead, hand selecting sentences that match the word-sense inferred from the Binder feature scores should help reduce this noise and improve performance.

4.2 Material

Same materials as Experiment 1a.

4.3 Method

For each word in the Binder data-set, ten sentences were hand-picked from the 250 randomly selected BWB sentences used in Experiment 1a. Sentences were picked by matching them to the word-sense

MEAN R-SQUARED	MODEL									
	BASELINE		GPT-2		RoBERTa		XL-Net		BERT	
	Base	*Large*	*Small*	*Med.*	*Base*	*Large*	*Base*	*Large*	*Base*	*Large*
Combined	.678	.692	.656	.670	**.736**	**.755**	.707	.730	.725	.741
Best Layer	.667	.679	.638	.643	.723	**.741**	.697	.714	.718	.729

Table 2: Mean R-squared scores for the models using selected sentences vs BERT baseline from Experiment 1a (randomly selected sentences)

inferred from the Binder feature scores. Following this, the exact same method as Experiment 1a was used, this time using the average embedding across the ten hand-selected sentences.

4.4 Results

Table 2 above gives the mean R-squared scores for the models. BERT scores from Experiment 1a are used as a baseline. (Individual feature results can be found in Figure c of the Appendix). Except from GPT-2, all embeddings from Experiment 1b outperformed the baseline from Experiment 1a.

4.5 Discussion

Using hand selected rather than purely randomly selected sentences improved the performance as expected. This was likely due to removing noise from unrelated uses of the word in the averaged embedding. Importantly, this shows to some degree that context can be captured in the derived semantic features as using more appropriate contexts improved performance. However, since the Binder data-set lacks explicit context for its words this experiment still falls short of a true ground-truth test of deriving contextualised semantic features from transformer word embeddings. To investigate how well semantic features can be predicted for words in specific contexts, it is necessary to look at other data-sets.

5 Experiment 2: Predicting Contextualised Features

5.1 Introduction

Together Experiments 1a and 1b demonstrate that semantic features ratings can be derived from transformer embeddings and that introducing some degree of context improves the performance. But the Binder data-set unfortunately lacks explicit context for its words.

An alternative data-set (Van Dantzig et al., 2011) of contextualised semantic features for words in context pairs can be used. In each context pair a property word e.g. *abrasive* is paired an object word e.g. *lava* and participants scored the property word across five semantic features in a similar way to the Binder dataset. In each case, the object should influence the meaning of the property word, in turn influencing its feature scores. Each property is paired with two different objects giving two word-pairs for each property and with different semantic feature scores for each one (see Table 3). By feeding the property-object pairs into the transformer models, the extracted embedding for the property word should capture its specific feature values influenced by its context object word. Since each property word is paired with two different objects, a static version of its embedding can be created by taking the mean of its embeddings across both of its context pairs. If the models successfully capture the specific feature values of the property words in the individual contexts, the individual contextual embeddings should outperform the static property embeddings in predicting semantic feature scores.

Due to its poor performance GPT-2 was dropped and only the better performing LARGE versions of BERT, XLNet and RoBERTa were used.

5.2 Materials

The Van Dantzig et al. (2011) data-set consists of 774 property-object pairs. Each word pair con-

PROPERTY	OBJECT	FEATURE				
		Visual	Auditory	Haptic	Gustatory	Olfactory
Abrasive	Lava	3.83	1.27	2.37	0.07	0.46
Abrasive	Sandpaper	3.37	2.35	4.81	0.26	0.09

Table 3: Feature scores for Property word *Abrasive* with its two different Object word pairs.

FEATURE	PROPERTY-MEAN			CONTEXTUALISED		
	BERT	XL-Net	RoBERTa	BERT	XL-Net	RoBERTa
Visual	0.532	0.448	0.456	**0.652**	0.583	0.633
Auditory	0.722	0.668	0.680	**0.793**	0.733	0.772
Haptic	0.556	0.512	0.505	**0.660**	0.616	0.634
Gustatory	0.611	0.531	0.591	0.800	0.704	**0.813**
Olfactory	0.610	0.587	0.597	**0.740**	0.736	0.731
MEAN	0.607	0.549	0.556	**0.729**	0.674	0.717

Table 4: Mean R-squared scores for the five features for mean and contextualised embeddings from the three different models, compared to a Numberbatch baseline.

sists of a property and object word, and has a rating across five semantic features: Visual, Auditory, Haptic, Gustatory and Olfactory. The ratings are between 0-5 for each. The same pre-trained $\text{BERT}_{\text{LARGE}}$, $\text{XL-Net}_{\text{LARGE}}$ and $\text{ROBERTA}_{\text{LARGE}}$ models from Experiment 1a and b were used and the pre-trained Numberbatch embeddings.

5.3 Method

The property-object word pairs were fed into the transformer models as the input sequences and the embedding for the property word was extracted. Embeddings from all 24 layers and the embedding layer were extracted. The different layer embeddings were then fed into a simple 4 hidden-layer (300, 200, 100, 50) neural network for training prediction with each of the five semantic features used separately as the target variable.

For the *Property-mean* condition, for each property word, the extracted embeddings across both of its object context pairs were averaged. For the *contextualised* condition, the extracted property embeddings were left unique for each object context pair.

Like Experiment 1, the data-set was split into ten-folds with 90% of the data for training and the reaming 10% for evaluation. The mean r-squared scores across the ten-folds was calculated for each of the five semantic features.

5.4 Results

Table 4 shows the R-squared scores for the best performing layer from each model. (See Appendix Figure d for per layer results). The contextualised transformer embeddings outperform both the mean transformer embeddings. Overall, the BERT model performed best.

5.5 Discussion

The purpose of experiment 2 was demonstrate the ability to derive contextual semantic features from transformer embeddings. As predicted, the contextual transformer embeddings performed better than the "static" ones. This suggests that, for each context pair, the model representations of the property words were able to capture the specific semantic features as influenced by the object it was paired with. Taking the mean across both object pairs was detrimental for performance as the embedding was no longer unique to the context pair.

Whilst this experiment demonstrates it is possible to derive contextualised semantic features from transformer embeddings, it only involves a small number of features for words in short word-pair contexts. Ideally, we would be able to predict the full 65 semantic features in the Binder embedding space for words contextualised in longer, more natural sequences.

6 Experiment 3: Evaluation of Contextualised Binder Embeddings

6.1 Introduction

Experiment 1a and b demonstrated that Binder features can be derived from various transformer embedding spaces and that some effects of context can be picked up, whilst Experiment 2 demonstrated that the embeddings can be used to derive contextualised semantic features, but for a very limited number of features and only in word-pair sequences. The lingering issue is the lack of a data-set of the full 65 Binder semantic features for words context which would provide a ground-truth test for deriving contextualised semantic features from transformer embeddings.

To address this, this experiment used the word-sense disambiguation (WSD) task as an indirect evaluation of derived semantic features for words

METRIC	Raw BERT$_{\text{LARGE}}$	Experiment 2	BERT Binder 1a	BERT Binder 1b
Accuracy	0.68	0.60	0.67	0.67
F1-Score	0.71	0.66	0.70	0.71

Table 5: Accuracy & F1 score of raw BERT & BERT-derived Binder embeddings on the validation set.

in context. WSD is an open problem in NLP where the task is to determine which sense of word is being used in a sequence (Navigli, 2009). Models that perform well on this task are able to separate the different semantic meanings of a word, depending on the context it is used in. By evaluating how well derived Binder embeddings perform at this task, it should indicate how good the embeddings are at representing the contextualised semantic features of the words. In this experiment the Binder embeddings are compared to raw BERT embeddings which have shown reasonable performance in the task (Pilehvar and Camacho-Collados, 2019).

For comparison, the different approaches for deriving Binder embeddings from Experiments 1a and 1b were used as well as the much smaller Van Dantzig feature set from Experiment 2.

6.2 Materials

The Word in Context (WiC) WSD data-set (Pilehvar and Camacho-Collados, 2019) was used. It consists of sentence pairs each containing the same target word and a binary classification (True/False) of whether the target word has the same word-sense or not between them. The data-set is already divided into a training (5429) and separate validation (639) set.

The same BERT$_{\text{LARGE}}$ model and trained neural networks from Experiment 1a, 1b and 2 were used to predict semantic feature values.

6.3 Method

Using the pre-trained BERT$_{\text{LARGE}}$ model, word embeddings from all 24 layers + the embedding layer were extracted for the target word in each of the sentences of the WiC dataset. Using the neural networks trained in Experiment 1a and 1b the Binder features were predicted using the optimal BERT$_{\text{LARGE}}$ layer for each of the 65 features and for the smaller Van Dantzig feature set from Experiment 2.

For each sentence pair, the cosine similarity was calculated between the embeddings for the target words, either using the raw BERT$_{\text{LARGE}}$ embeddings or the derived Binder or Van Dantzig embeddings. For evaluation a logistic regression model was used with the cosine similarity scores as input. The model was trained on the train set and evaluated on the validation set using accuracy and F1 Score.

6.4 Results

Table 5 shows the performance of the best performing layer (21) raw BERT$_{\text{LARGE}}$ embeddings, Binder and Van Dantzig embeddings on the WiC dev set (see Appendix Figure e for all layer performances). Overall the Binder embeddings performed comparatively to the raw BERT$_{\text{LARGE}}$ embeddings. The five feature Van Dantzig embeddings (from Exp. 2) performed worst.

6.5 Discussion

The purpose of this final experiment was to evaluate contextualised Binder embeddings. In the absence of a ground-truth data-set for contextualised Binder features, the WSD task was used as an indirect measure. The contextualised Binder embeddings performed comparatively to raw BERT embeddings

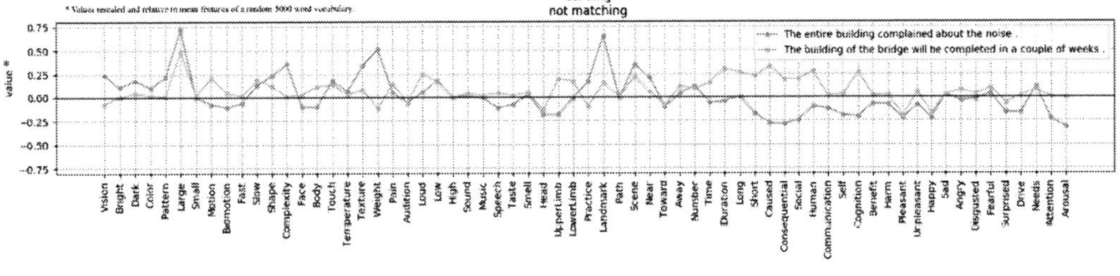

Figure 4: Example of predicted semantic features for the word *building* in two different context sentences

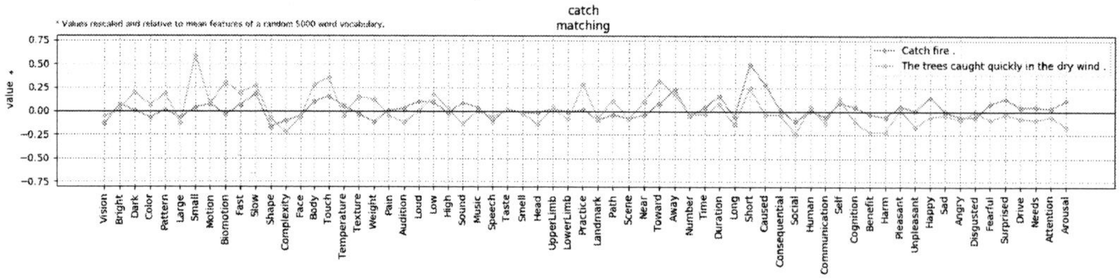

Figure 5: Example of predicted semantic features for the word *catch* in two different context sentences

which have been shown to capture contextualised semantics (Reif et al., 2019; Pilehvar and Camacho-Collados, 2019). This suggests that the Binder embeddings also capture contextualised semantic features to some extent. The improved performance of the approach in experiment 1b did not meaningfully contribute to improved performance in this downstream task. But, the Binder embeddings did outperform the smaller Van Dantzig feature-set embeddings from Experiment 2, suggesting that the larger Binder feature set is a more complete semantic representation of words.

Importantly, the nature of the Binder feature space makes interpreting the embeddings easier. Figure 4 below illustrates how the meaning of the word *building* differs in the two different context sentences from the WiC data-set.

However, Binder features predicted from transformer embeddings did not always match what would be expected. Figure 5 illustrates this, where the representation of *catch* in the second sentence appears closer to the *physical act of catching* rather than the intended meaning of *to catch fire*. Qualitative evaluation of the embeddings like this is powerful for understanding their quality, but comes at the cost of being time consuming.

7 Conclusion

The overarching aim of this work was to demonstrate that Binder style semantic feature embeddings can be derived from the BERT embedding space in the same way that previous research (Utsumi, 2018, 2020; Turton et al., 2020) has shown for static embeddings. It also offered the opportunity to probe how semantic information is represented across the different layers of BERT. Treating the embeddings as static, Experiment 1a supported this aim with BERT and other transformer embeddings outperforming the best performing static embeddings model Numberbatch. The results also supported the findings of Jawahar et al. (2019) that semantic information tends to be represented in the later layers of BERT. Hand-picking sentences in Experiment 1b lead to better performance indicating that some degree of context is represented in the derived semantic features.

Experiment 2 provided further evidence of the ability of transformer models to derive contextualised semantic features but was limited by the small set of features and the short word-pair context sequences.

Finally, the ability of Binder embeddings to perform comparatively to raw BERT embeddings in Experiment 3 suggests that they do capture, to some degree, contextualised semantic features when derived from transformer embeddings.

In conclusion, within the limitations of the Binder dataset, this paper suggests that it is possible to derive contextualised semantic features from contextualised word embeddings as a proof of concept. However, without a ground-truth test, it is not able to demonstrate this conclusively. To do this would likely require the production of a Binder feature set for words explicitly in context, and this may be a necessary next step if the Binder feature set is considered useful for further use. Furthermore, as the Binder dataset focuses on general use words, for researchers wishing to derive semantic features useful for specific domains, they likely would need to construct datasets of domain-specific features for a domain-specific vocabulary.

Beyond the direct findings of this paper, we also hope that this work highlights the usefulness of using existing psychological research data to improve the understanding and interpretability of what can otherwise be somewhat opaque deep learning models.

References

Cindy Aloui, Carlos Ramisch, Alexis Nasr, and Lucie Barque. 2020. Slice: Supersense-based lightweight interpretable contextual embeddings. In *Proceedings of the 28th International Conference on Computational Linguistics*, pages 3357–3370.

Yonatan Belinkov and James Glass. 2019. Analysis methods in neural language processing: A survey. *Transactions of the Association for Computational Linguistics*, 7:49–72.

Jeffrey R Binder, Lisa L Conant, Colin J Humphries, Leonardo Fernandino, Stephen B Simons, Mario Aguilar, and Rutvik H Desai. 2016. Toward a brain-based componential semantic representation. *Cognitive neuropsychology*, 33(3-4):130–174.

Gemma Boleda. 2020. Distributional semantics and linguistic theory. *Annual Review of Linguistics*, 6:213–234.

Davide Castelvecchi. 2016. Can we open the black box of ai? *Nature News*, 538(7623):20.

Ciprian Chelba, Tomas Mikolov, Mike Schuster, Qi Ge, Thorsten Brants, Phillipp Koehn, and Tony Robinson. 2014. One billion word benchmark for measuring progress in statistical language modeling. In *Fifteenth Annual Conference of the International Speech Communication Association*.

Kevin Clark, Urvashi Khandelwal, Omer Levy, and Christopher D Manning. 2019. What does bert look at? an analysis of bert's attention. In *Proceedings of the 2019 ACL Workshop BlackboxNLP: Analyzing and Interpreting Neural Networks for NLP*, pages 276–286.

Janez Demšar. 2006. Statistical comparisons of classifiers over multiple data sets. *The Journal of Machine Learning Research*, 7:1–30.

Jacob Devlin, Ming-Wei Chang, Kenton Lee, and Kristina Toutanova. 2019. Bert: Pre-training of deep bidirectional transformers for language understanding. In *Proceedings of the 2019 Conference of the North American Chapter of the Association for Computational Linguistics: Human Language Technologies, Volume 1 (Long and Short Papers)*, pages 4171–4186.

Allyson Ettinger. 2020. What bert is not: Lessons from a new suite of psycholinguistic diagnostics for language models. *Transactions of the Association for Computational Linguistics*, 8:34–48.

Ganesh Jawahar, Benoît Sagot, and Djamé Seddah. 2019. What does bert learn about the structure of language? In *ACL 2019-57th Annual Meeting of the Association for Computational Linguistics*.

Shusen Liu, Peer-Timo Bremer, Jayaraman J Thiagarajan, Vivek Srikumar, Bei Wang, Yarden Livnat, and Valerio Pascucci. 2017. Visual exploration of semantic relationships in neural word embeddings. *IEEE transactions on visualization and computer graphics*, 24(1):553–562.

Yinhan Liu, Myle Ott, Naman Goyal, Jingfei Du, Mandar Joshi, Danqi Chen, Omer Levy, Mike Lewis, Luke Zettlemoyer, and Veselin Stoyanov. 2019. Roberta: A robustly optimized bert pretraining approach. *arXiv preprint arXiv:1907.11692*.

Tomas Mikolov, Ilya Sutskever, Kai Chen, Greg Corrado, and Jeffrey Dean. 2013. Distributed representations of words and phrases and their compositionality. In *Proceedings of the 26th International Conference on Neural Information Processing Systems-Volume 2*, pages 3111–3119.

Roberto Navigli. 2009. Word sense disambiguation: A survey. *ACM computing surveys (CSUR)*, 41(2):1–69.

Abhishek Panigrahi, Harsha Vardhan Simhadri, and Chiranjib Bhattacharyya. 2019. Word2sense: sparse interpretable word embeddings. In *Proceedings of the 57th Annual Meeting of the Association for Computational Linguistics*, pages 5692–5705.

Jeffrey Pennington, Richard Socher, and Christopher D Manning. 2014. Glove: Global vectors for word representation. In *Proceedings of the 2014 conference on empirical methods in natural language processing (EMNLP)*, pages 1532–1543.

Matthew Peters, Mark Neumann, Mohit Iyyer, Matt Gardner, Christopher Clark, Kenton Lee, and Luke Zettlemoyer. 2018. Deep contextualized word representations. In *Proceedings of the 2018 Conference of the North American Chapter of the Association for Computational Linguistics: Human Language Technologies, Volume 1 (Long Papers)*, pages 2227–2237.

Mohammad Taher Pilehvar and Jose Camacho-Collados. 2019. Wic: the word-in-context dataset for evaluating context-sensitive meaning representations. In *Proceedings of the 2019 Conference of the North American Chapter of the Association for Computational Linguistics: Human Language Technologies, Volume 1 (Long and Short Papers)*, pages 1267–1273.

Alec Radford, Jeffrey Wu, Rewon Child, David Luan, Dario Amodei, and Ilya Sutskever. Language models are unsupervised multitask learners.

Emily Reif, Ann Yuan, Martin Wattenberg, Fernanda B Viegas, Andy Coenen, Adam Pearce, and Been Kim. 2019. Visualizing and measuring the geometry of bert. *Advances in Neural Information Processing Systems*, 32:8594–8603.

Jennifer Rodd, Gareth Gaskell, and William Marslen-Wilson. 2002. Making sense of semantic ambiguity: Semantic competition in lexical access. *Journal of Memory and Language*, 46(2):245–266.

Tobias Schnabel, Igor Labutov, David Mimno, and Thorsten Joachims. 2015. Evaluation methods for unsupervised word embeddings. In *Proceedings of the 2015 conference on empirical methods in natural language processing*, pages 298–307.

Lütfi Kerem Şenel, İhsan Utlu, Furkan Şahinuç, Haldun M Ozaktas, and Aykut Koç. 2020. Imparting interpretability to word embeddings while preserving semantic structure. *Natural Language Engineering*, pages 1–26.

Lütfi Kerem Şenel, Ihsan Utlu, Veysel Yücesoy, Aykut Koc, and Tolga Cukur. 2018. Semantic structure and interpretability of word embeddings. *IEEE/ACM Transactions on Audio, Speech, and Language Processing*, 26(10):1769–1779.

Robyn Speer, Joshua Chin, and Catherine Havasi. 2017. Conceptnet 5.5: An open multilingual graph of general knowledge. In *Proceedings of the AAAI Conference on Artificial Intelligence*, volume 31.

Ian Tenney, Dipanjan Das, and Ellie Pavlick. 2019. Bert rediscovers the classical nlp pipeline. In *Proceedings of the 57th Annual Meeting of the Association for Computational Linguistics*, pages 4593–4601.

Jacob Turton, David Vinson, and Robert Smith. 2020. Extrapolating binder style word embeddings to new words. In *Proceedings of the second workshop on linguistic and neurocognitive resources*, pages 1–8.

Akira Utsumi. 2018. A neurobiologically motivated analysis of distributional semantic models. In *Proceedings of the 40th Annual Conference of the Cognitive Science Society*, pages 1147–1152.

Akira Utsumi. 2020. Exploring what is encoded in distributional word vectors: A neurobiologically motivated analysis. *Cognitive Science*, 44(6):e12844.

Saskia Van Dantzig, Rosemary A Cowell, René Zeelenberg, and Diane Pecher. 2011. A sharp image or a sharp knife: Norms for the modality-exclusivity of 774 concept-property items. *Behavior Research Methods*, 43(1):145–154.

Yuxuan Wang, Yutai Hou, Wanxiang Che, and Ting Liu. 2020. From static to dynamic word representations: a survey. *International Journal of Machine Learning and Cybernetics*, pages 1–20.

Zhilin Yang, Zihang Dai, Yiming Yang, Jaime Carbonell, Russ R Salakhutdinov, and Quoc V Le. 2019. Xlnet: Generalized autoregressive pretraining for language understanding. *Advances in Neural Information Processing Systems*, 32:5753–5763.

Ka Yee Yeung and Walter L Ruzzo. 2001. Details of the adjusted rand index and clustering algorithms, supplement to the paper an empirical study on principal component analysis for clustering gene expression data. *Bioinformatics*, 17(9):763–774.

Appendix

	MODEL							
	BERT		GPT-2		XLNet		RoBERTA	
	Base	*Large*	*Small*	*Medium*	*Base*	*Large*	*Base*	*Large*
Parameters	110M	340M	117M	345M	110M	340M	125M	355M
Layers	12	24	12	24	12	24	12	24
Attention Heads	12	16	12	16	12	16	12	16
Hidden state size	768	1024	768	1024	768	1024	768	1024

Table a. Selected properties of the different transformer models used (large models shaded).

	MODEL											
	$\text{BERT}_{\text{BASE}}$			$\text{GPT-2}_{\text{SMALL}}$			$\text{XLNet}_{\text{BASE}}$			$\text{RoBERTa}_{\text{BASE}}$		
R-sq.	*First*	*Last*	*Mean*	*First*	*Last*	*Mean*	*First*	*Last*	*Mean*	*First*	*Last*	*Mean*
Comb.	.668	**.678**	.677	.548	**.630**	.611	.655	.660	**.665**	.660	.670	**.673**
Best	.657	**.671**	.667	.520	**.615**	.591	.645	.652	**.657**	.647	.652	**.658**

Table b. Mean R-squared across all Binder features for different subword embedding approaches (first subword, last subword or mean across all subwords). Comb. = combined best layer per feature. Best = best single layer overall.

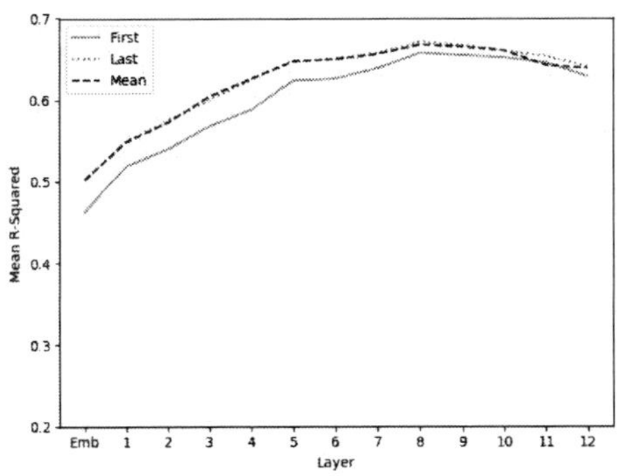

(a)

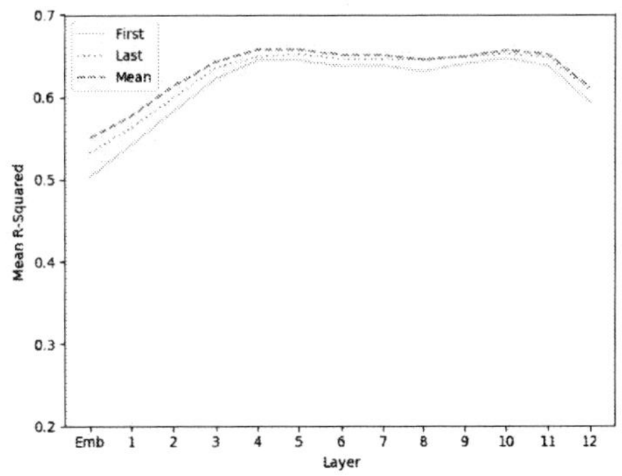

(b)

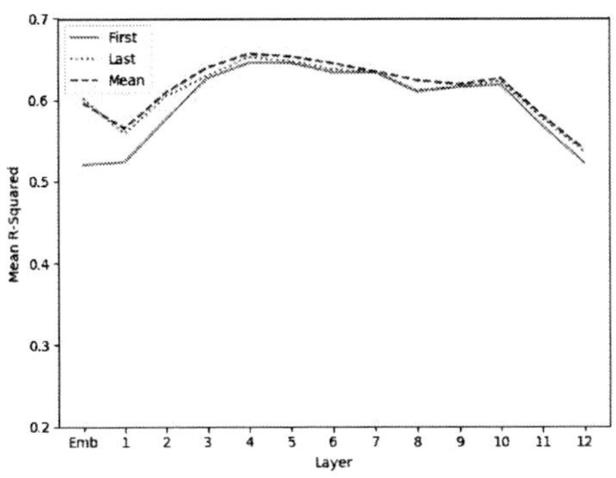

(c)

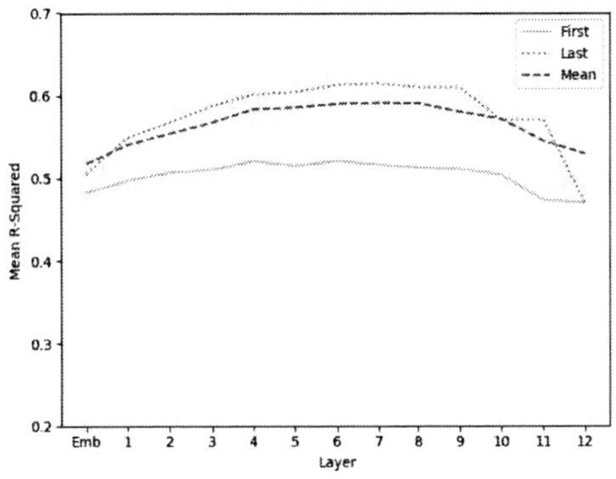

(d)

Figure a. performance of different subword embeddings across the 12 layers for (a) $\text{BERT}_{\text{BASE}}$ (b) $\text{RoBERTA}_{\text{BASE}}$ (c) $\text{XLNet}_{\text{BASE}}$ and (d) $\text{GPT-2}_{\text{SMALL}}$

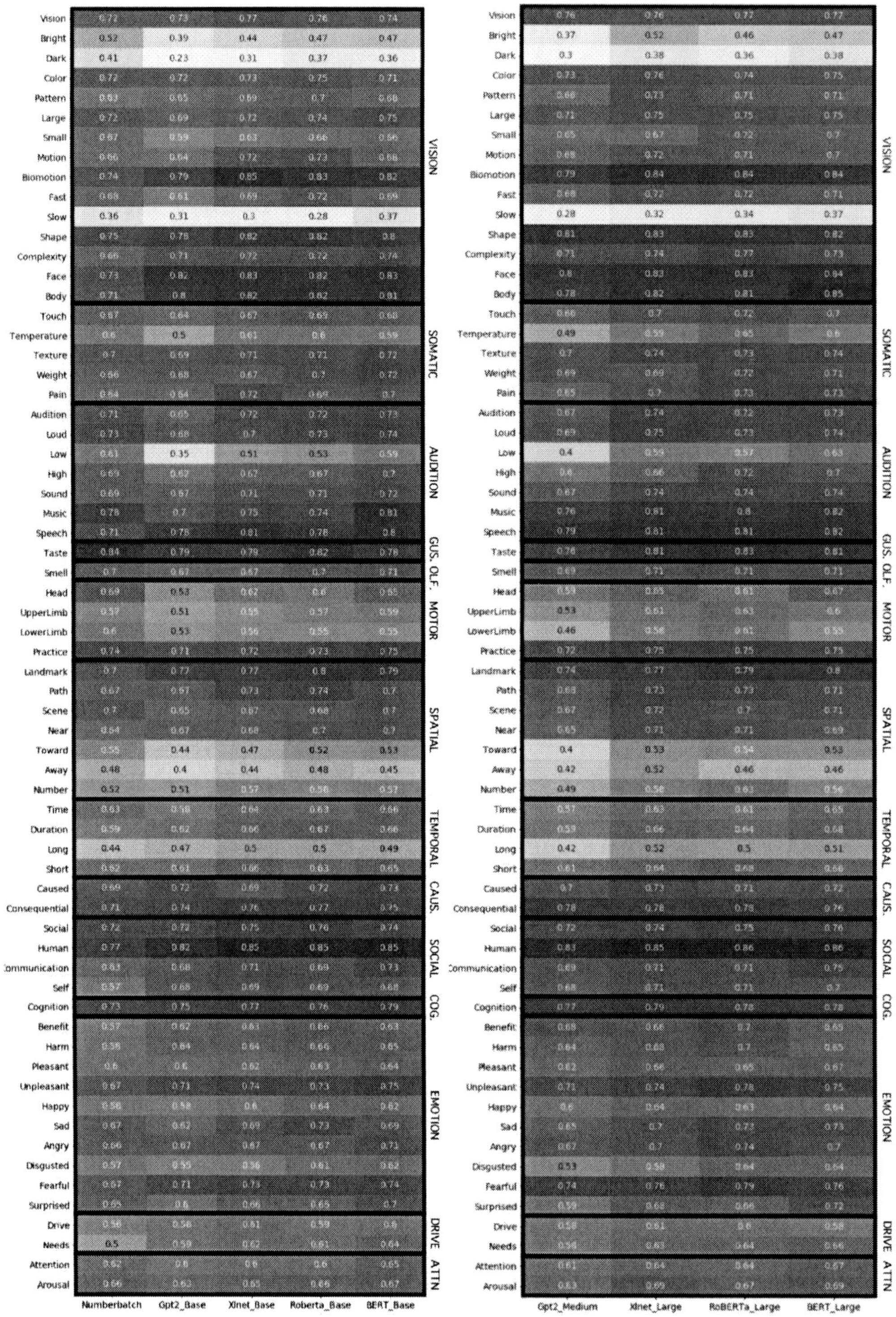

(a) (b)

Figure b. All feature R-squared scores for the Numberbatch baseline and (a) small models (b) large models, with Binder et al (2016) categories indicated.

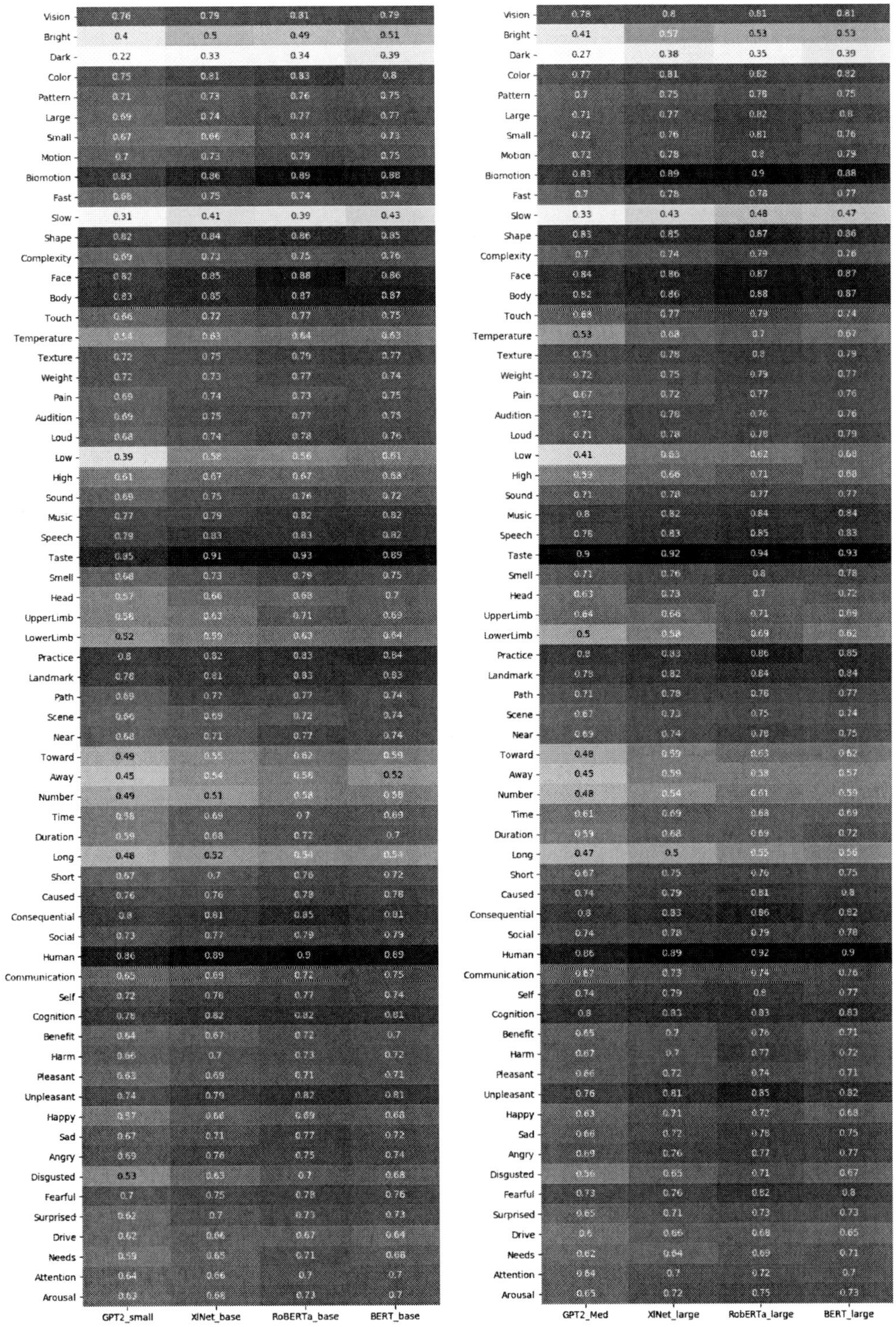

(a) (b)

Figure c. All feature R-squared scores for the (a) small and (b) large models for selected sentences of Experiment 1b.

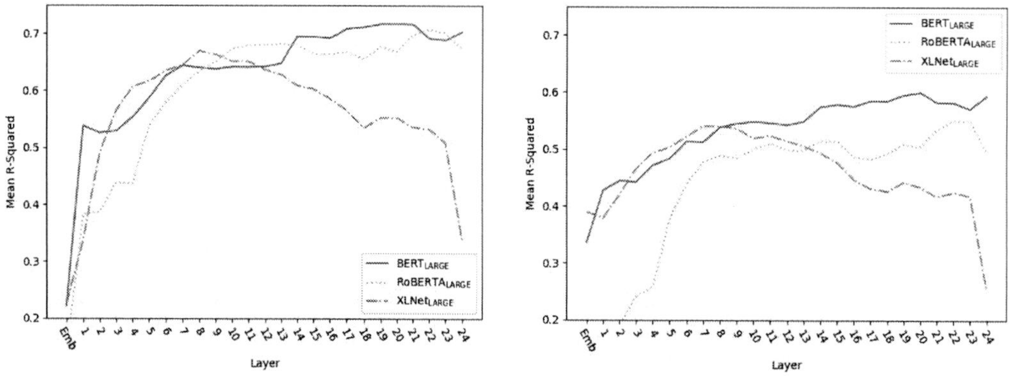

(a) (b)

Figure d. Model per-layer mean R-squared scores for Experiment 2 using (a) individual word-pair property embedding and (b) mean across word-pairs property embedding.

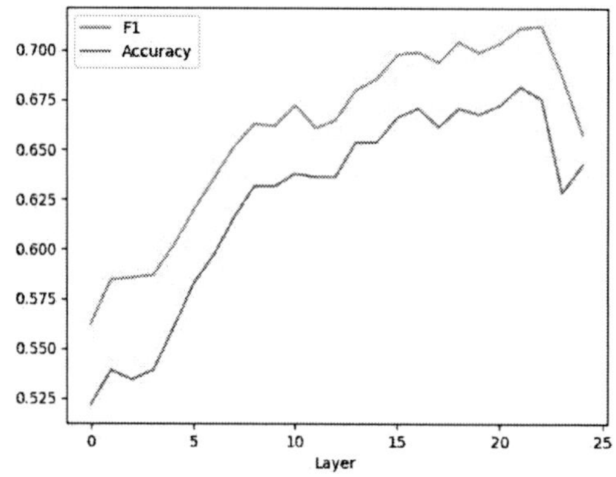

Figure e. Raw $\text{BERT}_{\text{LARGE}}$ Accuracy and F1 scores on WiC dataset

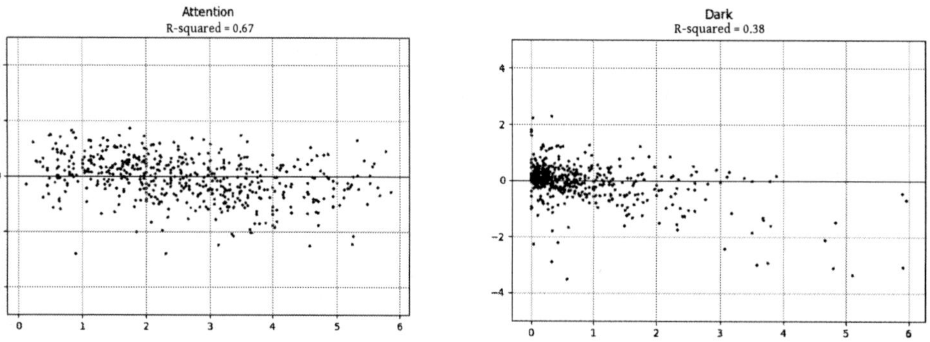

(a) (b)

Figure f. Residual plots for features (a) *Attention* and (b) *Dark*

Syntactic Perturbations Reveal Representational Correlates of Hierarchical Phrase Structure in Pretrained Language Models

Matteo Alleman[†] **Jonathan Mamou**[‡] **Miguel A Del Rio**[◇]
Hanlin Tang[‡] **Yoon Kim**[⋆,◇,•] **SueYeon Chung**[†,◇,•]

[†]Columbia University [‡]Intel Labs
[⋆]MIT-IBM Watson AI [◇]Massachusetts Institute of Technology

Abstract

While vector-based language representations from pretrained language models have set a new standard for many NLP tasks, there is not yet a complete accounting of their inner workings. In particular, it is not entirely clear what aspects of sentence-level syntax are captured by these representations, nor how (if at all) they are built along the stacked layers of the network. In this paper, we aim to address such questions with a general class of interventional, input perturbation-based analyses of representations from pretrained language models. Importing from computational and cognitive neuroscience the notion of representational invariance, we perform a series of probes designed to test the sensitivity of these representations to several kinds of structure in sentences. Each probe involves swapping words in a sentence and comparing the representations from perturbed sentences against the original. We experiment with three different perturbations: (1) random permutations of n-grams of varying width, to test the scale at which a representation is sensitive to word position; (2) swapping of two spans which do or do not form a syntactic phrase, to test sensitivity to global phrase structure; and (3) swapping of two adjacent words which do or do not break apart a syntactic phrase, to test sensitivity to local phrase structure. Results from these probes collectively suggest that Transformers build sensitivity to larger parts of the sentence along their layers, and that hierarchical phrase structure plays a role in this process. More broadly, our results also indicate that structured input perturbations widens the scope of analyses that can be performed on often-opaque deep learning systems, and can serve as a complement to existing tools (such as supervised linear probes) for interpreting complex black-box models [1]

[1]Datasets, extracted features and code will be publicly available upon publication.

• Correspondence

1 Introduction

It is still unknown how distributed information processing systems encode and exploit complex relational structures in data, despite their ubiquitous use in the modern world. The fields of deep learning (Saxe et al., 2013; Hewitt and Manning, 2019), neuroscience (Sarafyazd and Jazayeri, 2019; Stachenfeld et al., 2017), and cognitive science (Elman, 1991; Kemp and Tenenbaum, 2008; Tervo et al., 2016) have given great attention to this question, including a productive focus on the potential models and their implementations of hierarchical tasks, such as predictive maps and graphs. In this work, we provide a generic means of identifying input structures that deep language models use to "chunk up" vastly complex data.

Natural (human) language provides a rich domain for studying how complex hierarchical structures are encoded in information processing systems. More so than other domains, human language is unique in that its underlying hierarchy has been extensively studied and theorized in linguistics, which provides source of "ground truth" structures for stimulus data. Much prior work on characterizing the types of linguistic information encoded in computational models of language such as neural networks has focused on supervised readout probes, which train a classifier on top pretrained models to predict a particular linguistic label (Belinkov and Glass, 2017; Liu et al., 2019a; Tenney et al., 2019). In particular, Hewitt and Manning (2019) apply probes to discover linear subspaces that encode tree-distances as distances in the representational subspace, and Kim et al. (2020) show that these distances can be used even without any labeled information to induce hierarchical structure. However, recent work has highlighted issues with correlating supervised probe performance with the amount of language structure encoded in such representations (Hewitt and Liang, 2019). Another popular approach to analyzing deep models is through the

Proceedings of the 6th Workshop on Representation Learning for NLP (RepL4NLP-2021), pages 263–276
Bangkok, Thailand (Online), August 6, 2021.

lens of geometry (Reif et al., 2019; Gigante et al., 2019). While geometric interpretations provide significant insights, they present another challenge in summarizing the structure in a quantifiable way. More recent techniques such as replica-based mean field manifold analysis method (Chung et al., 2018; Cohen et al., 2019; Mamou et al., 2020) connects representation geometry with linear classification performance, but the method is limited to categorization tasks.

In this work, we make use of an experimental framework from cognitive science and neuroscience to probe for hierarchical structure in contextual representations from pretrained Transformer models (i.e., BERT (Devlin et al., 2018) and its variants). A popular technique in neuroscience involves measuring change in the population activity in response to controlled, input perturbations (Mollica et al., 2020; Ding et al., 2016). We apply this approach to test the characteristic scale and the complexity (Fig. 1) of hierarchical phrase structure encoded deep contextual representations, and present several key findings:

1. Representations are distorted by shuffling small n-grams in early layers, while the distortion caused by shuffling large n-grams starts to occur in later layers, implying the scale of characteristic word length increases from input to downstream layers.

2. Representational distortion caused by swapping two constituent phrases is smaller than when the control sequences of the same length are swapped, indicating that the BERT representations are sensitive to hierarchical phrase structure.

3. Representational distortion caused by swapping adjacent words across phrasal boundary is larger than when the swap is within a phrasal boundary; furthermore, the amount of distortion increases with the syntactic distance between the swapped words. The correlation between distortion and tree distance increases across the layers, suggesting that the characteristic complexity of phrasal subtrees increases across the layers.

4. Early layers pay more attention between syntactically closer adjacent pairs and deeper layers pay more attention between syntactically distant adjacent pairs. The attention paid in each layer can explain some of the emergent sensitivity to phrasal structure across layers.

Our work demonstrates that interventional tools such as controlled input perturbations can be useful for analyzing deep networks, adding to the growing, interdisciplinary body of work which profitably adapt experimental techniques from cognitive neuroscience and psycholinguistics to analyze computational models of language (Futrell et al., 2018; Wilcox et al., 2019; Futrell et al., 2019; Ettinger, 2020).

2 Methods

Eliciting changes in behavioral and neural responses through controlled input perturbations is a common experimental technique in cognitive neuroscience and psycholinguistics (Tsao and Livingstone, 2008; Mollica et al., 2020). Inspired by these approaches, we perturb input sentences and measure the discrepancy between the resulting, perturbed representation against the original. While conceptually simple, this approach allows for a targeted analysis of internal representations obtained from different layers of deep models, and can suggest partial mechanisms by which such models are able to encode linguistic structure. We note that sentence perturbations have been primarily utilized in NLP for representation learning (Hill et al., 2016; Artetxe et al., 2018; Lample et al., 2018), data augmentation (Wang et al., 2018; Andreas, 2020), and testing for model robustness (e.g., against adversarial examples) (Jia and Liang, 2017; Belinkov and Bisk, 2018). A methodological contribution of our work is to show that input perturbations can complement existing tools and widens the scope of questions that could be asked of representations learned by deep networks.

2.1 Sentence perturbations

In this work we consider three different types of sentence perturbations designed to probe for different phenomena.

n-gram shuffling In the n-gram shuffling experiments, we randomly shuffle the words of a sentence in units of n-grams, with n varying from 1 (i.e., individual words) to 7 (see Fig. 2a for an example). While the number of words which change absolute position is similar for different n, larger n will better preserve the local context (i.e., relative position) of more words. Thus, we reason that n-gram swaps affect the representations selective to the context

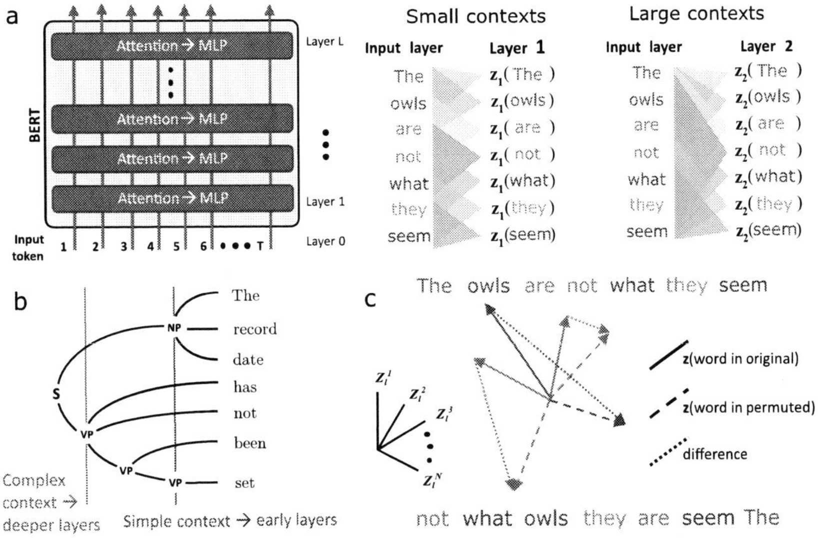

Figure 1: Do Transformers build complexity along their layers? (**a**) The representation of a word is a function of its context, and this cartoon illustrates an hypothesis that deeper representations use larger contexts. (**b**) An example parse tree, illustrating our notion of phrase complexity. (**c**) Cartoon of the distortion metric, where vectors are the z-scored feature vectors $\mathbf{z}$, and color map vectors to words.

with size n or higher within the sentence, and that lower n will result in greater distortion in sentence representations.

Phrase swaps The n-gram shuffling experiments probe for sensitivity of representations to local context without taking into account syntactic structure. In the phrase swap experiments, we perturb a sentence by swapping two randomly chosen spans. We explore two ways of swapping spans. In the first setting, the spans are chosen such that they are valid phrases according to its parse tree.[3] In the second setting, the spans are chosen that they are invalid phrases. Importantly, in the second, control setting, we fix the length of the spans such that the lengths of spans that are chosen to be swapped are the same as in the first setting (see Fig. 3a for an example). We hypothesize that swapping invalid phrases will result in more distortion than swapping valid phrases, since invalid swaps will result in greater denigration of syntactic structure.

Adjacent word swaps In the adjacent word swapping experiments, we swap two adjacent words in a sentence. We again experiment with two settings – in the first setting, the swapped words stay within the phrase boundary (i.e., the two words share the same parent), while in the second setting, the swapped words cross phrase boundaries. We also perform a more fine-grained analysis where we condition the swaps based on the "syntactic distance" between the swapped words, where syntactic distance is defined as the distance between the two words in the parse tree (see Fig. 6c). Since a phrase corresponds to a subtree of the parse tree, this distance also quantifies the number of nested phrase boundaries between two adjacent words. Here, we expect the amount of distortion to be positively correlated with the syntactic distance of the words that are swapped.

2.2 Contextual representations from Transformers

For our sentence representation, we focus on the Transformer-family of models pretrained on large-scale language datasets (BERT and its variants). Given an input word embedding matrix $\mathbf{X} \in \mathbb{R}^{T \times d}$ for a sentence of length T, the Transformer applies self attention over the previous layer's representation to produce a new representation,

$$\mathbf{X}_l = f_l([\mathbf{H}_{l,1}, \ldots, \mathbf{H}_{l,H}]), \;\; \mathbf{H}_{l,i} = \mathbf{A}_{l,i}\mathbf{X}_{l-1}\mathbf{V}_{l,i},$$
$$\mathbf{A}_{l,i} = \text{softmax}\left(\frac{(\mathbf{X}_{l-1}\mathbf{Q}_{l,i})(\mathbf{X}_{l-1}\mathbf{K}_{l,i})^\top}{\sqrt{d_k}}\right), \quad (1)$$

where f_l is an MLP layer, H is the number of heads, $d_H = \frac{d}{H}$ is the head embedding dimension, and $\mathbf{Q}_{l,i}, \mathbf{K}_{l,i}, \mathbf{V}_{l,i} \in \mathbb{R}^{d \times d_k}$ are respectively the learned query, key, and value projection matrices at layer l for head i. The MLP layer consists of a residual layer followed by layer normalization and a nonlinearity. The 0-th layer representation

[3]We use constituency parse trees from the English Penn Treebank (Marcus et al., 1994).

$\mathbf{X}_0$ is obtained by adding the position embeddings and the segment embeddings to the input token embeddings $\mathbf{X}$, and passing it through normalization layer.[4]

In this paper, we conduct our distortion analysis mainly on the intermediate Transformer representations $\mathbf{X}_l = [\mathbf{x}_{l,1}, \ldots, \mathbf{x}_{l,T}]$, where $\mathbf{x}_{l,t} \in \mathbb{R}^d$ is the contextualized representation for word t at layer l.[5] We analyze the trend in distortion as a function of layer depth l for the different perturbations. We also explore the different attention heads $\mathbf{H}_{l,i} \in \mathbb{R}^{T \times d_H}$ and the associated attention matrix $\mathbf{A}_{l,i} \in \mathbb{R}^{T \times T}$ to inspect whether certain attention heads specialize at encoding syntactic information.

2.3 Distortion metric

Our input manipulations allow us to specify the distortion at the input level, and we wish to measure the corresponding distortion in the representation space (Fig. 1). Due to the attention mechanism, a single vector in an intermediate layer is a function of the representations of (potentially all) the other tokens in the sentence. Therefore, the information about a particular word might be distributed among the many feature vectors of a sentence, and we wish to consider all feature vectors together as a single sentence-level representation.

We thus represent each sentence as a matrix and use the distance induced by matrix 2-norm. Specifically, let $\mathbf{P} \in \{0,1\}^{T \times T}$ be the binary matrix representation of a permutation that perturbs the input sentence, i.e., $\tilde{\mathbf{X}} = \mathbf{P}\mathbf{X}$. Further let $\tilde{\mathbf{X}}_l$ and $\mathbf{X}_l$ be the corresponding sentence representations for the l-th layer for the perturbed and original sentences. To ignore uniform shifting and scaling, we also z-score each feature dimension of each layer (by subtracting the mean and dividing by the standard deviation where these statistics are obtained from the full Penn Treebank corpus) to give $\tilde{\mathbf{Z}}_l$ and $\mathbf{Z}_l$. Our distortion metric for layer l is then defined as $\|\mathbf{Z}_l - \mathbf{P}^{-1}\tilde{\mathbf{Z}}_l\|/\sqrt{Td}$, where $\|\cdot\|$ is the matrix 2-norm (i.e., Frobenius norm).[6] Importantly, we invert the permutation of the perturbed representation to preserve the original ordering, which allows us to measure the distortion due to structural change, rather than distortion due to simple differences in surface form. We divide by $\sqrt{Td}$ to make the metric comparable between sentences (with different T) and networks (with different d).

Intuitively, our metric is the scaled Euclidean distance between the z-scored, flattened sentence representations, $\mathbf{z}_l \in \mathbb{R}^{Td}$. Because each dimension is independently centered and standardized, the maximally unstructured distribution of $\mathbf{z}_l$ is an isotropic Td-dimensional Gaussian. The expected distance between two such vectors is approximately $\sqrt{2Td}$. Therefore, we can interpret a distortion value approaching $\sqrt{2}$ as comparable to if we had randomly redrawn the perturbed representation.

3 Experimental Setup

We apply our perturbation-based analysis on sentences from the English Penn Treebank (Marcus et al., 1994), where we average the distortion metric across randomly chosen sentences. We analyze the distortion, as measured by length-normalized Frobenius norm between the perturbed and original representations, as a function of layer depth. Layers that experience large distortion when the syntactic structure is disrupted from the perturbation can be interpreted as being more sensitive to hierarchical syntactic structure.

As we found the trend to be largely similar across the different models, in the following section, we primarily discuss results from BERT (`bert-base-cased`). We replicate key results with other pretrained and randomly-initialized Transformer-based models as well (see A.1).

4 Results

4.1 Sensitivity to perturbation size increases along BERT layers

When we shuffle in units of larger n-grams, it only introduces distortions in the deeper BERT layers compared to smaller n-gram shuffles. The n-gram sized shuffles break contexts larger than n, while preserving contexts of size n or smaller. Interestingly, smaller n-gram shuffles diverge from the original sentence in the early layers (Fig. 2b, top curve), implying that only in early layers are representations built from short-range contexts. Larger n-gram shuffles remain minimally distorted for 'longer' (Fig. 2b, bottom curve), implying that long-

[4] However, the exact specification for the MLP and $\mathbf{X}_0$ may vary across different pretrained models.

[5] BERT uses BPE tokenization (Sennrich et al., 2015), which means that some words are split into multiple tokens. Since we wish to evaluate representations at word-level, if a word is split into multiple tokens, its word representation is computed as the average of all its token representations.

[6] There are many possible ways of measuring distortion, induced by different norms. We observed the results to be qualitatively similar for different measures, and hence we focus on the Frobenius norm in our main results. We show the results from additional distortion metrics in the A.2

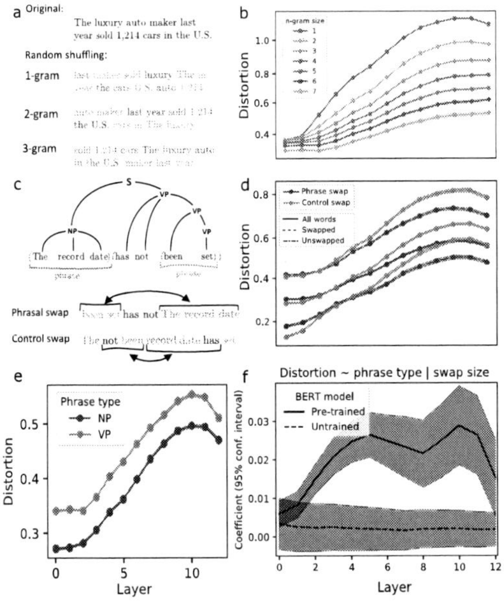

Figure 2: Swapping n-grams and phrases. (**a**) Examples of basic n-gram shuffles, where colors indicate the units of shuffling. (**b**) Distortion metric computed at each layer, conditioned on n-gram size. Error bars hereafter represent standard error across 400 examples. (**c**) An example parse tree, with phrase boundaries shown as grey brackets, and two low-order phrases marked; and examples of a phrasal and control swap, with colors corresponding to the phrases marked above. (**d**) Distortion, computed at each layer, using either the full sentence, the subsentence of unswapped words, or the subsentence of swapped words, conditioned on swap type. (e) Full-sentence distortion for VP and NP phrase swaps. (f) Partial linear regression coefficients (see A.4) for pre-trained and untrained BERT models after controlling for swap size.

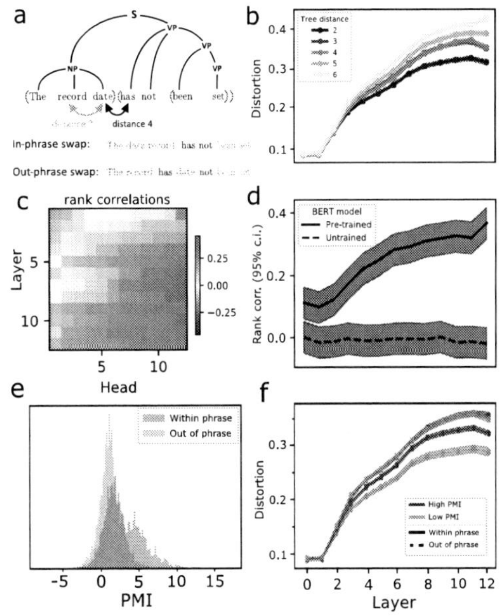

Figure 3: Syntactic distance affects representational distortion. (**a**) An example of adjacent swaps which do and do not cross a phrase boundary, with low-order phrases colored. Phrase boundaries are drawn in red. (**b**) Distortion in each layer, but conditioned on the tree distance. (**c**) For each head (column) of each layer (row), the (Spearman) rank correlation between distortion and tree distance of the swapped words. Colors are such that red is positive, blue negative. (**d**) Rank correlations between distortion (of the full representation) in the trained and untrained BERT models. (**e**) Histogram of PMI values, for pairs in the same phrase and not. (**f**) Similar to **b**, but averaging all out-of-phrase swaps, and separating pairs above ('high') or below ('low') the median PMI.

range contexts play a larger role deeper layer representations.

Effects of phrasal boundaries Since BERT seems to build larger contexts along its layers, we now ask whether those contexts are structures of some grammatical significance. A basic and important syntactic feature is the constituent phrase, which BERT has previously been shown to represented in some fashion (Goldberg, 2019; Kim et al., 2020). We applied two targeted probes of phrase structure in the BERT representation, and found that phrasal boundaries are indeed influential.

If we swap just two n-grams, the BERT representations are less affected when phrases are kept intact. We show this by swapping only two n-grams per sentence and comparing the distortion when those n-grams are phrases to when they cross phrase boundaries (Fig. 3a), where we control for the length of n-grams that are swapped in both settings. There is less distortion when respecting phrase boundaries, which is evident among all feature vectors, including those in the position of words which did not get swapped (Fig. 2d). The global contextual information, distributed across the sentence, is affected by the phrase boundary.

To see if the role of a phrase impacts its salience, we distinguish between verb phrases (VP) and noun phrase (NP) swaps. Swapping VP results in more distortion than swapping NP (Fig. 2e). Since VP are in general larger than NP, this effect could in principle be due simply to the number of words being swapped. Yet that is not the case: Using a partial linear regression (see details in A.4), we can estimate the difference between the VP and NP distortions conditional on any smooth function of the swap size, and doing this reveals that there is still a strong difference in the intermediate layers (Fig. 2f).

4.2 Sensitivity depends on syntactic distance of the perturbation

Having seen that representations are sensitive to phrase boundaries, we next explore whether that sensitivity is proportional to the number of phrase boundaries that are broken, which is a quantity related to the phrase hierarchy. Instead of swapping entire phrases, we swap two adjacent words and analyze the distortion based on how far apart the two words are in the constituency tree (Fig. 3a)[7]. This analysis varies the distance in the deeper tree structure while keeping the distance in surface form constant (since we always swap adjacent words).

If the hierarchical representations are indeed being gradually built up along the layers of these pretrained models, we expect distortion to be greater for word swaps that are further apart in tree distance. We indeed find that there is a larger distortion when swapping syntactically distant words (Fig. 3b). This distortion grows from earlier to later BERT layers. Furthermore, when looking at the per-head representations of each layer, we see that in deeper layers there are more heads showing a positive rank correlation between distortion and tree distance (Fig. 3c). In addition to a sensitivity to phrase boundaries, deeper BERT layers develop a sensitivity to the number of boundaries that are broken.

Controlling for co-occurrence Since words in the same phrase may tend to occur together more often, co-occurrence is a potential confound when assessing the effects of adjacent word swaps. Co-occurrence is a simple statistic which does not require any notion of grammar to compute – indeed it is used to train many non-contextual word embeddings (e.g., word2vec (Mikolov et al., 2013), GloVe (Pennington et al., 2014)). So it is natural to ask whether BERT's resilience to syntactically closer swaps goes beyond simple co-occurrence statistics. For simplicity, let us focus on whether a swap occurs within a phrase (tree distance = 2) or not.

As an estimate of co-occurrence, we used the pointwise mutual information (PMI). Specifically, for two words w and v, the PMI is $\log \frac{p(w,v)}{p(w)p(v)}$, which is estimated from the empirical probabilities. We confirm that adjacent words in the same phrase do indeed have a second mode at high PMI (Fig. 3e). Dividing the swaps into those whose words have high PMI (above the marginal median) and low PMI (below it), we can see visually that the difference between within-phrase swaps and out-of-phrase swaps persists in both groups (Fig. 3f). When quantitatively accounting for the effect of PMI with a partial linear regression (see A.4), there remains a significant correlation between the breaking of a phrase and the subsequent distortion. This indicates that the greater distortion for word swaps which cross phrase boundaries is not simply due to surface co-occurrence statistics.

Relation to linguistic information Do our input perturbations, and the resulting the distortions, reflect changes in the encoding of important linguistic information? One way to address this question, which is popular in computational neuroscience (DiCarlo and Cox, 2007) and more recently BERTology (Liu et al., 2019a; Tenney et al., 2019), is to see how well a linear classifier trained on a linguistic task generalizes from the (representations of the) unperturbed sentences to the perturbed ones. With supervised probes, we can see how much the representations change with respect to the subspaces that encode specific linguistic information.

Specifically, we relate representational distortion to three common linguistic tasks of increasing complexity: part of speech (POS) classification; grandparent tag (GP) classification (Tenney et al., 2019); and a parse tree distance reconstruction (Hewitt and Manning, 2019)[8]. The probe trained on each of these tasks is a generalized linear model, mapping a datapoint $\mathbf{x}$ (i.e. representations from different layers) to a conditional distribution of the labels, $p(y|\theta^T\mathbf{x})$ (see A.5 for model details). Thus a ready measure of the effect of each type of swap, for a single sentence, is $\log p(y|\theta^T\mathbf{x}_i) - \log p(y|\theta^T\tilde{\mathbf{x}}_i)$, where $\tilde{\mathbf{x}}_i$ is same datum as $\mathbf{x}_i$ in the perturbed representation[9]. Averaging this quantity over all datapoints gives a measure of content-specific distortion within a representation, which we will call "inference impairment".

Based on the three linguistic tasks, the distortion we measure from the adjacent word swaps is more strongly related to more complex information. The inverted L shape of Fig. 4a suggests that increasing distortion is only weakly related to impairment of POS inference, which is perhaps unsurprising given that POS tags can be readily predicted from

[7] Note that for adjacent words, the number of broken phrase boundaries equals the tree distance minus two.

[8] While the original paper predicted dependency tree distance, in this paper we instead predict the constituency tree distance.

[9] POS- and GP-tag prediction outputs a sequence of labels for each sentence, while the distance probe outputs the constituency tree distance between each pair of words. Then $\log p(y|\theta^T\mathbf{x}_i)$ is simply the log probability of an individual label.

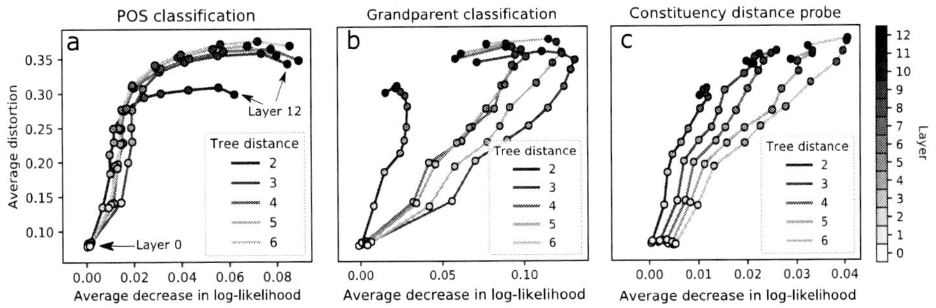

Figure 4: Distortion and inference impairment for increasing linguistic complexity. In each plot, a point is the average (distortion, 'impairment') for a given layer and a given class of word swap distance. Points are connected by lines according to their swap type (i.e. tree distance). The circles are colored according to layer (see right for a legend). Averages are taken over 600 test sentences, with one of each swap type per sentence, and both distortion and log-likelihood are computed for every word in the sentence.

local context. A deeper syntactic probe, the GP classifier (4b), does show a consistent positive relationship, but only for swaps which break a phrase boundary (i.e. distance >2). Meanwhile, impairment of the distance probe (4c), which reconstructs the full parse tree, has a consistently positive relationship with distortion, whose slope is proportionate to the tree distance of the swap. Thus, when specifically perturbing the phrasal boundary, the representational distortion is related to relatively more complex linguistic information.

4.3 Sensitivity to perturbations is mediated by changes in attention

In the transformer architecture, contexts are built with the attention mechanism. Recall that attention is a mechanism for allowing input vectors to interact when forming the output, and the ultimate output for a given token is a convex combination of the features of all tokens (Eq. 1). It has been shown qualitatively that, within a layer, BERT allocates attention preferentially to words in the same phrase (Kim et al., 2020), so if our perturbations affect inference of phrase structure then the changes in attentions could explain our results. Note that it is not guaranteed to do so: the BERT features in a given layer are a function of the attentions and the "values" (each token's feature vector), and both are affected by our perturbations. Therefore our last set of experiments asks whether attention alone can explain the sensitivity to syntactic distance.

To quantify the change in attention weights across the whole sentence, we compute the distance between each token's attention weights in the perturbed and unperturbed sentences, and average across all tokens. For token i, its vector of attention weights in response to the unperturbed sentence is a^i, and for the perturbed one $\tilde{a}^i$ (such that $\sum_j a^i_j = 1$). Since each set of attention weights are non-negative and sum to 1 due to softmax, we use the relative entropy[10] as a distance measure. This results in the total change in attention being:

$$\Delta a = \frac{1}{T}\sum_{i=1}^{T}\sum_{j=1}^{T} a^i_j \log \frac{a^i_j}{\tilde{a}^i_j}$$

which is non-negative and respects the structure of the weights. We confirmed that other measures (like the cosine similarity) produce results that are qualitatively similar.

First, we observe that the changes in the attention depend on the layer hierarchy when adjacent word swaps break the phrase boundary. Like the distortion, attention changes little or not at all in the early layers, and progressively more in the final layers (Fig. 5b). Furthermore, these changes are also positively correlated with syntactic distance in most cases, which suggests that representation's sensitivities to syntactic tree distance may primarily be due to changes in attention.

To see whether the changes in attention can in fact explain representational sensitivity to syntactic distance, we turned to the same partial linear regression model as before (A.4) to compute the the correlation between the representation's distortion and the tree distance between the swapped adjacent words, after controlling for changes in attention (Δa). The correlations substantially reduced in the controlled case (Fig. 5c), which suggests that attention weights contribute to the representational sensitivity to syntactic tree distance; but the correlations are not eliminated, which suggests that distortions from the previous layer also contribute.

[10] Also called the KL divergence.

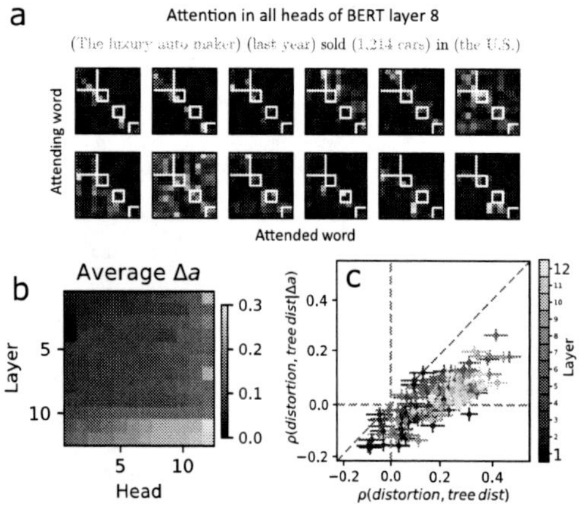

Figure 5: Attention changes explain part of the sensitivity to tree distance. **(a)** An example of the attention matrices for all heads in a single layer (layer 8), given the above sentence as input. Phrases in the sentence are drawn as blocks in the matrix. **(b)** The change in attention between the unperturbed and perturbed attention weights, averaged over all out-of-phrase swaps. Columns are sorted independently by their value. **(c)** The head/layer-wise rank correlations ($\pm 95\%$ confidence intervals) between distortion and tree distance after controlling for changes in attention, plotted against the uncontrolled rank correlations. Being below the diagonal indicates that the relationship between distortion and tree distance is partially explained by Δa.

5 Discussion and Conclusion

In this paper, we used the representational sensitivity to controlled input perturbation as a probe of hierarchical phrasal structure in deep linguistic representations. The logic of our probe is the representations which respect phrase structure should less sensitive to perturbations which preserve the phrasal unit, and more sensitive to those which disrupt a phrase. We hope that our results demonstrate the versatility and utility of perturbation-based approaches to studying deep language models.

We showed that BERT and its variants build representations which are sensitive to the phrasal unit, as demonstrated by greater invariance to perturbations preserving phrasal boundaries compared to control perturbations which break the phrasal boundaries (Fig. 2-5). We also find that while the representational sensitivity to broken phrase boundaries grows across layers, this increase in sensitivity is more prominent when the breakage occurs between two words that are syntactically distant (i.e., when the broken phrase is more complex). Using the same methods to show that changes in attention provide a partial explanation for perturbation-induced distortions.

While our distortion metric is a task-agnostic measure of change in the neural population activity, this may or may not reflect changes in the encoding of specific linguistic information. To relate our metric with specific kinds of information, we measured the change in the performance of supervised linear probes trained on top of the representation (Fig. 4). The probe sensitivity measure also bears a suggestive resemblance to the saliency map analysis (Simonyan et al., 2014) in machine learning, which is used to highlight the most output-sensitive regions within the input. To draw an analogy with that work, one way of characterizing our results is that phrasal boundaries are regions of high saliency in hidden representations and that, in deep layers, complex phrase boundaries are more salient than simple phrase boundaries. Further exploring the use of supervised probes and our input perturbations as a tool for layerwise probing of syntactic saliency is a promising direction for future work.

Finally, several studies (Sinha et al., 2021; Gupta et al., 2021; Pham et al., 2020), have recently found that masked language models pretrained or fine-tuned on sentences that break natural word order (e.g. via n-gram shuffling) still perform quite well across various tasks, even on supervised probes of syntactic phenomena. It would be interesting to apply our perturbative analyses on such models to see if they exhibit less sensitivity to the experimental vs. control setups (e.g. n-gram vs. phrase swaps). This may indicate that such models do not capture representational correlates of phrase structure in their representations despite their good performance on supervised probing tasks. In such a case, what tasks would actually require the "linguistic knowledge" that we are probing for? In similar vein, applying our perturbative analyses on models that explicitly incorporate syntax into their representations (Sundararaman et al., 2019; Wang et al.; Zanzotto et al., 2020; Kuncoro et al., 2020) might provide further insights.

Our method and results suggest many interesting future directions. We hope that this work will motivate: (1) a formal theory of efficient hierarchical data representations in distributed features; (2) a search for the causal connection between attention structure, the representational geometry, and the model performance; (3) potential applications in network pruning studies; (4) an extension of the current work as a hypothesis generator in neuroscience to understand how neural populations implement tasks with an underlying compositional structure.

References

Jacob Andreas. 2020. Good-Enough Compositional Data Augmentation. In *Proceedings ACL*.

Mikel Artetxe, Gorka Labaka, Eneko Agirre, and Kyunghyun Cho. 2018. Unsupervised neural machine translation. In *Proceedings of ICLR*.

Yonatan Belinkov and Yonatan Bisk. 2018. Synthetic and natural noise both break neural machine translation. In *Proceedings of ICLR*.

Yonatan Belinkov and James Glass. 2017. Analyzing hidden representations in end-to-end automatic speech recognition systems. In *Advances in Neural Information Processing Systems*, pages 2441–2451.

SueYeon Chung, Daniel D Lee, and Haim Sompolinsky. 2018. Classification and geometry of general perceptual manifolds. *Physical Review X*, 8(3):031003.

Uri Cohen, SueYeon Chung, Daniel D Lee, and Haim Sompolinsky. 2019. Separability and geometry of object manifolds in deep neural networks. *bioRxiv*, page 644658.

Jacob Devlin, Ming-Wei Chang, Kenton Lee, and Kristina Toutanova. 2018. Bert: Pre-training of deep bidirectional transformers for language understanding. *arXiv preprint arXiv:1810.04805*.

James J DiCarlo and David D Cox. 2007. Untangling invariant object recognition. *Trends in cognitive sciences*, 11(8):333–341.

Nai Ding, Lucia Melloni, Hang Zhang, Xing Tian, and David Poeppel. 2016. Cortical tracking of hierarchical linguistic structures in connected speech. *Nature neuroscience*, 19(1):158.

Jeffrey L Elman. 1991. Distributed representations, simple recurrent networks, and grammatical structure. *Machine learning*, 7(2-3):195–225.

Allyson Ettinger. 2020. What bert is not: Lessons from a new suite of psycholinguistic diagnostics for language models. *Transactions of the Association for Computational Linguistics*, 8:34–48.

Richard Futrell, Ethan Wilcox, Takashi Morit, and Roger Levy. 2018. RNNs as psycholinguistic subjects: Syntactic state and grammatical dependency. *arXiv:1809.01329*.

Richard Futrell, Ethan Wilcox, Takashi Morita, Peng Qian, Miguel Ballesteros, and Roger Levy. 2019. Neural language models as psycholinguistic subjects: Representations of syntactic state. In *Proceedings of the 2019 Conference of the North American Chapter of the Association for Computational Linguistics: Human Language Technologies, Volume 1 (Long and Short Papers)*, pages 32–42, Minneapolis, Minnesota. Association for Computational Linguistics.

Scott Gigante, Adam S Charles, Smita Krishnaswamy, and Gal Mishne. 2019. Visualizing the phate of neural networks. In *Advances in Neural Information Processing Systems*, pages 1840–1851.

Yoav Goldberg. 2019. Assessing bert's syntactic abilities. *arXiv preprint arXiv:1901.05287*.

Ashim Gupta, Giorgi Kvernadze, and Vivek Srikumar. 2021. Bert family eat word salad: Experiments with text understanding. *AAAI*.

Bruce Hansen. 2000. *Econometrics*. `https://www.ssc.wisc.edu/~bhansen/econometrics/`.

John Hewitt and Percy Liang. 2019. Designing and Interpreting Probes with Control Tasks. In *Proceedings of EMNLP*.

John Hewitt and Christopher D Manning. 2019. A structural probe for finding syntax in word representations. In *Proceedings of the 2019 Conference of the North American Chapter of the Association for Computational Linguistics: Human Language Technologies, Volume 1 (Long and Short Papers)*, pages 4129–4138.

Felix Hill, Kyunghyun Cho, and Anna Korhonen. 2016. Learning distributed representations of sentences from unlabelled data. In *Proceedings of the 2016 Conference of the North American Chapter of the Association for Computational Linguistics: Human Language Technologies*, pages 1367–1377, San Diego, California. Association for Computational Linguistics.

Robin Jia and Percy Liang. 2017. Adversarial examples for evaluating reading comprehension systems. In *Proceedings of EMNLP*, Copenhagen, Denmark. Association for Computational Linguistics.

Charles Kemp and Joshua B Tenenbaum. 2008. The discovery of structural form. *Proceedings of the National Academy of Sciences*, 105(31):10687–10692.

Taeuk Kim, Jihun Choi, Daniel Edmiston, and Sang goo Lee. 2020. Are Pre-trained Language Models Aware of Phrases? Simple but Strong Baselines for Grammar Induction. In *Proceedings of ICLR*.

Adhiguna Kuncoro, Lingpeng Kong, Daniel Fried, Dani Yogatama, Laura Rimell, Chris Dyer, and Phil Blunsom. 2020. Syntactic Structure Distillation Pretraining for Bidirectional Encoders. *Transactions of the Association for Computational Linguistics*, 8:776–794.

Guillaume Lample, Alexis Conneau, Ludovic Denoyer, and Marc'Aurelio Ranzato. 2018. Unsupervised machine translation using monolingual corpora only. In *Proceedings of ICLR*.

Zhenzhong Lan, Mingda Chen, Sebastian Goodman, Kevin Gimpel, Piyush Sharma, and Radu Soricut. 2019. Albert: A lite bert for self-supervised learning of language representations.

Nelson F. Liu, Matt Gardner, Yonatan Belinkov, Matthew E. Peters, and Noah A. Smith. 2019a. Linguistic knowledge and transferability of contextual representations. *CoRR*, abs/1903.08855.

Yinhan Liu, Myle Ott, Naman Goyal, Jingfei Du, Mandar Joshi, Danqi Chen, Omer Levy, Mike Lewis, Luke Zettlemoyer, and Veselin Stoyanov. 2019b. Roberta: A robustly optimized bert pretraining approach.

Jonathan Mamou, Hang Le, Miguel A Del Rio, Cory Stephenson, Hanlin Tang, Yoon Kim, and SueYeon Chung. 2020. Emergence of separable manifolds in deep language representations. *arXiv preprint arXiv:2006.01095*.

Mitchell Marcus, Grace Kim, Mary Ann Marcinkiewicz, Robert MacIntyre, Ann Bies, Mark Ferguson, Karen Katz, and Britta Schasberger. 1994. The penn treebank: Annotating predicate argument structure. In *Proceedings of the Workshop on Human Language Technology*, HLT '94, pages 114–119, Stroudsburg, PA, USA. Association for Computational Linguistics.

Tomas Mikolov, Ilya Sutskever, Kai Chen, Greg S Corrado, and Jeff Dean. 2013. Distributed representations of words and phrases and their compositionality. In *Advances in neural information processing systems*, pages 3111–3119.

Francis Mollica, Matthew Siegelman, Evgeniia Diachek, Steven T Piantadosi, Zachary Mineroff, Richard Futrell, Hope Kean, Peng Qian, and Evelina Fedorenko. 2020. Composition is the core driver of the language-selective network. *Neurobiology of Language*, 1(1):104–134.

Ari Morcos, Maithra Raghu, and Samy Bengio. 2018. Insights on representational similarity in neural networks with canonical correlation. In S. Bengio, H. Wallach, H. Larochelle, K. Grauman, N. Cesa-Bianchi, and R. Garnett, editors, *Advances in Neural Information Processing Systems 31*, pages 5732–5741. Curran Associates, Inc.

Jeffrey Pennington, Richard Socher, and Christopher D. Manning. 2014. Glove: Global vectors for word representation. In *Empirical Methods in Natural Language Processing (EMNLP)*, pages 1532–1543.

Thang M. Pham, Trung Bui, Long Mai, and Anh Nguyen. 2020. Out of order: How important is the sequential order of words in a sentence in natural language understanding tasks?

Maithra Raghu, Justin Gilmer, Jason Yosinski, and Jascha Sohl-Dickstein. 2017. Svcca: Singular vector canonical correlation analysis for deep learning dynamics and interpretability. In I. Guyon, U. V. Luxburg, S. Bengio, H. Wallach, R. Fergus, S. Vishwanathan, and R. Garnett, editors, *Advances in Neural Information Processing Systems 30*, pages 6076–6085. Curran Associates, Inc.

Emily Reif, Ann Yuan, Martin Wattenberg, Fernanda B Viegas, Andy Coenen, Adam Pearce, and Been Kim. 2019. Visualizing and Measuring the Geometry of BERT. In *Advances in Neural Information Processing Systems*, pages 8592–8600.

Victor Sanh, Lysandre Debut, Julien Chaumond, and Thomas Wolf. 2019. Distilbert, a distilled version of bert: smaller, faster, cheaper and lighter.

Morteza Sarafyazd and Mehrdad Jazayeri. 2019. Hierarchical reasoning by neural circuits in the frontal cortex. *Science*, 364(6441):eaav8911.

Andrew M Saxe, James L McClellans, and Surya Ganguli. 2013. Learning hierarchical categories in deep neural networks. In *Proceedings of the Annual Meeting of the Cognitive Science Society*, volume 35.

Rico Sennrich, Barry Haddow, and Alexandra Birch. 2015. Neural machine translation of rare words with subword units. *arXiv preprint arXiv:1508.07909*.

Karen Simonyan, Andrea Vedaldi, and Andrew Zisserman. 2014. Deep inside convolutional networks: Visualising image classification models and saliency maps.

Koustuv Sinha, Robin Jia, Dieuwke Hupkes, Joelle Pineau, Adina Williams, and Douwe Kiela. 2021. Masked language modeling and the distributional hypothesis: Order word matters pre-training for little.

Kimberly L Stachenfeld, Matthew M Botvinick, and Samuel J Gershman. 2017. The hippocampus as a predictive map. *Nature neuroscience*, 20(11):1643.

Dhanasekar Sundararaman, Vivek Subramanian, Guoyin Wang, Shijing Si, Dinghan Shen, Dong Wang, and Lawrence Carin. 2019. Syntax-Infused Transformer and BERT models for Machine Translation and Natural Language Understanding. *arXiv:1911.06156*.

Ian Tenney, Dipanjan Das, and Ellie Pavlick. 2019. BERT Rediscovers the Classical NLP Pipeline. In *Proceedings of ACL*.

D Gowanlock R Tervo, Joshua B Tenenbaum, and Samuel J Gershman. 2016. Toward the neural implementation of structure learning. *Current opinion in neurobiology*, 37:99–105.

Doris Y Tsao and Margaret S Livingstone. 2008. Mechanisms of face perception. *Annu. Rev. Neurosci.*, 31:411–437.

Wei Wang, Bin Bi, Ming Yan, Chen Wu, Zuyi Bao, Jiangnan Xia, Liwei Peng, and Luo Si. StructBERT: Incorporating Language Structures into Pre-training for Deep Language Understanding.

Xinyi Wang, Hieu Pham, Zihang Dai, and Graham Neubig. 2018. SwitchOut: an efficient data augmentation algorithm for neural machine translation. In *Proceedings of EMNLP*.

Ethan Wilcox, Roger Levy, and Richard Futrell. 2019. Hierarchical representation in neural language models: Suppression and recovery of expectations. *arXiv preprint arXiv:1906.04068*.

Zhilin Yang, Zihang Dai, Yiming Yang, Jaime Carbonell, Ruslan Salakhutdinov, and Quoc V. Le. 2019. XLNet: Generalized Autoregressive Pretraining for Language Understanding. In *Proceedings of NeurIPS*.

Fabio Massimo Zanzotto, Andrea Santilli, Leonardo Ranaldi, Dario Onorati, Pierfrancesco Tommasino, and Francesca Fallucchi. 2020. KERMIT: Complementing transformer architectures with encoders of explicit syntactic interpretations. In *Proceedings of the 2020 Conference on Empirical Methods in Natural Language Processing (EMNLP)*.

A Appendix

Here we go into further detail on our methods and data to aid in reproducibility.

A.1 Model details

Here we give the details for all models considered in this paper. The majority of results are from BERT, but we also tested other variants.[11]

- **BERT** (Devlin et al., 2018) `bert-base-cased`. 12-layer, 768-hidden, 12-heads, 110M parameters.
- **RoBERTa** (Liu et al., 2019b) `roberta-base`. 12-layer, 768-hidden, 12-heads, 125M parameters.
- **ALBERT** (Lan et al., 2019) `albert-base-v1`. 12 repeating layers, 128 embedding, 768-hidden, 12-heads, 11M parameters.
- **DistilBERT** (Sanh et al., 2019) `distilbert-uncased`. 6-layer, 768-hidden, 12-heads, 66M parameters. The model distilled from the BERT model `bert-base-uncased` checkpoint.
- **XLNet** (Yang et al., 2019) `xlnet-base-cased`. 12-layer, 768-hidden, 12-heads, 110M parameters.

Note that the hidden size is 768 across all the models. For each pre-trained model, input text is tokenized using its default tokenizer and features are extracted at token level.

[11]We use the implementation from `https://github.com/huggingface/transformers`.

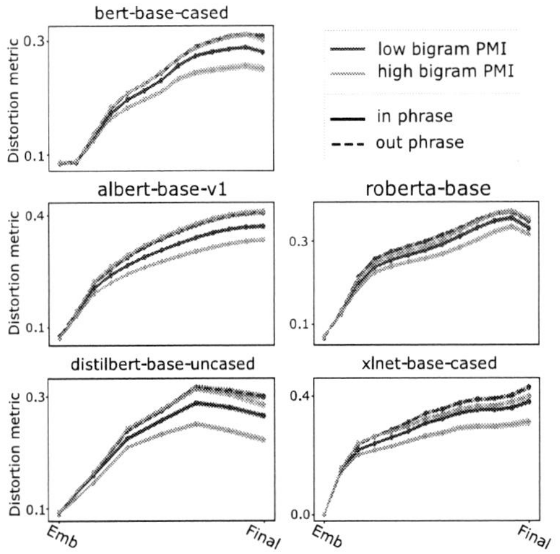

Figure 6: Replicating the adjacent word swapping experiments using different transformer architectures. Lines are the mean Frobenius distance, and the shading is ± 1 standard error of the mean.

A.2 Additional metrics

In addition to the scaled Frobenius distance, we also considered other ways of measuring distortion in the representation. We will briefly report results for two other metrics, and describe them here.

CCA Canonical correlations analysis (CCA) (Raghu et al., 2017) measures the similarity of two sets of variables using many samples from each. Given two sets of random variables $\mathbf{x} = (x_1, x_2, ..., x_n)$ and $\mathbf{y} = (y_1, y_2, ..., y_m)$, CCA finds linear weights $\mathbf{a} \in \mathbb{R}^n$ and $\mathbf{b} \in \mathbb{R}^m$ which maximise $\text{cov}(\mathbf{a} \cdot \mathbf{x}, \mathbf{b} \cdot \mathbf{y})$. In our context, we treat the representation of the original sentence as $\mathbf{x}$, and the representation of the perturbed sentence as $\mathbf{y}$, and the resulting correlation as a similarity measure.

Since CCA requires many samples, we use the set of all word-level representations across all perturbed sentences. For example, to construct the samples of $\mathbf{x}$ from S perturbed sentences, we get use $[\mathbf{X}_1|\mathbf{X}_2|...|\mathbf{X}_S]$, where each $\mathbf{X}_i \in \mathbb{R}^{768 \times T_i}$. Unless specified otherwise, $S = 400$. For good estimates, CCA requires many samples (on the order of at least the number of dimensions), and we facilitate this by first reducing the dimension of the matrices using PCA. Using 400 components preserves $\sim 90\%$ of the variance. Thus, while CCA gives a good principled measure of representational similarity, its hunger for samples makes it unsuitable as a per-sentence metric.

We also measured distortion using Projec-

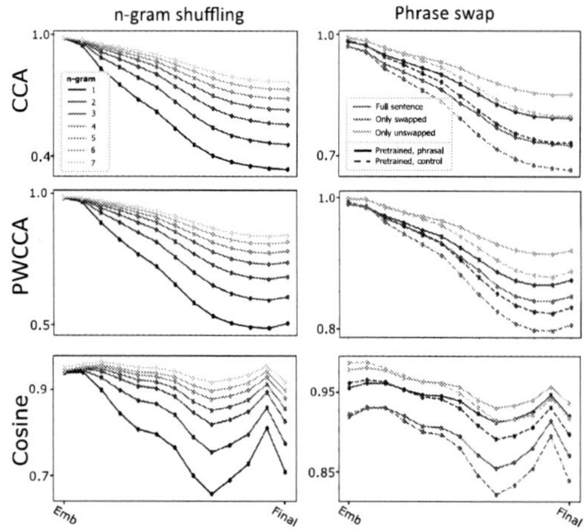

Figure 7: Results from the pretrained BERT model using alternative distortion metrics, on the n-gram shuffling and phrase swap experiments.

tion Weighted Canonical Correlation Analysis (PWCCA), an improved version of CCA to estimate the true correlation between tensors (Morcos et al., 2018).[12]

As reported in Figure 7, we did not find any qualitative differences between PWCCA and CCA in our experiments.

Cosine A similarity measure defined on individual sentences is the cosine between the sentence-level representations. By sentence-level representation, we mean the concatenation of the word-level vectors into a single vector $\mathbf{s} \in \mathbb{R}^{NT}$ (where N is the dimension of each feature vector). Treating each dimension of the vector as a sample, we can then define the following metric: $\text{corr}\left(\mathbf{s}_i^{original}, \mathbf{s}_i^{swapped}\right)$. This is equivalent to computing the cosine of the vectors after subtracting the (scalar) mean across dimensions, hence we will refer to it as 'cosine'.

A.3 Additional details on the dataset

In this section, we describe additional details of the manipulations done on the datasets.

n-gram shuffling For a given a sentence, we split it into sequential non-overlapping n-gram's from left to right; if the length of the sentence is not a multiple of n, the remaining words form an additional m-gram, $m < n$. The list of the n-gram's is randomly shuffled. Note that the 1-gram case is equivalent to a random shuffling of the words. In our analysis, we consider n-grams, with n varying from 1 (i.e., individual words) to 7 and all the sentences have at least 10 words.

We provide here an example of n-gram shuffling.

- Original: The market 's pessimism reflects the gloomy outlook in Detroit
- 1-gram : market pessimism the 's Detroit in The gloomy reflects outlook
- 2-gram : 's pessimism in Detroit The market reflects the gloomy outlook
- 3-gram : The market 's gloomy outlook in pessimism reflects the Detroit
- 4-gram : in Detroit The market 's pessimism reflects the gloomy outlook
- 5-gram : the gloomy outlook in Detroit The market 's pessimism reflects
- 6-gram : outlook in Detroit The market 's pessimism reflects the gloomy
- 7-gram : in Detroit The market 's pessimism reflects the gloomy outlook

Phrase swaps Using constituency trees from the Penn Treebank(Marcus et al., 1994), we define phrases as constituents which don't contain any others within them. (See Fig. 2c or Fig. 3a in the main text.) Phrase swaps thus consist of swapping one phrase with another, and leaving other words intact.

To provide an appropriate control perturbation, we swap two disjoint n-grams, which are the same size as true phrases but cross phrase boundaries.

Adjacent word swaps To better isolate the effect of broken phrase boundaries, we used adjacent word swaps. Adjacent words were chosen randomly, and one swap was performed per sentence.

A.4 Partial linear regression

In order to control for uninteresting explanations of our results, we often make use of a simple method for regressing out confounds. Generally, we want to assess the linear relationship between X and Y, when accounting for the (potentially non-linear) effect of another variable Z. In our experiments, X is always the swap-induced distortion and Y is the swap type, like integer-valued tree distance

[12]For both CCA and PWCCA, we use the implementation from `https://github.com/google/svcca`.

or binary-valued in/out phrase. We wish to allow $\mathbb{E}[Y|Z]$ and $\mathbb{E}[X|Z]$ to be any smooth function of Z, which is achieved by the least-squares solution to the following partially linear model:

$$Y \sim \beta_x X + \beta_{\mathbf{z}} \cdot \mathbf{f}(Z)$$

where $\mathbf{f}(z)$ is a vector of several (we use 10) basis functions (we used cubic splines with knots at 10 quantiles) of Z. Both regressions have the same optimal β_x, but the one on the left is computationally simpler (Hansen, 2000). The standard confidence intervals on β_x apply.

Intuitively, the β_x obtained by the partially linear regression above is related to the conditional correlation of X and Y given Z: $\rho(X, Y|Z)$. Like an unconditonal correlation, it will be zero if X and Y are conditionally independent given Z, but not necessarily *vice versa* (both X and Y must be Gaussian for the other direction to be true). To compute conditional rank correlations (which assess a monotonic relationship between X and Y), we rank-transform X and Y (this changes the confidence interval calculations).

We apply this method to swap size in Fig. 2 and attentions in Fig. 5. In these supplemental materials, we will also report the results when X is the binary in/out phrase variable, and Z is PMI. The full p-values and coefficients of the uncontrolled and controlled regressions can be found in Table 1, where we observe that past layer 2, the p-value on phrase boundary is very significant ($p < 10^{-12}$).

A.5 Supervised probes

In this section, we describe the experiments based on the three linguistic tasks: parts of Speech (POS); grandparent tags (GP); and constituency tree distance.

The POS and GP classifiers were multinomial logistic regressions trained to classify each word's POS tag (e.g. 'NNP', 'VB') and the tag of its grandparent in the constituency tree, respectively. If a word has no grandparent, its label is the root token 'S'. The probes were optimized with standard stochastic gradient descent, 50 sentences from the PTB per mini-batch. 10 epochs, at 10^{-3} learning rate, were sufficient to reach convergence.

The distance probe is a linear map $\mathbf{B}$ applied to each word vector w in the sentence, and trained such that, for all word pairs i, j, $\mathrm{TreeDist}(i, j)$ matches $\|\mathbf{B}(\mathbf{w}_i - \mathbf{w}_j)\|_2^2$ as closely as possible. Unlike the classifiers, there is freedom in the output dimension of $\mathbf{B}$; we used 100, although performance and results are empirically the same for any choice greater than ~ 64. Our probes are different from (Hewitt and Manning, 2019) in two ways: (1) we use constituency trees, instead of dependency trees, and (2) instead of an L1 loss function, we use the Poisson (negative) log-likelihood as the loss function. That is, if $\lambda_{i,j} = \|\mathbf{B}(\mathbf{w}_i - \mathbf{w}_j)\|_2^2$, and $y_{i,j} = \mathrm{TreeDist}(i, j)$

$$-l_{i,j} = y_{i,j} \log \lambda_{i,j} - \lambda_{i,j} - \log y_{i,j}!$$

Otherwise, the probes are trained exactly as in (Hewitt and Manning, 2019). Specifically, we used standard SGD with 20 sentences from the PTB in each mini-batch, for 40 epochs.

Evaluation A linear model is fit to maximize $p(y|\theta(\mathbf{x}))$, with p a probability function (multinomial for classifiers, Poisson for distance), and $\mathbf{x}$ coming from the unperturbed transformer representation. We evaluate the model on $\tilde{\mathbf{x}}$, which are the representations of the data when generated from a perturbed sentence. We take the average of $\log p(y|\theta(\mathbf{x}_i)) - \log p(y|\theta(\tilde{\mathbf{x}}_i))$ over all the data i in all sentences. For example, all words for the classifiers, and all pairs of words for the distance probe. Concretely, we are just measuring the difference in validation loss of the same probe on the $\mathbf{x}$ data and the $\tilde{\mathbf{x}}$ data. But because the loss is an appropriate probability function, we can interpret the same quantity as a difference in log-likelihood between the distribution conditioned on the regular representation and that conditioned on the perturbed representation. Distortion is similarly computed using the full sentence, providing a number for each swap in each sentence.

	Without PMI		With PMI	
Layer	Coeff.$\times 10^{-2}$	p-value	Coeff. $\times 10^{-2}$	p-value
Emb.	-0.21	5.6×10^{-5}	-0.11	9.4×10^{-2}
1	-0.11	3.4×10^{-2}	-0.05	4.2×10^{-1}
2	-0.74	$< 10^{-16}$	-0.53	2.12×10^{-8}
3	-1.6	$< 10^{-16}$	-1.3	2.2×10^{-16}
4	-2.0	$< 10^{-16}$	-1.4	4.4×10^{-16}
5	-2.1	$< 10^{-16}$	-1.5	8.8×10^{-16}
6	-2.4	$< 10^{-16}$	-1.7	$< 10^{-16}$
7	-2.6	$< 10^{-16}$	-1.7	1.6×10^{-15}
8	-3.4	$< 10^{-16}$	-2.3	$< 10^{-16}$
9	-3.8	$< 10^{-16}$	-2.7	$< 10^{-16}$
10	-4.1	$< 10^{-16}$	-3.0	$< 10^{-16}$
11	-3.8	$< 10^{-16}$	-2.8	$< 10^{-16}$
12	-4.2	$< 10^{-16}$	-3.1	$< 10^{-16}$

Table 1: Coefficients and p-values of the regular ('without PMI') and controlled ('with PMI') regressions of distortion against phrase boundary.

Box-To-Box Transformations for Modeling Joint Hierarchies

Shib Sankar Dasgupta, Xiang Lorraine Li, Michael Boratko
Dongxu Zhang, Andrew McCallum
College of Information and Computer Sciences
University of Massachusetts, Amherst
{ssdasgupta,xiangl,mboratko,dongxu,mccallum}@cs.umass.edu

Abstract

Learning representations of entities and relations in structured knowledge bases is an active area of research, with much emphasis placed on choosing the appropriate geometry to capture the hierarchical structures exploited in, for example, ISA or HASPART relations. Box embeddings (Vilnis et al., 2018; Li et al., 2019; Dasgupta et al., 2020), which represent concepts as n-dimensional hyperrectangles, are capable of embedding hierarchies when training on a subset of the transitive closure. In Patel et al. (2020), the authors demonstrate that only the transitive reduction is required and further extend box embeddings to capture joint hierarchies by augmenting the graph with new nodes. While it is possible to represent joint hierarchies with this method, the parameters for each hierarchy are decoupled, making generalization between hierarchies infeasible. In this work, we introduce a learned box-to-box transformation that respects the structure of each hierarchy. We demonstrate that this not only improves the capability of modeling cross-hierarchy compositional edges but is also capable of generalizing from a subset of the transitive reduction.

1 Introduction

Representation learning for hierarchical relations is crucial in natural language processing because of the hierarchical nature of common knowledge, for example, <Bird ISA Animal> (Athiwaratkun and Wilson, 2018; Vendrov et al., 2016; Vilnis et al., 2018; Nickel and Kiela, 2017). The ISA relation represents meaningful hierarchical relationships between concepts and plays an essential role in generalization for other relations, such as the generalization of <organ PARTOF person> based on <eye PARTOF of person>, and <organ ISA eye>. The fundamental nature of the ISA relation means that it is inherently involved in a large amount of compositional reasoning involving other relations.

Modeling hierarchies is essentially the problem of modeling a *poset*, or *partially ordered set*. The task of inferring missing edges that requires learning a transitive relation, was introduced in Vendrov et al. (2016). The authors also introduce a model based on the *reverse product order* on $\mathbb{R}^n$, which essentially models concepts as *infinite cones*. Region-based representations have been effective in representing hierarchical data, as containment between regions is naturally transitive. Vilnis et al. (2018) introduced axis-aligned hyperrectangles (or *boxes*) that are provably more flexible than cones, and demonstrated state-of-the-art performance in multiple tasks.

Thus far, not as much effort has been put into modeling joint hierarchies. Patel et al. (2020) proposed to simultaneously model ISA and HASPART hierarchies from Wordnet (Miller, 1995). In order to do so, they effectively augmented the graph by duplicating the nodes to create a single massive hierarchy. Their model assigns two separate box embeddings B_{ISA} and B_{HASPART} for each node n, where these two do not share any common parameter between them, and therefore misses out on a large amount of semantic relatedness between ISA and HASPART .

In this paper we propose a box-to-box transformation which translates and dilates box representations between hierarchies. Our proposed model shares information between the ISA and HASPART hierarchies via this transformation as well as cross-hierarchy containment training objectives. We compare BOX-TRANSFORM MODEL with multiple strong baselines under different settings. We substantially outperform the prior TWO-BOX MODEL while training with only the transitive reduction (which is informally the minimal graph with the same connectivity as the original hierarchy) of both hierarchies and predicting inferred composition

Proceedings of the 6th Workshop on Representation Learning for NLP (RepL4NLP-2021), pages 277–288
Bangkok, Thailand (Online), August 6, 2021. ©2021 Association for Computational Linguistics

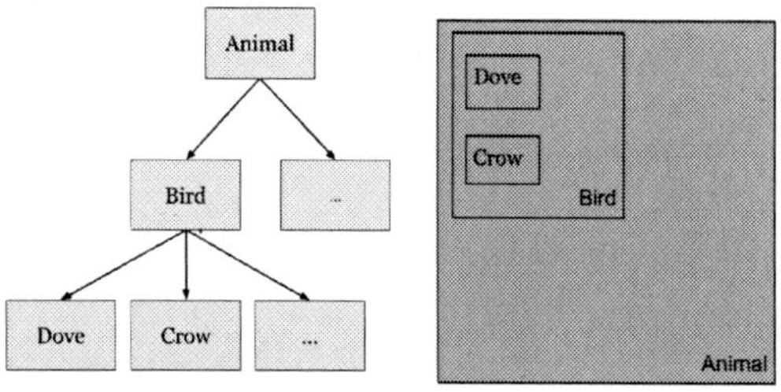

Figure 1: An example Box Embedding representation of the IsA hierarchy where

edges. As mentioned above, our model's shared learned features should allow for more generalization, and we test this by training on a subset of the transitive reduction, where we find we are able to outperform strong baselines. Finally, we perform a detailed analysis of the model's capacity to predict compositional edges and transitive closure edges, both from an overfitting and generalization standpoint, identifying subsets where further improvement is needed. The source code for our model and the dataset can be found in `https://github.com/iesl/box-to-box-transform.git`.

2 Related Work

Recent advances in representing one single hierarchy mainly fall in two categories: 1) representing hierarchies in non-Euclidian space (eg. hyperbolic space, due to the curvature's inductive bias to model tree-like structures) 2) using region-based representations instead of vectors for each node in the hierarchy (Erk, 2009). Hyperbolic space has been shown to be efficient in representing hierarchical relations, but also encounters difficulties in training (Nickel and Kiela, 2017; Ganea et al., 2018b; Chamberlain et al., 2017).

Categorization models in psychology often represent a concept as a region (Nosofsky, 1986; Smith et al., 1988; Hampton, 1991). Vilnis and McCallum (2015) and Athiwaratkun and Wilson (2018) use Gaussian distributions to embed each word in the corpus, the latter of which uses thresholded divergences which amount to region representations. Vendrov et al. (2016) and Lai and Hockenmaier (2017) make use of the reverse product order on $\mathbb{R}_{+}^{n}$, which effectively results in cone representations. Vilnis et al. (2018) further extend this cone representation to axis-aligned hyperrectangles (or *boxes*), and demonstrate state-of-the-art performance on modeling hierarchies. Various training improvement methods for box embeddings have been proposed (Li et al., 2019; Dasgupta et al., 2020), the most recent of which, *GumbelBox*, use a latent noise model where box parameters are represented via Gumbel distributions to improve on the loss landscape by making the gradient smooth for the geometric operations involved with box embeddings.

Region representations are also used for tasks which do not require modeling hierarchy. In Vilnis et al. (2018), the authors also model conditional probability distributions using box embeddings. Abboud et al. (2020) and Ren et al. (2020) take a different approach, using boxes for their capacity to contain many vectors to provide slack in the loss function when modeling knowledge base triples or representing logical queries, respectively. Ren et al. (2020) also made use of an action on boxes similar to ours, involving translation and dilation, however our work differs in both the task (i.e. representing logical queries vs. joint hierarchies) and approach, as their model represents entities using vectors and a loss function based on a box-to-vector distance. The inductive bias of hyperbolic space is also exploited to model multiple relations, Ganea et al. (2018a) learn hyperbolic transformations for multiple relations using Poincare embeddings, and show model improvement in low computational resource settings. Patel et al. (2020), which our work is most similar to, represent joint hierarchies using box embeddings. However, they represent each concept with two boxes ignoring the internal semantics of the concepts.

Modeling joint hierarchies shares some similarities with knowledge base completion, however the goals of the two settings are different. When modeling joint hierarchies you are attempting to learn simultaneous transitive relations, and potentially learn relevant compositional edges involving these relations. For knowledge base completion, on the other hand, you may be learning many different relations, and primarily seek to recover edges which were removed rather than inferring new compositional edges. Still, the models which perform knowledge base completion can be applied to this task, as the data can be viewed as knowledge base triples with only 2 relations. There have been multiple works that aim to build better knowledge representation (Bordes et al., 2013; Trouil-

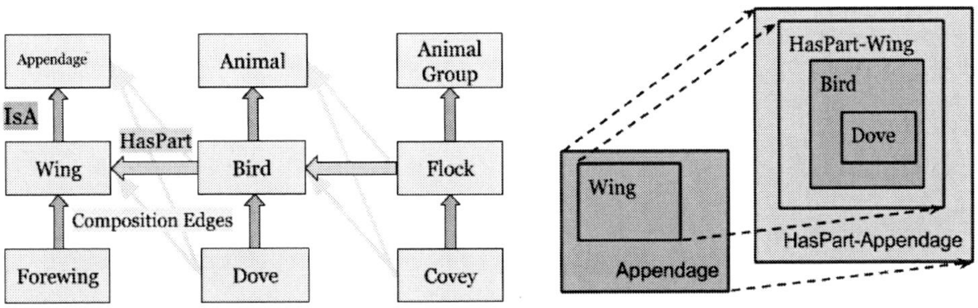

Figure 2: An overview of BOX-TRANSFORM MODEL on joint ISA and HASPART hierarchies. Composition edges are created following certain rules and it should be correctly inferred for a well-trained model. The ISA Wing box is transformed into a HASPART Wing box representing concepts that has wings, and Bird is a subset of it. Same follows for Appendage, and the monotonicity in the ISA space is preserved in HASPART space.

lon et al., 2016; Sun et al., 2019; Balazevic et al., 2019b). Most relevant, (Chami et al., 2020; Balazevic et al., 2019a) recently proposed KG embedding methods which embeds entities in the Poincaré ball model of hyperbolic space. These models are intended to capture relational patterns present in multi-relational graphs, with a particular emphasis on hierarchical relations.

3 Background

3.1 Box Lattice Model

Introduced in (Vilnis et al., 2018), a *box lattice model* (or *box model*) is a geometric embedding which captures partial orders and lattice structure using n-dimensional hyper-rectangles. Formally, we define the set of boxes $\mathcal{B}$ in $\mathbb{R}^n$ as

$$\mathcal{B}(\mathbb{R}^n) = \{[x_1, x^1] \times \cdots \times [x_d, x^d]\}, \quad (1)$$

where $x_i, x^j \in \mathbb{R}$, and we represent all degenerate boxes where $x_i > x^i$ with $\emptyset$. A box model for a set S is a function $\mathrm{Box} : S \to \mathcal{B}(\mathbb{R}^n)$ which captures some desirable properties of the set S. As the name implies, the box lattice model is particularly suited to representing partial orders and lattice structures.

Definition 1 (Poset)**.** A *partially ordered set*, or *poset*, is a set P along with a relation $\preceq$ such that, for each $a, b, c \in P$, we have

1. $a \preceq a$ (reflexivity)
2. if $a \preceq b$ and $b \preceq a$ then $a = b$ (antisymmetry)
3. if $a \preceq b$ and $b \preceq c$ then $a \preceq c$ (transitivity)

Definition 2 (Lattice)**.** A *lattice* is a poset where each pair of elements have a unique upper bound called the *join*, denoted by $\wedge$, and a unique lower bound called the *meet*, denoted by $\vee$.

The authors note that there are natural geometric operations which form a lattice structure on $\mathcal{B}$:

$$\mathrm{Box}(x) \wedge \mathrm{Box}(y) := \prod_i [\max(x_i, y_i), \min(x^i, y^i)], \quad (2)$$

$$\mathrm{Box}(x) \vee \mathrm{Box}(y) := \prod_i [\min(x_i, y_i), \max(x^i, y^i)], \quad (3)$$

In other words, the *meet* of two boxes is the smallest containing box, and the *join* is the intersection, or $\emptyset$ if the boxes are disjoint. These geometric operations map very neatly to hierarchies, where the meet of two nodes is their closest common ancestor and the join is the closest common descendent (or $\emptyset$ if no such node exists). The ability of this model to capture lattice structure using geometric operations makes it a natural choice to embed hierarchies.

3.2 Probabilistic Box Model Training

In Vilnis et al. (2018), the authors also introduced a *probabilistic* interpretation of box embeddings and a learning method which was improved upon in Li et al. (2019) and Dasgupta et al. (2020). By using a probability measure μ on $\mathbb{R}^d$ (or by constraining the space to $[0, 1]^d$), one can calculate box volumes as $\mu(\mathrm{Box}(X))$. The pullback of this measure yields a probability measure on S, and thus the box model can be imbued with valid probabilistic semantics. In particular, since the box space $\mathcal{B}$ is closed under intersection, we can calculate joint probabilities by computing $P(X,Y) = \mu(\text{Box}(X) \wedge \text{Box}(Y))$ and similarly compute conditional probabilities as

$$P(X \mid Y) = \frac{\mu(\text{Box}(X) \wedge \text{Box}(Y))}{\mu(\text{Box}(Y))}. \quad (4)$$

The conversion from a poset or lattice structure to probabilistic semantics is accomplished by assigning conditional probabilities, namely $a \preceq b$ if and only if $P(b \mid a) = 1$. We note that the properties required of the relation $\preceq$ follow as a natural consequence of the axioms for conditional probability. Apart from providing rigor and interpretability, the calibrated probabilistic semantics also inform and facilitate the training procedure for box embeddings, which is accomplished via gradient descent using KL-divergence with respect to the aforementioned probability distribution as a loss function.

As one might expect, care must be taken to handle the case when boxes are disjoint, as there is no gradient. In Vilnis et al. (2018) the authors made use of the lattice structure to derive a lower bound on the probability, and Li et al. (2019) introduced an approximation to Gaussian convolution over the boxes which similarly handled the case of disjoint boxes. Dasgupta et al. (2020) improves this further by taking a random process perspective, ensembling over an entire family of box models. The endpoints of boxes are represented using Gumbel distributions, that is

$$\begin{aligned} \text{GumbelBox}(X) &= \prod_i [X_i, X^i], \\ X_i &\sim \text{MaxGumbel}(\mu_i, \beta), \\ X^i &\sim \text{MinGumbel}(\mu^i, \beta), \end{aligned} \quad (5)$$

where μ, β are the location and scale parameters of the Gumbel distribution respectively. The MaxGumbel distribution is given by

$$f(x; \mu, \beta) = \frac{1}{\beta} \exp(-\tfrac{x-\mu}{\beta} - e^{-\frac{x-\mu}{\beta}}), \quad (6)$$

and the MinGumbel distribution given by negating x an μ. The Gumbel distribution was chosen due to it's min/max stability, making the set of Gumbel boxes closed under intersection, i.e. the intersection of two Gumbel boxes is another Gumbel box. We denote the space of all such boxes as $\mathcal{G}$. The expected volume of a Gumbel box can be efficiently calculated analytically, and in Dasgupta et al. (2020) the authors use this expected volume to calculate the conditional probabilities mentioned in equation (4). This training method leads to improved performance on many tasks, and is particularly beneficial when embedding trees, thus we will use *GumbelBox* in our setting.

3.3 Modeling Joint Hierarchies

Many existing methods have been proposed for modeling a single hierarchy, however entities are often simultaneously part of multiple hierarchies, for example *hypernymy* (i.e. ISA) and *meronomy* (i.e. HASPART). Furthermore, useful information can be shared across inferred compositional edges between the two hierarchies. For example, as shown in 2, based on <Bird,HASPART ,Wing> and <Dove,ISA ,Bird>, we can infer <Dove,HASPART ,Wing>. Due to the compositional nature of these relations, we can infer not only the per-relation transitive closure edges but also the compositional edges, i.e <Dove, HASPART , Wing>.

Formally, for two hierarchical relations r_1 and r_2, composition edges can be formulated following certain rules. In figure 2, the rules are designed as follows: for <Head,HASPART ,Tail>, < x_1, ISA , Head> represent the sub-class of Head, and <Tail, ISA , x_2 > is the super-class of Tail. Composition edges can be generated as < x_1,HASPART ,x_2 >, < x_1,HASPART ,Tail> or < Head ,HASPART ,x_2 >. These compositional edges are identified in Patel et al. (2020), where it is observed that a model which effectively captures both hierarchies should correctly predict not only over the transitive closure of each individual relation but also on these compositional edges.

4 Methods

4.1 Box-to-Box Transformation

As mentioned previously, our goal is to not only capture intra-relation transitivity, but also require the model to capture cross-hierarchy compositional edges; that is, for a set S with two partial orders $\preceq_1$, $\preceq_2$, we want a model capable of learning $(a \preceq_1 b) \wedge (b \preceq_2 c) \implies a \preceq_2 c$ and $(a \preceq_2 b) \wedge (b \preceq_1 c) \implies a \preceq_2 c$. Furthermore, we hope to do so without including these compositional edges in our training data, with the expectation that the embedding parameters capture relevant structure which allows us to recover them.

As shown in Dasgupta et al. (2020), Gumbel boxes are able to model hierarchies, we would like to benefit from this capability, particularly for modeling the ISA hierarchy, and thus we seek to learn a function $f_1 : S \to \mathcal{G}$, where

$$a \preceq_1 b \iff \frac{E[\mu(f_1(a) \cap f_1(b))]}{E[\mu(f_1(a))]} = 1. \quad (7)$$

For a given Gumbel box,

$$f(x) = \prod_{i=1}^{d} [X_i, X^i],$$
$$X_i \sim \text{MaxGumbel}(\mu_i, \beta),$$
$$X^i \sim \text{MinGumbel}(\mu_i + \Delta_i, \beta). \quad (8)$$

where the free parameters are μ_i and Δ_i. To simultaneously model a second relation, we train a function $\varphi : \mathcal{G} \to \mathcal{G}$ such that

$$a \preceq_2 b \iff \frac{E[\mu(\varphi(f_1(a)) \cap f_1(b))]}{E[\mu(\varphi(f_1(a)))]} = 1. \quad (9)$$

For notational simplicity, we abbreviate $f_2 = \varphi \circ f_1$.

We choose the transformation φ to operate on the "min" coordinate of a Gumbel box and the "side-lengths", that is, we transform a given Gumbel box

$$f(x) = \prod_{i=1}^{d} [X_i, X^i],$$
$$X_i \sim \text{MaxGumbel}(\mu_i, \beta),$$
$$X^i \sim \text{MinGumbel}(\mu_i + \Delta_i, \beta). \quad (10)$$

to

$$\varphi\,(\text{GumbelBox}(X)) = \prod_{i=1}^{d} [Y_i, Y^i], \quad (11)$$

where

$$Y_i \sim \text{MaxGumbel}(\theta_i \mu_i + b_i, \beta)$$
$$Y^i \sim \text{MinGumbel}(\theta_i \mu_i + b_i + \text{softplus}(\theta^i \Delta_i + b^i), \beta)$$

and the $\theta_i, \theta^i, b_i, b^i$ are learned parameters. This effectively translates and dilates the location parameters of the Gumbel distributions which represent the "corners" of a given Gumbel box. We call this model the BOX-TRANSFORM MODEL .

The softplus function is used here as a way to ensure the max coordinate remains larger than the min, and it also provides a simple overflow protection for the expected box volume, as might happen with side-lengths larger than one in high dimensions. While mathematically simple, this transformation allows for parameter sharing between the embedding of a concept with respect to $\preceq_1$ and with respect to $\preceq_2$. Importantly, the transformation is capable of capturing both a global translation and dilation as well as a scaled transformation of the existing learned representation, allowing the absolute position in space (which, for previous box embedding models, was irrelevant) to potentially capture relevant features of the entities.

Remark 1. The lack of a transformation on $f_1(b)$ is not an oversight. Using figure 2 as an example, if we consider the Bird box as representative of "all things which are birds", and the HASPART Wing box as the representative of "all thing which have wings", then encouraging containment of the Bird box inside the HASPART Wing box is quite natural. This conceptual motivation is precisely captured by the lack of a transformation on $f_1(b)$. This also coincides with the probabilistic semantics discussed in section 3.2, and is also the method employed by (Patel et al., 2020), where this cross-hierarchy containment objective is soley responsible for any flow of information between hierarchies in the TWO-BOX MODEL .

4.2 Connection to Two-Box Model

There are two main differences between our model and the model introduced in Patel et al. (2020), the TWO-BOX MODEL . First, the TWO-BOX MODEL preceded the Gumbel box model, and instead uses the Soft box model from (Li et al., 2019). To ensure that the benefits from our model are not conflated with the improvements from using Gumbel boxes we also train a TWO-BOX MODEL from (Patel et al., 2020) which makes use of Gumbel boxes.

Second, both models use different boxes to represent different relations, however, TWO-BOX MODEL allows both boxes to have free parameters, relying on containment between boxes representing different relations to pass information. Under the framework we have currently presented, this would be equivalent to learning two functions, f_1 and f_2, both of which have separate parameters for the min and side length of the boxes for each entity. While such a model has significant representational capacity, we would expect that it would suffer greatly from a lack of generalization. We evaluate this hypothesis by creating a second test, discussed in section 5.4, which removes edges from the transitive reduction of the training data.

5 Experiments

5.1 Dataset

We demonstrate the efficacy of BOX-TRANSFORM MODEL by using the joint hierarchy that has been created by Patel et al. (2020) from WordNet (Miller, 1995). In this dataset, *hypernymy* (ISA) and *meronymy* (HASPART) are two hierarchical relations of WordNet over noun sysnets, which are $82,114$ in total. Individually, the *hypernymy* part of the hierarchy contains $82,114$ nodes (i.e., all the synsets) with $84,363$ edges in its transitive reduction and the *meronymy* portion has $11,235$ synsets (out of $82,114$ synsets) with $9,678$ edges in its transitive reduction.

Joint Hierarchy In order to evaluate the performance on the joint hierarchy, Patel et al. (2020) created composition edges using the inter-relational semantics between *hypernymy* and *meronymy*. In particular they use the following composition rules:

$$\underbrace{\text{IsA} \circ \text{IsA} \cdots \text{IsA}}_{\text{0 or 1 or 2 times}} \circ \text{HasPart} \circ \underbrace{\text{IsA} \circ \text{IsA} \cdots \text{IsA}}_{\text{0 or 1 or 2 times}} = \text{HasPart}. \tag{12}$$

To illustrate from Figure 2, *<Dove* ISA *Bird>* $\wedge$ *<Bird* HASPART *Wing>* $\wedge$ *<Wing* ISA *Appendage>* implies that *<birds* HASPART *appendage>*. In total, $189,613$ composition edges are generated by the method described above for evaluation of the model on the joint hierarchy task. For each test/validation edge, a fixed set of negative samples of size 10 was generated by corrupting the head and tail 5 times each. The overall statistics for the dataset is provided in Table 1.

We have also created a second training dataset which further removes part of the transitive reduction to evaluate the models on their generalization capability (refer to Section 5.4 & 5.5). The dataset used for those section has different statistics and they are reported in the respective sections.

5.2 Baseline Models and Training Details

We compare BOX-TRANSFORM MODEL against geometric embedding methods as well as knowledge base completion methods. We give a brief description for each baseline below.

1. **TWO-BOX MODEL :** As mentioned in 4.2, Patel et al. (2020) extends the idea of Box embeddings (Vilnis et al., 2018; Li et al., 2019) to model joint hierarchies by defining two boxes per node, one for each relation.

2. **Order Embeddings:** (Vendrov et al., 2016) treats each concept as axis parallel cones in positive orthant. We considered two different cone parameters for each entity following the TWO-BOX MODEL (Patel et al., 2020).

3. **Poincaré Embeddings:** (Nickel and Kiela, 2017) & **Hyperbolic Entailment Cones** (Ganea et al., 2018b): Tree-structured data are best captured in hyperbolic space (Chamberlain et al., 2017). Thus in Nickel and Kiela (2017), the authors learn embedding on n-dimensional Poincaré ball. For similar reasons, Ganea et al. (2018b) uses the hyperbolic space however they extend the hyperbolic point embeddings to entailment cones. Again, for these models, two separate parameters are considered for each entity.

4. **TransE and RotatE** (Bordes et al., 2013; Sun et al., 2019): This task can be posed as knowledge base completion for a KB with only two relations. Thus we evaluate TransE and RotatE which are simple yet effective methods for knowledge base embeddings, which achieve state-of-the-art for many knowledge base embedding tasks. Unlike the TWO-BOX MODEL (Patel et al., 2020) or the other baselines, these methods have shared representation for each entity, and thus they are expected to generalise better on missing edges.

5. **Hyperbolic KG Embeddings** (Balazevic et al., 2019a; Chami et al., 2020): We also compared our method against recently proposed KG embedding methods based on hyperbolic embeddings to model hierarchical structures present in KGs. The Multi-Relational Poincaré model (MuRP) (Balazevic et al., 2019a) learns relation-specific transforms of the entities that are embedded in hyperbolic space. The RoTH (Chami et al., 2020) parameterize the relation specific transformations as hyperbolic rotation, where as the AttH (Chami et al., 2020) combines hyperbolic reflection and rotation using attention. More training details are in Appendix A.2.

Table 1: Details of the hypernymy, meronymy hierarchies and the composition edges.

	Transitive Reduction	Transitive Closure	Validation (pos/neg)	Test (pos/neg)
Hypernym	84,363	661,127	28,838/ 288,380	28,838/ 288,380
Meronym	9,678	30,333	5,164/ 51,640	5,164/ 51,640
Composite Edge	-	-	94,807/ 948,070	94,806/ 948,070

Table 2: Test F1 scores(%)of various methods for predicting the Composition edges.

Methods	F1 score
Poincaré Embeddings	43.8
Hyperbolic Entailment Cones	44.0
TransE	57.0
RotatE	51.0
Order Embeddings	68.5
MuRP	21.4
AttH	51.3
RotE	51.5
RotH	55.8
TWO-BOX MODEL (Patel et al., 2020)	68.1
TWO-BOX MODEL (with GumbelBox)	73.7
BOX-TRANSFORM MODEL	**82.2**

Table 3: Test F1 scores(%) of various methods for generalization capability.

Methods	F1 score
Poincaré Embeddings	33.5
Hyperbolic Entailment Cones	36.0
TransE	57.0
RotatE	55.0
Order Embeddings	54.5
MuRP	20.1
AttH	27.0
RotE	48.8
RotH	46.7
TWO-BOX MODEL (with GumbelBox)	58.9
BOX-TRANSFORM MODEL	**63.9**

5.3 Composition Edges from Transitive Reduction

In order to demonstrate the ability of the model to capture partially ordered (tree-like) data most embedding methods (Ganea et al., 2018b; Nickel and Kiela, 2017; Patel et al., 2020) train their model on the transitive reduction and predict on the transitive closure. For an evaluation on modeling the joint hierarchy, therefore, it is natural to train the models only on the transitive reduction of *hypernymy* and *meronymy* and evaluate on the composition edges, as done in Patel et al. (2020). We report the F1 score (with 1:10 negatives) for those edges in table 2. The threshold used for the classification is determined by maximizing the F1 score on the validation set.

From Table 2, we observe that BOX-TRANSFORM MODEL outperforms the other baselines by a significant margin. As mentioned in Patel et al. (2020) and so do we observe that in the next section 5.4 that the Poincaré embeddings and Hyperbolic entailment cones do face difficulty in learning when presented only with transitive reduction edges. However, the hyperbolic KG method Atth RoTH are able to learn the composite edges to a certain extent. The performance gain of RotH over its euclidean counterpart RotE can be attributed to its inductive bias towards modeling hierarchies. The performance of Box embedding method as proposed by Patel et al. (2020) performs at par order embedding method. However using GumbelBox formulation (Dasgupta et al., 2020), we observe significant performance boost as GumbelBox improves the local identifiability of the parameter space. Still, the capability of the BOX-TRANSFORM MODEL to benefit from shared cross-hierarchy features allows it to substantially outperform even this improved version of the TWO-BOX MODEL . This is likely due to the fact that the inductive bias provided by the transformation is more in line with the data; the model can benefit from the containments learned as a result of the ISA relation, and learn a HASPART transformation which potentially preserves these containments.

5.4 Learning from Incomplete Transitive Reduction

In Patel et al. (2020), and also in our previous experiment, we already observe that box embedding methods are highly capable of to recovering the transitive closure (in our case, composition edges) given the transitive reduction only. In this experiment, we train with even less of the transitive reduction, moving some of these edges to the test

Table 4: Single hierarchy F1 score (%) analysis on ISA and HASPART . The overall dataset is the combination of overfitting, generalization and extended generalization

	Type	Overall TC(X)	Overfitting TC(X1)	Generalization X-X1	Extended Generalization TC(X) - TC(X1) -(X-X1)
TransE	ISA	52.9	52.1	66.5	46.0
Two Box Model		47.8	58.9	19.9	22.9
BOX-TRANSFORM MODEL		**57.3**	60.0	65.9	44.4
TransE	HASPART	**59.9**	63.0	56.1	48.3
Two Box Model		51.6	54.8	40.8	37.8
BOX-TRANSFORM MODEL		58.8	64.2	33.4	25.4

Table 5: Joint hierarchy F1 score (%) analysis. The overall data is the combination of overfitting and generalization.

	Overall COMP(X, Y)	Overfitting COMP(X1, Y1)	Generalization COMP(X, Y) - COMP(X1, Y1)
TransE	58.8	70.1	68.6
Two Box Model	62.5	72.7	63.6
BOX-TRANSFORM MODEL	**69.6**	86.1	70.0

set. Now, reconstruction of the closure and the composition edges require models to generalize over the missing parts of the graph. We train on 9175 *meronymy* edges and 80372 *hypernymy* edges and test/validate on an aggregated pool of 251783 edges. Please refer to the Appendix A.1 for details on dataset creation and statistics.

From Table 3, we observe that BOX-TRANSFORM MODEL outperforms all the baseline methods by a large extent. Although the two box model is performing worse than BOX-TRANSFORM MODEL , it is able to beat other baselines. Out of the two Knowledge base completion methods TransE performs the best and achieves comparative performance to two box model. Although the hyperbolic KG embeddings were able to perform well on the composite edges, their generalization performance is relatively lower than other KG embedding methods. We also observe that the RotE model that was under performing in composite edges, outperforms RotH by some margin in this generalization setting. We select the top three best performing methods for further analysis for each type of edges in the graph.

5.5 Performance analysis on different splits

Training on a subset of the transitive reduction showed that our model could generalize to composition edges even with the absence of essential edges to make such prediction. We further perform evaluation analysis using the same training data with the best-performed model selected by maximizing the f1 score on composition edges. We evaluate the model performance on the transitive closure for each hierarchy (ISA and HASPART), and the composition edges on the joint hierarchy.

For each single hierarchy, some edges are removed from the transitive reduction X to create the incomplete transitive reduction training data $X1$. Evaluating the transitive closure of X directly evaluates the model's performance on each hierarchy, denoted as $\text{TC}(X)$. This can be further divided into three categories: dataset that evaluates model ability to capture transitive closure of $X1$, $\text{TC}(X1)$, dataset that evaluates model generalization ability on missing edges $X - X1$, and dataset that evaluates model's extended generalization ability on $\text{TC}(X) - \text{TC}(X1)$.

Composition edges from the joint hierarchy can be analyzed the same way. $\text{COMP}(X, Y)$ represent all the composition edges in the full wordnet dataset, composed by ISA transitive reduction X and HASPART transitive reduction Y. It can be further divided into two categories: data that evaluate model overfitting ability to capture $\text{COMP}(X_1, Y_1)$ where X_1 and Y_1 is the corresponding training ISA and HASPART data in section 5.4, and data that evaluate model generalization ability on learning logical operations $\text{COMP}(X, Y) - \text{COMP}(X_1, Y_1)$. The detailed statistics on each of these splits are provided in Appendix A.4. The evaluation dataset is created by randomly creating negative examples with the pos: neg ratio 1:10. We select the top 3 best models from section 5.4, then choose the threshold that maximized the F1 score for the validation data of each split and report the test F1. As shown in table 4 and table 5, our model performs the best overall across different dataset splits. BOX-TRANSFORM MODEL performs much better on the full transitive closure of ISA , and all the composition edges. In general, BOX-TRANSFORM MODEL performs much better on transitive closure and composition edges by a large margin in all overfitting settings. TransE does better on predicting removed edges from the transitive reduction (which serves more as an analysis of the model's capability, as it is not a typical evaluation for partial order completion), however we note that our model does surprisingly well on the ISA missing edges, which we attribute to the shared semantics between the hierarchy made possible by this box-to-box transformation.

6 Conclusion

We proposed a box-to-box transformation that facilitates sharing of learned features across hierarchies when modeling joint hierarchies. We demonstrate the BOX-TRANSFORM MODEL is capable of achieving state-of-the-art performance compared with other strong baseline models when predicting compositional edges across a joint hierarchy. Furthermore, the model also outperforms other models when modeling the transitive closure of each relation independently. In the future, we aim to extend the current model from two relations to multiple relations in order to obtain more generalization from hierarchical ISA edges.

Acknowledgments

We the anonymous reviewers for their constructive feedback. This work was supported in part by the Center for Intelligent Information Retrieval and the Center for Data Science, in part by the Chan Zuckerberg Initiative, in part by the National Science Foundation under Grant No. IIS-1763618, in part by University of Southern California subcontract no. 123875727 under Office of Naval Research prime contract no. N660011924032, and in part by University of Southern California subcontract no. 89341790 under Defense Advanced Research Projects Agency prime contract no. FA8750-17-C-0106. Any opinions, findings and conclusions or recommendations expressed in this material are those of the authors and do not necessarily reflect those of the sponsor.

References

Ralph Abboud, İsmail İlkan Ceylan, Thomas Lukasiewicz, and Tommaso Salvatori. 2020. Boxe: A box embedding model for knowledge base completion. In *Proceedings of the 34th Annual Conference on Neural Information Processing Systems NeurIPS*.

Ben Athiwaratkun and Andrew Gordon Wilson. 2018. Hierarchical density order embeddings. In *International Conference on Learning Representations*.

Ivana Balazevic, Carl Allen, and Timothy Hospedales. 2019a. Multi-relational poincaré graph embeddings. In *Advances in Neural Information Processing Systems*, volume 32, pages 4463–4473. Curran Associates, Inc.

Ivana Balazevic, Carl Allen, and Timothy Hospedales. 2019b. TuckER: Tensor factorization for knowledge graph completion. In *Proceedings of the 2019 Conference on Empirical Methods in Natural Language Processing and the 9th International Joint Conference on Natural Language Processing*.

Lukas Biewald. 2020. Experiment tracking with weights and biases. Software available from wandb.com.

Antoine Bordes, Nicolas Usunier, A. Garcia-Duran, Jason Weston, and Oksana Yakhnenko. 2013. Translating embeddings for modeling multi-relational data. In *Neural Information Processing Systems*.

Benjamin Paul Chamberlain, James R. Clough, and Marc Peter Deisenroth. 2017. Neural embeddings of graphs in hyperbolic space. *13th international workshop on mining and learning from graphs held in conjunction with KDD*.

Ines Chami, Adva Wolf, Da-Cheng Juan, Frederic Sala, Sujith Ravi, and Christopher Ré. 2020. Low-dimensional hyperbolic knowledge graph embeddings. *arXiv preprint arXiv:2005.00545*.

Shib Sankar Dasgupta, Michael Boratko, Dongxu Zhang, Luke Vilnis, Xiang Lorraine Li, and Andrew McCallum. 2020. Improving local identifiability for probabilistic box embeddings. In *Neural Information Processing Systems*.

Katrin Erk. 2009. Representing words as regions in vector space. In *Proceedings of the Thirteenth Conference on Computational Natural Language Learning*.

Octavian Ganea, Gary Bécigneul, and Thomas Hofmann. 2018a. Hyperbolic neural networks. In *Advances in neural information processing systems*, pages 5345–5355.

Octavian-Eugen Ganea, Gary Bécigneul, and Thomas Hofmann. 2018b. Hyperbolic entailment cones for learning hierarchical embeddings. In *International Conference on Machine Learning*.

James A Hampton. 1991. The combination of prototype concepts. *The psychology of word meanings*, pages 91–116.

Alice Lai and Julia Hockenmaier. 2017. Learning to predict denotational probabilities for modeling entailment. In *Proceedings of the 15th Conference of the European Chapter of the Association for Computational Linguistics*.

Xiang Li, Luke Vilnis, Dongxu Zhang, Michael Boratko, and Andrew McCallum. 2019. Smoothing the geometry of probabilistic box embeddings. In *International Conference on Learning Representations*.

George A Miller. 1995. WordNet: a lexical database for English. *Communications of the ACM*.

Maximilian Nickel and Douwe Kiela. 2017. Poincaré embeddings for learning hierarchical representations. In *Neural Information Processing Systems*.

Robert M Nosofsky. 1986. Attention, similarity, and the identification–categorization relationship. *Journal of experimental psychology: General*, 115(1):39.

Dhruvesh Patel, Shib Sankar Dasgupta, Michael Boratko, Xiang Li, Luke Vilnis, and Andrew McCallum. 2020. Representing joint hierarchies with box embeddings. *Automated Knowledge Base Construction*.

Hongyu Ren, Weihua Hu, and Jure Leskovec. 2020. Query2box: Reasoning over knowledge graphs in vector space using box embeddings. *International Conference on Learning Representations*.

Edward E Smith, Daniel N Osherson, Lance J Rips, and Margaret Keane. 1988. Combining prototypes: A selective modification model. *Cognitive science*, 12(4):485–527.

Zhiqing Sun, Zhi-Hong Deng, Jian-Yun Nie, and Jian Tang. 2019. Rotate: Knowledge graph embedding by relational rotation in complex space. *International Conference on Learning Representations*.

Théo Trouillon, Johannes Welbl, Sebastian Riedel, Éric Gaussier, and Guillaume Bouchard. 2016. Complex embeddings for simple link prediction. In *International Conference on Machine Learning*.

Ivan Vendrov, Ryan Kiros, Sanja Fidler, and Raquel Urtasun. 2016. Order-embeddings of images and language. In *International Conference on Learning Representations*.

Luke Vilnis, Xiang Li, Shikhar Murty, and Andrew McCallum. 2018. Probabilistic embedding of knowledge graphs with box lattice measures. In *Association for Computational Linguistics*.

Luke Vilnis and Andrew McCallum. 2015. Word representations via gaussian embedding. *International Conference on Learning Representations*.

A Appendix

A.1 Dataset creation steps from Section 5.4

In order to remove edges from the transitive reductions, we iterate through the transitive reduction edges of meronymy. With 0.5 probability we choose the edge for further processing. For each chosen HASPART edge, we select an outgoing ISA edge and pair them. We drop the ISA edge from the pair with 0.9 probability (the ratio of HASPART to ISA transitive reduction) and drop the HASPART edge in case the ISA is not dropped already. This procedure ensures that all the edge removals happen around the composition edges, thus, the results reflect the models true capacity to generalize well for this joint hierarchy task. We evaluate the model on the composition edges, the removed reduction edges, and the closure edges with 251783 in numbers which we split into two parts for validation and test. In Table 3, we report the F1 score on this aggregated evaluation data with 1:10 fixed true negatives.

A.2 Training Details

In our experiments, we have kept the number of parameters same across all the methods. We use 5 dimensional box embeddings for the Two Box Model (Patel et al., 2020). Since box embeddings are specified using min and side length in the same dimension. Thus we compare with 10 dimensional order embeddings, Poincaré embeddings, and hyperbolic entailment cones. However, since the above mentioned methods has two different number of parameters for each node, we use 20 dimensional vectors for RotatE, TransE to account for that. Our BOX-TRANSFORM MODEL uses 10 dimension box embeddings for similar reason.

Hyperparameter range: We use Bayesian hypermeter optimizer with Hyperband algorithm for all the methods using the web interface (Biewald, 2020). The hyperparameter ranges are $Gumbel\beta \in [0.001, 3]$, Softplus temperature for box volume $T \in [1, 30]$, $lr \in [0.0005, 1]$, batch size $\in \{8096, 2048, 1024, 512\}$, number of negative samples $\in [2, 30]$ for all the methods. For max margin trainging we searched for the $margin \in [1, 50]$.

The best hyperparameters for our method and a few competitive baselines are provided in appropriate **config** files along with the source code. We will make the code public after the anonymity period.

In order to remove edges from the transitive reductions, we iterate through the transitive reduction edges of *meronymy*. With 0.5 probability we choose the edge for further processing. For each chosen HASPART edge, we select an outgoing ISA edge and pair them. We drop the ISA edge from the pair with 0.9 probability (the ratio of HASPART to ISA transitive reduction) and drop the HASPART edge in case the ISA is not dropped already.

This procedure ensures that all the edge removals happen around the composition edges, thus, the results reflect the models true capacity to generalize well for this joint hierarchy task. We evaluate the model on the composition edges, the removed reduction edges, and the closure edges with 251783 in numbers which we split into two parts for validation and test. In Table 3, we report the F1 score on this aggregated evaluation data with 1:10 fixed true negatives.

A.3 Visualization

We plot 2-dimensional box embeddings to inspect the quality of our proposed BOX-TRANSFORM MODEL . Please refer to Figure 3. Here, we use the box embedding parameters of the best performing model from experiment 5.3 (Table 2). Note that, the model is 10 dimensional. However, for a perfectly trained model for the hierarchical tree-like data, we should observe more numbers of full containments, i.e., containment along each dimension. Thus, we pick two dimensions randomly out of the 10-d to visualize the box embeddings.

In the example in Figure 3 (next page), the facts that <Car,HASPART ,CarDoor> and <CarDoor,ISA ,Door> would enable us to infer that <Car,HASPART , Door>. This is a particular example of the compositional edges. We observe from the Figure 3 that the HASPART transformation of the "Car Door" and "Door" successfully encloses the ISA transformation of the "Car", thus our model is able infer that composition edge . All the other composite edges such as <Sedan,HASPART , CarDoor >, <Sedan,HASPART , Door> etc. can be similarly inferred from the visualization.

A.4 Details of the splits from Section 5.5

We report the performance of our method on different splits which are qualitatively different from each other. The detailed statistics of these splits can be found in Table 6 & 7.

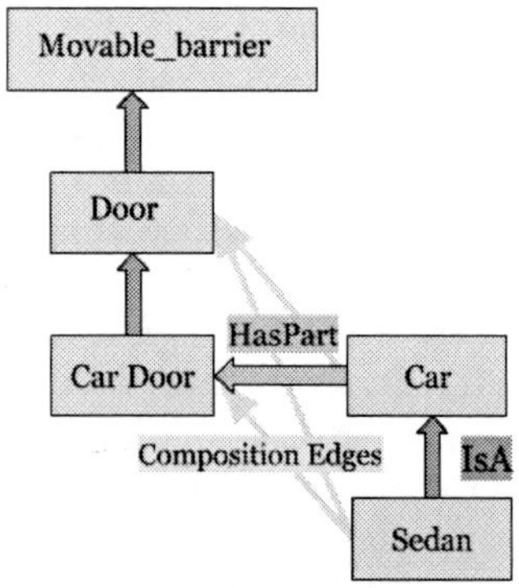

(a) Example of Joint Hierarchy extracted from the WordNet dataset.

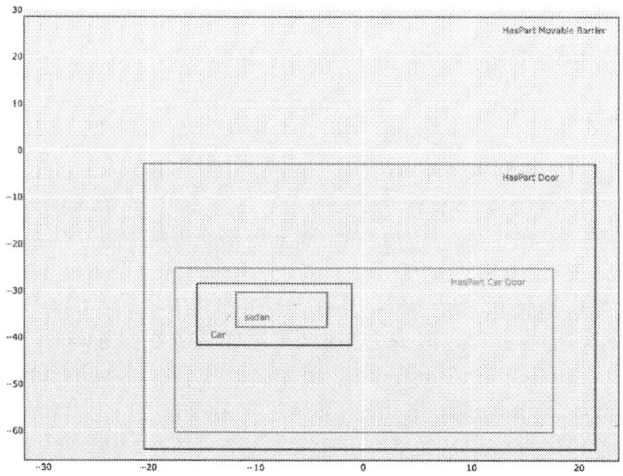

(b) We plot the transformed ISA box for "Sedan" & "Car" and transformed HASPART box for "Door", "Car Door", "Movable Barrier" on the same space. The transformations do preserve the containment and provide an consistent assignment of box embedddings for the example on left.

Figure 3: 2-dimensional visualization of proposed Box embedding model.

Table 6: Dataset statistics for different parts of individual ISA and PARTOF hierarchy.

Hierarchy	TC(X)	TC(X1)	X-X1	TC(X) - TC(X1) - (X-X1)
IsA	61,667	51,195	3,991	6,481
HasPart	30,335	26,388	503	3,444

Table 7: Dataset statistics for different composition edges in Joint Hierarchy.

Hierarchy	Comp(X, Y)	COMP(X1, Y1)	COMP(X, Y1) - COMP(X1, Y1)
Joint Hierarchy	189,613	146,867	42,746

An Overview of Uncertainty Calibration for Text Classification and the Role of Distillation

Han Guo **Ramakanth Pasunuru** **Mohit Bansal**
UNC Chapel Hill
hanguo@cs.cmu.edu {ram, mbansal}@cs.unc.edu

Abstract

Recent advances in NLP systems, notably the pretraining-and-finetuning paradigm, have achieved great success in predictive accuracy. However, these systems are usually not well calibrated for uncertainty out-of-the-box. Many recalibration methods have been proposed in the literature for quantifying predictive uncertainty and calibrating model outputs, with varying degrees of complexity. In this work, we present a systematic study of a few of these methods. Focusing on the text classification task and finetuned large pretrained language models, we first show that many of the finetuned models are not well calibrated out-of-the-box, especially when the data come from out-of-domain settings. Next, we compare the effectiveness of a few widely-used recalibration methods (such as ensembles, temperature scaling). Then, we empirically illustrate a connection between distillation and calibration. We view distillation as a regularization term encouraging the student model to output uncertainties that match those of a teacher model. With this insight, we develop simple recalibration methods based on distillation with no additional inference-time cost. We show on the GLUE benchmark that our simple methods can achieve competitive out-of-domain (OOD) calibration performance w.r.t. more expensive approaches. Finally, we include ablations to understand the usefulness of components of our proposed method and examine the transferability of calibration via distillation.

1 Introduction

The recent success of NLP systems, notably the pretraining-and-finetuning paradigm has led to widespread applications (Peters et al., 2018; Devlin et al., 2019; Radford et al., 2019). However, these systems are not always well-calibrated; in many high-stake decision-making scenarios such as medical diagnosis, even small errors would have large damage. Suppose an ML system predicts a 20% probability a patient has cancer whereas the reality is 40%, diagnosis relying on inaccurate estimates could lead to devastating consequences (Kumar et al., 2019). Further, interpreting and communicating these uncertainties facilitates better trust between humans and ML systems (Bansal et al., 2020; Wilder et al., 2020; Ribeiro et al., 2016, 2018).

Hence, it is increasingly important for users to understand not only when the systems would succeed, but also when they could fail. One seemingly straightforward approach is to have the systems output predictions and some measure of their confidence/uncertainty. Users could then use both the predictions and associated uncertainties to decide how much they would trust the prediction. For example, one might decide to take an umbrella to work only if the confidence of the rain prediction is more than 50%. For many statistical methods, confidence/uncertainty is either part of the system by design (e.g., Bayesian methods) or could be efficiently estimated (e.g., linear regressions). Unfortunately, for large-scale DNNs, estimating uncertainty becomes a challenge (Gal, 2016): e.g., nominal probabilities from the softmax function are shown to be uncalibrated estimates of model uncertainty (Platt, 1999; Niculescu-Mizil and Caruana, 2005; Guo et al., 2017; Ovadia et al., 2019).

In this work, we present a systematic study on recalibrating current NLP systems, particularly those that fall in the recent popular pretraining-and-finetuning paradigm (Hendrycks et al., 2020; Desai and Durrett, 2020), as they are widely deployed in recent state-of-the-art systems and hence it is important that they are well calibrated for safety and transparency. However, the methods discussed in this work could generalize to a broader range of systems. We focus on the calibration not only of the task itself, but also under dataset distributional

Proceedings of the 6th Workshop on Representation Learning for NLP (RepL4NLP-2021), pages 289–306
Bangkok, Thailand (Online), August 6, 2021.

shift (Ovadia et al., 2019).

We start by introducing uncertainty and calibration, and cover related advances in the deep learning literature. In addition to widely-used maximum calibration error and expected calibration error, we follow previous works (Ovadia et al., 2019; Kumar et al., 2019) and include additional calibration evaluation metrics for better comparisons (e.g., Brier scores and ℓ_p calibration error).

We conduct experiments on GLUE classification tasks (Wang et al., 2019) and show that finetuned language models are usually not calibrated out-of-the-box, especially when the data comes from *a distribution different from the training data*. We use the term "out-of-domain" (or "out-of-distribution", OOD) to refer to the setting where the train and evaluation data come from different "distributions". Related works in NLP have considered data from similar tasks but from different datasets as OOD (Ovadia et al., 2019; Hendrycks and Gimpel, 2017). Next, in order to make models more calibrated, we study some of the widely-used recalibration methods, with various degrees of effectiveness and computational cost. For example, ensembling models has been shown to be very effective in out-of-domain settings (Ovadia et al., 2019), but the cost of computation scales with the size of ensembles. On the other hand, distillation (Hinton et al., 2015) is a widely-known method for improving the system's performance by learning from a stronger teacher model. In this work, we empirically examine the connection between distillation and calibration. Notably, we view the objective function of distillation as a regularization term that encourages the student model to match the predictive uncertainty of a stronger, more calibrated teacher model.

We conduct analysis experiments to show that the teacher's calibration performance could be distilled into the student model, even when the teacher model's accuracy remains similar. With this insight, we show that simple methods based on distillation could achieve competitive performance in out-of-domain calibration, without introducing extra computation at inference time. Finally, we also conduct ablation experiments to understand the usefulness of components of the method. In summary, our contributions are listed as follows:

- We present a systematic study on the performance of various recalibration methods on finetuned language models for both in-domain and out-of-domain settings.
- We empirically examine the connection between distillation and calibration, and conduct experiments showing that distillation can distill calibration performance.
- We describe two simple recalibration methods, and experimental results demonstrate their competitiveness in the out-of-domain settings; finally, we also ablate method's components and measure the extent to which distillation transfers teachers' calibration improvement.

2 Background and Related Works

Due to space constraints, we present some of the most relevant materials in the main paper. Please see the appendix (Sec. A) for extended background and related works.

The quality of the uncertainty measurement is usually measured via calibration (Kendall and Gal, 2017). In the context of calibration, the uncertainties often refer to predictive probabilities. The model is calibrated if the predictive probabilities match the empirical frequency of the data (Gal, 2016). Let $\hat{Y}$ and $\hat{P}$ be the predicted class and its associated confidence of a neural network. We would like the confidence estimates $\hat{P}$ to be calibrated, which intuitively means that we want $\hat{P}$ to represent true probabilities (Guo et al., 2017):

$$\mathbb{P}(\hat{Y} = Y|\hat{P} = p) = p, \forall p \in [0, 1]. \quad (1)$$

Suppose a classification model is given N input examples, and made predictions $\hat{y}_1, ..., \hat{y}_N$, each with $\hat{p} = 0.35$. We would expect 35% of the predictions would be correct. The problem of uncertainty/confidence calibration and confidence scores have been studied and applied in various settings such as structured prediction problems (Kuleshov and Liang, 2015), online recalibration (with potentially adversarial/OOD input) (Kuleshov and Ermon, 2017), model regularization (Pereyra et al., 2017), and misclassified/OOD examples detection (Hendrycks and Gimpel, 2017). In practice, however, perfect calibration is almost impossible (Guo et al., 2017), and estimating the first term in Eq. 1 is not straightforward using finite samples, because in most cases $\hat{P}$ is a continuous random variable (Guo et al., 2017; Kumar et al., 2019). In Sec. 3, we describe ways to estimate the calibration performance.

It has been widely observed that modern neural networks are usually not calibrated out of the box (Platt, 1999; Zadrozny and Elkan, 2001; Guo et al., 2017; Ovadia et al., 2019). Recalibration methods improve calibration by transforming un-calibrated outputs into calibrated outputs/probabilities, and they include scaling-based methods (Platt, 1999; Guo et al., 2017), histogram-binning-based methods (Guo et al., 2017; Zadrozny and Elkan, 2001), and ensembles (Lakshminarayanan et al., 2017). Recently, Kumar et al. (2019) proposed the scaling-binning calibrator and a more sample-efficient estimator of calibration error. In our work, we describe simple approaches that combine the strength of ensembles and temperature scaling without introducing computation at inference time; we further apply the scaling-binning calibrator to ensure calibration.

Ensemble-based methods work by aggregating multiple networks trained independently on the entire dataset, and has been shown to achieve strong performance in out-of-domain calibration (Ovadia et al., 2019; Lakshminarayanan et al., 2017). More generally, there are randomization-based ensembles and boosting-based ensembles. Within the randomization-based ensembles, we use the entire training dataset to train each model instead of different bootstrap samples of the original training set (Lakshminarayanan et al., 2017).

Temperature scaling is an extension of Platt scaling (Guo et al., 2017). It uses a single scalar parameter $T > 0$ for all classes. Given output z_i, the confidence prediction is:

$$\hat{p}_i = \max_k \sigma(z_{i,k}/T). \quad (2)$$

An extension, called heteroscedastic regression, is used in our work, which replaces the constant scalar with learned values (Kendall and Gal, 2017; Kendall et al., 2018).

Knowledge distillation (Hinton et al., 2015) is a compression technique in which a compact model (usually referred to as the student model) is trained to mimic the behavior of a more powerful teacher model. In the context of classification, knowledge distillation works by augmenting the loss function with an additional term $D_{KL}(p_i \| p_j)$ where $p_i = \text{softmax}(z_i/T)$ and $p_j = \text{softmax}(z_j/T)$ with z_i and z_j the logits from two models, and T controls the smoothness of the output distribution. In this work, we show that distillation can also be used to distill calibration performance, and use it to build simple yet competitive recalibration methods.

Concurrently, Desai and Durrett (2020) studied the calibration of pretrained transformers when finetuned to downstream tasks, and Hendrycks et al. (2020) studied the out-of-distribution robustness of pretrained transformers. We are different from them in that first we present a systematic study on the out-of-distribution calibration; second we draw insights from the connection between distillation and temperature scaling to design simple yet competitive recalibration methods; third, we conduct experiments to understand the connection between them empirically; finally, we also include a more comprehensive set of calibration evaluations following Ovadia et al. (2019) and Kumar et al. (2019).

3 Measuring Calibration Errors

3.1 Calibration Error Metrics

Let $\mathcal{X}$ be the input space, and $\mathcal{Y} = \{1, ..., K\}$ be the label space, and $X \in \mathcal{X}$ and $Y \in \mathcal{Y}$ be random variables denoting the input and the label, respectively. Further, let $f : \mathcal{X} \to [0,1]^K$ be a neural network that outputs the model's confidence for each class. For simplicity of notation, we define $\hat{Y} = \arg\max_j f(X)_j$, and $\hat{P} = \max_j f(X)_j$.

Expected Calibration Error. One notion of miscalibration is the expected difference between confidence and accuracy,

$$\text{ECE}(f) = \mathbb{E}\left[\left|\mathbb{P}\big(Y{=}\hat{Y}|P{=}\hat{P}\big) - \hat{P}\right|\right]. \quad (3)$$

As mentioned in Sec. 2, this cannot be estimated using finitely many samples if $\hat{P}$ is a continuous random variable. Expected Calibration Error (Naeini et al., 2015; Guo et al., 2017), or ECE, approximates this via partitioning predictions into multiple bins and computing the weighted average.

Maximum Calibration Error. In high-risk scenarios, we might be interested in measuring the worst-case performance. Maximum Calibration Error (Naeini et al., 2015; Guo et al., 2017), or MCE, estimates the following quantity via binning,

$$\text{MCE}(f) = \max\left|\mathbb{P}\big(\hat{Y}{=}Y|P{=}\hat{P}\big) - \hat{P}\right|. \quad (4)$$

Brier Score. Calibration alone is not sufficient. We could construct cases in which the outputs of the model are calibrated but not useful. An example includes always outputting 50% in a binary classification task containing 50% of both labels (Kumar et al., 2019). An alternative measure is the Brier score (Brier, 1950), $\mathbb{E}[(f(X)-Y)^2]$. Note that the Brier Score is a proper scoring rule, thus the optimum score corresponds to a system with perfect calibration. We refer a more detailed discussion on proper scoring rule to Lakshminarayanan et al. (2017) (Sec 2.2). An extension of Brier Score is Brier Skill Scores (BSS). BSS is favored when the classes are imbalanced. In our early experiments, we did not observe significant ranking changes between these two measures, so we report Brier Score for simplicity.[1]

ℓ_p Calibration Error. A generalized notion of the calibration error is described in Kumar et al. (2019),

$$\mathrm{CE}(f) = \left(\mathbb{E}\left[|\mathbb{P}(Y{=}\hat{Y}|P{=}\hat{P}) - \hat{P}|^p\right]\right)^{1/p}. \quad (5)$$

This recovers the MCE when $p = \infty$ and ECE when $p = 1$ (Kumar et al., 2019). When $p = 2$, we refer to it as Squared Calibration Error (SCE).[2] This is estimated via binning the outputs and labels in practice similar to ECE and MCE. The plugin estimate for each term in the calibration error has been shown to be a biased estimate in Kumar et al. (2019), and the authors encouraged the use of a debiased estimator for the calibration error. We refer to this as the debiased Squared Calibration Error.

3.2 Underestimation of Calibration Errors for Model with Continuous Outputs

As noted in Sec. 2, the key to estimating the calibration error is estimating the conditional expectation $\mathbb{E}[Y|f(X)]$. However, if $f(X)$ is continuous, without smoothness assumptions on $\mathbb{E}[Y|f(X)]$, this is impossible (Kumar et al., 2019). An approximation could be made via binning the outputs into B intervals, as is done in most of the metrics aforementioned. However, Kumar et al. (2019) showed that the binned version always has a lower calibration error. The authors introduced the scaling-binning calibrator, which first fits a parametric function and then bins the function values to ensure calibration. Thus, in addition to reporting results using the metrics described in Sec. 3.1, we report results by running the scaling-binning calibrator on top of each method that we considered.[3] We further include ECE results with multiple bin-values in order to reduce the gap.

4 Methods

4.1 Baseline Model

Our baseline model follows the general finetuning of large pretrained language models on downstream tasks: we finetune RoBERTa-base (Liu et al., 2019) on downstream tasks.

4.2 Distillation and Uncertainty

Despite the strong empirical performance of many calibration methods (e.g., ensembles), their usefulness in practice is limited due to increased computation and/or memory costs at inference time (Ovadia et al., 2019). In Sec. 4.3, we describe a simple baseline: recalibrate, ensemble, and distill.

Distillation has been shown to mostly "preserve" performance in terms of accuracy – stronger teacher models tend to translate to stronger students (Hinton et al., 2015). However, whether distillation could also "preserve" calibration performance is less studied. A model with better performance does not necessarily translate to better calibration (Guo et al., 2017). Here, we briefly look at the distillation's objective from an angle of uncertainty matching, and show that they are related intuitively. Sec. 6.1 provides empirical evidence showing that the teacher model's calibration performance could be distilled into the student model.

There are two ways to see the connection. First, note that distillation tries to minimize the KL-divergence between the teacher output distribution and the student output distribution. This intuitively regularizes the student model to output confidence values that would be close to the confidence values from the teacher model. Later in Sec. 6.1, experimental results show that the confidences from two models indeed correlate positively. Another perspective, which we elaborate below, considers distillation as encouraging the students to output uncertainty close to that of teacher models.

[1] One can further include negative log-likelihood score. However, we want to avoid overcrowding the results table with too many numbers (which is already large, please see the supplementary materials Table 3-6). Since both Brier Score and NLL are proper-scoring rules (see Sec.3 in Ovadia et al. (2019)), we believe the results would be qualitatively similar.

[2] Technically, this is 2-norm Calibration Error. But we refer to this as the Squared Calibration Error for notation simplicity.

[3] The top-label variant of scaling-binning calibrator we use outputs calibrated probabilities of the top predictions, whereas Brier Scores require full probability vectors. Thus we exclude Brier Scores when using the scaling-binning calibrator.

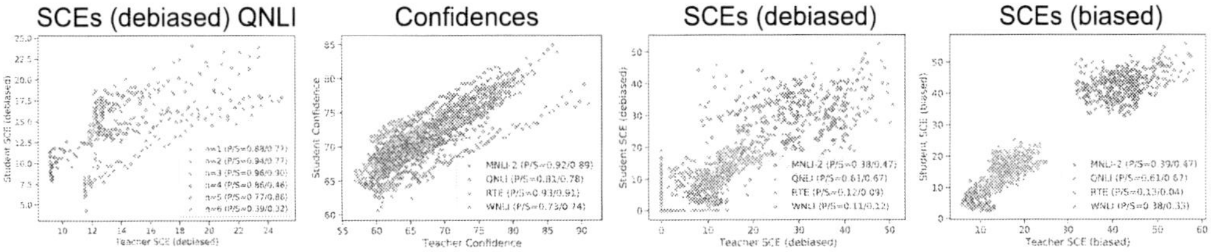

Figure 1: **Left-most Figure:** Visualization of calibration performance, measured by SCEs (debiased), between teacher and student models, trained on RTE and evaluated on QNLI. The n in the legend refers to the size of ensemble(s). *One metric/task, emphasizing different ensemble sizes.* **The Other Three Figures:** These are zoomed-out versions of the left-most figure, along with other tasks. Instead of using color to imply the ensemble size, here the color refers to the task in which the models are evaluated, and points of different ensemble sizes but the same evaluation task are aggregated and represented by the same color. Each sub-figure represents the evaluation metric. *More tasks/metrics, less emphasis on ensemble sizes.* **All Figures:** The X-axis refers to the teacher model performance, and the Y-axis refers to the student model performance. Each dot represents a different configuration used in the teacher model. The P/S in the legends refer to the Pearson/Spearman correlations.

We start by defining a loss function as a weighted combination of the regular cross entropy loss function and a regularization term that measures the difference in the uncertainty between the student model, θ, and the teacher model, $\theta^\star$,

$$L(\theta) = (1-\alpha)L_{XE}(\theta)+\alpha|H(\theta)-H(\theta^\star)|, \quad (6)$$

where H refers to predictive entropy (Gal, 2016), and is defined as (θ is ignored for simplicity),

$$H(y|x,\mathcal{D})=-\sum_c p(y{=}c|x,\mathcal{D}) \log p(y{=}c|x,\mathcal{D}). \quad (7)$$

Gal (2016) showed that $H(y|x,\mathcal{D})$ could be approximated using samples from the (approximate) posterior distribution of the parameters. In practice, this could be satisfied, for example, if the student model is trained using dropout, and the teacher model uses either MC-dropout or ensembles.[4] Next, suppose we approximate one of the predictive entropy terms using cross entropy. This turns the second term in Eq. 6 into KL-divergence, and hence recovers the distillation objective.[5]

4.3 Recalibrate, Ensemble, and Distill

This simple algebraic manipulation shows that distillation has the effect of encouraging the student model to match the teacher model's uncertainty, and motivates us to build a simple recalibration method **"recalibrate, ensemble, and distill"** by first building an expensive yet calibrated teacher model (an ensemble of models each of which is re-calibrated using temperature scaling),[6] and then distilling the expensive teacher model into a cheaper student model.

The training cost is roughly $(N+1)C_0 + C_1$, where N is the ensemble size, C_0 the cost of training the baseline, $+1$ comes from distillation, and C_1 comes from training the temperature scaling model (which is relatively cheap). However, the inference cost is almost the same as a single model (i.e., small overhead), which is very useful when inference is the primary concern (e.g., deployment).

4.4 Choosing the Distillation Temperature

The distillation term is often written as:

$$D_{\mathrm{KL}}\Big(P(x;\theta^\star,T) \;||\; P(x;\theta,T)\Big), \quad (8)$$

where $P(x;\theta,T) = \mathrm{softmax}(f(x;\theta)/T)$ and T is usually a hyperparameter to be tuned. One might notice that this is similar to the equation of temperature scaling (Eq. 2). This, together with the uncertainty matching viewpoint, motivates a small change to the distillation: we can remove the T from the student, and choose the constant $\hat{T}$ for the teacher that minimizes the calibration error,

$$D_{\mathrm{KL}}\Big(P(x;\theta^\star, \arg\min_{\hat{T}} \mathrm{CE}(\theta^\star,\hat{T})) \;||\; P(x;\theta)\Big), \quad (9)$$

[4]Note that the samples from a model using dropout (MC-dropout) or ensemble could be used to approximate the posterior distribution (Gal, 2016; Lakshminarayanan et al., 2017).

[5]Note that the approximation error equals the KL divergence, the term that the objective function seeks to minimize. As KL-divergence decreases, the approximation error also decreases.

[6]There are many ways to construct a powerful/expensive teacher model, and we choose the popular ensemble method for simplicity. Alternatives includes MC-dropout (with multiple forward passes) and SWA (Izmailov et al., 2018).

which is similar to performing another temperature scaling. The motivation is that we want the student model to produce calibrated probabilities rather than the scaled version of the student. If we simultaneously scale the student by T, then $f(x;\theta)/T$ would be calibrated, but the student model itself would not. We want to emphasize here that we are not the first ones to describe the connection between distillation and calibration, related findings have been presented in previous works (Tang et al., 2020; Müller et al., 2019). However, we believe our view from the angle of predictive entropy is novel. More importantly, we conduct extensive experiments and analyses in the context of finetuned language models for several text classification tasks, to empirically verify that calibration performance between student and teacher model is correlated.

5 Setup

We include additional details in the supplementary materials. Also included are expanded experiment results, such as figures evaluated on more tasks using more evaluation metrics (Sec. 6.1), and detailed/expanded results tables as well as accuracy and ECEs with multiple bin-sizes (Sec. 6.2).

Model. Our codebase is largely based on HuggingFace `Transformers` (Wolf et al., 2019). When applicable, we use an ensemble size 2, and choose $\hat{T}$ (Eq. 9) based on the Brier Scores on the validation dataset. The baseline model has 125.2M parameters, the temperature-scaling model (heteroscedastic variant) has 125.8M, and our method has 125.2M (same as the baseline model).

Data. We perform experiments on the classification tasks from the GLUE Benchmark (Wang et al., 2019), and we refer readers to Wang et al. (2019) regarding dataset statistics. Because the calculation of calibration errors requires access to the ground truth data, which is not available for GLUE data, we split the validation dataset into two halves, one for validation and the other for test, following Desai and Durrett (2020). For MultiNLI, we merge the results for both MultiNLI matched and mismatched sections. When computing the out-of-domain performance between the 3-label MultiNLI and other 2-label NLI tasks, we follow `jiant` (Pruksachatkun et al., 2020) and merge the predictions/labels that correspond to "neutral" and "contradiction" into a single category.

Evaluation. Our evaluation follows Guo et al. (2017), Ovadia et al. (2019), and Kumar et al. (2019). The train and evaluation data come from the same task for in-domain evaluations, but they come from different tasks of the same type for out-of-domain evaluations. We group MRPC and QQP (paraphrase tasks), and group MNLI (2-label version), QNLI, RTE, and WNLI (NLI tasks). We leave SST-2 (sentiment), CoLA (acceptability), and MNLI (3-label version, NLI) as separate groups. We use the in-domain validation data to train the scaling-binning calibrator.[7]

Analysis Experiments Details. We conduct experiments on RTE, in which we distill teacher models with different ensemble-sizes (from 1 to 6) and the temperature scaling constant (from 0.50 to 2.00 with a step size of 0.02) to student models. Each model is then evaluated on both in-domain task (RTE) and out-of-domain tasks (MNLI-2, QNLI, WNLI) using confidence, ECE, MCE, Brier Scores, SCE (debiased) and SCE (biased). The numbers represent performances on the validation dataset.

6 Experiments

6.1 Analysis Experiments

Sec. 4.2 shows the connection between distillation and uncertainty regularization. In this section, we perform analysis experiments examining the correlation between the calibration performance of the teacher models and student models. We conduct experiments on RTE, in which we distill teacher models with different ensemble-sizes and the temperature scaling constant to student models. Each model is then evaluated on both in-domain and out-of-domain tasks. Numbers here represent performances on the validation dataset.

We start by examining the calibration performances of teacher and student models, where we vary the calibration performance of the teacher model while holding the accuracy almost the same.[8] Fig. 1 (left) shows the debiased Squared Calibration Error of models trained on RTE and

[7]We only use the 2-label version of MNLI for evaluation. We use accuracy for CoLA evaluation so that calibration error computations would be more consistent across tasks.

[8]Note the accuracy of teacher models with the same ensemble size but different temperature scaling constants would be almost the same, as for each model, temperature scaling constant sharpens/flattens the probabilities but usually does not change their relative ranking. The motivation here is to reduce external influences, as comparing calibration performance might not be very meaningful if the predictions/accuracies change significantly.

	Without Scaling-Binning Calibrator					With Scaling-Binning Calibrator			
	MCE	ECE	Brier Score	SCE (d)	SCE (b)	MCE	ECE	SCE (d)	SCE (b)
				In Domain					
Baseline	24.51	5.80	12.20	**6.28**	12.18	9.11	3.78	1.71	5.95
Ensemble	23.96	6.10	**11.83**	7.81	12.03	11.81	**2.94**	4.36	7.46
TempScale	23.49	**4.39**	11.87	7.31	**10.75**	**8.81**	3.91	**0.93**	**5.41**
Ours	17.19	5.66	12.19	8.18	12.28	12.94	3.24	4.39	7.51
Ours ($\hat{T}$)	**16.21**	4.93	12.09	8.58	11.91	10.78	3.43	4.66	8.11
				Out of Domain					
Baseline	29.66	19.30	29.00	20.06	23.92	30.16	17.83	19.44	21.40
Ensemble	30.71	16.61	27.60	18.95	22.95	**23.77**	**14.39**	**13.45**	**17.17**
TempScale	**26.45**	16.35	27.53	18.71	22.35	33.60	17.55	18.61	20.65
Ours	28.26	17.17	28.08	17.63	22.15	25.11	14.50	15.55	17.92
Ours ($\hat{T}$)	29.79	**15.52**	**27.21**	**17.20**	**21.28**	28.95	14.62	15.97	18.82

Table 1: In-domain and out-of-domain experiment results averaged across tasks. **SCE(d)/SCE(b)**: Squared Calibration Errors (debiased/biased). Lower scores indicate better calibration. Bold/underscored numbers are the best/second-best among comparisons, respectively.

evaluated on QNLI. We can observe that, by varying the teacher model's calibration performance, the calibration performance of the student model also changes in similar directions.

Next, Fig. 1(right) depicts the calibration performances of each teacher-student pair across multiple calibration metrics. Similarly, these figures indicate that correlation of calibration performance between teacher/student models are in general positive. This confirms the intuition described in Sec. 4.2 that calibration performance of the teacher model could be distilled into the student model.

6.2 Main Experiments

Next, we show our experimental results comparing the following four models: Baseline (**Baseline**, Sec. 4.1), Ensemble (Lakshminarayanan et al., 2017) (**Ensemble**, Sec. 2), Temperature Scaling (Guo et al., 2017) (**TempScale**, Sec. 2), our method (**Ours**, Sec. 4.2), and its variant with automatic distillation temperature selection (**Ours ($\hat{T}$)**, Sec. 4.4). For each table, we report results with and without running the scaling-binning calibrator following the description in Sec. 3.2. Due to space constraints, we discuss and display the average performances in here (please see Sec. 5).

Baseline Performances. Results are shown in Table 1; here, we can see that the baseline has relatively high calibration errors. Notably, the out-of-domain ECE values are around $18-19$, interpreted as over/under-estimating the probability by about $18-19\%$ in expectation.

Ensemble and Temperature Scaling. Next, we add ensembles/temperature scaling to the baseline. Results in Table 1 show that performances improve in general, especially in the out-of-domain settings: $3/9$ in-domain metrics improve ($2/9$ metrics similar) and $8/9$ out-of-domain metrics improve for ensembles, $6/9$ in-domain metrics improve ($2/9$ metrics similar) and $7/9$ out-of-domain metrics improve ($1/9$ metrics similar) for temperature-scaling. The results are largely consistent with previous observations that temperature-scaling performed better when the data come from in-domain (it out-performs ensembles among $7/9$ metrics and $1/9$ similar in in-domain settings), whereas ensembles are more competitive in out-of-domain settings at the cost of extra computation (it out-performs temperature scaling in $4/9$ metrics in out-of-domain settings while being similar in $3/9$).

Our Methods. Then, we apply our method, which has the same computation at inference time as the baseline. Table 1 showed that performances improve as well despite having no extra inference-time computation cost: $2/9$ metrics improve ($3/9$ metrics similar) in-domain and $9/9$ metrics improve out-of-domain. Applying the automatic temperature selection on top of our method further improves out-of-domain performance in 4 metrics. However, using automatic temperature does not further improve the performance when we additionally apply the scaling-binning calibrator. We hypothesize that this is because temperature values are chosen based on evaluation metrics before applying the scaling-binning calibrator, thus fail to take it into account. Also, comparing our method to ensembles and temperature scaling, our method improves upon temperature scaling in $5/9$ metrics in out-of-domain settings ($1/9$ similar), but out-performs the more expensive ensembles in just $3/9$

	Without Scaling-Binning Calibrator					With Scaling-Binning Calibrator			
	MCE	ECE	Brier Score	SCE (d)	SCE (b)	MCE	ECE	SCE (d)	SCE (b)
				In Domain					
Ours	17.19	5.66	12.19	8.18	12.28	12.94	3.24	4.39	7.51
−**Ensemble**	18.10	5.90	12.20	10.11	13.19	17.09	5.48	6.40	9.33
−**TempScale**	21.70	6.13	12.28	8.33	12.58	10.49	3.79	4.45	8.26
−**Distillation**	13.04	4.51	11.58	4.40	10.09	6.14	2.61	4.30	7.38
				Out of Domain					
Ours	28.26	17.17	28.08	17.63	22.15	25.11	14.50	15.55	17.92
−**Ensemble**	27.25	17.40	27.96	18.75	22.89	32.20	16.70	19.86	21.81
−**TempScale**	29.18	19.89	29.50	21.28	24.89	30.68	17.40	20.76	22.63
−**Distillation**	21.74	15.39	26.71	15.85	20.58	19.89	14.82	13.05	16.85

Table 2: In-domain/out-of-domain ablation results averaged across tasks. **SCE(d)/SCE(b)**: Squared Calibration Errors (debiased/biased). Lower scores indicate better calibration.

metrics ($1/9$ similar). Comparing our method with automatic temperature selection, we can see $8/9$ metrics in out-of-domain settings improves compared to temperature scaling, and $5/9$ compared to ensembles ($1/9$ similar). This shows that our methods are competitive in out-of-domain settings with little extra computation.

6.3 Ablation Experiments

In this section, we (1) ablate our method by removing components to gain insights into how each of the components contribute to the final performance,[9] and (2) measure how well distillation transfers calibration performance.

First, we remove ensembles (or temperature scaling), and include only temperature scaling (or ensembles) and distillation (−**Ensembles** and −**TempScale**, respectively). We can see from the results in Table 2 that removing either of them leads to worse performances in general: $7/9$ in-domain ($2/9$ being similar) and $6/9$ ($2/9$ being similar) out-of-domain for removing ensembles, $4/9$ in-domain ($4/9$ similar) and $9/9$ out-of-domain for removing temperature scaling. This shows that the additional calibration gains from the teacher model can be effectively distilled into the student models.

Next, we compare the models before/after distillation (−**Distillation**).[10] As expected, the teacher model (before distillation) achieved strong performance at the expense of extra inference-time computation. We then study to what extent distillation transfers calibration performance. Let A_t and B_t be two different teacher models (before distillation) with difference in only one of the components (e.g., ensemble or temperature-scaling), and let A_s and B_s be the corresponding student models (after distillation). Then, we compute the *relative* percentage of improvement because of a component from teacher to student model (assuming A is more powerful than B), denoted as ρ_{AB}:

$$\rho_{AB} = \frac{\varepsilon(A_s) - \varepsilon(B_s)}{\varepsilon(A_t) - \varepsilon(B_t)} \times 100, \qquad (10)$$

where $\varepsilon(\cdot)$ denotes the out-of-domain calibration performance. We compute ρ_{AB} for each metric, and use the median of percentages as the summary statistic. We found 40.8% (111.2%) of the improvements from adding ensembles (temperature scaling) as extra components in teacher models are transferred to students models via distillation.[11]

7 Conclusion and Discussion

We presented a study of calibration of finetuned language models in the context of text classification, where models are evaluated on in-domain and out-of-domain data. We showed the effectiveness of a few widely-used calibration methods. We illustrated the intuitive connection between distillation and calibration, and described simple yet competitive calibration methods. We conducted experiments to empirically understand whether distillation can be used to distill calibration performance, and showed that the simple methods we described achieved competitive out-of-domain calibration performances. We further presented ablation studies on the usefulness of components of

[9] For ease of comparison, we only ablate the system without the automatic temperature selection.

[10] The −**Distillation** in Table 2 is the result of combining ensembles and temperature-scaling. In Table 1, we showed that distillation (especially when combined with automatic temperature) could be helpful compared to either ensembles or temperature-scaling alone.

[11] We chose median as it is simple and less affected by outliers. Please see the supplementary materials Sec. C for more details.

the proposed method and examined the transferability of calibration via distillation. However, our method is limited in that it requires an overhead cost involved in training the student model, which could be expensive in some settings. We leave it to future works to investigate more efficient inference-time recalibration techniques.

Acknowledgments

We thank the reviewers for their helpful comments. This work was supported by DARPA YFA17-D17AP00022, ONR Grant N00014-18-1-2871, and Microsoft PhD Fellowship. The views contained in this article are those of the authors and not of the funding agency.

References

Eneko Agirre, Llu'is M'arquez, and Richard Wicentowski, editors. 2007. *Proceedings of the Fourth International Workshop on Semantic Evaluations (SemEval-2007)*. Association for Computational Linguistics, Prague, Czech Republic.

Jimmy Ba and Rich Caruana. 2014. Do deep nets really need to be deep? In *NeurIPS*.

Gagan Bansal, Besmira Nushi, Ece Kamar, Eric Horvitz, and Daniel S Weld. 2020. Optimizing ai for teamwork. *arXiv:2004.13102*.

Roy Bar-Haim, Ido Dagan, Bill Dolan, Lisa Ferro, Danilo Giampiccolo, Bernardo Magnini, and Idan Szpektor. 2006. The second pascal recognising textual entailment challenge. In *RTE*.

Luisa Bentivogli, Ido Dagan, Hoa Trang Dang, Danilo Giampiccolo, and Bernardo Magnini. 2009. The fifth PASCAL recognizing textual entailment challenge. In *TAC*.

Avrim Blum and Tom Mitchell. 1998. Combining labeled and unlabeled data with co-training. In *COLT*.

Glenn W Brier. 1950. Verification of forecasts expressed in terms of probability. *Monthly weather review*.

Cristian Buciluǎ, Rich Caruana, and Alexandru Niculescu-Mizil. 2006. Model compression. In *KDD*.

Kevin Clark, Minh-Thang Luong, Urvashi Khandelwal, Christopher D Manning, and Quoc Le. 2019. Bam! born-again multi-task networks for natural language understanding. In *ACL*.

Ido Dagan, Oren Glickman, and Bernardo Magnini. 2006. The PASCAL recognising textual entailment challenge. In *Machine learning challenges. evaluating predictive uncertainty, visual object classification, and recognising tectual entailment*. Springer.

Shrey Desai and Greg Durrett. 2020. Calibration of pre-trained transformers. In *EMNLP*.

Jacob Devlin, Ming-Wei Chang, Kenton Lee, and Kristina Toutanova. 2019. Bert: Pre-training of deep bidirectional transformers for language understanding. In *NAACL*.

William B Dolan and Chris Brockett. 2005. Automatically constructing a corpus of sentential paraphrases. In *IWP*.

Pedro Domingos. 1997. Knowledge acquisition from examples via multiple models. In *ICML*.

Hady Elsahar and Matthias Gallé. 2019. To annotate or not? predicting performance drop under domain shift. In *EMNLP*.

Tommaso Furlanello, Zachary Lipton, Michael Tschannen, Laurent Itti, and Anima Anandkumar. 2018. Born again neural networks. In *ICML*.

Yarin Gal. 2016. *Uncertainty in Deep Learning*. Ph.D. thesis, University of Cambridge.

Danilo Giampiccolo, Bernardo Magnini, Ido Dagan, and Bill Dolan. 2007. The third PASCAL recognizing textual entailment challenge. In *RTE*.

Chuan Guo, Geoff Pleiss, Yu Sun, and Kilian Q Weinberger. 2017. On calibration of modern neural networks. In *ICML*.

Corina Gurau, Alex Bewley, and Ingmar Posner. 2018. Dropout distillation for efficiently estimating model confidence. *arXiv:1809.10562*.

Dan Hendrycks and Kevin Gimpel. 2017. A baseline for detecting misclassified and out-of-distribution examples in neural networks. In *ICLR*.

Dan Hendrycks, Xiaoyuan Liu, Eric Wallace, Adam Dziedzic, Rishabh Krishnan, and Dawn Song. 2020. Pretrained transformers improve out-of-distribution robustness. In *ACL*.

Geoffrey Hinton, Oriol Vinyals, and Jeffrey Dean. 2015. Distilling the knowledge in a neural network. In *NeurIPS Deep Learning and Representation Learning Workshop*.

Pavel Izmailov, Dmitrii Podoprikhin, Timur Garipov, Dmitry Vetrov, and Andrew Gordon Wilson. 2018. Averaging weights leads to wider optima and better generalization. In *UAI*.

Alex Kendall and Yarin Gal. 2017. What uncertainties do we need in bayesian deep learning for computer vision? In *NeurIPS*.

Alex Kendall, Yarin Gal, and Roberto Cipolla. 2018. Multi-task learning using uncertainty to weigh losses for scene geometry and semantics. In *CVPR*.

Yoon Kim and Alexander M Rush. 2016. Sequence-level knowledge distillation. In *EMNLP*.

Volodymyr Kuleshov and Stefano Ermon. 2017. Estimating uncertainty online against an adversary. In *AAAI*.

Volodymyr Kuleshov and Percy S Liang. 2015. Calibrated structured prediction. In *NeurIPS*.

Ananya Kumar, Percy S Liang, and Tengyu Ma. 2019. Verified uncertainty calibration. In *NeurIPS*.

Balaji Lakshminarayanan, Alexander Pritzel, and Charles Blundell. 2017. Simple and scalable predictive uncertainty estimation using deep ensembles. In *NeurIPS*.

Hector J Levesque, Ernest Davis, and Leora Morgenstern. 2011. The Winograd schema challenge. In *AAAI Spring Symposium: Logical Formalizations of Commonsense Reasoning*, volume 46.

Yinhan Liu, Myle Ott, Naman Goyal, Jingfei Du, Mandar Joshi, Danqi Chen, Omer Levy, Mike Lewis, Luke Zettlemoyer, and Veselin Stoyanov. 2019. Roberta: A robustly optimized bert pretraining approach. *arXiv:1907.11692*.

Rafael Müller, Simon Kornblith, and Geoffrey E Hinton. 2019. When does label smoothing help? In *NeurIPS*.

Mahdi Pakdaman Naeini, Gregory Cooper, and Milos Hauskrecht. 2015. Obtaining well calibrated probabilities using bayesian binning. In *AAAI*.

Alexandru Niculescu-Mizil and Rich Caruana. 2005. Predicting good probabilities with supervised learning. In *ICML*.

Yaniv Ovadia, Emily Fertig, Jie Ren, Zachary Nado, David Sculley, Sebastian Nowozin, Joshua Dillon, Balaji Lakshminarayanan, and Jasper Snoek. 2019. Can you trust your model's uncertainty? evaluating predictive uncertainty under dataset shift. In *NeurIPS*.

Gabriel Pereyra, George Tucker, Jan Chorowski, Łukasz Kaiser, and Geoffrey Hinton. 2017. Regularizing neural networks by penalizing confident output distributions. In *ICLR Workshop*.

Matthew Peters, Mark Neumann, Mohit Iyyer, Matt Gardner, Christopher Clark, Kenton Lee, and Luke Zettlemoyer. 2018. Deep contextualized word representations. In *NAACL*.

John C. Platt. 1999. Probabilistic outputs for support vector machines and comparisons to regularized likelihood methods. In *ADVANCES IN LARGE MARGIN CLASSIFIERS*.

Yada Pruksachatkun, Phil Yeres, Haokun Liu, Jason Phang, Phu Mon Htut, Alex Wang, Ian Tenney, and Samuel R Bowman. 2020. jiant: A software toolkit for research on general-purpose text understanding models. In *Proceedings of ACL (demonstration track)*.

Alec Radford, Jeffrey Wu, Rewon Child, David Luan, Dario Amodei, and Ilya Sutskever. 2019. Language models are unsupervised multitask learners. *OpenAI Blog*.

Pranav Rajpurkar, Jian Zhang, Konstantin Lopyrev, and Percy Liang. 2016. SQuAD: 100,000+ questions for machine comprehension of text. In *EMNLP*.

Siddharth Reddy, Anca D Dragan, Sergey Levine, Shane Legg, and Jan Leike. 2019. Learning human objectives by evaluating hypothetical behavior. *arXiv:1912.05652*.

Marco Tulio Ribeiro, Sameer Singh, and Carlos Guestrin. 2016. " why should i trust you?" explaining the predictions of any classifier. In *KDD*.

Marco Tulio Ribeiro, Sameer Singh, and Carlos Guestrin. 2018. Anchors: High-precision model-agnostic explanations. In *AAAI*.

Victor Sanh, Lysandre Debut, Julien Chaumond, and Thomas Wolf. 2019. Distilbert, a distilled version of bert: smaller, faster, cheaper and lighter. *EMC2*.

Jonathan Schwarz, Wojciech Czarnecki, Jelena Luketina, Agnieszka Grabska-Barwinska, Yee Whye Teh, Razvan Pascanu, and Raia Hadsell. 2018. Progress & compress: A scalable framework for continual learning. In *ICML*.

Jiaxi Tang, Rakesh Shivanna, Zhe Zhao, Dong Lin, Anima Singh, Ed H Chi, and Sagar Jain. 2020. Understanding and improving knowledge distillation. *arXiv:2002.03532*.

Yee Teh, Victor Bapst, Wojciech M Czarnecki, John Quan, James Kirkpatrick, Raia Hadsell, Nicolas Heess, and Razvan Pascanu. 2017. Distral: Robust multitask reinforcement learning. In *NeurIPS*.

Alex Wang, Amanpreet Singh, Julian Michael, Felix Hill, Omer Levy, and Samuel Bowman. 2019. Glue: A multi-task benchmark and analysis platform for natural language understanding. In *ICLR*.

Tongzhou Wang, Jun-Yan Zhu, Antonio Torralba, and Alexei A Efros. 2018. Dataset distillation. *arXiv:1811.10959*.

Alex Warstadt, Amanpreet Singh, and Samuel R Bowman. 2019. Neural network acceptability judgments. *TACL*.

Bryan Wilder, Eric Horvitz, and Ece Kamar. 2020. Learning to complement humans. *ACL*.

Adina Williams, Nikita Nangia, and Samuel R. Bowman. 2018. A broad-coverage challenge corpus for sentence understanding through inference. In *NAACL*.

Thomas Wolf, Lysandre Debut, Victor Sanh, Julien Chaumond, Clement Delangue, Anthony Moi, Pierric Cistac, Tim Rault, R'emi Louf, Morgan Funtowicz, and Jamie Brew. 2019. Huggingface's transformers: State-of-the-art natural language processing. *ArXiv*, abs/1910.03771.

Li Yuan, Francis EH Tay, Guilin Li, Tao Wang, and Jiashi Feng. 2020. Revisit knowledge distillation: a teacher-free framework. In *CVPR*.

Sukmin Yun, Jongjin Park, Kimin Lee, and Jinwoo Shin. 2020. Regularizing class-wise predictions via self-knowledge distillation. In *CVPR*.

Bianca Zadrozny and Charles Elkan. 2001. Obtaining calibrated probability estimates from decision trees and naive bayesian classifiers. In *ICML*.

Xinchuan Zeng and Tony R. Martinez. 2000. Using a neural network to approximate an ensemble of classifiers. *Neural Processing Letters*.

A Background and Related Works

A.1 Epistemic and Aleatoric Uncertainty

Two types of uncertainty commonly appear in machine learning literature: epistemic uncertainty and aleatoric uncertainty (Gal, 2016; Kendall and Gal, 2017). **Epistemic uncertainty** accounts for uncertainty in model parameters, and tends to decrease as the amount of observed data increases. **Aleatoric uncertainty** conveys the noise inherent in the observations, and thus cannot be explained away with an increasing amount of data available. In the case of classification, examples of aleatoric uncertainty include the probability of the top class,[12] and the entropy of the probability distribution over classes (Kendall et al., 2018); examples of epistemic uncertainties include the mutual information.[13] In the literature of uncertainty calibration, we usually calibrate aleatoric uncertainty measured by the probability of the prediction. In Sec. 4.2, we also view distillation from the angle of matching another uncertainty between teacher model and student model, the predictive entropy (Gal, 2016).

A.2 Uncertainty Calibration

The quality of the uncertainty measurement is usually measured via calibration (Kendall and Gal, 2017). In the context of calibration, the uncertainties often refer to predictive probabilities. The model is calibrated if the predictive probabilities match the empirical frequency of the data (Gal, 2016). Let $\hat{Y}$ and $\hat{P}$ be the predicted class and its associated confidence (probability of correctness) of a neural network. We would like the confidence estimates $\hat{P}$ to be calibrated, which intuitively means that we want $\hat{P}$ to represent true probabilities (Guo et al., 2017):

$$\mathbb{P}(\hat{Y} = Y | \hat{P} = p) = p, \forall p \in [0, 1]. \tag{11}$$

Suppose a classification model is given N input examples, and made predictions $\hat{y}_1, ..., \hat{y}_N$, each with $\hat{p} = 0.35$. We would expect 35% of the predictions would be correct. The problem of uncertainty/confidence calibration and confidence scores have been studied and applied in various settings (Kuleshov and Liang, 2015; Kuleshov and Ermon, 2017; Pereyra et al., 2017; Hendrycks and Gimpel, 2017; Elsahar and Gallé, 2019; Reddy et al., 2019). In practice, however, perfect calibration is almost impossible (Guo et al., 2017), and estimating the first term in Eq. 11 is not straightforward using finite samples, because in most cases $\hat{P}$ is a continuous random variable (Guo et al., 2017; Kumar et al., 2019). In Sec. 3, we describe ways to estimate the calibration performance.

It has been widely observed that modern neural networks are usually not calibrated out of the box (Platt, 1999; Zadrozny and Elkan, 2001; Guo et al., 2017; Ovadia et al., 2019). Recalibration methods improve calibration by transforming un-calibrated outputs into calibrated outputs/probabilities, and they include scaling-based methods (Platt, 1999; Guo et al., 2017), histogram-binning-based methods (Guo et al., 2017; Zadrozny and Elkan, 2001), and ensembles (Lakshminarayanan et al., 2017). Recently, Kumar et al. (2019) proposed the scaling-binning calibrator and a more sample-efficient estimator of calibration error. In our work, we describe simple approaches that combines the strength of ensembles and temperature scaling without introducing computation at inference time; we further apply the scaling-binning calibrator to ensure calibration.

Ensembles work by aggregating multiple networks trained independently on the entire dataset, and has been shown to achieve strong performance in out-of-domain calibration (Ovadia et al., 2019; Lakshminarayanan et al., 2017).[14] Temperature

[12]More specifically, it is one minus the probability/confidence of the top class.

[13]Please see page 54 in Gal (2016) for details.

[14]More generally, there are randomization-based ensembles and boosting-based ensembles. Within the randomization-based ensembles, in our work we use the entire training dataset to train each model instead of different bootstrap samples of the original training set (Lakshminarayanan et al., 2017).

scaling is an extension of Platt scaling (Guo et al., 2017). It uses a single scalar parameter $T > 0$ for all classes. Given output z_i (usually logits vectors), the confidence prediction is:

$$\hat{p}_i = \max_k \sigma(z_{i,k}/T). \quad (12)$$

An extension, called heteroscedastic regression, is used in our work, which replaces the constant scalar with learned values (Kendall and Gal, 2017; Kendall et al., 2018).

A.3 Distillation

Knowledge distillation (Hinton et al., 2015; Domingos, 1997; Blum and Mitchell, 1998; Zeng and Martinez, 2000; Ba and Caruana, 2014) is a compression technique in which a compact model (usually referred to as the student model) is trained to mimic the behavior of a more powerful teacher model. In the context of classification, knowledge distillation works by augmenting the loss function with an additional term $D_{KL}(p_i \| p_j)$ where $p_i = \text{softmax}(z_i/T)$ and $p_j = \text{softmax}(z_j/T)$ with z_i and z_j the logits from two models, and T controls the smoothness of the output distribution. Knowledge distillation has been used in a wide range of applications (Buciluă et al., 2006; Wang et al., 2018; Kim and Rush, 2016; Furlanello et al., 2018; Clark et al., 2019; Teh et al., 2017; Schwarz et al., 2018; Sanh et al., 2019). In this work, we show that distillation can also be used to distill calibration performance, and use it to build simple yet competitive recalibration methods.

A related area of research is label smoothing (Yuan et al., 2020). Label smoothing replaces the hard/one-hot targets y_k with modified targets $y_k(1-\alpha)+\alpha/K$, where K is the number of classes and α is a hyper-parameter. Pereyra et al. (2017) showed that label smoothing provides consistent gains across many tasks and proposed a new regularizer, termed confidence penalty. Müller et al. (2019) studied when label smoothing is helpful , and found that label smoothing can implicitly calibrate model's predictions. Instead, our use of a teacher model can be seen as adaptively deciding how much smoothing is needed (Tang et al., 2020).

A.4 Recent Related Works

Finally, there are also a few recent related works in the computer vision literature, e.g., Yun et al. (2020) proposed to distill the predictive distribution between different samples of the same label during training to improve calibration performance, Gurau et al. (2018) proposed Distilled Dropout Network which distills knowledge from multiple MC samples from the teacher to improve the reliability of its uncertainty scores. In our work, we mainly focus on language tasks. Concurrent to our work, Desai and Durrett (2020) studied the calibration of pretrained transformers when finetuned to downstream tasks, and Hendrycks et al. (2020) studied the out-of-distribution robustness of pretrained transformers. We are different from these two works in that first we present a systematic study on the out-of-distribution calibration; second we draw insights from the connection between distillation and temperature scaling to design simple yet competitive recalibration methods; third, we conduct experiments to understand the connection between these two concepts empirically; finally, we also include a more comprehensive set of calibration evaluations following Ovadia et al. (2019) and Kumar et al. (2019).

B Setup Details

Model Details and Hyperparameter Search. Our codebase is largely based on the `Transformers` library from HuggingFace (Wolf et al., 2019).[15] We used RoBERTa-base (Liu et al., 2019) for the language model backbone and used most of the default/recommended hyperparameters in the `Transformers` library. We tried two values of the learning rate in our initial experiments: $2e{-}5$ and $1e{-}5$; these numbers are chosen based on the hyperparameter search described in the library, and we stick to one of them ($1e{-}5$) based on accuracy. For experiments that involve ensembles, we use an ensemble size 2. For experiments that involve distillation, we set $T = 1.0$ (i.e., no scaling) for models without automatic temperature selection unless we explicitly mention otherwise. When automatic temperature selection is used, we chose $\hat{T}$ based on the Brier Scores on the validation dataset. All of our experiments ran on a single V100 GPU. The baseline model has 125.2M parameters, the temperature-scaling (heteroscedastic variant) has 125.8M parameters, and our method has 125.2M (same as the baseline model). We train multiple models using different random seeds before ensembling them, but otherwise run the training

[15] `https://github.com/huggingface/transformers`. We used `v2.4.1`.

and inference once. The runtime varies among tasks, but most of them could finish within a day.

Data. We perform experiments on the classification tasks from the GLUE Benchmark (Wang et al., 2019; Warstadt et al., 2019; Dolan and Brockett, 2005; Agirre et al., 2007; Williams et al., 2018; Rajpurkar et al., 2016; Dagan et al., 2006; Bar-Haim et al., 2006; Giampiccolo et al., 2007; Bentivogli et al., 2009; Levesque et al., 2011).[16][17], and we refer readers to Wang et al. (2019) regarding dataset statistics. Because the calculation of calibration errors requires access to the ground truth data, which is not available for GLUE data, we split the validation dataset into two halves, one for validation and the other for test, following the approach of Desai and Durrett (2020). For MultiNLI, we merge the results for both MultiNLI matched and mismatched sections. When computing the out-of-domain performance between the 3-label MultiNLI and other 2-label NLI tasks, we follow the approach used in the `jiant` library (Pruksachatkun et al., 2020) and merge the predictions/labels that correspond to "neutral" and "contradiction" into a single category. We follow the `Transformers` library for the rest of the data preprocessing.

Evaluation Details. Our evaluation follows Guo et al. (2017), Ovadia et al. (2019), and Kumar et al. (2019). For MCE, ECE, and Brier Score, our implementation follows Ovadia et al. (2019),[18] and we use the default bin-size of 10 (in the tables below, we additionally include the performances when evaluating using bin-sizes of 15 and 50). For squared calibration errors (debiased or biased), we use the `uncertainty-calibration` library from Kumar et al. (2019) and follow default configurations whenever possible.[19]

For in-domain evaluations, the train data and evaluation data come from the same task. For out-of-domain evaluations, the train data and evaluation data come from different tasks of the same type. We group MRPC and QQP (paraphrase tasks), and group MNLI (2-label version),[20] QNLI, RTE, and WNLI (NLI tasks). We leave SST-2 (sentiment), CoLA[21] (acceptability), and MNLI (3-label version, NLI) as separate groups. We use the in-domain validation data to train the scaling-binning calibrator.

Analysis Experiments Details. We conduct experiments on RTE, in which we distill teacher models with different ensemble-sizes (from 1 to 6) and the temperature scaling constant (from 0.50 to 2.00 with a step size of 0.02) to student models. Each model is then evaluated on both in-domain task (RTE) and out-of-domain tasks (MNLI-2, QNLI, WNLI) using confidence, ECE, MCE, Brier Scores, SCE (debiased) and SCE (biased). The numbers represent performances on the validation dataset.

C Further Experiment Details

Distillation Transferability of Calibration. We compute ρ_{AB} based on both Table 1 and Table 2 of the main paper. The percentage of improvement presented in Sec. 6.3 of the main paper on ensembles is computed based on temperature scaling + ensembles ($-$**Distillation** in main paper Table 2) as A_t, ensembles only (**Ensemble** in main paper Table 1) as B_t, temperature scaling + ensembles + distillation (**Ours** in main paper Table 2) as A_s, and ensembles + distillation ($-$**TempScale** in main paper Table 2) as B_s. The percentage of improvement on temperature scaling is computed similarly with temperature scaling component as the main difference between the teacher/student models.

D Expanded Analysis Experiments

Please see Fig. 2 for the expanded visualization of the analysis experiments.

E Detailed Main Experiment Results

Please see Table 3 and Table 4 for detailed in-domain and out-of-domain experiment results.

F Detailed Ablation Experiment Results

Please see Table 5 and Table 6 for detailed in-domain and out-of-domain ablation experiment results.

[16] `https://gluebenchmark.com/`

[17] QQP dataset: `https://www.quora.com/q/quoradata/First-Quora-Dataset-Release-Question-Pairs`

[18] `https://github.com/google-research/google-research/tree/master/uq_benchmark_2019`

[19] `https://github.com/p-lambda/verified_calibration`

[20] We only use the 2-label version of MNLI for evaluation.

[21] We use accuracy for CoLA evaluation so that calibration error computations would be more consistent across tasks.

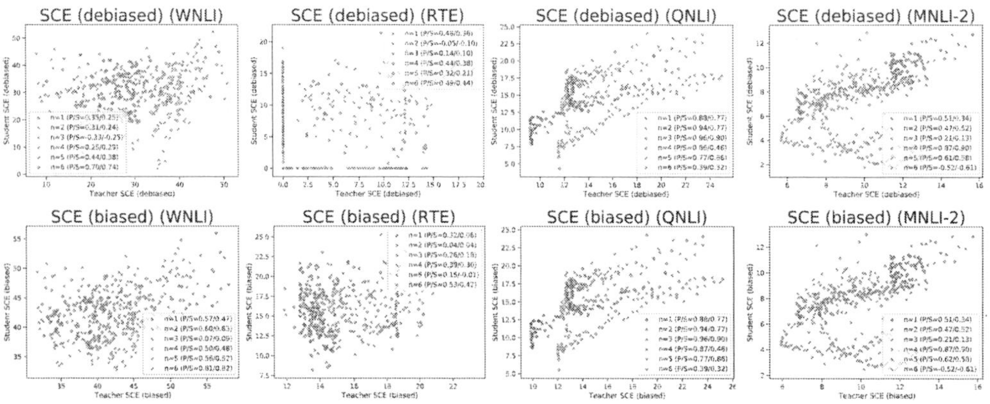

(a)

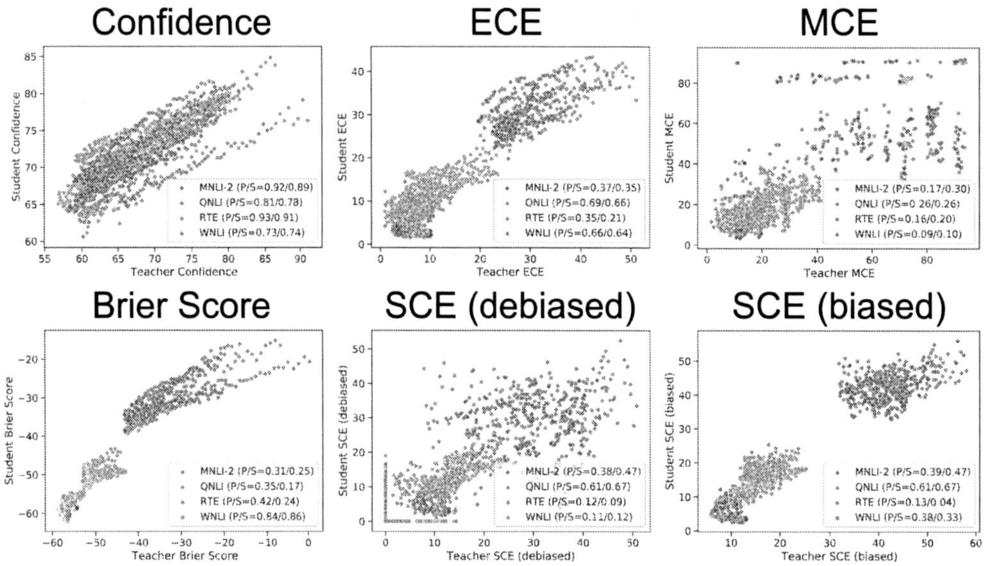

(b)

Figure 2: **Figure (a):** Visualization of calibration performance, measured by SCEs (debiased and biased), between teacher models and student models, trained on RTE evaluated on RTE (in-domain), WNLI, QNLI, and 2-label version of MNLI (out-of-domain). The n in the legend refers to the size of ensemble(s). **Figure (b):** This is a zoomed-out version of Figure (a). Instead of using color to imply the ensemble size, here the color refers to the task in which the models are evaluated, and points of different ensemble sizes but the same evaluation task are aggregated and represented by the same color. Here each sub-figure represents the evaluation metric. **All Figures:** The X-axis refers to the performance of the teacher model, and the Y-axis refers to the performance of the student model. Within each sub-figure, each dot represents a different configuration used in the teacher model. The P/S in the legends refer to the Pearson/Spearman correlations.

Train	SST-2	CoLA	MNLI	MRPC	QQP	QNLI	RTE	WNLI	Average	SST-2	CoLA	MNLI	MRPC	QQP	QNLI	RTE	WNLI	Average
	Accuracy									**Accuracy (+SBC)**								
Baseline	93.1	80.3	87.2	86.8	91.0	92.3	64.7	55.6	81.38	/	/	/	/	/	/	/	/	/
Ensemble	93.8	79.9	87.4	85.8	91.2	92.4	66.2	55.6	81.54	/	/	/	/	/	/	/	/	/
TempScale	93.1	80.3	87.2	86.8	91.0	92.3	64.7	55.6	81.38	/	/	/	/	/	/	/	/	/
Ours	93.3	79.7	87.4	84.8	91.0	92.2	65.5	55.6	81.19	/	/	/	/	/	/	/	/	/
Ours ($\hat{T}$)	93.6	79.7	87.3	86.3	91.0	92.4	64.0	55.6	81.24	/	/	/	/	/	/	/	/	/
	Maximum Calibration Error									**Maximum Calibration Error (+SBC)**								
Baseline	49.7	32.1	38.6	19.6	12.9	21.5	17.6	4.1	24.51	1.6	7.9	4.1	5.1	2.6	6.3	14.3	31.0	9.11
Ensemble	74.0	29.2	16.3	21.5	12.6	14.6	19.0	4.5	23.96	6.6	9.5	4.9	8.7	3.2	3.9	17.9	39.8	11.81
TempScale	33.0	12.3	24.2	16.7	3.3	13.2	80.5	4.7	23.49	1.0	11.8	3.3	5.0	2.5	4.2	12.8	29.9	8.81
Ours	34.0	20.8	14.3	16.6	9.3	14.0	24.0	4.5	17.19	2.8	13.5	3.8	22.8	2.9	3.8	17.2	36.7	12.94
Ours ($\hat{T}$)	44.3	20.4	11.9	11.7	7.3	8.9	21.1	4.1	16.21	1.2	10.5	3.8	15.4	1.9	3.9	12.7	36.8	10.78
	Expected Calibration Error (bin size = 10)									**Expected Calibration Error (bin size = 10) (+SBC)**								
Baseline	5.5	11.5	6.3	5.2	4.2	4.1	5.5	4.1	5.80	1.0	3.3	0.8	1.5	0.4	1.2	7.3	14.7	3.78
Ensemble	4.6	11.9	5.5	4.2	3.4	3.3	11.4	4.5	6.10	1.6	4.0	0.9	2.3	0.6	0.9	7.5	5.7	2.94
TempScale	3.4	8.2	3.9	4.2	1.7	1.9	7.1	4.7	4.39	0.2	4.0	0.8	2.0	0.5	1.2	8.2	14.4	3.91
Ours	4.6	11.6	5.2	4.1	3.0	3.5	8.8	4.5	5.66	0.6	4.0	1.1	3.3	0.5	0.8	7.7	7.9	3.24
Ours ($\hat{T}$)	3.6	9.3	4.1	4.0	2.4	2.2	9.7	4.1	4.93	0.2	5.5	0.8	4.5	0.4	0.7	9.6	5.7	3.43
	Expected Calibration Error (bin size = 15)									**Expected Calibration Error (bin size = 15) (+SBC)**								
Baseline	5.5	11.6	6.3	6.3	4.2	4.1	5.5	4.1	5.95	1.0	4.6	1.1	1.7	0.4	1.5	6.8	16.3	4.18
Ensemble	4.7	11.9	5.5	4.4	3.4	3.3	8.5	4.5	5.78	1.6	5.4	1.0	3.1	0.6	1.0	10.6	5.7	3.63
TempScale	3.6	8.6	3.9	5.4	1.7	1.9	9.0	4.7	4.85	0.2	4.6	0.8	2.4	0.7	1.5	7.4	16.0	4.20
Ours	4.8	12.1	5.2	5.2	3.1	3.5	9.4	4.5	5.98	0.6	4.0	1.4	4.4	0.5	1.3	9.4	7.9	3.69
Ours ($\hat{T}$)	3.7	9.4	4.1	5.1	2.4	2.2	9.7	4.1	5.09	0.3	4.9	1.1	4.5	0.4	1.4	8.5	5.7	3.35
	Expected Calibration Error (bin size = 50)									**Expected Calibration Error (bin size = 50) (+SBC)**								
Baseline	6.2	12.6	6.4	7.9	4.2	4.3	11.2	4.1	7.11	2.1	3.9	1.1	2.2	0.5	1.5	9.9	19.7	5.11
Ensemble	5.2	12.6	5.6	6.9	3.5	3.6	16.8	4.5	7.34	3.3	5.2	1.5	3.8	0.6	1.2	11.9	16.2	5.46
TempScale	5.0	9.7	4.1	9.5	1.8	2.6	11.3	4.7	6.09	0.7	5.0	1.2	3.3	0.7	1.5	8.3	19.3	5.00
Ours	5.7	12.9	5.2	11.6	3.1	3.7	15.5	4.5	7.78	1.8	5.6	1.6	5.2	0.6	1.4	11.9	13.0	5.14
Ours ($\hat{T}$)	4.4	10.7	4.4	10.0	2.4	2.6	16.6	4.1	6.90	1.7	6.0	1.5	5.5	0.4	1.5	11.1	8.2	4.49
	Brier Score									**Brier Score (+SBC)**								
Baseline	5.80	15.25	6.63	10.35	7.00	6.20	21.45	24.90	12.20	/	/	/	/	/	/	/	/	/
Ensemble	5.10	15.20	6.43	10.05	6.70	5.85	20.35	24.95	11.83	/	/	/	/	/	/	/	/	/
TempScale	5.15	14.35	6.37	10.35	6.65	5.85	21.35	24.90	11.87	/	/	/	/	/	/	/	/	/
Ours	5.50	15.85	6.43	10.45	6.75	6.15	21.45	24.90	12.19	/	/	/	/	/	/	/	/	/
Ours ($\hat{T}$)	5.20	15.35	6.37	10.60	6.70	5.95	21.65	24.90	12.09	/	/	/	/	/	/	/	/	/
	Squared Calibration Error (debiased)									**Squared Calibration Error (debiased, +SBC)**								
Baseline	9.4	12.0	8.2	3.6	6.0	5.5	5.5	0.0	6.28	1.3	1.5	1.3	0.0	0.7	1.8	7.1	0.0	1.71
Ensemble	5.7	13.7	7.2	0.0	5.0	4.7	9.7	16.5	7.81	2.6	4.1	1.7	0.0	1.0	0.7	8.9	15.9	4.36
TempScale	5.1	8.4	5.0	7.4	2.0	1.9	0.0	28.7	7.31	0.0	3.9	1.2	0.0	0.9	1.4	0.0	0.0	0.93
Ours	7.3	13.0	6.8	0.0	4.2	4.7	13.0	16.4	8.18	0.0	4.8	1.9	5.3	0.9	1.1	8.4	12.7	4.39
Ours ($\hat{T}$)	4.8	11.7	5.6	4.2	3.3	3.1	12.6	23.3	8.58	0.0	5.5	1.5	1.1	0.6	1.4	14.4	12.8	4.66
	Squared Calibration Error (biased)									**Squared Calibration Error (biased, +SBC)**								
Baseline	10.2	13.5	8.3	9.2	6.1	5.8	15.6	28.7	12.18	3.3	5.2	1.6	3.1	0.9	2.3	13.9	17.3	5.95
Ensemble	7.0	15.0	7.3	8.1	5.0	5.0	17.0	31.8	12.03	4.0	6.3	2.0	5.2	1.1	1.6	14.4	25.1	7.46
TempScale	6.5	10.5	5.2	11.2	2.2	2.6	10.6	37.2	10.75	1.6	6.3	1.5	4.2	1.0	2.0	11.6	15.1	5.41
Ours	8.3	14.5	6.9	8.3	4.2	5.0	19.2	31.8	12.28	2.2	6.9	2.1	8.5	1.1	1.8	14.6	22.9	7.51
Ours ($\hat{T}$)	6.3	13.3	5.7	9.6	3.4	3.5	19.0	34.5	11.91	2.1	7.4	1.8	7.2	0.8	2.0	18.8	24.8	8.11

Table 3: In-domain performances on SST-2 (S), CoLA (C), MultiNLI (MN), MRPC (MR), QQP (QQ), QNLI (QN), RTE (R), WNLI (W). Note that for the metrics we considered here, lower scores indicate better calibration.

Train	MR	QQ	QN			R			W			Average
Eval	QQ	MR	M2	R	W	M2	QN	W	M2	QN	R	
	Accuracy											
Baseline	68.3	68.1	55.2	56.8	38.9	67.6	55.4	44.4	35.1	50.1	48.2	53.46
Ensemble	67.9	65.2	58.5	54.7	47.2	67.7	57.7	44.4	35.1	50.1	48.2	54.25
TempScale	68.3	68.1	55.2	56.8	38.9	67.6	55.4	44.4	35.1	50.1	48.2	53.46
Ours	68.4	68.1	58.6	57.6	47.2	67.3	61.0	44.4	35.1	50.1	48.2	55.09
Ours ($\hat{T}$)	67.2	71.1	61.1	59.7	38.9	66.2	61.2	44.4	35.1	50.1	48.2	54.84
	Maximum Calibration Error											
Baseline	35.8	24.3	37.3	34.6	68.4	18.5	19.7	67.2	16.2	1.2	3.1	29.66
Ensemble	36.9	46.7	35.6	34.7	94.7	9.6	16.9	42.7	16.0	1.1	2.9	30.71
TempScale	34.5	35.0	35.0	34.6	61.1	9.9	20.0	41.8	15.7	0.8	2.6	26.45
Ours	35.7	33.5	33.2	31.2	70.9	11.3	11.4	64.1	15.9	0.9	2.8	28.26
Ours ($\hat{T}$)	39.2	22.7	30.3	30.7	94.0	11.2	12.6	66.2	16.3	1.3	3.2	29.79
	Expected Calibration Error (bin size = 10)											
Baseline	19.5	22.9	26.4	29.9	40.0	9.5	8.4	35.2	16.2	1.2	3.1	19.30
Ensemble	20.6	22.9	21.7	28.4	22.9	3.5	10.6	32.1	16.0	1.1	2.9	16.61
TempScale	20.4	17.6	21.6	24.6	34.3	6.9	5.5	29.8	15.7	0.8	2.6	16.35
Ours	18.3	19.3	21.2	24.5	38.7	3.7	9.0	34.6	15.9	0.9	2.8	17.17
Ours ($\hat{T}$)	20.4	17.3	15.5	19.4	32.1	4.8	7.5	32.9	16.3	1.3	3.2	15.52
	Expected Calibration Error (bin size = 15)											
Baseline	19.5	22.9	26.4	31.5	40.0	10.6	8.5	35.2	16.2	1.2	3.1	19.55
Ensemble	21.0	24.3	21.7	28.4	22.9	4.9	10.8	32.1	16.0	1.1	2.9	16.92
TempScale	20.8	18.5	21.6	24.9	34.3	8.5	5.4	29.8	15.7	0.8	2.6	16.63
Ours	18.3	19.9	21.3	24.5	38.7	4.6	9.1	34.6	15.9	0.9	2.8	17.33
Ours ($\hat{T}$)	20.5	17.5	15.5	18.7	34.7	5.3	7.5	32.9	16.3	1.3	3.2	15.76
	Expected Calibration Error (bin size = 50)											
Baseline	19.8	25.7	26.4	32.4	45.4	10.7	8.5	35.2	16.2	1.2	3.1	20.42
Ensemble	21.4	24.9	21.7	31.9	41.3	5.4	11.0	32.1	16.0	1.1	2.9	19.06
TempScale	21.1	19.6	21.6	26.1	44.2	9.6	6.8	31.6	15.7	0.8	2.6	18.15
Ours	18.5	21.2	21.4	27.4	43.5	5.2	9.1	38.4	15.9	0.9	2.8	18.57
Ours ($\hat{T}$)	21.0	21.5	15.6	23.6	45.3	5.8	7.5	38.5	16.3	1.3	3.2	18.15
	Brier Score											
Baseline	26.20	26.50	33.00	33.00	40.65	22.40	24.70	37.05	25.45	25.00	25.05	29.00
Ensemble	26.85	26.40	30.55	33.35	29.80	21.60	24.45	35.25	25.35	25.00	25.05	27.60
TempScale	26.15	23.95	30.65	30.65	36.00	22.35	24.45	33.35	25.25	25.00	25.05	27.53
Ours	26.20	24.45	29.90	31.05	39.40	21.95	23.85	36.75	25.30	25.00	25.05	28.08
Ours ($\hat{T}$)	27.55	23.80	27.00	28.90	34.70	22.50	23.45	35.95	25.45	25.00	25.05	27.21
	Squared Calibration Error (debiased)											
Baseline	24.2	21.5	28.9	27.3	39.1	12.0	10.0	30.5	16.3	1.1	9.8	20.06
Ensemble	25.6	22.5	25.2	28.1	21.2	7.0	14.3	43.0	16.3	1.4	3.9	18.95
TempScale	24.3	17.7	24.5	23.4	33.6	10.7	8.9	37.3	15.8	0.0	9.6	18.71
Ours	23.0	18.5	24.1	26.4	33.8	6.9	9.4	34.0	15.9	1.9	0.0	17.63
Ours ($\hat{T}$)	26.9	16.6	18.6	21.3	39.0	7.7	7.9	32.8	16.3	2.1	0.0	17.20
	Squared Calibration Error (biased)											
Baseline	24.2	25.0	29.0	31.6	48.6	12.2	10.7	43.1	16.4	3.9	18.4	23.92
Ensemble	25.7	25.7	25.2	32.4	35.8	7.2	14.8	49.0	16.4	3.9	16.3	22.95
TempScale	24.3	21.5	24.6	28.3	44.3	10.8	9.6	45.2	15.9	3.0	18.3	22.35
Ours	23.1	22.3	24.2	30.6	45.5	7.2	10.1	44.6	16.0	4.2	15.9	22.15
Ours ($\hat{T}$)	26.9	20.8	18.7	26.5	46.6	7.9	8.6	43.7	16.4	4.3	13.7	21.28

Train	MR	QQ	QN			R			W			Average
Eval	QQ	MR	M2	R	W	M2	QN	W	M2	QN	R	
	Accuracy (+SBC)											
Baseline	/	/	/	/	/	/	/	/	/	/	/	/
Ensemble	/	/	/	/	/	/	/	/	/	/	/	/
TempScale	/	/	/	/	/	/	/	/	/	/	/	/
Ours	/	/	/	/	/	/	/	/	/	/	/	/
Ours ($\hat{T}$)	/	/	/	/	/	/	/	/	/	/	/	/
	Maximum Calibration Error (+SBC)											
Baseline	33.3	19.7	33.2	32.3	58.7	7.4	19.8	31.4	37.8	26.5	31.7	30.16
Ensemble	34.7	17.3	33.9	38.8	33.7	6.5	20.5	34.4	21.6	11.2	8.9	23.77
TempScale	32.5	26.1	34.2	33.7	55.8	8.4	22.2	65.9	35.8	25.9	29.1	33.60
Ours	33.9	22.8	27.4	32.1	52.7	4.3	13.7	30.1	26.9	15.0	17.3	25.11
Ours ($\hat{T}$)	37.5	19.8	26.4	40.5	91.0	4.1	8.2	35.6	26.0	15.7	13.6	28.95
	Expected Calibration Error (bin size = 10) (+SBC)											
Baseline	18.2	13.7	14.7	17.1	25.4	5.8	9.1	30.6	27.2	16.3	18.0	17.83
Ensemble	21.3	15.2	12.2	18.2	12.9	5.3	9.3	28.5	21.3	5.4	8.7	14.39
TempScale	14.8	12.9	16.3	18.0	26.4	6.5	8.5	31.6	26.2	15.6	16.3	17.55
Ours	15.8	12.1	12.8	15.5	22.4	3.7	5.2	27.6	23.7	9.1	11.6	14.50
Ours ($\hat{T}$)	20.4	12.3	9.9	11.4	27.6	2.2	7.6	26.2	23.4	8.6	11.2	14.62
	Expected Calibration Error (bin size = 15) (+SBC)											
Baseline	18.2	13.7	14.7	17.1	25.4	8.6	9.0	30.6	27.2	16.7	18.0	18.11
Ensemble	21.3	15.2	12.2	18.2	12.9	3.4	8.6	28.5	21.3	5.4	8.7	14.15
TempScale	17.7	12.9	16.3	18.0	26.4	7.9	8.5	31.6	26.2	15.6	16.4	17.95
Ours	15.8	12.1	12.8	15.5	22.4	2.1	5.2	27.6	23.7	9.1	13.0	14.48
Ours ($\hat{T}$)	20.4	12.3	9.9	11.4	27.6	3.0	7.0	26.2	23.4	8.6	11.2	14.64
	Expected Calibration Error (bin size = 50) (+SBC)											
Baseline	18.2	13.7	14.7	17.1	25.4	9.0	9.1	32.4	27.2	16.7	18.4	18.35
Ensemble	21.3	15.2	12.2	18.2	12.9	5.4	9.5	28.5	21.3	5.4	8.7	14.42
TempScale	17.7	12.9	16.3	18.0	26.4	8.1	8.7	31.6	26.2	15.6	17.3	18.07
Ours	15.8	12.1	12.8	15.5	22.4	4.3	5.5	32.4	23.7	9.1	13.0	15.15
Ours ($\hat{T}$)	20.4	12.3	9.9	11.4	27.6	3.0	7.6	28.4	23.4	8.6	12.6	15.02
	Brier Score (+SBC)											
Baseline	/	/	/	/	/	/	/	/	/	/	/	/
Ensemble	/	/	/	/	/	/	/	/	/	/	/	/
TempScale	/	/	/	/	/	/	/	/	/	/	/	/
Ours	/	/	/	/	/	/	/	/	/	/	/	/
Ours ($\hat{T}$)	/	/	/	/	/	/	/	/	/	/	/	/
	Squared Calibration Error (debiased, +SBC)											
Baseline	22.2	15.2	19.4	17.4	28.9	10.2	11.0	23.9	28.7	18.3	18.6	19.44
Ensemble	24.3	13.0	18.5	20.5	0.0	6.2	13.2	15.9	21.4	6.5	8.5	13.45
TempScale	21.5	14.3	19.8	18.7	28.6	9.2	10.3	22.6	27.5	17.6	14.6	18.61
Ours	21.1	11.6	17.0	16.5	25.5	4.9	6.8	29.1	23.9	10.1	4.5	15.55
Ours ($\hat{T}$)	26.1	12.6	14.5	14.2	22.4	5.9	10.3	27.5	23.6	9.6	9.0	15.97
	Squared Calibration Error (biased, +SBC)											
Baseline	22.3	17.2	19.5	20.5	31.0	10.3	11.3	33.4	28.7	18.6	22.6	21.40
Ensemble	24.3	15.6	18.6	23.1	13.8	6.4	13.4	29.9	21.4	7.1	15.3	17.17
TempScale	21.5	16.4	19.8	21.4	30.8	9.3	10.6	32.4	27.5	17.8	19.6	20.65
Ours	21.1	14.3	17.0	19.2	29.3	5.1	7.4	35.1	23.9	10.5	14.2	17.92
Ours ($\hat{T}$)	26.2	15.2	14.6	19.3	29.6	6.1	10.6	36.1	23.6	10.0	15.7	18.82

Table 4: Out-of-domain performances on MRPC (MR), QQP (QQ), QNLI (QN), RTE (R), WNLI (W). We use M2 to denote the 2-label version of MultiNLI task. Note that for the metrics we considered here, lower scores indicate better calibration.

Train	SST-2	CoLA	MNLI	MRPC	QQP	QNLI	RTE	WNLI	Average	SST-2	CoLA	MNLI	MRPC	QQP	QNLI	RTE	WNLI	Average
	Accuracy									**Accuracy (+SBC)**								
Ours	93.3	79.7	87.4	84.8	91.0	92.2	65.5	55.6	81.19	/	/	/	/	/	/	/	/	/
−Ensemble	93.3	79.5	87.4	85.3	91.0	92.5	66.2	55.6	81.35	/	/	/	/	/	/	/	/	/
−TempScale	93.1	79.1	87.3	86.3	91.1	92.3	65.5	55.6	81.29	/	/	/	/	/	/	/	/	/
−Distillation	94.0	79.9	87.4	86.3	91.2	92.3	66.9	55.6	81.70	/	/	/	/	/	/	/	/	/
	Maximum Calibration Error									**Maximum Calibration Error (+SBC)**								
Ours	34.0	20.8	14.3	16.6	9.3	14.0	24.0	4.5	17.19	2.8	13.5	3.8	22.8	2.9	3.8	17.2	36.7	12.94
−Ensemble	49.6	25.3	15.5	14.3	8.6	11.3	16.4	3.8	18.10	2.3	11.9	3.5	26.3	2.8	9.6	6.7	73.6	17.09
−TempScale	58.7	34.3	16.7	7.6	15.6	16.6	19.8	4.3	21.70	12.5	9.9	3.7	3.8	3.8	4.0	5.5	40.7	10.49
−Distillation	28.3	22.8	8.4	12.8	3.1	8.2	15.9	4.8	13.04	4.5	9.7	3.0	9.3	2.1	3.1	15.7	1.7	6.14
	Expected Calibration Error (bin size = 10)									**Expected Calibration Error (bin size = 10) (+SBC)**								
Ours	4.6	11.6	5.2	4.1	3.0	3.5	8.8	4.5	5.66	0.6	4.0	1.1	3.3	0.5	0.8	7.7	7.9	3.24
−Ensemble	4.5	11.8	5.3	3.8	3.0	3.3	11.7	3.8	5.90	0.7	4.5	1.0	6.0	0.5	1.2	6.4	23.5	5.48
−TempScale	5.4	13.3	6.2	3.6	4.0	3.6	8.6	4.3	6.13	1.8	3.5	0.9	1.5	0.5	0.7	5.5	15.9	3.79
−Distillation	3.2	9.3	3.1	2.4	1.3	1.3	10.7	4.8	4.51	1.2	4.3	0.8	1.7	0.6	0.8	9.8	1.7	2.61
	Expected Calibration Error (bin size = 15)									**Expected Calibration Error (bin size = 15) (+SBC)**								
Ours	4.8	12.1	5.2	5.2	3.1	3.5	9.4	4.5	5.98	0.6	4.0	1.4	4.4	0.5	1.3	9.4	7.9	3.69
−Ensemble	4.5	11.8	5.3	4.7	3.0	3.3	11.7	3.8	6.01	0.7	3.8	1.4	5.4	0.5	1.6	8.9	23.5	5.73
−TempScale	5.5	13.3	6.2	5.6	4.0	3.7	8.9	4.3	6.44	2.7	4.4	1.2	2.1	0.4	1.3	5.5	18.0	4.45
−Distillation	3.4	9.4	3.0	4.3	1.3	1.7	12.6	4.8	5.06	1.2	4.4	0.8	2.0	0.6	0.8	12.1	1.7	2.95
	Expected Calibration Error (bin size = 50)									**Expected Calibration Error (bin size = 50) (+SBC)**								
Ours	5.7	12.9	5.2	11.6	3.1	3.7	15.5	4.5	7.78	1.8	5.6	1.6	5.2	0.6	1.4	11.9	13.0	5.14
−Ensemble	5.5	12.7	5.5	10.7	3.1	3.5	15.5	3.8	7.54	1.7	5.5	1.7	6.7	0.5	1.6	10.2	27.5	6.93
−TempScale	6.3	13.7	6.3	9.7	4.1	4.0	11.9	4.3	7.54	4.3	4.1	1.4	2.6	0.5	1.4	5.5	18.9	4.84
−Distillation	4.7	11.6	3.2	7.3	1.4	2.0	17.2	4.8	6.53	2.1	5.2	1.0	2.7	0.6	1.0	12.5	4.8	3.74
	Brier Score									**Brier Score (+SBC)**								
Ours	5.50	15.85	6.43	10.45	6.75	6.15	21.45	24.90	12.19	/	/	/	/	/	/	/	/	/
−Ensemble	5.25	15.65	6.47	10.15	6.80	6.05	22.35	24.85	12.20	/	/	/	/	/	/	/	/	/
−TempScale	5.75	16.05	6.57	10.75	6.90	6.10	21.25	24.90	12.28	/	/	/	/	/	/	/	/	/
−Distillation	4.70	14.40	6.20	10.05	6.45	5.65	20.25	24.95	11.58	/	/	/	/	/	/	/	/	/
	Squared Calibration Error (debiased)									**Squared Calibration Error (debiased, +SBC)**								
Ours	7.3	13.0	6.8	0.0	4.2	4.7	13.0	16.4	8.18	0.0	4.8	1.9	5.3	0.9	1.1	8.4	12.7	4.39
−Ensemble	7.4	14.6	7.3	0.0	4.2	4.0	10.3	33.1	10.11	0.0	7.2	1.8	8.2	0.8	2.9	11.7	18.6	6.40
−TempScale	9.7	14.8	8.1	0.0	5.6	5.0	0.0	23.4	8.33	4.8	6.2	1.5	0.0	1.1	1.1	10.4	10.5	4.45
−Distillation	3.7	12.1	3.8	0.0	1.5	1.8	12.3	0.0	4.40	0.0	3.8	1.1	0.0	0.7	0.0	10.1	18.7	4.30
	Squared Calibration Error (biased)									**Squared Calibration Error (biased, +SBC)**								
Ours	8.3	14.5	6.9	8.3	4.2	5.0	19.2	31.8	12.28	2.2	6.9	2.1	8.5	1.1	1.8	14.6	22.9	7.51
−Ensemble	8.4	15.9	7.4	7.9	4.2	4.4	17.8	39.5	13.19	2.5	8.7	2.0	10.5	1.0	3.3	16.9	29.7	9.33
−TempScale	10.5	16.1	8.2	7.7	5.7	5.3	12.5	34.6	12.58	5.8	7.9	1.8	3.4	1.2	1.8	16.4	27.8	8.26
−Distillation	5.4	13.5	3.9	6.5	1.7	2.5	18.4	28.8	10.09	2.6	6.1	1.4	4.5	0.9	1.3	15.6	26.6	7.38

Table 5: In-domain ablation performances on SST-2 (S), CoLA (C), MultiNLI (MN), MRPC (MR), QQP (QQ), QNLI (QN), RTE (R), WNLI (W). Note that for the metrics we considered here, lower scores indicate better calibration.

Train	MR	QQ	QN			R			W			Average	MR	QQ	QN			R			W			Average
Eval	QQ	MR	M2	R	W	M2	QN	W	M2	QN	R		QQ	MR	M2	R	W	M2	QN	W	M2	QN	R	
Accuracy													**Accuracy (+SBC)**											
Ours	68.4	68.1	58.6	57.6	47.2	67.3	61.0	44.4	35.1	50.1	48.2	55.09	/	/	/	/	/	/	/	/	/	/	/	/
–Ensemble	66.3	66.2	59.7	59.0	44.4	67.5	55.7	44.4	35.1	50.1	48.2	54.24	/	/	/	/	/	/	/	/	/	/	/	/
–TempScale	66.6	67.2	56.0	56.1	47.2	68.0	54.6	44.4	35.1	50.1	48.2	53.95	/	/	/	/	/	/	/	/	/	/	/	/
–Distillation	67.8	65.2	58.7	54.7	50.0	67.8	57.9	44.4	35.1	50.1	48.2	54.54	/	/	/	/	/	/	/	/	/	/	/	/
Maximum Calibration Error													**Maximum Calibration Error (+SBC)**											
Ours	35.7	33.5	33.2	31.2	70.9	11.3	11.4	64.1	15.9	0.9	2.8	28.26	33.9	22.8	27.4	32.1	52.7	4.3	13.7	30.1	26.9	15.0	17.3	25.11
–Ensemble	39.3	27.4	32.5	40.7	58.6	8.7	27.1	43.5	16.7	1.7	3.5	27.25	37.3	21.4	28.5	28.6	17.5	15.5	27.4	28.0	56.5	45.6	47.9	32.20
–TempScale	39.1	31.5	37.0	38.3	54.6	11.6	21.1	67.3	16.2	1.2	3.1	29.18	37.7	16.6	31.9	30.5	61.8	3.0	16.4	26.6	38.4	31.0	43.6	30.68
–Distillation	35.8	25.6	33.2	36.7	34.6	4.8	17.4	31.9	15.7	0.8	2.6	21.74	33.5	18.3	30.9	27.6	14.8	4.7	18.4	31.5	22.3	7.7	9.1	19.89
Expected Calibration Error (bin size = 10)													**Expected Calibration Error (bin size = 10) (+SBC)**											
Ours	18.3	19.3	21.2	24.5	38.7	3.7	9.0	34.6	15.9	0.9	2.8	17.17	15.8	12.1	12.8	15.5	22.4	3.7	5.2	27.6	23.7	9.1	11.6	14.50
–Ensemble	18.9	20.6	20.9	24.7	31.9	3.3	15.2	34.0	16.7	1.7	3.5	17.40	18.4	13.2	10.6	12.6	17.2	3.6	15.5	28.0	24.9	17.9	21.8	16.70
–TempScale	23.9	22.4	27.5	31.1	40.6	3.4	14.6	34.8	16.2	1.2	3.1	19.89	21.2	12.7	18.9	22.5	26.7	3.0	16.4	26.6	23.3	9.5	10.6	17.40
–Distillation	20.1	18.4	18.0	25.4	26.7	3.7	8.8	29.1	15.7	0.8	2.6	15.39	20.6	15.2	13.6	21.0	11.8	3.8	9.3	28.6	22.3	7.7	9.1	14.82
Expected Calibration Error (bin size = 15)													**Expected Calibration Error (bin size = 15) (+SBC)**											
Ours	18.3	19.9	21.3	24.5	38.7	4.6	9.1	34.6	15.9	0.9	2.8	17.33	15.8	12.1	12.8	15.5	22.4	2.1	5.2	27.6	23.7	9.1	13.0	14.48
–Ensemble	20.5	21.2	20.9	24.7	31.9	4.4	15.2	35.5	16.7	1.7	3.5	17.84	20.8	13.2	10.6	12.6	17.2	4.4	15.6	28.0	24.9	17.9	21.8	17.00
–TempScale	24.0	22.9	27.5	30.4	39.4	5.6	14.6	34.8	16.2	1.2	3.1	19.97	21.2	12.7	18.9	22.5	26.7	3.0	16.4	26.6	23.3	10.1	13.3	17.70
–Distillation	20.9	18.8	18.0	25.4	28.4	3.7	8.9	29.1	15.7	0.8	2.6	15.66	20.6	15.2	13.6	21.0	11.8	3.1	8.8	28.6	22.3	7.7	9.1	14.71
Expected Calibration Error (bin size = 50)													**Expected Calibration Error (bin size = 50) (+SBC)**											
Ours	18.5	21.2	21.4	27.4	43.5	5.2	9.1	38.4	15.9	0.9	2.8	18.57	15.8	12.1	12.8	15.5	22.4	4.3	5.5	32.4	23.7	9.1	13.0	15.15
–Ensemble	21.2	23.3	21.0	27.5	35.2	4.8	15.2	34.0	16.7	1.7	3.5	18.55	20.8	13.8	10.6	12.6	17.2	3.6	16.7	28.0	25.1	17.9	21.8	17.10
–TempScale	24.5	24.2	27.7	34.1	46.2	5.9	14.6	41.0	16.2	1.2	3.1	21.70	21.2	12.7	18.9	22.5	26.8	3.0	16.4	26.6	23.3	10.1	16.5	18.00
–Distillation	21.8	20.0	18.1	29.8	35.6	4.5	9.1	31.6	15.7	0.8	2.6	17.24	20.6	15.2	13.6	21.0	11.8	4.0	9.3	28.6	22.3	7.7	9.1	14.84
Brier Score													**Brier Score (+SBC)**											
Ours	26.20	24.45	29.90	31.05	39.40	21.95	23.85	36.75	25.30	25.00	25.05	28.08	/	/	/	/	/	/	/	/	/	/	/	/
–Ensemble	27.90	25.70	29.35	30.45	33.75	21.70	26.10	36.95	25.55	25.05	25.10	27.96	/	/	/	/	/	/	/	/	/	/	/	/
–TempScale	28.60	25.25	33.45	34.15	42.00	21.50	26.25	37.70	25.40	25.05	25.10	29.50	/	/	/	/	/	/	/	/	/	/	/	/
–Distillation	26.75	24.25	28.80	31.45	28.25	21.45	24.15	33.40	25.25	25.00	25.05	26.71	/	/	/	/	/	/	/	/	/	/	/	/
Calibration Error (debiased)													**Calibration Error (debiased, +SBC)**											
Ours	23.0	18.5	24.1	26.4	33.8	6.9	9.4	34.0	15.9	1.9	0.0	17.63	21.1	11.6	17.0	16.5	25.5	4.9	6.8	29.1	23.9	10.1	4.5	15.55
–Ensemble	27.3	21.0	23.4	24.4	28.9	6.9	17.6	30.2	16.7	0.5	9.4	18.75	26.2	15.2	16.2	19.2	12.3	8.1	19.7	24.7	30.5	21.5	24.9	19.86
–TempScale	28.7	20.0	30.0	30.1	40.6	6.8	16.1	35.6	16.2	2.9	7.1	21.28	26.2	11.9	22.0	23.0	32.4	8.9	19.3	29.4	24.8	12.7	17.8	20.76
–Distillation	25.4	16.2	21.5	24.5	17.9	4.9	13.0	23.2	16.0	1.9	9.8	15.85	23.5	13.5	18.2	20.4	0.0	4.7	12.9	20.2	22.5	7.7	0.0	13.05
Calibration Error (biased)													**Calibration Error (biased, +SBC)**											
Ours	23.1	22.3	24.2	30.6	45.5	7.2	10.1	44.6	16.0	4.2	15.9	22.15	21.1	14.3	17.0	19.2	29.3	5.1	7.4	35.1	23.9	10.5	14.2	17.92
–Ensemble	27.3	24.5	23.5	29.0	40.8	7.1	18.0	42.9	16.8	3.7	18.2	22.89	26.2	17.0	16.3	21.3	17.2	8.2	19.9	33.9	30.5	21.7	27.7	21.81
–TempScale	28.7	23.6	30.0	34.0	49.8	7.0	16.5	45.9	16.3	4.7	17.3	24.89	26.3	14.3	22.1	25.2	36.6	9.0	19.5	36.1	24.8	13.0	22.0	22.63
–Distillation	25.4	20.5	21.6	29.2	34.0	5.2	13.5	38.3	16.1	4.2	18.4	20.58	23.5	15.6	18.3	23.3	11.9	4.9	13.2	31.5	22.6	8.3	12.2	16.85

Table 6: Out-of-domain ablation performances on MRPC (MR), QQP (QQ), QNLI (QN), RTE (R), WNLI (W). We use M2 to denote the 2-label version of MultiNLI task. Note that for the metrics we considered here, lower scores indicate better calibration.

Entity and Evidence Guided Document-Level Relation Extraction

Anonymous ACL-IJCNLP submission

Abstract

Document-level relation extraction is a challenging task, requiring reasoning over multiple sentences to predict a set of relations in a document. In this paper, we propose a novel framework *E2GRE* (Entity and Evidence Guided Relation Extraction) that jointly extracts relations and the underlying evidence sentences by using large pretrained language model (LM) as input encoder. First, we propose to guide the pretrained LM's attention mechanism to focus on relevant context by using attention probabilities as additional features for evidence prediction. Furthermore, instead of feeding the whole document into pretrained LMs to obtain entity representation, we concatenate document text with head entities to help LMs concentrate on parts of the document that are more related to the head entity. Our *E2GRE* jointly learns relation extraction and evidence prediction effectively, showing large gains on both these tasks, which we find are highly correlated. Our experimental result on DocRED, a large-scale document-level relation extraction dataset, is competitive with the top of the public leaderboard for relation extraction, and is top ranked on evidence prediction, which shows that our *E2GRE* is both effective and synergistic on relation extraction and evidence prediction.

1 Introduction

Relation Extraction (RE), the problem of predicting relations between pairs of entities from text, has received increasing research attention in recent years [Zhang *et al.*, 2017; Zhao *et al.*, 2019; Guo *et al.*, 2019]. This problem has important downstream applications to numerous tasks, such as automatic knowledge acquisition from web documents for knowledge graph construction [Trisedya *et al.*, 2019], question answering [Yu *et al.*, 2017] and dialogue systems [Young *et al.*, 2018]. While most

Document: [0] The Legend of Zelda : The Minish Cap ( ) is an action - adventure game and the twelfth entry in The Legend of Zelda series. [1] Developed by Capcom and Flagship , with Nintendo overseeing the development process , it was released for the Game Boy Advance handheld game console in Japan and Europe in 2004 and in North America and Australia the following year . [2] In June 2014 , it was made available on the Wii U Virtual Console . [3] The Minish Cap is the third Zelda game that involves the legend of the Four Sword , expanding on the story of and . [4] A magical talking cap named Ezlo can shrink series protagonist Link to the size of the Minish , a bug - sized race that live in Hyrule . [5] The game retains some common elements from previous Zelda installments , such as the presence of Gorons , while introducing Kinstones and other new gameplay features . [6] The Minish Cap was generally well received among critics . [7] It was named the 20th best Game Boy Advance game in an IGN feature , and was selected as the 2005 Game Boy Advance Game of the Year by GameSpot .
Head Entity: Link
Tail Entity: The Legend of Zelda
Relation: "Present in Work"
Evidence Sentences: 0,3,4

Figure 1: An example document in the DocRED dataset, where a head and tail entity pair span across multiple sentences.

previous work focus on relation extraction at the sentence level, in real world applications, e.g predicting relations from web articles, the majority of relations are expressed across multiple sentences. Figure 1 shows an example from the recently released DocRED dataset [Yao *et al.*, 2019], which requires reasoning over three evidence sentences to predict the relational fact that "Link" is present in the work "The Legend of Zelda". In this paper, we focus on the more challenging task of *document-level* relation extraction task and design a method to facilitate *document-level* reasoning.

Aside from extracting entity relations from a document, it is often useful to also highlight the evidence that a system uses to predict them, so that a human or second system can verify them for consistency. What is more, evidence prediction can potentially supplement RE performance by restricting the model's focus on the correct context. In preliminary experiments, we find that current models are able to achieve around 87% RE F1 on DocRED by only keeping the gold evidence sentences when trained and evaluated only on the gold evidence sentences, which is a significant im-

Proceedings of the 6th Workshop on Representation Learning for NLP (RepL4NLP-2021), pages 307–315
Bangkok, Thailand (Online), August 6, 2021. ©2021 Association for Computational Linguistics

provement on current leaderboard DocRED RE F1 numbers ($\sim 63\%$ RE F1). However, evidence prediction is a challenging task, and most existing relation extraction (RE) approaches ignore the task of evidence prediction entirely.

Most recent approaches for relation extraction fine-tune large pretrained Language Models (LMs) (e.g.,BERT [Devlin *et al.*, 2019], RoBERTa [Liu *et al.*, 2019]) as input encoder. However, naively adapting pretrained LMs for document-level RE faces an issue which limits its performance. Due to the length of a given document, many more entities and relations exist in document-level RE than in intra-sentence RE. A pretrained LM has to simultaneously encode information regarding all pairs of entities for relation extraction, making the task more difficult, and limiting the pretrained LM's effectiveness.

In this paper we propose a new framework: Entity and Evidence Guided Relation Extraction (*E2GRE*), which jointly solves relation extraction and evidence prediction. For evidence prediction, we take a pretrained LM as input encoder and use its internal attention probabilities as additional features to predict evidence sentences. As a result, we use supporting evidence sentences to provide direct supervision on which tokens the LM should attend to during finetuning, which in turn helps improve relation extraction in a joint training framework. To further help LMs focus on a smaller set of relevant word context from a long document, we also introduce entity-guided input sequences as the input to these models, by appending each head entity to the document text, one at a time. This allows the LM encoder to explicitly model relations involving a specific head entity while ignoring all other entity pairs, thus simplifying the task for the LM encoder. The joint training framework helps the model locate the correct semantics that are required for each relation prediction. To the best of our knowledge[1], we are the first to present an effective joint training framework for relation extraction and evidence prediction.

Each of these ideas gives a significant boost in performance, and by combining them, we are able to achieve highly competitive results on the DocRED leaderboard. We obtain 62.5 relation extraction F1 and 50.5 evidence prediction F1 from our E2GRE trained RoBERTa$_{\text{LARGE}}$ model, which is the current state-of-the-art performance on evidence prediction. Our proposed *E2GRE* framework is a simple joint training approach that effectively incorporates information from evidence prediction to guide the pretrained LM encoder, boosting performance on both relation extraction and evidence prediction.

Our main contributions are summarized as follows:

- We propose to generate multiple new entity-guided inputs to a pretrained language model: for every document, we concatenate every entity with the document and feed it as an input sequence to a pretrained LM encoder.
- We propose to use internal attention probabilities of the pre-trained LM encoder as additional features for the evidence prediction.
- Our joint training framework of *E2GRE* which receives the guidance from entity and evidence, improves the performance on both relation extraction and evidence prediction, showing that the two tasks are mutually beneficial to each other.

2 Related Work

Early work attempted to solve RE with statistical methods with different feature engineering [Zelenko *et al.*, 2003; Bunescu and Mooney, 2005]. Later on, neural models have shown better performance at capturing semantic relationships between entities. These methods include CNN-based approaches [Zeng *et al.*; Wang *et al.*, 2016] and LSTM-based approaches [Cai *et al.*, 2016].

On top of using CNNs/LSTM encoders, previous models added additional layers to model semantic interactions. For example, Han *et al.* [2018] introduced using hierarchical attentions in order to generate relational information from coarse-to-fine semantic ideas; Zhang *et al.* [2017] applied GCNs over pruned dependency trees, and Guo *et al.* [2019] introduced Attention Guided Graph Convolutional Networks (AG-GCNs) over dependency trees. These models have shown good performance on intra-sentence relation extraction, but are not easily adapted for document-level RE.

Many approaches for document-level RE are graph-based neural network methods. Quirk and Poon [2017] first introduced a document graph being used for document-level RE; In [Jia *et al.*, 2019], an entity-centric, multi-scale representation

[1]Based on published papers on DocRED.

learning on entity/sentence/document-level LSTM model was proposed for document-level n-ary RE task. Christopoulou *et al.* [2019] recently proposed a novel edge-oriented graph model that deviates from existing graph models. Nan *et al.* [2020] proposed an induced latent graph and Li *et al.* [2020] used an explicit heterogeneous graph for DocRED. These graph models generally focus on constructing unique nodes and edges, and have the advantage of connecting and aggregating different granularities of information. Zhou *et al.* [2021] pointed out multi-entity and multi-label issues for document-level RE, and proposed two techniques: adaptive thresholding and localized context pooling, to address these problems.

Pretrained Language Models [Radford *et al.*, 2019; Devlin *et al.*, 2019; Liu *et al.*, 2019] are powerful NLP tools trained with enormous amounts of unlabelled data. In order to take advantage of the large amounts of text that these models have seen, finetuning on large pretrained LMs has been shown to be effective on relation extraction [Wadden *et al.*, 2019]. Generally, large pretrained LMs are used to encode a sequence and then generate the representation of a head/tail entity pair to learn a classification [Eberts and Ulges, 2019; Yao *et al.*, 2019]. Baldini Soares *et al.* [2019] introduced a new concept similar to BERT called "matching-the-black" and pretrained a Transformer-like model for relation learning. The models were finetuned on SemEval-2010 Task 8 and TACRED achieved state-of-the-art results. Our framework aims to improve the effectiveness of pretrained LMs for document-level relation extraction, with our entity and evidence guided approaches.

3 Method

In this section, we introduce our *E2GRE* framework. First, we describe how to generate entity-guided inputs. Then we present how to jointly train RE with evidence prediction, and finally show how to combine this with our evidence-guided attentions. We use BERT as our pretrained LM when describing our framework.

3.1 Entity-Guided Input Sequences

The goal of relation extraction is to predict *relation* label between every head/tail (*h*/*t*) pair of given entities in a given *document*. Most standard models approach this problem by feeding in an entire document and then extracting all of the head/tail pairs to predict relations.

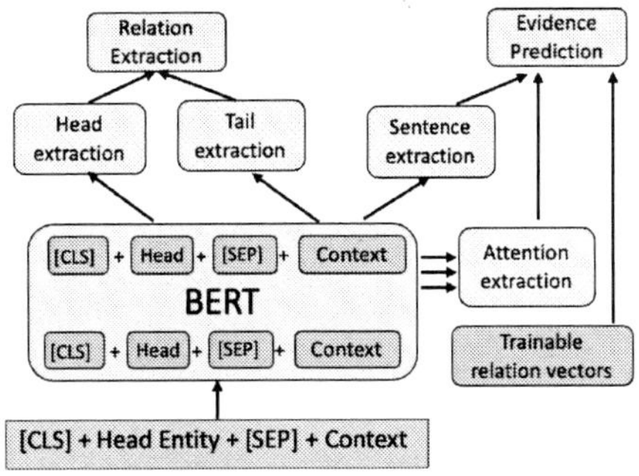

Figure 2: Diagram of our *E2GRE* framework. As shown in the diagram, we pass an input sequence consisting of an entity and document into BERT. We extract head and tails for relation extraction. We show the learned relation vectors in grey. We extract out sentence representation and BERT attention probabilities for evidence predictions.

Instead, we design entity-guided inputs to give BERT more guidance towards the entities during training. Each training input is organized by concatenating the tokens of the first mention of a head entity, denoted by H, together with the document tokens D, to form: "[CLS]"+ H + "[SEP]" + D + "[SEP]", which is then fed into BERT.[2]

We generate these input sequences for each entity in the given document. Therefore, for a document with N_e entities, N_e new entity-guided input sequences are generated and fed into BERT separately.

Our framework predicts $N_e - 1$ different sets of relations for each training input, corresponding to $N_e - 1$ head/tail entity pairs.

After passing a training input through BERT, we extract the *head entity* embedding and a set of *tail entity* embeddings from the BERT output. After obtaining the head entity embedding $\boldsymbol{h} \in \mathbb{R}^d$ and all tail entity embeddings $\{\boldsymbol{t}_k | \boldsymbol{t}_k \in \mathbb{R}^d\}$ in an entity-guided sequence, where $1 \leq k \leq N_e - 1$, we feed them into a bilinear layer with the sigmoid activation function to predict the probability of i-th relation between the head entity h and the k-th tail

[2]Since the max input length for BERT is 512, for any input length longer than 512, we make use of a sliding window approach over the input and separate it into two chunks (DocRED does not have documents longer than 1024): the first chunk is the input sequence up to 512 tokens; the second chunk is the input sequence with an offset, such that offset + 512 reaches the end of the sequence. This is shown as "[CLS]"+ H + "[SEP]" + D[offset:end] + "[SEP]". We combine these two input chunks in our model by averaging the embeddings and BERT attention probabilities of the overlapping tokens in the model.

entity t_k, denoted by $\hat{y}_{ik}$, as follows

$$\hat{y}_{ik} = \delta(\boldsymbol{h}^T \boldsymbol{W}_i \boldsymbol{t}_k + b_i) \quad (1)$$

where δ is the sigmoid function, $\boldsymbol{W}_i$ and b_i are the learnable parameters corresponding to i-th relation, where $1 \leq i \leq N_r$, and N_r is the number of relations. Finally, we finetune BERT with multi-label cross-entropy loss.

During inference, we group the $N_e - 1$ predicted relations for each entity-guided input sequence from the same document, to obtain the final set of predictions for a document.

3.2 Evidence Guided Relation Extraction

3.2.1 Evidence Prediction

Evidence sentences are sentences which contain important facts for predicting the correct relationships between head and tail entities. Therefore, evidence prediction is a very important auxiliary task to relation extraction and also provides explainability for the model. We build our evidence prediction upon the baseline introduced by Yao *et al.* [2019], which we will describe next.

Let N_s be the number of sentences in the document. We first obtain the sentence embedding $\boldsymbol{s} \in \mathbb{R}^{N_S \times d}$ by averaging all the embeddings of the words in each sentence (i.e., *Sentence Extraction* in Fig. 2). These word embeddings are derived from the BERT output embeddings.

Let $\boldsymbol{r}_i \in \mathbb{R}^d$ be the relation embedding of i-th relation r_i ($1 \leq i \leq N_r$), which is learnable and initialized randomly in our model. We employ a bilinear layer with sigmoid activation function to predict the probability of the j-th sentence s_j being an evidence sentence w.r.t. the given i-th relation r_i as follows.

$$\begin{aligned} \boldsymbol{F}^i_{jk} &= \boldsymbol{s}_j \boldsymbol{W}^r_i \boldsymbol{r}_i + b^r_i \\ \hat{\boldsymbol{y}}^i_{jk} &= \delta(\boldsymbol{F}^i_{jk} \boldsymbol{W}^r_o + b^r_o) \end{aligned} \quad (2)$$

where $\boldsymbol{s}_j$ represents the embedding of j-th sentence, $\boldsymbol{W}^r_i / b^r_i$ and $\boldsymbol{W}^r_o / b^r_o$ are the learnable parameters w.r.t. i-th relation. We define the loss of evidence prediction under the given i-th relation as follows:

$$\begin{aligned} L_{Evi} = &-\tfrac{1}{N_e - 1} \tfrac{1}{N_s} \textstyle\sum_{k=1}^{N_e - 1} \sum_{j=1}^{N_s} (y^i_{jk} \log(\hat{\boldsymbol{y}}^i_{jk}) \\ &+ (1 - y^i_{jk}) \log(1 - \hat{\boldsymbol{y}}^i_{jk})) \end{aligned} \quad (3)$$

where $y^j_{ik} \in \{0, 1\}$, and $y^j_{ik} = 1$ means that sentence j is an evidence for the i-th relation. It should be noted that in the training stage, we use the embedding of true relation in Eq. 2. In testing/inference stage, we use the embedding of the relation predicted by the relation extraction model.

3.2.2 Baseline Joint Training

In [Yao *et al.*, 2019] the baseline relation extraction loss L_{RE} and the evidence prediction loss are combined as the final objective function for the joint training:

$$L_{baseline} = L_{RE} + \lambda * L_{Evi} \quad (4)$$

where $\lambda > 0$ is the weight factor to make trade-offs between two losses, which is data dependent. In order to compare to our models, we utilize a BERT-baseline to predict relation extraction loss and evidence prediction loss.

3.2.3 Guiding BERT Attention with Evidence Prediction

Pretrained language models have been shown to be able to implicitly model semantic relations internally. By looking at internal attention probabilities, Clark *et al.* [2019] has shown that BERT learns coreference and other semantic information in later BERT layers. In order to take advantage of this inherent property, our framework attempts to give more guidance to where correct semantics for RE are located. For each pair of head h and tail t_k, we introduce the idea of using internal attention probabilities extracted from the last l internal BERT layers for evidence prediction.

Let $\boldsymbol{Q} \in \mathbb{R}^{N_h \times L \times (d/N_h)}$ be the query and $\boldsymbol{K} \in \mathbb{R}^{N_h \times L \times (d/N_h)}$ be the key of the Multi-Head Self Attention layer, N_h be the number of attention heads as described in [Vaswani *et al.*, 2017], L be the length of the input sequence and d be the embedding dimension. We first extract the output of multi-headed self attention (MHSA) $\boldsymbol{A} \in \mathbb{R}^{N_h \times L \times L}$ from a given layer in BERT as follows. These extraction outputs are shown as *Attention Extractor* in Fig. 2.

$$\text{Attention} = \text{softmax}(\frac{\boldsymbol{Q}\boldsymbol{K}^T}{\sqrt{d/N_h}}) \quad (5)$$

$$\text{Att-head}_i = \text{Attention}(\boldsymbol{Q}\boldsymbol{W}^Q_i, \boldsymbol{K}\boldsymbol{W}^K_i) \quad (6)$$

$$\boldsymbol{A} = \text{Concat}(\text{Att-head}_1, \cdots, \text{Att-head}_n) \quad (7)$$

For a given pair of head h and tail t_k, we extract the attention probabilities corresponding to head and tail tokens to help relation extraction. Specifically, we concatenate the MHSAs for the last l BERT layers extracted by Eq. 7 to form an attention probability tensor as: $\tilde{\boldsymbol{A}}_k \in \mathbb{R}^{l \times N_h \times L \times L}$.

Then, we calculate the attention probability representation of each sentence under the given head-tail entity pair (h, t_k) as follows.

1. We first apply maximum pooling layer along the attention head dimension (i.e., second dimension) over $\tilde{\boldsymbol{A}}_k$. The max values are helpful to show where a specific attention head might be looking at. Afterwards we apply mean pooling over the last l layers. We obtain $\tilde{\boldsymbol{A}}_s = \frac{1}{l}\sum_{i=1}^{l} \text{maxpool}(\tilde{\boldsymbol{A}}_{ki})$, $\tilde{\boldsymbol{A}}_s \in \mathbb{R}^{L \times L}$ from these two steps.

2. We then extract the attention probability tensor from the head and tail entity tokens according to the start and end positions of in the document. We average the attention probabilities over all the tokens for the head and tail embeddings to obtain $\tilde{\boldsymbol{A}}_{sk} \in \mathbb{R}^{L}$.

3. Finally, we generate sentence representations from $\tilde{\boldsymbol{A}}_{sk}$ by averaging over the attentions of each token in a given sentence from the document to obtain $\boldsymbol{a}_{sk} \in \mathbb{R}^{N_s}$

Once we get the attention probabilities $\boldsymbol{a}_{sk}$, we pass the sentence embeddings $\hat{\boldsymbol{F}}_k^i$ from Eq. 2 through a transformer layer to encourage inter-sentence interactions and form the new representation $\hat{\boldsymbol{Z}}_k^i$. We combine $\boldsymbol{a}_{sk}$ with $\hat{\boldsymbol{Z}}_k^i$ and feed it into a bilinear layer with sigmoid (δ) for evidence sentence prediction as follows:

$$\hat{\boldsymbol{Z}}_k^i = \text{FFN}(\text{LayerNorm}(\text{Multi-Head}(\hat{\boldsymbol{F}}_k^i))) \quad (8)$$

$$\hat{\boldsymbol{y}}_k^{ia} = \delta(\boldsymbol{a}_{sk}\boldsymbol{W}_i^a \hat{\boldsymbol{Z}}_k^i + b_i^a) \quad (9)$$

Finally, we define the loss of evidence prediction under a given i-th relation based on attention probability representation as follows:

$$L_{Evi}^a = -\frac{1}{N_e - 1}\frac{1}{N_s}\sum_{k=1}^{N_e-1}\sum_{j=1}^{N_s}(y_{jk}^{ia}\log(\hat{\boldsymbol{y}}_{jk}^{ia}) + (1 - y_{jk}^{ia})\log(1 - \hat{\boldsymbol{y}}_{jk}^{ia})), f \quad (10)$$

where $\hat{\boldsymbol{y}}_{jk}^{ia}$ is the j-th value of $\hat{\boldsymbol{y}}_k^{ia}$ computed by Eq. 8.

3.2.4 Joint Training with Evidence Guided Attention Probabilities

Here we combine the relation extraction loss and the attention guided evidence prediction loss as the final objective function for the joint training:

$$L_{E2GRE} = L_{RE}^e + \lambda_a * L_{Evi}^a \quad (11)$$

where $\lambda_a > 0$ is the weight factor to make trade-offs between two losses, which is data dependent.

4 Experiments

4.1 Dataset

DocRED [Yao *et al.*, 2019] is a large document-level dataset for the tasks of relation extraction and evidence prediction. It consists of 5053 documents, 132375 entities, and 56354 relations mined from Wikipedia articles. For each (head, tail) entity pair, there are 97 different relation types as candidates to predict. The first relation type is an "NA" relation between two entities, and the rest correspond to a WikiData relation name. Each of the head/tail pair that contains valid relations also includes a set of evidence sentences.

We follow the same setting in [Yao *et al.*, 2019] to split the data into Train/Development/Test for model evaluation for fair comparisons. The number of documents in Train/Development/Test is 3000/1000/1000, respectively. The dataset is evaluated with the metrics of relation extraction **RE F1**, and evidence **Evi F1**. There are also instances where relational facts may occur in both the development and train set, so we also evaluate **Ign RE F1**, which removes these relational facts.

4.2 Experimental Setup

Hyper-parameter Setting. The configuration for the $\text{BERT}_{\text{BASE}}$ model follows the setting in [Devlin *et al.*, 2019]. We set the learning rate to 1e-5, λ_a to 1e-4, the hidden dimension of the relation vectors to 108, and extract internal attention probabilities from last three BERT layers.

We conduct our experiments by fine-tuning the $\text{BERT}_{\text{BASE}}$ model. The implementation is based on the HuggingFace [Wolf *et al.*, 2020] PyTorch [Paszke *et al.*, 2017] implementation of BERT[3]. The DocRED baseline and our *E2GRE* model have 115M parameters[4]. We implement a RoBERTa-large model for the public leaderboard.

Baseline models. We compare our framework with the following published models.

1. *Context Aware BiLSTM.* [Yao *et al.*, 2019] introduced the original baseline to DocRED in their paper. They used a context-aware BiLSTM (+ additional features such as entity type, coreference and

[3]https://github.com/huggingface/pytorch-pretrained-BERT

[4]We will release the code after paper review.

Model	Dev			Test		
	Ign F_1	RE F_1	Evi F_1	Ign F_1	RE F_1	Evi F_1
Baseline Models						
BiLSTM [Yao *et al.*, 2019]	45.12	50.95	-	44.73	51.06	-
$\text{BERT}_{\text{BASE}}$ [Wang *et al.*, 2019]	-	54.16	-	-	53.20	-
Transformer-based Models						
$\text{BERT-TS}_{\text{BASE}}$ [Wang *et al.*, 2019]	-	54.32	-	-	53.92	-
$\text{HIN-BERT}_{\text{BASE}}$ [Tang *et al.*, 2020]	54.29	56.31	-	53.70	55.60	-
$\text{CorefBERT}_{\text{BASE}}$ [Ye *et al.*, 2020]	55.32	57.51	-	54.54	56.96	-
$\text{BERT-LSR}_{\text{BASE}}$ [Nan *et al.*, 2020]	52.43	59.00	-	56.97	59.05	-
$\text{CorefRoBERTa}_{\text{LARGE}}$ [Ye *et al.*, 2020]	57.84	59.93	-	57.68	59.91	-
$\text{RoBERTa-ATLOP}_{\text{LARGE}}$[Zhou *et al.*, 2021]	**61.32**	**63.18**	-	**61.39**	**63.40**	-
Joint Frameworks						
$\text{BERT}_{\text{BASE}}$-Joint Training	-	55.04	43.13	-	-	-
BiLSTM-Joint Training [Yao *et al.*, 2019]	-	-	-	44.60	51.10	43.8
Ours						
$\text{E2GRE-BERT}_{\text{BASE}}$	55.22	58.72	47.14	55.4	57.80	48.35
$\text{E2GRE-RoBERTa}_{\text{LARGE}}$	59.55	62.91	**51.11**	60.29	62.51	**50.51**

Table 1: **Main results (%) on the development and test set of DocRED.** We report the official test score of the best checkpoint on the development set. Our *E2GRE* framework is competitive with the top of the current DocRED leaderboard, and is the best on the public leaderboard for evidence prediction.

distance) to encode the document. Head and tail entities are then extracted for relation extraction.

2. *BERT Two-Step*. [Wang et al., 2019] introduced finetuning BERT in a two-step process, where the model first does predicts the NA relation, and then predicts the rest of the relations.

3. *HIN*. [Tang *et al.*, 2020] introduced using a hierarchical inference network to help aggregate the information from entity to sentence and further to document-level in order to obtain semantic reasoning over an entire document.

4. *CorefBERT*. [Ye et al., 2020] introduced a way of pretraining BERT in order to encourage the model to look more at relations between the coreferences of different noun phrases.

5. *BERT+LSR*. [Nan *et al.*, 2020] introduced an induced latent graph structure to help learn how the information should flow between entities and sentences within a document.

6. *ATLOP*. [Zhou *et al.*, 2021] introduced adaptive thresholding and localized context pooling to help alleviate multi-label and multi-entity issues in document-level RE.

4.3 Main Results

Table 1 presents the main results of our proposed *E2GRE* framework, compared with other published results. From this table, we observe that:

- Our RE result is highly competitive with the best published models using $\text{BERT}_{\text{BASE}}$ model. Our proposed framework is also the only one which solves the dual task of evidence prediction, while taking advantage of evidence sentences for relation extraction.
- By replacing $\text{BERT}_{\text{BASE}}$ with $\text{RoBERTa}_{\text{LARGE}}$, we obtain SOTA performance on the DocRED leaderboard. Our test result ranks top 3 on the public leaderboard for relation extraction, and top 1 for evidence prediction [5], which shows that our *E2GRE* is both effective and mutually beneficial for relation extraction and evidence prediction.

We see that our framework significantly boosts F1 scores on both relation extract and evidence prediction compared to previous $\text{BERT}_{\text{BASE}}$ models. Even though we do not have the state-of-the-art performance on relation extraction, we are the first paper to show that with appropriate joint training of RE and evidence prediction we can effectively improve performance for both. [6]

Table 2 compares our proposed *E2GRE* with the joint-training BERT baseline, as described in our

[5]At the time of the submission date

[6]The original DocRED paper [Yao *et al.*, 2019] did not report improvement of RE from joint training.

Models	Multi-Mention			Multi-Evidence		
	R	P	F1	R	P	F1
Relation Extraction						
$\text{BERT}_{\text{BASE}}$-Joint Training	52.42	43.88	47.77	51.20	37.55	43.33
E2GRE-$\text{BERT}_{\text{BASE}}$	55.84	47.75	**51.47**	53.04	40.78	**46.11**
Evidence Predictions						
$\text{BERT}_{\text{BASE}}$-Joint Training	42.59	31.21	36.02	40.44	34.68	37.34
E2GRE-$\text{BERT}_{\text{BASE}}$	42.04	37.78	**39.79**	38.34	40.83	**39.54**

Table 2: Analysis of how Evidence Prediction (EP) impact on Relation Extraction (RE) in the joint training framework. Results on recall, precision and F1 are shown on the dev set with BERT base model.

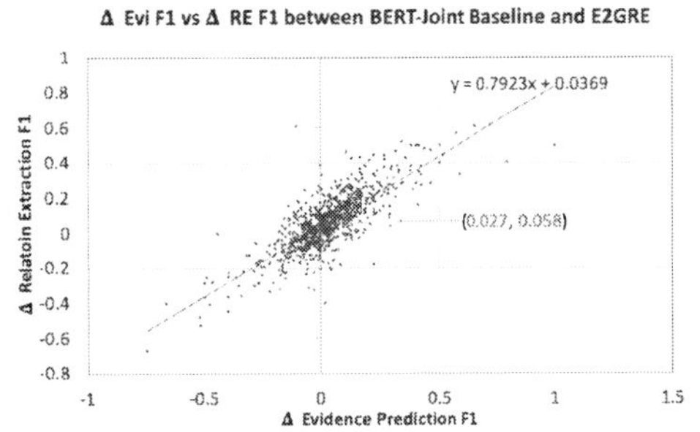

Figure 3: Plot showing the change in RE F1 and EVI F1 from $\text{BERT}_{\text{BASE}}$-Joint Training to our E2GRE-$\text{BERT}_{\text{BASE}}$ model for each document in the dev set.

model section on evidence prediction. We examine the comparison under two challenging scenarios in the dev set: 1) entity pairs which consists of multiple mentions in a document; and 2) entity pairs with multiple evidence sentences for evidence prediction.

From Table 2, we observe that: *E2GRE* shows consistent improvement in terms of F1 on both settings. This is due to the evidence guided attention probabilities from the pretrained LM which helps extract relevant contexts from the document. These relevant contexts further benefit the relation extraction and thus result in significant F1 improvement comparing to the baseline. In summary, our implementation of evidence prediction enhances the performance of relation extraction, and the utilization of a pretrained LM's internal attention probability is a more effective way for joint training.

4.4 Ablation Study

To explore the contribution of different components in our *E2GRE*, we conduct an ablation study in Table 3. We start off with our full *E2GRE*, and consecutively remove the evidence-guided attention and entity-guided sequences. From this table, we observe that: both entity-guided sequences and evidence-guided attentions play a significant role in improving F1 on relation extraction and evidence prediction: entity-guided sequences improve RE by about 2 $F1$ and evidence prediction by about 3.5 $F1$. Evidence-guided attentions improve RE by about 1.7 $F1$ and evidence prediction by about 1 $F1$.

We also observe that entity-guided sequences tend to help more on precision in both tasks of RE and evidence prediction. Entity-guided sequences help by grounding the model to focus on the correct entities, allowing it to be more precise in its information extraction. In contrast, evidence-guided attentions tend to help more on recall in both tasks of RE and evidence prediction.These attentions help by giving more guidance to locate relevant contexts, therefore increasing the recall of RE and evidence prediction.

Model	Recall	Precision	F1
Relation Extraction			
E2GRE-$\text{BERT}_{\text{BASE}}$	**59.09**	56.95	**58.72**
− Evidence-guided attentions	54.07	**60.43**	57.08
− Entity-guided inputs	55.06	55.02	55.04
Evidence Prediction			
E2GRE-$\text{BERT}_{\text{BASE}}$	**44.83**	49.75	**47.14**
− Evidence-guided attentions	43.10	**49.66**	46.15
− Entity-guided inputs	47.50	38.91	43.13

Table 3: Ablation study on evidence guided attentions and entity guided input sequence components, by removing attention extraction module in Figure 2, and entity-guided input sequences consecutively on the dev set.

4.5 Analysis on number of BERT layers

Table 4 shows the impact of the number of BERT layers from which the attention probabilities are extracted on evidence prediction and relation extraction. We observe that using the last 3 layers is better than using the last 6 layers. This is because later layers in pretrained LMs tend to focus more on semantic information, whereas earlier layers focus more on syntactic information [Clark *et al.*, 2019]. We hypothesize that the last 6 layers may include noisy information related to syntax.

4.6 Analysis on Evidence/Relation Interdependence

In Fig. 3, we plot the change in RE F1 and EVI F1 between $\text{BERT}_{\text{BASE}}$-Joint Training and our E2GRE-$\text{BERT}_{\text{BASE}}$. We observe that RE F1 and EVI F1 are closely linked, with a coefficient of

Model	Recall	Precision	F1
Relation Extraction			
w/o attention	54.07	60.43	57.08
Last 3 Layers	59.09	56.95	**58.72**
Last 6 Layers	61.87	54.14	58.51
Evidence Prediction			
w/o attention	43.10	49.05	46.15
Last 3 Layers	44.83	49.75	**47.14**
Last 6 Layers	46.34	48.19	46.90

Table 4: Analysis on the number of BERT layers for relation extraction and evidence prediction. Results are shown on dev set.

Model	10%	30%	50%
Relation Extraction			
$\text{BERT}_{\text{BASE}}$-Joint Training	40.00	47.12	52.88
E2GRE-$\text{BERT}_{\text{BASE}}$	**47.37**	**53.48**	**56.55**
Evidence Prediction			
$\text{BERT}_{\text{BASE}}$-Joint Training	21.15	30.70	38.25
E2GRE-$\text{BERT}_{\text{BASE}}$	**36.27**	**41.92**	**44.82**

Table 5: Analysis on how our E2GRE model performs on 10%, 30%, and 50% data for relation extraction.

0.7923, showing that when EVI F1 improves, RE F1 also improves. We observe that the centroid of the points lies in the first quadrant $(2.7\%, 5.8\%)$, showing the overall improvement of our model.

Furthermore, we analyze the effectiveness of our E2GRE model with smaller amounts of training data. Table. 5 shows that our model achieves much larger gains on RE F1 when training with 10, 30 and 50% of the data. E2GRE-$\text{BERT}_{\text{BASE}}$ is able to achieve bigger improvements with less data, as attention probabilities used for evidence prediction provides a effective guidance for relation extraction.

5 Conclusion

In this paper we propose a simple, yet effective joint training framework *E2GRE* (Entity and Evidence Guided Relation Extraction) for relation extraction and evidence prediction on DocRED. In order to more effectively exploit pretrained LMs for document-level RE, we first generate new entity-guided sequences to feed into an LM, focusing the model on the relevant areas in the document. Then we utilize the internal attentions extracted from the last few layers to help guide the LM to focus on relevant sentences for evidence prediction. Our *E2GRE* method improves performance on both RE and evidence prediction, and achieves the state-of-the-art performance on the DocRED public leaderboard. We show that evidence prediction is an important task that helps RE models perform better.

References

Livio Baldini Soares, Nicholas FitzGerald, Jeffrey Ling, and Tom Kwiatkowski. Matching the blanks: Distributional similarity for relation learning. In *ACL*, 2019.

Razvan Bunescu and Raymond Mooney. A shortest path dependency kernel for relation extraction. In *EMNLP*, Vancouver, British Columbia, Canada, October 2005.

Rui Cai, Xiaodong Zhang, and Houfeng Wang. Bidirectional recurrent convolutional neural network for relation classification. In *ACL*, Berlin, Germany, August 2016.

Fenia Christopoulou, Makoto Miwa, and Sophia Ananiadou. Connecting the dots: Document-level neural relation extraction with edge-oriented graphs. In *EMNLP*, Hong Kong, China, November 2019.

Kevin Clark, Urvashi Khandelwal, Omer Levy, and Christopher D. Manning. What does BERT look at? an analysis of BERT's attention. In *ACL*, 2019.

Jacob Devlin, Ming-Wei Chang, Kenton Lee, and Kristina Toutanova. BERT: Pre-training of deep bidirectional transformers for language understanding. In *NAACL*, 2019.

Markus Eberts and Adrian Ulges. Span-based joint entity and relation extraction with transformer pre-training. 09 2019.

Zhijiang Guo, Yan Zhang, and Wei Lu. Attention guided graph convolutional networks for relation extraction. In *ACL*, Florence, Italy, July 2019.

Xu Han, Pengfei Yu, Zhiyuan Liu, Maosong Sun, and Peng Li. Hierarchical relation extraction with coarse-to-fine grained attention. In *EMNLP*, Brussels, Belgium, October-November 2018.

Robin Jia, Cliff Wong, and Hoifung Poon. Document-level n-ary relation extraction with multiscale representation learning. In *NAACL*, Minneapolis, Minnesota, June 2019.

Bo Li, Wei Ye, Zhonghao Sheng, Rui Xie, Xiangyu Xi, and Shikun Zhang. Graph enhanced dual attention network for document-level relation extraction. In *Proceedings of the 28th International Conference on Computational Linguistics*, 2020.

Yinhan Liu, Myle Ott, Naman Goyal, Jingfei Du, Mandar Joshi, Danqi Chen, Omer Levy, Mike Lewis, Luke Zettlemoyer, and Veselin Stoyanov. Roberta: A robustly optimized bert pretraining approach, 2019.

Guoshun Nan, Zhijiang Guo, Ivan Sekulić, and Wei Lu. Reasoning with latent structure refinement for document-level relation extraction. In *ACL*, 2020.

Adam Paszke, Sam Gross, Soumith Chintala, Gregory Chanan, Edward Yang, Zachary DeVito, Zeming Lin, Alban Desmaison, Luca Antiga, and Adam Lerer. Automatic differentiation in pytorch. 2017.

Chris Quirk and Hoifung Poon. Distant supervision for relation extraction beyond the sentence boundary. In *ACL*, Valencia, Spain, April 2017. ACL.

Alec Radford, Jeff Wu, Rewon Child, David Luan, Dario Amodei, and Ilya Sutskever. Language models are unsupervised multitask learners. 2019.

Hengzhu Tang, Yanan Cao, Zhenyu Zhang, Jiangxia Cao, Fang Fang, Shi Wang, and Pengfei Yin. Hin: Hierarchical inference network for document-level relation extraction. In *PAKDD*, 2020.

Bayu Distiawan Trisedya, Gerhard Weikum, Jianzhong Qi, and Rui Zhang. Neural relation extraction for knowledge base enrichment. In *ACL*, Florence, Italy, July 2019. ACL.

Ashish Vaswani, Noam Shazeer, Niki Parmar, Jakob Uszkoreit, Llion Jones, Aidan N. Gomez, Lukasz Kaiser, and Illia Polosukhin. Attention is all you need. *NeurIPS*, 2017.

David Wadden, Ulme Wennberg, Yi Luan, and Hannaneh Hajishirzi. Entity, relation, and event extraction with contextualized span representations. In *EMNLP*, Hong Kong, China, November 2019.

Linlin Wang, Zhu Cao, Gerard de Melo, and Zhiyuan Liu. Relation classification via multi-level attention CNNs. In *ACL*, Berlin, Germany, August 2016. ACL.

Hong Wang, Christfried Focke, Rob Sylvester, Nilesh Mishra, and William Wang. Fine-tune bert for docred with two-step process, 2019.

Thomas Wolf, Lysandre Debut, Victor Sanh, Julien Chaumond, Clement Delangue, Anthony Moi, Pierric Cistac, Tim Rault, Rémi Louf, Morgan Funtowicz, Joe Davison, Sam Shleifer, Patrick von Platen, Clara Ma, Yacine Jernite, Julien Plu, Canwen Xu, Teven Le Scao, Sylvain Gugger, Mariama Drame, Quentin Lhoest, and Alexander M. Rush. Huggingface's transformers: State-of-the-art natural language processing, 2020.

Yuan Yao, Deming Ye, Peng Li, Xu Han, Yankai Lin, Zhenghao Liu, Zhiyuan Liu, Lixin Huang, Jie Zhou, and Maosong Sun. DocRED: A large-scale document-level relation extraction dataset. In *ACL*, 2019.

Deming Ye, Yankai Lin, Jiaju Du, Zhenghao Liu, Maosong Sun, and Zhiyuan Liu. Coreferential reasoning learning for language representation. *ArXiv*, abs/2004.06870, 2020.

Tom Young, Erik Cambria Cambria, Iti Chaturvedi, Minlie Huang, Hao Zhou, and Subham Biswas. Augmenting end-to-end dialog systems with commonsense knowledge. In *AAAI*, 2018.

Mo Yu, Wenpeng Yin, Kazi Saidul Hasan, Cicero dos Santos, Bing Xiang, and Bowen Zhou. Improved neural relation detection for knowledge base question answering. In *ACL*, July 2017.

Dmitry Zelenko, Chinatsu Aone, and Anthony Richardella. Kernel methods for relation extraction. *Journal of Machine Learning Research*, 3:1083–1106, 08 2003.

Daojian Zeng, Kang Liu, Siwei Lai, Guangyou Zhou, and Jun Zhao. Relation classification via convolutional deep neural network. In *COLING*.

Yuhao Zhang, Victor Zhong, Danqi Chen, Gabor Angeli, and Christopher D. Manning. Position-aware attention and supervised data improve slot filling. In *Proceedings of the 2017 Conference on Empirical Methods in Natural Language Processing (EMNLP 2017)*, 2017.

Yi Zhao, Huaiyu Wan, Jianwei Gao, and Youfang Lin. Improving relation classification by entity pair graph. In Wee Sun Lee and Taiji Suzuki, editors, *ACML*, volume 101, Nagoya, Japan, 2019.

Wenxuan Zhou, Kevin Huang, Tengyu Ma, and Jing Huang. Document-level relation extraction with adaptive thresholding and localized context pooling. In *AAAI*, 2021.

Scaling Deep Contrastive Learning Batch Size under Memory Limited Setup

Luyu Gao[1], **Yunyi Zhang**[2], **Jiawei Han**[2], **Jamie Callan**[1]
[1] Language Technologies Institute, Carnegie Mellon University
[2] Department of Computer Science, University of Illinois Urbana-Champaign
[1]{luyug, callan}@cs.cmu.edu [2]{yzhan238, hanj}@illionis.edu

Abstract

Contrastive learning has been applied successfully to learn vector representations of text. Previous research demonstrated that learning high-quality representations benefits from batch-wise contrastive loss with a large number of negatives. In practice, the technique of in-batch negative is used, where for each example in a batch, other batch examples' positives will be taken as its negatives, avoiding encoding extra negatives. This, however, still conditions each example's loss on all batch examples and requires fitting the entire large batch into GPU memory. This paper introduces a gradient caching technique that decouples backpropagation between contrastive loss and the encoder, removing encoder backward pass data dependency along the batch dimension. As a result, gradients can be computed for one subset of the batch at a time, leading to almost constant memory usage. [1]

1 Introduction

Contrastive learning learns to encode data into an embedding space such that related data points have closer representations and unrelated ones have further apart ones. Recent works in NLP adopt deep neural nets as encoders and use unsupervised contrastive learning on sentence representation (Giorgi et al., 2020), text retrieval (Lee et al., 2019), and language model pre-training tasks (Wu et al., 2020). Supervised contrastive learning (Khosla et al., 2020) has also been shown effective in training dense retrievers (Karpukhin et al., 2020; Qu et al., 2020). These works typically use batch-wise contrastive loss, sharing target texts as in-batch negatives. With such a technique, previous works have empirically shown that larger batches help learn better representations. However, computing loss and updating model parameters with respect to a big batch require encoding all batch data and storing all activation, so batch size is limited by total available GPU memory. This limits application and research of contrastive learning methods under memory limited setup, e.g. academia. For example, Lee et al. (2019) pre-train a BERT (Devlin et al., 2019) passage encoder with a batch size of 4096 while a high-end commercial GPU RTX 2080ti can only fit a batch of 8. The gradient accumulation technique, splitting a large batch into chunks and summing gradients across several backwards, cannot emulate a large batch as each smaller chunk has fewer in-batch negatives.

In this paper, we present a simple technique that thresholds peak memory usage for contrastive learning to almost constant regardless of the batch size. For deep contrastive learning, the memory bottlenecks are at the deep neural network based encoder. We observe that we can separate the back-propagation process of contrastive loss into two parts, from loss to representation, and from representation to model parameter, with the latter being independent across batch examples given the former, detailed in subsection 3.2. We then show in subsection 3.3 that by separately pre-computing the representations' gradient and store them in a cache, we can break the update of the encoder into multiple sub-updates that can fit into the GPU memory. This pre-computation of gradients allows our method to produce the *exact same* gradient update as training with large batch. Experiments show that with about 20% increase in runtime, our technique enables a single consumer-grade GPU to reproduce the state-of-the-art large batch trained models that used to require multiple professional GPUs.

2 Related Work

Contrastive Learning First introduced for probablistic language modeling (Mnih and Teh, 2012),

[1]Our code is at `github.com/luyug/GradCache`.

Proceedings of the 6th Workshop on Representation Learning for NLP (RepL4NLP-2021), pages 316–321
Bangkok, Thailand (Online), August 6, 2021.

Noise Contrastive Estimation (NCE) was later used by Word2Vec (Mikolov et al., 2013) to learn word embedding. Recent works use contrastive learning to unsupervisedly pre-train (Lee et al., 2019; Chang et al., 2020) as well as supervisedly train dense retriever (Karpukhin et al., 2020), where contrastive loss is used to estimate retrieval probability over the entire corpus. Inspired by SimCLR (Chen et al., 2020), constrastive learning is used to learn better sentence representation (Giorgi et al., 2020) and pre-trained language model (Wu et al., 2020).

Deep Network Memory Reduction Many existing techniques deal with large and deep models. The gradient checkpoint method attempts to emulate training deep networks by training shallower layers and connecting them with gradient checkpoints and re-computation (Chen et al., 2016). Some methods also use reversible activation functions, allowing internal activation in the network to be recovered throughout back propagation (Gomez et al., 2017; MacKay et al., 2018). However, their effectiveness as part of contrastive encoders has not been confirmed. Recent work also attempts to remove the redundancy in optimizer tracked parameters on each GPU (Rajbhandari et al., 2020). Compared with the aforementioned methods, our method is designed for scaling over the batch size dimension for contrastive learning.

3 Methodologies

In this section, we formally introduce the notations for contrastive loss and analyze the difficulties of using it on limited hardware. We then show how we can use a Gradient Cache technique to factor the loss so that large batch gradient update can be broken into several sub-updates.

3.1 Preliminaries

Under a general formulation, given two classes of data $\mathcal{S}, \mathcal{T}$, we want to learn encoders f and g for each such that, given $s \in \mathcal{S}, t \in \mathcal{T}$, encoded representations $f(s)$ and $g(t)$ are close if related and far apart if not related by some distance measurement. For large $\mathcal{S}$ and $\mathcal{T}$ and deep neural network based f and g, direct training is not tractable, so a common approach is to use a contrastive loss: sample anchors $S \subset \mathcal{S}$ and targets $T \subset \mathcal{T}$ as a training batch, where each element $s_i \in S$ has a related element $t_{r_i} \in T$ as well as zero or more specially sampled hard negatives. The rest of the random samples in T will be used as in-batch negatives.

Define loss based on dot product as follows:

$$\mathcal{L} = -\frac{1}{|S|} \sum_{s_i \in S} \log \frac{exp(f(s_i)^\top g(t_{r_i})/\tau)}{\sum_{t_j \in T} exp(f(s_i)^\top g(t_j)/\tau)} \tag{1}$$

where each summation term depends on the *entire* set T and requires fitting *all* of them into memory.

We set temperature $\tau = 1$ in the following discussion for simplicity as in general it only adds a constant multiplier to the gradient.

3.2 Analysis of Computation

In this section, we give a mathematical analysis of contrastive loss computation and its gradient. We show that the back propagation process can be divided into two parts, from loss to representation, and from representation to encoder model. The separation then enables us to devise a technique that removes data dependency in encoder parameter update. Suppose the function f is parameterized with Θ and g is parameterized with Λ.

$$\frac{\partial \mathcal{L}}{\partial \Theta} = \sum_{s_i \in S} \frac{\partial \mathcal{L}}{\partial f(s_i)} \frac{\partial f(s_i)}{\partial \Theta} \tag{2}$$

$$\frac{\partial \mathcal{L}}{\partial \Lambda} = \sum_{t_j \in T} \frac{\partial \mathcal{L}}{\partial g(t_j)} \frac{\partial g(t_j)}{\partial \Lambda} \tag{3}$$

As an extra notation, denote normalized similarity,

$$p_{ij} = \frac{exp(f(s_i)^\top g(t_j))}{\sum_{t \in T} exp(f(s_i)^\top g(t))} \tag{4}$$

We note that the summation term for a particular s_i or t_i is a function of the batch, as,

$$\frac{\partial \mathcal{L}}{\partial f(s_i)} = -\frac{1}{|S|} \left(g(t_{r_i}) - \sum_{t_j \in T} p_{ij} g(t_j) \right), \tag{5}$$

$$\frac{\partial \mathcal{L}}{\partial g(t_j)} = -\frac{1}{|S|} \left(\epsilon_j - \sum_{s_i \in S} p_{ij} f(s_i) \right), \tag{6}$$

where

$$\epsilon_j = \begin{cases} f(s_k) & \text{if } \exists\, k \text{ s.t. } r_k = j \\ 0 & \text{otherwise} \end{cases} \tag{7}$$

which prohibits the use of gradient accumulation. We make two observations here:

- The partial derivative $\frac{\partial f(s_i)}{\partial \Theta}$ depends only on s_i and Θ while $\frac{\partial g(t_j)}{\partial \Lambda}$ depends only on t_j and Λ; and

- Computing partial derivatives $\frac{\partial \mathcal{L}}{\partial f(s_i)}$ and $\frac{\partial \mathcal{L}}{\partial g(t_j)}$ requires only encoded representations, but not Θ or Λ.

These observations mean back propagation of $f(s_i)$ for data s_i can be run independently with its own computation graph and activation if the *numerical* value of the partial derivative $\frac{\partial \mathcal{L}}{\partial s_i}$ is known. Meanwhile the derivation of $\frac{\partial \mathcal{L}}{\partial s_i}$ requires only *numerical* values of two sets of representation vectors $F = \{f(s_1), f(s_2), .., f(s_{|S|})\}$ and $G = \{g(t_1), g(t_2), ..., g(t_{|T|})\}$. A similar argument holds true for g, where we can use representation vectors to compute $\frac{\partial \mathcal{L}}{\partial t_j}$ and back propagate for each $g(t_j)$ independently. In the next section, we will describe how to scale up batch size by pre-computing these representation vectors.

3.3 Gradient Cache Technique

Given a large batch that does not fit into the available GPU memory for training, we first divide it into a set of sub-batches each of which can fit into memory for gradient computation, denoted as $\mathbb{S} = \{\hat{S}_1, \hat{S}_2, ..\}, \mathbb{T} = \{\hat{T}_1, \hat{T}_2, ..\}$. The full-batch gradient update is computed by the following steps.

Step1: Graph-less Forward Before gradient computation, we first run an extra encoder forward pass for each batch instance to get its representation. Importantly, this forward pass runs without constructing the computation graph. We collect and store all representations computed.

Step2: Representation Gradient Computation and Caching We then compute the contrastive loss for the batch based on the representation from Step1 and have a corresponding computation graph constructed. Despite the mathematical derivation, automatic differentiation system is used in actual implementation, which automatically supports variations of contrastive loss. A backward pass is then run to populate gradients for each representation. Note that the encoder is not included in this gradient computation. Let $\mathbf{u}_i = \frac{\partial \mathcal{L}}{\partial f(s_i)}$ and $\mathbf{v}_i = \frac{\partial \mathcal{L}}{\partial g(t_i)}$, we take these gradient tensors and store them as a *Representation Gradient Cache*, $[\mathbf{u}_1, \mathbf{u}_2, .., \mathbf{v}_1, \mathbf{v}_2, ..]$.

Step3: Sub-batch Gradient Accumulation We run encoder forward one sub-batch at a time to compute representations and build the corresponding computation graph. We take the sub-batch's representation gradients from the cache and run back propagation through the encoder. Gradients are accumulated for encoder parameters across all sub-batches. Effectively for f we have,

$$\begin{aligned}\frac{\partial \mathcal{L}}{\partial \Theta} &= \sum_{\hat{S}_j \in \mathbb{S}} \sum_{s_i \in \hat{S}_j} \frac{\partial \mathcal{L}}{\partial f(s_i)} \frac{\partial f(s_i)}{\partial \Theta} \\ &= \sum_{\hat{S}_j \in \mathbb{S}} \sum_{s_i \in \hat{S}_j} \mathbf{u}_i \frac{\partial f(s_i)}{\partial \Theta}\end{aligned} \tag{8}$$

where the outer summation enumerates each sub-batch and the entire internal summation corresponds to one step of accumulation. Similarly, for g, gradients accumulate based on,

$$\frac{\partial \mathcal{L}}{\partial \Lambda} = \sum_{\hat{T}_j \in \mathbb{T}} \sum_{t_i \in \hat{T}_j} \mathbf{v}_i \frac{\partial g(t_i)}{\partial \Lambda} \tag{9}$$

Here we can see the *equivalence* with direct large batch update by combining the two summations.

Step4: Optimization When all sub-batches are processed, we can step the optimizer to update model parameters as if the full batch is processed in a single forward-backward pass.

Compared to directly updating with the full batch, which requires memory linear to the number of examples, our method fixes the number of examples in each encoder gradient computation to be the size of sub-batch and therefore requires constant memory for encoder forward-backward pass. The extra data pieces introduced by our method that remain persistent across steps are the representations and their corresponding gradients with the former turned into the latter after representation gradient computation. Consequently, in a general case with data from S and T each represented with d dimension vectors, we only need to store $(|S|d + |T|d)$ floating points in the cache on top of the computation graph. To remind our readers, this is several orders smaller than million-size model parameters.

3.4 Multi-GPU Training

When training on multiple GPUs, we need to compute the gradients with all examples across all GPUs. This requires a single additional cross GPU communication after *Step1* when all representations are computed. We use an all-gather operation to make all representations available on all GPUs. Denote F^n, G^n representations on n-th GPU and a total of N device. *Step2* runs with gathered representations $F^{\text{all}} = F^1 \cup .. \cup F^N$ and $G^{\text{all}} = G^1 \cup .. \cup G^N$. While F^{all} and G^{all} are used

Method	Top-5	Top-20	Top-100
DPR	-	78.4	85.4
Sequential	59.3	71.9	80.9
Accumulation	64.3	77.2	84.9
Cache	68.6	79.3	86.0
- BSZ = 512	68.3	79.9	86.6

Table 1: Retrieval: We compare top-5/20/100 hit accuracy of small batch update (Sequential), accumulated small batch (Accumulation) and gradient cache (Cache) systems with DPR reference.

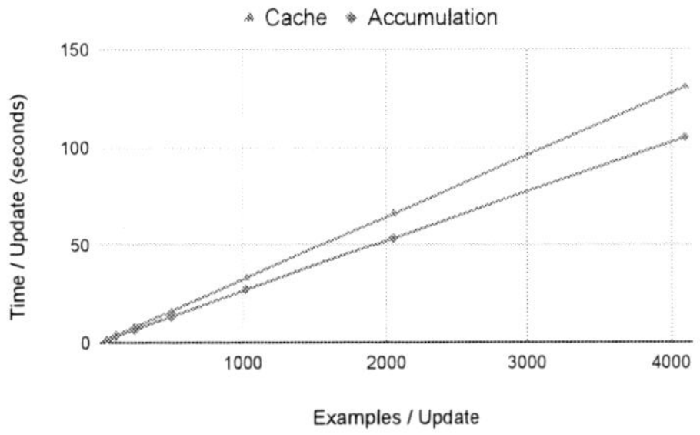

Figure 1: We compare training speed versus the number of examples per update for gradient cache (Cache) and gradient accumulation (Accumulation).

to compute loss, the n-th GPU only computes gradient of its local representations F^n, G^n and stores them into cache. No communication happens in *Step3*, when each GPU independently computes gradient for local representations. *Step4* will then perform gradient reduction across GPUs as with standard parallel training.

4 Experiments

To examine the reliability and computation cost of our method, we implement our method into dense passage retriever (DPR; Karpukhin et al. (2020))[2]. We use gradient cache to compute DPR's supervised contrastive loss on a single GPU. Following DPR paper, we measure top hit accuracy on the Natural Question Dataset (Kwiatkowski et al., 2019) for different methods. We then examine the training speed of various batch sizes.

4.1 Retrieval Accuracy

Compared Systems 1) **DPR**: the reference number taken from the original paper trained on 8 GPUs, 2) **Sequential**: update with max batch size that fits into 1 GPU, 3) **Accumulation**: similar to Sequential but accumulate gradients and update until number of examples matches DPR setup, 4) **Cache**: training with DPR setup using our gradient cache on 1 GPU. We attempted to run with gradient checkpointing but found it cannot scale to standard DPR batch size on our hardware.

Implementations All runs start with the same random seed and follow DPR training hyperparameters except batch size. Cache uses a batch size of 128 same as DPR and runs with a sub-batch size of 16 for questions and 8 for passages. We also run Cache with a batch size of 512 (BSZ=512) to examine the behavior of even larger batches. Sequential uses a batch size of 8, the largest that fits into memory. Accumulation will accumulate 16 of size-8 batches. Each question is paired with a positive and a BM25 negative passage. All experiments use a single RTX 2080ti.

Results Accuracy results are shown in Table 1. We observe that Cache performs better than DPR reference due to randomness in training. Further increasing batch size to 512 can bring in some advantage at top 20/100. Accumulation and Sequential results confirm the importance of a bigger batch and more negatives. For Accumulation which tries to match the batch size but has fewer negatives, we see a drop in performance which is larger towards the top. In the sequential case, a smaller batch incurs higher variance, and the performance further drops. In summary, our Cache method improves over standard methods and matches the performance of large batch training.

4.2 Training Speed

In Figure 1, we compare update speed of gradient cache and accumulation with per update example number of $\{64, 128, 256, 512, 1024, 2048, 4096\}$. We observe gradient cache method can steadily scale up to larger batch update and uses 20% more time for representation pre-computation. This extra cost enables it to create an update of a much larger batch critical for the best performance, as shown by previous experiments and many early works. While the original DPR reports a training time of roughly one day on 8 V100 GPUs, in practice, with improved data loading, our gradient cache code can train a dense retriever in a practical 31 hours on a single RTX2080ti. We also find gradient checkpoint only runs up to batch of 64 and consumes

[2]Our implementation is at: `https://github.com/luyug/GC-DPR`

twice the amount of time than accumulation[3].

5 Extend to Deep Distance Function

Previous discussion assumes a simple parameter-less dot product similarity. In general it can also be deep distance function Φ richly parameterized by Ω, formally,

$$d_{ij} = d(s_i, t_j) = \Phi(f(s_i), g(t_j)) \tag{10}$$

This can still scale by introducing an extra *Distance Gradient Cache*. In the first forward we collect all representations as well as all distances. We compute loss with d_{ij}s and back propagate to get $w_{ij} = \frac{\partial \mathcal{L}}{\partial d_{ij}}$, and store them in Distance Gradient Cache, $[w_{00}, w_{01}, .., w_{10}, ..]$. We can then update Ω in a sub-batch manner,

$$\frac{\partial \mathcal{L}}{\partial \Omega} = \sum_{\hat{S} \in \mathbb{S}} \sum_{\hat{T} \in \mathbb{T}} \sum_{s_i \in \hat{S}} \sum_{t_j \in \hat{T}} w_{ij} \frac{\partial \Phi(f(s_i), g(t_j))}{\partial \Omega} \tag{11}$$

Additionally, we *simultaneously* compute with the constructed computation graph $\frac{\partial d_{ij}}{\partial f(s_i)}$ and $\frac{\partial d_{ij}}{\partial g(t_j)}$ and accumulate across batches,

$$\mathbf{u}_i = \frac{\partial \mathcal{L}}{\partial f(s_i)} = \sum_j w_{ij} \frac{\partial d_{ij}}{\partial f(s_i)} \tag{12}$$

and,

$$\mathbf{v}_j = \frac{\partial \mathcal{L}}{\partial g(t_j)} = \sum_i w_{ij} \frac{\partial d_{ij}}{\partial g(t_j)} \tag{13}$$

with which we can build up the Representation Gradient Cache. When all representations' gradients are computed and stored, encoder gradient can be computed with *Step3* described in subsection 3.3. In philosophy this method links up two caches. Note this covers early interaction $f(s) = s, g(t) = t$ as a special case.

6 Conclusion

In this paper, we introduce a gradient cache technique that breaks GPU memory limitations for large batch contrastive learning. We propose to construct a representation gradient cache that removes in-batch data dependency in encoder optimization. Our method produces the exact same gradient update as training with a large batch. We show the method is efficient and capable of preserving accuracy on resource-limited hardware. We believe a critical contribution of our work is providing a large population in the NLP community with access to batch-wise contrastive learning. While many previous works come from people with industry-grade hardware, researchers with limited hardware can now use our technique to reproduce state-of-the-art models and further advance the research without being constrained by available GPU memory.

Acknowledgments

The authors would like to thank Zhuyun Dai and Chenyan Xiong for comments on the paper, and the anonymous reviewers for their reviews.

[3] We used the gradient checkpoint implemented in Huggingface transformers package

References

Wei-Cheng Chang, Felix X. Yu, Yin-Wen Chang, Yiming Yang, and Sanjiv Kumar. 2020. Pre-training tasks for embedding-based large-scale retrieval. In *8th International Conference on Learning Representations, ICLR 2020, Addis Ababa, Ethiopia, April 26-30, 2020*. OpenReview.net.

T. Chen, B. Xu, C. Zhang, and Carlos Guestrin. 2016. Training deep nets with sublinear memory cost. *ArXiv*, abs/1604.06174.

Ting Chen, Simon Kornblith, Mohammad Norouzi, and Geoffrey E. Hinton. 2020. A simple framework for contrastive learning of visual representations. *ArXiv*, abs/2002.05709.

Jacob Devlin, Ming-Wei Chang, Kenton Lee, and Kristina Toutanova. 2019. BERT: Pre-training of deep bidirectional transformers for language understanding. In *Proceedings of the 2019 Conference of the North American Chapter of the Association for Computational Linguistics: Human Language Technologies, Volume 1 (Long and Short Papers)*, pages 4171–4186, Minneapolis, Minnesota. Association for Computational Linguistics.

John Michael Giorgi, Osvald Nitski, Gary D Bader, and Bo Wang. 2020. Declutr: Deep contrastive learning for unsupervised textual representations. *ArXiv*, abs/2006.03659.

Aidan N. Gomez, Mengye Ren, R. Urtasun, and Roger B. Grosse. 2017. The reversible residual network: Backpropagation without storing activations. In *NIPS*.

Vladimir Karpukhin, Barlas Oguz, Sewon Min, Patrick Lewis, Ledell Wu, Sergey Edunov, Danqi Chen, and Wen-tau Yih. 2020. Dense passage retrieval for open-domain question answering. In *Proceedings of the 2020 Conference on Empirical Methods in Natural Language Processing (EMNLP)*, pages 6769–6781, Online. Association for Computational Linguistics.

Prannay Khosla, Piotr Teterwak, Chen Wang, Aaron Sarna, Yonglong Tian, Phillip Isola, Aaron Maschinot, Ce Liu, and Dilip Krishnan. 2020. Supervised contrastive learning. *arXiv preprint arXiv:2004.11362*.

T. Kwiatkowski, J. Palomaki, Olivia Redfield, Michael Collins, Ankur P. Parikh, C. Alberti, D. Epstein, Illia Polosukhin, J. Devlin, Kenton Lee, Kristina Toutanova, Llion Jones, Matthew Kelcey, Ming-Wei Chang, Andrew M. Dai, Jakob Uszkoreit, Q. Le, and Slav Petrov. 2019. Natural questions: A benchmark for question answering research. *Transactions of the Association for Computational Linguistics*, 7:453–466.

Kenton Lee, Ming-Wei Chang, and Kristina Toutanova. 2019. Latent retrieval for weakly supervised open domain question answering. In *Proceedings of the 57th Annual Meeting of the Association for Computational Linguistics*, pages 6086–6096, Florence, Italy. Association for Computational Linguistics.

Matthew MacKay, Paul Vicol, Jimmy Ba, and Roger B. Grosse. 2018. Reversible recurrent neural networks. In *NeurIPS*.

Tomas Mikolov, Ilya Sutskever, Kai Chen, G. Corrado, and J. Dean. 2013. Distributed representations of words and phrases and their compositionality. In *NIPS*.

A. Mnih and Y. Teh. 2012. A fast and simple algorithm for training neural probabilistic language models. In *ICML*.

Yingqi Qu, Yuchen Ding, Jing Liu, Kai Liu, Ruiyang Ren, Xin Zhao, Daxiang Dong, Hua Wu, and Haifeng Wang. 2020. Rocketqa: An optimized training approach to dense passage retrieval for open-domain question answering.

Samyam Rajbhandari, Jeff Rasley, Olatunji Ruwase, and Yuxiong He. 2020. Zero: Memory optimizations toward training trillion parameter models.

Z. Wu, Sinong Wang, Jiatao Gu, Madian Khabsa, Fei Sun, and Hao Ma. 2020. Clear: Contrastive learning for sentence representation. *ArXiv*, abs/2012.15466.

Direction is what you need: Improving Word Embedding Compression in Large Language Models

Klaudia Bałazy[†*], Mohammadreza Banaei[‡*], Rémi Lebret[‡], Jacek Tabor[†] and Karl Aberer[‡]

[†]Jagiellonian University

klaudia.balazy@doctoral.uj.edu.pl, jacek.tabor@uj.edu.pl

[‡]EPFL

[mohammadreza.banaei, remi.lebret, karl.aberer]@epfl.ch

Abstract

The adoption of Transformer-based models in natural language processing (NLP) has led to great success using a massive number of parameters. However, due to deployment constraints in edge devices, there has been a rising interest in the compression of these models to improve their inference time and memory footprint. This paper presents a novel loss objective to compress token embeddings in the Transformer-based models by leveraging an AutoEncoder architecture. More specifically, we emphasize the importance of the direction of compressed embeddings with respect to original uncompressed embeddings. The proposed method is task-agnostic and does not require further language modeling pre-training. Our method significantly outperforms the commonly used SVD-based matrix-factorization approach in terms of initial language model Perplexity. Moreover, we evaluate our proposed approach over SQuAD v1.1 dataset and several downstream tasks from the GLUE benchmark, where we also outperform the baseline in most scenarios. Our code is public.[1].

1 Introduction

Pretraining deep Transformer models (Vaswani et al., 2017) with language modeling and fine-tuning these models over downstream tasks have led to great success in recent years (Devlin et al., 2018; Liu et al., 2019; Yang et al., 2019), and even enabled researchers to design models that outperform human baselines in the GLUE benchmark (Wang et al., 2018). Although these models are empirically powerful in many natural language understanding (NLU) tasks, they often require a massive number of parameters, making them hard to use for memory-constrained applications (e.g., edge devices). Therefore, there have been efforts to compress BERT-like models while preserving comparable performance with the original model.

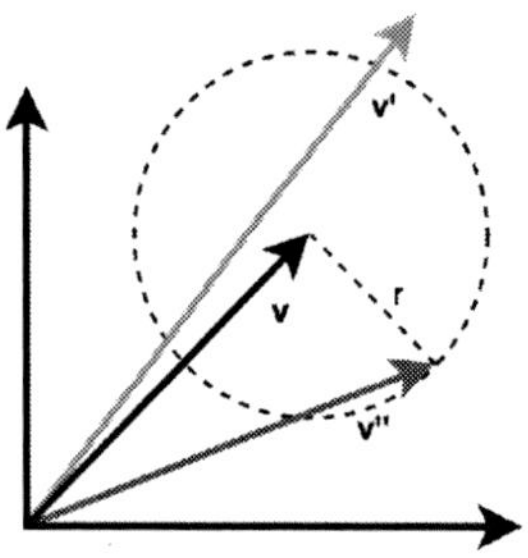

Figure 1: This figure presents a two-dimensional visualization of a token embedding vector v with its two approximations: v' and v''. Vector v' has a larger Euclidean distance error than v'', but its direction is more similar to the reference vector. Our experiments show that v' generally provides a better approximation of the original token compared to v''.

Many of these compression methods are based on knowledge distillation (Hinton et al., 2015) to help the compressed model (student) to perform close to the original model in different NLU tasks. However, these approaches often need high computation resources due to e.g., the necessity of retraining the expensive language modeling on a huge corpus (Sanh et al., 2019) or the use of expensive augmentation techniques to make the distillation effectively work (Jiao et al., 2019). Moreover, compression techniques that rely on training/fine-tuning language models are becoming less feasible due to its ever-increasing cost for current state-of-the-art architectures with hundreds

*Equal contribution

[1] https://github.com/MohammadrezaBanaei/orientation_based_embedding_compression

Proceedings of the 6th Workshop on Representation Learning for NLP (RepL4NLP-2021), pages 322–330
Bangkok, Thailand (Online), August 6, 2021.

of millions of parameters (He et al., 2020; Raffel et al., 2019; Brown et al., 2020).

More recently, there have been efforts to compress Transformer-based models for more resource-constrained scenarios (Mao et al., 2020) by using offline methods, such as matrix factorization (Winata et al., 2019; Lan et al., 2019; Wang et al., 2019), weight pruning (Li et al., 2016; Han et al., 2015), and also weight quantization (Zhou et al., 2016; Hubara et al., 2016).

This paper focuses on token embedding matrix compression due to being one of the largest matrices in BERT-based architectures. We specifically question the effectiveness of current low-rank matrix factorization methods in recent literature (Lan et al., 2019; Wang et al., 2019) by comparing them with the performance of a linear AutoEncoder over different compression ratios[2]. We define a new loss objective which is not only dependent on the commonly used Mean Absolute Error (MAE) or Mean Squared Error (MSE) loss between input embeddings and AutoEncoder reconstruction, but is also sensitive to the noise in reconstructed embeddings "direction" (measured by cosine distance). We present the intuition behind the importance of embedding vector direction in the Figure 1. In the following sections we show that cosine distance indeed plays a more critical role than MAE/MSE (Figure 3) as measured by the Perplexity of the entire model in language modeling.

In Section 4, we demonstrate that our compression algorithm is superior or competitive to the Singular Value Decomposition (SVD) baseline over several natural language understanding tasks from GLUE (Wang et al., 2018) benchmark, as well as the SQuAD dataset (Rajpurkar et al., 2016) for question answering. We also compare our performance with the SVD-based compression over different compression ratios, and specifically show that our model performs consistently better in higher compression ratios.

Our contribution can be summarized as follows:

- We demonstrate the importance of direction (measured by cosine distance) in token embeddings compression.
- We leverage the AutoEncoder architecture to explore various multi-objective optimization functions.
- We outperform the SVD-based baseline in terms of Perplexity and over various downstream tasks.

[2]Number of parameters in the original embedding matrix, over the sum of the parameters in factorized matrices.

2 Related work

The current mostly used compression methods can be roughly categorized into four classes, namely knowledge distillation (Hinton et al., 2015), weight pruning (Li et al., 2016; Han et al., 2015), matrix factorization (Lan et al., 2019; Wang et al., 2019; Mao et al., 2020) and weight quantization (Zhou et al., 2016; Hubara et al., 2016). This section focuses on matrix factorization-based methods that are currently used for token embedding compression in the literature.

2.1 Background: Low-rank matrix factorization

This section describes the baseline method that we are comparing our approach with throughout the paper. Let A be $n \times m$ embedding matrix representing m-dimensional embedding for each n different input tokens. The truncated version of the matrix factorization aims to find a low-rank approximation $\widetilde{A}$ of input matrix A (Halko et al., 2011):

$$\widetilde{A} = BC, \quad (1)$$

where B is the size of $n \times k$ and C is the size of $k \times m$. When the inner dimension k is smaller than $min(n, m)$, then the approximation is less expensive for storing it and performing further computations. The objective of this approximation is:

$$L_2(A, \widetilde{A}) = \left\| A - \widetilde{A} \right\|_2, \quad (2)$$

where $\|\cdot\|_2$ denotes the l_2 operator norm. In this paper, we use the SVD method as a low-rank matrix factorization baseline to compare our approach.

2.2 Matrix factorization for token embeddings compression

Lan et al. (2019) proposed to use matrix factorization to limit the number of parameters in the token embedding matrix, which also separates the Transformer hidden layer dimension from the size of vocabulary embedding. It is especially important as token embeddings are supposed to be *context-independent*, but hidden layer representation should be a *context-dependent* representation and hence needs more parameters. Moreover, reducing the vocabulary embedding dimension reduces the chance of overfitting, as many of the tokens are rarely used in downstream tasks.

There have been more recent efforts that use matrix factorization idea to compress different matrices in the Transformer architecture (Wang et al., 2019; Mao et al., 2020). For instance, Mao et al. (2020) proposed an iterative hybrid approach that uses matrix factorization together with weight pruning (while distilling knowledge from a teacher model) until reaching the final desired compression ratio. Lioutas et al. (2019) also proposed using a non-linear AutoEncoder model with knowledge distillation to compress word embeddings. However, we later demonstrate that only adding non-linearity indeed results in a minor improvement to the resulting compressed language model quality.

In this paper, we specifically focus on the effectiveness of SVD for compression of the token embedding matrix and show that Root Mean Square Error (RMSE) is not an optimal function to minimize the zero-shot Perplexity of the language model, which is the main criterion when language models are trained. We propose a new loss objective for linear matrix factorization using AutoEncoder to achieve a task-agnostic compressed language model with reasonable Perplexity without further fine-tuning the language model. In this work, we mainly investigate the effectiveness of SVD, and other complementary methods such as knowledge distillation can be used later to further boost the performance.

3 Model Description

Although SVD matrix-factorization is one of the most popular methods for matrix compression, we believe it is not an optimal method for compressing token embeddings in BERT-like architectures. The objective of SVD is to minimize the l_2 norm between the original matrix and the reconstructed one; however, focusing on l_2 norm optimization prioritizes the reduction of larger errors, and it may end up ignoring more minor vector differences. It is also sensitive to the influence of outliers. The most crucial reason for the l_2 norm not being the best choice is that it only considers the distance between the original and reconstructed token vector, and it does not necessarily pay attention to the orientation difference between them. In section 4, we demonstrate that vectors representing language tokens are more sensitive to noise in their direction rather than to changes in Euclidean distance from the reference vector. We also discuss the motivation behind it further in this section.

In order to mitigate the problem of focusing only on the largest errors between two vectors, we propose replacing the l_2 norm objective with the l_1 norm raised to the power of α:

$$L_1^{\alpha}(A, \widetilde{A}) = \left\| A - \widetilde{A} \right\|_1^{\alpha}, \tag{3}$$

where A denotes the original embedding matrix, $\widetilde{A}$ denotes the reconstructed embedding matrix, and $\|\cdot\|_1$ denotes the l_1 operator norm. Due to the flexibility in our defined loss objective, by decreasing the α parameter, we can control how much we want to focus on smaller error differences. We may set the α parameter to be a constant value, or linearly decrease it during the training. We denote linearly decreasing strategy for α as:

$$[t_1, t_2], \tag{4}$$

where t_1 is a starting value of α and t_2 is the target value to be reached at the end. The intuition behind using a decreasing α is to sequentially make the reconstruction harder for the model during training (as when the α becomes smaller, small reconstruction errors will also be magnified).

Since we believe that enforcing direction similarity between the original and the reconstructed embedding vectors is crucial for better language model performance, we introduce the second loss objective component, namely, cosine distance. Cosine distance can be interpreted as a measure of the difference in orientation of two vectors. This measure has been widely used in NLP for finding similar words (Mikolov et al., 2013), document clustering (Muflikhah and Baharudin, 2009), detecting plagiarism (Foltýnek et al., 2019), and many more. The goal of introducing cosine distance loss as a part of our objective is to enforce direction similarity of each pair of vectors from the original and reconstructed matrix.

Taking into consideration all points above, we propose to replace the l_2 norm objective with a new multi-objective function consisting of l_1 norm (raised to the power of α, where α is a hyper-parameter that can be changed during

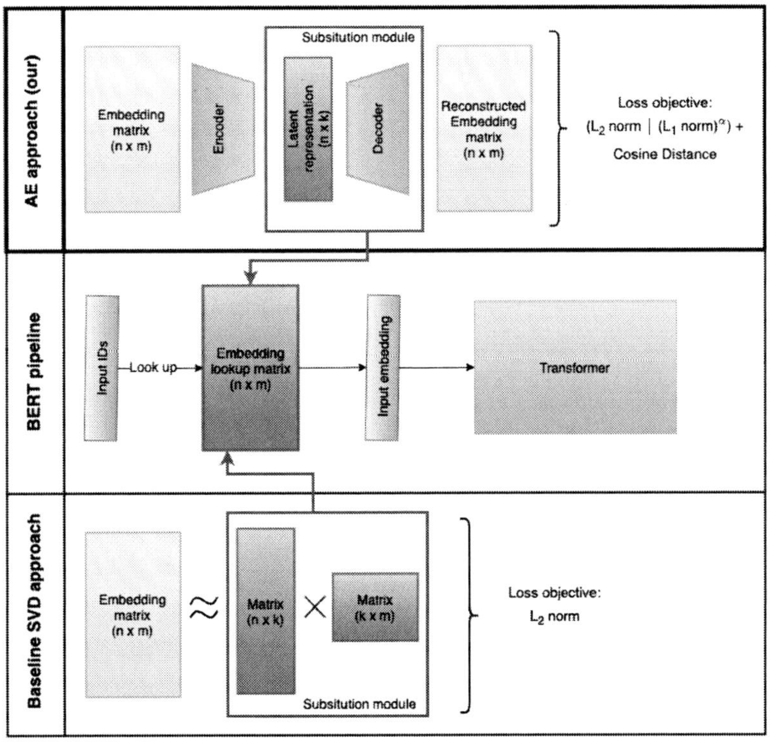

Figure 2: Overview of our AutoEncoder (ours) approach for BERT-like embedding matrix compression.

training) and cosine distance:

$$\Phi_{\alpha,\beta}(A,\widetilde{A}) = L_1^{\alpha}(A,\widetilde{A}) + \beta * CD(A,\widetilde{A}), \quad (5)$$

where A denotes the original embedding matrix, $\widetilde{A}$ denotes the reconstructed embedding matrix, and $CD(A,\widetilde{A})$ represents the mean cosine distance of all embedding vector pairs. It is worth noting that it is the combination of these two functions that gives a powerful tool which allows both to optimize the distance and direction of the reconstructed vectors to the reference. Focusing only on one of these functions may lead to suboptimal results. For comparison, we also define another multi-objective function which is the combination of l_2 norm with cosine distance loss:

$$\Psi_{\beta}(A,\widetilde{A}) = L_2(A,\widetilde{A}) + \beta * CD(A,\widetilde{A}). \quad (6)$$

In addition to the new loss function, we propose leveraging Auto-Encoder architecture for $\Phi_{\alpha,\beta}$ and Ψ_{β} loss optimization (Equation 5 and 6). We use a simple AutoEncoder consisting of a one-layer Encoder/Decoder without any activation function in order to have a fair comparison with the SVD baseline. Using Auto-Encoder enables efficient multi-objective optimization, but it also allows to select the appropriate level of model complexity when needed. At the end of the Auto-Encoder training, we extract an approximation of the original matrix, as shown in Figure 2. We substitute the original embedding matrix with a new module consisting of latent representation of vocabulary tokens along with the Decoder module.

4 Results

In this section, we evaluate our approach, which is based on using AutoEncoder model with a multi-objective loss function that incorporates cosine distance with l_1 or l_2 norm (Equation 5 and Equation 6) on the task of BERT-like token embedding matrix compression. We compare our results versus the commonly used randomized SVD method (Halko et al., 2011) to perform low-rank matrix factorization. We have implemented our token embeddings compression with the PyTorch backend (Paszke et al., 2019) and as an extension of Huggingface's Transformers library (Wolf et al., 2019), enabling researchers to apply our compression method in most of the existing Transformer architectures. It is worth noting that

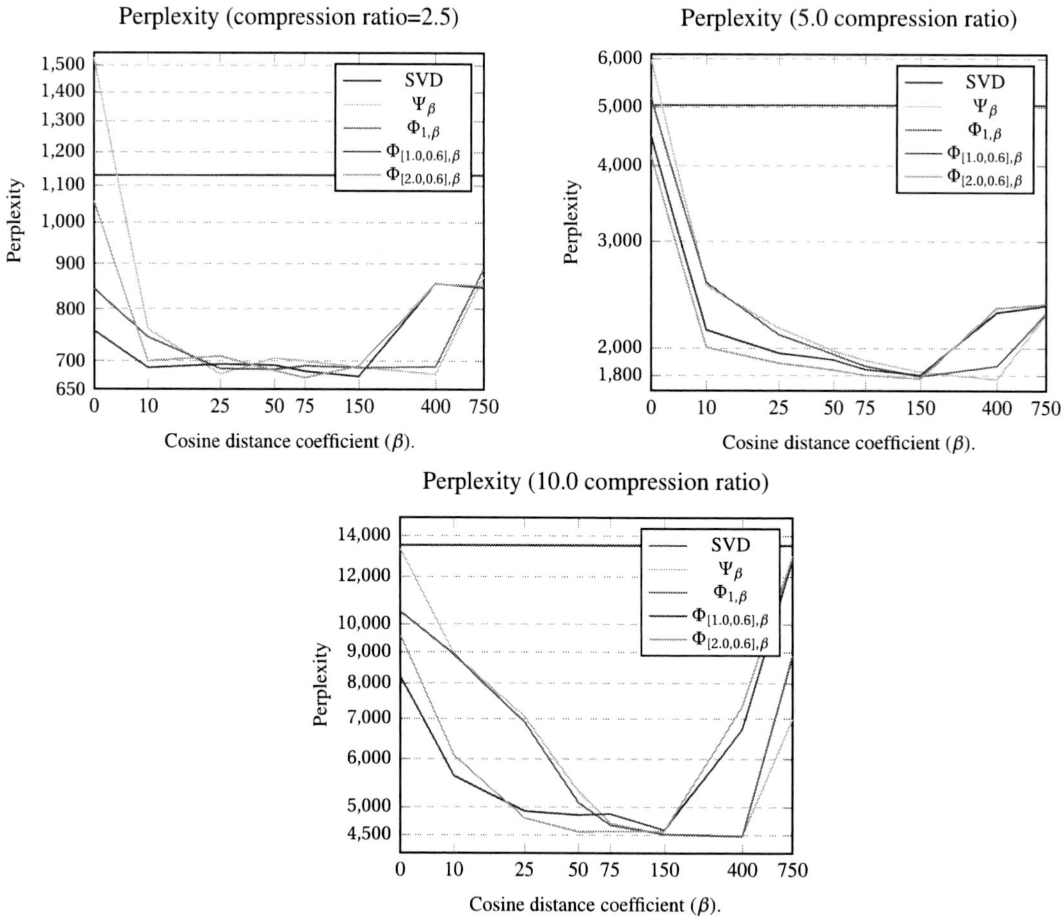

Figure 3: The impact of the β coefficient on Perplexity metric (lower is better) in the linear AutoEncoder loss functions: $\Phi_{\alpha,\beta}$ (Equation 5) and Ψ_β (Equation 6). In all configurations we select a final model based on the best Perplexity achieved during training. The term $[t_1, t_2]$ indicates linearly decreasing α parameter (Equation 4). Setting $\beta = 0$ represents not including cosine distance component in the loss function. We may observe that not including cosine distance in the loss function as well as making it a too dominant component (very big β) is not optimal for achieving good Perplexity. We also present the best Perplexity achieved by the baseline SVD method for three compression ratios: 2.5, 5.0, 10.0. Our approach significantly outperforms the baseline in the studied scenarios.

the offline training of our compression method on BERT-base (Devlin et al., 2018) token embedding matrix takes only few minutes on a single GPU device.

4.1 Experiments

In this paper, we perform our experiments over BERT-base model, but the general idea can be applied to the vocabulary embeddings of any other similar transformer-based architecture. The BERT-Base token embedding matrix consists of more than 23 Million parameters which is around 21% of all parameters in the model. We evaluate the quality of our final compressed embeddings on the masked (Devlin et al., 2018) language modeling task (using WikiText-103 test dataset), GLUE benchmark (Wang et al., 2018) downstream tasks and SQuAD v1.1 dataset (Rajpurkar et al., 2016). We also analyze results on other metrics, namely RMSE, MAE and Cosine Distance.

In Figure 3, we compare the Perplexity score achieved by SVD[3] method versus the results

[3]For SVD training, we select an iteration that minimizes Perplexity over our language modeling dataset.

achieved by a linear AutoEncoder model with different loss configurations, when compressing BERT token embeddings. We specifically examine the importance of cosine distance coefficient (β) in our studied loss functions over three different compression ratios: 2.5, 5, 10. The loss objective $\Phi_{t,\beta}$ (Equation 5) denotes constant (during the entire training) α parameter (equals to t) and $\Phi_{[t_1,t_2],\beta}$ denotes linearly decreasing α parameter (from t_1 to t_2). We present results when $\alpha = 0$, which represents combination of l_1 norm with cosine distance, and also when α linearly decreases from 1.0 or from 2.0 to 0.6 ($[1.0, 0.6]$ and $[2.0, 0.6]$ respectively). These values have been selected experimentally.

Table 1 presents more metrics to compare SVD method with our AutoEncoder-based approach. We show the results of the model with the best performing objective function (in terms of Perplexity) for a given compression ratio. Additionally, we examine the effect of adding non-linear activation function to this selected AutoEncoder model, where it can be seen that the improvements due to addition of non-linearity is marginal.

We further validate the quality of our compressed token embeddings by inserting it into the BERT-base architecture and fine-tuning the model on different downstream tasks from the GLUE benchmark (Wang et al., 2018) and on the SQuAD v1.1 (Rajpurkar et al., 2016) dataset. Table 2 presents an extensive comparison between our best (in terms of perplexity) linear AE and the SVD baseline on eight different downstream tasks and over different compression ratios. More specifically, we can see that our proposed method is superior or competitive to the SVD baseline and performs relatively better (compared to baseline) on higher compression ratios. The original BERT (without compression) performance is also added for a better comparison of studied scenarios.

Figure 4 presents learning curves for three selected NLU downstream tasks: SST-2 (Socher et al., 2013), MRPC (Dolan and Brockett, 2005) and SQuAD 1.1 (Rajpurkar et al., 2016). We show results for the compression ratio of 10, as we observed more significant gain for higher compression ratios.

4.2 Discussion

The experiments presented in Figure 3 confirm our claim that the l_2 norm alone is not an optimal measure for evaluating the quality of reconstructed token embeddings in a Transformer-based architecture. We observe that adding cosine distance objective function correlates positively with a better Perplexity metric (Figure 3) and also with higher performance on downstream tasks (Table 2). Figure 3 demonstrates that the best results are achieved when the cosine distance coefficient β is a dominant component of the loss function. However, if the β factor becomes too large, the quality of the solution decreases. Hence, we conclude that taking into account both the commonly used L1/L2 distance and focusing on the direction of the token vectors are indispensable. We show that combining the l_2 or l_1 norm with the cosine distance into one multi-objective loss function and optimizing it by AutoEncoder model outperforms the baseline SVD Perplexity for all tested compression ratios (Figure 3). Our experiments show that depending on the compression ratio l_2 or l_1 norm may be a better choice. However, they are conclusive that adding cosine distance is the key factor.

Moreover, our approach outperforms SVD in terms of accuracy for most GLUE benchmark downstream tasks and on SQuAD v1.1 (Table 2). We also observe that for higher compression ratios, our approach outperforms the SVD approach more significantly. More importantly, Figure 4 demonstrates that using our linear AutoEncoder compressed module in the BERT model generally converges faster than SVD-based compressed module, which is especially important in few-shot learning scenarios.

Looking at the results presented in Table 1, we may also reflect on the importance of preserving the token vector orientation and its effect on Perplexity. More specifically, the mean cosine distance measures for SVD and our approach are pretty close, but its effect on Perplexity metric is significant. Our approach indeed provides a compressed submodule with a much better (lower) Perplexity.

We also show that only adding a non-linear activation function to the studied AutoEncoder model has a little effect on improving Perplexity. Table 1 presents the effect of modifying the original linear AutoEncoder architecture by adding

CR (#Params)	Architecture	Objective	RMSE	Cosine Distance	MAE	Perplexity
2.5 (~9.38M)	SVD	l_2	**0.02233**	0.10300	**0.01734**	1130
	Linear AE (+ ELU)	$\Phi_{[2.0,0.6],75}$	0.02427 (0.02431)	**0.1024 (0.1028)**	0.01896 (0.01902)	**669.8 (664.0)**
5.0 (~4.69M)	SVD	l_2	**0.02848**	0.17490	**0.02216**	5035
	Linear AE (+ ELU)	Ψ_{400}	0.03101 (0.03061)	**0.17390 (0.17410)**	0.02433 (0.02401)	**1776 (1730)**
10.0 (~2.34M)	SVD	l_2	**0.03215**	0.23050	**0.02506**	13501
	Linear AE (+ ELU)	$\Phi_{1,400}$	0.03680 (0.03707)	**0.22900 (0.22910)**	0.02909 (0.02934)	**4478 (4387)**

Table 1: Additional metrics for comparing the performance of SVD baseline and the best performing linear AutoEncoder model (we select the configuration that minimizes Perplexity, as presented in Figure 3) for different compression ratios (CR). For each AutoEncoder model, we also present (in parentheses) the results after adding non-linearity. Bold values indicate best results between SVD and linear AutoEncoder in each compression ratio.

CR	Architecture	SST-2 (Acc)	MRPC (F1/Acc)	STS-B (Pearson/Spearman correlation)	QQP (Acc/F1)	MNLI (Acc)	QNLI (Acc)	RTE (Acc)	SQuAD v1.1 (F1/EM)
-	Original BERT	91.74	88.12/83.58	88.71/88.55	90.67/87.43	84.04	90.96	65.34	81.97/73.42
2.5	SVD	89.22	82.37/75.25	86.27/85.72	89.88/86.39	82.83	**89.46**	**62.92**	80.75/72.34
	Linear AE	**90.83**	**86.64/80.88**	**87.35/86.88**	**90.04/86.72**	**83.13**	89.16	62.58	**81.29/72.85**
5.0	SVD	87.04	83.95/77.70	84.88/84.2	**89.79/86.45**	**81.39**	87.33	59.21	80.37/71.67
	Linear AE	**88.07**	**86.67/81.37**	**85.9/85.43**	89.2/85.66	81.11	**87.53**	**64.26**	**80.53/72.00**
10.0	SVD	82.0	83.95/72.55	80.93/80.67	87.6/83.57	76.59	83.51	54.51	74.15/65.0
	Linear AE	**84.29**	**84.06/77.7**	**84.7/84.16**	**88.32/84.38**	**79.26**	**86.09**	**58.48**	**75.70/66.75**

Table 2: Performance comparison of the best SVD and the best linear AutoEncoder objective configuration on several NLU tasks from GLUE benchmark (Wang et al., 2018) and for SQuAD v1.1 in different compression ratios (CR).

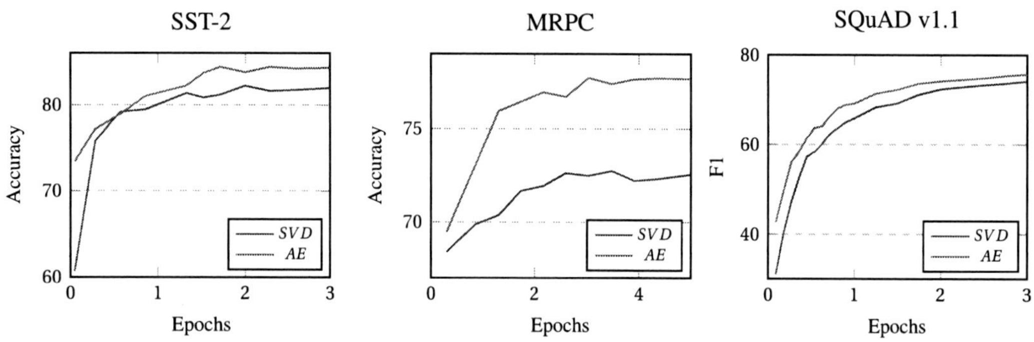

Figure 4: Comparing the learning curves of the best SVD baseline and the best-selected configuration of the AutoEncoder model for SST-2 (Socher et al., 2013), MRPC (Dolan and Brockett, 2005), and SQuAD v1.1 (Rajpurkar et al., 2016) during fine-tuning for compression ratio=10.0 .

ELU (Clevert et al., 2015) as this activation shows a better impact on Perplexity than other activations in our experiments. It can be seen that the improvements in Perplexity due to the addition of non-linearities are marginal (as previously observed by Lioutas et al. (2019) in a distillation-based approach for token embeddings compression). Hence, we focused only on the linear AutoEncoder in all our downstream tasks experiments.

5 Conclusion

In this work, we propose a simple linear AutoEncoder model with a multi-objective loss function for BERT-like token embeddings compression. We emphasize the importance of the direction component (measured by the cosine distance between the original and the reconstructed token embeddings) in the compression objective function. We challenge the commonly used SVD-based matrix-factorization method and show that our approach achieves significantly better zero-shot language model Perplexity. Moreover, we show that BERT-like models with our compressed token embeddings submodule converge much faster and outperform the SVD baseline on SQuAD v1.1 and on GLUE benchmark tasks in most scenarios.

References

Tom B Brown, Benjamin Mann, Nick Ryder, Melanie Subbiah, Jared Kaplan, Prafulla Dhariwal, Arvind Neelakantan, Pranav Shyam, Girish Sastry, Amanda Askell, et al. 2020. Language models are few-shot learners. *arXiv preprint arXiv:2005.14165*.

Djork-Arné Clevert, Thomas Unterthiner, and Sepp Hochreiter. 2015. Fast and accurate deep network learning by exponential linear units (elus). *arXiv preprint arXiv:1511.07289*.

Jacob Devlin, Ming-Wei Chang, Kenton Lee, and Kristina Toutanova. 2018. Bert: Pre-training of deep bidirectional transformers for language understanding. *arXiv preprint arXiv:1810.04805*.

William B Dolan and Chris Brockett. 2005. Automatically constructing a corpus of sentential paraphrases. In *Proceedings of the Third International Workshop on Paraphrasing (IWP2005)*.

Tomáš Foltýnek, Norman Meuschke, and Bela Gipp. 2019. Academic plagiarism detection: a systematic literature review. *ACM Computing Surveys (CSUR)*, 52(6):1–42.

Nathan Halko, Per-Gunnar Martinsson, and Joel A Tropp. 2011. Finding structure with randomness: Probabilistic algorithms for constructing approximate matrix decompositions. *SIAM review*, 53(2):217–288.

Song Han, Jeff Pool, John Tran, and William J Dally. 2015. Learning both weights and connections for efficient neural networks. *arXiv preprint arXiv:1506.02626*.

Pengcheng He, Xiaodong Liu, Jianfeng Gao, and Weizhu Chen. 2020. Deberta: Decoding-enhanced bert with disentangled attention. *arXiv preprint arXiv:2006.03654*.

Geoffrey Hinton, Oriol Vinyals, and Jeff Dean. 2015. Distilling the knowledge in a neural network. *arXiv preprint arXiv:1503.02531*.

Itay Hubara, Matthieu Courbariaux, Daniel Soudry, Ran El-Yaniv, and Yoshua Bengio. 2016. Binarized neural networks. In *Proceedings of the 30th International Conference on Neural Information Processing Systems*, pages 4114–4122.

Xiaoqi Jiao, Yichun Yin, Lifeng Shang, Xin Jiang, Xiao Chen, Linlin Li, Fang Wang, and Qun Liu. 2019. Tinybert: Distilling bert for natural language understanding. *arXiv preprint arXiv:1909.10351*.

Zhenzhong Lan, Mingda Chen, Sebastian Goodman, Kevin Gimpel, Piyush Sharma, and Radu Soricut. 2019. Albert: A lite bert for self-supervised learning of language representations. *arXiv preprint arXiv:1909.11942*.

Hao Li, Asim Kadav, Igor Durdanovic, Hanan Samet, and Hans Peter Graf. 2016. Pruning filters for efficient convnets. *arXiv preprint arXiv:1608.08710*.

Vasileios Lioutas, Ahmad Rashid, Krtin Kumar, Md Akmal Haidar, and Mehdi Rezagholizadeh. 2019. Distilled embedding: non-linear embedding factorization using knowledge distillation. *arXiv preprint arXiv:1910.06720*.

Yinhan Liu, Myle Ott, Naman Goyal, Jingfei Du, Mandar Joshi, Danqi Chen, Omer Levy, Mike Lewis, Luke Zettlemoyer, and Veselin Stoyanov. 2019. Roberta: A robustly optimized bert pretraining approach. *arXiv preprint arXiv:1907.11692*.

Yihuan Mao, Yujing Wang, Chufan Wu, Chen Zhang, Yang Wang, Yaming Yang, Quanlu Zhang, Yunhai Tong, and Jing Bai. 2020. Ladabert: Lightweight adaptation of bert through hybrid model compression. *arXiv preprint arXiv:2004.04124*.

Tomas Mikolov, Kai Chen, Greg Corrado, and Jeffrey Dean. 2013. Efficient estimation of word representations in vector space. *arXiv preprint arXiv:1301.3781*.

Lailil Muflikhah and Baharum Baharudin. 2009. Document clustering using concept space and cosine similarity measurement. In *2009 International Conference on Computer Technology and Development*, volume 1, pages 58–62. IEEE.

Adam Paszke, Sam Gross, Francisco Massa, Adam Lerer, James Bradbury, Gregory Chanan, Trevor Killeen, Zeming Lin, Natalia Gimelshein, Luca Antiga, et al. 2019. Pytorch: An imperative style, high-performance deep learning library. *arXiv preprint arXiv:1912.01703*.

Colin Raffel, Noam Shazeer, Adam Roberts, Katherine Lee, Sharan Narang, Michael Matena, Yanqi Zhou, Wei Li, and Peter J Liu. 2019. Exploring the limits of transfer learning with a unified text-to-text transformer. *arXiv preprint arXiv:1910.10683*.

Pranav Rajpurkar, Jian Zhang, Konstantin Lopyrev, and Percy Liang. 2016. Squad: 100,000+ questions for machine comprehension of text. *arXiv preprint arXiv:1606.05250*.

Victor Sanh, Lysandre Debut, Julien Chaumond, and Thomas Wolf. 2019. Distilbert, a distilled version of bert: smaller, faster, cheaper and lighter. *arXiv preprint arXiv:1910.01108*.

Richard Socher, Alex Perelygin, Jean Wu, Jason Chuang, Christopher D Manning, Andrew Y Ng, and Christopher Potts. 2013. Recursive deep models for semantic compositionality over a sentiment treebank. In *Proceedings of the 2013 conference on empirical methods in natural language processing*, pages 1631–1642.

Ashish Vaswani, Noam Shazeer, Niki Parmar, Jakob Uszkoreit, Llion Jones, Aidan N Gomez, Lukasz Kaiser, and Illia Polosukhin. 2017. Attention is all you need. *arXiv preprint arXiv:1706.03762*.

Alex Wang, Amanpreet Singh, Julian Michael, Felix Hill, Omer Levy, and Samuel R Bowman. 2018. Glue: A multi-task benchmark and analysis platform for natural language understanding. *arXiv preprint arXiv:1804.07461*.

Ziheng Wang, Jeremy Wohlwend, and Tao Lei. 2019. Structured pruning of large language models. *arXiv preprint arXiv:1910.04732*.

Genta Indra Winata, Andrea Madotto, Jamin Shin, Elham J Barezi, and Pascale Fung. 2019. On the effectiveness of low-rank matrix factorization for lstm model compression. *arXiv preprint arXiv:1908.09982*.

Thomas Wolf, Lysandre Debut, Victor Sanh, Julien Chaumond, Clement Delangue, Anthony Moi, Pierric Cistac, Tim Rault, Rémi Louf, Morgan Funtowicz, et al. 2019. Huggingface's transformers: State-of-the-art natural language processing. *arXiv preprint arXiv:1910.03771*.

Zhilin Yang, Zihang Dai, Yiming Yang, Jaime Carbonell, Ruslan Salakhutdinov, and Quoc V Le. 2019. Xlnet: Generalized autoregressive pretraining for language understanding. *arXiv preprint arXiv:1906.08237*.

Shuchang Zhou, Yuxin Wu, Zekun Ni, Xinyu Zhou, He Wen, and Yuheng Zou. 2016. Dorefa-net: Training low bitwidth convolutional neural networks with low bitwidth gradients. *arXiv preprint arXiv:1606.06160*.

Author Index

Association for Computational Linguistics
209 N. Eighth Street
Stroudsburg, Pennsylvania 18360

CURRAN ASSOCIATES INC.
proceedings.com

ISBN 978-1-7138-3384-0
9 781713 833840